Muslim-Christian Polemic during the Crusades

The Letter from the People of Cyprus and
Ibn Abī Ṭālib al-Dimashqī's Response

Edited by

Rifaat Y. Ebied
David Thomas

BRILL
LEIDEN · BOSTON
2005

This book is printed on acid-free paper.

Christians and Muslims have been involved in exchanges over matters of faith and morality since the founding of Islam. Attitudes between the faiths today are deeply coloured by the legacy of past encounters, and often preserve centuries-old negative views. The History of Christian-Muslim Relations, Texts and Studies presents the surviving record of past encounters in authoritative, fully introduced text editions and annotated translations, and also monograph and collected studies. It illustrates the development in mutual perceptions as these are contained in surviving Christian and Muslim writings, and makes available the arguments and rhetorical strategies that, for good or for ill, have left their mark on attitudes today. The series casts light on a history marked by intellectual creativity and occasional breakthroughs in communication, although, on the whole beset by misunderstanding and misrepresentation. By making this history better known, the series seeks to contribute to improved recognition between Christians and Muslims in the future.

Library of Congress Cataloging-in-Publication Data

Muslim-Christian polemic during the Crusades : the letter from the people of Cyprus and Ibn Abi Talib al-Dimashqi's response / edited by Rifat Y. Ebied, David Thomas.
    p. cm. — (The history of Christian-Muslim relations, ISSN 1570-7350 ; v. 2)
English and Arabic.
Includes bibliographical references (p.) and index.
ISBN 90-04-13589-8
    1. Apologetics-Early works to 1800. 2. Christianity and other religions-Islam-Early works to 1800. 3. Islam-Relations-Christianity-Early works to 1800. 4. Letter from the people of Cyprus. 5. Koran-Criticism, interpretation, etc. -Early works to 1800. 6. Dimashqī, Shams al-Dīn Muḥammad ibn Abī Ṭālib, 1256 or 7-1327. Response to the letter from the people of Cyprus. 7. Church history-Middle Ages, 600-1500. I. Ebied, R. Y. II. Thomas, David (David Richard), 1948- III. Dimashqi, Shams-al-Din Muhammad ibn Abi Talib, 1256 or 7-1327. Response to the letter from the people of Cyprus. English & Arabic. IV. Letter from the people of Cyprus. English & Arabic. V. Series.

BT1100.M83 2004
261.2'7'09023-dc22

                                                                            2004058526

ISSN   1570–7350
ISBN   90 04 13589 8

CONTENTS

FOREWORD

We publish here an edition and translation of one of the most substantial exchanges of ideas between Christian and Muslim scholars that has survived from the medieval period. Our hope is that it will both inform students and scholars about aspects of inter-faith relations at the time the letters that comprise it were sent, and will also assist those who are engaged in the crucial task of building constructive relations between the faiths to avoid repeating past mistakes. It is the second volume in the History of Christian-Muslim Relations series, which is intended to make accessible in reliable editions and translations the record of encounters between members of the two faiths.

We acknowledge with gratitude the assistance we have received from the librarians of the University Library, Utrecht, the Bodleian Library, Oxford, and the Bibliothèque Nationale, Paris, in supplying photocopies of the manuscripts, responding to queries and granting permission to publish the texts. In addition, Rifaat Ebied acknowledges the generous financial support he has received from the Australian Research Council which has enabled him to travel to Europe to examine the manuscripts and to consult with his co-editor, while David Thomas acknowledges the support he has received from the University of Birmingham which has enabled him to travel to Australia for the same purpose.

THE LETTERS AND THEIR AUTHORS

In the spring of 721/1321, the Damascus scholar Shams al-Dīn Abū 'Abdallāh Muḥammad Ibn Abī Ṭālib al-Anṣārī al-Ṣūfī was presented with a letter from Christians in Cyprus. He quickly perceived its provocative nature and set about composing a response, completing it by the early summer of the same year, and so bringing to a conclusion a correspondence that had originally started maybe a century earlier. This complicated episode in Christian-Muslim relations is unparalleled for the knowledge of one another's faith displayed by authors on both sides, and also for their readiness to manipulate information to their own advantage and to argue from behind a façade of decorum with vehement ferocity.

The story begins with neither the Cypriot author of the Christian letter nor al-Dimashqī in the eighth/fourteenth century, but with the monk Paul of Antioch, Melkite Bishop of Sidon, about a century before. The little that is known about this personality comes from his own correspondence, and it is not even possible to fix the period of his activity with much certainty. He may have lived any time between the mid fifth/eleventh century, since he draws on the works of Elias of Nisibis who died in 437-8/1046, and the early seventh/thirteenth century, when the first known copy was made of his *Letter to a Muslim Friend*, one of the works we are concerned with here. This was a subversive piece of writing, as we shall see, and it is unlikely that its arguments would have long been unanswered. In fact, the Egyptian jurist Shihāb al-Dīn Aḥmad b. Idrīs al-Qarāfī (626/1228-684/1285) appears to have done this in the mid or late seventh/thirteenth century in his *Al-ajwiba al-fākhira 'an al-as'ila al-fājira*, 'Proud Answers to Insolent Questions'. So it may not be too inaccurate to date Paul's main period of activity and his composition of this letter to the early seventh/thirteenth century.[1]

---

[1] Cf. P. Khoury, *Paul d'Antioche, évêque melkite de Sidon (xiie s.)*, Beirut, 1964, pp. 8-18, for a discussion of the facts relating to his biography, and also S.K. Samir, 'Notes sur la "Lettre à un musulman de Sidon" de Paul d'Antioche', *Orientalia Lovaniensia Periodica* 24, 1993, pp. 180-90, who corrects some of Khoury's facts; also more briefly, D. Thomas, 'Paul of Antioch's *Letter to a Muslim Friend* and *The Letter from Cyprus*', in D. Thomas, ed., *Syrian Christians under Islam, the first thousand years*, Leiden, 2001, pp. 203-4.

Paul's *Letter to a Muslim Friend* forms the basis of *The Letter from the People of Cyprus* which was sent to al-Dimashqī and elicited his passionate response. The anonymous Cypriot Christian responsible edited Paul's work in a number of ways, so in order to understand the background and intention of this later letter, it is important to know something about Paul's original letter and why he wrote it.[2]

Paul makes clear the circumstances of his writing at the very outset. He tells how he has been on a journey through the Byzantine empire and to Constantinople, to Amalfi in southern Italy, through 'Frankish' territory, *baʿḍ aʿmāl al-Ifranj*, and to Rome. He was able to meet the leaders among the people of these regions and to confer with their experts, and he sought their opinion about Muḥammad. Now, in response to a request from a Muslim friend in Sidon, he will explain what they said.[3]

This professed intention, then, is to pass on to a Muslim friend the views about the Prophet that were held by Christian experts in different parts of Europe. Such an idea does not strain credibility entirely. Links between Constantinople, Italy, other parts of Europe and the eastern Mediterranean were, of course, firmly established, and would have been intensified since the start of the Crusades in the late fifth/eleventh century. And thus it would not be strange for the bishop of a Melkite see within an area of Crusader rule to travel to major centres of the church,[4] or for European and Byzantine Christians to know enough about Islam and the Prophet to be able to express an informed opinion about him. But when we discover more about these Christians and their knowledge of Islam, it becomes extremely difficult to think of them as the figures the bishop says they were.

Paul continues to explain that these experts had obtained a Qurʾan, and on reading it had discovered a range of reasons to dissuade them from accepting Islam. And so the main body of the letter goes on to lay out a long series of arguments which are supposedly found in the Qurʾan itself in favour of Christian doctrines and against any require-

---

[2] Ed. Khoury, *Paul d'Antioche*, pp. 59-83 (Arabic) and 169-87 (French); also pp. 54-147 below in parallel with *The Letter from the People of Cyprus*. (Earlier editions of the *Letter* were published by L. Buffat, 'Lettre de Paul, évêque de Saïda', *Revue de l'Orient Chrétien* 8, 1903, pp. 388-425, with a French translation; and by L. Cheikho, *Vingt traités théologiques d'auteurs arabes chrétiens*, Beirut, 1920, pp. 15-26).

[3] Paul's *Letter* in Khoury, *Paul d'Antioche*, §§ 1-3.

[4] Khoury, *Paul d'Antioche*, p. 13, n. 25, suggests that if this journey was historical it may have been for the Third Lateran Council.

ment to abandon them. These begin with a proof that Muḥammad and his message were sent solely for the Arabs, and proceed to show how the Qur'an endorses Christian beliefs in Christ, the Apostles, the Gospels, Christian monotheism and religious services. The Qur'an even acknowledges the doctrine of the Trinity, which is anyway based on reason, the Incarnation, the two natures of Christ and the death of his human nature alone.

The character of the approach adopted in Paul's letter is made patently clear here, where verses from the Qur'an are mustered together with Biblical quotations and rational arguments to make the point that Muslim scripture is not only not intended for Christians but actually approves their position.

The letter goes on to defend the use of apparently anthropomorphic language about God but in a figurative manner, and also the philosophical meaningfulness of calling God substance, and the logic of the Incarnation as the supreme expression of God's generosity to his creation in communing with them through one of their own. It concludes with Paul suggesting innocently that these arguments remove contention between the two faiths, though if the situation is otherwise his Muslim friend should inform him and he will relay his difficulties to the experts.

This relatively brief letter offers a spirited defence of Christianity based on both reason and revelation. And it is the use of the latter that occasions most surprise. For these experts appear able to choose from the Arabic Qur'an verses and parts of verses that they can at will use to bolster their own beliefs. For example, they serenely say:

> Then we find in the book also glorification of the lord Christ and his mother and that God made them a sign to the worlds, for its words are, 'And she who was chaste, therefore we breathed into her of our Spirit and made her and her son a token for all peoples'.[5]

They clearly take this as signifying that Christ was divine, although there is no explicit indication of that here and there are many denials elsewhere in the Qur'an, and thus effectively Christianise the verse.

But they go further than relatively mild reinterpretation of verses. From time to time they make changes to the actual text of the Qur'an in order to make it support Christian doctrine, as when they represent it recounting the sending out of Christ's Apostles with the Gospel:

---

[5] *Ibid.*, § 8, quoting S XXI: 91.

> [The Apostles] were glorified in this book and exalted: 'We sent our mes-
> sengers with clear proofs, and with them the Book, *wa-maʿahum al-kitāb*,
> that mankind might observe right measure'. It means his Apostles the
> disciples, for if it had meant Abraham, Moses, David and Muḥammad
> it would have said 'with them the Books', and would not have said 'the
> Book' which is the Gospel.[6]

This seems persuasive until we see that they have changed the verse
which they quote from the original '… with clear proofs, and revealed
with them the Book and the Balance', *wa-anzalnā maʿahum al-kitāb wa-
al-mīzān*. The net effect is that the verse is made to assert the Christian
teaching that the Apostles were sent out with a single common scripture, rather than the Muslim teaching that God revealed a separate
scripture upon each of the messengers he sent before Muḥammad.

Most flagrant of all these re-readings and alterations of the text of the
Qur'an is the interpretation of the opening words of *Sūrat al-baqara*:

> Concerning the Gospel, [the Qur'an] witnesses that it is guidance for
> the God-fearing, in its words, 'Alif Lam Mim. That is the book, *dhālika
> al-kitāb*, in which is no doubt, guidance for the God-fearing'. Now, Alif
> Lam Mim is a part, which is Al-Masīḥ. And 'that book' is the Gospel …
> because 'that' cannot be 'this', *li-anna dhālika lā yakūnu hadhā*.[7]

This is creative exegesis at its most unrestrained, showing clearly
a disregard for the Qur'an as a whole and an unabashed readiness
to take verses in isolation and read them from a purely Christian
perspective.

But this kind of approach to the Qur'an also suggests that whoever
is responsible for this inventiveness is not only thoroughly acquainted
with the text but also fully proficient in Arabic, and therefore much less
likely to be unspecified Byzantine or European experts, among whom
deep knowledge of the Qur'an is not attested in the sixth/twelfth or
seventh/thirteenth centuries, than an Eastern Christian who spoke and
wrote in Arabic as his first language, and was immersed in Muslim
culture. It is difficult to avoid identifying Paul himself as the originator
or compiler of these challenging exegetical arguments, in which case
the experts he introduces become convenient literary mouthpieces who

---

[6] *Ibid.*, § 13, quoting S LVII: 25.

[7] *Ibid.*, § 16, quoting S II: 1-2. The interpretation of *dhālika al-kitāb* as a scripture
other than the Qur'an is known from the Muslim exegete Abū Jaʿfar al-Ṭabarī and
from earlier Christians; cf. B. Roggema, 'A Christian Reading of the Qur'an: the
legend of Sergius-Baḥīrā and its use of Qur'an and Sīra', in Thomas, *Syrian Christians
under Islam*, p. 62 and n. 20.

can take the responsibility and blame for these interpretations and allow Paul to preserve a demeanour of politeness and cooperativeness while effectively undermining Islam.

Given the subversive character and its implicit criticism that Islam is subordinate to Christianity, there is no surprise that Paul's letter circulated widely after it was written. Three copies made in the seventh/thirteenth century have survived,[8] it was refuted by Shihāb al-Dīn al-Qarāfī in his *Al-ajwiba al-fākhira 'an al-as'ila al-fājira*,[9] and in the early eighth/fourteenth century Ibn Taymiyya knew it under the title *Al-kitāb al-manṭiqī al-dawla khānī al-mubarhan 'an al-iʿtiqād al-ṣaḥīḥ wa-al-ra'y al-mustaqīm*, 'The most eloquent treatise of [?] weighty authority which proves sound belief and correct discernment',[10] and described it as a familiar source upon which Christian scholars had depended for some years, passing it down among them so that old copies of it were available.[11]

Sometime in the early eighth/fourteenth century Paul's letter became known to a Christian scholar in Cyprus. He revised it, removing some elements, altering others, and adding copious quotations from the Bible and Qur'an, and in this new form it was sent to the two Muslim scholars in Damascus, Tāqī al-Dīn Aḥmad Ibn Taymiyya in 716/1316, and Shams al-Dīn Muḥammad Ibn Abī Ṭālib al-Anṣārī al-Dimashqī four or so years later in 721/1321.

This *Letter from the People of Cyprus* inaugurated the second stage in this protracted correspondence, and provoked two of the longest refutations by Muslims against Christianity that have survived. So it is pertinent to ask in particular how it differs from Paul of Antioch's original, and what its author's intention may have been.

Although we are given to believe that the *Letter* contains the views of leading Christians in Cyprus, we must assume that there was one editor who took Paul's earlier work and fashioned from it his own. But we are not provided with any personal information about him,

---

[8] Cf Khoury, *Paul d'Antioche*, pp. 21-3, MSS Sinai Arabic 531 (1232 AD), Bodleian Greaves 30 (thirteenth century) and Mingana Christian Arabic 44 (1254 AD). Samir, 'Notes', pp. 180-90, shows that Sinai Arabic 448, which Khoury dates to 1221, was in fact copied in 1530.

[9] Ed. B.Z. 'Awaḍ, Cairo, 1987.

[10] Ibn Taymiyya, *Al-jawāb al-ṣaḥīḥ li-man baddala dīn al-Masīḥ*, Cairo, 1905, vol. I, p. 20, and also ed. 'A.B. Ḥasan b. Nāṣir *et al*, Riyāḍ, 1999, vol. I, p. 101, according to which, n. 2, *khānī* is a Persian word meaning 'important'. The grammar of this title presents some difficulties, and should maybe read *Al-kitāb al-manṭiqī li-dawla khānī...*

[11] *Jawāb* (Cairo edition), p. 19.

and must accept that this inventive though careful scholar remains anonymous. In neither the three extant copies of the *Letter* nor in the versions quoted by the Muslim respondents is anything said to identify him. In the earliest copy the Christian who purportedly writes it is introduced as 'our master, the revered teacher, the head, lord, distinguished, unique and unparalleled professor',[12] though there is no guarantee that this esteemed personage is any more real than Paul of Antioch's European experts. The other witnesses are silent. So all we can say is that he was a Melkite Christian living in Cyprus, maybe a native, maybe a refugee from the Levant or Palestine, though it must be significant that he was so thoroughly acquainted with the text of the Qur'an that he could not only add proof-texts to the ones given by Paul but also correct Paul's revisions of the text and supply the names of the *sūras* quoted by Paul and the ones he himself adds. His knowledge of the Qur'an was prodigious. We will return to this point below.

If we take P1 (MS Arabe 204) as the nearest version we have to the original,[13] we see immediately how the editor recast Paul's opening while remaining true to its inspiration. He is first introduced as a great scholar, in the fulsome words quoted above, and then explains that in response to a request from an unnamed person, who is clearly his friend since he feels 'deep attachment and great affection' for him, he has made 'a full inquiry' of what Christians in their world-wide diversity believe. Thus, he has travelled to Cyprus, met their leaders and conferred with 'their distinguished and learned individuals', and he now promises to present their doctrines and beliefs.

The relationship between this and the opening of Paul's letter is immediately obvious. Both authors say they write in response to a request from a friend, both make journeys (presumably from their homeland on the Mediterranean seaboard) in order to discover what foreign Christians believe, and both have been given access to leading religious intellectuals. But there are also differences. Paul makes it clear that he as a Christian is writing for a Muslim friend, but the Cypriot leaves the identity of both author and recipient unstated. Paul states plainly that he is allowed to meet leading people wherever he goes because he is a bishop, while in the absence of clear indications, one must infer that access is granted to the Cypriot's protagonist because of

---

[12] Cf. p. 55 below.
[13] Cf. pp. 37-9 below.

his scholarly standing. And thirdly, Paul sets out ascertain his experts' opinions about Muḥammad, while the Cypriot's scholar is engaged in a survey of Christian beliefs.

The Cypriot editor apparently intends by these changes to remove not only the precise circumstantial details of Paul's letter, but also any hint that might point to the faith allegiance of the main figure. The result is that this scholarly personage can be taken as a neutral inquirer, or even a Muslim, an identity well suited to his role as prompt and cross-examiner of the Christians in the *Letter from the People of Cyprus* proper. This might make a Muslim reader more likely to sympathise with him, and thus maybe to read his questions and the answers given without hostility or suspicion. Here we see the editor quietly excising an element that might impede his work in realising its aim.

Throughout his revision, the Cypriot editor judiciously removes or changes parts of Paul's letter, often the most pointed and contentious. For example, Paul draws attention to the approval given to Jesus' followers in the Qur'an:

> We also find in it that God raised Christ to him, and placed those who followed him above those who did not believe until the day of resurrection; these are his words, '[And] when Allah said: O Jesus [son of Mary], Lo! I am gathering thee and causing thee to ascend unto me, and am cleansing thee of those who disbelieve and am setting those who follow thee above those who disbelieve until the day of resurrection'. And also, 'We caused Jesus, son of Mary, to follow, and gave him the Gospel, and placed compassion and mercy in the hearts of those who followed him'.[14]

He implies strongly that the Qur'an signals approval to all who follow Jesus, including Christians at the time he wrote his letter. The Cypriot editor tones this down by leaving out Paul's reference to Christians, and also by adding further verses from the Qur'an:

> We also find in it that God raised him up to himself. He says in *The Family of 'Imrān*, 'O Jesus [son of Mary]! Lo! I am gathering thee and causing thee to ascend unto me, and am cleansing thee of those who disbelieve and am setting those who follow thee above those who disbelieve until the day of resurrection'; he says in *The Cow*, 'And we gave unto Jesus, son of Mary, clear proofs, and we supported him with the Holy Spirit'; he also says in *Iron*, 'And we caused Jesus, son of Mary, to follow, and gave him the Gospel, and placed compassion and mercy in the hearts of

---

[14] Paul's *Letter*, § 10, quoting SS III: 55 and LVII: 27.

those who followed him. But monasticism they invented—we ordained it not for them—only seeking Allah's pleasure, and they observed it not with right observance. So we gave those of them who believe their reward';[15] and he also says in *The Family of 'Imrān*, 'Of the people of the Scripture there is a staunch community who recite the revelations of Allah in the night season, falling prostrate. They believe in Allah and the last day, and enjoin right conduct and forbid indecency, and vie with one another in good works. These are of the righteous'.[16]

The result here is that the focus remains on the person of Jesus, and any contention about his followers being Christians from the author's own time rather than Jesus' first followers before later distortions set in is avoided.

In the same way, when he comes to Paul's argument discussed above that the Qur'an extols the disciples, the editor restores the full text of S LVII: 25, which Paul altered to suit his purpose, and makes his point by means of another verse which he is able to quote without having to cut it:

And in *The Cow* he says, 'And Allah sent prophets as bearers of good tidings and as warners, and revealed therewith the scripture with the truth that it might judge between mankind concerning that wherein they differed', more or less meaning by his words his 'prophets, bearers of good tidings' the disciples, who spread through the seven regions of the world and proclaimed the one book, the holy Gospel. For if he had meant Abraham, David, Moses and Muḥammad he would have said, 'and with them the scriptures', because each of them brought a scripture different from others. But he only refers to the one scripture, which is the holy Gospel.[17]

He makes exactly the same point as Paul, but without violating the scriptural text, and therefore more eirenically and with greater prospect of success.

In conformity with this more conciliatory and persuasive approach, the editor excises completely Paul's exegesis of S II: 1-2 quoted above, that the letters Alif Lam Mim refer to *al-Masīḥ* and that *dhālika al-kitāb* must be the Gospel, and elsewhere omits some of Paul's more direct comments.[18] His most extensive re-editing is to §§ 33-42 of Paul's letter, in Paul's main explanation of the two natures of Christ. He

---

[15] The last clause of the verse, 'but many of them are evil-livers', is tacitly omitted.

[16] Pp. 63-5 below.

[17] P. 67 below.

[18] E.g. Paul's *Letter*, § 24, the last sentence beginning *wa-li-annā na'lamu*, an

removes completely Paul's attempt in §§ 33-5 at a reasoned justification for Christ being eternal Son of God and not separated from him
when he was incarnate, and for Mary's conception of him not being
carnal, moves §§ 36-8 and 40 to a later stage in the *Letter*, and removes
completely §§ 39 and 41-2, the metaphors Paul coins in order to show
how Christ could possess two natures. It is not that he disagrees with
Paul's line of thought, because he re-employs two sections from §§ 36-8
and 40 later on. Rather, his reason for removing that substantial block
of material must be that it is speculative and thus open to a range of
criticisms and counter arguments, and also that it is not directly based
on scripture, which as we shall see below is his primary concern in
the material he himself adds to Paul's letter. He appears intent on
gaining acceptance by the Muslims, rather than being rejected for
polemical contentiousness.

A last excision shows most clearly of all the editor's concern to tone
down Paul's acerbity and to make a sympathetic gesture towards his
Muslim readers. Paul's one justification for using only selected parts
of the Qur'an to make his case comes in §§ 45-8. Here he explains
rather tortuously that it is justifiable to use some parts and not others
because the situation is like a debtor who holds a cancelled bill of debt,
to whom his creditor comes and demands the payment on grounds
that even though the bill now bears the note of cancellation it still
carries the original statement of debt. Paul argues here by analogy that
the statements positive towards Christianity in the Qur'an which he
feels free to use cancel negative statements, and he goes on to quote a
number of these. But the editor cuts the whole section, apart from two
quotations in § 47 which refer to God recognising Christians above
unbelievers, S III: 55, and to Jesus as spirit and word of God, S IV:
171. Clearly, he thinks that omitting any defence of this procedure is
preferable to risking indignation among Muslim readers by hinting
that some parts of the Qur'an are more authentic than others, and that
Christians know what these are better than Muslims do themselves.

---

undisguised justification for not accepting Islam; § 29, the last sentence, in which
Paul implies that S II: 255, 'Allah, there is no god save he, the Alive, the Eternal',
with its threefold mention of God is a reference to the Trinity; § 31, S XL: 68, 'He
it is who quickeneth and giveth death. When he ordaineth a thing, He saith unto
it only: Be! And it is', which Paul reads as a reference to God possessing a Word,
ignoring such verses as SS III: 47 and XIX: 35, which talk of Jesus being created
by this same fiat; § 32, where Paul reads the opening *basmallah* of the Qur'an as an
affirmation of the Trinity.

In these instances where we see the Cypriot editor carefully removing parts of Paul's letter it is clear that he wishes to cut out passages that might disturb Muslim sensitivities and unduly increase indignation. He also seems to want to avoid arguments based solely on logic and reason, presumably because these could be countered in kind and cause further contention rather than accord.

Nevertheless, the editor supports Paul's general intention to show that Muslim scripture endorses Christian beliefs. But his approach has a different emphasis, which can be seen clearly from the alterations and additions he makes to Paul's text.

There are alterations to Paul's prose in all parts of the work, where the editor softens the original language, substitutes proof verses from the Qur'an that in his view better suit the argument, and generally presents a less combative approach than his predecessor, showing confidence in a sympathetic reception that Paul does not. A single example will illustrate this point.

When Paul summarises the miracles of Jesus referred to in the Qur'an he describes the miracle of the clay birds in subtly dualistic language: 'He made, 'amala, from clay the likeness of a bird and breathed into it and it flew by God's permission' (§ 9). This is close to the two versions in the Qur'an, SS III: 49 and V: 110, but it differs from both in one striking aspect, the substitution of the verb 'amala for the curious khalaqa, 'he created', in the sacred text. Paul might have been expected to favour a verb used elsewhere only of God, so he must have had a reason to change this. He does not give this, of course, but it could well be that he wanted to emphasise the close cooperation of the human and divine in this miracle, the human shaping the bird rather than creating it, and the divine causing it to fly in a miraculous manner. In fact, he may well be implying that it was accomplished by the divine and human natures of Christ acting in concert.[19]

The Cypriot editor will have none of this. He quotes the verse faithfully, reinstating khalaqa, and thereby sacrifices any opportunity to find tacit support in the Qur'an for Christian doctrines. But while he loses subtlety, he increases the chances of a sympathetic hearing.

The Cypriot's additions to Paul's original are extensive and increase its length considerably. But they are easy to account for since they nearly all comprise extra quotations from the Qur'an and two long

---

[19] Cf. Thomas, 'Paul of Antioch's *Letter*', pp. 210-11.

series of quotations from the Old Testament prophets. These betray the editor's intention more clearly than any other element in his rewriting of Paul's letter.

The starting point for these is the editor's amplification of Paul's argument in §§ 14-17. Paul shows by means of quotations that the Qur'an sanctioned the authority of the Torah and Gospel at the time it itself was revealed, and goes on to argue that their texts cannot have been corrupted since that time because they are widespread and in diverse languages. He offers further evidence that the Qur'an accepts the Bible, and finishes by showing that it is the Jews and not the Christians who are identified as unjust in what the Qur'an says. His whole argument is characteristically brief and to the point.

The Cypriot editor, however, adds a whole string of Qur'anic verses to the few that Paul gives to show that it accepts Christian scripture, and goes to some lengths to respond to the allegation that the Biblical texts may have been corrupted in the period since the Qur'an. In fact, he shows at this point uncharacteristic warmth of feeling:

> [The narrator] said to [the Cypriot experts]: What if someone should say that substitution and alteration could have taken place after this declaration? They said, We would be amazed at how these people, despite their knowledge, intelligence and perceptiveness, could confront us with such a remark. For if we were to argue with them in the same way, and say that they had made alterations and substitutions in the book which they possess today, and had written in it what they wanted and desired, would they tolerate our words?'[20]

And he proceeds to argue in detail that since the Biblical books are widespread in seventy-two languages it is quite impractical to think of anyone being able to have them changed. When he comes to Paul's comment about the Jews being unjust he fires off a second volley of verses from the Old Testament prophets that attest to their perfidy and abandonment by God.

In this amplification the editor preserves Paul's structure but adds many supporting verses from the Qur'an and Old Testament, and also adds detail to the point that the Bible has not been corrupted. This allows him later on to use Biblical proof-texts extensively, particularly in his amplification of Paul's § 36, where he employs them to prove the divinity of Christ and the Trinity, and also to explain why the Jews do not accept them despite knowing them.

---

[20] Pp. 71-3 below.

The editor evidently favours scriptural proofs as the most acceptable way of presenting and proving his case. And, having now established that the Biblical text has not been violated, he can legitimately use it as a strong source of argument. He clearly prefers it to Paul's logical proofs, since he habitually removes these or pares them down. The final result is that the *Letter* he prepares to be sent from Cyprus bases the claims for Christianity on firm scriptural foundations, Biblical and Qur'anic, and employs scripture with respect in its original form.[21] Considering the evident care with which the unknown editor made these various kinds of changes to Paul's letter and the purpose he had in mind, it should no longer be thought that the *Letter from the People of Cyprus* is little more than the result of light re-editing, as Erdmann Fritsch and Paul Khoury remark.[22] In fact, he deserves considerable respect for the efforts he made to find a way of attracting Muslims to some degree of agreement with Christians, while staunchly defending his own faith. The title 'editor' does him little justice.

It appears, then, that the Cypriot author hoped to receive a hearing not simply through the intellectual force of his arguments but through their persuasive appeal. This was his immediate design in altering Paul of Antioch's *Letter to a Muslim Friend* in the careful way that he did. But beneath this attempted eirenical surface lurks a deeper intention that links the Cypriot *Letter* with Paul's earlier composition in threatening the very validity of Islam. It is this that provoked the Damascus scholars to their impassioned refutations as they detected, in al-Dimashqī's words, 'a letter exemplary in politeness but alien in intention and shocking in purpose'[23] and that may link the Cypriot *Letter* with wider aspirations and strategies current at the time it was written.

This intention is expressed at the outset of the *Letter*, where the Cypriot experts with whom the author engages explain that although they have heard about Muḥammad and know that he claimed to come from God, they did not see any reason to doubt their own faith and follow him. Their central reason is that the Qur'an itself, as they read it, makes it clear that Muḥammad was not a universal prophet

---

[21] Cf. T. Michel, *A Muslim Theologian's Response to Christianity, Ibn Taymiyya's al-Jawab al-Sahih*, Delmar, New York, 1984, p.96.

[22] E. Fritsch, *Islam und Christentum im Mittelalter: Beiträge zur Geschichte der Muslimischen Polemik gegen das Christentum in arabischer Sprache*, Breslau, 1930, p. 30; Khoury, *Paul d'Antioche*, p. 10 n. 9.

[23] Al-Dimashqī's *Response*, § 3 below.

but one sent with a particularly Arabic message to the pagans among whom he lived.[24] In support of this they show in the rest of the *Letter* that Christianity is both endorsed by the Qur'an and demonstrably sound on both Biblical and rational grounds.

Although the author does not say so directly, the implication of this logic is that Muḥammad was no more than a local preacher, maybe sent with divine approval but directed only towards a particular pagan group in order to bring them the monotheistic rudiments of true religion. Furthermore, proper study of the book he gave them will point them towards Christianity and the fullness of truth to be found there. Islam is thus a kind of *praeparatio evangelica*, and far from Christians abandoning their faith to follow what came after, Muslims would be wise to move on from their faith in order to seek the complete truth.

With this deeper intention at its centre the *Letter* can thus be seen as an audacious, if conciliatory, effort to assert the proper relationship between Christianity and Islam, and to overturn the received wisdom of the day among Muslims and maybe some disheartened Eastern Christians.[25] It could be read by many of the latter as, in fact, an essay in theodicy in that it explains the origin and development of Islam as a divinely inspired movement to bring a particular people out of darkness and nearer the truth, while clearly confirming Christianity as the embodiment of that truth, attested even in the Qur'an itself. Thus, the *Letter* encourages Christians to adhere to their own faith despite the current supremacy of Islam and its continuing triumphs. As we have said, there is no explicit statement in the *Letter* to support this interpretation, but when we look at events in the eastern Medi-

---

[24] *The Letter from the People of Cyprus*, § ii below.

[25] It actually resumes attitudes that are detectable among Christians in early 'Abbasid times, particularly the anonymous authors of the Baḥīrā legend who portrayed the Christian monk's coaching of Muḥammad as intended to promote a simplified form of true faith among unlettered and unbelieving people (cf. Roggema, 'A Christian Reading of the Qur'an', pp. 57-73), and the Patriarch Timothy I who famously said in his dialogue with the Caliph al-Mahdī that Muḥammad 'walked in the path of the prophets' (on which cf. S.K. Samir, 'The Prophet Muḥammad as seen by Timothy I and some other Arab Christian Authors', in Thomas, *Syrian Christians*, pp. 91-106). Nearer in time is the observation by the pilgrim Burchard of Mount Zion, who wrote in 1283 that Muslims say Muḥammad 'was sent by God only to them (*ad se tantum a Deo missum*); I read this in the Alchoran, which is their book', *Descriptio Terrae Sanctae* § 15, ed. C.J. Lauren in *Perigrinationes medii aevi quatuor*, Leipzig, 1864 (ref. in J.V. Tolan, *Saracens, Islam in the Medieval European Imagination*, New York, 2002, pp. 208-9).

terranean around the time it was composed we see how this reading of the author's intention may be validated, and come to see why at this particular juncture he thought of redeploying Paul of Antioch's arguments of maybe a century earlier.

Christian fortunes in the Holy Land and Syria had taken severe blows in the latter decades of the seventh/thirteenth century. Under the leadership of the sultan al-Ẓāhir Baybars the Mamlūks had gradually brought back areas of Crusader possessions under Muslim rule, until in 690/1291 they took Acre and so ended Crusader claims upon the mainland. From this time Cyprus became a refuge for Christians who feared reprisals, and from the latter years of the seventh/thirteenth century it became the main Christian stronghold in the east. The enlargement of the Franciscan friary in Nicosia in 691/1292 to house refugees[26] is a single testimony to the influx experienced at this time, while slightly earlier the re-establishment on the island of monastic communities from Jerusalem and elsewhere[27] is indicative of the Christians' recognition of their failure. In succeeding decades nobles and religious invested their energies (and maybe sense of frustration) in building fortresses and monasteries throughout the island.

This reversal of military and territorial fortunes does not appear to have subdued the Christians' impulse to plan new expeditions to regain what had been lost, for a number of proposals for new crusading movements were put forward. It might be that despite visible failure many minds were encouraged by what appears to have been a widespread expectation that Islam was nearing extinction, and by the news that it was threatened by a powerful enemy from the east.

The expectation of the extinction of Islam is confidently expressed by a number of authors from the seventh/thirteenth century, as J.V. Tolan has shown.[28] William of Tripoli, for example, writing in 670/

---

[26] N. Coureas, *The Latin Church of Cyprus, 1195-1312*, Aldershot, 1997, p. 207. After withdrawing from the mainland following the sack of Acre, the Knights Hospitaller had by 1301 established new headquarters at Limassol, with a hospice and personal lodgings; A. Luttrell, 'The Hospitallers in Cyprus after 1291', *Acts of the I International Congress of Cypriot Studies, II. Nicosia, 1972*, pp. 161-71, repr. in A. Luttrell, *The Hospitallers in Cyprus, Rhodes, Greece and the West 1291-1440*, Aldershot, Hampshire, 1978, no. II; *idem*, 'The Hospitallers in Cyprus: 1310-1378', *Kypriakai Spoudai* 50, 1986, p. 155, repr. in A. Luttrell, *The Hospitallers of Rhodes and their Mediterranean World*, Aldershot, Hampshire, 1992, no. IX.

[27] Coureas, *Latin Church of Cyprus*, pp. 189-90. It may be significant that the monastery of St Paul of Antioch had settled monks in Cyprus before 1268, p. 187.

[28] Tolan, *Saracens*, pp. 203-9, 225-9. Cf. also F. Schmeider, '*Nota sectam maometicam*

1271, detects the overthrow of the Muslims in the Qur'an itself:

> It is written in their laws that the Romans or Latins shall be defeated by them, but that shortly thereafter they themselves will be defeated and destroyed; no one denies this. Thus they all predict, expect, and believe that the age of the Saracens must quickly end, while that of the Christians will last until the end of the world, which is coming.[29]

Just a little later in 672/1273 the author of the anonymous *De Statu Saracenorum* claims that Muḥammad himself had foretold that Islam would come to an end when the caliphate was overthrown, which, he points out, happened in 656/1258 with the sack of Baghdad.[30]

A few years earlier in 665/1267 the English Franciscan Roger Bacon characteristically based his prediction of the downfall of Islam on what he saw as scientific certainty:

> According to what Abū Maʿshar said in the seventh chapter of his second book, the law of Muhammad cannot last beyond 693 years ... And now it is the year of the Arabs 665 from the time of Muhammad [1267 CE], and therefore it will soon be destroyed by the grace of God, and this will be a great relief for Christians.[31]

Here the authority of the third/ninth century astronomer Abū Maʿshar Jaʿfar b. Muḥammad al-Balkhī (Albumasar) replaces that of the Qur'an, but the argument is the same as in the other two predictions: Muslim sources themselves declare the end of Islam.

The precise manner in which such ideas originated and found their way into Christian minds in the latter seventh/thirteenth century is not easy to trace. But it takes little imagination to see how they would comfort and encourage those who had suffered defeat at Muslim hands and to whom Islam might appear invincible and divinely commissioned. If they continued to circulate into the eighth/fourteenth century, they may have seemed for a time to be borne out by events that were

---

atterendam a tartaris et christianis, The Mongols as non-believing apocalyptic friends around the year 1260', *Journal of Millenial Studies* 1, 1998, pp. 1-11.

[29] William of Tripoli, *Notitia de Machometo*, ed. P. Engels (*Corpus Islamo-Christianorum, Series Latina*), Wurzburg, 1992, p. 260 § 15; trans. Tolan, *Saracens*, p. 204.

[30] *De Statu Saracenorum*, ed. Engels, *Notitia*, pp. 302-4 § 14 (this work was at one time attributed to William of Tripoli); Tolan, *Saracens*, pp. 204, 206-8. From this time dates the 'prophecy' of the Muslim 'son of Agap', who foresaw the downfall of Islam. This is contained in the *Rothelin* continuation of William of Tyre's *Historia Hierosolymitana*, trans. J. Shirley, *Crusader Syria in the Thirteenth Century*, Aldershot, 1999, pp. 29-33.

[31] Roger Bacon, *Opus Maius*, ed. J. Bridges, Oxford, 1897-1900, vol. I, p. 266; Tolan, *Saracens*, p. 228.

taking place in the east, where the Mongols loomed as a threat to Mamlūk survival.

The Mongols had been engaged in attacks on Muslim possessions in Syria for nearly fifty years before 700/1300,[32] and attempts had been made by Christian leaders to combine with them in a united front. This had never been realised, though again in 699/1299, 701/1301 and 703/1303, when they launched three fresh invasions, arrangements were made to send Crusader forces, but without successful coordination. Nevertheless, hopes for cooperation remained high, so much so that Mongol ambassadors made visits to the pope in 702/1302 and 704/1304. In 707/1307 the Knights Hospitaller suggested to Pope Clement V that a force should be stationed in Cyprus and Rhodes in readiness for an attack on Egypt in the event of a future Mongol invasion, a clear indication of the levels of expectancy in the early eighth/fourteenth century, and of the central role of Cyprus as a staging post.[33]

In defiant reaction to the Mamlūk successes of the latter seventh/thirteenth century and the Christian retreat from the mainland, a number of other plans were put forward for fresh invasions to retake what had returned into Muslim hands, many of them advocating Cyprus as the obvious point of launch. Thus, the Armenian John Hayton of Gorhigos in 707/1307 suggested an expedition via Cilicia, while in 711/1311 King Henry II of Cyprus advocated an attack on Egypt from his island,[34] and for years Pope Clement V (1305-14) encouraged plans for a full-scale crusade;[35] this was eventually launched in 710/1310 but achieved little.[36]

The repeated statements of intention to wrest back the Holy Land from Muslim possession, fuelled by grandiose designs to launch a concerted campaign with the Mongol power to remove Muslims once and for all, and rumours that the divinely decreed end of Islam was imminent, must all have been well known in Cyprus, and would

---

[32] Bacon, *Opus Maius*, *loc. cit.*; Tolan, *Saracens*, p. 229, expresses the hope that even before the predicted date of their downfall, 'the Saracens will be destroyed either by Tartars or by Christians'.

[33] P. Edbury, *The Kingdom of Cyprus and the Crusades, 1191-1374*, Cambridge, 1991, pp. 106-7.

[34] *Ibid.*, p. 106; J.R. Michot, *Ibn Taymiyya, Lettre à un roi croisé*, Louvain-la-Neuve and Lyons, 1995, introduction pp. 24-5, and n. 32 for further references to plans for attacks.

[35] Edbury, *The Kingdom of Cyprus*, p. 120.

[36] *Ibid.*, p. 123.

have been confirmed in part by the arrivals and departures of fighting men and fleets of ships.[37] In the atmosphere of buoyed-up hopes they must have created, it is not difficult to think of a scholar deciding to play his own small part, or being requested to, by writing about the superiority of Christianity over Islam, and the proofs to this effect that acute detection could discover in the Qur'an itself. This is the historical context in which the *Letter* was written, and one or more of its aspects may well be major influences behind the composition.

As we have said, the *Letter* contains no direct information or details that link it with anything in this wider context. All we know is that it was sent in one form to Ibn Taymiyya in 716/1316, and in a slightly different form to our author al-Dimashqī in 721/1321. Since it was clearly intended to provoke a response, it cannot have been written very long before it was sent off. Therefore, sometime around 715/1315 seems a reasonable date for its composition, slightly after all the events we have detailed above, but maybe close enough to them to have been influenced by all the confident hopes they evoked, and to have been written as a part of the effort to combat and contain Islam.

It has been suggested that the *Letter from the People of Cyprus* may have been prompted by Ibn Taymiyya's *Al-risālat al-Qubruṣiyya*, the letter he wrote to a Cypriot notable, Sire John, Lord of Gibelet, to vindicate his own faith and to ask for sympathetic treatment of Muslim prisoners on the island.[38] It is, indeed, attractive to think that the one letter resulted in the other, and if not it is strangely coincidental that the *Letter from the People of Cyprus* was first sent to the author of the *Risālat al-Qubruṣiyya*. However, it must be borne in mind that Ibn Taymiyya wrote his letter in 703/1304 at the latest, since his references to the Mongol ruler Ghāzān as though he was alive dictate a date of composition before his death in this year.[39] This separates the two letters

---

[37] Other examples of calls at this time for concerted efforts to recover the Holy Places could be multiplied. Three conveniently published together come from: Ramon Lull in his treatise *De fine* of 1305, in which he sets out his plan to establish academies for learning the oriental languages and for the nomination of a 'warrior-king' to coordinate the recovery effort; from Fulk of Villaret, Master of the Hospitallers, in a memorandum of *ca* 1305, in which he sets out a strategy for organising a crusading force like those of earlier times; and again from Ramon Lull in his *De acquisitione Terra Sanctae* of 1309, in which he advocates a two-pronged approach to the Holy Land through Constantinople and North Africa; all in N. Housley, *Documents on the Later Crusades, 1274-1580*, Basingstoke, Hampshire, 1996, pp. 35-49.

[38] Michot, *Ibn Taymiyya*, contains an edition and French translation.

[39] *Ibid.*, p. 91.

by at least ten years. Furthermore, the contents of the later letter do not correspond to the earlier, but arise almost entirely from Paul of Antioch's preceding composition. So, although it would seem natural to look for a link between the two this does not appear to be the case, and even T. Michel's suggestion that Ibn Taymiyya's *Risāla* established his connection with the court of Cyprus and may be the reason the *Letter from the People of Cyprus* was sent to him[40] is rather tenuous.

It seems we are on firmer ground if we look for the connection between Ibn Taymiyya and Cyprus not in the theologian's lobbying of a noble on the island but, strangely, in what the *Letter from the People of Cyprus* tells us about its author and his concerns. In the first place, it is important to note that this author read and wrote Arabic with ease, probably as his first language. Secondly, his knowledge of the Bible was of Arabic translations. And thirdly, he knew the Qur'an in its original form so well that he could correct Paul of Antioch's alterations, supply what his predecessor had omitted, and add his own quotations at will. These features would seem to indicate that the author was an Oriental Christian, a native Arabic speaker, who had immersed himself in the Qur'an; they also explain why he would know and be able to make ready use of Paul of Antioch's Arabic letter. Thus, the evidence from the text of the *Letter from the People of Cyprus* suggests that its author is more likely to have been an émigré to Cyprus from the eastern mainland than a native of the island, and suggests that he may have fled from his home when the Mamlūks dismantled the Crusader possessions and their religious institutions in the late seventh/thirteenth century. Was he, in fact, a convert from Islam? We could speculate and say that this would account for his thorough knowledge of the Qur'an, for his interest in showing how Islam is secondary to Christianity though with its own modest validity (and significantly not a heretical form or demonic innovation, as earlier Christian thinkers had judged), and also for his action of fleeing punishment for apostasy at home when Muslim rule was reimposed and he would have been left unprotected.

Whatever the case about conversion, if we accept that this Arabic-speaking Christian came from somewhere in the former Crusading possessions of Syria, then it is not difficult to understand why he would think of Ibn Taymiyya, the most renowned Muslim scholar of his day, as the obvious recipient of his composition. This accounts

---

[40] Michel, *A Muslim Theologian's Response to Christianity*, p. 78.

for the connection between the *Letter from the People of Cyprus* and the Damascus theologian, without any need to base a link on anything the Muslim had sent himself, or any reputation he may have left in Cyprus. Pursuing this thought further, the author's decision to send his *Letter* to al-Dimashqī, not so well known on a wide scale, may be explained by the local knowledge he possessed. And this would suggest that he came from near enough to Damascus to know who figured among its leading experts.

Summing up, the *Letter from the People of Cyprus* was written shortly before 716/1316 by a Christian who was at home in Arabic and knew the Qur'an intimately. He probably originated from Syria, showed his Melkite beliefs by accepting Paul of Antioch's Christology, and he wrote his *Letter* to demonstrate the supremacy of Christianity and the proofs in its favour given in the Qur'an. He wrote during a period of intense speculation about the demise of Islam, overthrown maybe by Christians and Mongols together, and of successive plans to send forces to recapture what Christians regarded as theirs. He might have written as part of the larger Crusading effort, in order to comfort and encourage fellow Christians in their alienated and dejected position, and to persuade Muslims that their scripture acknowledged the rightful place of Christianity.

The *Letter* itself, of course, contains little that will permit a firm decision about these suggestions, and substantially follows the argument of Paul of Antioch's *Letter to a Muslim Friend*, though with the changes we have noted above. It can be divided into eighteen linked sections. In the text and translation of the *Letter* presented later these are indicated by Roman numerals, as follows:

  i. Introduction: the author travels to Cyprus and converses with Christians there.
 ii. The scholars admit they have heard about Muḥammad and have read the Qur'an but concluded it was not intended for them but for the pagan Arabs.
iii. Furthermore, the Qur'an acknowledges that Mary was a virgin, and that Christ was divine,
 iv. and that he sent out disciples.
  v. It attests to the inspiration of the Gospel and other Christian scriptures,
 vi. and defends their integrity against accusations of corruption.
vii. It makes a distinction between Christians and Jews, as do the Old Testament prophets,

viii. and, together with the Old Testament, commends Christian worship including the eucharist.

ix. It makes clear that Muḥammad was not sent to the Christians.

x. The Trinity can be defended on both rational and scriptural grounds (Bible and Qur'an),

xi. and the Incarnation is supported by rational and copious scriptural proofs.

xii. The Jews were wrong to ignore the Old Testament prophecies about Christ.

xiii. The Old Testament supports the doctrine of the Trinity,

xiv. while both the Old Testament and the Qur'an support the doctrine of the Incarnation.

xv. The apparently anthropomorphic elements in Christian doctrine should be treated metaphorically, in the way that Muslims treat such elements in the Qur'an,

xvi. while it is philosophically valid to call God substance.

xvii. God's plan of revelation reaches its climax in Christ, as the Qur'an acknowledges, and there is no need of anything afterwards.

xviii. There is thus agreement in Christian and Muslim revelation, though if anyone differs let him speak out.

These eighteen sections fall into three main parts: 1. §§ i-ii, the setting of the Christians' defence, and explanation that the Qur'an is not directed at them; 2. §§ iii-ix, the main elements of Christian belief are confirmed by the Qur'an; 3. §§ x-xviii, the two major doctrines of the Trinity and Incarnation are attested by the Old Testament and Qur'an, as well as reason. Together, these build a tightly logical argument against abandoning Christianity, and in favour of its most contested doctrines. Starting from the claim that the Qur'an itself declares that Christians are not among those addressed by the teaching of Islam (§ ii), the argument moves on to show that the Qur'an itself endorses Christian beliefs (§§ iii-viii). Since these include the inspired and intact status of the Bible (§§ v-vii), which Christians interpret more correctly than the Jews, the Bible as well as the Qur'an can be employed as proof of the Christian case (§§ viii-ix). With this validation of Christian revelation, it defends the Trinity and Incarnation on scriptural and rational grounds (§§ x-xvi), and finally demonstrates that the appearance of Christ was the culmination of God's revelation, concluding that 'nothing can come after perfection and be superior' (§ xvii).

The key element in this argument is the proof that the Bible has not suffered corruption, and can thus be used as a support for the Christian case which both sides will accept. For, as we have said above, the author prefers to base his case on scriptural texts than on rational arguments, since the latter lack finality and lead to endless quibbles while the former, if authoritative, are final. This must be why in § vi, where the issue of the corruption of the text is raised, he comes as close as he ever does to abandoning his calm, controlled pose, and retorts with a direct rebuke to the Muslims if they ever made such an accusation: 'We would be amazed at how these people, despite their knowledge, intelligence and perceptiveness, could confront us with such a remark'. And in a series of rhetorical questions he proceeds to ask how all the widespread copies of the Bible, translated into seventy-two languages, could have been collected together and changed. The passionate note he strikes here betrays his dislike of any intimation that his cardinal source could in any way be impaired.

Here, then, is an exercise in persuasion, from which much of the acerbity and bright though brittle logic and Qur'anic juggling of Paul of Antioch's letter have been removed and replaced with a series of proof texts from the Bible and Qur'an, which are shown to be final authorities. In this toned down and strengthened form it was sent from Cyprus to Ibn Abī Ṭālib al-Dimashqī.

We should observe at this stage that the version of the *Letter* we have so far been considering differs in minor details from the version that al-Dimashqī quotes in his *Response*. The outlines and great majority of the arguments remain the same in both, but they differ at the beginning and end. At the beginning, the *Letter from the People of Cyprus* sets the scene with the writer's journey to the island and his meeting with the experts (§ i), while in his *Response* al-Dimashqī explains instead that a copy of the *Letter* was brought to him from the religious leaders of Cyprus by Kilyām the merchant (§ 3). After these different introductions, both versions agree in their main arguments until the end, where the two versions again differ considerably. Here the *Letter* contains two striking interpretations of Qur'anic verses that show the exaltedness of Christ (§ xvii, continuing from the references to God choosing Mary), which do not appear in al-Dimashqī's quoted version.

The change to the opening of the *Letter* can be explained by al-Dimashqī's explanation of how he came to receive it, on which we will say more below, and can hence be understood as his own intentional alteration. But his omission of the arguments at the end is uncharacteristic of an author who has picked up every point made by his correspondents so far, and not easily explicable in terms of his editorial judgement. When we consider that the version of the *Letter* which he quotes at this point preserves most of the parts in which the *Letter* itself agrees with Paul of Antioch's earlier version, we are caused to wonder whether the form in which the *Letter* was sent to al-Dimashqī did not contain these concluding interpretations of the Qur'an, but adhered more closely to Paul's underlying model.

This suspicion is supported by the evidence of MS P2, the version of the *Letter* which, according to its own witness, was sent to Ibn Taymiyya. This text begins in precisely the same way as P1, outlining the author's journey to Cyprus and his meeting with experts there (f. 48v). The two versions then substantially agree throughout, as far as the point at which al-Dimashqī's quotations of the *Letter* diverge from P1, where P2 preserves the same shorter form of the closing arguments as his. This agreement between al-Dimashqī and P2 against P1 at this point suggests strongly that the form in which the *Letter* was sent to the Damascus scholars did not include the long ending of P1. Incidentally, the agreement at the beginning of the *Letter* between P1 and P2 suggests that this account of the author's voyage to Cyprus was present in the version sent to al-Dimashqī, and that he excised it for his own reasons.

But how should the long ending of P1 be explained? It must either have been part of the original draft, or would have been inserted later after the two copies were sent to Damascus. The second alternative seems extremely unlikely, both because this ending is contained within two parts of the argument with which al-Dimashqī and P2 conclude rather being added to it, and because it is characterised by the same inventive exegesis of the Qur'an as the main body of the *Letter*. There seems no reason to think of it as an addition, and therefore we must assume that the author or whoever prepared the *Letter* for despatch in the two copies to Ibn Taymiyya and al-Dimashqī judged it advisable to omit these concluding points.

An examination of the arguments contained in the points suggests that if, as we have contended above, the Cypriot author was intent upon persuading his correspondents of the validity of his arguments, he would think twice before concluding with two exegetical exercises so obviously challenging to Muslims. In one he shows that when Jesus greeted himself in S XIX: 33, he was greeting the greatest being of whom he was aware, for otherwise he would have greeted that being, and hence he must be God himself; and in the other he intimates that if God made Mary and Jesus a sign to the worlds, S XIX: 91, then they must have outstripped other beings in rank (§ xvii). Both are individualistic interpretations that challenge anything a Muslim would construe in the verses, and they leave the impression that the author is attempting to tell Muslims how to read their own scripture, hardly the way to close a conciliatory and persuasive essay. So it would seem that while these innovative exegeses may have been part of the Cypriot author's original composition, they were excluded in the interests of the wider purpose of the *Letter*. In this carefully conceived form, it was then sent to Damascus.

Ibn Taymiyya received his copy in 716/1316, and responded with his voluminous *Al-jawāb al-ṣaḥīḥ li-man baddala dīn al-Masīḥ*. And in 721/1321 a second copy was sent to Shams al-Dīn Abū ʿAbdallāh Muḥammad Ibn Abī Ṭālib al-Anṣārī al-Ṣūfī al-Dimashqī. As he himself informs us, he received it on 10 Ṣafar 721/11 March 1321. He was only the second recipient of the *Letter*, as far as we know and to his own knowledge, since he mentions the single earlier version sent to his illustrious contemporary. He must thus have occupied a pre-eminent position in Damascus intellectual life, at least as far as the author in Cyprus knew. The question arises as to what singled him out for this attention.

Of course, we are unlikely ever to know the actual reason, though the elements of an answer are provided by someone who knew al-Dimashqī personally and wrote about him not long after his death. This is the biographer Ṣalāḥ al-Dīn Khalīl b. Aybak al-Ṣafadī (696/1297-764/1362), who in his *Al-wāfī bi-al-wafayāt* recalls how he spent long periods with al-Dimashqī in his home town of Ṣafad, where the latter was shaykh, and how he revised one of al-Dimashqī's poems at the author's request.[41] He also speaks in suggestive terms of al-Dimashqī's cleverness and omnivorous interests:

---

[41] Al-Ṣafadī, *Al-wāfī bi-al-wafayāt*, vol. III, ed. S. Dedering, Weisbaden, 1974, pp. 163-4. The author repeats this information in his later *Aʿyān al-ʿaṣr wa-aʿwān al-naṣr*, ed. ʿA. Abū Zayd *et al.*, Beirut/Damascus, 1998, vol. IV, pp. 475-80, which is longer than the entry in the *Wāfī* but does not differ from it materially except in the inclusion of some of al-Dimashqī's verses. The *Aʿyān* was evidently the basis of Ibn Ḥajar al-ʿAsqalānī's entry on al-Dimashqī in *Al-durar al-kāmina fī aʿyān al-miʾa al-thāmina*, Hyderabad, 1349, vol. III, pp. 458-9.

He was one of the cleverest people alive, *min adhkiyā' al-'ālam*, with the power to penetrate into every discipline and the boldness to write about every field. I have seen a number of writings of his, including diets and theology according to ways other than the I'tizāl, the Ashā'ira and the Hashwiyya, because he had no knowledge but was just clever. So on one day I found him following the views of the philosophers, on another I found him following the views of the Ashā'ira, on another those of the I'tizāl, on another those of the Hashwiyya, on another that of Ibn Sab'īn and imitating him.[42] He used to discourse on magic squares and wrote about them, he used to discourse on the arcana of the alphabet, and he had a thorough understanding of geomancy. He produced writings on everything about which he discoursed.[43]

Al-Ṣafadī goes on to talk about al-Dimashqī's poetic compositions, and about his claims to know alchemy. He observes, 'It seems that he understood what would outwit experts, and he could play with the minds of the inexperienced'.[44]

In this complimentary though not uncritical summary, al-Ṣafadī gives the impression of a sharp-minded enthusiast, eager to inquire into the branches of knowledge and known for his intellectual energy, though maybe lacking in true scholarly application and originality, and maybe something of a popularist. These characteristics are certainly evident in one of al-Dimashqī's earlier works, the *Kitāb al-maqāmāt al-falsafiyya wa-al-tarjamāt al-Ṣūfiyya*, dating from about 702/1302,[45] which comprises fifty sections devoted to a wide range of topics, including mathematics, theology, history and esoteric speculation (it is littered with diagrams, charts and maps). And they can also be witnessed in his *Nukhbat al-dahr fī 'ajā'ib al-barr wa-al-bahr*,[46] the geographical work in

---

[42] These represent a range of views, from the rationalism of the Mu'tazilites, through the theological traditionalism of the Ash'arites and the uncritical fideism of the Hashwiyya who accepted all that had been passed down from the time of Muhammad (on these cf. *Response* Section 13, n. 11), to the Aristotelian purism of the seventh/thirteenth century Andalusī philosopher Abū Muhammad 'Abd al-Haqq Ibn Sab'īn.

[43] Al-Ṣafadī, *Wāfī*, pp. 163.17-164.3. This is the basis of Khayr al-Dīn al-Ziriklī's comment in *Al-a'lām*, Beirut, 1999, vol. VI, p. 170, col. 3.

[44] Al-Ṣafadī, *Wāfī*, p. 164. 5-6.

[45] Cambridge University Library MS Qq: 19, unpublished. Its date can be deduced from the author's remark on f. 135r, at the end of a brief history, that with the departure of the Mamlūk Sultan Malik al-Nāṣir Muhammad b. al-Malik al-Manṣūr (second rule 698/1299-708/1309) from Damascus to Egypt in 702/1302, he has brought his account up to the present.

[46] Ed. A.F. Mehren, *Cosmographie de Chems-ed-Din Abou Abdallah Mohammad ed-Dimachqui*, St Petersburg, 1866; trans. Mehren, *Manuel de la Cosmographie du Moyen Age*, Copenhagen, 1874.

which he somewhat indiscriminately amasses details about the parts of the known world.[47] Such works reveal a diverse assortment of interests and knowledge presented one after another seemingly without a single direction. These characteristics are also clear in the *Response* we present here, where al-Dimashqī shows he is quite capable of marshalling a dizzying array of facts and references to combat the arguments of his Christian correspondents but, one often feels, without engaging with the intellectual points the Cypriot author presents for discussion. They are no more obvious than in the concluding Section 13, where, in an apparent attempt to correct the notion of divine indifference that is implicit in Ibn Sīnā's cosmology, he embarks upon an involved and inelegant philosophical proof to show God must be outside the contingent universe but still in touch with it. This is impressive in its show of philosophical awareness, but frequently lacking in cogency and sometimes in coherence of argument, the composition of an enthusiastic amateur but not a practised philosophical master.

Shows of brilliant information and clever learning would have made al-Dimashqī a most congenial companion and conversationalist—no wonder al-Ṣafadī says at the end of his account, 'He was cheerful in discourse and delightful on rare matters, and he shone out in cleverness'.[48] And they would undoubtedly bring him to the attention of people in Damascus and around. Hence, we might imagine that as a well-known intellect with a reputation for wide reading and writing, al-Dimashqī might strike anyone who was acquainted with the city as a suitable recipient of their *Letter*, and moreover someone who might be relied upon to respond.

For this reason, then, the *Letter* was sent to al-Dimashqī in his sixty-seventh/sixty-fifth year,[49] a man of standing among scholarly writers in his home city. He himself says that it was actually brought to him by a certain Kilyām (presumably Guillaume/William) whom he identifies as a merchant and *wazīr al-Marqab*, chamberlain of the 'Watch Tower'. He evidently knows this person since he asks the blessing of prolonged happiness upon him,[50] but despite mentioning him again

---

[47] D.M. Dunlop in *EI²*, art. 'Al-Dimashḳī', comments, 'Though the author's standpoint is conspicuously uncritical, his book contains a deal of information not to be found elsewhere.'

[48] Al-Ṣafadī, *Wāfī*, p. 164. 21-2.

[49] Al-Ṣafadī, *Aʿyān al-ʿaṣr*, vol, IV, p. 426 (repeated in Ibn Ḥajar, *Al-durar al-kāmina*, vol. III, p. 458) says he was born in 654/1256.

[50] Cf. *Response*, § 3 and n. 9.

several times in connection with quotations form the *Letter* he gives no more information about him except that he is a Christian,[51] and that he is a representative between the two sides.[52]

These references to this Kilyām are rather curious. In the first place, to identify him as a merchant at a time of frequent papal embargoes on trade between Christians and Muslims[53] suggests that he may have been something of a renegade, and a strange choice as courier of this *Letter*. And his identification as *wazīr al-Marqab* is extremely difficult to explain, given that the Hospitaller castle of al-Marqab/Margat had been captured by Muslims as long ago as 684/1295, thirty-five years before the *Letter* was sent.[54] Does this mean that he still retained the title as a sort of nickname from a position he had held many years previously, or could it mean that as a Christian he occupied a senior position in a sensitive Muslim stronghold? Neither seems likely.[55]

In the second place, al-Dimashqī makes Kilyām a participant in the debates that comprise the substance of the *Letter*. It will be recalled that the author frames the whole discourse by the Cypriot scholars within a narrative of a journey made by an unidentified individual, who recounts his visit and meeting in the first person. Even when the scholars take over and set out their arguments in detail he reappears from time to time to ask a question or briefly to put a point on behalf of the Muslims. We have no reason to suppose that the form of the *Letter* received by al-Dimashqī differed from this, since both MSS P1 and P2 preserve it. So it is a notable feature of his quotations in the *Response* that he substitutes Kilyām for the unnamed narrator and alters the grammar in order to accommodate him. Kilyām'a first appearance is the most telling: in place of the *Letter's* 'I said to them, What if someone should say...?', the *Response* has, 'Someone said to you in

---

[51] *Ibid.*, § 86, where Kilyām says to the Christian experts, 'They [the Muslims] criticise us...', indicating that he numbered himself among the Christians.

[52] *Ibid.*, § 59, where he represents Muslim views to the Christians, and § 90, where al-Dimashqī refers to him as a *safīr*, mediator, for the purpose of obtaining a reply to the Christians' *Letter*.

[53] Edbury, *Kingdom of Cyprus*, pp. 121, 139-40, 150.

[54] Cf. *Response*, Introduction n. 9.

[55] In the Arabic text of a treaty of 669/1271 between the Mamlūk Sultan al-Ẓāhir Baybars and the Hospitallers, the *wuzarā'*, 'ministers', are listed among officials from al-Marqab; cf. P. Holt, *Early Mamluk Diplomacy (1260-1290), Treaties of Baybars and Qalāwūn with Christian Rulers*, Leiden, 1995, p. 51: 'the Brethren, the knights, the ministers, the clerks, the representatives...'.

the presence of Kilyām, What if someone should say…?'.[56] Here and elsewhere[57] this merchant is portrayed not just as the messenger who brought the *Letter* to Damascus, but as the witness of the Christians' account of their reasons for not accepting Islam, and as the nearest to the author of the *Letter* itself.

Part of the reason for this change in the dramatic framework of the *Letter* is that al-Dimashqī omits entirely the introductory narrative in which the author gives his reason for going to Cyprus and meeting the Christian experts. Instead, he more directly tells how he received the *Letter* from 'the bishops and patriarchs, priests and monks, the foremost in the faith of Christ and leaders of the community of Jesus'[58] who had sent it via Kilyām. In the absence of the explanation given in this narrative the sudden appearance from time to time of an anonymous individual speaking in the first person would be jarring, and so al-Dimashqī makes the changes that turn Kilyām from messenger into participant and maybe author. But if he could do this, it is equally possible for him to have invented the person of Kilyām altogether, giving him the intriguing identity of merchant and castle 'minister'. He gives just enough verisimilitude to the character to leave the impression of reality, though the traces of his reworking keep alive the suspicion that the character was part of his literary reframing of the background of the *Letter*, maybe in order to give it more immediacy and therefore impact.

In accordance with his stated intention to answer the *Letter* in detail, al-Dimashqī divides it into a number of parts,[59] which he answers in thirteen sections, prefaced by a short introduction. His *Response* thus loosely follows the given structure of the *Letter from the People of Cyprus*, and ultimately of Paul's *Letter to a Muslim Friend*, though with a vast range of additional arguments and details that make his work an important source of Muslim attitudes towards Christianity at this time, and even more of knowledge of Christian doctrines, popular beliefs and the suppositions Christians had about them. They can be summarised as follows:

---

[56] Cf. *Letter*, § vii and *Response*, § 42 below.
[57] *Letter*, § x and *Response*, § 59; *Letter*, § xii and *Response*, § 69; *Letter*, § xv and *Response*, § 82.
[58] *Response*, § 3.
[59] *Ibid.*, § 4.

1. Introduction, §§ 1-4: al-Dimashqī received the *Letter* through Kilyām in 721, and saw that its senders were inviting a polemical reply.

2. Section 1, §§ 5-34: The Christians begin by saying there is no requirement on them to follow Muḥammad because the Qur'an explicitly states he was sent to the pagan Arabs alone (§ 5). *But* to start, the Cypriots have been impolite in the way they refer to Muḥammad (§ 6), and also wrong in their claim that he came without any earlier announcement. There are seven references to him in the Torah and Gospel (§§ 7-8), as well as in other Old Testament books (§§ 9-10), and among events that happened before and around the time of his coming, such as predictions by Daniel (§ 11), the expectation of his coming among the Sicilians (§ 12), Baḥīrā (§ 13), the inhabitants of Jerusalem (§ 14), and the Arab soothsayer Sawād Ibn Qārib (§ 15). Moreover, the first Christians waited for his coming to rebuke the world, and though at the time of Constantine the texts on which they based their hopes were given a mistaken interpretation (§§ 16-17), the various forms of rebuke in the Qur'an fulfil the initial expectation, particularly against the Christians who make Christ divine and the Jews who deny Muḥammad (§§ 18-22). Eight additional illustrations support his authenticity and the truth of what the Qur'an teaches, and prove that the Cypriots should follow him (§§ 23-33). And lastly, they have misinterpreted verses from the Qur'an which they cite in support of their case (§ 34).

3. Section 2, §§ 35-7: The Christians say the Qur'an extols Christ, Mary and the Gospels (§ 35). *But* the Cypriots are obstinate in refusing to follow Muḥammad, despite acknowledging the Qur'an (§ 36), for its contents show that he was sent to the whole world and that it is addressed to all people (§ 37).

4. Section 3, §§ 38-41: *Furthermore*, the Qur'an contains teachings that meet all situations (§ 38). By comparison the Torah has not been preserved intact (§ 39), while the Gospel has been transmitted in four differing versions (§ 40). The Qur'an was sent to correct the errors that have crept in (§ 41).

5. Section 4, §§ 42-7: The Christians cite verses which show that the Qur'an recognises the soundness of the Gospel and that it has not been corrupted, and argue that the Gospel is so widespread that it could not practically have been falsified (§ 42). *But* they misinterpret these verses, and they also know that the historical

Gospels are accounts written down after the time of Jesus (§ 43), when later Christians supplemented the Gospel teachings with rules about worship and living (§§ 44-5). Their claim that the Qur'an acknowledges the Gospel is false, as proper interpretation of the verses cited by the Christians shows (§ 46), and their claim that it is so widespread it cannot have been falsified is misdirected because until the time of Constantine it only existed in four versions (§ 47).

6. Section 5, §§ 48-58: The Christians say the Qur'an explicitly acknowledges them, and condemns the Jews in the same way that the prophets of the Old Testament did. The Qur'an also recognises Christian worship, as do the prophets, and also emphasises that Christians are accepted by God (§§ 48-9). *But* they are wrong in the interpretations they put on the verses they employ (§§ 50-2), and they must realise that they are guilty of polytheism (§ 53). The verses of the Qur'an they use in favour of themselves do not mean what they say, for reasons that can clearly be shown (§§ 54-5). And in particular their claim that the Qur'an refers to the disciples being sent out by Jesus is entirely wrong; it refers to the sending of prophets, which can be shown on grounds of reason to be necessary as guidance for humanity (§§ 56-7). In making this mistake the Christians are only adding to the many errors they commit in their doctrines, particularly the Trinity (§ 58).

7. Section 6, §§ 59-65: The Christians prove the doctrine of the Trinity by reason and by the Bible and the Qur'an (§ 59). *But* this is a wrong use of reason (§§ 60-2), especially when they make Christ divine, misunderstanding for divinity the tokens of esteem accorded to him as to other prophets (§ 63), and ignoring his many human traits (§ 64). The doctrine of the Incarnation is simple falsehood (§ 65).

8. Section 7, §§ 66-8: The Christians argue that the Incarnation of God's Word was his supreme act of communication with his creatures; the Old Testament prophets foretold his coming (§ 66). *But* only the Christians understand the prophets in this way, for the Jews disagree with them (§ 67), while the Muslims dismiss these interpretations as untrustworthy both scripturally and rationally (§ 68).

9. Section 8, §§ 69-77: The Christians say that although the Jews know of the prophecies about Jesus they reject them, because they wrongly look for the Messiah who is yet to come. God has

made it clear in the Old Testament that he is Trinitarian in nature, although the Jews reject the teachings they find there (§§ 69-70). *But* the Christians should not read these teachings literally (§ 71). A previous debater showed the lack of logic in saying Christ was divine, pointed out the contradictions between the Gospels and Creed (§ 72), compared Christ's miracles with those of other prophets to show they did not signal his divinity (§ 73), and pointed out the inconsistencies in a number of Christian doctrines, particularly in the very human Jesus, as the Gospels declare, being divine (§§ 74-5). It may be added to these earlier arguments that Paul came years after Christ and introduced many distortions, and there are later distortions as well (§§ 76-7).

10. Section 9, §§ 78-81: The Christians say that they base their doctrines of the Trinity and Incarnation upon the Old Testament, and that they are logically coherent and supported by the Qur'an (§ 78). *But* they are mistaken in both logical and scriptural inference (§ 79). Furthermore, they resemble the dualists in identifying two gods, one of whom was captured by Satan and killed (§ 80), and are philosophically incoherent in teaching about the uniting of the spiritual and physical in the Incarnation (§ 81).

11. Section 10, §§ 82-5: The Christians claim that their language about three Persons is metaphorical, just like apparently anthropomorphic references to God in the Qur'an (§ 82). *But* the doctrine of the Trinity has always been acknowledged by Christians as belief in three individuals (§ 83), although it is beyond question that Christ himself did not teach it and it was only introduced when the Gospels were circulated under Constantine (§ 84). On the other hand, the Qur'an when interpreted according to its main teachings speaks of the purest monotheism (§ 85).

12. Section 11, §§ 86-7: The Christians justify their calling God substance in theological terms (§ 86). But God is unlike other entities, and cannot be compared with substances or any other things in the contingent order (§ 87).

13. Section 12, §§ 88-9: The Christians say that after the first law of justice sent with Moses, the second law of grace was brought by the most perfect being, God's Word. After this perfect communication there was no need of anything further (§ 88). *But* this is wrong, for the two laws from God are of his will, which establishes the ways of the universe and of humankind, and of his command, which was brought by the prophets as a way for humankind to follow (§ 89).

14. Section 13, §§ 90-100: Still on the issue of there being no need for a messenger after Christ, the latter was sent to end the errors of his time although various groups misunderstood his significance and drew wrong conclusions about him (§§ 90-2). The truth that was brought later by Muḥammad, when expressed theologically and philosophically, states that God is entirely distinct from the contingent universe (§ 93), but is nevertheless the origin of all that exists (§ 94-5). He surrounds the universe, but is not affected in any way by it although he is not remote from what occurs within it (§§ 96-9). To conclude, the Christians should try to understand these arguments and not presume to teach the Muslims about truth (§ 100).

Al-Dimashqī's replies in these thirteen sections to the points made in the *Letter from the People of Cyprus* include a huge range of arguments, from reinterpretations of verses employed by the Cypriot author and demonstrations of the incoherence of his doctrines when seen in the light of monotheism, to poetry, proofs from popular piety, and stories and anecdotes that probably only ever held oral currency. His approach is not forensic in weighing arguments and judging their merits and disadvantages, but plainly polemical in revealing the possible danger in a point and marshalling all available resources to quash it. Thus, he never acknowledges any element of validity in the case his correspondent makes, but consistently rejects every one of the carefully framed arguments he encounters.

The Cypriot author could have wished for a less brutal reception. But here he found a Muslim who was incensed at the implied threats his *Letter* posed to Islam by diminishing the universal status of the Prophet and obscuring the distinctive nature of God in Trinitarian and Incarnational relationships, and was not prepared to concede the least credibility to his attempts to validate Christianity in Islamic terms. Al-Dimashqī responds with passion and rhetorical vehemence to what the Cypriot might have hoped would be considered with sympathy and measured patience. But, as T. Michel observes, he is not 'a theologian responding carefully to the adversaries' theologians; rather his perspective is that of a *khaṭīb* defending the truth of Islām from deviant challenges he has encountered in Christianity'.[60] And

---

[60] T. Michel, 'Ibn Taymiyya's *Al-Jawāb al-Ṣaḥīḥ*, a Muslim Theologian's Response

as such he employs the points and arguments that will bring down condemnation and ridicule upon his opponents, rather than those that might patiently convince them to revise their beliefs.

Al-Dimashqī composed his *Response* to the *Letter from the People of Cyprus* between Ṣafar II/March and Jumādā II/June 721/1321,[61] less than four months. The evident speed with which he completed it is suggestive of his indignation, and it maybe affected the precision of his argument in places, producing frequent anecdotal accumulations that cloud the central points, and the presence of some material that seems only marginally relevant. In such circumstances it is too much to hope for any references to sources, and nowhere in the *Response* is any mentioned. Comparison with earlier works in the genre shows that al-Dimashqī was fully abreast of many of the familiar arguments that had been used by Muslims against Christians in earlier centuries, though his indebtedness to any particular authorities cannot be ascertained. One is caused to wonder, however, whether he did expressly consult any written sources, rather than relying upon memory and hearsay. For nowhere does he give any indication of closely following arguments in a text he may have before him, but generally gives the impression of casually mentioning points as they occur to him and as they suit his argument. This is clearly evident in his references to Christian history and worship.

From early Christian history al-Dimashqī frequently mentions Paul and others, and he is firmly under the impression that Paul and Peter lived about 150 years after Christ.[62] On the other hand, he says that the emperor Constantine lived only about a 100 years after Christ.[63] He may not have known differently (though one would imagine he was aware that Peter was a disciple), but his mention of Paul burying the true cross for Constantine's mother to discover,[64] which is impossible according to this chronology, betrays simple carelessness. His close knowledge of Christian worship, however, contrasts with this. For not only can he talk movingly about the effects of the organ music played

---

to Christianity', PhD Dissertation, Chicago, 1978, p. 258. This is substantially the translation that Michel published under the title *A Muslim Theologian's Response to Christianity* in 1984, though it includes an examination of al-Dimashqī's *Response* which does not appear in the published work.

[61] Cf. *Response*, § 1.
[62] *Ibid.*, § 76.
[63] *Ibid.*, §§ 16, 47.
[64] *Ibid.*, § 76.

in Christian services,[65] but he can also recall word for word the prayers that are recited on specific festivals.[66] He evidently has no trouble remembering what he has almost certainly witnessed at first hand, but is less consistent when he has to remember facts he has come across at some time in books or by other second hand means.

Although it bears such signs of hasty composition as these, and also lack of care over details and traces of intemperateness, al-Dimashqī's *Response* is a document of considerable value for what it can tell about Muslim attitudes towards Christianity, and the factual basis that supported them, in the latter period of the Crusades.[67] It shows that Muslim minds had built up a considerable degree and range of knowledge about many aspects of this other faith, Biblical, historical and ecclesiastical, and had constructed systematic understandings of why Christians believed what they did and worshipped as they did. But everything was seen through the lens of the Qur'an and the absolute monotheism it focuses, so that Christian beliefs and practices were judged as deficient or deviant in accordance with the degree to which they diverged from this norm, rather than being appreciated for what they may have been in themselves. Another example well illustrates this point.

Al-Dimashqī is fully cognisant of the doctrines of the Incarnation and atonement, but in a form that pays little attention to their Christian versions or the beliefs they express. Thus he presents the account of the descent of the Word and the death of Jesus in a dualist form in which the god of heaven is powerless to prevent the god of the earth from seizing the Word incarnate and having him executed, explaining it as a belief derived from Ṣābianism.[68] In this way he can demonstrate that the original pure teachings of the faith have become corrupted under malign alien influence, as normative Muslim belief had long held, and avoid encounter with Christian concerns about sin or the need for redemption. His main emphasis remains firmly fixed on the difference between this strange belief and Qur'anic monotheism,

---

[65] *Ibid.*, § 45.

[66] *Ibid.*, §§ 20, 77.

[67] Michel, 'Ibn Taymiyya's *Jawāb*', p. 267, notes that many of the points included by Ibn Taymiyya in his reply are also present in al-Dimashqī's work, indicating that they 'were part of the body of polemical material known by learned *'ulamā'* of the day'.

[68] *Response*, §§ 31-2, 80.

and his interest extends only to the point where it departs from this unimpeachable source of truth.

The inflexible attitude al-Dimashqī shows here, of judging Christian beliefs according to his own Islamic norms, is typical of polemic from the earliest times, when, for example, we find the third/ninth century convert ʿAlī al-Ṭabarī presenting twelve principles about God with which he says both Muslims and Christians agree, that are patently Islamic,[69] or his contemporary the independently-minded theologian Abū ʿĪsā al-Warrāq similarly judging the doctrines of the Trinity and Incarnation according to strict monotheistic criteria that are not only compatible with Islam but ultimately derived from it.[70] Neither of these appears to understand Christianity in its own terms, and al-Dimashqī does not differ from them, though it must be acknowledged that in an atmosphere as patently hostile between the faiths as that in which he lived, and in a response to a systematic Christianisation of the Qurʾan, it would be almost a miracle if he showed more understanding than he does.

The *Letter to the People of Cyprus* then ranks alongside many other documents of Muslim and Christian origin from the early centuries of Islam in which vehement dislike and the intention to disparage and disprove are uppermost. However, it stands out among them for its length, and for the wide range of material it draws into its defences and proofs. While it lacks the theological mastery of the supreme examples of this genre, it is hardly rivalled for its verve and profuseness, and for the picture it gives of inter-religious attitudes at a time when enmity was hotter than almost any other.

A last word concerns the outcome of this *Response*, and of the protracted correspondence begun a century earlier by Paul of Antioch. But there is little to say. We do not know whether al-Dimashqī's reply to the *Letter from the People of Cyprus* ever reached the island, or indeed whether it was ever sent from Damascus. And we do not know whether it ever reached a substantial audience at all, either Muslim or Christian,

---

[69] ʿAlī al-Ṭabarī, *Al-radd ʿalā al-Naṣārā*, ed. I.-A. Khalifé and W. Kutsch, 'Ar-Radd ʿalā-n-Naṣārā de ʿAlī aṭ-Ṭabarī', *Mélanges de l'Université Saint Joseph* 36, 1959, pp. 128.19-129.2; trans. J.-M. Gaudeul, *Riposte aux Chrétiens par ʿAlī al-Ṭabarī*, Rome, 1995, pp.18-19.

[70] Abū ʿĪsā al-Warrāq, *Al-radd ʿalā al-thalāth firaq min al-Naṣārā*, ed. D. Thomas, *Anti-Christian Polemic in Early Islam, Abū ʿĪsā al-Warrāq's 'Against the Trinity'*, Cambridge, 1992, and D. Thomas, *Early Muslim Polemic against Christianity, Abū ʿĪsā al-Warrāq's 'Against the Incarnation'*, Cambridge, 2002, *passim*.

though the evidence of a single manuscript copy surviving from 772/
1370, about fifty years after the original composition, together with a
slavish copy of this actual version made many centuries afterwards, is
not suggestive of wide dissemination. So the unfortunate conclusion
could well be that all this effort was for little or nothing in the long
run. The sad fact remains that the misconceived Cypriot enterprise
to Christianise the Qur'an provoked al-Dimashqī to articulate Muslim
sentiments that had persisted for centuries. The lesson to be learnt is
that the correspondence betrays attitudes that were not at all atypical
of the times. The challenge it presents is to renounce them.

THE MANUSCRIPTS OF THE LETTERS

(i) *The Letter from the People of Cyprus*

The Arabic text containing the *Letter from the People of Cyprus* published here is taken from an eighth/fourteenth century manuscript preserved in the collection of Christian Arabic manuscripts in the Bibliothèque Nationale, MS Arabe 204[1] [hereafter = P1]. The manuscript in total comprises a number of pieces of varying content written in Arabic— polemical treatises, homilies and theological expositions.

P1 consists of 68 folios, some of which are mutilated or left blank (e.g. ff. 67-8). It was copied by the priest Ṣalībā Ibn Yuḥannā al-Mawṣilī in Famagusta, Cyprus, in A.G. 1647 = A.D. 1336 = A.H. 737. The part of the manuscript which comprises our *Letter* consists of ff. 49v–66r, written in a form of *ruqʿa* script in black ink, with headings and names of Sūras in red.

Incipit:

بسم الله الحيّ المحيي القديم الأزلي.أمّا بعد الذي يعلم مولانا الشيخ المكرّم الرئيس السيّد الفاضل الأوحد النفيس أطال الله في أتـمّ النعم بقاءه وحرسه من الأسواء وتولاه. سألتني أن أفحص لك فحصًا بينًا ما يعتقده النصارى المسيحيين.(*sic*)

Explicit:

فقد سألوني ذلك وجعلوني سفيرًا. والحمد لله ربّ العالمين.

This is followed by the colophon on f. 66v, which states the name of the scribe and date and place of writing. It reads:

لخّص هذه الرسالة وصحّحها أضعف عباد الله وأحوجهم إلى رحمته صليبا بن يوحنا القسّ الموصلي .بمحروسة مدينة الماغوصة من أعمال جزيرة قبرس حماها الله تعالى، ووافق الفراغ في العشر الأوسط من شهر آب سنة ألف وستماية وسبعة وأربعين

---

[1] G. Troupeau, *Catalogue des manuscrits Arabes*, Pt. 1 (manuscrits chrétiens). Tome 1, Paris, 1972, pp. 172-3.

لتاريخ الإسكندر اليوناني الموافق لسنة ألف وثلثماية وستة وثلاثين مسيحية المجانس
للمحرّم سنة سبعماية وسبعة وثلاثين هلالية. رحم مَن نظر فيه ودعا له بالمغفرة
وأصلح ما وجد من الزلل والخلل.

Two other versions of the *Letter* have survived in the same Bibliothèque
Nationale collection of Christian Arabic manuscripts, MS Arabe 214
and MS Arabe 215. Both these manuscripts are described by Troupeau in his *Catalogue*.[2]

MS Arabe 214 [hereafter = P2] comprises a number of pieces of
varying content written in Arabic—theological treatises and commentaries, polemical letters, extracts from various authors, etc. It consists
of 262 folios and was copied by Jirjis al-Ifranjī for Yuḥannā Ibn Isḥāq
al-Batanūnī in A.D. 1538. The portion which contains our *Letter* consists
of ff. 48r–65r, written in an oriental (Egyptian) script in black ink.

Incipit:

بسم الاب والابن والروح القدس اله واحد . نبتدي بعون الله تعالى وحسن توفيقه
بنسخ الرسالة التي وردت من جزيرة قبرص إلى الشيخ الفاضل تقي الدين ابن التيمية
بدمشق المحروسة. قال الذي يعلم به مولاي الشيخ الرئيس الفاضل الأوحد النفيس
أطال الله في أتم النعم بقاءه وحرسه من الاسواء وتولاه ...

Explicit:

فقد سألوني ذلك وجعلوني سفيرًا ومواسطًا فيه. و الحمد لله رب العالمين. تمت الرسالة
الذي (sic) حضرت من قبرص وجزاير البحر المحيط بمعونة الله تعالى.

MS Arabe 215 [hereafter = P3] also comprises a number of pieces of
varying content written in Arabic, including *inter alia* some anonymous
theological treatises and extracts from various authors. It consists of
262 folios and was copied by an anonymous scribe in A.M. 1306/1307
= A.D. 1590/1591. The part of the manuscript which comprises the
text of our *Letter* consists of ff. 203r–223r,[3] written in an oriental
(Egyptian) script in black ink.

---

[2] *Ibid.*, pp. 185-9.
[3] Troupeau, p. 188, is mistaken in stating that the *Letter* is contained in ff. 203-28.
In fact it ends on f. 223r and is followed by an extract on ff. 223r–228r from various
ancient philosophers, the *incipit* of which reads:

Incipit:

بسم الله الخالق الحي الناطق علينا رحمته آمين. نبتدي بعون الله وحسن ارشاده بكتب
نسخة الرسالة التي وردت من جزيرة قبرس إلى الشيخ الإمام تقي الدين ابن التيمية
بمدينة دمشق المحروسة في شهور سنة ستة عشر وسبع ماية العربية ولله المجد إلى
الأبد آمين.

Explicit:

فقد سألوني ذلك وجعلوني سفيرًا ومواسطًا. تمت الرسالة والمجد لله رب العالمين.

All variant readings, excluding minor orthographic readings, in P2
and P3 have been included in the critical apparatus of our edition
of the text of the *Letter*. Furthermore, we reproduce here, in parallel
columns, the text of Paul of Antioch's letter, as published by Paul
Khoury.[4]

(ii) *Al-Dimashqī's Response*

The Author

As we said in the previous chapter, Shams al-Dīn Muḥammad Ibn
Abī Ṭālib al-Anṣārī al-Ṣūfī al-Dimashqī was born in Damascus in
654/1256 and died in Ṣafad in 727/1327.[5] He was *shaykh* and *imām*

الذي وجد من أقوال الحكماء الفلاسفة القدماء من الألفاظ المطابقة لاقوال الأنبياء على ورود
السيد المسيح وتجسده وتصرفه في العالم وولادته (وولاده :MS) من السيدة الطاهرة العذرى
البتول.

Its *explicit* reads:

... هذا الذي يكون في منتهى الدهر آمين . والسبح لله دائمًا أبدًا

This colophon follows:

كمل هذا الكتاب المبارك يوم الخميس المبارك ثالث عشر شهر توت المبارك من شهور سنة ألف
وثلثماية وسبعة للشهداء الأطهار ، رزقنا الله بركتهم. آمين آمين آمين .

[4] Khoury, *Paul d'Antioche*, pp. 59-83.
[5] For an account of al-Dimashqī's life and works cf. D.M. Dunlop, art. "Al-
Dimashḳī", *EI²*, vol. II, p. 291; C. Brockelmann, *Geschichte der arabischen Literatur*,
Berlin, 1902, vol. II, p. 130, Supplement Band II, Leiden, 1938, p. 161; Khayr
al-Dīn al-Ziriklī, *Al-aʿlām*, Cairo, 1956, vol. VII, p. 40; M. Kurd ʿAlī, *Kunūz al-ajdād*,
Damascus, 1950, pp. 350-9; Ṣalāḥ al-Dīn al-Ṣafadī, *Al-wāfī bi-al-wafayāt*, vol. III,

at al-Rabwa, which is described by Ibn Baṭṭūṭa as a pleasant locality near Damascus. He is credited with the authorship of a number of unpublished legal works, several Ṣūfī treatises, and a geographical work, *Nukhbat al-dahr fī ʿajāʾib al-barr wa-al-baḥr*, for which he was best known. He became deaf ten years before his death.

The Jawāb

In addition to the above mentioned works, al-Dimashqī wrote a *Response* to the *Letter* sent to him by the Christians of Cyprus, entitled *Jawāb risālat ahl jazīrat Qubruṣ* [hereafter = *Jawāb*]. This work has survived in two manuscripts, Utrecht Codex No. 40 [1449], preserved in the University Library, Utrecht, The Netherlands [hereafter = A][6] and MS Marsh 40 [Uri Arab. Moh. 124(2)], preserved in the Bodleian Library, Oxford [hereafter = B].[7] The first, which is dated 772/1370, less than half a century after the death of its author, contains 214 pages (107 folios), while the Oxford manuscript consists of 255 folios and is dated A.D. 1645. We recently identified and discovered the Oxford manuscript in the course of searching for other copies of the work. It had been wrongly attributed to the copyist Abū Bakr Raʿūd al-Trūḥī by M. Steinschneider in his *Polemische und apologetische Literatur in arabischer Sprache*.[8]

Folio 1r of the Utrecht manuscript contains information regarding

---

Damascus, 1953, pp. 163-5; Ibn Ḥajar al-ʿAsqalānī, *Al-durar al-kāmina fī aʿyān al-miʾa al-thāmina*, Hyderabad, A.H. 1349, vol. III, pp. 458-9.

[6] This manuscript was bought by Christianus Ravinus, chronographer and professor of philosophy, in Constantinople in A.D. 1640; cf. M.J. de Goeje, *Catalogus Codicum Orientalium Bibliothecae Academiae Lugduno–Batavae*, vol. V, Leiden, 1873, p. 273; P. Tiele and A. Hulshof, *Catalogus Codicum Manu Scriptorum Bibliothecae Universitatis Rheno-Trajectinae*, Leiden, 1887, pp. 341-2; cf. P. de Jong, "Een arabisch Handschrift, behelzende eene Bestrijding van 't Christendom", *Verslagen en Mededeelingen der Koninklijke Akademie van Wetenschappen*, Afdeeling Letterkunde, Tweede Reeks, Achtste Deel, Amsterdam, 1878, pp. 232-3.

[7] J. Uri, *Bibliothecae Bodleianae Codicum Manuscriptorum Orientalium*, Oxford, 1787, Pt. 1, p. 62; A. Nicoll, *Catalogi Codicum Manuscriptorum Orientalium Bibliothecae Bodleianae pars secunda*, Oxford, 1835, p. 569.

[8] *Polemische und apologetische Literatur in arabischer Sprache, zwischen Muslimen, Christen und Juden nebst Anhangen verwandten Inhalts* (*Abhandlungen für die Kunde des Morgenlandes* 6, no. 3), Leipzig, 1877, p. 42. For a preliminary study of this work and these two manuscripts, cf. R. Ebied, 'Inter-religious attitudes: al-Dimashqi's (d. 727/1327) *Letter to the People of Cyprus*', *ARAM* (The Mamluks and the early Ottoman Period in Bilad al-Sham: History and Archaeology) 9 and 10, 1997-8, pp. 19-24.

the title of the work in question, its author and the date of its composition. It reads as follows:

كتاب فيه جواب رسالة أهل جزيرة قبرس، أجاب به العبد بالذات والصفات، الفقير
إلى الله تعالى من كل الوجوه والجهات، محمد بن أبي طالب الأنصاري الصوفي
الدمشقي، أثابه الله وأيّده بعون منه يمنه وبمنّه، وصلّى الله على سيدنا محمد وعلى
آله. أرسلت في أيام من صفر من سنة احدى وعشرين وسبعمائة، ورجع الجواب
إليهم في سلخ جمادى الآخرة من السنة المذكورة. غفر الله لمصنّفها ولكاتبها ولقارئها
ولسامعها ولجميع المسلمين.

After a brief *incipit*, al-Dimashqī sets out the purpose of his composition on folios 2r-v as follows:

... فإنه لما كان اليوم العاشر من شهر صفر سنة احدى وعشرين وسبعمائة للهجرة
النبوية الشريفة المحمدية، على صاحبها أفضل الصلاة والسلام، والثاني عشر من
مارس أو آذار سنة ألف وستمائة واثنين وثلاثين للاسكندر ذي القرنين اليوناني،
والسادس عشر من برمهات سنة ألف وسبعة وثلاثين لدقلطيانوس القبطي، والسابع
عشر من خردادماه سنة ستمائة وتسعين ليزدجرد بن شهريار بن كسرى أنو شروان
الفارسي، وردت على يد الأديب كليام التاجر، وزير المرقب كان أدام الله مسرته،
رسالة حسنة التلطف، غريبة المغزى، عجيبة المرمى...، أرسلها الأساقفة والبطارقة
القسيسون والرهابنة، أماثل الملة المسيحية وأكابر الأمة العيسوية، من جزيرة قبرس،
نسختين: احداهما إلى الشيخ الإمام قدوة الأنام، أبي العباس احمد بن تيميّة، أدام الله
النفع به وامتع ببقائه، والثانية إلى من ظنّوا أن عنده علمًا...

It is clear from this that he dates the receipt of the *Letter from the People of Cyprus* to precisely 12th March, 1321. His *Jawāb* was sent approximately four months later, at the end, *salkh*, of Jumādā al-ākhira in the same year.[9] The fact that he was one of the recipients of the *Letter from the People of Cyprus* is a measure of his standing as a scholar and well-known theologian at the time.

Folio i of the Oxford manuscript bears the following title: *Disputatio Ibn Idris Sunhazjita contra Christianos & Ivdaeos. Arabice & Muhammedani ad Christianorum Cypriorum Epistolam Responsio*. Thus the manuscript comprises the following two polemical works:

---

[9] F. 1r of MS Utrecht 40; cf. the quotation above.

(a) Folio ii:

كتاب الأجوبة الفاخرة عن الأسولة (sic) الفاجرة للشيخ الإمام العالم لسان المتكلمين
وسيف الناظرين شهاب الدين أبي العباس احمد ابن ادريس الصنهاجي المالكي.

i.e. Al-Qarāfī's (d. 684/1285) *Al-ajwiba al-fākhira 'an al-as'ila al-fājira*.[10]
The colophon of this work (ff. 160r-v) gives the name of the scribe,
Niqulāwus Ibn Buṭrus al-Ḥalabī, and the date of copying, Thursday,
16 Tishrīn al-thānī, 1645. It reads as follows:

تمت نساخته نهار الخميس السادس عشر من تشرين الثاني سنة الف وستمائة خمس
واربعون مسيحية على يد العبد الفقير نيقولاوس بن بطرس الحلبي رحم الله له ولوالديه
ولمن قرأ وترحم عليه آمين.

b) Folio iii: *Muhammedani ad Epistolam Christianorum Cypriorum Responsio*,
i.e. al-Dimashqī's *Jawāb* (ff. 161r-255r). The colophon of this work
(f. 255r) gives the name of the scribe, Abū Bakr 'Alī Ra'ūḍ al-Trūḥī,
and the date of copying, 25 Rabī' al-awwal, A.H. 772.[11] It reads as
follows:

ثم (sic) الجواب بالنفثات السبوحية عن رسالة أهل الملة المسيحية على يد العبد
الفقير إلى من هو بالعفو جدير ابي بكر علي رعوض التروحي في خامس عشرين
ربيع الأول من عام ٧٧٢.

A not only antedates B by approximately 275 years, but also contains
a superior text to that of B, which contains many erroneous readings.
There are a number of instances in B which indicate that it is an
inferior copy and that it may have been copied either directly from
A or from an otherwise lost version copied from it. A few examples
will suffice to illustrate this point:

---

[10] This work was printed in the margins of *Kitāb al-fāriq bayna al-makhlūq wa-al-Khāliq* of Bachahji-Zadah, Cairo, A.H. 1322, and was edited more recently by Bakr Zakī 'Awaḍ in *Min nawādir al-turāth, silsilat muqaranat adyān*, Cairo, 1987.

[11] This colophon is identical with that of the Utrecht manuscript, f. 109v. It can thus be safely concluded (with de Jong, *op. cit.*, pp. 232f.) that al-Dimashqī's *Jawāb* in the Oxford manuscript, which is dated 1645, was copied from the Utrecht manuscript, which is dated 1370, and that Steinschneider was mistaken in ascribing the work to the scribe Ra'ūḍ al-Trūḥī.

(1) F. 3v: ولا نذير; والنذير in B, f. 162v, thus misreading the ﻻof ولا as ال.

(2) F. 4v: لا نذكر; ألنذكر in B, f. 163v, thus misreading ﻻ as لأ.

(3) F. 8r: لا شريك; الشريك in B, f. 166r, thus misreading ﻻ as ال.

(4) F. 8r: سأبطل; ساء (sic) in B, f. 166r, being the first part of the word written in the body of the text in A, with the other part (بطل) written in its margin.

(5) F. 9r: ورس; ورس (لك) (sic) in B, f. 166v, being the latter half of the word available in A which is damaged on the right hand side of this folio, hence missing the first few consonants of words in the top five lines.

(6) F. 9v: الشأن; الشا in B, f. 167r, being a misreading of A which has the final *nūn* of the word at the end of the line above.

(7) F. 19v: الأرض; مرض in B, f. 175r, obviously being a misreading of الأرض the latter half of which, رض, is written in the line above in A.

In 1733, E. L. Vriemoet published a short extract from A, together with a Latin translation [hereafter = V], from the bottom of f. 5r (*incipit*: ... كان اسمه وبعثه مكتوبًا في التوراة) to the top of f. 9r (*explicit*: عند اليهود والفرس...).[12] As is noted in the critical apparatus of our edition of the *Jawāb*, Vriemoet's reproduction of this portion of the text is not entirely free from mistakes and inaccuracies.

---

[12] E.L. Vriemoet, *Arabismus; Exhibens Grammaticam Arabicam Novam & Monumenta Quaedam Arabica, cum Notis Miscellaneis & Glossario Arabico–Latino*, Franequerae, 1733, pp. 130–48.

THE LANGUAGE OF THE LETTERS: DIVERGENCES FROM CLASSICAL USAGE

The language of our text is Middle Arabic, that form of the language which by the time of the author(s) had diverged in orthography, morphology and syntax from the standard classical tongue. We here give details of the most important of these linguistic features, and where relevant we have drawn attention to discussions of them to be found in the following authorities:

J. Blau, *A Grammar of Christian Arabic* (CSCO, 267, 276, 279; *Subsidia*, 27, 28, 29), Louvain, 1966-7 [=Blau];

J. Fück, *Arabiya: Untersuchungen zur arabischen Sprach- und Stilgeschichte* (*Abhandlungen der Sachsischen Akademie der Wissenschaften zu Leipzig*, Phil. hist. Kl., Bd. 45, Ht. 1), Berlin, 1950 [=Fück];

I.-A. Khalifé, "*Makhṭūṭ al-'ilm al-ṭabī'ī wa-mīzātuh al-lughawiyya*", *Al-machriq* 62, 1968, pp. 485-94 [= Khalifé];

G. Rahmé, "*Risāla fī faḍīlat al-'afāf*", *Al-machriq* 62, 1968, pp. 3-74 [=Rahmé].

The following list represents an analysis of the chief divergences referred to above:

I. *Orthography*

1. *Dāl* and *dhāl*, *ḍād* and *ẓā'* are not distinguished in the MSS.

Examples: الدي اتاهم (P1, f. 50v); يدكر فيها (P1, f. 51r); الدي هو (P1, f. 51v); وأندرونا بدينا (A, f. 3v); ندير من قبلك (A, f. 1v); تنفيد مشيئة (A, f. 3v); ظلوا من الله; (A, f. 23v) والحاله الفضيعة (P1, f. 52r); وموعضه للمتقين (P1, f. 54r); ولا الظالين (P1, f. 55v).

2. Divergences in the employment of *hamza*:

a) Omission of *hamza* in medial and final positions [cf. Blau, pp. 92f.; Khalifé, p. 490; Rahmé, p. 12].

Examples: بما جا فيه (P1, f. 50v); فجاوهم بالبينات (P1, f. 1r); سالتني ان (P1,

الابا الافاضل (A, f. ; وقراناه وفهمناه (A, f. 3v); لاولى الالباب (A, f. 2r); f. 50v);
سورة الشعرا (A, f. 3v); سمّوا لنا أسما (A, f. 9r); على من يشا (A, f. 14v). 3r);

b) Replacement of *hamza* by *yā'* [cf. Blau, p.94; Rahmé, p.12].

Examples: عن النقايص (A, بجزاير البحر (P1, f. 49v); احجابوا قايلين (P1, f. 50r); f. 2r); وساير الملبين (A, f. 4v).

c) *Alif* marking *hamza* [cf. Blau, p.85].

Examples: هبأا (A, f.3r); مأا (A, f. 3r).

3. *Tā' marbūṭa*:

a) *Tā' marbūṭa* is often written without dots [cf. Blau, p. 122].

Examples: المخاطبه (P1, f. 1r); من اربعه زوايا (P1, f. 52v); المختلفه ألسنتهم والمكاتبه (A, f. 4v); الحمد والنعمه (A, f. 8r).

b) Confusion of *tā' marbūṭa* and *tā' maftūḥa* [cf. Blau, pp. 115f].

Example: التي تسمى الكهنوة (P1, f. 65r).

4. Confusion of *alif maqṣūra* and *alif mamdūda*.

Examples: الخطية العظما (A, f. ; يدعا الامين (A, f. 7r); أغنا عن قوله (A, f. 5r);
ملايكة العرش (A, f. 22v); وحكا بعضهم لبعض (A, f. 24v); على الطريقة المثلا 12v);
والسموات حزانا (A, f. 23r).

5. Confusion of *alif maqṣūra* and *alif hamza*.

Examples: من مريم العذرى (P1, f. 60v); ها هي العذرى (P1, f. 58r); يتهزى بادم (P1, ff. 61v and 62r).

6. Confusion of *alif maqṣūra* and *yā'*.

Examples: لقد حق القول علي (P1, f. 49v); ومن الجنوب إلي الشمال (P1, f. 50r);
يوبّخ العالم علي (A, f. ; والهدي إلي الحق (A, f. 3r); إلي يوم القيامة (P1, f. 51r);
11v).

7. Lengthening of short vowels.

Examples: هو وهم (P1, f. 51v)؛ ينحوا بذلك عن (P1, f. 50r)؛ يتلوا عليهم آياته
إجلالا منه للإلاه (A, f. 18r)؛ قولكم بسم الإلاه (A, f. 4v)؛ فيكي (P1, f. 57v)؛
فالتفت ذووا العقول (A, f. 23v).

8. Shortening of long vowels [cf. Blau, pp. 65f.].

Examples: نسا العلمين (P1, f. 53r)؛ ليس حيونات (P1, f. 51v)؛ فآمنت طيفة من
بني اسرايل (A, ff. 65r and v)؛ العبد الفقر (A, f. 3r)؛ آية للعلمين (P1, f. 66r)؛ (A,
رؤس الجبال (A, f. 7v)؛ يوم القيمة (A, ff. 13r and v). ff. 7v and 8r)؛

9. Fluctuation in the spelling of certain words of foreign origin, particularly proper nouns.

Examples: البترك؛ (A, f. 6v)؛ االوليا (A, ff. 6r and 15v)؛ التوراة for ,التورية
والأساقفة (A, f. 9v).

10. Repetition of a consonant instead of *tashdīd* [cf. Blau, p. 122f.].

Example: ولتجددن أقربهم (P1, f. 54r).

11. Coalescence of words [cf. Blau, p. 128f.].

Examples: وكلمن (P1, f. 55v؛ A, ff. 18r, 24v and 30v)؛ وكل ما for ,وكلما
وغيروا كلما أوصيتهم (A, f. 41r). يحمل ذلك (P1, f. 63r)؛

II. *Morphology*

1. Demonstrative pronouns: use of هولا and هاولا instead of هؤلاء [cf. Blau, pp. 136f.].

Examples: عما ينكرون هاولا (P1, ff. 64r and v)؛ يا هولا (A, f. 23v)؛ هولا القوم
بين هاولا وهاولا (A, f. 25v). (A, f. 24v)؛

2. Anomalous forms of plurals [cf. Blau, p. 230].

Examples: حزانا باكيين (A, f. 23r)؛ المساجد والمواذن (A, f. 9v).

3. Anomalous sound plural suffixes: the *nūn* of the plural ending is sometimes preserved even in the construct form [cf. Blau, p. 226].

Example: ذبحوا بنينهم (P1, f. 53r).

4. Confusion of the plurals of words from similar roots [cf. Blau, p. 230].

Examples: كالعجيبات (P1, f. 54r); القسوس والرهبان (P1, f. 54r); قسوس ورهبان (A, f. 35v); كالعجائب والمعجزات for الأناجيل, الإنجيلات for والمعاحز (A, f. 36r).

III. *Syntax*

1. Omission of the definite article from nouns [cf. Blau, pp. 364f.].

Examples: في سورة شورى (A, f. 35r); واعلموا أن رسول (A, f. 32v).

2. Divergence of the syntax of numerals from classical usage [cf. Blau, p. 368].

Examples: العشرة ضربات (P1, f. 57v); الى اربع مايه سنة واثنان وثمانون سنه (P1, f. 59r); ثلثة دفوع (A, f. 15r); اثنان وثلاثون سنة (P1, f. 60v); إلى أربعة فرق (A, f. 16v); سبع شياطين (A, f. 32v); ثلاث أقانيم (A, f. 16v).

3. Violation of the rules of construct forms: use of nouns in the absolute form [cf. Fück, p. 61].

Example: كانوا قريبين العهد (A, f. 21v).

4. Confusion in the use of cases [cf. Blau, pp. 317f.; Khalifé, p. 491; Rahmé, p.12].

Examples: سيأتي ... (P1, f. 55r); ومن بعد سابوعًا (P1, f. 54r); لم نعمل شيء (P1, f. 55v); فهذا أمرًا واضحًا بينًا ظاهرًا (P1, f. 55r); سبعين سابوعًا (A, f. 24r); لما كان لكل شيء وسطًا وطرفين (P1, f. 57v); ابنًا يكون للعالم الهين (A, f. 31v); لم تبق منهم ... إلا رجلًا واحدًا (A, f. 30v); اثنين قديمين ويكون ... (A, f. 37r) موقعًا عظيمًا.

5. Confusion of moods:

a) Indicative used for jussive after *lam* [cf. Blau, p. 263; Fück, p. 61; Khalifé, p. 492; Rahmé, p.12].

Examples: لم نسمّيه نحن (P1, f. 55r); و لم يعرفون (P1, f. 55r); لم يسمعون كلامي (A, f. 33v). لم تنقاد الأمم (A, f. 19v); فلم يرتاب الفاحصون (P1, f. 56r).

b) Subjunctive used for indicative [cf. Blau, p. 263; Fück, p. 61; Khalifé, p. 492; Rahmé, p. 12].

Examples: وتعرفي أني أنا (P1, f. 57v); ويكونوا له شعبًا (P1, f. 57v).

c) Irregular form of the imperative [cf. Blau, p. 194f.].

Example: اذهب قول (P1, f. 59v).

6. Violation of the rules of grammatical accord:

a) Lack of concord between verb and subject in a verbal clause [cf. Blau, p. 281].

Example: ويزول به دولة (A, f. 8v).

b) Lack of concord between relative pronoun and its antecedent [cf. Blau, p. 573].

Examples: كلمة الله الخالقه الذي (P1, f. 61v); جميع أفعاله الذي (P1, f. 57r); اليهود واللذين أشركوا (P1, ff. 51v and 52v); الذي في أيدينا (P1, f. 54r).

c) Lack of concord between a noun and the demonstrative pronoun referring to it.

Examples: فأشرف هذه القسمين (P1, f. 64r); لهذه القسمين (P1, f. 64r).

d) Tendency to bring the preceding verb into strict concord in number with the subject [cf. Blau, pp. 275f.].

Examples: يرفعون الأمم (P1, f. 53v); ويهتدوا بها الظالين (P1, f. 58r); ويحمّلونه (A, f. 33r); يحسوا الغلاة (A, f. 32v); مما ساقوه الثلاثة (A, f. 18v); الأردال خشبته.

7. Substitution of dual for plural [cf. Blau, p. 72; Fück, p. 95].

Example: من يدي الرسل (P1, f. 59v).

8. Violation of the rules of diptotes.

Example: أَن يكون أبيضًا (P1, f. 54r).

In addition to such linguistic characteristics, there are a number of idiosyncratic features of the text of both the *Letter from the People of Cyprus* and the *Jawāb* which are probably to be attributed to scribal carelessness rather than to their reflecting genuine linguistic features of Middle Arabic.

The most noteworthy of these is the frequent disregard shown for the distinguishing of diacritical points of consonants: *ḥā'* appears for *jīm* (e.g. ينبتق من فيه for بحبال فاران ;(بجبال فاران *tā'* appears for *thā'* (e.g. الخطيه العظما ,ظهور سيدنا for طهور سيدنا ;(ينبثق من فيه for *ṭā'* for *ẓā'* (e.g. والله عفور for والله غفور), 'ayn for ghayn (e.g. الخطية العظمى ;(الخطية العظمى for *'ayn* for *ghayn* (e.g. والله عفور for والله غفور), while some consonants, e.g. *bā', qāf, nūn,* and *yā',* are occasionally written without any dots at all. *Dāl* and *dhāl, ḍād* and *ẓā'* are often not distinguished, as mentioned above. In all these cases the correct pointing has been restored in our edition.

Other examples of scribal carelessness are the many instances of fluctuation in the spelling of words, particularly those of foreign origin.

In the edition and translation of *The Letter from the People of Cyprus* that follows, Roman numerals indicate the eighteen sections into which it naturally falls. In addition, Arabic numbers in brackets indicate the correspondences between many of its paragraphs and those in Paul of Antioch's *Letter to a Muslim Friend* as they are numbered in Khoury's edition (the sequence is not complete because the Cypriot editor omits some of Paul's paragraphs and rearranges others).

In the edition and translation of al-Dimashqī's *Response*, Arabic numerals indicate the hundred sections into which it falls.

Translations from the Qur'an follow M.M. Pickthall, *The Glorious Qur'ān*. In some places where al-Dimashqī curtails a quotation on the assumption his readers will know what follows, the omitted part has been included in square brackets if it helps to clarify the continuing discussion.

The following abbreviations are used in the edition and translation:

A   Utrecht, University Library, MS 1449 [Or. 40]

B   Oxford, Bodleian Library, MS Marsh 40 [Uri Arab. Moh. 124 (2)]

P1   Bibliothèque Nationale, MS Arabe 204

P2   Bibliothèque Nationale, MS Arabe 214

P3   Bibliothèque Nationale, MS Arabe 215

S   Sūras of the Qur'an

V   E.L. Vriemoet, *Arabismus; Exhibens Grammaticam Arabicam Novam & Monumenta Quaedam Arabica, cum Notis Miscellaneis & Glossario Arabico–Latino* (1733), pp. 130-48 = ff. 5r–9r of the Utrecht MS (A)

THE LETTER FROM THE PEOPLE OF CYPRUS

TEXT AND TRANSLATION

THE LETTER FROM THE PEOPLE OF CYPRUS

Paul of Antioch's Letter

(1) بسم الاب والابن والروح القدس

(3) أما بعد اطال الله في اتم النعم بقاك ، وحرسك من الاسوا وتولاك! واني لما اهلته من المنزلة—اعني الاسقفية– اجتمعت باجلا اهل تلك الديار وروسايهم وفاوضت افاضلهم وعلماهم، سالتني ان اشرح لك شرحا بينا ما عرفته من راي القوم الذين رايتهم وخاطبتهم في محمد عليه السلام. فاجبت الى مسلتك ، لاجل افراط مودتك وكثرة محبتك، قايلا:

The Letter from the People of Cyprus (P1)

* i. * بسم الله الحيّ المحيي القديم الأزلي.

(3) أمّا بعد الذي يعلم مولانا[1] الشيخ المكرّم[2] الرئيس السيّد الفاضل الأوحد النفيس أطال الله في أتـمّ النعم بقاءه وحرسه من الأسواء وتولاه.

سألتني أن أفحص لك فحصًا بيّنًا[3] ما يعتقده[4] النصارى المسيحيون[5] المختلفة ألسنتهم المتفرّقة في أربع[6] زوايا العالم، من المشرق إلى المغرب ومن الجنوب إلى الشمال والقاطنون[7] بجزائر البحر والمقيمون[8] في البرّ[9] المتصل إلى مغيب الشمس[10].

وإنني لمّا وصلت إلى جزيرة قبرص اجتمعت ببعض أجــلاء تلك البلاد ورؤسائهم وفاوضت أفاضلهم وعلماءهم. وما علمت من رأي القوم الذين رأيتهم وخاطبتهم عن دينهم وما يعتقدونه[11] وما يحتجّون به عن أنفسهم،

---

[1] P2: أعلم به مولاي ; P3: يعلم به مولاي   [2] P2 and 3 om.   [3] P2: تبيّنًا   [4] P2: عمّا يعتقدوه ; P3: يعتقدوه   [5] P1, 2 and 3: المسيحيين   [6] P1: أربعة   [7] P1, 2 and 3: والقاطنين   [8] P1, 2 and 3: والمقيمين   [9] P2 and 3: بالبرّ   [10] P2 and 3: البحر   [11] P2: يعتقدوه   المحيط

THE LETTER FROM THE PEOPLE OF CYPRUS

i. (49v) In the name of the living, life-giving God, eternal and everlasting.

(3) To our purpose. This is what our master, the revered teacher, the head, lord, distinguished, unique and unparalleled professor, may God prolong his life in the most perfect favour, protect him from ill and care for him, taught:

You have asked me to make a full inquiry for you of what the Christians, followers of Christ, who are diverse in their languages and scattered over the four corners of the earth from east to west, south to north, inhabiting the islands of the sea and established on the dry land stretching as far as the setting of the sun, believe.

When I landed in the island of Cyprus, I met some of the great men of this land and their chiefs, and I conferred with their distinguished and learned individuals. What I learned about the thought of the people whom I saw and talked with about their faith, what they believe and what arguments they employ on their own behalf,

حيث سألتني[12] فأجبت إلى مساءلتك[13]
لأجل إفراط[14] مودّتك وكثرة محبتك
قائلاً:

ii. (4) إنّ القوم يقولون: "إنّا سمعنا أن
قد ظهر في العرب إنسان[15] اسمه محمّد،
يقول إنّه رسول الله[16] وإنّه أتى[17] بكتاب
يقول إنه منزل عليه من الله تعالى، فلم
نزل نجتهد[18] إلى أن حصل هذا[19] الكتاب
عندنا.

(4) ان القوم يقولون: انا لما سمعنا انه قد
ظهر في العرب انسان اسمه محمد يقول انه
رسول الله ، وانه اتى بكتاب يذكر انه
منزل عليه من الله تعالى ، توصلنا الى ان
حصل الكتاب عندنا.

(5) فقلت[20] لهم: إذا كنتم قد سمعتم
بهذا الإنسان واجتهدتم على تحصيل هذا
الكتاب الذي أتى به عندكم، فلأيّ حال
لم تتبعوه؟ ولا سيّما في[21] الكتاب يقول
في سورة آل عمران[22]: ﴿ومن يبتغ غير
الإسلام دينًا فلن[23] * يقبل منه وهو في
الآخرة من الخاسرين﴾. أجابوا[24] قائلين:
لأحوال شتّى، فقلت: وما هي؟

(5) قلت: فاذ كنتم قد سمعتم بهذا
الرسول ، واجتهدتم على تحصيل
الكتاب الذي اتى به عندكم ، فلاي
حال لم تتبعوه ؟ لا سيما وفي الكتاب
يقول : " ومن يبتغي غير الاسلام دينا
فلن يقبل منه ، وهو في الاخرة من
الخاسرين". – اجابوا : لاحوال شتى.
– قلت: وما هي؟

(6) قالوا: منها أنّ الكتاب عربي
وليس بلساننا[25]، حسب ما جاء فيه
يقول: ﴿وأنزلناه[26] قرآنا عربيًّا﴾ وأيضًا
وجدنا فيه[27] يقول في سورة الشعراء:
﴿ولو نزّلناه على بعض الأعجمين

(6) قالوا: منها ان الكتاب عربي وليس
بلساننا ، حسب ما جا فيه ، وهو:
"وانزلنا القران عربيا". وايضا: "لتنذر
قوما ما انذر اباوهم ، فهم غافلون" .
وايضا : " وانذر عشيرتك الاقربين".

---

12 P2 and 3: حسب ما سألتني 13 P2 and 3: سؤالك 14 P2 and 3: فرط 15 P2 and 3: إنسانًا 16 P3: أرسل من الله 17 P2 and 3: وأتى 18 P1 om. 19 P2 في سورة آل عمران P2 and 3 om. 20 P2 and 3: قلت 21 P2: وفي 22 P2 and 3 om: و 26 P1, 2 and 3: وأنزلنا 27 P2 and لساننا 25 P2: هو فلم :P2 23 أجابوه :P2 24 3 om: وجدنا فيه

since you have asked me, I will respond to your request because of deep attachment and great affection for you. So I say:

ii. *(4)* The people say: We heard that a man by the name of Muḥammad appeared among the Arabs, saying that he was the messenger of God and bringing a book which he said had been revealed to him from God the exalted. So we did not rest until this book was obtained for us.

(5) I said to them: If you have heard about this man, and made efforts to obtain for yourselves this book which he brought, then for what reason do you not believe in him, especially since in the book it says in *The Family of ʿImrān*, 'And whoso seeketh a religion other than the Surrender it will not (50r) be accepted from him, and he will be a loser in the Hereafter'? They replied, saying: For many reasons. I said: What are they?

(6) They said: One is that the book is in Arabic and not in our language, according to what is stated in it, 'And we have revealed it, a Lecture in Arabic'. Also, we have found what is said in *The Poets*, 'And if we had revealed it unto one of any other nation than the Arabs,

فقرأه عليهم فما كانوا به مؤمنين[28]﴾.
وقال في سورة البقرة: ﴿كما أرسلنا
فيكم رسولاً[29] منكم يتلو عليكم أياتنا
ويزكّيكم ويعلّمكم الكتاب والحكمة
ويعلّمكم ما لم تكونوا تعلمون﴾. وقال
في سورة آل[30] عمران: ﴿إذ بعث فيهم
رسولاً من أنفسهم يتلو عليهم آياته
ويزكّيهم ويعلّمهم الكتاب والحكمة
وإن كانوا من قبل لفي ضلال[31] مبين﴾.
وقال في سورة القصص: ﴿لتنذر قومًا
ما أتاهم من[32] نذير من قبلك لعلّهم
يتذكّرون﴾. وقال في سورة السجدة[33]:
﴿لتنذر قومًا[34] ما أتاهم من[35] نذير من
قبلك لعلّهم يهتدون﴾. وقال في سورة[36]
يس: ﴿لتنذر قومًا ما أنذر آباؤهم فهم
غافلون لقد حقّ القول على أكثرهم فهم
لا يؤمنون﴾.

(7) فلما راينا هذا فيه ، علمنا انه لم يرسل الينا ، بل الى الجاهلية من العرب: الذي قال انه لم ياتهم من نذير من قبله. وانه لا يلزمنا اتباعه ، لانا نحن قد اتانا رسل من قبله خاطبونا بالسنتنا واندرونا وسلموا الينا التورية والانجيل بلغاتنا. واذ قد اتضح من الكتاب انه لم يرسل	(7) فلمّا رأينا هذا فيه علمنا أنه لم يأت إلينا بل إلى الجاهلية من العرب الذين[37] قال إنّه لم[38] يأتهم رسول ولا نذير[39] من قبل، وأنّه لا يلزمنا اتباعه لأننا نحن[40] قد أتانا رسل من قبله خاطبونا بألسنتنا وأنذرونا *بديننا الذي[41] نحن متمسّكون[42] به يومنا[43] هذا، وسلّموا

and if he had read it unto them, they would not have believed in it';
in *The Cow*, 'Even as we have sent unto you a messenger from among
you, who reciteth unto you our revelations and causeth you to grow,
and teacheth you the Scripture and wisdom, and teacheth you that
which ye knew not'; in *The Family of 'Imrān*, 'By sending unto them a
messenger of their own who reciteth unto them his revelations, and
causeth them to grow, and teacheth them the Scripture and wisdom;
although before (he came to them) they were in flagrant error'; in *The
Stories*, 'That thou mayest warn a folk unto whom no warner came
before thee, that haply they may give heed'; in *The Prostration*, 'That
thou mayest warn a folk to whom no warner came before thee, that
haply they may walk aright'; and in *Ya Sin*, 'That thou mayest warn
a folk whose fathers were not warned, so they were heedless. Already
hath the word proved true of most of them, for they believe not'.

(7) When we noticed this in it, we knew that he had not been sent
to us but to the pagan Arabs, about whom it says that no messenger or
warner had come to them before him, and that it was not obliging us
to follow him because messengers had come to us before, addressing us
in our own tongues and warning us (50v) about our religion, to which
we adhere today. They delivered

إلينا التوراة والإنجيل بلغاتنا على ما يشهد لهم⁴⁴ الكتاب الذي أتى به هذا الرجل حيث يقول في سورة ابراهيم: ﴿وما أرسلنا من رسول⁴⁵ إلا بلسان قومه﴾. وقال أيضًا⁴⁶ في سورة⁴⁷ النحل: ﴿ولقد بعثنا في كلّ أمة رسولاً﴾. وقال أيضًا⁴⁸ في سورة الروم: ﴿ولقد أرسلنا من قبلك رسلاً إلى قومهم فجاؤوهم بالبيّنات﴾. فقد صحّ من هذا الكتاب أنّه لم يأت إلا إلى الجاهلية⁴⁹ من العرب. وقوله⁵⁰: ﴿ومن يبتغ غير الإسلام دينًا فلن يقبل منه وهو في الآخرة من الخاسرين﴾، فيريد بحسب مقتضى العدل قومه الذين⁵¹ أتاهم بلغتهم لا غيرهم ممّن لم يأتهم بما جاء فيه.

ولنعلم⁵² أنّ الله تعالى عدل وليس من عدله أن يطلب⁵³ يوم القيامة أمّة من الأمم بإتباع إنسان لم يأت إليهم ولا وقفوا⁵⁴ على كتابه⁵⁵ بلسانهم ولا من جهة⁵⁶ داع من قبله.

iii. (8) ثمّ وجدنا⁵⁷ في هذا الكتاب أيضًا من تعظيم السيّد المسيح وأمّه حيث يقول في سورة التحريم⁵⁸: ﴿ومريم التي⁵⁹ أحصنت فرجها فنفخنا فيها من روحنا

الا الى الجاهلية من العرب ، فقوله "ومن يبتغي غير الاسلام دينا فلن يقبل منه، وهو في الاخرة من الخاسرين" ، فيريد به ، حسب مقتضى العدل ، قومه الذين اتاهم بلغتهم ، لا غيرهم ممن لم ياتهم ، حسب ما جا فيه.

(8) ثم وجدنا في الكتاب ايضا من تعظيم السيد المسيح وامه ، وان الله جعلهما اية للعالمين، وذلك قوله: "والتي احصنت فرجها ، فنفخنا فيها من روحنا

---

⁴⁴ P2 and 3: به ⁴⁵ P2: رسولاً ⁴⁶ P2 and 3 om. ⁴⁷ P2: صورة (sic) ⁴⁸ P2 and 3 om. ⁴⁹ P3: للجاهلية ⁵⁰ P2 and 3: وأمّا قوله ⁵¹ P1, 2 and 3: الذي ⁵² P2 and 3: وليعلم ⁵³ P2 and 3: لم يطالب ⁵⁴ P2 and 3 add: له ⁵⁵ P2 and 3: كتاب ⁵⁶ P2 and 3: من جهته ولا أتاهم من جهته ⁵⁷ P2 add: أيضًا ⁵⁸ Corrected in the margin of P1 from ومريم ابنة عمران P3: ; ابنة عمران P2: ⁵⁹ P2 and 3: الأنبياء ; الأنبياء

to us the Torah and Gospel in our languages, in accordance with what the book brought by this man attests about them. For in *Abraham* it says, 'And we never sent a messenger save with the language of his folk'; in *The Bee*, 'And verily we have raised in every nation a messenger'; and in *The Romans*, 'Verily we sent before thee messengers to their own folk. They brought them clear proofs'. So it has been shown correctly according to this book that he was sent only to the pagan Arabs. Its words: 'And whoso seeketh as religion other than the Surrender it will not be accepted from him, and he will be a loser in the Hereafter', according to the demands of what is just it means: his people to whom he brought it in their language, and not others to whom he did not come, as is stated in it.

We know that God the exalted is just, and it is not part of his justice to require on the day of resurrection that any community should have followed a man who had not come to them, or whose book they were not familiar with in their language or without the authority of any summoner preceding him.

iii. *(8)* Further, we also find in this book eulogies of the lord Christ and his mother in what he says in *Banning*, 'And Mary, she who was chaste, therefore we breathed into her of our Spirit

، وجعلناها وابنها آية للعالمين". وايضا:
"واذ قالت الملايكة : يا مريم : ان الله
اصطفاك وطهرك على نسا العالمين".

وجعلناها وابنها آية للعالمين﴾. وقال في
سورة آل عمران: ﴿وإذ قالت الملائكة
يا مريم إنّ الله اصطفاك[60] وطهّرك[61]
واصطفاك[62] على نساء العالمين﴾.

(9) مع الشهادات للسيّد المسيح
بالمعجزات، وانه حبل به لا من مباضعة
رجل بل ببشارة ملاك الله لامه ، وانه
تكلم في المهد واحيا الميت وابرا الاكمه
ونقى الابرص ، وعمل من الطين كهية
الطير ونفخ فيها فطارت باذن الله.

(9) مع الشهادات للسيّد[63] المسيح
بالمعجزات وأنّه حبل به لا من مباضعة
رجل بل * ببشارة ملاك الله لأمّه، وأنّه
تكلّم في المهد وأحيا الميت وأبرأ الأكمه
ونقى الأبرص[64] وأنّه خلق من الطين
كهيئة الطير[65] ونفخ فيه وكان طيرًا[66]
بإذن الله[67].

(10) ووجدنا فيه ايضا ان الله رفع
المسيح اليه، وذلك قوله:" واذ قال الله:
يا عيسى بن مريم، اني متوفيك ورافعك
الي، ومطهرك من الذين كفروا وجاعل
الذين اتبعوك فوق الذين كفروا، الى يوم
القيامة."وايضا:" وقفينا بعيسى بن مريم،
واتيناه الانجيل ، وجعلنا في قلوب الذين
اتبعوه رافة ورحمة" .

(10) ووجدنا أيضًا فيه أنّ الله رفعه
إليه[68]. قال[69] في سورة آل عمران[70]:
﴿يا عيسى (ابن مريم) إني متوفّيك
ورافعك إليّ ومطهّرك من الذين كفروا
وجاعل الذين اتبعوك فوق الذين كفروا
إلى يوم القيامة﴾. وقال في سورة البقرة:
﴿وآتينا عيسى ابن مريم البيّنات وأيّدناه
بروح القدس﴾. وقال أيضًا[71] في سورة
الحديد: ﴿وقفينا بعيسى[72] ابن مريم
وآتيناه الإنجيل وجعلنا في قلوب الذين
اتبعوه رأفة ورحمة ورهبانية ابتدعوها ما
كتبناها عليهم إلا ابتغاء رضوان الله فما

---

60 P2: لسيّدنا 61 P3: قد اصطفاك ; P3: مصطفيك P2: 62 P2 and 3 om. 63 P3: ومطهّرك P2: لسيّدنا 64 P3: البرص P2: 65 الطائر P2: 66 فكان طائرًا ; P3: فكان طيرًا P2: 67 P2 and 3 add: أي 68 P2 and 3 om: ووجدنا أيضًا فيه بإذن اللاهوت الذي هو كلمة الله المتحدة في الناسوت (wrongly). 71 P2 and 3 om. 69 P2 and 3: وقال 70 P3: سورة النساء أنّ الله رفعه إليه 72 P2 and 3 add: على آثارهم

and made her and her son a token for peoples'. And in *The Family of 'Imrān* he says, 'And when the angels said: O Mary! Lo! Allah hath chosen thee and made thee pure, and hath preferred thee above the women of creation'.

(9) There are also the testimonies to the lord Christ in the miracles, that he was conceived not through the intercourse of a man but (51r) by the annunciation of an angel of God to his mother,[1] that he spoke in the cradle,[2] brought the dead back to life, healed those born blind, made lepers whole,[3] created from clay the likeness of a bird, breathed into it, and it was a bird by the permission of God.[4] *(10)* We also find in it that God raised him up to himself. He says in *The Family of 'Imrān*, 'O Jesus [son of Mary]! Lo! I am gathering thee and causing thee to ascend unto me, and am cleansing thee of those who disbelieve and am setting those who follow thee above those who disbelieve until the day of resurrection'; he says in *The Cow*, 'And we gave unto Jesus, son of Mary, clear proofs, and we supported him with the Holy Spirit'; he also says in *Iron*, 'And we caused Jesus, son of Mary, to follow, and gave him the gospel, and placed compassion and mercy in the hearts of those who followed him. But monasticism they invented—we ordained it not for them—only seeking Allah's pleasure, and they

---

[1] SS. XIX: 16-22; III: 45.
[2] SS. XIX: 29-33; III: 46; V: 110.
[3] SS. III: 49; V: 110.
[4] SS. III: 49; V: 110.

رعوها حقّ رعايتها فآتينا الذين آمنوا
منهم أجرهم﴾ . وقال أيضًا[73] في سورة
آل عمران: ﴿من[74] أهل الكتاب أمّة
قائمة يتلون آيات الله آناء الليل[75] وهم
يسجدون يؤمنون[76] بالله واليوم الآخر
ويأمرون بالمعروف وينهون عن المنكر
ويسارعون في الخيرات وأولئك[77] من
الصالحين﴾ .

(11) ثمّ وجدناه أيضًا[78] يعظّم إنجيلنا
ويقدّم صوامعنا ويشرّف بيعنا[79] ويشهد
بأنّ اسم الله يذكر فيها كثيرًا، وذلك
قوله[80] في سورة الحجّ[81]: ﴿ولولا دفع الله
الناس بعضهم ببعض لهدمت صوامع وبيع
وصلوات ومساجد[82] يذكر فيها اسم الله
كثيرًا﴾ .

iv. (12) فهذا[83] وغيره أوجب لنا
التمسّك بديننا * وأن لا نهمل مذهبنا[84]
ولا نرفض ما معنا[85] ولا نتبع غير السيّد
المسيح كلمة الله[86] وحوارييه الذين[87]
أرسلهم إلينا وأنذرونا[88] بلغاتنا،

(13) الذين قد عظّموا في هذا الكتاب
بقوله في سورة[89] الحديد: ﴿لقد[90] أرسلنا

---

(11) ثم وجدناه ايضا يعظم انجيلنا،
ويقدم صوامعنا وبيعنا على المساجد،
ويشهد لها بان اسم الله يذكر فيها
كثيرا. وذلك قوله : "ولولا دفع الله
الناس بعضهم ببعض ، لهدمت صوامع
وبيع وصلوات ومساجد يذكر فيها اسم
الله كثيرا".

(12) وهذا وغيره اوجب لنا التمسك
بديننا، وان لا نهمل مذهبنا ولا نرفض
ما معنا، ولا نتبع غير السيد المسيح
كلمة الله وحواريه الذين ارسلهم الينا
لينذرونا،

(13) الذين قد عظموا في هذا الكتاب
وبجلوا بقوله:" وارسلنا رسلنا بالبينات ،

---

[73] P2 and 3 om. [74] P1 and 3: ومن [75] P2 add: وأطراف النهار [76] P1, 2 and 3:
مساجدنا [77] P1, 2 and 3: أُولئك [78] P2 and 3 om. [79] P2 and 3:
مساجدنا [80] P2: وقال أيضًا [81] P2 and 3 om: في سورة الحجّ [82] P2: ومساجدًا (sic). [83] P2 and 3:
هذا [84] P2 and 3: مذهبنا [85] P2 and 3: ما معنا [86] P2 and 3 add : وروحه [87] P1:
الذي (wrongly). [88] P2 and 3: أنذرونا [89] P2: صورة (sic). [90] P1, 2 and 3: ولقد

observed it not with right observance. So we gave those of them who believe their reward';[5] and he also says in *The Family of 'Imrān*, 'Of the people of the Scripture there is a staunch community who recite the revelations of Allah in the night season, falling prostrate. They believe in Allah and the last day, and enjoin right conduct and forbid indecency, and vie with one another in good works. These are of the righteous'.

(11) Then we also find him extolling our Gospel, favouring our hermitages, honouring our churches, and bearing witness that the name of God is mentioned in them often. This is his word in *The Pilgrimage*, 'For had it not been for Allah's repelling some men by means of others, cloisters and churches and oratories and mosques, wherein the name of Allah is oft mentioned'.

iv. *(12)* This and other things oblige us to keep to our religion and not to neglect our doctrine, abandon what we have or follow anyone other than the lord Christ, the Word of God, and his disciples whom he sent to us to warn us in our languages. *(13)* They are extolled in his words in *Iron*, 'We verily sent

---

[5] The last clause of the verse, 'but many of them are evil-livers', is tacitly omitted.

رسلنا بالبيّنات وأنزلنا[91] معهم الكتاب
والميزان ليقوم[92] الناس[92] بالقسط[93]. وقال
في سورة[94] البقرة: ﴿فبعث[95] الله النبيين
مبشّرين ومنذرين وأنزل معهم الكتاب
بالحقّ ليحكم بين الناس[96] فيما اختلفوا
فيه﴾، فأعنى بقوله أنبياءه المبشّرين ينحو
بذلك عن الحواريين[97] الذين داروا
في سبعة[98] أقاليم العالم وبشّروا بالكتاب
الواحد الذي هو الإنجيل المقدّس[99] لأنه
لو كان أعنى عن ابراهيم وداود وموسى
ومحمّد لكان قال[100]: "ومعهم الكتب"،
لأنّ كلّ واحد منهم جاء بكتاب دون
غيره، ولم يقل[101] إلا الكتاب الواحد
الذي هو الإنجيل المقدّس[102].

ثمّ يشهد لهم أنهم أنصار الله،
إذ يقول في سورة الصفّ[103]: ﴿وإذ
قال عيسى ابن مريم للحواريين[104] من
أنصاري إلى الله قال[105] الحواريون نحن
أنصار الله فآمنت طائفة من بني إسرائيل
وكفرت طائفة فأيّدنا[106] الذين آمنوا
على عدوّهم فأصبحوا ظاهرين[107]﴾.

v. (14) وأمّا تعظيم إنجيلنا وكتبنا
التي[108] في أيدينا[109] فإنه يقول[110]

معهم الكتاب ، ليقوم الناس بالقسط ".
لأنه لو كان عنى ابراهيم وموسى
وداوود ومحمد ، لكان قال: "معهم
الكتب" ولم يقل "الكتاب"، الذي هو
الانجيل.

ثم شهد لهم انهم انصار الله ، اذ
يقول :"واذ قال عيسى بن مريم : من
انصاري الى الله؟ قال الحواريون : نحن
انصار الله. فامنت طائفة من بني اسرائيل
وكفرت طائفة. فايدنا الذين امنوا على
عدوهم ، فاصبحوا ظاهرين".

(14) فاما تعظيمه لانجيلنا وكتبنا التي
في ايدينا، فقوله: "انزلنا عليك الكتاب

---

91 P1, 2 and 3: وأنزل   92 P2 and 3: ليقوموا   93 P3: للناس   94 P2: صورة (sic).
95 P1: بعث   96 P2 and 3 add: بالحقّ which is crossed out in P1.   97 P1 and 2: الحواريون
98 P2: سبع   99 P2 and 3: الطاهر   100 P2 and 3: فكان يقول   101 P2: يقول   102 P2 and
3 om: لأن ما أتى جماعة مبشرين بكتاب واحد غير and add: الذي هو الإنجيل المقدّس
104 P2 في سورة الصف   103 P2 and 3 om: الحوارين (الحواريون P3: الذين أتوا بالإنجيل الطاهر
and 3 om.   105 P2 and 3: قالت   106 P1 and 2: وأيّدنا   107 P2: طاهرين (sic).   108 P1
and 3: الذي   109 P2 and 3: بأيدينا   110 P2 and 3: فيقول

our messengers with clear proofs, and revealed with them the scripture and the balance, that mankind may observe right measure'. And in *The Cow* he says, 'And Allah sent prophets as bearers of good tidings and as warners, and revealed therewith the Scripture with the truth that it might judge between mankind concerning that wherein they differed', more or less meaning by his words his 'prophets, bearers of good tidings' the disciples, who spread through the seven regions of the world and proclaimed the one book, the holy Gospel. For if he had meant Abraham, David, Moses and Muḥammad he would have said, 'and with them the scriptures', because each of them brought a scripture different from others. But he only refers to the one scripture, which is the holy Gospel.

Then he bears witness to them that they are helpers of God, for he says in *The Ranks*, 'Even as Jesus son of Mary said unto the disciples: Who are my helpers for Allah? The disciples said: We are Allah's helpers. And a party of the Children of Israel believed, while a party disbelieved. Then we strengthened those who believed against their foe, and they became the uppermost'.

v. *(14)* As for extolling our Gospel and the books which we possess, he says

مصدقا لما بين يديه من التورية والانجبل".

في سورة المائدة¹¹¹: ﴿وأنزلنا¹¹² إليك الكتاب مصدّقاً لما بين يديه¹¹³ من التوراة والإنجيل﴾. * وقال في أوّل¹¹⁴ سورة آل عمران: ﴿ألم الله لا إله إلا هو الحيّ القيوم نزّل عليك¹¹⁵ الكتاب بالحقّ مصدّقاً لما بين يديه وأنزل التوراة والإنجيل من قبل هدى للناس¹¹⁶﴾. وقال أيضًا¹¹⁷ في سورة¹¹⁸ البقرة: ﴿ذلك الكتاب لا ريب فيه هدى للمتقين الذين يؤمنون بالغيب ويقيمون الصلاة وممّا رزقناهم ينفقون﴾. فأعنى بالكتاب الإنجيل والذين يؤمنون بالغيب نحن النصارى.¹¹⁹ ثمّ أتبع بالقول¹²⁰: ﴿والذين يؤمنون بما أنزل إليك من قبلك﴾. فأعنى بهذا القول عن¹²¹ المسلمين الذين آمنوا بما أتى به¹²² وما أتى¹²³ من قبله. وقال أيضًا¹²⁴ في سورة¹²⁵ المائدة: ﴿وقفينا على آثارهم¹²⁶ بعيسى ابن مريم مصدّقاً لما بين يديه من التوراة وآتيناه الإنجيل فيه هدى ونور¹²⁷ ومصدّقاً لما بين يديه من التوراة¹²⁸ وهدى وموعظة¹²⁹ للمتقين وليحكم أهل الإنجيل بما أنزل الله¹³⁰ فيه

---

¹¹¹ P2 and 3 om: في سورة المائدة   ¹¹² P2 and 3: وأنزل   ¹¹³ P2: لما في التوراة   ¹¹⁴ P2 and 3 om this word which is added above the line in P1.   ¹¹⁵ P2 and 3: عليه   ¹¹⁶ P2: الناس   ¹¹⁷ P2 and 3 om.   ¹¹⁸ P2: صورة (sic).   ¹¹⁹ P2 and 3 add: المسيح ومارأيناه   ¹²⁰ P2 and 3: القول عن المسلمين   ¹²¹ These words are omitted in P1 and 2 which read instead: فهذا قول ظاهر لأن المسلمين هم الذين أمنوا   الذين آمنّا بالسيّد (P3: بيسوع)   ¹²² P2: أنزل إليه   ¹²³ P2: أنزل   ¹²⁴ P2 and 3 om.   ¹²⁵ P2: صورة (sic).   ¹²⁶ P2 and 3 om: على   ¹²⁷ P2: ونورًا   ¹²⁸ P3 om: التوراة ... وآتيناه الإنجيل فيه   ¹²⁹ P1 and 2: وموعضة (sic).   ¹³⁰ P2 and 3 om.

in *The Table Spread*, 'And unto thee have we revealed the scripture, confirming [the Torah and Gospel that were] before it'. (52r) And he says at the beginning of *The Family of 'Imrān*, 'Alif. Lām. Mīm. Allah! There is no god save him, the alive, the eternal. He hath revealed unto thee the Scripture with truth, confirming that which was before it, even as he revealed the Torah and the Gospel aforetime, for a guidance to mankind'. He also says in *The Cow*, 'This is the scripture whereof there is no doubt, a guidance to those who ward off evil who believe in the unseen and establish worship, and spend of that we have bestowed upon them'. By 'the scripture' he means the Gospel, and by 'who believe in the unseen' us Christians. Then he follows with the words, 'And who believe in that which is revealed unto thee '. By these words he means the Muslims who believed in what he brought and what came before him. He also says in *The Table Spread*, 'And we caused Jesus, son of Mary, to follow in their footsteps, confirming that which was (revealed) before him in the Torah, and we bestowed on him the Gospel wherein is guidance and light, confirming that which was (revealed) before him in the Torah—a guidance and an admonition unto those who ward off (evil). Let the People of the Gospel judge by that which Allah hath revealed therein.

ومن لم يحكم بما أنزل الله فأولئك[131] هم الفاسقون﴾. وقال في سورة[132] آل عمران: ﴿فإن كذّبوك فقد كذّب رسل من قبلك جاؤوا بالبيّنات[133] والزبر[134] والكتاب المنير﴾ الذي[135] هو الإنجيل المقدّس. وقال أيضًا في سورة يونس:[136] ﴿فإن[137] كنت في شكٍّ ممّا أنزلنا إليك[138] فاسأل الذين يقرأون[139] الكتاب من قبلك لقد[140] جاءك الحقّ من ربّك فلا تكونن من الممترين ولا تكونن من الذين كذّبوا بآيات الله فتكونن من الخاسرين﴾. *فثبت بهذا[141] ما معنا. نعم ونفى عن إنجيلنا وكتبنا التي[142] في أيدينا التهم والتبديل لها والتغيير لما فيها بتصديقه لما فيها.[143]

وايضا : "وان كنت في شك مما انزلنا عليك، فاسل الذين يقرون الكتاب من قبلك". فثبت بهذا ما معنا – نعم – ونفى عن إنجيلنا وكتبنا التهمة بالتبديل لها والتغيير لما فيها، بتصديقه لها.

5 *

vi. (15) فقلت لهم[144]: إن قال قائل[145] إنّ التبديل والتغيير قد يجوز أن يكون بعد هذا القول. قالوا[146]: إنّا نعجب[147] من هؤلاء القوم مع علمهم ومعرفتهم وذكائهم[148] كيف يحتجّون علينا بهذا القول؟[149] وذلك أنا إذا احتججنا نحن أيضًا عليهم بمثل هذا[150] وقلنا: إنّ الكتاب الذي في أيديهم يومنا

(15) – قلت: فان قال قايل ان التبديل قد يجوز ان يكون بعد هذا القول. – قالوا: هذا ما لا يجوز لقايل ان يقوله. لان كتبنا قد جاز عليها نحو ستماية سنة، وصارت في ايدي الناس يقرونها باختلاف السنتهم، على تشاسع بلدانهم.

---

[131] P1 and 2: فإن أولئك   [132] P2: صورة (sic).   [133] P2: البيّنات   [134] P1, 2 and 3: والزبور   [135] P2: أعنى الذي   [136] P2 and 3 om: في سورة يونس   [137] P2: وإن   [138] P2: أنزل الله عليك ؛ P3: أنزل عليك   [139] P3: أتوا   [140] P2 and 3 om: لقد جاءك ... الخاسرين   [141] P2 and 3 add: صحّة   [142] P1 and 3: الذي   [143] P2 and 3: إياها   [144] P2 om.   [145] P2: قائلاً   [146] P2: أجابوا قائلين ؛ P3: فأجابوا قائلين   [147] P2 and 3: لنعجب   [148] P2 and 3: كيف يقولون هذا الكلام ويحتجون به بما عندهم من العلم والمعرفة والذكاء 3: بما عندهم من العلم والمعرفة والذكاء   [149] P2 and 3:   [150] P2 and 3 add: القول علينا

Whoso judgeth not by that which Allah hath revealed: such are evil-livers';
and he says in *The Family of 'Imrān*, 'And if they deny thee, even so did
they deny messengers who were before thee, who came with miracles
and with the Psalms and with the scripture giving light', which is the
holy Gospel. He also says in *Jonah*, 'And if thou art in doubt concerning that which we reveal unto thee then question those who read the
scripture before thee. Verily the truth from thy Lord hath come unto
thee. So be not thou of the waverers. And be not thou of those who
deny the revelations of Allah, for then wert thou of the losers'. (52v) By
this it confirms what we possess, and indeed by giving assent to what is
in them it rejects any suspicions about the Gospel and books which we
possess, and any substitution or alteration to what they contain.

vi. *(15)* I said to them: What if someone should say that substitution
and alteration could have taken place after this declaration? They said,
We would be amazed at how these people, despite their knowledge,
intelligence and perceptiveness, could confront us with such a remark.
For if we were to argue with them in the same way, and say that they
had made alterations and substitutions in the book which they possess
today,

هذا[151] غيّروه وبدّلوه وكتبوا فيه ما
أرادوا واشتهوا، هل كانوا يجوّزون[152]
كلامنا؟ فقلت لهم: هذا ما لا يجوز ولا
يمكن لأحد[153] أن يقوله أبدًا ولا يمكن
أن يتغيّر منه[154] حرف واحد.[155]

فقالوا[156]: إذا كان الكتاب الذي
لهم الذي هو باللسان الواحد العربي
وكان في بقعة واحدة[157] لا يمكن تبدّله
ولا تغيّر حرف واحد منه، فكيف يمكن
تغيّر كتبنا التي هي مكتوبة[158] باثنين
وسبعين لسانًا وفي كلّ لسان منها كذا
ألف ألف[159] مصحف وجاز عليها
إلى مجيء محمّد أكثر من[160] ستمائة
سنة وصارت في أيدي الناس يقرأونها
باختلاف ألسنتهم[161] على سعة بلدانهم
وتباعدها،[162] فمن هو الذي تكلّم باثنين
وسبعين لسانًا؟ أو من هو الذي حكم
على جمعها[163] من أربع زوايا العالم
حتى غيّرها؟ وإن كان غيّر بعضها وتُرك
* بعضها[164] فهذا ما لا يمكن لأنّ جميعها * 5
قول واحد[165] في جميع الألسن، فهذا ما لا
يجوز لقائل أن يقوله أبدًا.

(17)   ثمّ وجدنا ما هو أعظم   (17)   ثمّ وجدنا[166] ما هو أعظم برهانا مما

---

[151] هذا (sic). [152] P2 and 3: ولا لأحد ; P3: كانوا يجوز كان يجوز P2: [153] أجابوا قائلين: سبحان الله العظيم P2 and 3: قد P3 add: [156] حرفًا واحدًا P3: [155] فيه P2 and 3: [154] [157] P2 and 3 om: وكان في بقعة واحدة which is added in the margin of P1. [158] P2 and 3 om: باختلاف ألسنتهم P2 om: [161] كثيرًا فوق P2: [160] كذا كذا ألف P2 and 3: [159] [162] P2: وتباعدها على الدنيا جميعها ملوكها وقساتها [163] P2: في تشاسع بلدانهم P3; على تشاسع بلدانهم [164] P2 and 3: وإن كان ما أمكنه جمعها كلها ولكن بعضها وعالمها حتى حكم على جميعها [165] P2 and 3 add: ونص واحد واعتقاد واحد في هذا الكتاب [166] P2 and 3 add:

and had written in it what they wanted and desired, would they tolerate our words?' I said to them, 'This would not be tolerated, nor could
anyone ever say it. It is impossible for a single jot of it to have been
altered.'

So they said, 'If the book which they have in the one language of
Arabic and is in one location cannot have been altered and not one
letter of it substituted, how can our books which are written in seventy-
two languages be altered?[6] In each one of them there are thousands of
copies, which were accepted for six hundred years before the coming
of Muḥammad. They came into people's hands, and they read them
in their different languages despite the size of their countries and the
distance between them. Who can speak seventy-two languages? Or
who could take the decision to collect them from the four corners of
the earth in order to change them? If some of them were changed and
some were left—this was not possible because they are all (53r) one
message, all the languages. So such a thing cannot ever be said.

(17) Indeed, we have found a proof that is more impressive

---

[6] For a discussion of the origin of this number, cf. Section 4, n. 4, in al-Dimashqī's
Response.

من هذا¹⁶⁷ برهانًا قوله في سورة
الشورى:¹⁶⁸ ﴿وقل آمنت بما أنزل الله
من كتاب¹⁶⁹ وأمرت لأعدل بينكم الله
ربّنا وربّكم لنا أعمالنا ولكم أعمالكم
لا حجّة بيننا وبينكم الله يجمع بيننا وإليه
المصير﴾. وأمّا لغير أهل الكتاب يقول
في سورة الكافرون:¹⁷⁰ ﴿قل يا أيها
الكافرون لا أعبد ما تعبدون ولا أنتم
عابدون ما أعبد ولا أنا عابد ما عبدتم
ولا أنتم عابدون ما أعبد¹⁷¹ لكم دينكم
ولي دين﴾.¹⁷²

(18) وقال أيضًا في سورة¹⁷³
العنكبوت: ﴿ولا تجادلوا¹⁷⁴ أهل الكتاب
إلا بالتي هي أحسن إلا الذين ظلموا
منهم وقولوا¹⁷⁵ آمنا بالذي أنزل إلينا
وأنزل إليكم وإلهنا وإلهكم واحد ونحن
له مسلمون﴾، و لم يقل: "كونوا له
مسلمين"¹⁷⁶ لكن¹⁷⁷ "ونحن" أي¹⁷⁸ عنه
وعن العرب التابعين لما أتى به.¹⁷⁹

vii. (19) وأمّا الذين ظلموا فما
يشكّ¹⁸⁰ أحد في¹⁸¹ أنهم اليهود الذين
سجدوا لرأس العجل وكفروا بالله

تقدم، وهو قوله: "آمنت بما انزل الله
من كتاب. وامرت لاعدل بينكم. الله
ربنا وربكم. لنا اعمالنا ولكم اعمالكم.
لا حجة بيننا وبينكم. الله يجمع بيننا
وبينكم. واليه المصير". واما لغير اهل
الكتاب، فقال فيهم: "قل: يا ايها
الكافرون، لا اعبد ما تعبدون ولا انتم
عابدون ما اعبد. ولا انا عابد ما عبدتم
ولا انتم عابدون ما اعبد. لكم دينكم
ولي ديني".

(18) وقوله ايضا للذين جاهم: "ولا
تجادلوا اهل الكتاب الا بالتي هي احسن،
الا الذين ظلموا منهم. وقولوا: امنا بما
انزل الينا وانزل اليكم. والهنا والهكم
واحد. ونحن له مسلمون". و لم يقل
"كونوا له مسلمين".

(19) فاما "الذين ظلموا"، فما يشك
احد في انهم اليهود، الذين سجدوا
لراس العجل وكفروا بالله، وقتلوا

---

¹⁶⁷ P2 and 3 om: من هذا ¹⁶⁸ P2: صورة الشعري (sic); P3: سورة الشعري (sic).
¹⁶⁹ P3 add: مكتوب ¹⁷⁰ P2 and 3 om: في سورة الكافرون ¹⁷¹ ولا أنتم عابدون ما
أعبد: these words are added in the margin in P2. ¹⁷² P1: ديني ¹⁷³ P2: صورة (sic).
¹⁷⁴ P2: تجادلون; P3: يجادلون ¹⁷⁵ P1: وقالوا ¹⁷⁶ P2 om: كونوا له مسلمين و لم يقل:
¹⁷⁷ P2: لكن قال; P3: ولكن قال ¹⁷⁸ P3: فأعنى بذلك ¹⁷⁹ P2 and 3: التابعين له
وعن العرب ¹⁸⁰ P2: شكّ ¹⁸¹ P3: فيهم

than this in his words in *Counsel*, 'Say: I believe in whatever scripture Allah hath sent down, and I am commanded to be just among you. Allah is our Lord and your Lord. Unto us our works and unto you your works; no argument between us and you. Allah will bring us together, and unto him is the journeying'. As for those who are not People of the Book, it says in *The Disbelievers*, 'Say: O disbelievers! I worship not that which ye worship; nor worship ye that which I worship. And I shall not worship that which ye worship. Nor will ye worship that which I worship. Unto you your religion, and unto me my religion.' *(18)* It also says in *The Spider*, 'And argue not with the People of the Scripture unless it be in (a way) that is better, save with such of them as do wrong; and say: We believe in that which hath been revealed unto us and revealed unto you; our God and your God is one, and we surrender unto him'. It does not say: You surrender to him, but 'and we', i.e. himself and the Arabs who followed what he brought.

vii. *(19)* As for 'such of them as do wrong', there can be no doubt at all that they are the Jews who bowed down before the heifer's head, and refused to believe in God

انبيايه ورسله، وعبدوا الاصنام، وذبحوا
للشياطين ليس حيوانات غير ناطقة
فقط بل بنيهم وبناتهم، حسب ما شهد
الله عليهم به، على لسان داوود النبي
في مزمور مابة وخمسة، اذ يقول: "وذبحوا
بنيهم وبناتهم للشياطين. واراقوا دما
زكيا، دم بنيهم وبناتهم الذي ذكوه
لمنحوتات كنعان. وتنجست الارض
بالدما وتدنست باعمالهم".

مرارًا[182] كثيرة ليس واحدة وقتلوا
أنبياءه[183] وعبدوا الأصنام وذبحوا
للشياطين ليس حيوانات غير ناطقة
فقط بل بنيهم وبناتهم، حسب ما شهد
الله عليهم قائلًا على لسان داوود النبي
في كتابه[184] المسمّى الزبور في مزمور
5 * ماية وخمسة يقول[185]: "ذبحوا بنيهم[186] *
وبناتهم للشياطين وأراقوا دمًا زكيًا، دم
بنيهم وبناتهم الذين[187] ذبحوا لأوثان[188]
كنعان وتدنّست الأرض بالدماء
وتنجّسوا[189] بأعمالهم وزنوا بصنائعهم
وسخط الربّ بغضبه[190] على شعبه
وأرذل[191] ميراثه".

وقال[192] أيضًا على لسان أشعيا
النبي: "يقول الله في بني إسرائيل
لم تسمعوا كلامي ووصاياي لم تحفظوا
وغيّرتم كلّ ما أوصيتكم به فنقضتم[193]
الميثاق الذي كنت جعلته لكم[194] إلى
الأبد، فلذلك أجلسهم على الخزي
والخراب وأهلكهم وأقطع ممّن يبقى[195]
منهم الفرح والسرور. هكذا[196] قال الله
على بني إسرائيل سكان بيت المقدس
سأبدّدهم بين الأمم وفي تلك الأيام
يرفعون الأمم أصواتهم ويمجّدون الله
ويسبّحونه بأصوات عالية ويجتمعون من

حيث : P2 and 3 [182] مرار : P2 [183] P2 and 3 add : ورسله [184] P2 : كتابهم [185] P2 and 3 : يقول [186] P1 : بنينهم [187] P1, 2 and 3 : الذي [188] P2 and 3 : لمنحوتات [189] P2 and 3 : وتنجّست [190] P2 : بغضب ; P3 : بغضبًا (sic). [191] P2 and 3 : ورذل [192] P2 add: الله [193] P2 and 3: كلامي لم يسمعوا ووصاياي لم يحفظوا وغيّروا كلّ ما أوصيتم به ونقضوا [194] P2 om ; P3: لهم [195] P3: تبقى [196] P2: وهكذى

many times not just once, killed his prophets, worshipped idols and offered to satans in sacrifice not just creatures without reason but their sons and daughters, according to what God declares against them, saying on the tongue of the prophet David in his book named Psalms, in Psalm 105, 'They sacrificed their sons (53v) and daughters to satans, and shed pure blood, the blood of their own sons and daughters which they sacrificed to the hewn images of Canaan. The earth was polluted with blood and they became polluted by their deeds, they committed fornication by their deeds, and the Lord's anger was stirred up against his people and he repudiated his heritage'.

Also on the tongue of the prophet Isaiah he says, 'God says concerning the People of Israel: You do not listen to my words, and my injunctions you do not keep. You alter everything I have given you in instruction, and you cancel the covenant which I made for you for ever. For this I will make them dwell in shame and desolation; I will put an end to them, and I will cut off joy and happiness from those of them that are left. Thus says God about the People of Israel, the inhabitants of Jerusalem: I will scatter them among the nations, and in these days the nations will raise their voices and will give glory to God and praise him with loud voices. They will gather from

أقطار الأرض ومن جزائر البحر ومن
البلدان البعيدة ويقدّسون¹⁹⁷ اسم الله
ويرجعون إلى الله إله إسرائيل ويكونون
شعبه وأمّا بنو¹⁹⁸ إسرائيل فيكونون
مبدّدين في الأرض".

وقال أيضًا أشعيا النبي: "يقول الله
يا بني إسرائيل نجّستم جبلي¹⁹⁹ المقدّس
فإني سأفنيكم بالحرب²⁰⁰ وتموتون وذلك
لأني دعوتكم فلم تجيبوني وكلّمتكم فلم
تسمعوني وعملتم الشرّ بين يديّ".

وقال أيضًا أشعيا:²⁰¹ "إنّ²⁰² الله
قد بغض بني إسرائيل ومن بيتهم قد
أخرجهم ولا يغفر²⁰³ لهم لأنهم لعنة.
وقد جعلوا لعنة للناس فلذلك أهلكهم

5 * الله * وبدّدهم بين الأمم ولا يعود
يرحمهم ولا ينظر إليهم برحمته²⁰⁴ إلى أبد
الآبدين. ولا يقرّبون لله قربانًا ولا ذبيحة
في ذلك الزمان²⁰⁵ ولا تفرح بنو²⁰⁶
إسرائيل ولا تهلّل²⁰⁷ كالأمم لأنهم قد
ضلّوا من²⁰⁸ الله".

وقال إرميا النبي: "قال الله²⁰⁹ كما
أنّ الحبشي²¹⁰ لا يستطيع أن يكون
أبيض²¹¹ وكذلك²¹² بنو إسرائيل
لا يتركون عاداتهم القبيحة²¹³ الخبيثة
ولذلك إني لا أرحم ولا أشفق ولا أرقّ

---

197 P2: ويقدّمون   198 P1, 2 and 3: بني   199 P2 and 3: هيكلي   200 P2: بالحروب؛
201 P2 and 3 add : النبي   202 P2 and 3 om.   203 P2: يغضّ   204 P2:
P3: بالجروب   205 P2 and 3: في ذلك الزمان ولا ذبيحة (trsp).   206 P1 and 3: بني   207 P2: برحمة
يتهلّلوا؛ P3: يتهلّلون   208 P1: ظلوا من (sic); P2 and 3: ظلوا عن (sic).   209 P2 and 3 om.
الله 210 P2: الزنجي   211 P1 and 2: أبيضًا   212 P2 and 3: فلذلك   213 P2 and 3 om.

the ends of the earth, from the islands of the sea and from the distant lands, and will praise the name of God, and they will return to God the God of Israel and will be his people. As for the People of Israel, they will be scattered over the earth.'

The prophet Isaiah also says, 'God says: People of Israel, you have defiled my holy mountain, therefore I will destroy you with war and you will die; this is because I called you and you did not answer me; I spoke to you and you did not listen to me, but you did evil in my sight.'

Isaiah also says, 'Indeed God has hated the People of Israel, he has expelled them from his house, and he will not forgive them because they are accursed and they have been made a curse to the people. Because of this, God has destroyed them (54r) and scattered them among the nations. He will no longer have compassion on them and he will never again look on them with his compassion. They will not be able to draw near to God with offering or sacrifice in those days. The People of Israel will not be gladdened and they will not rejoice like the nations, for they have erred from God.'

The prophet Jeremiah says, 'God says: Just as the Ethiopian cannot be white, so the People of Israel will not abandon their foul, evil ways. Because of this I will not show them compassion, nor have pity on them, nor will I relent

على الأمّة الخبيثة²¹⁴ ولا أرثي لها قال
الربّ الله²¹⁵".

وقال حزقيال النبي: "قال الله إنما
رفعت يدي عن بني إسرائيل وبدّدتهم
بين الأمم لأنهم لم يعملوا بوصاياي ولم
يطيعوني²¹⁶ وخالفوني فيما قلت لهم ولم
يسمعوني".

ومثل هذا القول²¹⁷ في التوراة
وكتب الأنبياء وزبور داوود شيء كثير
عند اليهود²¹⁸ يقرؤونها²¹⁹ في كنائسهم
ويقرّون بها²²⁰ ولم ينكروا منها كلمة
واحدة.²²¹

(20) وأمّا نحن النصارى لم²²² نعمل
شيئاً ممّا عملته اليهود، ولذلك جاء
في القرآن²²³ يقول: ﴿لتجدنّ أشدّ
الناس عداوة للذين آمنوا اليهود والذين
أشركوا ولتجدنّ أقربهم مودّة للذين
آمنوا الذين قالوا إنا²²⁴ نصارى ذلك
بأنّ منهم قسّيسيناً ورهباناً²²⁵ وأنهم²²⁶
لا يستكبرون﴾. فقد ذكر القسّيسين²²⁷
والرهبان لئلا يُقال إنّ هذا قيل عن
غيرنا، ودلّ بهذا على جميل أفعالنا²²⁸
وحسن نيّاتنا. (21) نعم ونفى عنّا
اسم²²⁹ الشرك بقوله: "اليهود والذين

(20) فاما نحن النصارى، فلم نفعل شيا
مما فعلته اليهود. ولذلك جا في الكتاب:
"لتجدن اشد الناس عداوة للذين امنوا
اليهود والذين اشركوا. ولتجدن اقربهم
مودة للذبن امنوا الذين قالوا انا نصارى،
ذلك بان منهم قسيسين ورهبان وانهم لا
يستكبرون". فذكر القسيسين والرهبان
ليلا يقال: ان هذا قيل عن غيركم. ودل
بهذا على جميل افعالنا وحسن نياتنا.
نعم. (21) ونفى عنا اسم الشرك بقوله
"اليهود والذين اشركوا اشد عداوة للذين
امنوا، والنصارى اقربهم مودة".

---

²¹⁴ P3 om: على الأمّة الخبيثة   ²¹⁵ P2 and 3 om. ولذلك إني لا أرحم ولا أشفق ولا أرقّ
يقرؤوه :P2 and 3   ²¹⁹ (trsp).   ²¹⁸ P2 and 3: عند اليهود شيء كثير   ²¹⁷ P2 and 3 om.   ²¹⁶ P2: ولا
²²⁰ P2 and 3: به   ²²¹ P2 and 3: منه حرفًا واحدًا ; :P2 and 3 add ومثل هذا هو عندهم   ²²² P2 and 3: فلم   ²²³ P2 and 3: الكتاب   ²²⁴ P1 and وكذلك عندنا في جميع الألسن
جميع جميلنا :P2   ²²⁵ P1: قسوس ورهبان   ²²⁶ P2: وهم   ²²⁷ P1: القسوس   ²²⁸ P2: لأنّ :2
وأفعالنا   ²²⁹ P2 and 3 om.

towards the evil nation or feel sorrow towards them, says the Lord God.'

The prophet Ezekiel says, 'God says: Indeed I have withdrawn my hand from the People of Israel and have scattered them among the nations, because they have not acted according to my injunctions and have not obeyed me. They have offended me in what I said to them and they have not listened to me.'

There are many things in the Torah, the books of the prophets and Psalms of David like these words in the possession of the Jews. They read them in their synagogues, and they believe them and do not deny a single word. *(20)* But we Christians have never done a single thing such as the Jews did. And for this reason in the Qur'an occurs what it says, 'Thou wilt find the most vehement of mankind in hostility to those who believe the Jews and the idolaters. And thou wilt find the nearest of them in affection to those who believe those who say: Lo! We are Christians. That is because there are among them priests and monks, and because they are not proud'. He mentions priests and monks, so that it cannot be said that this is said about anyone other than us. In this he points to our fine deeds, presents the goodness of our intentions positively, *(21)* and denies the name of polytheism with regard to us, in his words, 'The Jews and the

٥ * أشركوا أشدّ عداوة * للذين آمنوا
والنصارى أقربهم مودّة".

(22) "ان الذين امنوا والذين هادوا
والنصارى والصابيين، من امن بالله
وباليوم الاخر وعمل صالحا، فلهم
اجرهم عند ربهم ولا خوف عليهم ولا
هم يحزنون". فساوا بهذا القول بين ساير
الناس، المسلمين وغيرهم.

viii. ‏(22) وقال أيضًا[230] في سورة
البقرة: ﴿إنّ الذين آمنوا والذين هادوا
والنصارى[231] والصابئين من آمن بالله
واليوم الآخر[232] وعمل صالحا فلهم
أجرهم عند ربّهم ولا خوف عليهم ولا
هم يحزنون﴾. وأفصل[233] في هذا[234]
القول بين سائر[235] الناس المسلمين[236]
وغيرهم.

(23) ثم مدح قرابيننا وتواعدنا، ان
اهلنا ما معنا وكفرنا بما انزل الينا،
يعذبنا عذابا لا يعذبه احدا من العالمين،
بقوله: "واذ قال الحواريون : يا عيسى
بن مريم، هل يستطيع ربك ان ينزل
علينا مايدة من السما؟ قال: اتقوا الله
ان كنتم مومنين. قالوا: نريد ان ناكل
منها وتطمين قلوبنا ونعلم ان قد صدقتنا
ونكون عليها من الشاهدين. قال عيسى
بن مريم: اللهم ربنا، انزل علينا مايدة من
السما تكون لنا عيدا لاولنا واخرنا واية
منك. وارزقنا، وانت خير الرازقين. قال
الله: اني منزلها عليكم. فمن يكفر بعد
منكم. فاني اعذبه عذابا لا اعذبه احدا

(23) ثمّ إنه[237] مدح قرابيننا وتوعّدنا
إن أهلنا ما معنا أو كفرنا[238] بما أنزل
إلينا يعـذّبنا عذابًا لم يُعـذّب به أحد
من العالمين بقوله في سورة المائدة: ﴿إذ
قال الحواريون يا عيسى ابن مريم هل
يستطيع ربّك أن ينزل علينا مائدة من
السماء قال[239] اتقوا الله إن كنتم مؤمنين
قالوا نريد أن نأكل منها وتطمئن قلوبنا
ونعلم أن قد صدقتنا ونكون عليها من
الشاهدين قال عيسى ابن مريم اللهم
ربّنا أنزل علينا مائدة من السماء تكون
لنا عيدًا لأوّلنا وآخرنا[240] وآية منك
وأرزقنا[241] وأنت خير الرازقين قال الله
إني منزلها عليكم فمن يكفر بعد[242]

---

[230] P2 om.　[231] P2 add in the margin; P3 om.　[232] P2 add: واليوم الآخر in the margin;
P3 om.　[233] P1: أفيشكوا (?)　[234] P2 and 3: بهذا　[235] P2 om.　[236] P3: والمسلمين　[237] P2
and 3 om.　[238] P2 and 3: وكفرنا　[239] P3 add: يا قوم　[240] P2: ولآخرنا　[241] P2 and 3:
ترزقنا　[242] P3: يكفر من بعد ذلك

idolaters are the most vehement in hostility to those who believe, and the Christians are closest to them in affection.'

viii. *(22)* Furthermore he says in *The Cow*, 'Those who believe, and those who are Jews, and Christians, and Sabaeans—whoever believeth in Allah and the Last Day and doeth right—surely their reward is with their Lord, and there shall no fear come upon them neither shall they grieve'. Here he makes all people, Muslims and others, equal. *(23)* And then he commends our communions and warns us that if we abandon what we have or do not believe in what was revealed to us, he will punish us with a punishment which he has not meted out to any being of the worlds. These are his words in *The Table Spread*, 'When the disciples said: O Jesus, son of Mary! Is thy Lord able to send down for us a table spread with food from heaven? He said: Observe your duty to Allah, if ye are true believers. (They said:) We wish to eat thereof, that we may satisfy our hearts and know that thou hast spoken truth to us, and that thereof we may be witnesses. Jesus, son of Mary, said: O Allah, Lord of us! Send down for us a table spread with food from heaven, that it may be a feast for us, for the first of us and for the last of us, and a sign from thee. Give us sustenance, for thou art the best of sustainers. Allah said: Lo! I send it down for you. And whoso disbelieveth of you

من العالمين". فالمايدة هي القربان الذي
نتقربه في كل قداس.

منكم فإني أعذّبه عذابًا لا أعـــذّبـّه[243]
أحدًا من العالمين﴾. فالمائدة[244] هي
القربان[245] الذي نتقرّب منه[246] في كلّ
قدّاس.[247]

(24) ولما تقدم به القول، ولانه غير لايق
عند ذوي الالباب ان نهمل روح الله
وكلمته – الذي شهد له في هذا الكتاب
بالعظايم وقال عنه: "ان منهم الا ليومنن
به قبل موته، ويوم القيامة يكون عليهم
شهيدا"

(24) ولما تقدّم به القول لأنه غير لائق
عند ذوي الألباب أن يهمل روح القدس
وكلمة الله الذين[248] شهد لهم في هذا[249]
الكتاب بالعظايم. وقال عنه[250] إنّ أيّا
منهم[251] لا يؤمن به قبل موته يوم القيامة
يكون عليهم شهيدًا.

ثمّ يشهد لقرابيننا وذبائحنا أنها
تقدمة مقبولة لدى الله تعالى من كتب
اليهود * التي في أيديهم يومنا هذا[252]
المنزّلة[253] على أفواه الأنبياء.[254] قال
أشعيا النبي: "قال الله إني أعرف بني
إسرائيل وقلوبهم القاسية الخبيثة، فإذا
أنا ظهرت إلى الأمم[255] فنظروا[256] إلى
كرامتي أقيم منهم أنبياء وأبعث منهم[257]
مخلّصين يخلّصون الأمم من البلدان
القاصية الذين لم يسمعوا سماعي ولم
يعرفوا من قبل كرامتي ويكون اسمي
فيهم ويجلبون إخوتهم من الأمم كلّها
ويجيبون[258] قرابين الله[259] على الدواب

243 P2 and 3: يتقرّب   244 P2 and 3: والمائدة   245 P3: القرابين   246 P2: به   247 P3: يتقرّب
248 P2 and 3: الذي   249 P2 om.   250 P2 and 3: عنهم   251 P2 and 3: مَن   مَن
المرسلين   252 P2 om; P3: اليوم هذا   253 P2 and 3 add: من الله تعالى   254 P2 and 3 add: المرسلين
255 P3: للأمم   256 P2 and 3: ونظروا   257 P2 and 3: فيهم   258 P3: ويقدّمون   259 P2 and 3:
على أيديهم ويحملوها ; P3 add: لله

afterward, him surely will I punish with a punishment wherewith I have not punished any of (my) creatures'. For the table is the holy communion which we receive in every communion service.

(24) Thus, in the light of these arguments, it is not appropriate for reasonable people to abandon the Holy Spirit and Word of God, whom he witnesses to in this book with great exaltations. For he says about him, 'There is not one of them but will believe in him before his death, and on the day of resurrection he will be a witness against them'.

Then he witnesses that our communions and sacrifices were guaranteed as acceptable before God the exalted by the books of the Jews (55r) which they possess today, and which have come down through the mouths of the prophets. The prophet Isaiah says, 'God says: Indeed I know the People of Israel and their hard and evil hearts. But when I appear to the nations they will see my glory. I will raise up from them prophets, and from them I will send liberators who will liberate the nations from the distant lands, who have never heard tell of me and have never before acknowledged my glory, and my name will be among them. They will win friends from all the nations and will bring offerings to God on riding animals

والمراكب إلى جبل قدسي[260] بيت
المقدس فيقرّبون لي القرابين بالسميد كما
كانوا بنو إسرائيل من قبل وكذلك تأتي
الأمم وتقرّب القرابين بين يديّ هم[261]
وزرعهم إلى الأبد ويحجّون في كلّ شهر
ومن سنة إلى سنة إلى بيت المقدس بيت
الله كلّهم ويقرّبون لله ربّهم فيه قرابين
ذكيّة نقيّة وينظرون إلى الأمّة الخبيثة
الماردة بني إسرائيل لا يلى خزيها[262] ولا
ينقطع بلاها إلى الأبد".

وقال دانيال النبي: "سيأتي على
شعبك وقرية قدسك سبعون[263] سابوعًا
وتنقضي الذنوب وتفنى الخطايا وغفران
الإثم وليؤتى بالحقّ الذي لم يزل من قبل
ولتتمّ[264] نبوءات الأنبياء وكتب الرسل
وتفسد قرية القدس[265] وتخرب مع مجيء
المسيح ويفنى الميثاق العتيق من الناس
ومن بعد سابوع[266] ونصف تبطل ذبائح
اليهود وقرابينهم وتصير على كنف[267]
النجاسة والفساد إلى انقضاء الجرم[268]" .

وقال ميخا النبي: "قال الله
5 * في آخر الزمان إذا أتى المسيح * يدعو
الأمم المبدّدة ويجعلهم[269] شعبًا واحدًا
وأبطل قتال[270] بني إسرائيل وسلاحهم
وملكهم[271] وقرابينهم إلى الأبد".

---

[260] P2 and 3 om. [261] P2 and 3: أيديهم [262] P2 and 3: حزنها [263] P1, 2 and
3: سابوعًا; [264] P2: ويقيم ويتمّ; P3: وتتمّ [265] P2 and 3: بيت المقدس [266] P1: سبعين
3: ويصنعهم [267] P2 and 3: كف [268] P2 and 3: الخربة [269] P2 and 3: أسبوع P2 and 3:
[270] P2: مثال (sic); P3: ويبطل قتال [271] P2 and 3 om.

and carriages to the mountain of my holiness, Jerusalem, and they will make grain offerings to me as the People of Israel did before. And the nations will likewise come; they will make offerings before me, they and their seed for ever. They will all make pilgrimage in every month and year after year to the holy house, the house of God. And they will make pure, clean offerings to God their Lord there, and they will look on the evil rebellious nation, the People of Israel, whose shame never lightens, whose affliction is never relieved.'

The prophet Daniel says, 'Seventy weeks will be completed for your people and holy city, and offences will come to an end, transgression will cease, there will be forgiveness of sin, truth will be introduced as never before, the prophecies of the prophets and books of the messengers will be fulfilled, and the holy city will be ruined and destroyed with the coming of the Messiah. The old covenant will be brought to an end before the people, and after a week and a half the sacrifices and offerings of the Jews will cease and will be on the wing of impurity and iniquity until there is an end of sin.'

The prophet Micah says, 'God says: In the latter time behold the Messiah will come; (55v) he will call the scattered nations and will make them into one people; he will abolish the murderousness of the People of Israel, their weapons, dominion and offerings for ever.'

وقال عاموص النبي: "لا تذبحوا بعد العجول، فإنّ الربّ سيأتي إلى صهيون ويحدث وصيّة جديدة طاهرة[272] من الخبز النقي والخمر الزكي[273] ويصير بنو[274] إسرائيل مطرودين".[275] وهذا أيضًا يقرّون به اليهود ويقرأونه في[276] كنائسهم و لم ينكروا منه حرفًا واحدًا.

ix. وأيضًا من قول هذا الرجل[277] حيث أتبع القول إنه لم يرسل إلينا مع تشككه فيما أتى به بقوله في هذا الكتاب[278] في سورة سبأ[279] حيث يقول: ﴿وإنا أو إيّاكم[280] لعلى هدى[281] أو في ضلال[282] مبين﴾. وأيضًا قال[283] في سورة الأحقاف:[284] ﴿وما أدري ما يفعل [الله][285] بي ولا بكم﴾ مع الأمر له في فاتحة الكتاب أن يسأل الهداية إلى الصراط المستقيم ﴿صراط الذين أنعمت عليهم غير المغضوب عليهم ولا الضالّين﴾[286]. فأعني بقوله هذا عن الثلاث[287] أمم الذين[288] كانوا في عصره وهم النصارى واليهود وعبّاد الأصنام. فالمنعم عليهم نحن النصارى والمغضوب عليهم فلا يشكّ[289] في[290] أنهم اليهود

— ثم نتبع من لم يرسل الينا، مع تشككه فيما اتى به، بقوله في هذا الكتاب: "واني واياكم لعلى هدى او في ضلال مبين"، مع الامر له، في فاتحة الكتاب، ان يسل الهداية الى "السراط المستقيم، سراط الذين انعمت عليهم، غير المغضوب عليهم، ولا الضالين" — فالذي انعم عليهم نحن النصارى، و"المغضوب عليهم" اليهود، و"الضالين" عباد الاصنام، والسراط الطريق اي المذهب.

---

[272] P2 and 3 om.   [273] P2 and 3: الذكي   [274] P1: بني (sic); P2 and 3: ويصيروا بني   [275] P2 and 3 add: فماذا يكون أعظم برهانًا وأقوى شهادة إذ قد أوردنا أعدائنا المخالفين لديننا من كتب (trsp.).   [276] P3 add: جميع   [277] P2 and 3: الإنسان   [278] P2: بقوله في هذا الكتاب   [279] P2 and 3: النساء (sic).   [280] P2 and 3: وإني وإيّاكم   [281] P2: في هدا   [282] P3: ظلال   [283] P2: وقال   [284] P2 and 3: الأحقاب   [285] P1, 2 and 3 add.   [286] P2: الظاليين; P3 add: آمين   [287] P1 and 2: الثلاثة   [288] P2 and 3: التي   [289] P2 and 3: فبلا شك   [290] P2 and 3 om.

The prophet Amos says, 'Do not sacrifice heifers any more. For the Lord will come to Zion and he will make a new, pure covenant in unblemished bread and clear wine, and he will drive out the People of Israel in exile.' The Jews also confirm this and read it in their synagogues, and they do not deny a single jot of it.

ix. Also among the words of this man is where he next says that he was not sent to us and his own doubts about what he was bringing, in his words in this book in *Sabā'* where he says, 'Lo! we and you assuredly are rightly guided or in error manifest', and also in *The Wind-Curved Sandhills*, 'Nor know I what [God will do] with me or with you', together with the command to him in *The Opening of the Book* to ask for guidance on the straight path, 'The path of those whom thou hast favoured; not the (path) of those who earn thine anger nor of those who go astray'. By these words of his he means the three communities that existed in his day, Christians, Jews and idol worshippers. Now, 'those who are favoured' are we Christians, 'those who are the object of anger' are without doubt the Jews,

الذين غضب الله عليهم في التوراة

وكتب²⁹¹ الأنبياء والضالّون²⁹² فهم عبّاد

الأصنام الذين ضلّوا²⁹³ عن معرفة الله

تعالى. فهذا أمر²⁹⁴ واضح بيّن ظاهر²⁹⁵

* عند كلّ أحد * ولا²⁹⁶ سيّما عند ذوي

العقل والمعرفة. والسراط²⁹⁷ المذهب

أي الطريق وهذه لفظة يونانية²⁹⁸ لأن

الطريق باليونانية أسطراط.²⁹⁹

(25) – قلت: فانهم ينكرون علينا قولنا ابا وابنا وروح القدس. – قالوا: لو علموا ان قولنا هذا، انما نريد به تصحيح القول ان الله تعالى شي حي ناطق، لما انكروا ذلك علينا.	**x.** (25) فقلت لهم: فإنهم³⁰⁰ ينكرون عليكم في قولكم:³⁰¹ آب وابن وروح قدس، وأيضًا في قولكم³⁰² إنهم³⁰³ ثلاثة أقانيم، وأيضًا في قولكم في المسيح³⁰⁴ إنه ربّ وإله وإنه خالق.³⁰⁵ أجابوا قائلين:³⁰⁶ لو³⁰⁷ علموا قولنا هذا إنّما نريد به تصحيح القول إنّ الله تعالى³⁰⁸ حيّ ناطق لما أنكروا ذلك علينا.
(26) لانا، معشر النصارى، لما راينا حدوث الاشيا، علمنا ان شيا غيرها احدثها، اذ لا يمكن حدوثها من ذواتها،	(26) لأننا معشر النصارى لمّا رأينا حدوث الأشياء علمنا أنّ شيئاً غيرها أحدثها إذ لا يمكن حدوثها من ذاتها

²⁹¹ P2 and 3 om.   ²⁹² P1 and 3:والضالين   ²⁹³ P2:ظلوا   ²⁹⁴ P2:شيء
²⁹⁵ P1:أمرًا واضحًا بيّنًا ظاهرًا   ²⁹⁶ P2 and 3: لا   ²⁹⁷ P2 and 3 add: هو   ²⁹⁸ P2 and 3:
²⁹⁹ P2 and 3: بالرومي سراطا   ³⁰⁰ P2 and 3: إنهم   ³⁰¹ P2 and 3: علينا في قولنا   رومية
³⁰² P2 and 3: قولنا   ³⁰³ P2 and 3 om.   ³⁰⁴ P2 and 3: قولنا في السيّد المسيح   ³⁰⁵ P2
³⁰⁶ P2 and 3 add: وأيضًا طلبوا منّا إيضاح تجسّده   and add: وخالق   أمّا قولنا آب: and 3:
³⁰⁷ P2 and 3: فلو   ³⁰⁸ P2 and 3 om.   وابن وروح قدس

upon whom God directed anger in the Torah and books of the prophets, and 'those who go astray' are the idol worshippers who went astray
from knowing about God the exalted. This is a clear, evident and
manifest fact to everyone, (56r) particularly intelligent, knowledgeable
people. And 'the path' which is followed is a highway: it is a Greek
word, for 'highway' in Greek is *isṭirāṭ*.

x. *(25)* I said to them: They disapprove of you saying 'Father, Son
and Holy Spirit'; and also 'They are three hypostases'; and also 'Christ
is Lord, God and Creator'.

They replied saying:

If only they knew these teachings of ours, that we only intend by
this to affirm the teaching that God the exalted is living and articulate, they would not disapprove of us saying this.[7] *(26)* For when we
Christians see that things come into being, we know that something
other than them has brought them into being, since they could not
come into being of themselves

---

[7] This argument is found in 'Ammār al-Baṣrī, *K. al-Burhān*, in M. Hayek, *'Ammār
al-Baṣrī, théologie et controverses*, Beirut, 1977, pp.46-65 and particularly pp. 48.18-49.2,
in the third/ninth century, one of the first generation of known Arabic-speaking
Christian theologians. Cf. Section 6, n. 2, in al-Dimashqī's *Response*.

لما فيها من التضادد. فقلنا انه شي
لا كالاشيا المخلوقة، اذ هو الخالق لكل
شي. وذلك لننفي العدم عنه.

لما فيها من التضادّ[309] والتقلّب. فقلنا
إنه شيء لا كالأشياء المخلوقة إذ هو
الخالق[310] لكلّ[311] شيء وذلك[312] لينفي
العدم عنه.[313]

(27) ورأينا الاشيا تنقسم قسمين: شي
حي وشي غير حي. فوصفناه باجل
القسمين. فقلنا انه حي، لننفي الموتانية
عنه.

(27) ورأينا الأشياء[314] تنقسم قسمين:
شيء حيّ وشيء غير حيّ، فوصفناه
بأجلّ القسمين فقلنا إنه حيّ لينفى الموت
عنه.[315]

(28) ورأينا الحي ينقسم قسمين: حي
ناطق وحي غير ناطق. فوصفناه باجل
القسمين. فقلنا انه ناطق، لننفي الجهل
عنه. (29) والثلثة الاسما، فهي الاله
الواحد الذي لم يزل ولا يزال شيا حيا
ناطقا. فالذات عندنا الاب، الابن النطق،
والحياة الروح القدس.

(28) ورأينا الحيّ ينقسم قسمين: حيًّا
ناطقًا وحيًّا غير ناطق، فوصفناه بأفضل
القسمين[316]، فقلنا إنه ناطق لننفي الجهل
عنه.[317] (29) والثلاثة أسماء فهي[318]
إله واحد لم يزل ولا[319] يزول، شيء
حيّ ناطق:[320] الذات والنطق والحياة،
فالذات عندنا الآب[321] والنطق الابن[322]
والحياة[323] روح القدس.

(30) وهذه الاسما، فلم نسمه نحن
النصارى بها من ذوات انفسنا، بل الله
تعالى اسما لاهوته بها. وذلك قوله على

(30) وهذه الأسماء لم نسمّه نحن
النصارى بها[324] من ذات[325] أنفسنا
5 * بل الله * تعالى سمّى لاهوته بها وذلك

---

309 التضادد :P1, 2 and 3   310 خالق :P2 and 3   311 كلّ :P3   312 P2 and 3: om.
313 عنه العدم (trsp) :P2 and 3   314 المخلوقة :P2 and 3 add   315 لننفي عنه :P2 and 3
(trsp).   316 الموت :P2 and 3 om   317 عنه الجهل :P2 and 3   318 هي :P2 and 3
319 ولم :P2   320 أي :P2 and 3 add   321 أي ابتداء :P2 and 3 add   322 الذي هو مولود منه كولادة النطق من العقل :P2 and 3 add   323 P2 and 3
الشيئين :add   324 هي :P3 om.   325 ذوات :P3

because of the contradictions and inconstancy within them. So we say that he is a thing unlike created things because he is the Creator of all things. This is in order to deny non-existence of him.

(27) And we see things divided into two kinds: Things living and things not living. So we ascribe to him the more exalted of the two kinds and we say he is living in order to deny death of him.

(28) We see living things divided into two kinds: Living things that are articulate and living things that are not. So we ascribe to him the more superior of the two kinds and we say that he is articulate in order to deny ignorance of him. (29) The three names are one eternal and everlasting God: thing, living and articulate, the essence, speech and life. As we see it, the essence is the Father, the speech is the Son and the life is the Holy Spirit.

(30) We Christians have not called him by these names on our own authority, but rather God the exalted calls his divine nature by them. He actually

قوله326 على لسان موسى النبي مخاطبًا لبني إسرائيل قائلاً: "أليس هذا الآب الذي صنعك وبراك واتقنك327 واقتناك؟". وعلى لسانه أيضًا328 قائلاً: "وكان روح الله ترفرف على وجه الماء".329 وقوله330 على لسان داوود النبي: "روحك القدوس لا تنزع مني". وأيضًا قال:331 "بكلمة الله خلقت332 السماوات والأرض333 وبروح فيه جميع جنوده".334 وقوله على لسان أيوب الصديق: "روح الله خلقني وهو يعلّمني". وقوله على لسان أشعيا النبي: "ييبس القتاد335 ويجفّ العشب وكلمة الله باقية إلى الأبد". وقال على لسان داوود النبي: "أنت الربّ إلى الأبد وكلمتك ثابتة في السماء". وقال أيضًا: "لكلمة الله أسبّح".336 وقال السيّد337 المسيح في الإنجيل المقدّس لتلاميذه الأطهار: "إذهبوا إلى جميع الأمم وتلمذوا338 وأعمدوهم339 باسم الآب والابن وروح القدس إله واحد340 وعلّموهم أن يحفظوا جميع ما أوصيتكم به".

لسان موسى النبي مخاطبا لبني اسراييل: "اليس هذا الاب الذي صنعك وبراك واقتناك؟ " وايضا على لسان موسى النبي: "وكان روح الله يرف على الما". وقوله على لسان داوود النبي: "روحك القدوس لا تنزع مني". وايضا على لسان داوود النبي: "بكلمة الله تشددت السموات، وبروح فيه جميع قواهن". وقوله على لسان ايوب الصديق: "روح الله خلقني وهو يعلمني". وقوله على لسان اشعيا النبي: "ييس القتاد ويجف العشب، وكلمة الله باقية الى الابد". وقول السيد المسيح في الانجيل المقدس لتلاميذه الاطهار: "اذهبوا الى ساير الامم، واعمدوهم باسم الاب والابن والروح القدس، وعلموهم ان يحفظوا جميع ما اوصيتكم به".

---

326 P2: وقال ; P3: وذلك قال الله   327 P2 and 3 om.   328 P2: وقال أيضًا على لسانه   329 P2: وأيضًا على ; P3: وقوله على لسان داوود النبي   330 P2: وقال   331 P2: يرفّ على المياه ; P3: يرفّ على الماء   335 P3: القبار   332 P2 and 3: تشدّدت   333 P2 and 3 om.   334 P2 and 3: قواتهن   336 P2 and 3 om: وقال على لسان ... أسبّح   337 P3: سيّدنا   338 P2 and 3 om.   339 P2 and 3: وعمّدوهم   340 P2 om: إله واحد ; P3: الإله الواحد

says on the tongue of the prophet Moses, speaking to the People of Israel, 'Is this not the Father who formed you, created you, made you and got you for his own?'; also on his tongue, 'The Spirit of God was hovering over the face of the water'; his words on the tongue of the prophet David, 'Do not take your Holy Spirit from me'; he also says, 'By the Word of God were the heavens and the earth created and by the breath of his mouth all his hosts'; on the tongue of Job the upright, 'The Spirit of God created me and he teaches me'; on the tongue of the prophet Isaiah, 'The bush dries up and the grass withers away, but the word of the Lord remains for ever'; on the tongue of the prophet David, 'You are the Lord for ever and your Word is established in the heaven'; he also says, 'I give praise to the Word of God'; and the lord Christ says in the holy Gospel to his pure disciples, 'Go to all the nations, make them disciples and baptize them in the name of the Father and of the Son and of the Holy Spirit, one God, and teach them to observe all that I have commanded you'.

(31) وقد قال في هذا الكتاب:[341] ﴿ولقد سبقت كلمتنا لعبادنا المرسلين﴾[342]. وأيضًا قال:[343] ﴿يا عيسى ابن مريم أذكر نعمتي عليك وعلى والدتك إذ أيّدتك بروح القدس﴾. وأيضًا قال:[344] ﴿وكلّم الله موسى تكليمًا﴾. وأيضًا قال[345] في سورة التحريم: ﴿ومريم ابنة عمران التي أحصنت فرجها فنفخنا فيه[346] من روحنا وصدقت بكلمات ربّها وكتبه[347] وكانت من القانتين﴾. وسائر المسلمين يقولون إنّ الكتاب كلام الله ولا يكون كلام إلا لحيّ ناطق.

(32) وهذه صفات جوهرية تجري مجرى أسماء وكلّ صفة منها غير الأخرى وهو إله واحد[348] خالق[349] واحد.[350]

xi. (36) وأمّا اتحاد[351] كلمة الله الخالقة بإنسان[352] مخلوق[353] فإنه لم يخاطب الباري تعالى أحدًا من الأنبياء إلا وحيًا[355] أو من وراء حجاب حسب ما جاء في هذا الكتاب قوله[356] في سورة

---

(31) وقد قال في هذا الكتاب: "ولقد سبقت كلمتنا الى عبادنا الصالحين". وايضا : "واذ قال الله: يا عيسى بن مريم، اذكر نعمتي عليك وعلى والدتك، اذ ايدتك بروح القدس". وايضا: "وكلم الله موسى تكليما". وايضا: "مريم ابنة عمران التي احصنت فرجها، فنفخنا فيه من روحنا. وصدقت بكلمات ربها وكتبه. وكانت من القانتين". وساير المسلمين يقولون ان الكتاب كلام الله، ولا يكون كلام الا الحي ناطق.

(32) وهذه فصفات جوهرية تجري مجرى اسما. وكل صفة منها غير الاخرى، والاله واحد.

(36) فاما تجسم كلمة الله انسانا تاما، فلانه لم يخاطب الباري تعالى احدا من الانبيا الا من ورا حجاب، حسب ما جا في الكتاب: "وما كان لبشر ان يكلمه الله الا وحيا او من ورا حجاب".

---

341 P2: وقد ; P2 and 3: أيضًا   342 P1: لعبادنا الصالحين ; P2 and 3: إلى عبادنا الصالحين   343 P2:
(trsp). وقال أيضًا :P2 344   (trsp). وقال أيضًا :P2 345   خالق :P1 346   وقال أيضًا :P2 347 P2 om.   348 P2
and 3: فالإله هو واحد   349 P2 and 3: وخالق   350 P2 and 3 add: واحد لا يتبعّض ولا يتجزّأ
ولادتهما معًا مع أي الكلمة مع :P2 351 تجسّم :P3   352 P3: بإنسانًا (sic)   353 P2 and 3 add: إذ يقول
الناسوت :P3 354   بالوحي :P3 355 P2 and 3 om.   356 P2 and 3: إذ يقول

(31) And he says in this book, 'And verily our word went forth of old unto our bondmen sent'; he also says, 'O Jesus, son of Mary! Remember my favour unto thee and unto thy mother; how I strengthened thee with the holy Spirit'; he also says, 'And God spake directly unto Moses'; and he also says in *Banning*, 'And Mary, daughter of 'Imrān, whose body was chaste, therefore we breathed therein something of our Spirit. And she put faith in the words of her Lord and his scriptures, (57r) and was of the obedient.' All the Muslims say that the book is the word of God, and only one who is living and articulate possesses word.

(32) These are attributes of the substance which are just like names, and each one of the attributes is different from the other, and he is one God, one Creator.

xi. *(36)* As for the Word of God, which is creator, uniting with a created human, the exalted Creator never addressed any of the prophets except through revelation or from behind a veil, as is given in this book where it says in

الشورى:³⁵⁷ ﴿وما³⁵⁸ كان لبشر أن
يكلّمه الله إلا وَحيًا أو من وراء حجاب
أو³⁵⁹ يرسل رسولاً فيوحي بإذنه ما
يشاء إنه عليّ حكيم﴾. فقد جوّز القرآن
ظهور الله في حجاب، والمسيح بناسوته
حجاب الله الذي كلّم الله الخلق منه.
وقوله في سورة النساء: ﴿إنّما [المسيح]
عيسى ابن مريم رسول الله وكلمته ألقاها
إلى مريم وروح منه﴾ أي من ذاته.
وقوله: ﴿ألقاها إلى مريم﴾ أي أحلّها في
الذات البشرية المتبشّرة فيها.

واذا كانت اللطايف لا تظهر الا في
الكثايف، افكلمة الله تعالى التي خلقت
اللطايف تظهر في غير كثيف؟ - كلا!
ولذلك ظهر في عيسى بن مريم، اذ
الانسان اجل ما خلقه الله، ولهذا خاطب
الخلق الذي شاهده منه، كما خاطب
موسى النبي من العوسجة.

وإذا³⁶⁰ كانت اللطائف لا تظهر
إلا في الكثائف،³⁶¹ فكلمة الله تعالى³⁶²
التي بها خُلقت اللطائف تظهر في غير
كثيف كلا. ولذلك ظهر في عيسى ابن
مريم، إذ³⁶³ الإنسان أجلّ ما خلقه الله،
ولهذا³⁶⁴ خاطب الخلق منه³⁶⁵ وشاهدوا
منه ما شاهدوا.
وقد قال الله تعالى على أفواه
الأنبياء المرسلين الذين³⁶⁶ تنبّأوا على
ولادته³⁶⁷ وعلى جميع أفعاله التي فعلها
في الأرض.³⁶⁸ * وكذلك هي³⁶⁹ عند
اليهود وهم مقرّون معترفون بها³⁷⁰ ولم

* 5

---

³⁵⁷ P2 and 3 om: في سورة الشورى   ³⁵⁸ P1: ما   ³⁵⁹ P2 and 3 om from: أو يرسل :to
³⁶⁰ P2: وإذ   ³⁶¹ P2 and 3 add: وغيرها مثل الروح   ³⁶² P2 and 3 om.   ³⁶³ P2: إذا
³⁶⁴ P2: فلهذا ; P3: وبهذا   ³⁶⁵ P2 and 3 om.   ³⁶⁶ P1 and 3: الذي   ³⁶⁷ P2 and 3 add: من المتبشّرة فيها
³⁶⁸ P2 and 3 add: وصعوده إلى السماء   ³⁶⁹ P2 and 3: وهذه النبوءات جميعها   العذراء الطاهرة مريم
³⁷⁰ P2: ومعترفين ومقرّين بها ; P3: مقرّين بها ; ومقرّين معترفين

Counsel, 'And it was not (vouchsafed) to any mortal that Allah should speak to him unless by revelation or from behind a veil, or (that) he sendeth a messenger to reveal what he will by his leave. Lo! He is exalted, wise'. So the Qur'an approves of God appearing through a veil, and Christ in his humanity is God's veil, through whom God spoke to creation. His words in *Women*: 'The Messiah, Jesus son of Mary, was only a messenger of Allah, and his word which he conveyed unto Mary, and a spirit from him', that is, from his essence, and his words 'which he conveyed unto Mary' mean that he established it in the human essence, which rejoiced in it.

If refined things are only made manifest in physical things, then the Word of God the exalted, by which refined things were created, could not possibly be made manifest in anything other than a physical thing. Thus it was made manifest in Jesus, son of Mary, because humankind is the most noble thing that God the exalted has created, and in this way he spoke to creation from him and they beheld something of him.[8]

God the exalted spoke through the mouths of the prophets who had been sent, who prophesied about his birth and all his actions that he performed on earth. (57v) Thus the Jews possess them, and they acknowledge and confess them and do not

---

[8] This argument is also found in ʿAmmār al-Baṣrī, *K. al-Burhān*, pp. 62.15-68.10.

ينكروا منها[371] حرفًا واحدًا[372] وسبيلنا
أن[373] نذكر بعض ما قال[374] الأنبياء
الذين تنبّأوا على ولادة[375] السيّد[376]
المسيح ونزوله إلى[377] الأرض.

قال عزرا الكاهن[378] حيث سباهم
بخت نصر إلى أرض بابل قال: "إلى
أربعماية سنة واثنتين وثمانين سنة[379] يأتي
المسيح ويخلّص الشعوب والأمم".[380]

قال[381] إرميا النبي: "في ذلك
الزمان[382] يقوم لداوود ابن[383] وهو
ضوء[384] النور يملك الملك ويعلّم ويفهم
ويقيم الحقّ والعدل في الأرض ويخلّص
من آمن به من اليهود ومن إسرائيل[385]
ويبقي بيت المقدس بغير مقاتل واسمه
الإله".[386]

وقال أشعيا النبي: "قل لصهيون
هناك تفرح وتتهلّل[387] بأنّ[388] الله يأتي
ويخلّص من آمن به من شعبه ويخلّص
مدينة بيت المقدس ويظهر الله ذراعه
الطاهر فيها[389] لجميع الأمم المبدّدين
ويجعلهم أمّة واحدة ويبصرون جميع أهل
الأرض[390] خلاص الله لأنه يمشي معهم

---

[371] P2: كلمة ؛ [372] P2 and 3: ولم يقدروا أن ينكروا منها ; P3: ولم ينكروا منه P2: [373] ولنذكر ؛ [374] P2: أقوال [375] P2 and 3 om. [376] P3: سيّدنا [377] P2 and 3: واحدة [378] P2: الكاتب [379] P2: واثنين وثمانين سنة ؛ P1 and 3: وثمانون [380] P2 and 3: على [381] P2 and 3: وقال [382] P2 and 3: add: وعند كمال هذه السنين المذكورة أتى المسيح [383] P1, 2 and 3: ابنًا [384] P3: ضياء [385] P2: بني اسرائيل [386] P2 and 3 add: اليوم وأمّا قوله ابن داوود لأنّ مريم كانت من نسل داوود لأجل ذلك قال النبي يقوم لداوود ابنًا (sic) جميع الأمم [387] P3: يفرح ويتهلّل [388] P2 and 3: فإنّ [389] P2 om. [390] P2 and 3:

deny a single word of them. We will now proceed to cite some of the utterances of the prophets which they prophesied about the birth of the lord Christ and his descent to earth.

When Nebuchadnezzar led them into exile in the land of Babylon, Ezra the priest said, 'In four hundred and eighty-two years the Christ will come to free the people and the nations'.

The prophet Jeremiah says, 'At this time a son of David will rise up, the brightness of light; he will rule the kingdom, he will teach and instruct, he will establish truth and justice on the earth and he will redeem those who believe in him among the Jews and Israel, and Jerusalem will remain without warriors, and his name will be God.'

The prophet Isaiah says, 'Say to Zion, behold, be happy and rejoice, for God is coming and will liberate those who believe in him amongst his people. He will liberate the city of Jerusalem and God will show there his holy arm to all the scattered nations, and he will make them a single nation. All the people of the earth will behold the salvation of God, for he will walk with them

وبين أيديهم ويجمعهم إله اسرائيل".

وقال[391] زكريا[392] النبي: "إفرحي
يا ابنة صهيون لأني آتيك وأحلّ فيك
وأتراءى قال الله ويؤمن بالله في ذلك
اليوم الأمم الكثيرة ويكونون له شعبًا
واحدًا ويحلّ هو وهم فيك[393] وتعرفين
أني[394] أنا الله القوي الساكن فيك
ويأخذ الله في ذلك اليوم الملك من

* 5 *يهوذا ويملك عليهم إلى الأبد".

وقال عاموص النبي: "ستشرق
الشمس على[395] الأرض ويهتدي[396]
بها الضالّون[397] ويضلّ[398] عنها بنو
إسرائيل[399]".

وقال في السفر الثالث من أسفار
الملوك: "والآن[400] يا ربّ إله إسرائيل[401]
لتحقّق كلامك لداوود أبي[402] لأنه[403]
حقّ أن يكون آية[404]، سيسكن الله مع
الناس على الأرض. إسمعوا أيّتها الشعوب
كلّكم ولتنصت الأرض وكلّ من فيها
ويكون[405] الربّ عليها شاهدًا، الربّ من
بيته المقدّس[406] ويخرج من موضعه وينزل

---

391 P2: قال   392 P3: زخاريا   393 P2: فيهم ويتمّ فيك; P3: وهو يتمّ فيك   394 P3 om.   395 P3
om. (sic). 396 P1, 2 and 3: ويهتدوا   397 P1: الظالين بها; P2: الظاليين بها (sic); P3: بها الظالين (sic); 398 P1: ويظلون; P2: ويضلوا; P3: ويظلوا (sic). 399 P2 and 3 add: [P3 : فالشمس والشمس
هي السيّد المسيح والضالين [والظاليين :P2] الذين اهتدوا هم النصارى المختلفة ألسنتهم الذين
كانوا من قبل عابدي [عابدين :P2] الأصنام والضالين [هم الظاليين :P2] عن معرفة الله فلمّا أتوهم
التلاميذ [الحواريين :P3 add] وأنذروهم بما أوصاهم السيّد [سيّدنا :P3] المسيح [:P3 add
وما عاينوه منهم من العجائب العظيمة] وتركوا عبادة الأصنام واهتدوا باتّباعهم السيّد
المسيح [يسوع : P3 add] : الآن 400 P2 and 3 om: إله إسرائيل :P2 401 P2 and 3: 402 P2: عبدك;
P3 om. 403 P2 and 3: أنه   404 P2 and 3: أنه   405 P2 and 3: فيكون   406 P2: مدينة المقدس;
P3: بيته القدوس

and before them; the God of Israel will unite them.'

The prophet Zechariah says, 'Rejoice, O daughter of Zion, for I am coming to you, and will dwell among you and show myself. God says: Many nations will believe in God that day, and they will become one people before him, and he and they will dwell within you, and you will know that I, God the almighty, am residing within you. On that day God will appoint a king from (58r) Judah, and he will rule over them for ever.'

The prophet Amos says, 'The sun will rise over the earth, and those who are astray will be guided by it, but the children of Israel will stray from it.'

In the third Book of Kings it says, 'Lord God of Israel, now may your word to David my father be confirmed. For it is true that the sign will be that God will reside with mankind on the earth; all you peoples take heed of it, and let the earth and all who are in it give ear, and the Lord will be a witness against it; the Lord from his holy house, he will leave his place and come down

ويطأ على مشارق⁴⁰⁷ الأرض في شأن
خطيئة بني يعقوب"، هذا كله.

وقال ميخا النبي: "وأنت بيت⁴⁰⁸
لحم قرية يهوذا بيت أفراتا منك يخرج
لي رئيس⁴⁰⁹ الذي يرعى شعبي إسرائيل
وهو من قبل أن تكون الدنيا لكنه
لا⁴¹⁰ يظهر إلا في الأيام التي تلد فيها
الوالدة وسلطانه من أقاصي الأرض إلى
أقاصيها.^{"411}

وقال حبقوق النبي: "إنّ الله يتراءى
في الأرض⁴¹² ويختلط بالناس ويمشي
معهم".

وقال⁴¹³ إرميا النبي: "الله بعد هذا
يظهر في الأرض ويتقلّب مع البشر
يقول⁴¹⁴ الله ربّ الأرباب".

وقال⁴¹⁵ أشعيا النبي: "ها
هي⁴¹⁶ العذراء تحبل وتلد ابنًا ويدعى
اسمه عمانوئيل"، وعمانوئيل كلمة عبرانية
وتفسيرها بالعربي⁴¹⁷: إلهنا معنا.⁴¹⁸

وقال أيضًا: "أن ولدًا⁴¹⁹ ولد لنا
وابن أعطيناه الذي رئاسته على عاتقه
ومنكبيه⁴²⁰ * ويدعى اسمه ملكًا عظيم

5 *

---

⁴⁰⁷ P2 and 3 om. ⁴⁰⁸ P2 and 3: يا بيت ⁴⁰⁹ P1 and 3: رئيسًا ⁴¹⁰ P2 and 3: لم
⁴¹⁵ P3: ⁴¹⁴ P3: ويقول ⁴¹³ P3: قال ⁴¹² P2 and 3: على الأرض يتراءى ⁴¹¹ P2: أقصائها
قال ⁴¹⁶ P3: هوذا ⁴¹⁷ P2: تفسيرها بالعبراني ; P3: تفسيرها بالعربي ⁴¹⁸ P2 and 3 add:
فقد شهد النبي أنّ مريم ولدت اللاهوت المتجسّد بالناسوت [الناسوت المتحد باللاهوت :P3]
أعني منكبيه :P2; منكبيه :P3 420 غلامًا :P2 and 3 419 كلاهما

to subjugate the eastern parts of the earth because of the sins of the children of Jacob.' All of this.

The prophet Micah says, 'And you, O Bethlehem, city of Judah, house of Ephrātā, from you will come out for me a leader; he will shepherd my people Israel. He existed before the earth was, but he will only appear in the days when a woman with child gives birth to him. And his rule will be from one end of the earth to another.'

The prophet Habakkuk says, 'God will appear on earth; he will mingle with the people and will walk with them.'

The prophet Jeremiah says, 'After this God will appear on the earth; he will commune closely with man; he will say, "God, the Lord of lords".'

The prophet Isaiah says, 'Behold, the virgin will be with child and will give birth to a son, and he will be called Emmanuel'. 'Emmanuel' is a Hebrew word, the meaning of which in Arabic is 'our God with us'.

He also says, 'A child has been born to us, a son we have been given. His government is on his neck and shoulders, (58v) and his name will be called king mighty

المشيئة مشيرًا ملكًا[421] عجيبًا إلهًا قويًا مسلّطًا رئيس السلامة أب كلّ الدهور سلطانه كامل ليس له فناء".

وقال أشعيا أيضًا: [422] " تخرج عصاه من أصل يسّي وينبت نورًا منها[423] ويحلّ فيه روح الله[424] روح[425] الحكمة والفهم روح الحيل والقوّة روح[426] العلم وخوف الله. وفي تلك الأيام يكون أصل يسّي آية للأمم وبه يؤمنون وعليه يتوكّلون ويكون لهم النياح[427] والكرامة إلى دهر الداهرين".

وقال أشعيا أيضًا:[428] " ومن أعجب الأعاجيب أنّ ربّ الملائكة سيولد من البشر".

ومثل هذا القول عندنا[429] في كتب الله[430] المنزّلة على أفواه الأنبياء[431] شيء كثير.[432] وإنّما ذكرنا بعضه[433] لنجد[434] الحجّة لتثبيت ديننا وما نعتقده. وهذه النبوءات جميعها عند اليهود وهم مقرّون معترفون لنا بذلك ولم ينكروا منها حرفًا واحدًا.[435]

---

[421] P2 and 3 om. [422] P2: أشعيا النبي أيضًا ; P3: أيضًا أشعيا النبي [423] P2 and 3: منها [424] P2: القدس [425] P2 and 3: وروح [426] P2 and 3: وروح [427] P3: التاج [424 نورًا (trsp). [428] P2 and 3: أشعيا النبي أيضًا [429] P2 and 3 om. [430] P2: الأنبياء ; P3: الكتب كتب الله [431] P2 and 3 add: والرسل [432] P2 and 3 add: في المتفرقين ألسنتهم المختلفة جميعهم النصارى عند سبعة أقاليم الدنيا [P3: العالم] المتمسّكين بدين النصرانية قول واحد ونصّ واحد على ما تسلّموه من الرسل الحواريين حين أنذروهم وردّوهم عن عبادة الأصنام إلى معرفة الله تعالى، سلّموها إليهم كلّ أمّة بلسانها وهي على هيئتها إلى يومنا هذا. وكذلك هذه الكتب عند اليهود على هذا اللفظ والنصّ على ما تسلّموه من موسى النبي وباقي الأنبياء مقرّين بذلك جميعه ولم ينكروا منه كلمة واحدة [433] P2 and 3: القليل هذا أوردنا وإنما الأنبياء كتب في ما بعض ذكرنا الذي وهذا [434] P2 and 3 add: ذلك [435] This phrase is omitted in P2 and 3. Cf. n. 432 above.

in will, counsellor, wonderful king, powerful and mighty God, prince of peace, father of all times. His dominion is perfect and will know no decline.'

Isaiah also says, 'A rod will go forth from the root of Jesse, and a shoot will spring up from it. In him will dwell the Spirit of God, the Spirit of wisdom and understanding, the Spirit of strength and power, the Spirit of knowledge and the fear of God. In those days the root of Jesse will be a sign for the nations: in him they will believe and on him they will depend. He will be to them tranquillity and honour for ever and ever.'

Isaiah also says, 'It is the greatest miracle that the Lord of the angels should be born of humankind.'

We have many things similar to these in the books of God sent down through the mouths of the prophets, though we have only mentioned some so that we may establish the argument to validate our religion and what we believe. The Jews possess all these prophecies: they acknowledge them and confess them to us, and they do not deny a single word of them.

xii. فقلت لهم: "إن كانت هذه النبوءات عند اليهود وهم مقرّون ومعترفون[436] بها أنها حقّ وأنها عتيدة أن تكمل عند مجيء المسيح[437] فأيّ حجة لهم عن الإيمان به؟

قالوا:[438] " إنّ الله تعالى[439] اختار بني إسرائيل واصطفاهم له شعبًا في ذلك الزمان دون كلّ العالم[440] وحيث كانوا في أرض مصر في عبودية فرعون أرسل[441] إليهم موسى * النبي دلّهم على معرفة الله تعالى وأوعدهم أنّ الله يخلّصهم من عبودية فرعون ويخرجهم من مصر ويورثهم أرض الميعاد التي هي أرض بيت المقدس، فطلب[442] موسى من الله[443] وعمل العجائب[444] أمامهم[445] وضرب أهل مصر العشر ضربات[446] وهم يرون ذلك جميعه.[447] وأخرجهم من مصر بيد قوية وشقّ لهم البحر وأدخلهم فيه وصار لهم الماء حائطًا[448] عن يمينهم وحائطًا عن شمالهم[449] ودخل فرعون وجميع جنوده[450] خلفهم فلمّا برزوا بنو إسرائيل من البحر أمر الله لموسى أن يردّ عصاه

* 5

---

[436] P1, 2 and 3 مقرّين ومعترفين | [437] P2: قد جاء السيّد المسيح والسيّد المسيح | [438] P2: أجابوا قائلين | P3: أجابوه قائلين | [439] P2 and P3: قد جاء مجيء المسيح والمسيح | [440] P2 om: دون كلّ الأمم الذين كانوا | P3: دون الأمم الذين كانوا في الأرض | 3 om. | [441] P2 and 3: رحمهم وأرسل | [442] P2 and 3: وطلب | [443] P2 adds: تعالى | [444] P2 and 3 add: والآيات | [445] P2 and 3: قدّام عيونهم | [446] P2 adds: على ما يشهد في ما تشهد به التوراة | P3 adds: على ما تشهد به التوراة ؛ به موسى في كتاب التوراة | [447] P2 and 3 add: حافظًا عن يمينهم وعن | [448] P3 adds: كالنور | [449] P2: ويعلموا أنّ الله تعالى (P3 om) يصنعه لأجلهم | [450] P3: شمالهم عساكره وجنوده

xii. I said to them: If the Jews possess these prophecies, and they acknowledge and confess that they are true and they will be fulfilled when Christ comes, what pretext do they have for not believing in him?

They said: God the exalted chose the People of Israel and made them a people for himself from all the world at that time. When they were in the land of Egypt in slavery to Pharaoh, he sent the prophet Moses to them (59r) to lead them to the knowledge of God the exalted, and to promise them that God would free them from slavery to Pharaoh and lead them out of Egypt and would give them the promised land, which is the land of Jerusalem. Moses prayed to God and he worked miracles before them: he struck the people of Egypt with the ten plagues, and they saw it all; he led them out of Egypt with a mighty hand and parted the sea for them; he led them through it and the water became a wall for them on their right and on their left. Pharaoh and all his armies went in behind them, and when the People of Israel came out of the sea God ordered Moses to strike his staff

على الماء فعاد الماء مثلما كان وغرق

فرعون وجميع جنوده[451] في الماء وبنو

إسرائيل ينظرون ذلك.[452]

فلمّا غاب عنهم موسى[453] إلى

الجبل ليناجي الله تعالى وأخذ لهم التوراة

من يد الله تعالى[454] تركوا عبادة الله

ونسوا جميع أفعاله[455] وعبدوا رأس

العجل.

ثمّ بعد هذا[456] عبدوا الأصنام. ليس

مرّة واحدة[457] فقط بل مرارًا كثيرة

وذبحوا لهم الذبائح ليس حيوانات غير

ناطقة فقط بل بنيهم وبناتهم حسب

ما تنبّأت عليهم الأنبياء[458] وأفعالهم

جميعها[459] مكتوبة[460] في أخبار بني

إسرائيل.[461]

فلمّا رأى الله سبحانه وتعالى

قساوة قلوبهم وغلظ رقابهم وكفرهم

وأفعالهم النجسة الخبيثة سخط[462] عليهم

5 * وجعلهم * مرذولين منهانين[463] في جميع

الأمم وليس لهم[464] ملك ولا كاهن[465]

ولا نبي[466] إلى الأبد حسب ما تنبّأت

عليهم الأنبياء وتشهد[467] به كتبهم التي في

---

451 P3: الحيّ   452 P2 and 3 add: عساكره وجنوده   453 P2 and 3 add: جميعه   454 P2 and 3 add: النبي

455 P3 adds: وما عمله قدّامهم من العجائب   456 P2 and 3: ذلك   457 P2 om.   458 P2 and 3 add:

مكتوب جميعه   459 P2 and 3 add: وكفرهم وعبادتهم الأصنام   460 P2 and 3: وقد ذكرناه قبل ذلك

غضب   462 P2 and 3: عندهم وعندنا على قول واحد ونصّ واحد   461 P2 and 3 add:

463 P2: ومنهانين مبدّدين ; P3: ومهانين ومبدّدين   464 P2: لها   465 P2 and 3:

ولا بلاد   466 P2 and 3: وبطل منهم الكهنوت والقربان   467 P3: وما تشهد

on the water; the water returned to where it had been, and Pharaoh and all his armies were drowned in the water; the People of Israel witnessed this.

When Moses withdrew from them onto the mountain to converse with God the exalted, and took the Torah from the hand of God the exalted for them, they abandoned the worship of God and forgot all his acts, worshipping a heifer's head.

Then after this they worshipped idols, not once but many times. They made sacrifices to them, not inarticulate animals but their sons and daughters. This is according to what the prophets prophesied against them. All their acts are written in the chronicles of the People of Israel.

When God, blessed and exalted, saw the hardness of their hearts, their stubbornness and their disbelief in him, and their vile, abominable acts, he grew angry with them and made them (59v) contemptible and insignificant among all the nations, and they have had no king, priest or prophet ever again. This is as the prophets prophesied about them, and as their books, which they have in

أيديهم يومنا هذا.

فمن ذلك468 ما قال الله لأشعيا469

النبي: "إذهب وقل لهذا الشعب

سيسمعون سمعًا470 ولا471 يفهمون

وينظرون نظرًا ولا يتصوّرون472 لأن

قلب هذا الشعب قد غلظ473 وقد سمعوا

بأفهامهم474 سمعًا ثقيلاً. وقد غمضوا

عيونهم لئلا يبصروا475 بأعينهم ويسمعوا

بآذانهم ويفهموا بقلوبهم ويرجعوا إليّ

فأخلّصهم".476

وقال أيضًا أشعيا:477" هكذا478

مقتت نفسي سبوتكم ورؤوس شهوركم

صارت عندي مرذولة، قال الله:" وفي

ذلك اليوم يقول الله سأبطل479 السبوت

والأعياد كلّها وأعطيهم480 سنّة جديدة

مختارة لا كالسنّة التي أعطيتها لموسى

عبدي يوم حوريب يوم الجمع الكثير،

بل سنّة جديدة مختارة آمر481 بها

وأخرجها من صهيون". فصهيون هي

أورشليم والسنّة الجديدة المختارة هي

السنّة التي تسلّمناها نحن معشر النصارى

من أيدي الرسل الحواريين الأطهار.482

فأيّ بيان يكون أوضح483 من هذا البيان

سمعًا يسمعون :P3 ; سماعًا :P2 470 قال أشعيا :P3 ; وقد قال أشعيا :P2 469 وذلك :P3 ;om P2 468
بآذانهم :P2 474 حدّا :add P2 and 3 473 فلا ينظرون :P2 and 3 472 فلا :P2 and 3 471 سماعًا
وقال أشعيا النبي :P3 ; "أشعيا" :om P2 477 فأرحمهم :P2 and 3 476 ينظرون :P2 475
أيضًا 478 قال الله هكذا :P2 and 3 479 أبطل :P2 and 3 480 وأعطيكم :P2 481 آمرها :P3
الذين خرجوا من أورشليم وداروا في سبعة أقاليم العالم وأنذروا :adds P2 482 (sic) آمرها :P3
بهذه السنّة الجديدة . P3 omits ca 3 lines of this added text in P2 owing to dittography.
وأصح :adds P2 483

their possession today, bear witness.

To this effect is what God said to the prophet Isaiah, 'Go, say to this people: You will hear but not understand, you will look but not see, because the minds of this people have been dulled and they understand little of what they hear; they have closed their eyes so that they cannot see or hear with their ears or understand with their minds or turn to me to save them.'

Isaiah also said, 'Likewise your sabbaths and new moons are abominable to me and have become despicable in my eyes; God said: 'On that day I will put an end to all sabbaths and festivals, and I will give you a new chosen law, not like the law I gave to my servant Moses on the day of Horeb, the day of the great assembly, but a new chosen law which I will enjoin and will send out from Zion.' Now Zion is Jerusalem, and the new chosen law is the law which we Christians have received from the hands of the Apostles, the holy disciples. What demonstration could be clearer than this

إذ قد أوردناه من قول الله تعالى؟ ولا

سيّما وأعداؤنا اليهود[484] يشهدون لنا

* بصحّة ذلك،[485] وإن * أنكروا فينكروا

عند مَن ليس له معرفة بكتبهم وذلك

لخبثهم وتغبيتهم وتعنّتهم. وهذه النبوءات

مثلما هي عندنا وكذلك عند اليهود

وكذلك عند النصارى جميعهم المتفرّقين

في جميع الدنيا وفي الألسن جميعها على

ما تسلّموها من الرسل الأطهار إلى يومنا

هذا قولاً واحدًا.[486]

وأمّا حجّة اليهود في هذه النبوءات

فإنهم[487] يقولون ويعتقدون أنها[488] حقّ

ولم ينكروا أنها قول الله سبحانه وتعالى،

ولكن يقولون[489] إنها عتيدة أن تكمل

وتتمّ عند مجيء المسيح لكن المسيح[490] ما

قد جاء بعد وإنّ الذي جاء ليس كان[491]

المسيح، حتى أنهم يكفرون ويتجرأون

بكفرهم[492] ويقولون إنه كان مضلّ وإنّ

المسيح[493] عتيد أنه[494] يأتي ويكمل[495]

نبوءات الأنبياء، فإذا ما أتى تبعناه.[496]

وهذا رأيهم واعتقادهم في السيّد

المسيح. فماذا يكون أعظم من هذا

الكفر الذي هم عليه؟ ولأجل ذلك

---

[484] P2 and 3 add: المخالفين   [485] P2 and 3 add: جميعه   [486] Ca 3 lines of text: وإن أنكروا ... are omitted in P2 and 3.   [487] P2 and 3 om.   [488] P2: بأنها   [489] P2 and 3 om: وهذا المسيح التي (sic) :P3؛ وينكرون بمجيئه ويقولون :P2   [490] ولم ينكروا أنها ... ولكن يقولون هو المسيح الذي تنبئوا :P3   [491] نحن النصارى مؤمنين به أنكروا به ويقولون الحقّ   [492] P2 and 3 add: ويتبجحون بقوة كفرهم   [493] P2 and 3: عليه الأنبياء   [494] P2 and 3: أن   [495] P1: وتكمّل   [496] P1: أتبعناه

that we have quoted from the word of God the exalted, particularly since our enemies the Jews acknowledge to us that this is correct? If (60r) they did make a denial, this would be a denial among those who had no knowledge of their books, and this is due to their wickedness, ignorance and stubbornness. Just as these prophecies are in our possession, so they are in the possession of the Jews and also of all the Christians scattered over all the world and in all their languages, as they received them from the pure Apostles, to this day a single message.

As for the Jews' argument concerning these prophecies, they say and believe that they are true, and they do not deny that they are the word of God, blessed and exalted. But they say that they will be fulfilled and completed when the Messiah comes, though the Messiah has not come and is far off, and he who has come is not the Messiah. And not only do they not believe, but they wantonly compound their unbelief by saying that he was a deceiver, for the Messiah is still to come, and the prophecies of the prophets will be fulfilled. 'And when he comes, we will follow him'.

This is what they think and believe about the lord Christ, though what greater disbelief could there be than theirs? It is because of this

سمّاهم القرآن[497] "المغضوب عليهم"

لأجل خلافهم لقول الله الذي أنطقه[498]

على أفواه[499] الأنبياء. وأمّا نحن[500] لأجل

قبولنا قول الأنبياء ولأننا متمسّكون[501]

بما أمرونا به الرسل الأطهار[502] سمّانا

"المنعم عليهم".

xiii. وأمّا قولنا في الله تعالى:[503]

ثلاثة أقانيم[504] إله واحد فهو أنّ الله

* تعالى[505] نطق به * وأوضحه لنا في كتب

الأنبياء[506] وفي التوراة. وذلك في السفر

الأوّل من التوراة إذ يقول:[507] " حين[508]

شاء الله أن يخلق آدم قال الله: لنخلق

إنسانًا على شبهنا ومثالنا". فمن هو

شبهه ومثاله[509] غير كلمته[510] وروحه؟

وحين خالف آدم وعصى ربّه قال الله:

" ها آدم قد صار كواحد منّا". وهذا

قول واضح أنّ الله تعالى قال هذا القول

لابنه[511] أي كلمته وروح قدسه. وقال

هذا القول يتهزّأ بآدم[512] أي أنه طلب

أن يصير إلهًا كواحد منّا،[513] صار هكذا

عريانًا منفضحًا.[514]

---

[497] لسان :P2 [498] نطق به :P2 and 3 [499] هذا الإنسان في الكتاب :P2 and 3 [500] P2 في أنّ الله :P2 [501] P2 and 3: الحواريين [502] P3 adds: وماسكين :P2 and 3 add: النصارى and 3 add: [503] P2 تعالى :P3 om); (om [504] P2 and 3 add: جوهرًا واحدًا [505] P2 and 3 om. [506] إذ يقول :P2 and 3 om [507] وأوضحه على أفواه الأنبياء :P3; على أفواه الأنبياء وأوضحه :P2 كلمة الله :P2 [508] هو شبيه الله وتمثاله :P3; يشبه الله وبمائله :P2 [509] حيث :P2 and 3 [510] P2 عني بذلك للابن المتحد :P3 adds [512] يتهم أن آدم :P2 [513] لذلك قال الله لابنه :P2 and 3 [511] به أي كلمته وروح قدسه وكان هذا القول من الله توبيخ لآدم على مخالفته أمر الله وتصديقه ما أشارت به حواء عليه من طغيان الشيطان لها أن الله ما منعكم أن تأكلوا من هذه الشجرة إلا أنكم مفتضح [514] P2 and 3: إذا أكلتم منها صرتم آلهة مثله وأن آدم لمّا أكل من الشجرة

that the Qur'an has called them 'those who earn thine anger', because of their dispute over the word of God which he uttered through the mouths of the prophets. And since we Christians adhere to the word of the prophets, and since we hold to what the pure Apostles commanded us, it calls us 'those whom thou hast favoured'.

xiii. Turning to our teaching about God the exalted, three hypostases, one God, this is because God the exalted spoke about it (60v) and made it clear to us in the books of the prophets and in the Torah. There is what he says in the first book of the Torah, 'When God willed to create Adam, God said, "Let us make a human in our own image and likeness"', and what are his image and likeness other than his Word and Spirit? And when Adam disobeyed and defied his Lord, God said, 'Adam has become like one of us'; these words are clearly spoken by God the exalted to his Son, that is, his Word, and his Holy Spirit. He said them in derision of Adam, that he should seek to be a god 'like one of us', and he thus became naked and exposed.

وقال أيضًا عندما أخسف الله

بسدوم وعامور،[515] قال الكتاب الذي

هو التوراة"[516]: وأمطر الربّ من عند

الربّ من السماء نارًا وكبريتاً على

سدوم وعامور"[517]. أوضح بهذا[518]

ربوبية الآب والابن.

وقال أيضًا في السفر الثاني من

التوراة: "وكلّم الله موسى[519] النبي

من[520] العلّيقة قائلاً: أنا إله ابراهيم وإله

اسحاق وإله يعقوب". ولم يقل: أنا إله

ابراهيم واسحاق ويعقوب، بل كرّر

اسم الإله[521] ثلاث دفوع قائلاً: أنا إله

وإله وإله ليحقّق مساواة الثلاثة أقانيم في

اللاهوتية.[522]

وقال داود النبي في المزمور الثاني:

" الربّ قال لي : أنت ابني وأنا اليوم

ولدتك". وأيضًا قال[523] في مزمور ماية

€ * * وتسعة * :" قال الربّ لربّي إجلس

عن يميني حتى أضع أعداءك تحت موطأ

قدميك".

وكذلك يشهد[524] أشعيا النبي

بتحقيق الثالوث ووحدانية جوهره

بقوله"[525]: إني سمعت الملائكة لا يزالون

يسبّحون[526] قائلين: قدّوس قدّوس

---

515 P2 and 3: وغامورا   516 P2 and 3: قال الله في التوراة   517 P2 and 3: وغامورا   518 P2
and 3 add: القول   519 P1: لموسى   520 P2 and 3: في   521 P2 and 3 om: اسم الإله ... ولم يقل
522 P2 and 3: لاهوتيته   523 P2: وقال أيضًا (trsp.).   524 P2 and 3: شهد   525 P2 and 3:
قائلاً   526 P2 and 3 add: الله

And also he said when God caused Sodom and Gomorrah to be destroyed, the book which is the Torah said, 'And the Lord rained down from the Lord from heaven fire and brimstone on Sodom and Gomorrah', thus making clear the lordship of the Father and the Son.

He also says in the second book of the Torah, 'God spoke to the prophet Moses from the burning bush saying, "I am the God of Abraham, I am the God of Isaac, I am the God of Jacob".' He did not say, 'I am the God of Abraham, Isaac and Jacob', but he repeated the name 'God' three times saying, 'I am God, and God, and God' in order to substantiate the issue of three as hypostases in his divinity.

The prophet David says in Psalm 2, 'The Lord said to me, "You are my son, today I have begotten you".' He also says in Psalm 109, (61r) 'The Lord said to my Lord, "Sit at my right hand until I cast your enemies beneath your footstool".'

In the same way the prophet Isaiah witnesses to the reality of the Trinity and the singleness of his substance when he says, 'I heard the angels giving praise and saying, "Holy, holy, holy

قدّوس، ربّ القوّات. جميع السماوات
والأرض ممتلئة من مجدك". أسماء تحقّق
أقانيمه الثلاثة بالتقديس المثلّث ووحدانية
جوهره بقوله: "ربّ القوّات"، وبقوله:
"السموات والأرض ممتلئة من مجدك".[527]
ومثل هذا القول في التوراة
والمزامير شيء كثير، حتى أنّ اليهود إلى
هذا الوقت[528] يقرأون هذه النبوءات
جميعها[529] في وسط كنائسهم[530] أكثر
من جميع النبوءات ولا يعرفون لها تأويلاً.
وهم يقرّون[531] بذلك ولا ينكرون
كلمة منه.[532] وإنما قلوبهم مغلوقة عن
فهمه، لأنّ الله[533] غلقها لقساوتهم[534]
على ما ذكرنا من قبل.[535]
وإنّهم إذا اجتمعوا في كنيستهم كلّ
سبت يقف الحزّان قدّامهم ويقول كلامًا
عبرانيًا هذا تفسيره ولا يجحدونه:[536]
نقدّسك ونعظّمك ونثلّث لك تقديسًا
مثلثًا كالمكتوب على لسان نبيّك
أشعيا،[537] فيصرخ الجميع[538] مجاوبين له:
قدّوس قدّوس قدّوس ربّ القوّات، جميع
6 * السماوات * والأرض ممتلئة من مجدك.
فما أوضح إقرارهم هذا في الثالوث!
فنحن لأجل هذا البيان الواضح

---

[527] P2 and 3 om: أسماء تحقّق ... من مجدك　[528] P2 and 3: يومنا هذا　[529] P2 and 3 om.
[530] P2 and 3: كنيستهم　[531] P2 and 3: مقرّون　[532] P2 and 3: منه كلمة واحدة　[533] P2 adds:
تعالى قد　[534] P2 and 3 adds: وكفرهم　[535] P2: ذكرناه قبل ذلك; P3: قد ذكرنا قبل ذلك; P3 adds: قد
كلّهم　[536] P2: يجحدوه　[537] P2: أشعيا نبيّك　[538] P2 and 3 add: (trsp).

is the Lord of hosts, all the heavens and earth are filled with your glory".' The names indicate the reality of his three hypostases by the triple repetition of 'holy', and of the oneness of his substance by his word, 'Lord of hosts', and by his word, 'The heavens and earth are filled with your glory'.

There are many things like this in the Torah and Psalms. Thus the Jews even now read all these prophecies within their synagogues, and more than all the prophecies, and do not recognise the interpretation of them, though they acknowledge them and do not deny a single word. But their minds are obscured from understanding it because God has hardened them through their mercilessness, as we have said above.

When they assemble in their synagogues each sabbath, the cantor[9] stands before them and says in Hebrew (of which this is a version), and they do not object to it, 'We glorify you, we exalt you, and we confess three times your threefold holiness, as is written on the tongue of your prophet Isaiah.' And the whole assembly cries out in response to him: 'Holy, holy, holy, Lord of hosts, all the heavens (61v) and earth are filled with your glory.' How openly do they acknowledge the Trinity in this way!

So, on the basis of this clear demonstration

---

[9] *Al-ḥazzān* is a direct transliteration of the Hebrew *ḥazzān*.

الذي قاله الله تعالى في التوراة والأنبياء
نجعله ثلاثة أقانيم جوهرًا واحدًا طبيعة
واحدة إلهًا واحدًا.[539] وهذا الذي
نقوله: آب وابن وروح قدس.

(43) وقد[540] علمنا أنه لا يلزمنا إذا قلنا
هذا عبادة ثلاثة آلهة بل إله واحد. كما
لا يلزمنا إذا قلنا الإنسان ونطقه وروحه
ثلاثة أناس أو ثلاثة أشخاص،[541] ولا
إذا[542] قلنا لهيب النار وضوء النار
وحرارة النار ثلاث نيران، ولا إذا قلنا
قرص الشمس وضوء الشمس وشعاع
الشمس ثلاث شموس.

(44) وإذا كان هذا رأينا في الله،
تقدّست أسماؤه وجلّت آلاؤه،[543] فلا
لوم علينا ولا ذنب لنا إذا لم نهمل ما
تسلّمناه ولا نرفض ما تقلّدناه ونتبع ما
سواه، ولا سيّما إذ لنا هذه الشهادات
البيّنات والدلائل الواضحات من الكتاب
الذي أتى به هذا الرسول.[544]

(43) وعلمنا انه لا يلزمنا، اذا قلنا
هذا، عبادة ثلثة الهة ، كما لا يلزمنا، اذا
قلنا عقل الانسان ونطق الانسان وروح
الانسان: ثلثة اناسي، ولا اذا قلنا لهيب
النار وضو النار وحرارة النار، ثلثة نيران،
ولا اذا قلنا قرص الشمس وضو الشمس
وسخونة الشمس، ثلثة شموس.

(44) واذا كان هذا راينا في الله-
تقدست اسماوه وجلت الاوه!-فلا لوم
علينا ولا ذنب لنا اذا لم نهمل ما تسلمناه
ولم نرفض ما تقلدناه ونتبع ما سواه ، لا
سيما اذ لنا مثل هذه الشهادات البينات
والدلايل الواضحات من الكتاب الذي
اتى به هذا الرسول .

[539] P2 and 3 add: ربًا واحدًا خالقًا واحدًا [540] P2 and 3: فقد [541] P2 and 3 om:
وجلّت :P3 ؛ وجلّ ثناؤه :P2 [543] وإذا :P2 [542] بل إنسان واحد :and add أو ثلاثة أشخاص
إلهيته [544] P2 and 3: الرجل and add the following passage from Paul of Antioch's
Letter (Khoury, *Paul d'Antioche*, p. 76, §§ 45-6): فقلت لهم إن كانوا (sic) المسلمون يحتجون
علينا قائلين إذا كنتم تحتجون علينا ببعض ما في كتبنا فيلزمكم قبوله كله. قالوا ليس الأمر
على هذه الصورة لأنه (لأن :P2) إذا كان لإنسان على إنسان كتاب بمائة دينار وكان مكتوب
(P2: om) في ظهر (على ظاهر :P3) الكتاب أنه استوفى، فإذا أظهر صاحب الدين الكتاب وطلب
من المديون المائة دينارًا يجوز للمديون أن يحتج بما في ظهر (قفى :P3) الكتاب أنه قد أوفاه المائة
دينارًا أم لا، أو يقول له صاحب الدين كما تقبل هذه المائة دينارًا لموفيه إقبل أيضًا هذه المائة
الدين بل يدفع عنه المائة دينار التي (الذي :P2) في الكتاب بما في الكتاب أيضًا من أنه قد أوفاه
ولم يبق له عليه شيء. وكذلك أي شيء قيل عنّا أو احتج به علينا من هذا الكتاب دفعناه من
هذا الكتاب أيضًا، ولهذا قلنا إنّ.

that God the exalted gives in the Torah and Books of the Prophets, we make him three hypostases and one substance, one nature, one God, and this is what we say: Father, Son and Holy Spirit. *(43)* We know that it does not follow for us from saying this that it is the worship of three gods but of one God, just as it does not follow from our saying a man, his speech and his spirit, that they are three people or three individuals, nor from our saying a fire's flame, heat and radiance, that they are three fires, nor from our saying the sun's disk, brightness and beams, that they are three suns.[10]

(44) If this is our view concerning God, holy be his names and great his divinity, no blame or offence attaches to us for not abandoning what we have received, or rejecting what we have been given to hold, and following something else, especially since we have these clear witnesses and obvious proofs from the book which this messenger brought.

---

[10] Analogies of this kind can be traced back to Patristic authors and are known among Muslim polemicists from the time of the earliest encounters with Christians; cf. e.g. al-Qāsim b. Ibrāhīm, '*Al-radd ʿalā al-Naṣārā*', ed. I. di Matteo, 'Confutazione contro i Cristiani dello zaydita al-Qāsim b. Ibrāhīm', *Rivista degli Studi Orientali* 9, 1921-2, p. 315.7-22, and Abū ʿĪsā al-Warrāq's passing reference to them in Thomas, *Anti-Christian Polemic*, pp. 68. 1-3, and 196, n. 8.

(47) وأعظم⁵⁴⁵ حجّتنا ما وجدنا فيه الشاهد لنا بأنّ الله⁵⁴⁶ جعلنا فوق الذين كفروا إلى يوم القيامة باتباعنا السيّد المسيح روح الله وكلمته.

xiv. وأمّا اتحاد⁵⁴⁷ كلمة الله الخالقة التي بها خلق كلّ شيء بالإنسان المخلوق⁵⁴⁸ الذي أخذ من مريم العذراء المصطفاة⁵⁴⁹ التي فُضّلت على نساء العالمين واتّحد به اتحادًا بريئاً من اختلاط أو تغيّر،⁵⁵⁰ وخاطب الناس منه⁵⁵¹ كما خاطب الله تعالى⁵⁵² موسى⁵⁵³ النبي⁵⁵⁴ من⁵⁵⁵ العوسجة. (37) ففعل المعجز⁵⁵⁶ بلاهوته⁵⁵⁷ وأظهر العجز⁵⁵⁸ بناسوته كالألم والموت وغير ذلك. والفعلان هما في⁵⁵⁹ المسيح الواحد.

وقد جاء أيضًا في هذا⁵⁶⁰ الكتاب الذي أتى به هذا الرسول⁵⁶¹ يقول في سورة آل عمران: ﴿يا عيسى إني متوفيك ورافعك إليّ﴾.⁵⁶² وقال أيضًا في سورة المائدة، إذ قال عيسى ابن مريم ﴿وكنت عليهم شهيدًا ما دمت فيهم فلمّا توفيتني كنت أنت الرقيب عليهم﴾. فأعني بتوفيه عن موت ناسوته الذي

---

(47) ولهذا قلنا ان اعظم حججنا ما وجدناه في الكتاب الذي اتى به هذا الرسول، الشاهد لنا بان الله جعلنا "فوق الذين كفروا الى يوم القيامة"، باتباعنا السيد المسيح "روح الله وكلمته".

(37) ففعل المعجز بلاهوته واظهر العجز بناسوته، والفعلان فللسيد المسيح الواحد.

---

⁵⁴⁵ P2 and 3: أعظم   ⁵⁴⁶ P2 add: تعالى   ⁵⁴⁷ P2 and 3: تجسيم   ⁵⁴⁸ P1, 2 and 3: إنسان مخلوق   ⁵⁴⁹ P2 and 3 add: نساء العالمين   ⁵⁵⁰ P2 and 3: تغيير   من (على) (P3: على)   ⁵⁵¹ P3 om.   ⁵⁵² P2 and 3 om.   ⁵⁵³ P1: لموسى   ⁵⁵⁴ P2 om.   ⁵⁵⁵ P2 and 3: في   ⁵⁵⁶ P3: المعجزات   ⁵⁵⁷ P2: بناسوته (wrongly).   ⁵⁵⁸ P2 and 3 om: وغير ذلك   وأظهر العجز ...   ⁵⁵⁹ P2 and 3 add: السيّد   ⁵⁶⁰ P2 and 3 om.   ⁵⁶¹ P2 and 3: الإنسان   ⁵⁶² The text in both P2 and 3 is out of sequence here. Some of the Qur'anic quotations are either omitted or transposed.

(47) Our most important proof is the witness in our favour that we find in it, that God has placed us above those who disbelieve until the day of resurrection because we follow the Lord Christ, God's Spirit and Word.

xiv. On the matter of the uniting of God's creative Word, by which God created all things, with the created man taken from the Virgin Mary, the chosen one (62r) who was honoured 'above the women of creation', it united with him in a union free from mixing or altering, and addressed people from him as God the exalted addressed the prophet Moses from the thorn bush. *(37)* He performed miracles by his divine nature and exhibited weakness, such as pain, death and so on, by his human nature, both actions being in the one Christ.

Furthermore, in this book which this messenger brought occur his words in *The Family of 'Imrān*, 'O Jesus! Lo! I am gathering thee and causing thee to ascend unto me'; and it also says in *The Table Spread* when Jesus son of Mary said, 'I was a witness of them while I dwelt among them, and when thou tookest me thou wast the watcher over them'—by his being taken it means the death of his human nature which

اتخذ من مريم العذراء. وقال أيضًا[563] في سورة النساء: ﴿وما قتلوه وما[564] صلبوه ولكن شبّه لهم﴾. فأشار بهذا القول إلى اللاهوت الذي هو كلمة الله الخالقة.[565]

(38)) وعلى هذا القياس نقول: "إنّ المسيح صُلب[566] بناسوته ولم يُصلب[567] بلاهوته". وقد جاء في هذا الكتاب أيضًا شيء يوافق قولنا[568] إذ يقول في سورة النساء: ﴿إنّما المسيح عيسى ابن مريم رسول الله وكلمته ألقاها إلى مريم وروح منه﴾. وقال في موضع آخر:[569] ﴿وإنّما مثل عيسى ابن مريم[570] كمثل آدم﴾. فأعني بقوله "عيسى" إشارة[571] إلى البشرية المأخوذة من مريم[572] الطاهرة.[573] وكما أنّ آدم خُلق من غير جماع ومباضعة وكذلك ناسوت[574] المسيح[575] خُلق من غير جماع ومباضعة. وكما أنّ جسد آدم ذاق الموت وكذلك جسد المسيح ذاق الموت.

(38)) وعلى هذا القياس نقول ان المسيح صلب، يعني انه صلب بناسوته وانه لم يصلب بلاهوته.

---

[563] P2 and 3 om.   [564] P1, 2 and 3: ولا   [565] P2 and 3: كلمة الله الذي لم يدخل عليه   [566] P2 and 3 add: وتألّم   [567] P2 and 3 add: ولم يؤلّم   [568] This phrase is transposed in P2 and 3 which also add the following at the end of the Qur'anic quotation: إذ قد شهد أنه إنسان مثلنا أي بالناسوت الذي أخذ من مريم وكلمة الله وروحه المتحدة به وحاشا كلمة الله وروحه. (المتحدة ... وروحه P2 om:) الخالقة مثلنا نحن المخلوقين   [569] P1: وقال في سورة followed by a blank in the text; the reading في موضع آخر is supplied from P2 and 3. The reference is to Sūrat Āl ʿImrān (S III: 59).   [570] P2: إن مثل عيسى عند الله ; P3: مثال عيسى   [571] P2 and 3: أشار   [572] P2 and 3 om.   [573] P2 and 3 add: جسد   [574] P2 and 3: ''لأنه لم يذكر هاهنا اسم المسيح إلا عيسى فقط''   [575] P2 and 3 om: خُلق من غير ... جسد المسيح, possibly due to dittography.

was derived from the Virgin Mary; it also says in *Women*, 'They slew him not nor crucified, but it appeared so unto them'—by these words it refers to the divine nature which is the creative Word of God, *(38)* by analogy with which we say that Christ was crucified in his human nature and not crucified in his divine nature. There also occurs in this book in agreement with our statement what is said in *Women*, 'The Messiah, Jesus son of Mary, was only a messenger of Allah, and his word which he conveyed unto Mary, and a spirit from him'. In another place it says, 'Lo, the likeness of Jesus son of Mary is as the likeness of Adam'—by his word 'Jesus' he intends to refer to the human nature derived from Mary the pure one (62v); just as Adam was created without intercourse or intimacy, so the human body of Christ was created without intercourse or intimacy; and just as the body of Adam tasted death, so the body of Christ tasted death.

وقد برهن بقوله[576] رأينا[577] قائلاً:[578]
"إنّ الله ألقى كلمته إلى مريم"، وذلك
حسب[579] قولنا معشر النصارى إنّ
كلمة الله[580] الأزلية حلّت في مريم
واتّحدت[581] بإنسان كامل. وعلى
هذا المثال نقول في السيّد المسيح
جوهران،[582] جوهر لاهوتي الذي هو
جوهر كلمة الله وروحه وجوهر ناسوتي
الذي أخذه من مريم العذراء واتّحد به.
وأمّا ما تقدّم به القول من الله تعالى
على لسان موسى النبي، إذ يقول:
"أليس[583] هذا الآب الذي خلقك وبراك
واقتناك؟"، وعلى لسان داود النبي:
"روحك القدّوس لا تنزع مني"،[584]
وأيضًا: " بكلمة الله تشدّدت[585]
السماوات وبروح فيه جميع قواهن"[586] –
فليس يدلّ هذا القول على ثلاثة خالقين
بل خالق واحد: الآب وكلمته أي نطقه
وروحه أي حياته.

xv. (49) فقلت لهم:[587] إذا
كان اعتقادكم في البارئ تعالى أنه
واحد،[588] فما حملكم على أن تقولوا:
آب وابن وروح قدس؟ فتوهمون
السامعين أنكم تعتقدون في الله[589]

(49) قلت: فانهم يقولون: اذا كان
اعتقادكم في الباري تعالى انه واحد،
فما حملكم على ان تسموه ثلثة اقانيم،
وتوهمون السامعين انكم تعتقدون ان
الله ثلثة اشخاص مركبة او ثلثة الهة

---

[576] P2 add: وعلى حسب   [577] P2: ثانيا أيضًا   [578] P2 om.   [579] P2 and 3:
حسب   [580] P2 and 3 add: الخالقة   [581] P2 and 3: وتجسّدت   [582] P2 and 3 om: جوهران ... ناسوتي.
[583] P2 and 3 om.   [584] P2 and 3 om this quotation.   طبيعتان: طبيعة لاهوتية التي هي كلمة P3: ; طبيعة من طبيعتين لاهوته وناسوته Instead P2:
الله وروحه وطبيعة ناسوتية الجسد   [585] P3: قامت   [586] P2 and 3: قواتهن   [587] P2 and 3 add: إنهم يقولون لنا   [588] P2 om:
أنه   [589] P2 and 3 add: تعالى أنه واحد

His words prove our view when he says, 'God conveyed his Word unto Mary.' This is in agreement with the teaching of us Christians that the eternal Word of God came to dwell in Mary and was united with a complete human. Accordingly, we say that there were two substances in the Lord Christ, the substance of the divine nature which is the Word and Spirit of God, and the substance of the human nature which he took from the Virgin Mary and united with it.

And concerning the earlier words of God the exalted about him on the tongue of the prophet Moses, when he says, 'Is not this the Father who created you, restored you and made you his own?'; and also on the tongue of the prophet David, 'Do not take your Holy Spirit from me'; and also, 'By the Word of God were the heavens set fast, and by the breath of his mouth all their strength'—these do not imply three creators but one Creator, the Father with his Word, that is his speech, and his Spirit, that is his life.

xv. *(49)* I said to them: If your belief about the exalted Creator is that he is one, what has made you say 'Father, Son and Holy Spirit'? You have made those who hear think that you believe that God

ثلاثة أشخاص مركّبة أو ثلاثة آلهة أو ثلاثة أجزاء وأنّ له ابنًا. ويظنّ من لا يعرف اعتقادكم *أنكم تريدون بذلك ابن المباضعة والتناسل فتطرقون على أنفسكم[590] تهمة أنتم[591] منها بريئون.

او ثلثة اجزا، وان له ابنا ويظن من لا يعرف اعتقادكم انكم تريدون بذلك ابن المباضعة والتناسل، فتطرقون على انفسكم تهمة انتم منها بريون ؟

(50) قالوا: والمسلمون[592] أيضًا لمّا كان اعتقادهم في الباري جلّت قدرته أنه غير ذي جسم وغير ذي جوارح وأعضاء وغير محصور في مكان، ما[593] حملهم على أن يقولوا إنّ له عينين يبصر بهما، ويدين يبسطهما، وساقًا ووجهًا يوليه[594] إلى كلّ مكان وجنب، وإنه يأتي[595] في ظلّ من[596] الغمام؟ فتوهمون السامعين أنّ الله تعالى ذو جسم وذو أعضاء وجوارح وأنه ينتقل من مكان إلى مكان في ظلّ من الغمام،[597] فيظنّ مَن لا يعرف اعتقادهم أنّهم يجسّمون الباري، حتى أنّ قومًا منهم اعتقدوا ذلك واتخذوه مذهبًا. ومَن لا يتحقّق اعتقادهم يتهمهم بما هم منه[598] بريئون.

(50) قالوا: وهم ايضا، لما كان اعتقادهم في الباري – جلت قدرته! – انه غير ذي جسم وغير ذي جوارح واعضا وغير محصور في مكان، ما حملهم على ان يقولوا ان له عينين يبصر بهما ويدين يبسطهما وساق يكشفها ووجه يوليه الى كل الجهات وجنب، وانه ياتي في ظلل من الغمام، ويوهمون السامعين ان الله تعالى جسم ذو اعضا وجوارح، وانه ينتقل من مكان الى مكان في ظلل من الغمام، فيظن من يسمع ولا يعرف اعتقادهم انهم يجسمون الباري تعالى – حتى ان قوما منهم اعتقدوا ذلك واتخذوه مذهبا – ومن لا يتحقق اعتقادهم يتهمهم بما هم منه بريون ؟

(51) قلت: إنهم يقولون إنّ العلّة في قولنا[599] هذا[600] إنّ الله له عينان

(51) قلت: فانهم يقولون: ان العلة في قولنا ان لله عينين ويدين ووجه وساق

590 P2: نفوسكم فتطرقون 591 P2: وأنتم 592 P2 and 3: وهم 593 P2 and 3: فما 594 P2 om: وجنب مكان كلّ إلى 595 P2: مكان إلى مكان من ينتقل and add: وجوارح 596 P2 om. 597 P2 and 3 om: الغمام من ظلّ ... السامعين فتوهمون, possibly due to ditto-graphy. 598 P3 om. 599 P2 and 3: قولهم 600 P2 om.

is three composite individuals, or three gods, or three parts, and that he has a son. Someone who did not know your belief might imagine (63r) that by this you mean a son by intimacy and reproduction, laying you open to a charge of which you are innocent.

(50) They said, The Muslims as well, since their belief about the Creator, great is his might, is that he has no body, limbs or organs, nor is limited in one place, what has made them say that he has two eyes by which he sees, two hands which he spreads wide, a leg, a face which he turns in every direction, and a side, and that he comes in the darkness of clouds, so that people hearing might imagine that God the exalted has a body, limbs and organs, and that he moves from place to place in the darkness of clouds?[11] Someone who did not know their belief might think that they give a body to the Creator—indeed, people among them have believed this and taken it as their doctrine—and someone who had not verified their belief might charge them with things of which they are innocent.

(51) I said, They say: The reason for our saying this, that God has two eyes,

---

[11] Al-Dimashqī identifies these Qur'an references in § 85 of his *Response.*

ويدان ووجه وساق وجنب وإنه يأتي
في ظلّ من الغمام هو أنّ[601] القرآن نطق
به والمراد بذلك[602] غير ظاهر اللفظ،
وكلّ مَن يحمل ذلك على ظاهر اللفظ
ويعتقد أنّ الله له عينان ويدان ووجه
وجنب وجوارح وأعضاء[603] وأنّ ذاته
تنتقل من مكان إلى مكان وغير ذلك
ممّا يقتضي التجسيم والتشبيه *فنحن
نلعنه ونكفّره.[604] وإذا كفّرنا[605] من
يعتقد ذلك[606] فليس لمخالفينا أن يلزمونا
بذلك[607] بعد أن لا نعتقده.

وجنب وانه ياتي في ظلل من الغمام،
هي ان القران نطق به. والمراد بذلك
غير ظاهر اللفظ. وكل من يحمل ذلك
على ظاهره، ويعتقد ان لله عينين ويدين
ووجه وجنب وساق –وهي جوارح
واعضا– وان ذاته تنتقل من مكان الى
مكان، وغير ذلك مما يقتضي التجسم
والتشبيه، فنحن نلعنه ونكفره. فاذا
كفرنا من يعتقد ذلك وما جانسه، فليس
لمخالفنا ان يلزمناه بعد ان لا نعتقده .

(52) قالوا: وكذلك نحن[608] أيضًا العلّة
في قولنا إنّ الله ثلاثة أقانيم: آب وابن
وروح قدس أنّ[609] الإنجيل نطق به،
والمراد بالأقانيم غير الأشخاص المركّبة
والأجزاء والأبعاض وغير ذلك ممّا يقتضي
الشرك والتكثير. فالآب[610] والابن غير
أبوّة وبنوّة نكاح أو تناسل أو جماع[611]
أو مباضعة. (53) وكلّ من يعتقد أنّ
الثلاثة أقانيم[612] ثلاثة آلهة مختلفة أو ثلاثة
آلهة متفقة أو ثلاثة أجسام مؤلّفة أو
ثلاثة أجزاء متفرّقة[613] أو ثلاثة أشخاص

(52) قالوا: فكذلك العلة في قولنا ان الله
ثلثة اقانيم، اب وابن وروح القدس، هي
ان الانجيل نطق بذلك. فالمراد بالاقانيم
غير الاشخاص المركبة والاجزا والابعاض
وغير ذلك مما يقتضي الشرك والتكثير،
وبالاب والابن غير ابوة وبنوة نكاح
وتناسل وجماع ومباضعة. (53) فكل من
يعتقد ان الثلثة اقانيم هي ثلثة الهة مختلفة
او متفقة، او ثلثة اجسام مولفة، او ثلثة
اجزا متفرقة، او ثلثة اشخاص مركبة، او
اعراض او قوى او غير ذلك مما يقتضي
الاشراك والتبعيض والتشبيه، وان المراد

601 P2 and 3: فهو   602 P2: وإذاً كان ذلك ; P3: وإذاً ذلك   603 P2: وأعظاء (sic).
604 P2 and 3: فهم يلعنوه ويكفّروه   605 P2 and 3: كفّروا   606 P2 and 3: هذا   607 P2
and 3: فليس لمخالفيهم أن يلزموهم به   608 P2 and 3 add: النصارى   609 P2 and 3 om.
610 P1: وبالآب   611 P2 and 3: تناسل اجتماع   612 P2 and 3 om.   613 P3: مفترقة

two hands, a face, leg and side, and that he comes in the darkness of clouds, is that the Qur'an speaks of it, though the intention in this is not literal. Anyone who takes it literally and believes that God has two eyes, two hands, a face, a side, limbs and organs, and that his essence moves from place to place, etc., as corporealism and anthropomorphism entail, (63v) we condemn him and declare him an unbeliever. And if we declare as an unbeliever anyone who believes this, our opponents are not in a position to impose it upon us, since we do not believe it.

(52) They said, It is exactly the same with us. The reason we say that God is three hypostases, Father, Son and Holy Spirit, is that the Gospel speaks about it. What is intended by 'hypostases' is not composite individuals, parts and divisions and so on, as partnership and plurality entail. For the Father and Son are not the fatherhood and sonship of wedlock, procreation or reproduction. (53) We excommunicate, curse and accuse of unbelief everyone who believes that the three hypostases are three different or coincident gods, three physical objects brought together, three separate parts, three composite

مرّكبة أو أعراض أو قوى أو غير ذلك
ممّا يقتضي الإشراك والتكثير⁶¹⁴ والتبعيض
والتشبيه أو بنوّة نكاح أو تناسل أو
مباضعة أو جماع أو ولادة زوجة أو من
بعض الأجسام أو من بعض الملائكة أو
من بعض المخلوقين فنحن نحرمه ونلعنه
ونكفّره.⁶¹⁵ وإذا لعنّا وكفّرنا من يعتقد
ذلك فليس لمخالفينا أن يلزمونا به بعد
أن⁶¹⁶ لا نعتقده.

بذكر الاب والابن ابوة وبنوة نكاح او
تناسل او مباضعة او جماع، او ولادة
من زوجة او من بعض الاجسام او من
بعض الملايكة او من بعض المخلوقين،
فنحن نلعنه ونحرمه ونكفره. واذا كفرنا
من يعتقد ذلك وما جانسه مما يودي
الى الشرك والتشبيه، فليس لمخالفنا ان
يلزمناه بعد ان لا نعتقده .

(54) فإن⁶¹⁷ ألزمونا الشرك والتشبيه
لأجل قولنا إنّ الله تعالى جوهر واحد
ثلاثة أقانيم:⁶¹⁸ آب وابن وروح قدس
لأنّ ظاهر ذلك⁶¹⁹ يقتضي * التكثير⁶²⁰
والتشبيه ألزمناهم أيضًا⁶²¹ التجسيم
والتشبيه لقولهم: إنّ الله له عينان ويدان
ووجه وساق وجنب، وإنّ ذاته تنتقل
من مكان إلى مكان وإنه استوى على
العرش من⁶²² بعد أنه لم يكن عليه،
وغير هذا⁶²³ ممّا يقتضي ظاهر التجسيم
والتشبيه.

(54) فان الزمونا الشرك والتشبيه لاجل
قولنا ان الله تعالى جوهر واحد، ثلثة
اقانيم، اب وابن وروح القدس، لان
ظاهر ذلك يقتضي التكثير والتشبيه،
الزمناهم التجسم والتشبيه لقولهم ان لله
عينين ويدين ووجه وساق وجنب، وانه
استوى على العرش بعد ان لم يكن عليه،
وغير هذا مما يقتضي ظاهر التجسم
والتشبيه.

xvi. (55) قلت: فإنهم ينكرون عليكم في
قولكم⁶²⁴ إنّ الله تعالى جوهر. قالوا:⁶²⁵

(55)   قلت: فانهم ينكرون علينا قولنا ان
الله تعالى جوهر. – قالوا : انا نسمع عن

* 6

614 التكثير والإشراك :P2. 615 P2 and 3: نلعنه ونكفّره ونحرمه (trsp). 616 P3: أن نحن
(trsp). 617 P2 and 3: وإن 618 P2 and 3 om: أقانيم ... إن الله 619 P2: ظاهر اللفظ 620 P2 and
3: الشرك والتكثير 621 نحن أيضًا :P2 and 3 622 P2 and 3 om. 623 P1: هذه 624 P2
علينا في قولنا :P2 and 3 625 فقالوا :and 3

individuals, accidents or powers, or anything entailed by partnership, plurality, division or anthropomorphism, sonship through wedlock, intimacy, procreation, reproduction or birth from a wife, or a physical object, an angel or a creature. And if we curse and accuse of unbelief anyone who believes this, our opponents are not in any position to impose upon us what we do not believe.

(54) Thus, if they force us to acknowledge polytheism and anthropomorphism on account of our teaching that God the exalted is one substance and three hypostases, Father, Son and Holy Spirit, because this literally entails (64r) plurality and anthropomorphism, we in turn force them to acknowledge corporealism and anthropomorphism because of their teaching that God has two eyes, two hands, a face, a leg and a side, that his essence moves from place to place, that he was seated on the throne after not being on it,[12] and other things that literally entail corporealism and anthropomorphism.

xvi. *(55)* I said, They criticise you for saying that God the exalted is a substance. They said,

---

[12] Verses such as SS. VII: 54, X: 3 and XIII: 2 appear to suggest that God mounted the heavenly throne after completing the creation.

العجب من هؤلاء القوم الذين قد نسمع
عنهم أنّ فيهم كثيرين من ذوي الفضل
والأدب والمعرفة،[626] ومَن هذه[627]
صورته وقد قرأ شيئا من كتب المنطق
والفلسفة،[628] فما حقّهم ينكرون[629] هذا
علينا؟

هولا القوم انهم ذو فضل وادب ومعرفة.
ومن هذه صورته وقد قرا شيا من كتب
الفلاسفة ومن المنطق، فما ينكر هذا.

(56) وذلك إن ليس في الوجود شيء[630]
إلا وهو إمّا جوهر وإمّا عرض، لأنّ[631]
أي أمر نظرنا فيه وجدناه إمّا قائمًا بنفسه
غير مفتقر في وجوده إلى غيره وهو
الجوهر، وإمّا مفتقرًا في وجوده إلى غيره
لا قوام له بنفسه وهو العرض، ولا يمكن
أن يكون لهذين القسمين قسم ثالث،
فأشرف هذين القسمين القائم بذاته الغير
مفتقر في وجوده إلى غيره وهو الجوهر.

(56) اذ ليس في الوجود شي الا وهو
اما جوهر واما عرض. لان اي امر نظرنا
فيه، وجدناه اما قائم بنفسه، غير مفتقر
في وجوده الى غيره، وهو الجوهر، واما
مفتقر في وجوده الى غيره، لا قوام له
بنفسه، وهو العرض. ولا يمكن ان يكون
لهذين القسمين قسم ثالث. فاشرفهما
القائم بذاته، الغير مفتقر في وجوده الى
غيره. وهو الجوهر.

(57) ولمّا كان البارئ تقدّست أسماؤه
أشرف الموجودات إذ هو سبب
سائرها، أوجب أن يكون أشرف
الأمور * وأعلاها الجوهر.[632] ولهذا[633]
قلنا: إنه جوهر لا كالجواهر المخلوقة
كما يقولون[634] إنه شيء لا كالأشياء
المخلوقة، وإلا لزم أن يكون قوامه بغيره
ومفتقر في وجوده إلى غيره. وهذا

6 *

(57) ولما كان الباري-تقدست
اسماوه!- اشرف الموجودات، اذ هو
سبب سايرها، وجب ان يكون اشرف
الامور. واشرفها الجوهر. ولهذا قلنا
انه جوهر لا كالجواهر المخلوقة، كما
نقول انه شي لا كالاشيا المخلوقة ايضا.
والا لزم ان يكون قوامه بغيره، ومفتقر
في وجوده الى غيره. وهذا فمن القبيح ان

---

626 P2 and 3: أنهم القوم هؤلاء أنّ نسمع إنّا :P2 627 هذا :P2 and 3 628 إنّ القوم هؤلاء أنّ نسمع إنّا والمنطق الفلاسفة .(trsp) 629 P2 and 3: ينكروا أن 630 P2 and 3: الوجود في شيء 631 P2: وإنّ; P3: فإنّ (trsp). 632 P2 add: واحدًا 633 P2 om. 634 P2 and 3: يقول

This is amazing from these people, many of whom we have heard are refined, cultured and experienced. People of this character will have done some reading of logic and philosophy, so can they really criticise us for this?

(56) The point is that there is no thing in existence that is not substance or accident. For, whatever entity we examine we find either that it subsists of itself without need of anything else for its existence, and this is a substance, or that it does need something else for its existence and it has no subsistence in itself, and this is an accident. There cannot be a third category in addition to these two. The more noble of these two categories is what subsists in itself without need of anything else for its existence, and this is a substance.

(57) Since the Creator, holy be his names, is the most noble of existent things, for he is the reason for all others, it necessarily follows that he is the most noble of entities (64v) and the highest of them, substance. Thus we say that he is a substance unlike created substances, as they say that he is a thing unlike created things. Otherwise his subsistence would have to derive from something else and he would need something else for his existence. This

فمن القبيح⁶³⁵ أن يُقال على⁶³⁶ الباري ⁣⁣⁣⁣⁣⁣⁣⁣⁣⁣⁣⁣⁣⁣ يقال عن الباري تعالى.
سبحانه وتعالى.

(58) قلت⁶³⁷ لهم: إنهم يقولون (58) قلت: فانهم يقولون لنا: انما نمتنع
إنّا⁶³⁸ إنّما نمتنع من⁶³⁹ أن نسمّيه جوهرًا من ان نسميه جوهرا، لان الجوهر ما
لأن الجوهر ما قبل عرضًا وما شغل⁶⁴⁰ قبل عرضا وشغل حيزا. ولهذا ما نطلق
حيّزًا. ولهذا ما نطلق⁶⁴¹ عليه القول بأنه عليه القول بانه تعالى جوهر. –قالوا
تعالى⁶⁴² جوهر. : ان الذي يقبل عرضا ويشغل حيزا

قالوا: إنّ الذي يقبل عرضًا ويشغل الجوهر الكثيف. فاما الجوهر اللطيف،
حيّزًا الجوهر الكثيف، فأمّا⁶⁴³ الجوهر فما يقبل عرضا ولا يشغل حيزا، مثل
اللطيف فما يقبل عرضًا ولا يشغل حيّزًا جوهر النفس وجوهر العقل وجوهر
مثل جوهر النفس وجوهر العقل وجوهر الضو وما يجري هذا المجرى من الجواهر
الضوء وما يجري هذا المجرى من الجواهر اللطايف. واذا كانت الجواهر اللطيفة
اللطيفة المخلوقة. وإذا⁶⁴⁴ كانت الجواهر المخلوقة لا تقبل عرضا ولا تشغل حيزا،
اللطيفة المخلوقة⁶⁴⁵ لا تقبل عرضًا ولا افيكون خالق الجواهر اللطايف والكثايف
تشغل حيّزًا، فيكون خالق الجواهر ومركب اللطايف والكثايف يقبل عرضا
اللطائف⁶⁴⁶ والكثائف ومركّب اللطائف ويشغل حيزا؟ كلا!
بالكثائف⁶⁴⁷ يقبل عرضًا ويشغل حيّزًا⁶⁴⁸
كلا من ذلك.⁶⁴⁹

(59) ثمّ قالوا: إنّا نعجب **xvii.** (59) ثم قالوا: انا نعجب من هولا
من هؤلاء القوم الذين مع أدبهم وما القوم، الذين مع ادبهم وما ياخذون به
يريضون⁶⁵⁰ به أنفسهم من الفضل كيف انفسهم من الفضل، كيف لم يعلموا
لم يعلموا⁶⁵¹ أنّ الشرائع شريعتان: ان الشرايع شريعتان، شريعة عدل

---

⁶³⁵ P2: وهذا الشيء قبيح ⁶³⁶ P2: عن ⁶³⁷ P2 and 3: فقلت ⁶³⁸ P2 and 3 om.
⁶³⁹ P2 and 3 om. ⁶⁴⁰ P2 and 3: وشغل ⁶⁴¹ P2: يطلق ⁶⁴² P2 om. ⁶⁴³ P2 and 3:
وأمّا ⁶⁴⁴ P2 and 3: فإذا ⁶⁴⁵ P2 and 3: المخلوقة اللطيفة ⁶⁴⁶ P2: اللطيفة (trsp). ⁶⁴⁷ P2:
يقبل العرض ويشغل الحيّز ⁶⁴⁸ P2: والكثائف ⁶⁴⁹ P2 and 3 om: كلاً من ذلك ⁶⁵⁰ P2 and
3: يجدون ⁶⁵¹ P2 and 3: لا يعلمون

is one of the most infamous things that can be said about God the Creator, blessed and exalted.[13]

(58) I said to them, They say: We refuse to call him substance, because a substance is what receives an accident and occupies space, and thus we do not utter the words 'The exalted One is a substance'.

They said, That which receives an accident and occupies space is indeed a physical substance. But refined substance, on the other hand, does not receive accidents or occupy space, for example the substance of the soul, the substance of the intellect, the substance of brightness, and other refined, created substances to which the same applies. So if there are refined, created substances which do not receive an accident or occupy space, then it can be that the Creator of refined and physical substances who sets the refined in the physical does not at all receive an accident or occupy space.

xvii. *(59)* Then they said, We are surprised why these people, in spite of their culture and the merit they have attracted to themselves, do not know that there are two revealed laws,

---

[13] Christians were accustomed to calling God substance for the reason given here, that the term denoted a self-subsistent entity. But Arabic-speaking Christians encountered difficulties when they employed the term *jawhar* to translate it because this was used in *kalām* to designate the fundamental composite of matter that bore and was characterised by accidents. For an earlier instance of the disagreement that arose from the two different understandings of the term, cf. al-Bāqillānī, *Kitāb al-tamhīd*, ed. R.J. McCarthy, Beirut, 1957, pp. 75.5-79.3.

شريعة عدل وشريعة فضل ، لأنه لمّا كان
الباري[652] عدل وجوّاد وجب أن يظهر
عدله على خلقه، فأرسل موسى النبي
إلى بني إسرائيل بوضع شريعة العدل
وأمرهم[653] بفعلها[654] إلى أن استقرّت
في نفوسهم.

(60) ولمّا كان الكمال الذي هو الفضل
لا يمكن أن يضعه إلا أكمل الكمال،
وجب أن يكون هو[655] تقدّست أسماؤه
وجلّت آلاؤه الذي يضعه لأنه ليس شيء
أكمل منه.

(61) ولأنه جوّاد وجب أن يجود بأجلّ
الموجودات. وليس في الموجودات أجود
من كلمته. فلذلك وجب أن يجود
بكلمته.[656]

(62) فعلى هذا وجب أن يتخذّ له[657]
ذاتاً محسوسة ويحلّ فيها[658] ليظهر
منها[659] قدرته وجوده. ولمّا لم يكن في
المخلوقات في عالم الكون[660] أشرف من
طبيعة[661] الإنسان وجب[662] أن يتّصل
بها أشرف المخلوقات من الباقيات الغير

وشريعة فضل! لانه لما كان الباري تعالى
عدلا وجوادا، وجب ان يظهر عدله
على خلقه، فارسل موسى النبي الى بني
اسرائيل بوضع شريعة العدل، وامرهم
بفعالها الى ان استقرت في نفوسهم.

(60) ولما كان الكمال، الذي هو
الفضل، لا يمكن ان يضعه الا اكمل
الكمال، وجب ان يكون هو —تقدست
اسماوه وجلت الاوه!— الذي يضعه ،
لانه ليس شي اكمل منه.

(61) ولانه جواد، وجب ان يجود باجل
الموجودات. وليس في الموجودات اجود
من كلمته، يعني نطقه. ولذلك وجب ان
يجود بكلمته.

(62) فعلى هذا وجب ان يتخذ ذاتا
محسوسة يظهر منها قدرته وجوده. ولما
لم يكن في المخلوقات منه اشرف من
الانسان، اتخذ الطبيعة البشرية من السيدة
مرتمريم المطهرة، المصطفاة على نسا
العالمين.

---

6 *

[652] P2 and 3 add: تعالى   [653] P2 and 3: وأمر   [654] P1: بفعالها   [655] P2 om.   [656] P2
om: ولذلك ; P3: فلذلك وجب أن يجود بكلمته   [657] P2 and 3 om.   [658] P2 and 3 om:
ويحلّ فيها   [659] P2 and 3: يظهر فيها   [660] P2 and 3 om: في عالم الكون   [661] P2 and 3 om.
[662] P2 and 3: اتخذ الطبيعة البشرية من السيّدة (P3: العذراء) الطاهرة مرتمريم (مريم :P3)
البتول المصطفاة على سائر نساء العالمين. Both P2 and 3 omit the remaining text in section
(62), [up to: وجب أن يكون هو الكمال].

the law of justice and the law of grace.[14] For since the exalted Creator
is just and generous, he must reveal (65r) his justice to his creatures.
So he sent the prophet Moses to the People of Israel to institute the
law of justice and to order them to implement it until it became
established in their souls.

(60) When perfection came, which was grace, only the most perfect
of the perfect could institute it. And so he himself, holy be his names
and great his divinity, was necessarily the one to institute it, because
there is nothing more perfect than he. (61) And since he is generous, he necessarily showed his generosity through the most glorious
of existing things. And there is nothing among existing things more
generous than his Word, and thus he necessarily showed his generosity through his Word. (62) For this purpose, he necessarily took an
essence perceptible to the senses and inhered in it in order to reveal
through it his power and generosity. And since among created things
in the existing world there is nothing more noble than human nature,
he necessarily combined with this most noble among created things,

---

[14] Cf. Jn I: 17.

فاسدات وهي النفس الناطقة والعقل.
ولمّا لم يكن في نوع الإنسان أشرف من
البشري المأخوذ من السيّدة مريم العذراء
الطاهرة المصطفاة على نساء العالمين
الرفيعة الشريفة النسبين التي من أبيها
من سبط الملك، أعني داود الملك والنبي
من جانب الله وخليقته في الأرض كما
شهد الإنجيل والقرآن، ومن أمّها من
سبط بيت الإمامة التي تُسمّى الكهنوت
أعني بيت هارون أخي موسى، استحقّ
أن تحلّ فيه أشرف الموجودات الذي   6 *
لا شرف بعده وهو روح الله وكلمته.
ولهذا ورث المسيح الملك والإمامة
وسلّمها إلى أهل نحلته.
وممّا يدلّ على شرفه من هذا
الكتاب ما ورد في سورة آل عمران:
﴿وإذا قالت الملائكة يا مريم إنّ الله
اصطفاك وطهّرك واصطفاك على نساء
العالمين﴾. ومعلوم أنّ مريم اصطفاها الله
على نساء العالمين لأجل المسيح. ومَن
تحصل أمه أفضل نساء العالمين لأجله
فهو أفضل الناس جميعهم. ولمّا أرسل الله
تعالى جبريل رئيس الأجناد السماوية
إلى مريم العذراء، ليبشّرها به قال لها:
"السلام عليك أيتها المباركة من النساء
سيّدنا معك" ولم يقل "سيّدي"، لكنه
جمع جميع أجناد الملائكة العليين فجعله
سيّدهم. وبالحريّ إذا كان سيّد العليين
الروحانيين فالأولى أن يكون والبشريين
السفليين.

permanent and incorruptible, and this is the articulate, rational soul. And since among the human species there was nothing more noble than the man taken from the lady Mary the pure virgin, who was chosen above the women of the world, aristocratic and noble in ancestry—on her father's side from the royal tribe, I mean David the king and prophet who was at the side of God, and his representative on earth, as the Gospel and Qur'an attest;[15] and on her mother's side from the tribe of the House of the religious leader who was called priestly, I mean the House of Aaron, brother of Moses[16]—he deserved (65v) to have dwelling in him the most noble of existent things, beyond which there is no nobility, the Spirit and Word of God. For this reason Christ was heir to kingship and religious leadership and he surrendered it to the people of his faith.

In this book, one of the things that demonstrate his nobility is what is mentioned in *The Family of 'Imrān*, 'And when the angels said: O Mary! Allah hath chosen thee and made thee pure, and hath preferred thee above the women of creation'. It is well-known that God chose Mary above the women of the world for the sake of Christ, and he whose mother was found to be the most excellent of the women of the world because of him was the most excellent of all humankind. When God the exalted sent Gabriel the captain of the hosts of heaven to the Virgin Mary to give her news of him, he said to her, 'Peace be upon you, O blessed among women, our Lord is with you.' He did not say 'my Lord', but united together all the hosts of the highest angels and made him their Lord. To be precise, if he was the Lord of the highest spiritual beings then how much the more should he be of lower humans.

---

[15] Cf. e.g. 2 Samuel VII: 8-16, and S. XXXVIII: 17-26.

[16] Mary's descent from Aaron was commonly inferred from her relationship with her cousin Elizabeth, often identified as the daughter of her mother's sister, who according to Lk I: 5 was 'of the daughters of Aaron' (cf. SS. XIX: 28 and LXVI: 12).

وقال لها: "روح القدس تأتيك
وأيدي العليّ تحلّ عليك من أجل هذا
الذي يولد منك قدّوسًا وعظيمًا".

وقد شهد القرآن أنه تكلّم في المهد
وسلّم على نفسه وقال: ﴿السلام عليّ
يوم ولدت ويوم أموت ويوم أبعث
حيًّا﴾، فتأمّلوا أمر طفل يعظم إلى أن
يسلّم على نفسه خاصّة، فلو أنّ غيره
أمثل منه سلّم على غيره. هيهات ما
أعمق هذا الخطاب حتى يفتخر على

٦ * الخلق ويصلّي على نفسه ويسلّم * فلو
كان بشري قبله أو بعده أجلّ منه كان
يسلّم عليه ثمّ يعطف بالسلام على نفسه.

وأيضًا فإنّ القرآن ينطق بأنّ الله جعل
مريم وابنها آية للعالمين، وهذا يؤيّد ما
تقدّم شرحه. وإذا كان الإنسان الكامل
المولود من مريم بلغت منزلته في العلوّ
على منازل الناس جميعهم حتى الأنبياء
والأصفياء والملائكة إلى هذا الحدّ الذي
وصفته من اتحاده بكلمة الله الخالقة
وروحه وجب أن يكون هو الكمال.

(63) وبعد هذا الكمال ما يبقى شي
يوضع. لان جميع ما تقدمه يقتضيه،
وما ياتي بعده غير محتاج اليه، لان ليس
شي ياتي بعد الكمال فيكون فاضلا، بل

(63) وبعد هذا الكمال[663] لم يبق شيء
يوضع لأنّ جميع ما تقدّمه يقتضيه وما
يأتي بعده غير محتاج إليه، لأن ليس
يأتي[664] شيء بعد الكمال فيكون فاضلاً
بل يكون[665] دونه أو آخذًا منه، والآخذ
منه فهو ما لا يحتاج إليه.

---

[663] P2 om.   [664] P2 and 3: أيّ شيء   [665] P1 and 3 om.

He said to her, 'The Holy Spirit will come to you and the power of the Most High will rest upon you, and for this reason he who is born of you will be holy and mighty.'

The Qur'an witnesses that he spoke in the cradle[17] and wished peace upon himself, 'Peace on me the day I was born, and the day I die, and the day I shall be raised alive!' Consider this instance of a child being made mighty enough to wish peace upon his own self alone; if there had been any other who was more prominent than him he would have wished peace upon this other. Observe how profound this address is, in that he was pre-eminent over creation and wished blessings and peace to himself, (66r) for if there had been any human before or after him more glorious than he, he would have wished peace upon him and then followed with a greeting on himself.

The Qur'an also says that God made Mary and her son a sign to the worlds,[18] which supports the preceding explanation. If the rank of the complete man born from Mary outstrips the ranks of all humans in exaltedness, including the prophets, the blessed and the angels, to the limit I have described of the creative Word of God and his Spirit uniting with him, then he must be perfection. (63) After such perfection there was nothing left to institute, because everything that preceded it necessitated it, and there was no need for what came after it. For nothing can come after perfection and be superior, but it will be inferior or derivative from it, and there is no need for what is derivative.

---

[17] SS. III: 46, V.110, etc.
[18] S. XXI: 91.

وفي هذا القول مقنع. والسلام على من
اتّبع الهدى.

دون او اخذ منه، والاخذ منه فهو فضل
لا يحتاج اليه. وفي هذا القول مقنع.
والسلام على من اتبع الهدى.

---

xviii. (64) وهذا ما عرفت من رأي
القوم الذين رأيتهم وفاوضتهم وما
يحتجّون به عن أنفسهم. وللّه[666] الحمد
والمنّة إذ قد[667] وفّق الآراء وأزال التهم[668]
من بين[669] عباده النصارى والمسلمين
حرسهم اللّه[670] جميعًا.
وإن كان يوجد شيء[671] بخلاف[672]
ذلك فيبيّنه مولانا الشيخ المعظّم[673]، أدام
اللّه[674] حراسته وفسّح في مدّته، لأوقفهم
عليه وأنظر ما عندهم فيه. فقد سألوني
ذلك وجعلوني سفيرًا[675]. والحمد[676] للّه
ربّ العالمين .

(64) وهذا ما عرفته من القوم الذين
رايتهم وفاوضتهم ، وما يحتجون به عن
انفسهم. فللّه الحمد والمنة، اذ قد وفق
الارا وازال المرا من بين عبيده النصارى
والمسلمين–حرسهم اللّه اجمعين!–وان
كان بخلاف ذلك، فيبينه لي الاخ المكرم
والصديق المعظم–ادام اللّه حراسته وفسح
في مدته!– لاوقفهم عليه وانظر ما
عندهم فيه ، فقد سالوني ذلك وجعلوني
سفيرا. والحمد للّه رب العالمين.

---

[666] P2 and 3 add: فلله صحيحًا ذكروه ما يكون فإن [667] P2 and 3 : الذي [668] P3: الهمّ
[669] P2: عن [670] P3 adds: تعالى [671] P2 and 3 om: شيء يوجد [672] P2: خلاف [673] P2 and 3: الإمام
[674] P2 adds: تعالى [675] P2 adds: فيه ومواسطًا ; P3 adds: ومواسطًا [676] P3: الرسالة تمّت
والمجد

This statement is final, so peace be upon those who follow guidance.

xviii. *(64)* This is what I was able to ascertain about the views of the people I met and conferred with, and about the arguments they were using on their own behalf. Praise and blessing be to God, for he has brought unanimity of view and put an end to suspicion between his servants the Christians and Muslims, may God protect them all!

If he has found anything different from this, may our master the revered teacher (may God eternally protect him and prolong his existence) point it out so that I may inform them about it and determine what views they have on it. For they have asked me to do this and made me a mediator. Praise be to God, Lord of the worlds.

IBN ABĪ ṬĀLIB AL-DIMASHQĪ'S
RESPONSE TO THE LETTER FROM THE PEOPLE OF CYPRUS

TEXT AND TRANSLATION

IBN ABĪ ṬĀLIB AL-DIMASHQĪ'S

RESPONSE TO THE LETTER FROM THE PEOPLE OF CYPRUS

1. * كتاب فيه جواب رسالة أهل جزيرة قبرص ¹، أجاب به العبد بالذات والصفات ، الفقير إلى الله تعالى من كلّ الوجوه والجهات ، محمّد بن أبي طالب الأنصاري الصوفي الدمشقي ، أثابه الله وأيّده ، بعون منْه يُمنه وبمنّه ²، وصلّى الله على سيّدنا محمّد وعلى آله.

أرسلت في أيام من صفر من سنة إحدى وعشرين وسبعمائة، ورجع الجواب إليهم في سلخ جمادي الآخرة من السنة المذكورة. غفر الله لمصنّفها ولكاتبها ولقارئها ولسامعها ولجميع المسلمين.

---

¹ A: قبرس   ² A: وبمنه (sic)

1. (1r) The book which contains the Response to the Letter from the People of the Island of Cyprus, by which the servant of the Essence and Attributes responded, he who has need of God the exalted in every respect and aspect, Muḥammad Ibn Abī Ṭālib al-Anṣārī al-Ṣūfī al-Dimashqī, may God reward and strengthen him by help from him which he pours down and by his grace. And may God bless our lord Muḥammad and his house.

It was sent sometime in Ṣafar 721, and the reply was returned to them at the end of Jumādā II in the same year.[1] May God grant pardon to the one who composed it, the one who wrote it down, the one who reads it, the one who hears it, and to Muslims everywhere.

---

[1] This was in March 1321CE, with al-Dimashqī completing his response four months later in June; see further n.7 below.

* 1v

2.

* بسم الله الرحمن الرحيم

الحمد لله الذي ضوّأ بمصباح التوحيد قلوب المصطفين من العباد ، وزحزح
عنها ظلمات الشرك ، قتألّق كوكبها في أوج الشرف والإسعاد ، واستبصرت
بأنوار الرسالة المحمدية فنطقت ألسنتها بتنزيه مبدعها عن الشركاء والأنداد ،
ونفث روح القدس في روحها فقدّسته عن اتحاد الصاحبة والأولاد ، سبحانه
وتعالى عن الحلول بذوات الممكنات والاتحاد ، والتشبّث بناسوت تركّب عن
مجموع عناصر قضى العقل عليه بالاستحالة والنفاد ، وجلّ جلاله الأكمل عن
الاستعانة بمن خلقه وسواه على تنفيذ مشيئة وتحصيل مراد . وأشهد أنّ لا إله
إلّا الله وحده لا شريك له الذي انبهرت العقول في ضياء مجده ، وغرقت[1]
أفكار المقدسين في بحار معرفته ، وخرّت عقولها ساجدة لعلو حدّه.[2] وأشهد
أنّ محمّدًا عبده ورسوله الذي بشّرت برسالته التوراة * والإنجيل ، وسطعت
أشعة براهينها لما اتضح لأولي الألباب من معجزها الباهر الدليل ، وأشرقت
بأنوار بغيته المغارب والمشارق ، وخفقت بالبرّ والبحر أعلام كمال النفوس
البشرية لما نزهت عن النقائص الواحد الخالق ،

* 2r

---

[1] B: وعرفت (wrongly).   [2] A and B: جده

2. *[Introduction]*

(1v) In the name of God, the Compassionate, the Merciful.

Praise be to God, who has illumined the hearts of chosen mortals with the blaze of his unity, and chased the shades of polytheism from them, so their star beams out at the zenith of honour and good fortune; they have been made to see by the brilliance of Muḥammad's apostleship, so their tongues declare that he who made them is too exalted for partners and companions; the holy spirit[2] has inspired their spirits, so they confess he is too holy to unite with spouses and sons;[3] he is too blessed and exalted to dwell in or unite with the essences of ephemeral things,[4] or to combine with a humanity composed of all the many races, which intellect rules is prone to change and decay; his most perfect majesty is too great to seek help in executing his will and attaining his purpose from those he created and formed.[5]

I witness that there is no god but God alone with no partner, in the lustre of whose glory intellects are dazzled, in the oceans of whose wisdom the thoughts of the holy are engulfed, and before the grandeur of whose vastness their intellects fall in adoration.

I witness that Muḥammad is his servant and messenger, whose apostleship the Torah (2r) and Gospel announced;[6] the rays of its proofs spread abroad when the evidence was made plain to the leading minds by its dazzling miracle; it radiated with the brightness of its purpose over west and east; and the banners of the most perfect human souls billowed over land and sea when they proclaimed that the One, the Creator was free from faults.

---

[2] This is the familiar title of the angel Gabriel, in the Qur'an God's messenger to the prophets and to all who confess God's unity; cf. SS. XVI: 2, 102, XL: 15f.

[3] Cf. SS. VI: 101, LXXII: 3.

[4] The terms *ḥulūl* and *ittiḥād* were employed from an early stage by both Muslims and Christians to explain the doctrine of the uniting of the divine and human in Christ; cf. Thomas, *Anti-Christian Polemic*, pp. 68ff., §§ 10 and 11.

[5] At the very outset al-Dimashqī explains why Islam has disproved Christianity: the doctrine of divine unity negates any idea that God could have a son, come into contact with a human body in any way, or seek help from a creature in his purpose of perfecting humanity.

[6] Cf. SS. III: 81, LXI: 6.

وارتسم في جواهرها بحكم كتابه المنير رسوم المعارف والتعاليم ، ومحت³ آثار ما أدّى إلى الشرك الصريح في الربوبية من القول بالأقانيم، فكانت رسالته بمحمد الله هدى ورحمة للعالمين ، وبرهانًا قاطعًا حجج الجاحدين والمعاندين ، وسلطانًا قاهرًا لمن تمادى في كفره وألحد ، وتبيانًا أوضح فساد قول من جعل أنّ الواحد الأحد يتجزّأ⁴ وتعدّد ، فصلوات الله وسلامه عليه وعلى من اتّبع هداه وآمن بمن أرسله لإقامة منار التوحيد وارتضاه ، وبعد:

3. فإنه لمّا كان اليوم العاشر من شهر صفر سنة احدى وعشرين وسبعمائة للهجرة النبوية الشريفة المحمدية ، على صاحبها أفضل الصلاة والسلام ، والثاني عشرين من مارس⁵ وآذار سنة ألف * وستمائة واثنين وثلاثين للإسكندر⁶ ذي القرنين اليوناني ، والسادس عشر من برمهات سنة ألف وسبعة وثلاثين لدقلطيانوس القبطي⁷ ، والسابع عشر من خردادماه سنة ستمائة وتسعين ليزدجرد بن شهريار ابن كسرى أنو شروان الفارسي⁸ ، وردت على يد الأرتب الأديب كليام التاجر ، وزير المرقب كان أدام الله مسرّته ، رسالة حسنة التلطّف ، غريبة المغزى ، عجيبة المرمى كما قيل :

مريضة في حواشي مرطها بلل   يهدى لكلّ عليل منه ابلال

* 2v

---

³ B: محت   ⁴ A and B: يتجزي   ⁵ A and B: مرس   ⁶ B: لالاسكندر   ⁷ Thus in A and B for the Roman emperor, Diocletian, whose reign (AD 284 to 305) was darkened by the major persecution of the Christians of Egypt.   ⁸ A and B: الفرسي

Through the direction of his resplendent Book the patterns of insight and learning were traced in their substances,
and the remains of the teaching about the hypostases that led to open polytheism about the lordship of God were erased.

God be praised, his apostleship was guidance and mercy for the worlds, a final proof against the arguments of those who were opposing and obdurate, a victorious power over those who persisted in their unbelief and rejected the right, a demonstration that made clear the error in the words of those who asserted that the sole One can be divided and multiplied.

Therefore, may God's blessings and peace be upon him, and upon those who follow his guidance, who trust in the One who sent him to set up the beacon of divine unity, and find contentment in him.

To our purpose:

3. On 10 Ṣafar 721 of the Hijra of the noble prophethood of Muḥammad,[7] on whom be the most abundant blessing and peace, 22 March and Ādhār (2v) 1632 of Alexander of the two horns the Greek, 16 Baramhāt 1037 of Diocletian the Copt, and 17 Khurdādmāh 690 of Yazdagird, son of Shahrīyār, son of Chosroes Anūshirvān the Persian,[8] a letter came by the hand of the foremost in rank and culture, Kilyām the merchant, the chamberlain of the Watch-Tower (may God prolong his happiness),[9] a letter exemplary in politeness but alien in intention and shocking in purpose. As has been said:

> Feeble, though with moisture in the fringes of its clothes,
>   by which recovery is brought to all the infirm,[10]

---

[7] The exact date according to the Gregorian calendar is 11 March 1321 CE.

[8] The identification of the Roman emperor Diocletian (r. 284-305 CE) as a Copt is typical of many other inaccuracies in the *Response*.

[9] Kilyām is mentioned several times in the *Response*, though he is not identified any more fully: cf. below §§ 42, 59, 69, 82, 86, 89 and 90. The title *wazīr al-Marqab* indicates that al-Dimashqī has in mind the fortress of al-Marqab on the main Syrian coastal road between Latakia and Tartus, protecting a harbour from which ships could reach Cyprus within two days. The fortress was captured from the Knights Hospitaller in 684/1285 by the Mamlūk Sultan Qalāwūn, and remained in Muslim hands thereafter; cf. *EI²*, vol. VI, art. 'al-Markab', and C. Hillenbrand, *The Crusades, Islamic Perspectives*, Edinburgh, 1999, pp.539f. Al-Dimashqī himself briefly mentions it in the *Nukhba*, p.208, where he says that the Muslims captured and repaired it 'in our time'.

[10] As al-Dimashqī immediately explains, the point of this verse is that while the

متحلّية بقلادة من جواهر كلم من آيات القرآن المجيد ، الميسّر للذكر[9] والشفاء لما في الصدور[10] تنزيل الحكيم الحميد[11]، أرسلها الأساقفة والبطارقة القسيسون والرهابنة ، أماثل الملّة المسيحية وأكابر الأمّة العيسوية ، من جزيرة قبرص[12] نسختين احداهما إلى الشيخ الإمام قدوة الأنام ، أبي العباس أحمد بن تيميّة ، أدام الله النفع به وامتع[13] ببقائه ، والثانية إلى من ظنّوا أنّ عنده علمًا.

4. فلمّا وقف العبد الفقير المشار إليه عليها * وتدبّرها ، علم أنهم التمسوا عمّا تضمنته[14] جوابًا ، فاتّحين بذلك في طلب المناظرة أبوابًا ، ظانين بأنهم قد ظفروا بما تؤيّد لهم مقالة ، أو يسدد لدينهم بذكره دلالة. ووجد العبد الفقير المشار إليه جميع ما تمسّكوا به هباءً أو كسراب بقيعة يحسبه الظمآن ماءً[15] ، فحسن عندي ردّ الأجوبة عما أوردوه ، وإظهار البرهان على بطلان ما اعتقدوه ، بعد أن فصّلت رسالتهم تفصيلاً ، وأوضحت بإثبات الحقّ الجواب عن كلّ فصل لمن أراد إلى الحقّ سبيلاً ، دبئاً عن دين الله واتباع رضوانه[16] ، راجيًا أن يبوئني الله بذلك دار أمانة ، فاستخرت الله تعالى وسألته العصمة من الخطأ في الجواب ، وحسن التوفيق والهدى إلى الحقّ والصواب ، فقلت مبتدئًا وبالله تعالى مهتديًا:

* 3r

---

[9] Cf. S. LIV: 17, 22, 32.   [10] Cf. S. X: 57.   [11] Cf. S. XLI: 42.   [12] A and B: قبرس   [13] B: اتبع (wrongly).   [14] B: تضمينته (wrongly).   [15] Cf. S. XXIV: 39.   [16] Cf. S. III: 162, 174; S. V: 18.

adorned with a necklace of gem-like words from verses of the glorious Qur'an, 'made easy to remember', 'a balm for that which is in the breasts', 'a revelation from the Wise, the Owner of praise'. The bishops and patriarchs, priests and monks, the foremost in the faith of Christ and leaders of the community of Jesus, had sent two copies of it from the Island of Cyprus, one to the Shaykh the Imam the model of humanity Abū al-ʿAbbās Aḥmad Ibn Taymiyya, may God always afford benefit through him and give delight by his continuing life,[11] and the second to one whom they thought might have some knowledge.

4. When this poor soul read it (3r) and reflected upon it, he realised they were looking for a response to what it contained. For they were opening up means of seeking a confrontation through it, under the impression that they had mastered what they had been assured was teaching, or that this might lead straight to their religion by the mention of it.[12] But this poor soul found that everything they clutched at was dust, or 'as a mirage in a desert, which the thirsty one supposeth to be water'. So I thought it right to send back responses to what they had written, and to provide a proof that what they believed was false. After dividing their letter into sections, I have given as a confirmation of truth a clear response to each section for anyone who desires a way to the truth, observing the religion of God and following his pleasure, hoping that in return God will give me a place in the abode of safety. So I appeal for help from God the exalted, and in this response I implore his protection against error, and good success and guidance to what is true and right. Being guided by God the exalted, I say as I begin:

---

main argument of the Christian *Letter* is unsound, the copious quotations from the Qur'an in it give it some marginal beneficial effect.

[11] Ibn Taymiyya knows details about the *Letter* of which al-Dimashqī shows no awareness, such as its title and its connection with Paul of Antioch; cf. p. 5 above.

[12] This is a bluntly realistic summing up of what the Christian authors' intention may well have been.

5. أرسلتم أيها الآباء الأفاضل ، والمعلّمون الأماثل ، والرؤساء الكهّان ، جاثليقية هذا الزمان ، ألهمكم الله رشدكم ، وهدى إلى الحقّ قصدكم ، تقولون بطريق الأخبار:

* 3v

أننا لمّا * سمعنا أن قد ظهر إنسان في العرب اسمه محمّد يقول إنه رسول الله وأتى بكتاب يذكر فيه أنه منزل عليه من عند الله ، فلم نزل إلى أن حصلنا الكتاب عندنا وقرأناه وفهمناه وتدبّرناه، فتحقّقنا منه أنّ محمّدًا أرسل إلى[1] العرب دوننا ، إذ هو عربي وليس بلساننا حسب ما جاء فيه وهو قوله في سورة الشعراء: ﴿ولو نزّلناه على بعض الأعجمين﴾ الآيات[2] ، وقوله في سورة البقرة: ﴿كما أرسلنا فيكم رسولاً منكم﴾ الآيات[3] ، وقوله في سورة آل عمران: ﴿لقد منّ الله على المؤمنين إذ بعث فيهم رسولاً من أنفسهم﴾ الآية[4]. وقوله في القصص: ﴿لتنذر قومًا ما آتهم من نذير من قبلك﴾ الآية[5] ، وكذلك في سورة السجدة[6] ، وقوله في سورة يس: ﴿لتنذر قومًا ما أنذر آباؤهم﴾ الآية[7].

فلمّا رأينا هذا فيه علمنا أنه لم يرسل إلينا بل إلى جاهلية العرب الذي إنه لم يأتهم رسول ولا نذير[8] من قبله ، وأنه لا يلزمنا اتباعه لأننا قد أتانا رسل من قبله ، خاطبونا

* 4r

بألستنا وأنذرونا بديننا الذي نحن متمسّكون به يومنا هذا.* وسلّموا إلينا التوراة والإنجيل بلغاتنا على ما يشهد لهما الكتاب الذي أتى به هذا[9] حيث يقول في سورة ابراهيم[10]: ﴿وما أرسلنا من رسول إلا بلسان قومه ليبيّن لهم﴾ الآية[11] ، وقوله في سورة النحل: ﴿ولقد بعثنا في كلّ أمّة رسولاً﴾[12]. وقوله في سورة الروم: ﴿ولقد أرسلنا من قبلك رسلاً إلى قومهم﴾ الآية[13]. فقد صحّ في هذا الكتاب أنه لم يأت إلا إلى جاهلية العرب. وأما قوله ﴿ومن يبتغ غير الإسلام دينًا﴾ الآية[14] فيريد بحسب مقتضى العدل الذي جاءهم به بلغتهم لا غيرهم ممّن لم يأتهم ما جاء فيه.

---

[1] B omits this word. [2] S. XXVI: 198. [3] S. II: 151; Cf. *ibid.* 129 [Abraham's prayer]. [4] S. III: 164. [5] S. XXVIII: 46. [6] Cf. S. XXXII: 3. [7] S. XXXVI: 6. [8] B: والنذير (wrongly), evidently a misreading of A. [9] P1, P2 and P3: هذا الرجل [10] A and B: ابرهيم [11] S. XIV: 4. [12] S. XVI: 36. [13] S. XXX: 47. [14] S. III: 85.

5.   *[Section One]*

Most excellent fathers, exemplary scholars, senior priests and catholicoi of this age—may God inspire rectitude in you and guide your purposes to the truth—you say by way of informing:

> When (3v) we heard that a man by the name of Muḥammad had appeared among the Arabs, saying that he was the messenger of God and bringing a book in which was mentioned that it had been revealed to him from God, we did not rest until we obtained the book for ourselves. We read it, comprehended it, and reflected upon it, and we concluded from it that Muḥammad had been sent to the Arabs and not to us. For, according to what is stated in it, it is in Arabic and not our language. This is what it says in *The Poets*, 'And if we had revealed it unto one of any other nation than the Arabs' and the following verses; in *The Cow*, 'Even as we have sent unto you a messenger from among you' and the following verses; in *The Family of 'Imrān*, 'Allah verily hath shown grace to the believers by sending unto them a messenger of their own' and the rest of the verse; in *The Stories*, 'That thou mayest warn a folk unto whom no warner came before thee' and the rest of the verse, with the same in *The Prostration*; and in *Yā Sīn*, 'That thou mayest warn a folk whose fathers were not warned' and the rest of the verse.
>
> When we noticed this in it, we knew that he had not been sent to us but to the pagan Arabs, about whom it says that no messenger or warner had come to them before him, and that it was not obliging us to follow him because messengers had come to us before him, addressing us in our own tongues and warning us about our religion, to which we adhere today. (4r) They delivered to us the Torah and Gospel in our languages, in accordance with what the book brought by this individual attests about them. For in *Abraham* it says, 'And we never sent a messenger save with the language of his folk, that he might make it clear for them' and the rest of the verse; in *The Bee*, 'And verily we have raised in every nation a messenger'; and in *The Romans*, 'Verily we sent before thee messengers to their own folk' and the rest of the verse. So it has been shown correctly in this book that he was sent only to the pagan Arabs. As for its words, 'And whoso seeketh as religion other than the Surrender [it will not be accepted from him, and he will be a loser in the Hereafter]', according to the demands of what is just this means: those to whom he brought it in their language, and not others to whom he did not come, as is stated in it.[1]

---

[1] The Christians appear more than willing to use the Qur'an in their own favour, although they do not here reach the point of acknowledging explicitly that it is divinely inspired.

6. فغاب عنكم الصواب لمعنيين: أحدهما ترك الإقتداء بذوي الآداب ، مع أنكم أهل أدب ومعارف ورتب، وثانيهما عدم اللحاق بذوي الألباب مع صحّة أذهانكم وانقيادكم للحقّ إذا ظهر لكم. أمّا تركّكم الأدب فكونكم لم تمجّدوا رسول الله صلّى الله عليه وسلّم بما يليق بجليل قدره وكرامته عند ذكره ، وخاطبتم الواصلة رسالتكم إليه بالتمجيد لاسمه وهو ذرّة من ذرّات وجود الرسول * وواحد من مئين15 ألوف ألوف شعوب ربوات من أمّته وتابعيه وخدّام شريعته ، ولأنّ العادة الجارية في سنّة المخاطبة والمكاتبة ، ولو بين الأعداء والمجهول بعضهم عند بعض ، استعمال الأدب مع أنّ اسم الرسول صلّى الله عليه وسلّم يقتضي المدح والحمد من مسمّيه ، سواء قصد مسمّيه ذلك أو لم يقصده ، فإن الاسم محمّد ، ومحمّد ضد مذمم ، فمن سمّاه بمجرد اسمه مدحه وحمده ومجّده طوعًا وكرهًا.

4v

وإنّا معشر المسلمين لا نذكر16 نبيًّا من الأنبياء ولا نسمع بذكره إلا ونصلّي عليه ونسلّم ونمجّد الربّ تعالى بذكر اسمائه المقدّسة عن مزاحمة اشتراك الأسماء المتخلّق بها العباد في التسمية كالاسم الذي افتتحتم17 به رسالتكم وهو قولكم "باسم الإله الناطق"، والنطق18 إن أردتم به أنه العلم والادراك أو الكلام النفساني أو الكلام اللساني أو المسموع من المتكلّم بأدوات جسمية أو غير جسمية ، فإنه اسم مشترك وليس من الأسماء المقدّسات الحسنى. وما مثلنا نحن وأنتم وسائر الملّيّن في تمجيدنا * للرسل والأنبياء عليهم السلام إلا كمثل من يمدح الشمس فيقول: "إنها مشرقة الضياء نيّرة" ، سواء قال ذلك أو لم يقله فإن الشمس في عزّها أغنى عن قوله. وإنما تمجيدنا وصلاتنا وسلامنا على الأنبياء شرف لنا في الدنيا والآخرة ، وسيّما السيّد المسيح المهجور ذكره من النصارى الغالين فيه ومن اليهود الغالين19 له ، إذ هؤلاء يقولون عند ذكره: "له منّا السجود" ، وهؤلاء لا يذكرونه إلاّ بالسوء وبالجحود ، فإنا نصلّي عليه ونسلّم ونقول فيه ما

5r

---

15 A and B: مين   16 B: ألنذكر (wrongly), evidently a misreading of A.   17 A and B: افتحتم   18 B: والناطق   19 B: القالين

6. Decorum has deserted you, in two respects. The first is failing to be guided by those who have manners, despite the fact that you are people of manners, culture and standing. And the second is not emulating people of reason, despite the soundness of your intellects and your deference to truth when it appears to you. As for your failure in manners, this is because you do not show honour to the messenger of God (may God bless him and give him peace) when you mention him, as befits the importance of his status and esteem, while you address the one to whom your letter has come by giving honour to his name, even though he is no more than a speck beside the being of the messenger, (4v) one of the hundreds, thousands of thousands of people of the myriads in his community, followers and servants of his law. For it is a continuing custom in the practice of speaking and writing to employ manners, even between enemies unknown to one another. Nevertheless, the name of the messenger (may God bless him and give him peace) compels tribute and praise from the one who names him, whether the person naming him intends this or not. This is because the name is 'greatly praised', and 'greatly praised' is the opposite of 'greatly blamed', so whoever calls him by his name alone, willy-nilly gives him tribute, praise and honour.

Of course, we Muslims do not mention any prophet or hear one mentioned without asking blessing and peace upon him. And we glorify the exalted Lord by employing his holy names without striving to share any names which humans make up in their naming, like the name with which you begin your letter when you say, 'In the name of God who speaks'. For 'speech', whether you mean by it 'knowledge', 'perception', 'inner word' or 'word spoken or heard from a speaker through physical or non-physical organs', is in fact a shared name and not one of the holy, beautiful names. When we give honour to (5r) the messengers and prophets (peace be upon them), we, you and followers of other religions are only like someone who pays tribute to the sun and says, 'It is shining and brilliant with beams'. It does not matter whether he says this or not, because the sun in its majesty has no need of his words, and our honouring and asking blessings and peace on the prophets is only a dignity for ourselves in this world and the next. This is particularly so in the case of the lord Christ, about whom the Christians, who are too much in favour of him, and the Jews, who are too much against him, both say absurd things. For the former when they refer to him say, 'He is worthy of our worship', and the latter only refer to him offensively and contemptuously. But we ask blessings and peace upon him, and we say about him what

قال ربّنا عزّ وجلّ: ﴿إنّما المسيح عيسى ابن مريم رسول الله وكلمته ألقاها إلى مريم وروح منه﴾ الآية[20].

7. وأمّا عدم اللحاق بذوي الألباب الذين أوحى الله إليهم وحيه وأسمعهم كلامه بألسنة رسله فآمنوا به وبكتبه وبرسله فلكونكم زعمتم أنّ ظهور سيّدنا محمّد صلّى الله عليه وسلّم كان بغتة مفاجأة للناس من غير أن يبشّر به نبي متقدّم ولا رسول من الرسل ، ولا هتفت بنعته الجان وسجعت بوصفه الكهّان ، ولا كان اسمه وبعثه مكتوبًا في التوراة في * سبع مواضع وفي الإنجيل مثل ذلك. مع أنّكم واليهود تقرأون[21] يومنا هذا في التوراة ما ترجمته بالعربية: "جاء الله من سيناء وأشرق من ساعير واستعلى بجبال فاران"[22]. وتعلمون أنّ المراد بسيناء موسى والتوراة فإنّ سيناء طور المخاطبة ، وأنّ المراد بساعير المسيح والإنجيل إذ ساعير مدينة الناصرة موضع البشارة بالمسيح ، وأنّ المراد بجبال فاران محمّد والقرآن ، فإنّ فاران مكة وجبال فاران جبال الحجاز. وكذلك تقرأون[23] أنتم واليهود في التوراة ما ترجمته: قال الله لموسى: "قل لهم ، يعني بني اسرائيل ، نبي يقيمه الله لكم من اخوتكم مثلي ، ويجعل الله كلامه في فيه"[24]. وتعلمون[25] أنّ بني اسرائيل ليس لهم أخوة إلا بني اسماعيل و لم

* 5v

---

[20] S. IV: 171. [21] A and B: تقرون [22] Cf. Deut XXXIII: 2. [23] A and B: تقرون
[24] A reminiscence of Deut XVIII: 15, 17-18. [25] So in V; A and B: ويعلمون

our Lord, great and mighty says, 'The Messiah, Jesus son of Mary, was only a messenger of Allah, and his word which he conveyed unto Mary, and a spirit from him' and the rest of the verse.[2]

7. As for not emulating people of reason, to whom God sent down his revelation and addressed his word by the tongues of his messengers so that they believed in him, his books and his messengers, this is because you claim that the appearance of our lord Muḥammad (may God bless him and give him peace) was sudden and surprising to people, because no earlier prophet or messenger announced him, the jinns did not hail his qualities nor the soothsayers rhyme his traits, nor likewise were his name and mission written in seven places in the Torah (5v) and the Gospel.[3] Even so, you and the Jews read even today in the Torah, what in Arabic translation is, 'God came from Sinai and shone out from Seir and towered over the mountains of Paran'.[4] You know that what is meant by Sinai is Moses and the Torah, since Sinai was the mountain of direct address, that what is meant by Seir is Christ and the Gospel, since Seir is the town of Nazareth, the place of the annunciation of Christ, and that what is meant by the mountains of Paran is Muḥammad and the Qur'an, since Paran is Mecca and the mountains of Paran are those of the Ḥijāz.[5]

Similarly, you and the Jews read in the Torah, what in translation is, 'God said to Moses: Say to them (that is to the people of Israel), God will raise up for you from your brothers a prophet like me, and God will put his own word in his mouth'.[6] You know that the people of Israel have no brothers except the people of Ismāʿīl, and that no

---

[2] This is the first appearance of one of the recurrent themes of the *Response*, that Muslims are restrained and balanced compared with the extremes to which Jews and particularly Christians are prone.

[3] In what follows four quotations from the Pentateuch and three from the Gospels are discussed. Cf. the convert to Islam ʿAlī al-Ṭabarī, who in his *K. al-Dīn wa-al-dawla*, ed. A. Mingana, Manchester, 1923, trans. A. Mingana, *The Book of Religion and Empire*, Manchester, 1922, identifies numerous references to Muḥammad in the Torah and books of the New and Old Testaments. There are no signs of a direct relationship between al-Dimashqī's versions of this and the Biblical quotations that follow in §§ 7-9 and the versions in this earlier author.

[4] Cf. ʿAlī al-Ṭabarī, *Dīn wa-dawla*, p. 74.16f./*Religion and Empire*, pp. 86f.

[5] This symbolic interpretation bears no resemblance to the one given by ʿAlī al-Ṭabarī. But cf. the late seventh/thirteenth century Ibn Kammūna's, *Tanqīḥ al-abḥāth li-al-milal al-thalāth*, trans. M. Perlmann, *Ibn Kammūna's Examination of the Three Faiths*, Los Angeles and London, 1971, p. 142 (also pp. 138-9), where this interpretation is considered.

[6] Cf. ʿAlī al-Ṭabarī, *Dīn wa-dawla*, p. 73.15f./*Religion and Empire*, p 85.

يقم في بني اسماعيل وبني قيدر قائم بناموس عام وشريعة عظمى مثل موسى غير محمّد. ولمّا كان في التوراة أنه "لا يأتي²⁶ في بني اسرائيل نبي مثل موسى²⁷"، قال الله: "أقيم نبيًّا من أخوتكم²⁸"، ولم يقل منكم لئلا يتناقض²⁹ القول، فكان نبيّنا القائم من بني اسماعيل وكان كلام الله في فيه * يقوله قولاً وهو أمّي، لا تعلّم ولا كتب ولا سافر، فيظنّ الظان أنه تعلّم في السفر.

* 6r

وكذلك في التوراة أيضًا ما ترجمته: "قال الله لاسماعيل سمعتك³⁰ ها أنا نمّيته وباركته وجعلته لأمّة عظيمة مذمد يولد اثني عشر شريفًا³¹". وأنتم واليهود تعلمون أنه لم ينم ويبارك ويبعث للأمّة العظيمة ويولد اثني عشر شريفًا سوى محمّد المسمّى مذمد³² والمبارك جدًا جدًا صلّى الله عليه وسلّم.

وكذلك جاء في السفر الخامس من التوراة ما ترجمته: "قال الله لموسى سأقيم لبني اسرائيل

---

²⁶ V: اليأتي (wrongly), evidently a misreading of A. ²⁷ Deut XXXIV: 10. ²⁸ A reminiscence of Deut XVIII: 15, 17-18. ²⁹ V: ينتاقض (wrongly). ³⁰ A and B: سمعتد; V: سمعتها (wrongly). ³¹ Cf. Genesis XVII: 20. ³² A note in the margin, written in a different colour of ink, reads as follows: مع ان عدده بالعبراني 92، فهو يطابق عدد محمد صلعم

one has arisen among the people of Ismāʿīl and the people of Kedar[7] who upheld the general law and the supreme revealed Law in the way that Moses did except Muḥammad. And since it is stated in the Torah: 'A prophet like Moses will not come from among the people of Israel', God said, 'I will raise up a prophet from your brothers', not saying 'from you' so as not to contradict his own words. Hence our Prophet rose up from the people of Ismāʿīl. God's word was in his mouth, (6r) and he delivered it orally for he was illiterate,[8] he had not studied, he could not write, and he had not gone on journeys for anyone to think he had studied on a journey.

Similarly, there occurs in the Torah what again in translation is, 'God said to Ismāʿīl: I have heard you; listen, I will bring him up and bless him, and make him into a great nation. Mudhmadh will beget twelve princes'.[9] Both you and the Jews know that no one has been brought up, or been blessed, or sent forth to the great nation, or has engendered twelve princes[10] other than Muḥammad, who is called 'Mudhmadh'[11] and 'the very greatly blessed' (may God bless him and give him peace).

Similarly, in the fifth book of the Torah there occurs what in translation is, 'God said to Moses: I will raise up for the people of Israel

---

[7] According to Genesis XXV: 13 and Ezekiel XXVII:21, this was Ishmael's second son whose descendants inhabited Arabia.

[8] Cf. S. VII:157f.

[9] Cf. ʿAlī al-Ṭabarī, *Dīn wa-dawla*, p. 67.1-3/*Religion and Empire*, pp. 77f. Al-Dimashqī subtly alters Genesis XVII: 20, where Abraham is addressed and it is Ishmael about whom the promises are made, so that Ismāʿīl becomes the addressee and the unspecified 'he' can be identified as Muḥammad. The occurrence of 'Mudhmadh' (vocalised here in accordance with the MS and on the model of 'Muḥammad') can be explained by reference to the Hebrew of Genesis XVII: 20, which reads: 'I will bless him and make him fruitful and multiply him exceedingly, *be-me'odh me'odh*; he shall be the father of twelve princes, and I will make him a great nation'. Al-Dimashqī or his source has altered this sequence, and evidently reads the adverbial *be-me'odh me'odh* as a personal noun Mudhmadh. The marginal note attempts to clarify the significance of this by pointing out that, according to the standard numerical equivalents of the Hebrew letters, the values of *be-me'odh me'odh* ([2+40+1+4 = 47] + [40+1+4 = 45] = 92) and Muḥammad (40+8+40+4 = 92) are identical. On this calculation, cf. Perlmann, *Ibn Kammūna's Examination of the Three Faiths*, p. 139, and also U. Rubin, *The Eye of the Beholder, the Life of Muḥammad as viewed by the Early Muslims*, Princeton, 1995, p. 24.

[10] Most obviously, these would be the twelve Imams of Ithnā ʿAsharī Shiʿism.

[11] Cf. ʿAlī al-Ṭabarī, *Dīn wa-dawla*, pp. 119.12-120.2/*Religion and Empire*, p. 141, for analogous speculation about the equivalence of 'Paraclete' and 'Muḥammad', and further *Dīn wa-dawla*, pp. 117.6-118.11/*Religion and Empire*, p. 137-9.

نبيًا مثلك، فليسمعوا له ويطيعوه ، ومن خالفه فإني أعاقبه وأعرض عنه "³³. وهذا يقرأه³⁴ السامرة³⁵ واليهود وتعلمونه أنتم، وأنه ما جعل في آخر التوراة إلا للتوكيد والعهد ، و لم يأت مثل موسى سوى محمّد صلّى الله عليه وسلّم.

8. وممّا جاء من وصفه والتبشير به³⁶ من المسيح عليه السلام قوله في الأناجيل³⁷ الأربعة للتلاميذ ليلة الفصح ما معناه: "إني ذاهب عنكم وخير لكم أن أذهب لأن الفارقليطس³⁸ يرسله الله إليكم ، يعلّمكم كلّ شئ "³⁹، والفارقليطس * معناه الرسول. وقال أيضًا ما ترجمته: " إذا أنا ذهبت فإنّ أركون العالم يأتي إليكم يوبّخ العالم على العدل وعلى الخطيئة من أجلي وعلى الحكم "⁴⁰. و لم يأت بعد المسيح من وبّخ العالم على هذه الثلاثة وكان أركون العالم سوى محمّد صلّى الله عليه وسلّم. وقال المسيح أيضًا ما معناه: "حقّ حقّ أقول لكم أنّ الفارقليط الآتي بعدي ينبثق⁴¹ من فيه روح الحقّ ويوبّخ العالم لكونهم اتخذوني هزءًا وبغضوني مجانًا ، فاسمعوا له وأطيعوا ⁴²".

* 6v

---

³³ Deut XVIII: 18-19; cf. also Acts III: 22-4.   ³⁴ A, B and V: يقروه   ³⁵ V: السمارة
(wrongly).   ³⁶ B om. this word.   ³⁷ V: الإنجيل   ³⁸ A note at the bottom of the folio,
written in a different colour if ink, reads as follows: فيه عبث، يا ليته لم يكتب هذا حتى لا
يضحكون النصارى   ³⁹ Cf. Jn XIV: 25-6.   ⁴⁰ *Ibid.* XVI: 7-8.   ⁴¹ V: ينشق (wrongly)—corrected in the errata (p.197) to ينبثق, which is also wrong!   ⁴² Cf. Jn XV: 26.

a prophet like you; let them hear him and obey him. And whoever opposes him, I shall punish him and turn away from him.'[12] This is what the Samaritans and Jews read, and you yourselves know it, and that it was only put at the end of the Torah as an assurance and promise.[13] And there has come no one like Moses except Muḥammad (may God bless him and give him peace).

8.   Part of the description and declaration about him that was given by Christ (peace be upon him) are his words in the four Gospels to the disciples on the night of the Passover, the meaning of which is, 'I am going from you, and it is good for you that I go, because God will send to you the Paraclete who will teach you all things'.[14] The meaning (6v) of 'the Paraclete' is the messenger. He also said, what in translation is, 'When I have gone, the ruler of the world will come to you; he will rebuke the world about justice, about sin on my account and about judgement.'[15] No one has come after Christ who has rebuked the world about these three and has been ruler of the world except Muḥammad (may God bless him and give him peace). Christ also said, its meaning being, 'Truly, truly I say to you, the Paraclete who will come after me; from his mouth will pour forth the spirit of truth; he will rebuke the world because they held me in derision and were wilfully hateful towards me. So listen to him and obey him.'[16]

---

[12] Cf. ʿAlī al-Ṭabarī, *Dīn wa-dawla*, pp. 73.17-74.1/*Religion and Empire*, p. 85.

[13] This prophecy from Deut XVIII: 18-19 may be considered as coming at the end of the Torah because it occurs half way through the last of the five books.

[14] Cf. ʿAlī al-Ṭabarī, *Dīn wa-dawla*, p. 118.14f./*Religion and Empire*, p. 140. These words are recorded only in the fourth Gospel, not in all four. The tradition of iden- tifying the Paraclete as Muḥammad goes back at least as far as the second/eighth century; Ibn Isḥāq/Ibn Hishām, *Sīrat sayyidnā Muḥammad rasūl Allāh*, ed, F. Wüstenfeld, Göttingen, 1858-60, pp. 149f., trans. A. Guillaume, *The Life of Muhammad*, Oxford, 1955, pp. 103f.; A. Mingana, 'The Apology of Timothy the Patriarch before the Caliph Mahdi', *Bulletin of the John Rylands Library* 12, 1928, pp.169-71.

[15] Cf. ʿAlī al-Ṭabarī, *Dīn wa-dawla*, p. 119.3-5/*Religion and Empire*, p. 140. While the title *arkūn al-ʿālam*, which here is inserted into the verse, may suit Muḥammad as a political leader and founder of an empire, it might carry negative overtones for a reader acquainted with John's Gospel, since it recalls the title *ho tou kosmou archōn* which John alone among the evangelists uses, and refers to the devil; Jn XIV: 30, cf. XII: 31, XVI: 11. In § 18 al-Dimashqī explains Jesus' reference to the Paraclete rebuking the world about sin on his account by showing how the Qurʾan emphasises his humanity and denies his divinity.

[16] While this recalls Jn XV: 26, it subtly changes the original. Firstly, it starts with the typically Johannine avowal *ḥaqqan ḥaqqan = amen amen*, which does not,

وقال المسيح أيضًا حين كان مارًّا ببيت عيانا وسأله رئيسها قائلاً: "أنت ألوليا[43] أو أكمد" فقال: "لست ألوليا[44] ولا أكمد ، وإنما أنا ابن البشر الوحيد". وأنتم تعلمون أن أكمد أحمد باللغة اللاتينية[45] ، فإن حرف الحاء لا يوجد فيها. وهذا معنى ما جاء في كتابنا من قول المسيح ﴿ومبشِّرًا برسول يأتي من بعدي اسمه أحمد﴾[46].

9. وممَّا جاء في وصفه صلَّى الله عليه وسلَّم في المزامير وكتب النبوّات التي تقرأونها وتصدِّقون بها قول داود عليه السلام الذي معناه بالعربية:" اللهم أيِّد عبدك * الذي جعلته ملكًا ونبيًّا مباركًا كالشمس نورًا وكالمطر رحمة[47] وكالبحر علمًا ، تأتي[48] به من الأمّة الوحشية ، يملأ الأرض علمًا وعدلاً، بيده السيف ذو[49] الحدين وكلامك الحقّ في فمه ، يدعى الأمين في بني قيدر تخرّ له ملوك سبأ ، تهدي إليه ملوك الحبشة هدايا من الجزائر ، يسبِّح الله بالتسبيحة الجديدة ، يدعو[50] إلى الله وحده لا شريك له ، يكون نوره في الأرض كضياء[51] الشمس والقمر ، طوبى لبيت الربّ المسكينة المطهّرة[52]، يطهّرها من كلّ الأنجاس ولا يُبقي عليها صنمًا ، طوبى لك يا ثيربا يقوم بمجدك به إلى دهر الداهرين آمين[53]".

وهذه بمجموعها صفات نبيِّنا ونعوته[54] ، وبيت الربّ مكّة ، وثيربا[55] أرض مدينته صلَّى الله عليه وسلَّم التي هاجر إليها ، وسبأ بلدة باليمن ، ولم[56] يقم في اليمن وجزيرة العرب قائم دعا إلى الله تعالى وملأ الأرض علومًا وعدلاً ،

* 7r

---

43 *Sic* in A and B; V: الأولياء   44 *Sic* in A and B; V: الأولياء   45 A and V: اللاتية؛ B: اللاتيه   46 S. LXI: 6.   47 V: رحمته (wrongly).   48 A and B: يأتي   49 So also in V; A and B: ذا   50 A, B and V: يدعوا   51 V: لضياء (wrongly), apparently a misreading of the letter *kāf* in A.   52 A and B: المضطهرة؛ V: السكينة المتطهرة   53 Cf. Psalm LXXII: 1, 5, 6, 10, 11; Isaiah XLII: 10, 11 and XLIX: 2.   54 V: ونبوته   55 V: ويثرب   56 V: فلم

And when he was passing through Bethany and its headman questioned him saying, 'Are you Elijah or Akmad?', Christ also said, 'I am neither Elijah nor Akmad; I am only the Son of Man and no more.'[17] And you know that Akmad is Aḥmad in Latin, because it does not have the letter ḥā'. This is the meaning of what appears in our Book in the words of Christ, 'And bringing good tidings of a messenger who cometh after me, whose name is Aḥmad'.

9.   Among the descriptions of him (may God bless him and give him peace) in the Psalms and books of the prophets which you read and accept as true is the saying of David (peace be upon him), the meaning of which in Arabic is, 'O God, give help to your servant (7r) whom you make a blessed king and prophet, like the sun in giving light, like the rain in mercy and like the ocean in knowledge. You will bring him forth from the wild nation, and he will fill the earth with knowledge and justice; in his hand will be a two-edged sword and your word of truth will be in his mouth. He will be named the Trustworthy among the children of Kedar; the kings of Sheba will fall down before him, the kings of Ethiopia will bring him gifts from the isles. He will praise God with a new hymn of praise; he will call to God alone with no partner to him; his light will be in the earth like the radiance of the sun and moon; a blessing to the lowly, pure house of the Lord, which he will purify of all defilements, and he will not leave any image in it; a blessing to you, O Thirba, through him your glory will last for ever and ever. Amen.'[18]

These are all attributes and characteristics of our Prophet: 'the house of the Lord' is Mecca, Thirba is the region of his city (may God bless him and give him peace) to which he migrated,[19] and Sheba is a town in Yemen; and no one rose up in Yemen and Arabia calling to God the exalted, and filling the earth with knowledge and justice,

---

however, appear in this verse in any original witness. Secondly, it alters the received 'the Spirit of truth that issues from the Father' to 'from his mouth will pour forth the spirit of truth', which changes the intimate relationship between Spirit and Son to the relationship between Prophet and spirit/angel Gabriel-inspired speech.

[17] The nearest New Testament equivalent to this incident is the question put to John the Baptist in Jn I: 21 (cf. Mtt XVI: 14). Bethany is associated with Jesus in all four Gospels, though there is no record of an exchange between him and a headman. The curious mention of a Latinised form of Aḥmad in the Gospel shows how comparatively superficial al-Dimashqī's Biblical knowledge was.

[18] Cf. 'Alī al-Ṭabarī, *Dīn wa-dawla*, pp. 76.9-77.3/*Religion and Empire*, pp. 89f.

[19] This is not a Biblical name. Al-Dimashqī clearly identifies it as Yathrib/Medina, with which he would see an evident etymological connection.

وخرّت له ملوك الحبشة طائعة وملوك سبأ والعرب العرباء ، وطهّر الكعبة
من الأصنام والشرك وأخلى جزيرة العرب * من الأصنام ، ودعا إلى الإسلام
عشر سنين بالقرآن والمعجزات وثلاث[57] عشرة سنة بالقرآن والمعجزات
والسيف ذي الحدين ، ومات عنه[58] مائة ألف صحابي وأربعة عشر ألف
صحابي كلهم كالتلاميذ وكأنبياء بني إسرائيل ، سوى نبيّنا محمّد صلّى الله
عليه وسلّم.

10. وكذا قول أرميا في تنبيه بالمسيح وبه صلّى الله عليهما[59] حيث يقول:
"قال لي ملاك الله قم فانظر ماذا ترى ، فرأيت رجلاً أبيض أحمر راكبًا حمارًا
وبين يديه شعوب شعوب وربوات ربوات. ثم قال لي ملاك الله قم فانظر ماذا
ترى ثانية فنظرت فإذا رجل أسمر أحمر راكبًا جملاً كان وجهه القمر وبين
يديه ربوات وشعوب مئين وألوف[60] يسبّحون الله تسبيحًا جديدًا، يدعون
الله وحده وينادون في كلّ سنة بالبرية الموحشة من رؤوس الجبال وبطون
الأودية: أتيناك أتيناك ، ليأتي[61] معهم إلى دهر الداهرين[62]". فالذي رآه أرميا
أوّلاً هو المسيح عليه السلام ، والذي رآه ثانيًا هو نبيّنا محمّد صلّى الله عليه
وسلّم. * والتسبيح الجديد "أتيناك أتيناك" هو معنى قولنا في الحجّ: "لبّيك
اللهم لبّيك ، لا شريك[63] لك لبّيك ، إنّ الحمد والنعمة لك والملك،
لا شريك لك". والأمّة الوحشية هي العرب العرباء والمستعربة أهل مكّة
والمدينة ومن حولها[64] من العرب.

---

before whom the kings of Ethiopia, Sheba and the pure Arabs fell down willingly,[20] no one purified the Ka'ba of idols and polytheism, and emptied Arabia (7v) of idols, who called to Islam for ten years by the Qur'an and miracles, and thirteen years by the Qur'an, miracles and a two-edged sword,[21] on whose account died one hundred thousand companions and fourteen thousand companions, all of them like the disciples and the prophets of the people of Israel, other than our Prophet Muḥammad (may God bless him and give him peace).

10. Jeremiah's words in his prophecy about Christ and him (may God bless them both) are similar, when he says, 'The angel of God said to me, "Stand up and look; what do you see?" And I saw a man in bright red riding on an ass, and before him masses and masses, and myriad myriads. Then the angel of God said to me, "Stand up and look; what do you see a second time?" And I looked, and behold there was a man in dark red riding on a camel, his face was the moon and before him myriads and masses, hundreds and thousands, praising God with new praise, calling to God alone and shouting in every pathway of the wild desert, from the tops of the mountains and the valley bottoms, "We have come to you, we have come to you". May he be with them for ever and ever'.[22] The one whom Jeremiah saw the first time was Christ (peace be upon him), and the one whom he saw the second time was our Prophet Muḥammad (may God bless him and give him peace). (8r) 'The new praise, "We have come to you, we have come to you"', is actually our words on the pilgrimage, 'I am at your service, O God, I am at your service; you have no partner, I am at your service; praise and blessing and dominion are yours; you have no partner'. 'The wild nation' are the pure Arabs and the Arabicised, the people of Mecca and Medina and the Arabs around.[23]

---

[20] These are references to the sympathetic reception given to the Muslim refugees in Ethiopia during the period of Quraysh persecutions, when the Negus supposedly converted to Islam (to which al-Dimashqī returns below), and to the success of Islam in central and southern Arabia towards the end of the Prophet's life.

[21] The Prophet preached in Mecca from about 610 to 622, and preached and fought in Medina from 622 to 632, years 1 to 11 in the Muslim calendar.

[22] Cf. 'Alī al-Ṭabarī, *Dīn wa-dawla*, p. 82.9-12/ *Religion and Empire*, p. 96. The attribution of this popular proof-text to Jeremiah rather than Isaiah is another indication of al-Dimashqī's uncertain knowledge of the Bible. He returns to the prophecy in §§ 25 and 41 below.

[23] This most immediately refers to those in the prophecy who shout 'in every pathway of the wild desert', though it also echoes 'the wild nation' of the Psalm quoted above. Ibn Isḥāq, *Sīra*, pp. 3-6/ *Life*, pp. 3-4, identifies the *'Arab al-'arbā'* and

وكذا قول أشعياء عن الله تعالى يخبر عن أمّة[65] محمّد صلّى الله عليه وسلّم ، قائلاً : "ويحجّون في كلّ شهر ومن سنة إلى سنة إلى بيت الله الحرام ، ويقرّبون لله ربّهم قرابين زكية نقية ، وينظرون إلى الأمّة الخبيثة المارّدة بني اسرائيل ، لا يلى حزنها[66] ولا ينقطع[67] بلاها إلى الأبد"[68]. وقول أشعياء أيضًا : "في ذلك اليوم سأبطل[69] السبوت والأعياد كلها وأعطي المؤمنين بي[70] سنّة جديدة مختارة كالسنّة التي أعطيتها لموسى عبدي ، يوم حوريب يوم الجمع الكبير ، سنّة جديدة مختارة آمر بها وأخرجها من صهيون"[71]. وهذا القول من أشعياء ليس عن المسيح لأنه لا يقوم في بني اسرائيل مثل موسى ولأنّ الله تعالى قال على لسان أشعياء إنه يأمر بالسنّة الجديدة أمرًا من عنده[72]

* وليس دين النصرانية كذلك ، بل هو تقنين أهل المجامع أيام قسطنطين كما يتبيّن[73] بعد إن شاء الله تعالى.

‎* 8v

11. وكثير مثل ذلك في كتب النبوّات وسفر الملوك ما لو أوردته لزاد على المقصود ، ومنه رؤيا سنحاريب أوّل ملوك بابل للصنم الذي رآه ، وعبّر له رؤياه دانيال النبي قائلاً : "أمّا رؤيا الملك لرأس الصنم وعنقه من الذهب الخالص فهي[74] دولتك ودولة بنيك ، وأمّا كون صدره ويديه[75] فضة خالصة فهي دولة ثانية دون[76] الدولة الأولى ، وأمّا كون بطنه وفخذيه[77] من حديد فهي دولة شغبة عسوفة جائرة ، وأمّا كون ساقيه وقدميه من فخّار فهي دولة تأتي باضطراب وضعف وبها انقراض دولة الفرس"[78] ، وأمّا الحجر الذي أتى من الحجاز ودقّ قوائم الصنم فحطّمها وحطّم الصنم كله ونما حتى بلغ السماء وانتشر حتى ستر الأفق فهو[79] نبي يبعث من جزيرة العرب ، لا يقوم له شئ وتنشر دعوته[80] في مجموع الأرض ويزول

---

[65] This word is added in the margin in A, but is lacking in B and V.   [66] B om this word.   [67] V: يقطع   [68] Cf. Isaiah LXVI: 23-4.   [69] B: ساء (sic wrongly), being the first part of the word written in the body of the text in A, with the other part written in the margin.   [70] B: لي ; V: في   [71] Cf. Isaiah II: 3 and Micah IV: 2; Malachi IV: 4.   [72] V omits أمرًا من عنده ; B: امر أن عنده (sic).   [73] V: نبيّن   [74] B: وهي   [75] So in V; A and B: ويداه   [76] B: دول (wrongly), a misreading of A.   [77] So in V; A and B: فخذاه   [78] Cf. Daniel II: 31-5.   [79] V omits this word.   [80] V: دعوة

Isaiah's words from God the exalted are similar, telling about
the community of Muḥammad (may God bless him and give him
peace) when he says, 'They will make pilgrimage in every month and
from year to year to the sacred house of God; they will make pure,
unblemished offerings to God their Lord; and they will look on the
evil, rebellious nation, the people of Israel, whose sorrows will not
diminish, and whose tribulations will never come to an end.' There
are also Isaiah's words, 'On that day I will abolish all the sabbaths
and festivals, and I will give to those who believe in me a new, chosen
way, like the way which I gave to Moses my servant on the day of
Horeb, the day of the great assembly, a new, chosen way which I will
impart and bring forth from Zion'. These words from Isaiah are not
about Christ because there did not rise up among the people of Israel
one like Moses, and because God the exalted said on the tongue of
Isaiah that he would impart the new way as a command from himself.
(8v) The religion of Christianity is not like this, for it is legislation by
people in Councils from the time of Constantine, as will be shown
later if God the exalted wills.[24]

11.   There are many things like this in the writings of the Prophets
and the Book of Kings, though if I mentioned them they would go
beyond my intention. Among them is the dream of Sennacherib, the
foremost of the kings of Babylon, of the idol which he beheld. The
prophet Daniel interpreted his dream for him, saying, 'The king's
dream of the head and neck of the idol of pure gold are your own
and your sons' rule; his chest and hands of pure silver are a second
rule inferior to the first; his belly and thighs of iron are a turbulent,
tyrannous and despotic rule; his legs and feet of clay are a rule that
will bring unrest and insecurity, through which the rule of the Persians will be extinguished; the stone which comes from the Ḥijāz and
crushes the feet of the idol and shatters them and shatters the whole
idol, and grows until it reaches the heavens and expands until it covers the horizon, is a prophet who is sent from Arabia, whom nothing
will withstand, whose call will extend throughout the world, through

---

the *Mustaʿriba* as respectively Arabian Arabs of pure descent and Ḥijāzī Arabs who
traced their ancestry back to Ismāʿīl.

    [24] Cf. §§ 31 and 43-5 below. For a brief account of the accusation made by ʿAbd
al-Jabbār in the fourth/tenth century that the Church Councils were the main agents
in distorting Jesus' original teachings, cf. S.Griffith, 'Muslims and Church Councils:
the Apology of Theodore Abū Qurrah', *Studia Patristica* 25, Leuven, 1993, pp. 282-
3.

به دولة المخالفين له ، يملأ الأرض عدلاً وعلمًا وخيرًا.

وهذه[81] الرؤيا * (...)[82] عند اليهود والفرس. وفي كتاب الأنسيا لزرادشت الذي أخبر الفرس أيضًا في كتابه المسمّى بالأنسيا أنّ من (علا)مات[83] اتيان النبى العربي المشار إليه خمود النار الموقودة (لكو)رس[84] للعبادة من المجوس بولادته وغور بحيرة ساوة وفيض وادي السهاوة بالماء وانشقاق ايوان كسرى، فكان ذلك كما قال دانيال وزرادشت ، وسقطت منه أربعة عشر شرافة. وفسّرها سطيح الكاهن لإبن اخته عبد المسيح رسولٍ كسرى بأنّ دليل النبّوة الخاتمة وظهور الملّة الحنيفية بعد أربعة عشر ملكا يملكون من الفرس ، فملكوا الأربعة عشر في مدّة عشر سنين وانقرضوا بالإسلام وقصّة ذلك مشهورة في العرب والعجم.

12. وكذلك أيضًا لمّا وصلت مراكب المسلمين إلى جزيرة أصقلية وصاروا بها منازلين أهلها أرسل ملكها إلى أمير المسلمين بملاءة مرقومة خمس صور تماثيل وقال لهم: "سمّوا لنا أسماء من هذه تماثيلهم" ، فسمّوا اسم نبيّنا صلّى الله عليه وسلّم لمعرفتهم لتمثاله وسمّوا أسماء خلفائه الأربعة ،

---

[81] V: وهذا (wrongly). [82] A is damaged on the right hand corner of this folio, hence this word is illegible in it; B has a blank here; V: رضا which does not seem to provide any satisfactory meaning. Read perhaps: تعبيرها [83] B: العلامات [84] B: ورس (sic), being the latter half of the word available in A.

whom the rule of his opponents will decline, and who will fill the earth with justice, knowledge and goodness.'[25]

This is the dream, (9r) and its interpretation is in the possession of the Jews and Persians. It is in the *Avesta* of Zoroaster,[26] who further related to the Persians in his book the *Avesta* that among the signs of the coming of this Arabian prophet would be the quenching at his birth of the fire lit for Cyrus for Persian worship, the drying up of lake Sāwa, the flooding of the valley of Sihāwa, and the cracking of the arch of Chosroes; this did happen as Daniel and Zoroaster had said, and fourteen of its pinnacles fell. Saṭīḥ the soothsayer interpreted it for his nephew 'Abd al-Masīḥ, the messenger of Chosroes, as the sign that prophethood would reach its climax and the Ḥanīfite community would appear after fourteen kings of the Persians had ruled. The fourteen did rule within a span of ten years, and they came to an end with Islam, the account of this being well-known among Arabs and foreigners.[27]

12.   In the same way again, when the ships of the Muslims landed on the island of Sicily and they were about to fight with its people there, its king sent to the commander of the Muslims five representations, portraits in a striped sheet. He said to them, 'Tell us the names of the persons whose portraits these are.' So they gave the name of our Prophet (may God bless him and give him peace) because they recognised his image, and they gave the names of his four caliphs.

---

[25] Cf. 'Alī al-Ṭabarī, *Dīn wa-dawla*, pp. 113.5-114.6/ *Religion and Empire*, pp. 133f.

[26] This occurs in both MSS as *a.l.a.n.s.y.a*, which does not appear to correspond to any text associated with Zoroaster. However, if it is repointed as *a.l.a.b.s.t.a*, which requires a minimal alteration to the dots on two of the letters, it can be read as *al-abasta*, an Arabised form of *Avesta*, the major Zoroastrian scripture. In al-Mas'ūdī, *Murūj al-dhahab*, ed. and trans. C. Barbier de Meynard and Pavet de Courteille, Paris, 1861-77, vol. II, pp. 124 etc., this scripture is referred to as *Bastah*.

[27] Abū Ja'far al-Ṭabarī, *Ta'rīkh al-rusul wa-al-mulūk*, ed. M.J. de Goeje *et al.*, Leiden, 1879-1901, part I, pp. 981-4, refers to three of these portents (he does not mention the flooding of Sihāwa), and also to the fourteen last Sasanian kings. They are commonplace in later authors, and from al-Dimashqī's concluding comment it is unlikely that he took any single one as his direct source. A measure of their popularity is that they are mentioned in al-Būṣīrī's (d. 694/1294) famous *Burda*, which had been composed at the most no more than fifty years earlier; cf. A. Jeffery, *A Reader on Islam*, 's Gravenhage, 1962, p. 611, verses 63-6 (translation).

On the largely mythological figures of Saṭīḥ and 'Abd al-Masīḥ, cf. *EI²*, vols. IX, art 'Saṭīḥ b. Rabī'a', and III, art. 'Ibn Buḳayla'. A brief reference to Saṭīḥ, together with Sawād Ibn Qārib, whose story al-Dimashqī recounts below, appears in Perlmann, *Ibn Kammūna's Examination of the Three Faiths*, p. 129. Cf. also Rubin, *The Eye of the Beholder*, p. 54.

فسألهم الملك عن * الثالث ، فقالوا هو الخليفة ، فوادعهم على ما أرادوا
وسلّم إليهم الجزيرة وبنوا بها المساجد والمآذن[85] وأقاموا الصلاة وشعائر
الإسلام بها ، وذلك لعلم الملك بظهور سيّدنا رسول الله صلّى الله عليه وسلّم
وإعلاء دينه على كلّ دين.

13. وقصّة بحيرا ونسطور الراهبين ببصرى معه حين رأياه مع قافلة قريش
ومع عمّه أبي طالب وهو دون البلوغ فنزلا إليه وقبّلا يده وسألاه عن الشامة
التي بكاهله وعن أشياء أخبرهم بها وبشّرا عمّه بالنبوة والملك وعظمة الشأن[86]
وعرفا القافلة باخضرار الشجرة التي نزلوا بها من أجله وبتظليل الغمامة له في
جملة سفره ، وقالا إنّ المسيح بشّر به وهو أركون العالم فاحترزوا عليه من
اليهود فإنهم أعداؤه.

14. وقصّة فتح بيت المقدس مشهورة إذ حاصرها المسلمون ، وطال الحصار
حتى أرسل البطرك[87] والأساقف بها يقولون لا نسلّم البلد إلا إلى عمر أمير
المؤمنين ، فلمّا وصل من الحجاز وعليه ثوب فيه رقع مختلفة فأنزعوه إياه
أصحابه وألبسوه غيره ، وتراءى لأهل بيت المقدس فقالوا: "ليس هو
المطلوب". فنزعه ولبس الثوب المرقع

A and B: والمواذن   [86] B: الشا, being a misreading of A which has the final *nūn*
of the word at the end of the line above.   [87] A and B: البترك

Then the king asked them about the (9v) third, and they said, 'He is the caliph', whereupon he promised them what they wanted and surrendered the island to them. They built mosques and minarets there, and they established worship and the rites of Islam there. This was because the king had knowledge that our lord the messenger of God (may God bless him and give him peace) was to appear, and that his religion would rise above every religion.[28]

13.   There is the story of the monks Baḥīrā and Nestorius with him at Boṣrā, when they saw him before he had grown up with a caravan of Quraysh and with his uncle Abū Ṭālib. They came to him and kissed his hand, and they asked him about the birthmark on his back, and about things that he was able to relate to them.[29] They gave his uncle the good news of prophethood, kingship and great status, and they told the caravan about the tree near which they had halted sprouting green because of him, and about clouds shading him throughout his journey.[30] They said that Christ had announced him, and that he was the ruler of the world,[31] so they should guard him against the Jews, because they were his enemies.

14.   The story of the capture of Jerusalem when the Muslims besieged it is well-known. The siege went on, and then its patriarch and bishops sent a message saying, 'We will only surrender the city to 'Umar, Commander of the Faithful.' When he arrived from the Ḥijāz he had on a garment with patches of different kinds, so his companions took this off him (10r) and put another on him. He presented himself to the people of Jerusalem, but they said, 'He is not the one we demanded'. So he took it off and put on the patched garment.

---

[28] The first Muslim landing in Sicily was in 31-2/652, which agrees with the reference to the third caliph 'Uthmān. The story of the portraits recalls incidents in which early Muslims identify Muḥammad from among portraits of other prophets, as requested by the king of China, al-Masʿūdī, *Murūj*, vol. I, pp. 315-18, and by the Roman emperor Heraclius, al-Dhahabī, *Taʾrīkh al-Islām wa-ṭabaqāt al-mashāhīr wa-al-aʿlām*, Cairo, 1367, vol. I, pp. 298-300. The latter, vol. I, pp. 297f., also recounts the story of a contemporary of the Prophet identifying him and Abū Bakr from portraits held by Christians in Baṣra. Cf. also Rubin, *The Eye of the Beholder*, p. 49.

[29] Accounts of this meeting go back as far as John of Damascus, *De Haeresibus*, in D.J. Sahas, *John of Damascus on Islam, the "Heresy of the Ishmaelites"*, Leiden, 1972, p. 132, and Ibn Isḥāq, *Sīra*, pp. 115-17/*Life*, pp. 79-81. See also Roggema, 'A Christian Reading of the Qurʾan', pp. 57-73.

[30] These details appear in Ibn Isḥāq's account (see previous note), and in many later versions of the life of the Prophet.

[31] Cf. § 8 above, and n. 15.

وتراءى لهم فقالوا: "هذا الذي يفتح البلد وهو أمير المؤمنين وخليفة النبي
العربي". ثم وادعوه على الجزية وسلّموا البيت المقدّس لأهله ، ولم يكن ذلك
إلا عن علم منهم ببعثة[88] محمّد صلّى الله عليه وسلّم إلى الناس كافة وظهور
دينه على الدين كله ، وأنّ خليفته عمر يفتح البيت المقدّس من صفته كذا
ومن حاله كذا.

15. ومنه قصّة سواد بن قارب الكاهن[89] لمّا دخل على أمير المؤمنين عمر بن
الخطّاب رضي الله عنه وهو في مجلس خلافته فقال له عمر: "نشدتك الله يا
سواد ، هل تحسن اليوم من كهانتك[90] شيئاً؟". فخجل سواد وقال: "تالله يا
أمير المؤمنين ما استقبلت أحدًا من جلسائك بمثل ما استقبلتني به" ، فقال له
عمر: "والله ما أردت إلا أن أسمع ما اتفق وأسمعه" .

فقال سواد: " بينا[91] أنا ذات ليلة نائم إذ أتاني نجيي فأنبهني من نومي
وقال: "سواد اسمع أقل لك" فقلت: "هات" ، فقال:

---

[88] B: بعثه (wrongly).   [89] This word is added in the margin in the same hand in A
and is omitted in B.   [90] A and B: كهانيك   [91] B: نيناء (wrongly).

He presented himself to them and they said, 'This is the one who will take the city; he is the commander of the faithful and the caliph of the Arabian Prophet.' Then they pledged the poll-tax to him and they surrendered Jerusalem to his people. This would never have happened unless they had known about the mission of Muḥammad (may God bless him and give him peace) to all humankind and the pre-eminence of his religion over all others and, from his particular description and bearing, that his caliph ʿUmar would be the conqueror of Jerusalem.[32]

15. Among them is the story of Sawād Ibn Qārib the soothsayer, when he came before the Commander of the Faithful ʿUmar Ibn al-Khaṭṭāb (may God be pleased with him) in the caliphal assembly. ʿUmar said to him, 'By God, Sawād, I beg you, will you kindly practise some of your soothsaying today?' Disconcerted, Sawād said, 'By God, Commander of the Faithful, you have not received any of the members of your assembly in the way you have received me.' ʿUmar said to him, 'By God, I only wanted to hear what happened, so relate it'.[33]

Sawād said, 'In the middle of the night while I was sleeping, suddenly my familiar came to me, and rousing me from my sleep he said, "Sawād, listen to what I tell you." I said, "Go on", and he said:[34]

---

[32] Al-Ṭabarī, *Tāʾrīkh* I, pp. 2403-8, says almost nothing about this, though the tradition of ʿUmar being persuaded to change his clothes gradually grew among Muslim historians; cf. H. Busse, "Omar's Image as Conqueror of Jerusalem', *Jerusalem Studies in Arabic and Islam* 8, 1986, pp.149-68, esp. pp.161-3.

ʿUmar's pious reluctance to change his clothes depicted here contrasts with the Christian account given in the early third/ninth century by Theophanes Confessor, who explains that Bishop Sophronios of Jerusalem was revolted at the sight of the Caliph in his travelling gear and persuaded him to change into the clean clothes that he himself provided; *The Chronicle of Theophanes Confessor*, trans. C. Mango and R. Scott, Oxford, 1997, pp. 471-2. Al-Dimashqī and Theophanes' versions use ʿUmar's indifference to outward appearance in different ways to underline respectively his saintly simplicity and his uncultured awkwardness.

[33] A similar account of this meeting appears in al-Ṭabarī, *Taʾrīkh* I, pp. 1144f., who attributes it to Ibn Isḥāq.

[34] There are many versions of the following verses, from the second/eighth century onwards. Most preserve only two or three lines, and the only authors who recount the story in the same length and detail as here are Abū al-Qāsim Sulaymān al-Ṭabarānī from the fourth/tenth century (d. 360/971), *Al-muʿjam al-kabīr*, ed. H. ʿAbd al-Majīd al-Salafī, vol. VII, Beirut, 1985, pp. 92-6, and al-Dimashqī's Syrian contemporary Ṣalāḥ al-Dīn al-Ṣafadī (d.764/1362), *Al-wāfī bi-al-wafayāt (Bibliotheca Islamica* 6P), vol. XVI, ed. W. al-Qāḍī, Wiesbaden, 1982, pp. 35f.

Both these authors tell the story of Sawād and the caliph in more or less the same way as al-Dimashqī, and compared with the 14 lines he quotes, al-Ṭabarānī gives 15 lines (he repeats al-Dimashqī's line 7, with variations, after lines 2 and 4, and omits

"عجبت للجنّ وأجناسها   *   وحملها العيس بأحلاسها

تهوى إلى مكّة تبغي الهدى   ما مؤمنو الجنّ كأرجاسها".

قال: "فلم يحرّك قوله مني شيئاً، فلمّا كان في الليلة الثانية أتاني فوكزني برجله

وقال: "سواد اسمع أقل لك"، فقلت: "هات" فقال:

"عجبت للجنّ وتطلابها   وحملها العيس بأقتابها

تهوى إلى مكّة تبغي الهدى   ما مؤمنو الجنّ ككذّابها".

فحرّك قوله مني شيئاً، فلمّا كان في الليلة الثالثة أتاني فوكزني برجله

فأيقظني وقال: " سواد اسمع أقل لك"، فقلت: "هات" فقال:

"عجبت للجنّ وأدوارها   وحملها العيس بأكوارها

تهوى إلى مكّة تبغي الهدى   ما مؤمنو الجنّ ككفّارها

فارحل إلى الصفوة من هاشم   بين دوابها وأحجارها".

فقمت من ساعتي، فشديت على قلوص لي وسرت إلى مكّة فأتيت فسألت

عن النبي صلّى الله عليه وسلّم فأخبرت أنه في منزل خديجة فأتيت إليه

فطرقت الباب فخرج إليّ وقال لي: "سواد، إني رسول الله إليك وإلى سائر

الناس"، فقلت له: "وما آيتك؟" فقال: "آيتي[92] ما قال لك نجيك في الثلاث

ليال.

وكنت[93] يا أمير المؤمنين نظمت قصيدة في الطريق فاستنشدني سجع

نجيي وقال لي: "قل ما قلت أنت" فقلت:

"أتاني نجيي بعد هدوء ورقدة   ولم أك فيما قد تلوت بكاذب

ثلاث ليال قوله كلّ ليلة   أتاك رسول من لؤي بن غالب

---

92 B: ليتّي (wrongly), apparently a misreading of A.   93 B: وكتب (wrongly).

I was amazed at the jinn and their kinds, (10v)
 Fine camels on their saddle covers bore them,
They were making for Mecca, seeking the guidance;
 The believers in jinn are not like those who think them false.'

He said, 'What he said did not move me at all. Then on the second night he came to me, and kicking me with his foot said, "Sawād, listen to what I tell you." I said, "Go on", and he said:

I was amazed at the jinn and their insistence,
 Fine camels on their saddles bore them,
They were making for Mecca, seeking the guidance;
 The believers in jinn are not like those who deny them.

What he said moved me a little. Then on the third night he came to me and kicked me with his foot to wake me, and he said, "Sawād, listen to what I tell you." I said, "Go on", and he said:

I was amazed at the jinn and their agitation,
 Fine camels on their saddles bore them,
They were making for Mecca, seeking the guidance;
 The believers in jinn are not like those who reject them.
So be off to the elect among Hāshim,
 In among their greys and mares.

I got up directly, and calling out to a young camel "Here!", I set off in the night for Mecca. When I arrived, I inquired about the Prophet (may God bless him and give him peace), and I was told that he was in Khadīja's house, so I went there and knocked on the door. He came out to me and said to me, "Sawād, I am the messenger of God to you and to all people". So I said to him, "What is your sign?" and he said, "My sign is what your familiar told you on the three (11r) nights."

'Commander of the Faithful, I had composed a *qaṣīda* on the way, because my familiar had asked me to recite some rhyming prose, saying to me, "Say what I said". So I said:

My familiar came to me in the quiet of sleep—
 And I am not lying in what I have said—
On three nights, and his words each night were,
 "An apostle has come to you from Lu'ayy Ibn Ghālib".[35]

line 8), and al-Ṣafadī gives 10 lines (he omits al-Dimashqī's lines 3-6). Significant differences in wording in all three versions rule out any direct interdependence. Cf. Rubin, *The Eye of the Beholder*, p. 55 for further references.

The ultimate inspiration of the sentiments in the poem can be found in such verses as SS. XLVI: 29-32 and LXXII: 1-15, in the latter of which the jinn repeatedly refer to 'guidance', as in the poem.

[35] This is the Prophet's ancestor in the ninth generation; Ibn Isḥāq, *Sīra*, p. 3/*Life*,

بي الذعلب الوجناء عبر السباسب	فشمّرت عن ذيلي الإزار وأدلجت
وأنك مأمون على كلّ غائب	فاعلم أنّ الله لا ربّ غيره
إلى الله يا ابن[94] الأكرمين الأطايب	وأنك أدنى المرسلين وسيلة
ولو كان فيما جاءك شيب الذوائب	فمرنا بما يأتيك يا خير شافع
سواك بمغن عن سواد بن قارب"	وكن لي شفيعًا يوم لا ذي شفاعة

فأعرض عليّ الإسلام ، فأسلمت.

فقال له الإمام: "هل تحسن منها شيئاً اليوم؟" فقال سواد: "معاذ الله يا أمير المؤمنين ، أنسيتها منذ أسلمت؟".

فلم يكن إرسال محمّد صلّى الله عليه وسلّم مفاجأة بغتة من غير تقدّم تبشير به ولا إعلام ، بل ظهرت علامات نبوته وآيات رسالته في أقطار الأرض وبشّرت به الأنبياء والعلماء والكهّان وهتفت به الجان وكانت[95] اليهود * سكّان الحجاز أشدّ الناس انتظارًا لظهوره لينتصروا به على العرب الجاهلية ، فلمّا ظهر كانوا أوّل كافر به وأشدّ عداوة من كلّ عدو.

16. وكذلك كان الصدر الأوّل من النصارى ينتظرون مجيئه ويعلمون أنه إذا جاء يوبّخ العالم كما قال المسيح ، فلمّا ظهر قسطنطين الملك ورأى منام النصرة على الأعداء بالملائكة والأعلام والصلبان وسأل عن الصليب ، وأخبروه بأهل الناصرة[96] وتعظيمهم للصليب وأرسل إليهم وحضر منهم نحو الثمانين رجلاً وكان ذلك بدء ظهور دين النصرانية وهو دون المسيح بنحو من مائة عام أو دون ذلك وحبّب

* 11v

⁹⁴ B: لبن (wrongly), apparently a misreading of A.   ⁹⁵ B: وكاتب (wrongly), apparently a misreading of A.   ⁹⁶ B: النصره

So I pulled up the skirts of my clothes
  And the nimble mount took me bounding by night through the
  desert dust.
For I know that there is no lord but God,
  And that you are trustworthy about all that is unseen;
Of those sent you are the nearest means
  To God, O son of the noblest and best.
So command us from what has come to you, O best of intercessors,
  Although in what has come to you there may be grey hairs,
And be for me an intercessor on the day of no intercession;
  No one but you can stand for Sawād Ibn Qārib.

He presented Islam to me, so I became a Muslim.'

The Imam said to him, 'Can you still practise any of that?' Sawād
said, 'God save me, Commander of the Faithful, could I forget it since
I became a Muslim?'

Thus, the sending of Muḥammad (may God bless him and give him
peace) was not surprising or sudden without any previous announcement or intimation about him. The tokens of his prophethood and signs
of his apostleship appeared throughout the earth: prophets, sages and
soothsayers announced him; the jinn hailed him; the Jews (11v) living
in the Ḥijāz most eagerly awaited his appearance in order to overcome
the pagan Arabs through him, though when he appeared they were
the first to disbelieve in him and the fiercest of all enemies.

16.   In the same way, the early Christians awaited his coming and
knew that when he came he would rebuke the world, as Christ had
said.[36] Then when Constantine the king appeared and had the dream
of help against enemies from angels, signs and crosses,[37] and he asked
about the cross and they told him about the Christian people and their
exaltation of the cross, and he sent to them and about eighty of them
came before him, this was the start of the emergence of Christianity, about a hundred years or thereabouts after Christ.[38] It aroused

---

p. 3; al-Ṭabarī, *Taʾrīkh* I, p. 1101. His name evidently appears here because it
fits into the rhythm and rhyme scheme.

[36] Cf. §§ 8 above and 22 below, referring to the Paraclete verses in the Gospel
of John.

[37] This is a reference to Constantine's vision on the eve of his battle with Max-
entius in 312 CE, after which 'with the cross-shaped letter X with its top bent over
he marked Christ on the shields'; Lactantius, *On the Deaths of the Persecutors* 44, 5-6.

[38] More accurately, this was about 300 years after Christ. Al-Dimashqī's shakiness on early Christian history is exposed again in § 47 where he says Constantine

إلى قسطنطين إظهار دين النصرانية واجتمعت الكلمة من أهل مملكته على ذلك وترتّب الذي في المجامع السبعة وجمع الإنجيل من أفواه المخبرين الأربعة متى ولوقا ومرقس ويوحنا.

واطلع قسطنطين على ذكر البارقليطس وأركون العالم والذي ينبثق من فيه روح الحقّ والذي يعلّم التلاميذ ما لم يكن المسيح علّمهم إياه والذي يوبّخ العالم على العدل * والحكم والخطيئة من أجل المسيح وأجل بعضهم له مجاناً⁹⁷ ففحص قسطنطين عن هذا الآتي المنتظر من هو فخشي أصحاب القوانين على ما شرعوا فيه أن يتغيّر ويرجع عنه قسطنطين انتظارًا للآتي فقرّروا أنّ هذا الآتي هو المشار إليه من المسيح إنما هو روح القدس وأنه هو المتكلّم بجميع ما نحن قائلونه وفاعلونه وأنك إنما أنت متكلّم به وواجد ما أنت واجده به في نفسك فاستقرّ ذلك عند قسطنطين وكان من عبدة الأصنام وروحانيات الكواكب صابئيًا فجوز ما زعموه من أمر روح القدس لأنس نفسه باعتقاد الروحانيات .

* 12r

---

⁹⁷ B: محانا (wrongly), apparently a misreading of A; cf. f. 6v above.

in Constantine a desire to make the Christian religion known, and so the teaching about this was collected together from the people of his realm, what was in the seven Councils was put in order, and the Gospel was collected from the mouths of the four transmitters, Matthew, Luke, Mark and John.[39]

Constantine was told about the reference to the Paraclete and the ruler of the world, the one from whose mouth the spirit of truth would proceed, who would teach the disciples what Christ had never told them, and would also rebuke the world about justice, (12r) judgement and sin on account of Christ and on account of their wilfully hating him. So Constantine inquired about the expected one who was to come, who he might be. The canonical experts were afraid that what they had begun to do might be changed, and that Constantine might abandon this as he waited for the one who was to come. So they reassured him: 'This one who was to come, whom Christ spoke about, is none other than the Holy Spirit; he speaks through all that we say and do, and you yourself speak through him, and you experience all that you do through him in your soul.' This became Constantine's conviction, for he had been a Ṣābian, a worshipper of idols and the spiritual forces of the stars. So he accepted what they claimed about the matter of the Holy Spirit because he himself was familiar with belief in spiritual forces.[40]

---

ruled a century after Christ, and in § 76 where he says that there were 150 years between the time of Jesus and Paul.

[39] These three items may represent what al-Dimashqī thought was contained in the New Testament, though exactly what the 'teaching' was, as distinct from the Gospel, is not made clear. The seven generally accepted councils of the early church were Nicea (325), Constantinople I (381), Ephesus (431), Chalcedon (451), Constantinople II (553), Constantinople III (680) and Nicea II (787), all of which were convened during or after Constantine's lifetime.

[40] The Ṣābians are referred to three times in the Qur'an, SS. II: 62, V: 69 and XXII: 17. Muslim authors frequently identified them as the star-worshippers of Ḥarrān; e.g. al-Nadīm, *Kitāb al-Fihrist*, ed. M. Riḍā-Tajaddud, Tehran, 1971, pp. 383-91, al-Shahrastānī, *Kitāb al-milal wa-al-niḥal*, ed. W. Cureton, London, 1846, pp. 248-51, and al-Masʿūdī, *Murūj*, vol. I, pp. 198-201, who explicitly links Eastern Christian denominations with the Ṣābians as their spiritual descendants. Curiously, although in the *Response* al-Dimashqī refers to Ṣābian influences on Christianity a number of times, in the section of the *Nukhba* in which he lists religions that were influenced by the Ṣābians, pp. 45-7, he says nothing about Christians.

Interestingly, ʿAbd al-Jabbār al-Hamadhānī, *Tathbīt dalāʾil al-nubuwwa*, ed. ʿA.-K. ʿUthmān, Beirut, 1966, p. 159, links Constantine with Ḥarrān through his mother Helena, who he says was a native of the town (on this cf. S.M. Stern, "ʿAbd al-Jabbār's Account of how Christ's Religion was falsified by the Adoption of Roman Customs',

17. وكان هذا مبدأ الضلالة ومنشأ الجهالة ولازال الأمر على ذلك حتى جاء الحقّ وظهر أمر الله وهم كارهون وأرسل الله محمّدًا بالهدى ودين الحقّ الصحيح وأخذ في توبيخ العالم كما بشّر به المسيح. فكان من جملة توبيخه للنصارى قول الله تعالى له في القرآن الذي قلتم إنكم حصلتموه وقرأتموه[98] وفهمتموه قل: ﴿يا أهل الكتاب لا تغلوا في دينكم ولا تقولوا * على الله إلا الحقّ إنما المسيح عيسى ابن مريم رسول الله وكلمته ألقاها إلى مريم وروح منه فآمنوا بالله ورسله ولا تقولوا ثلاثة انتهوا خيرًا لكم إنما الله إله واحد سبحانه أن يكون له ولد له ما في السموات وما في الأرض وكفى بالله وكيلاً لن يستنكف المسيح أن يكون عبدًا لله ولا الملائكة المقرّبون ومن يستنكف عن عبادته ويستكبر فسيحشرهم إليه جميعًا﴾[99]. وكيف يستنكف وهو عبد مقرّب عارف بربّه؟

ومن قوله في الإنجيل: "لا تدعوني صالحًا، ليس صالحًا إلا وحده"[100]. ومن قوله أيضًا: "لست أفعل مشيئتي وإنما أفعل مشيئة الربّ الذي أرسلني"[101]. وفي تضرّعه ودعائه وسهره وتعبده واستغاثته بالله تعالى ليلة الفصح كفاية.

18. وكان من التوبيخ على الخطيئة العظمى أيضًا قوله تعالى على لسان الرسول الحقّ موبخًا للنصارى ومهدّدًا ومتواعدًا لهم: ﴿لقد كفر الذين قالوا إن الله ثالث ثلاثة وما من إله إلا إله واحد وإن لم ينتهوا عمّا يقولون ليمسّن الذين كفروا منهم

* 12v

---

[98] B: وقرأموه (wrongly).   [99] S. IV: 171-2.   [100] Mk X: 18; Lk XVIII: 19; the words: في الإنجيل...صالحًا are written in the margin in B.   [101] Cf. Jn V: 30.

17.   This was the beginning of error and the origin of ignorance. The situation did not change until truth came and God's command was manifest, although they disbelieved, and God sent Muḥammad with guidance and the authentic religion of truth, and he set about rebuking the world as Christ had declared he would. Among all his rebukes to the Christians was God the exalted's word to him in the Qurʾan, which you say you have obtained, read and comprehended:[41] Say, 'O People of the Scripture! Do not exaggerate in your religion nor utter aught (12v) concerning Allah save the truth. The Messiah, Jesus son of Mary, was only a messenger of Allah and his word which he conveyed unto Mary, and a spirit from him. So believe in Allah and his messengers, and say not "Three"—Cease! It is better for you!—Allah is only one God. Far is it removed from his transcendent majesty that he should have a son. His is all that is in the heavens and all that is in the earth. And Allah is sufficient as defender. The Messiah will never scorn to be a slave unto Allah, nor will the favoured angels. Whoso scorneth his service and is proud, all such will he assemble unto him.' How could he feel scorn when he was a favoured slave who confessed his Lord?

There are also his words in the Gospel, 'Do not call me good; one alone is good', and again his words, 'I do not perform my own will; I only perform the will of the Lord who sent me.' And there is quite enough in his supplicating, praying, keeping watch, worshipping and appealing to God the exalted on the night of the Passover.[42]

18.   As a rebuke of great sin,[43] there are also the exalted One's words on the tongue of the true messenger, rebuking, scaring and threatening the Christians, 'They surely disbelieve who say, Lo! Allah is the third of three; when there is no God save the one God. If they desist not from so saying a painful doom will fall on those of them who

---

Journal of Theological Studies new series 19, 1968, pp. 173-4), though he also relates, p. 162, how Constantine exterminated the Ḥarrānians and their religion.

   [41]   This is a reference back to the Christians' words at the beginning of their *Letter*, § 5 above.

   [42]   Cf. Mtt XXVI: 39-44. As with the two Gospel quotations, al-Dimashqī refers to this account of Jesus praying and weeping in the Garden of Gethsemane to prove his humanity and subordination to God. Muslim authors had used it in this way since at least the early fourth/tenth century; cf. D. Thomas, 'Abū Manṣūr al-Māturīdī on the Divinity of Jesus Christ', *Islamochristiana* 23, 1997, p. 52.23-5. Cf. also n. 67, and Section 5, n. 27 below.

   [43]   This is the sin of associating another being with God by attributing divinity to Christ.

* 13r عذاب أليم ، أفلا يتوبون102 إلى الله ويستغفرونه103 والله غفور * رحيم ما
المسيح ابن مريم إلا رسول قد خلت من قبله الرسل وأمّه كانا صديقة كانا يأكلان
الطعام أنظر كيف نبيّن لهم الآيات ثم أنظر أنى يؤفكون﴾104. وكان من
توبيخ النصارى أيضًا قوله تعالى: ﴿لقد كفر الذين قالوا إن الله هو المسيح
ابن مريم قل فمن يملك من الله شيئًا إن أراد أن يهلك المسيح ابن مريم وأمّه
ومن في الأرض جميعًا ولله ملك السموات والأرض وما بينهما يخلق ما يشاء
والله على كلّ شئ قدير﴾105.

19. وكان من التوبيخ للنصارى المجسّمة قوله تعالى: ﴿وقالوا اتخذ الرحمن
ولدًا لقد جئتم شيئاً إدًا تكاد السموات يتفطّرن منه وتنشقّ الأرض وتخرّ
الجبال هدًا أن دعوا للرحمن ولدًا. وما ينبغي للرحمن أن يتخذ ولدًا. إن كلّ
من في السموات والأرض إلا آتي الرحمن عبدًا. لقد أحصاهم وعدّهم عدًّا
وكلهم آتيه يوم القيامة فردًا﴾106 وقوله تعالى: ﴿وينذر107 الذين قالوا اتخذ
* 13v الله ولدًا ما لهم به من علم ولا لآبائهم كبرت كلمة تخرج من أفواههم * إن
يقولون إلا كذبًا﴾108.

20. وكان أيضًا من التوبيخ لعموم جاهلية النصارى القائلين بإلهية المسيح
وأمّه كفرًا فطيرًا والقائلين في الكنائس109 ليلة البشارة: " يا أمّ الإله يا ست
يا حنونة يا عروس يا من لا عرس لها يا من ولدت الله بلا زرع". فقال الله
تعالى إخبارًا عمّا يقول للمسيح يوم القيامة: ﴿وإذ قال الله يا عيسى ابن مريم
أأنت قلت للناس اتخذوني وأمّي إلهين من دون الله؟ قال سبحانك ما يكون لي
أن أقول ما ليس لي

---

102 A and B: تتوبون   103 A and B: وتستغفرونه   104 S. V: 73-5.   105 *Ibid.*: 17.
106 S. XIX: 88-95.   107 A: وننذر (wrongly).   108 S. XVIII: 4-5.   109 B: والكنائس (for
في الكنائس), apparently a misreading of A.

disbelieve. Will they not rather turn unto Allah and seek forgiveness of him? For Allah is forgiving, (13r) merciful. The Messiah, son of Mary, was no other than a messenger, messengers had passed away before him. And his mother was a saintly woman. And they both used to eat food. See how we make the revelations clear for them, and see how they are turned away!' A further rebuke to the Christians is the exalted One's words, 'They indeed have disbelieved who say, Lo! Allah is indeed the Messiah, son of Mary. Say, Who then can do aught against Allah, if he had willed to destroy the Messiah son of Mary, and his mother and everyone on earth? Allah's is the sovereignty of the heavens and the earth and all that is between them. He createth what he will. And Allah is able to do all things.'

19.   A rebuke to the corporealist Christians[44] is the words of the exalted One, 'And they say: The Compassionate hath taken unto himself a son. Assuredly ye utter a disastrous thing, whereby almost the heavens are torn, and the earth is split asunder and the mountains fall in ruins, that they ascribe unto the Compassionate a son, when it is not meet for the Compassionate that he should choose a son. There is none in the heavens and the earth but cometh unto the Compassionate as a slave. Verily he knoweth them and numbereth them with numbering. And each one of them will come unto him on the day of resurrection, alone'; and the word of the exalted One, 'And to warn those who say: Allah hath chosen a son, whereof they have no knowledge, nor their fathers. Dreadful is the word that cometh out of their mouths. (13v) They speak nought but a lie.'

20.   There is a further rebuke to the ignorant majority of Christians who speak of the divinity of Christ and his mother in some inchoate unbelief, and say in the churches on the Eve of the Annunciation, 'O mother of God, O lady, O gentle one, O bride, O you whom none has wed, O you who bore God without seed'.[45] For God the exalted has said, telling of what he will say to Christ on the day of resurrection, 'And when Allah saith, O Jesus, son of Mary! Didst thou say unto mankind: Take me and my mother for two gods beside Allah? he saith: Be glorified! It was not mine to utter that to which I had no

---

[44] If they are at all a distinct group, these Christians impute physical features to God by linking Jesus with him as his son.

[45] Cf. § 77 end. Like other references in the *Response*, this quotation of a Christian prayer serves to indicate that while al-Dimashqī may not have had first-hand acquaintance with the text of the Bible, he did apparently know about Christian worship.

بحقّ¹¹⁰ إن كنت قلته فقد علمته تعلم ما في نفسي ولا أعلم ما في نفسك إنك أنت علّام الغيوب. ما قلت لهم إلا ما أمرتني به أن اعبدوا الله ربّي وربّكم وكنت عليهم شهيدًا ما دمت فيهم فلمّا توفيتني كنت أنت الرقيب عليهم وأنت على كلّ شيء شهيد. إن تعذّبهم فإنهم عبادك وإن تغفر لهم فإنك أنت العزيز الحكيم﴾ ¹¹¹.

21. ومن التوبيخ للعالم المذموم اليهود وتهديدهم¹¹² وتواعدهم بالعذاب والسخط قوله تعالى: ﴿يسألك أهل الكتاب [يعني اليهود]¹¹³ أن تنزل¹¹⁴ عليهم كتابًا * من السماء فقد سألوا موسى أكبر من ذلك فقالوا أرنا الله جهرة فأخذتهم الصاعقة بظلمهم ثم اتخذوا العجل من بعد ما جاءتهم البيّنات فعفونا عن ذلك وآتينا موسى سلطانًا مبينًا. ورفعنا فوقهم الطور بميثاقهم وقلنا لهم أدخلوا الباب سجّدًا وقلنا لهم لا تعدوا في السبت وأخذنا منهم ميثاقًا غليظًا. فبما نقضهم ميثاقهم وكفرهم بآيات الله وقتلهم الأنبياء بغير حقّ وقولهم قلوبنا غلف بل طبع الله عليها بكفرهم فلا يؤمنون إلا قليلاً. وبكفرهم وقولهم على مريم بهتانًا عظيمًا. وقولهم إنّا قتلنا المسيح عيسى ابن مريم رسول الله وما قتلوه وما صلبوه ولكن شبّه لهم وإنّ الذين اختلفوا فيه لفي شكّ منه ما لهم به من علم إلا اتباع الظنّ وما قتلوه يقينًا. بل رفعه الله إليه وكان الله عزيزًا حكيمًا﴾ ¹¹⁵.

22. فهذا هو التوبيخ من الرسول الحقّ الموبّخ العالم على العدل وعلى الحكم وعلى الخطيئة من أجل المسيح ، وهو أركون العالم * المنبثق من فيه روح الحقّ أعني القرآن العظيم الذي هو روح من أمر الله كما قال الله تعالى: ﴿وكذلك أوحينا إليك روحًا من أمرنا﴾ ¹¹⁶ وقال تعالى: ﴿يلقي الروح من أمره على من يشاء من عباده لينذر يوم التلاق﴾ ¹¹⁷ يعني يوم القيامة. وقال تعالى: يلقي الروح ﴿من أمره على من يشاء من عباده أن أنذروا أنه لا إله إلا أنا فاتقون﴾ ¹¹⁸.

* 14r

* 14v

---

¹¹⁰ A and B: بحق and also om. لي   ¹¹¹ S. V: 116-18.   ¹¹² A and B: وتهديهم
¹¹³ These two words are a gloss by the author.   ¹¹⁴ A and B: ينزل   ¹¹⁵ S. IV: 153-
8.   ¹¹⁶ S. XLII: 52.   ¹¹⁷ S. XL: 15.   ¹¹⁸ S. XVI: 2.

right. If I used to say it, then thou knewest it. Thou knowest what is in my mind, and I know not what is in thy mind. Lo! thou, only thou art the knower of things hidden. I spake unto them only that which thou commandedst me: Worship Allah, my Lord and your Lord. I was a witness of them while I dwelt among them, and when thou tookest me thou wast the watcher over them. Thou art witness over all things. If thou punish them, lo! they are thy slaves, and if thou forgive them. Lo! thou, only thou art the mighty, the wise.'

21. A rebuke to the people who deserve blame, the Jews, and a scare to them and threat of torment and wrath, are the exalted One's words, 'The People of the scripture [meaning the Jews] ask of thee that thou shouldst cause a book to descend upon them (14r) from heaven. They asked a greater thing of Moses aforetime, for they said: Show us Allah plainly. The storm of lightning seized them for their wickedness. Then they chose the calf after clear proofs had come unto them. And we forgave them that! And we bestowed on Moses evident authority. And we caused the mount to tower above them at their covenant; and we bade them: Enter the gate, prostrate! and we bade them: Transgress not the Sabbath! and we took from them a firm covenant. Then because of their breaking of their covenant, and their disbelieving in the revelations of Allah, and their slaying of the prophets wrongfully, and their saying: Our hearts are hardened—Nay, but Allah hath set a seal upon them for their disbelief, so that they believe not save a few—And because of their disbelief and of their speaking against Mary a tremendous calumny; And because of their saying: We slew the Messiah Jesus son of Mary, Allah's messenger—They slew him not nor crucified, but it appeared so unto them; and lo! those who disagree concerning it are in doubt thereof; they have no knowledge thereof save pursuit of a conjecture; they slew him not for certain, but Allah took him up unto himself. Allah was ever mighty, wise.'

22. This rebuke comes from the true messenger, who rebuked the world concerning justice, judgement and sin on account of Christ. He was the ruler of the world, (14v) from whose mouth proceeded the spirit of truth, that is, the sublime Qur'an, which is a spirit from the command of God: as God the exalted says, 'And thus have we inspired in thee a spirit of our command'; and the exalted One says, 'He casteth the spirit of his command upon whom he will of his slaves, that he may warn whom he will of the day of meeting,' meaning the day of resurrection; and the exalted One says, He casts the spirit 'of his command upon whom he will of his bondmen: Warn that there is no god save me, so keep your duty unto me.'

والبارقليطس الرسول الحقّ صاحب البيان والتعريف والتشريع والقول العدل الذي نصّ عليه المسيح وليس هو روح القدس فإنها قوّة روحية روحانية ملكانية إلاهية لا جسم لها ولا أعضاء ولا فم تتكلّم منه وينبثق منه روح الحقّ ولا لها لسان توبّخ العالم به، ويقول كما قال المسيح عن أركون العالم الرسول الناطق بكلام الله والمرسل من عند الله وموبّخ العالم بلسانه وموضّح الحقّ لهم ببيانه وبشر شريف يوحى إليه ونبي كريم صلّى الله عليه وليس بقوّة متوهّمة تشتبه في العقل بقوى كثيرة وللخصوم عليها إيرادات وطعون.

23. وإذا * اتضح هذا وظهر برهانه فلنذكر نكتا حسانًا، نكثة: قوله "جاء الله من سيناء وأشرق من ساعير واستعلى بجبال[119] فاران[120] وأتى من ربوات قدس"، عنى بالمجيء إلى طول مدّة دولة موسى وثبوت[121] شريعته، وعنى بالإشراق إلى قصر مدّة المسيح وبهر نور ما جاء به من مفهوم قوله" كونوا سماويين، وأبونا الذي في السموات"، وقوله "إنما جعل السبت من أجلك ولم تجعل أنت من أجل السبت"، وقوله "إنكم تصيرون إلى حياة أبدية". وكانت دولته قبل احتجابه ورفعه إلى السماء سنتين ونصف، والعمر كله اثنتان وثلاثون سنة ونصف وذلك شروق ولمع لا مجيء. وعنى بالاستعلاء الاستواء على ذروة قوس البناء واعلاء فعل القنطرة في المثال وأنّ نبيّنا يستعلى دينه وشريعته على كلّ ما سواه ولا يخرج عن ظلّه الظليل واستشراقه شيء ممّا قبله. وعنى بالإتيان من ربوات قدس أنّ كلّ واحد من الثلاثة يكون من الملوكية والشرف، فكان موسى من بيت بطليموس فرعون ملك مصر، وكان المسيح من جهة أمّه من * ذرّية داوود الملك النبي وكان محمّد من أشرف قبيلة

* 15r *

* 15v *

[119] Cf. Deut XXXIII: 2; see also f. 5v above.   [120] A and B omit فاران   [121] B: وثبوب (wrongly).

The Paraclete was the true messenger, the giver of elucidation, instruction, legislation and just words, to whom Christ pointed.[46] He was not the Holy Spirit, for that is a spiritual, immaterial force, angelic and divine, without body, limbs, or mouth with which to speak or from which the spirit of truth could proceed, or tongue with which to rebuke the world. He spoke just as Christ said the ruler of the world would, the messenger who would utter the word of God, sent from God and rebuking the world with his tongue, making plain the truth to them by his elucidation, an honoured human to whom revelation was sent, a noble prophet (may God bless him), not an imaginary force which in the intellect is similar to many forces and which adversaries might object to and oppose.

23.   Now that (15r) this has been explained and its proof demonstrated, let us continue with some suitable illustrations.

Illustration: His words, 'God came from Sinai and shone out from Seir and towered over the mountains of Paran, coming from myriads of holy ones',[47] mean by 'the coming' the long period of Moses' pre-eminence and the enduring of his law. And by 'the shining' it means the short period of Christ's pre-eminence and the dazzling light which he brought in the significance of his words, 'Be heavenly' and 'Our Father who is in heaven', his words, 'The sabbath was made for you, not you for the sabbath', and his words, 'You will obtain eternal life'. His pre-eminence before he disappeared and ascended into heaven was two and a half years, and his entire span of life was thirty-two and a half years, a dawning glimmer, not a coming. By 'the towering' it figuratively means occupying the apex of the arch of the building and holding high the structure of the vault. Our Prophet made his religion and law tower over everything else, with nothing that was before it escaping its dense shadow or mounting height. And by 'coming from myriads of holy ones' it means that each of the three belonged to royalty and nobility. For Moses was from the house of Pharaoh Ptolemy, king of Egypt;[48] Christ on his mother's side was from (15v) the seed of King David the prophet;[49] and Muḥammad was from the noblest tribe

---

[46] Cf. S. LXI: 6, in addition to the Paraclete verses from John which are repeatedly alluded to here, as in §§ 8 and 16 above.

[47] Cf. § 7 above, where the verse is quoted without the last clause.

[48] While Moses is conventionally placed in the period around 1300 BCE, the first Ptolemy ruled from 323 BCE.

[49] Cf. al-Ṭabarī, *Ta'rīkh* I, p. 713 and al-Mas'ūdī, *Murūj*, vol. I, p. 120, who trace

وأشرف بيت في العرب، فكلّ واحد منهم أتى من ربوات شرف وقدس لا ما زعمته اليهود أنه آت من أرض بيت المقدس، وهو المسيح عندهم ينتظرونه وذلك محال.

24. نكتة: لمّا كان عند اليهود من كلام التوراة أنه لا يأتي في بني إسرائيل نبي مثل موسى وجاء المسيح بما جاء به من حل السبت ومن التشريع الجديد أنكره الفريسيون وقالوا لا يأتي في بني إسرائيل مثل موسى نبي مرسل ولا يقوم فيهم غيره، وفاتهم أنّ المسيح ليس من بني إسرائيل بل بشر وحيد مثله كمثل آدم في الخلق، قال الله له كن فكان. ولذلك لتمام النعمة وكمال القسمة الرباعية المقتضية[122] الحكمة فإنّ آدم مخلوق من غير أب ولا أمّ وسائر بنيه وذرّيته كلّ منهم مخلوق من أمّ وأب وخلقت حواء أمّ البشر من أب بلا أمّ وهو آدم فإنها خلقت من ضلعه وخلق المسيح من أمّ وهي مريم بلا أب فكملت القسمة ولا مزيد عليها.

ولمّا كان ذلك * كانت[123] مريم وعاء لخلق المسيح بكلمة كن فكان. فلم يكن من بني إسرائيل مثل موسى. * 16r

25. نكتة: قول إرميا في تنبيّه أنه رأى شعوب وربوات ربوات بين[124] يدي المسيح إشارة إلى أنه أرسل إلى الأمم الأربعة الذين كانوا في زمنه وهم المجوس واليهود والصابئة واليونان الفلاسفة، وكذلك رؤيته للشعوب والربوات بين يدي نبيّنا محمّد صلّى الله عليه وسلّم وعلى المسيح أيضًا فإنها إشارة إلى أنه[125] مرسل إلى العالمين كافة[126] اليهود والنصارى والمجوس والصابئة والمشركين الجاهلية والثقلين الإنس والجنّ لأنه خاتم النبيّين ومتمّم مكارم الأخلاق، وكما أنه ليس بعد التمام تمام فكذلك ليس بعد الختام ختام.

---

122 A and B: المقتضيها   123 A repeats this word.   124 B: من   125 A and B repeat: إشارة إلى أنه   126 B: كافر (wrongly), apparently a misreading of A.

and house among the Arabs. Thus, each of them came from myriads of noble and holy ones. It is not as the Jews claim, that he is to come, and will come from the land of Jerusalem; this is the Messiah as they regard him, the one for whom they wait, but it is impossible.

24. *Illustration*: According to the Jews, in the Torah occurs, 'There will not come among the people of Israel a prophet like Moses'. [50] When Christ brought his teachings, such as freeing the sabbath and giving new laws,[51] the Pharisees repudiated him and said, 'There will not come among the people of Israel a prophet sent like Moses, and no other like him will arise among them'. They failed to see that Christ was not from the people of Israel, but rather a unique individual whose origin was like that of Adam.[52] For God said to him 'Be' and he was, thus perfecting grace and completing the fourfold sequence that sound reasoning requires. For Adam was created without a father or mother; all of his children and progeny were created from a mother and father; Eve, the mother of mankind, was created from a father, Adam, without a mother, for she was created from his rib; and Christ was created from a mother, Mary, without a father. So the sequence was completed, and there can be no extension beyond it. When it happened (16r) Mary was the vessel for the creation of Christ by the word 'Be', and he was. So there never has been one like Moses among the people of Israel.

25. *Illustration*: The words of Jeremiah in his prophecy, that he saw nations upon nations and myriads upon myriads before Christ,[53] is an indication that the latter was sent to the four peoples of his time, Persians, Jews, Ṣābians and Greeks, the philosophers. And similarly, his vision of the nations and myriads before our Prophet Muḥammad (may God bless him and give him peace, and also Christ) is an indication that he was sent to all the world, Jews, Christians, Persians, Ṣābians, pagan polytheists, and the two species of humankind and jinn. For he was the Seal of the prophets, the perfecter of the noblest moral qualities. And since there is no perfection beyond perfection, in the same way there is no seal beyond the Seal.

Mary's descent from David through her father 'Imrān, following SS. III: 35, LXVI: 12. See also *The Catholic Encyclopaedia*, vol. XV, p. 464E, for mentions of Mary's Davidic descent among Eastern Church Fathers.

[50] Cf. § 7 above, referring to Deuteronomy XXXIV: 10.

[51] Cf. Mtt XII: 1-4 and parallels; Mtt V: 21-48.

[52] Cf. S. III: 59.

[53] Cf. §§ 10 above and 41 below, referring to Isaiah XXI: 7.

26. نكثة: لمّا افترقت النصارى في غلوّهم في المسيح إلى أربع[127] فرق:
فرقة ربّعت فقالت آب وابن وروح قدس والإنسان القديم طبيعتان ومشيئة
واحدة، وهؤلاء هم البطلانيون * فلاسفة النصارى، سمّوا العالم الأكبر إنسانًا   16v *
قديمًا ذا ذات كلية مجرّدة وعقل كلي ونفس كلية وصورة الصور، وسمّوا
الإنسان عالمًا أصغر ذا روح وعقل ونفس ناطقة وجسد، وقالوا المظاهر
والمباطن[128] الأربعة إله واحد طبيعة واحدة ومشيئة واحدة.

وفرقة ثلّثت فقالت الآب والابن والروح القدس ثلاثة[129] أقانيم جوهرية
إله واحد، فالآب موجود لذاته حيّ بالروح ناطق بالابن. والابن ناطق لذاته
موجود بالآب حيّ بالروح . والروح حيّة لذاتها موجودة بالآب ناطقة
بالابن طبيعتان مشيئتان .

وفرقة ثنّت وقالت لم يولد المسيح إذ ولد إلا مخلوق إنسان تام مهيًّا
لحلول الإله فيه . فلمّا عمّده يوحنا المعمدان حلّت فيه روح القدس وصار
من وقت التعميد إلهًا تامًّا وإنسانًا تامًّا من جوهر أبيه، وعاين يوحنا الروح
ترفرف عليه وسمع النداء من السماء[130] وشهد به وكذلك أمّه كانت ذاتًا
حساسية مهيّأة لقبول حلول * كلمة الله فيها فلمّا حلّت الكلمة فيها   17r *
تجسّمت بها واتحدت، فكانت كالابن في الإلهية مشيئة واحدة وطبيعتان .

وفرقة قالت بالوحدة وعدم المغايرة طبيعة واحدة ومشيئتان .

---

127 A and B: أربعة   128 B: والمباطر (wrongly), a misreading of A.   129 A and B:
ثلاث   130 B: السماق (wrongly), a misreading of A.

26. *Illustration*: In their exaggeration over Christ the Christians divided into four sects. There was a sect which affirmed four, saying, Father, Son, Holy Spirit and eternal man with two natures and one volition.[54] They were futile, (16v) the philosophers of the Christians, who called the macrocosm an eternal human, possessor of a general, simple essence, a general intelligence, a general soul, and a form of forms; and called the human being the microcosm, possessor of spirit, intelligence, rational soul and body. They said that the four externals and internals are one God, one nature and one volition.

There was a sect which affirmed three, saying, Father, Son and Holy Spirit, three substantial hypostases, one God; the Father is existent by his essence, living by the Spirit and articulate by the Son; the Son is articulate by his essence, existent by the Father and living by the Spirit; the Spirit is living by its essence, existent by the Father and articulate by the Son, two natures and two volitions.

There was a sect which affirmed two, saying, Christ was born only when he was born, and was nothing more than a perfect creature, ready for the indwelling of the Divinity within him. When John the Baptist baptized him the Holy Spirit came to dwell within him, and from the time of the baptism he became perfect God and perfect man, of the substance of his Father. John saw the Spirit hovering over him, and he heard the voice from heaven and bore witness to it.[55] Similarly, his mother was a most sensitive essence, prepared to receive the indwelling (17r) of the Word of God within her. When the Word came to dwell within her it took flesh and united through her, so she was like the Son in divinity, with one volition and two natures.

There was a sect which talked of one without any difference, with one nature and two volitions.[56]

---

[54] The Christology of this group recalls that attributed to the Nestorians by Abū ʿĪsā al-Warrāq, in Thomas, *Early Muslim Polemic*, pp. 90-3, § 14, and further pp. 202-19, §§ 248-73.

[55] Cf. Jn I: 32-4.

[56] This fourfold division reflects a theoretical working out of the doctrines of the triune Godhead and two natures of Christ, but does not correspond closely with historical facts. For example, it would be hard to identify a sect like the first which asserted four members of the Godhead, or like the third which held an adoptionist Christology but also believed that the divine Word united with the human in Mary's womb and effectively united with Mary. That being said, many individual elements can be found in earlier Muslim schematisations of Christian beliefs; see particularly Abū ʿĪsā al-Warrāq in Thomas, *Anti-Christian Polemic*, pp. 66-77. Cf. also § 76 below where al-Dimashqī gives another four-fold version of doctrinal divergence.

فردّ الله تعالى هذه المقالات الأربع وبيّن كفر قائلها ووبّخهم بلسان رسوله محمّد صلّى الله عليه وسلّم بقوله في القرآن: ﴿لقد كفر الذين قالوا إنّ الله هو المسيح ابن مريم﴾[131]، ﴿لقد كفر الذين قالوا إنّ الله ثالث ثلاثة﴾[132]، ﴿وينذر[133] الذين قالوا اتخذ الرحمن ولدًا ما لهم به من علم ولا لآبائهم﴾ الآية[134]، ﴿وقالوا اتخذ الرحمن ولدًا لقد جئتم شيئًا إدًّا﴾ الآية[135]، وقوله تعالى: ﴿يا عيسى ابن مريم أأنت قلت للناس اتخذوني وأمّي إلهين من دون الله قال سبحانك (أي تنزهت وتقدست)[136] ما يكون لي أن أقول ما ليس لي بحقّ﴾[137].

27. نكثة: لمّا يقال للمسيح ﴿أأنت قلت للناس﴾ الآية[138] ويقول ﴿ما قلت لهم إلا ما أمرتني به أن اعبدوا الله ربّي وربّكم﴾[139][140] ويسوق إلى قوله ﴿إن تعذّبهم فإنهم عبادك﴾[141] يكون مثله صلّى الله على نبيّنا * وعليه كمثل نائب ملك عظيم بلغه أنّ النائب دعا إلى طاعة نفسه دون الملك فقال له الملك تهديدًا: "أأنت دعوت الناس إلى طاعتك من دوني" فقال: "لا وإنّ الملك ليعلم منّي أنّي لم أدعهم إلا إلى طاعته". ثمّ تحمله الإذلال والقرب من الملك على الشفاعة فيهم.

فوافق المسيح عليه السلام نبيّنا صلّى الله عليه وسلّم في الرأفة بالعباد والرحمة لهم والشفقة عليهم وطلب المغفرة لهم والعفو عنهم حيث يقول نبيّنا صلّى الله عليه وسلّم يوم وقعة أحد وقد استشهد عمّه حمزة المسمّى أسد الله وشجّ جبينه وكسر بعض أسنانه وقتل سبعون من أصحابه واشتدّ بأس

* 17v

---

[131] S. V: 17. [132] *Ibid.*: 73. [133] A and B: وتنذر [134] S. XVIII: 4–5. [135] S. XIX: 88–9. [136] أي تنزهت وتقدست: these words are added by the author. [137] S. V: 116. [138] *Ibid.*; A and B: أنت [139] B: ضربكم (wrongly), a misreading of A. [140] S. V: 117. [141] *Ibid.*: 118.

Now, God the exalted has refuted these four opinions and has made clear the unbelief of those who express them. And he has rebuked them by the tongue of his messenger Muḥammad (may God bless him and give him peace) through his words in the Qurʾan, 'They surely disbelieve who say, Lo! Allah is the Messiah, son of Mary'; 'They surely disbelieve who say, Lo! Allah is the third of three'; 'And to warn those who say, Allah hath chosen a son, whereof they have no knowledge, nor their fathers' and the rest of the verse; 'And they say, The Beneficent hath taken unto himself a son. Assuredly ye utter a disastrous thing' and the next verse; and the exalted One's words, 'O Jesus, son of Mary! Didst thou say unto mankind, Take me and my mother for two gods beside Allah? he saith, Be glorified! [i.e., be pure and holy] It was not mine to utter that to which I had no right'.

27.   *Illustration*: When it was said to Christ, 'Didst thou say unto mankind: [take me and my mother for gods beside Allah? he saith: Be glorified! It was not mine to utter that to which I had no right. If I used to say it, then thou knewest it. Thou knowest what is in my mind. Lo! Thou, only thou, art the knower of all things hidden!], and he said, 'I spake unto them only that which thou commandedst me, Worship Allah, my Lord and your Lord' continuing to his words, 'If thou punish them, lo! they are thy slaves', he (may God bless our Prophet (17v) and him) was just like the representative of a great king, who was told that the representative was demanding obedience to himself and not the king. The king said to him in threat, 'Did you urge the people to obey you and not me?' and he said, 'No, and may the king surely know from me that I have only ever urged them to obey him.' Thus his readiness to be humble and nearness to the king enabled him to intercede for them.

Christ (may peace be upon him) was just like our Prophet (may God bless him and give him peace) as regards kindness to humans, mercy upon them, pity towards them, and seeking forgiveness for them and pardon on their behalf. For on the day of the Battle of Uḥud, when his uncle Ḥamza who was called the Lion of God was martyred, when his own forehead was split open and some of his teeth broken, when seventy of his companions were killed,[57] and the strength of the

---

[57] Ibn Isḥāq, *Sīra*, p. 609/*Life*, p. 403, gives this number as 65, though other sources agree with al-Dimashqī; cf. Ibn Kathīr, *Al-bidāya wa-al-nihāya*, Beirut-Riyadh, 1966, vol. IV, pp. 25f., trans. T. Le Gassick, *The Life of the Prophet Muḥammad*, Reading, 2000, vol. III, pp. 34f., and further *EI²*, vol. X, p. 782.

الكفّار على المسلمين وهو في تلك الحالة يقول: "اللهم اغفر لقومي فإنهم لا يعلمون" وهوٰ يكرّرها مرّات وأصحابه يمسحون دمه من على وجهه.

والمسيح يقول عند سماع التعنيف يقول: ﴿أأنت قلت للناس﴾[142] ، ﴿إن تعذّبهم فإنهم عبادك وأن تغفر لهم فإنك أنت العزيز الحكيم﴾[143] أي ربّ العزّة المنزّه عمّا يقول الظالمون * الجاهلون ، ولم يقل "أنت الغفور الرحيم" إجلالاً منه للإله تعالى وتعريضًا بالعزّة التي هي الامتناع والرفعة المنزّهة عن كلّ ما قالوه بأفواههم وظنّوه بعقولهم وجهلوه لقصر أفهامهم وأخطأوا فيه لقلّة العلم منهم ونسبوه إلى الله تعالى غلطًا وسفهًا بغير علم ولا تعقّل، فلم يصل إلى الله تعالى شيء من مقالتهم ولا يناله شيء من ادّعائهم وباطلهم[144]، فتعرّض للشفاعة مع حفظ الأدب وملاحظة العزّة والحكمة.

28. نكتة: لمّا أرسل الله نبيّنا بالهدى ودين الحقّ ووبّخ العالم على الخطيئة والعدل كما بشّر به المسيح وأنزل الله الخبر الحقّ عن طهارته ونزاهته وسلامته وعصمته من الذين كفروا وإنه لم يقتل ولم يصلب ولكنه شبّه لهم استيقظت فطن أولي الألباب وقالوا صدق الله ورسوله

* 18r

---

142 *Ibid.*: 116.   143 *Ibid.*: 118.   144 B: وباطلها

unbelievers was increasing against the Muslims, in this situation our Prophet (may God bless him and give him peace) said, 'O God, forgive my people, for they do not know.'[58] He repeated this over and over, as his companions were wiping his blood from his face.

And when Christ heard the reprimand, 'Didst thou say unto mankind?' he said, 'If thou punish them, lo! they are thy slaves, and if thou forgive them, lo! thou, only thou art the powerful, the wise', that is 'the Lord of power' who is above what the ignorant (18r) transgressors say. He did not say, 'You are the forgiving, the merciful',[59] but showed his reverence towards God the exalted and referred to power. This was to deny and stand far above all that they were saying with their mouths, were thinking in their minds, were ignorant of because of their limited understanding, were mistaken about because of the scant knowledge they had, and were ascribing to God the exalted in error and stupidity, without knowledge or understanding—but not one of their opinions reaches God the exalted, and not one of their presumptions or falsehoods touches him. Rather, he made intercession in compliance with propriety, and with deference towards power and wisdom.

28. *Illustration*: When God sent our Prophet with guidance and the religion of truth, and he rebuked the world for sinfulness and justice as Christ had announced, and God sent down the true account of the latter's holiness, purity, blamelessness and sinlessness against those who did not believe, and that he was not killed or crucified but was made unclear to them,[60] the perceptions of the chief intellects were aroused, and they said, 'God and his messenger have spoken true, and

---

[58] Cf. Lk XXIII: 34. Ibn Kathīr, *Bidāya*, vol. IV, p. 29/*Life of the Prophet*, vol. III, p. 40, relates from Aḥmad Ibn Ḥanbal that when the Prophet was hit he asked, 'How could any people prosper who struck their prophet and broke his front teeth while he called people to God?', in response to which was revealed, 'It is no concern at all of thee whether He relent toward them or punish them; for they are evil-doers. Unto Allah belongeth whatsoever is in the heavens and whatsoever is in the earth. He forgiveth whom he will, and punisheth whom he will. Allah is forgiving, merciful' (S III: 128-9). These verses more or less contain the same sentiments as the Gospel phraseology which al-Dimashqī attributes to Muḥammad himself.

[59] Cf. S. XIV: 36, where Abraham uses these words in a prayer for those who disobey him. However, in the more serious case of those who make claims of divinity about Jesus and Mary, Jesus does not presume that God will be forgiving and merciful, but simply acknowledges his power and wisdom, and implicitly accepts his own inferior status.

[60] Cf. S. IV: 157.

وصدق المسيح في خبره وبشارته بهذا الرسول المنبثق من فيه روح الحقّ .

* 18v * وما ينبغي للمسيح المصطفى المقرّب المنتقى الذي سمّاه الله كلمته * وروحًا منه أن يعذّب ويهان ويربط وتخلع ثيابه ويكلّل بالشوك بدلاً من تاج الملك ويحمّلونه الأرذال خشيته ليصلب عليها ويسحنونه سحنًا ويلطمونه بأيديهم لطمًا مبرحًا قائلين له: "أنت ملك يهودا، أنت كلمة الله، أنت ابن الله، أنت رسول الله"، ويلطمونه ويقولون له": إن كنت نبيًا فقل لنا من لطمك" ثم لم يزالوا معه على ذلك حتى أوصلوه إلى موضع الصلب فصلبوه .

وشنقوا عن يمينه ويساره شخصين وبقي مصلوبًا طول نهار الجمعة إلى العصر وبات عطشانًا يتلظّى ويسأل أن يسقى شربة ماء فبلّوا له أسفنجة بخلّ وماء حنظل حاذق ورفعوها إليه في رأس قصبة فلمّا امتصّ منها سعر وجهه ومات ولم يسمع من كلامه شيء سوى عند الموت قالت مريم المجدلانية وهي مع أمّه تحت صليبه وهما تبكيان سمعته يقول وقد اسودّت الدنيا وأظلمت: "ليما ثافاختاني" الذي ترجمته بالعربية يا إلهي لماذا تركتني؟

* 19r * وأمّه وخالته ومريم المذكورة وجماعة نسوة * تحت خشبته يبكين ويندبن، فلمّا كان آخر النهار أنزلوه إلى والي الشرطة بعد أن طعنوه بحربة في جنبه وضربوه بخشبة على ساقيه كسروهما ثمّ لفّوه في لفافة ودفنوه ببستان يعرف بالفاخوري موضع العمارة المعروفة الآن بالقيامة بالبيت المقدّس كما هو مكتوب مؤرّخ عند اليهود والنصارى.

Christ spoke true in his news and announcement of this messenger from whose mouth the spirit of truth proceeds'.

And it was not proper for Christ, the chosen, the favourite, the select, whom God called his word (18v) and a spirit from him,[61] to be tormented, humiliated, bound, stripped of his clothes, and crowned with thorns in place of a royal crown, for base men to force him to carry his cross to be crucified on it, to bruise his face and rain blows violently upon him with their hands, saying to him, 'You are the King of the Jews, you are the Word of God, you are the Son of God, you are the Messenger of God' as they struck him, and saying to him, 'If you are a prophet, tell us who is striking you'.[62] They did not stop doing this to him until they brought him to the place of crucifixion, and they crucified him.

On his right and left they hung two men, and he remained crucified all through Friday until the afternoon. He became thirsty and grew hot, and he asked to be given water to drink. So they moistened a sponge with vinegar and the juice of bitter gourd for him, and raised it up to him on the end of a reed. After taking some, his face grew livid and he died. Nothing of what he said could be heard, except that as he was dying Mary Magdalene, who was standing beneath his cross with his mother, the two weeping together, when the earth had grown dark and murky, said she heard him say '*Līmā thāfākhtānī?*', which when translated into Arabic is 'My God, why have you forsaken me?'[63] His mother, his aunt, this Mary and the group of women (19r) beneath his cross wept and wailed.[64] Then, when the day came to its end, they took him down to the chief of the guard, after piercing his side with a spear and striking his legs with a stave and breaking them.[65] Then they wrapped him in cloths and buried him in a garden known as the Potter's Field, the site of the structure in Jerusalem known today as the Resurrection, as is recorded among the Jews and Christians.[66]

---

[61] Cf. SS. III: 45, IV: 171.

[62] Cf. Mtt XXVI: 67-8.

[63] Cf. Mtt XXVII: 46, where Jesus' words are given as '*Eli, Eli, lema sabachthani?*' The implication contained in these circumstantial details of Jesus' face changing appearance, the women weeping, and the earth being dark, all of which would have made it difficult to identify him properly, is drawn in the next paragraph.

[64] Cf. Mtt XXVII: 55f.; Jn XIX: 25.

[65] John, the only Gospel writer who refers to any incident like this, expressly says that the guards did not break Jesus' legs because he was already dead, XIX: 32f.

[66] According to Mtt XXVII: 7-10 (cf. Acts I: 18f.), the chief priests used the

ثمّ فحص العلماء الربانيون عن الذي ألقى الله عليه شبه المسيح من هو
فوجدوا المسيح ليلة الفصح والعهد سهر سهرًا طويلاً وتضرّع إلى الله كثيرًا
وكان من جملة مسألته أسألك يا إلهي أنت تصرف عني هذا الكأس فإنك
القادر لا غيرك وأنت الربّ لا سواك والمشيئة مشيئتك لا مشيئتي ، ثمّ أوصى
تلاميذه ولوّح لهم بأنه ذاهب عنهم وقال لبطرس: "أنت تنكرني وتحلف أنك
ما تعرفني ولا صحبتني" وقال ليهودس[145] أسخريوطي التلميذ أيضًا:" وأنت
تدلّهم عليّ ويا شقاوتك وذلك يكون عند السحر إذا سمعتم صياح الديكة
صوتها * الأوّل".

* 19v

فلمّا جاء ذلك الوقت وأحاط بهم الفريسيون أنكر بطرس المسيح والتزم[146]
يهودس[147] بالدلالة لهم عليه ومن ذلك الحين لم ير ليهودس[148] صورة ولا أثر
ولا علم عالم ما فعل الله به وإلى يوم القيامة فلم يرتب[149] الفاحصون في أنه
هو المصلوب المهان المعذّب المقتول الشقي دون المسيح.

29. وممّا يوضّح ذلك ويؤيّده مسألة العاقب وكوز[150] الأخوين
أسقفي نجران اليمن وحاكميها حين سألا نبيّنا صلّى الله عليه وسلّم عن
المسيح وما جرى له في كلام طويل[151]، فأجابهما أمّا معنى المسيح فهو ممسوح
بالدهن وماسح

---

[145] A and B: ليهرودس (wrongly). [146] B: والتوم (wrongly). [147] A and B: هيرودس [148] A and B: لهيرودس [149] A and B: يرتاب [150] A and B: وكور [151] B adds: مرض, obviously a misreading of الأرض on the following line in A.

Scholars among the rabbis inquired about the one on whom God cast the likeness of Jesus. And they discovered that all through the night of the Passover and Covenant Christ was keeping watch and continually crying to God with the request, 'My God, I beg you to take this cup from me, though you alone are powerful, you are the Lord and no other, so may your will be done and not mine'.[67] Then he gave his charge to his disciples and intimated to them that he was departing from them, saying to Peter, 'You will deny me and swear that you do not know me and have not been my companion'. And to Judas Iscariot, who was also a disciple, he said, 'You will lead them to me, and how great will your wretchedness be. This will be about dawn, when you hear the first sound of the cocks (19v) crowing.'[68]

When this time came and the Pharisees surrounded them, Peter denied Christ, and Judas undertook to lead them to him. But from this point the figure of Judas was no longer seen nor any trace of him. And no one knew then, nor will until the day of resurrection, what God had done to him. So those inquiring did not suspect that he, in place of Christ, could have been the one crucified, humiliated, tortured and killed as a criminal.[69]

29. What makes this clear and confirms it is the question put by al-'Āqib and Kūz, the two brothers who were bishops and governors of Najrān in the Yemen, when in a long conversation they asked our Prophet (may God bless him and give him peace) about Christ and what happened to him.[70] He answered them, 'As for the meaning of "Messiah", it is one who is anointed with oil, and one who wanders

---

money which Judas returned to them to purchase the Potter's Field as a burial place for foreigners.

[67] This prayer is used frequently by Muslim authors to demonstrate Jesus' weakness and humanity (cf. n. 42 above, and also Section 5, n. 27 below); cf. Thomas, 'Miracles of Jesus', nn. 36, 47, 51. Al-Dimashqī's version does not obviously resemble any earlier Arabic translations, and in content it is closer to Mk XIV: 36 than either of the other Synoptics.

[68] Cf. Mtt XXVI: 34 and 24, and parallels.

[69] The interpretation of S. IV: 157 that a substitute was crucified in place of Jesus is known from at least the second/eighth century; cf. John of Damascus, *De Haeresibus*, in Sahas, *John of Damascus on Islam*, p. 132. It was elegantly elaborated by, among others, the late third/ninth century theologian Abū 'Alī al-Jubbā'ī in his lost *tafsīr*; cf. D. Gimaret, *Une lecture mu'tazilite du coran*, Louvain-Paris, 1994, pp. 252f.

[70] Cf. Ibn Ishāq, *Sīra*, pp. 401-2/*Life*, pp. 270-1, and Ibn Kathīr, *Bidāya*, vol. V, pp. 52-6/*Life of the Prophet*, vol. IV, pp. 71-6. They explain that al-'Āqib was the title of a political office, and that Kūz, or Kurz in Ibn Kathīr, was the brother of another of the leaders of the deputation.

الأرض سياحة بنفسه وبحوارييه والمسيح الصديق ، ومعنى الحواريين "المخلصون الخالصون".

وأمّا الرسالة لهم فبعدما رفع وصلب الذي شبّه به فجاءت مريم الصديقة والمرأة التي كانت مجنونة وأبرأها المسيح وقعدتا عند الجذع يبكيان وقد أصاب أمّه عليه من الحزن ما لا يعلمه إلا الله تعالى، فأهبط المسيح إليهما وقال: "علام[152] * تبكيان" فقالتا: "عليك" فقال: "إني لم أقتل ولم أصلب ولكن الله رفعني وكرّمني وشبّه عليهم في أمري، أبلغا عني الحواريين أمري أن يلقوني في موضع كذا ليلاً". فجاء الحواريون ذلك الموضع فإذا الجبل قد اشتعل نورًا لنزوله به ثمّ أمرهم أن يدعوا الناس إلى دينه وعبادة ربّهم فوجّههم إلى الأمم ثم كسى كسوة الملائكة فعرج معهم فصار ملكيًا أنسيًا سمائيًا أرضيًا.

* 20r

فآمن كوز[153] وجماعة من أهل نجران واتضح ما كان مشكوكًا ومنكورًا وقوعه في العقل فإنّ الله عدل محسن قادر صادق الوعد ﴿لا يظلم مثقال ذرّة﴾[154] ، والمسيح عبده وصفيه ورسوله المؤيّد بروح القدس والمنعم عليه بتعليمه الكتاب والحكمة والتوراة والإنجيل والمجعول هو وأمّه آية للعالمين والمسمّى كلمة الله وروح منه والمتكلّم في المهد صبيًا والمبرئ الأكمه والأبرص والمحيي الموتى بإذن الله والخالق من الطين كهيئة[155] الطير والنافخ فيها

---

[152] B: على   [153] A and B: كور   [154] Cf. S. IV: 40.   [155] B: هيئة (wrongly), a mis-reading of A.

over the earth journeying alone or with his disciples, and the authentic Messiah. The meaning of "disciples" is "those who are sincere and pure".[71]

'As for the mission to them, after he had ascended and the one who resembled him had been crucified, Mary the beloved and the woman who had been insane and was healed by Christ were sitting near the trunk[72] weeping. His mother was so deeply stricken with grief over him that none except God the exalted knew, so he sent Christ down to them. He said, "What are (20r) you weeping over?" and they replied, "Over you". He said, "I have not been killed or crucified, but God has taken me up and honoured me, and has caused doubt among them about me. Tell the disciples about me, that they will find me in a particular place at night." The disciples went to this place, and indeed the mountain was ablaze with light because of his alighting on it. Then he commanded them to call people to his religion and the worship of their Lord, and he sent them out to the nations. Then he donned the clothing of angels, and he ascended in their presence and became angelic and human, heavenly and earthly.'[73]

So Kūz and the group of people from Najrān believed,[74] and what was uncertain and denied in the mind became clear, that God is just, charitable, powerful, sincere in his promise, and does not commit even the least injustice; that Christ was his servant, chosen one and messenger, strengthened by the holy spirit and blessed by his teaching the Book, the Wisdom, the Torah and the Gospel to him;[75] that he and his mother were made a sign to the nations;[76] that he was named a word of God and a spirit from him;[77] that he spoke in the cradle as a baby,[78] healed the dumb and blind, raised the dead by the help of God, created the shape of a bird from clay and breathed into it

---

[71] On these derivations of the two terms, cf. Lane, *Lexicon*, pp. 2714 and 666. The reference to 'the authentic Messiah' distinguishes Jesus from *al-Masīḥ al-dajjāl*, the Antichrist.

[72] This is the wooden cross.

[73] Cf. Mtt XXVIII: 8-10 and 16-20, Lk XXIV: 50-1.

[74] Ibn Isḥāq, *Sīra*, p. 402/*Life*, p. 271, followed by Ibn Kathīr, *Bidāya*, vol. V, p. 56/*Life of the Prophet*, vol. IV, p. 76, says that Kūz became a Muslim after considering his brother the bishop of Najrān's open declaration that Muḥammad was the expected prophet.

[75] SS. V: 110, III: 48.

[76] S. XIX: 91.

[77] S. IV: 171.

[78] SS. III: 46, V: 110, XIX: 29-33.

فتكون طيرًا بإذن الله والمنبئ الناس بما يأكلون وما يدخرون في بيوتهم وما يعملون من عمل حتى * كأنه شهيد عليهم في خلواتهم والمعصوم عصمة أولي العزم الرسل الكرام.

فحاشاه من الهوان والعذاب والصلب والقتل ، حاشا الله وحاشا المسيح ، وما الله بغافل ولا ناس ولا مهمل ولا فاعل فعلاً عبثاً ، ولا يصيب عبدًا بمصيبة إلا بما كسبت يد ذلك العبد ما أوجبها ، فحاشا الله أن يلي المسيح بذلك عبثاً أو لأجل درجة لا ينالها إلا بذلك، فيكون القادر على كلّ شيء سبحانه عاجزًا عن إيصال المسيح إلى تلك الدرجة إلا بهذا الهوان من غير استحقاق ولا سابقة توجبه ، والله أكرم وأعزّ وأرحم.

وممّا يدلّ على أنّ المصلوب يهودس[156] اللابس شبه المسيح أنّ المسيح عليه السلام كان أعلم أهل زمانه بالتوراة والحكمة وأحجّهم جدلاً وأعرفهم بمواقع الكلام وأعظمهم صولة ومهابة ، ولمّا أمسكته اليهود وشحطوه للصلب على ما تقدّم ذكره من الهوان لم يسمع منه كلمة واحدة ولا مدافعة وإنما انقاد معهم حقيرًا ذليلاً لا يملك خطابًا ولا يردّ جوابًا مع أشدّ الهوان هونًا وأفحش الهلاك هلكة. وشهادة العقول بأنّ هذا لا يحسن أن * ينسب فعله إلى الله تعالى ولا أنّ للمسيح ذنبًا[157] استحق به ذلك ولا يقال إنه إنما وقع لمصلحة المسيح ولفائدة يعود إليه نفعها ، فإنّ الله ليس بعاجز[158] ولا محجور عليه ولا لأحد معه حكم ولا خلو ولا أمر إلا له وهو الحكيم العليم.

---

156 A and B: هيرودس   157 A and B: ذنب   158 B: بماجن. (wrongly), a misreading of A.

so that it became a bird by the help of God,[79] announced to people what they might eat and what they might store in their houses, and what deeds they might perform,[80] so that (20v) he became as it were a witness against them in their retreats, and sinless with the sinlessness of the resolute, the blessed messengers.

Far be humiliation, punishment, crucifixion and death from him, far be these from both God and Christ. And God is not negligent, forgetful or careless, and does not indulge in sport or visit any affliction upon a human except when this human hand has committed something that warrants it. So, far be it from God to have inflicted this upon Christ as sport or for the sake of a rank he could only be given through this. For it would make the One who is powerful over everything, may he be praised, incapable of elevating Christ to such a rank except through this humiliation, without deserving it or anything earlier having warranted it.[81] God is most gracious, powerful and merciful.

What proves that the one crucified was Judas bearing the resemblance of Christ, is that Christ (peace be upon him) was the most learned of the people of his time in the Torah and the Wisdom,[82] was the most nimble of them in debate, was the most experienced of them in points of argument, and was the most incisive and masterful of them. But when the Jews seized him and dragged him off for crucifixion, according to the account of the humiliation just given, not a single word or cry of defence was heard from him. Rather, he went with them humbly and submissively, incapable of any speech, offering no response, no matter how harsh the humiliation or naked the threat of death. This is evidence to intelligent minds that this man's actions could not be (21r) attributed to God the exalted, and that Christ had not done any wrong for which he deserved this, and that it cannot be said that it only happened as a benefit to Christ or as a gain whose profit might be returned to him. For God is not weak and has no constraint upon him, none has rule beside him, and he alone has freedom and command, for he is the all-wise and all-knowing. So it is proved

---

[79] SS. III: 49, V: 110.

[80] S. III: 49-50.

[81] Al-Dimashqī refers to a view of the atonement that seems close to Philippians II: 6-11, in which Christ's humbling of himself and death are the conditions for his elevation and glorification. For al-Dimashqī himself this suggests that God was unable to elevate Christ without inflicting suffering on a sinless man, contrary to SS. III: 55, IV: 158.

[82] SS. III: 48, V: 110.

فثبت بذلك أنّ المصلوب غير المسيح وهو يهودس[159] وأنّ الله حجب المسيح عن أعين اليهود وألقى شبهه على يهودس[160] بغتة وشعر يهودس[161] بذلك فاعترفت نفسه بالذنب وسكت مقهورًا محيّرًا.

30. وبقي أهل الكتاب الفريقان ، أعني اليهود والنصارى ، في شكّ وفي خلاف وظنون فاسدة حتى نزل القرآن المجيد بالخبر الحقّ عن المسيح وعن اختلاف الفريقين في أمره، وشهد بنزاهته وطهارته وسلامته من الصلب والقتل وبإجلاله ورفعه وعصمته من أن يكون ملعونًا مبعودًا من الرحمة بشهادة موسى ابن عمران عليه السلام حيث يقول: "إنّ خشبة الصلب ملعونة والمصلوب عليها ملعون".[162] وذلك هو اللائق الذي ينبغي أن يكون.

ولعمري إنّ طائفة من اليهود أنكرت الصلب جملة واحدة * وقالوا: "لم * 21v يقع ذلك ولم يكن" ، ولكن الفريسيون لمّا أنكروا ما أنكروا على المسيح وسجنوه وأرادوا صلبه لم يجدوه في السجن ووجدوا تلاميذه الذين سجنوا معه فأخرجوهم وودروهم نفيًا وتغييبًا. ثمّ أخرجوا من السجن ثلاثة أنفار أحدهم عليه شبه المسيح فصلبوه وشنقوا الاثنين عن يمينه ويساره وسكتوا عن اختفاء المسيح وغيبته لئلا يكون ذلك سببًا لافتتان بني إسرائيل به ، ويكاد هذا يقرب من الصحيح والله أعلم.

31. نكتة: ذهبت النصارى أصحاب القوانين إلى أنّ المسيح إنما صلب وقتل وذاق العذاب والهوان والموت لأجل خلاص آدم وذريّته من الجحيم فقبل[163] وغلب بزعمهم ولم يخلّصهم ولا خلّص واحدًا منهم ، والذي حملهم[164] على القول بذلك أنّ قسطنطين وأهل مملكته وأصحاب القوانين وأهل المجامع السبعة بجملتهم كانوا قريبي[165] العهد بدين الصابئة ومذهبهم كمذهب الثنوية القائلين بإلهين إثنين، إله السماء وإله الأرض، فالخيرات والأنوار والسعادات من إله السماء، والشرور والظلمات والشقاوات * من إله الأرض، وزعمهم * 22r مشهور.

---

[159] A and B: هيرودس   [160] A and B: هيرودس   [161] A and B: هيرودس   [162] Cf. Deut XXI: 23; Galatians III: 13.   [163] B: فقيل (wrongly).   [164] B: حملها   [165] A and B: قريبين

by this that the one crucified was not Christ but was Judas, and that God concealed Christ from the eyes of the Jews and suddenly placed his likeness upon Judas. Judas realised this and his soul confessed the sin, and he remained silent in perplexity and helplessness.

30. The two groups of the People of the Book, that is to say Jews and Christians, remained in doubt and disagreement, and maintained wrong views until the glorious Qur'an came down with the truthful report about Christ and the two groups' disagreement about him. It bore witness to his integrity and purity, to his being untouched by crucifixion and killing, to his being exalted and raised up, and to his innocence of being accursed and excluded from mercy, as Moses son of 'Imrān (peace be upon him) witnessed when he said, 'The wood of crucifixion is accursed and the one crucified on it is accursed', which aptly refers to someone to whom this may happen.

Indeed, a party of the Jews denied the crucifixion altogether (21v) and said, 'This never happened and never took place'. Indeed, when the Pharisees reproached Christ in the way they did and imprisoned him and were going to crucify him, they could not find him in the prison, but only his disciples who had been imprisoned with him. They brought these out and got rid of them by banishing and removing them. Then they brought out of the prison three individuals, one of whom bore Christ's likeness. Him they crucified, and they hanged the two on his right and his left. They kept silent about Christ's disappearance and vanishing, lest it should cause the people of Israel to riot over him. This more or less approximates to the truth, and God knows.

31. *Illustration*: The Christians, the canonical experts, believed that Christ had been crucified, killed, subjected to torture, humiliation and death, in order to save Adam and his seed from hell, and according to their claim he submitted to this and triumphed. But he did not save them, not even a single one of them. What induced them to say this is that Constantine, together with the people of his realm, the canonical experts, and the members of the seven Councils, were all near in time to the religion of the Ṣābians. The doctrines of these people were like those of the dualists, who taught about two gods, one of the heaven and one of the earth, with good things, illumination and good fortune coming from the god of the heaven, and disasters, injustices and misfortunes (22r) from the god of the earth. Their claims are well known.[83]

---

[83] Cf. n. 40 above.

وقسطنطين قد أظهر دين النصرانية وأدخل الناس فيه طوعًا وكرهًا ، وقد
بلغهم ما نسب إلى المسيح من الصلب والقتل والعذاب والهوان وما زعمته
أصحاب القوانين من الأبوّة والبنوّة والحلول والاتّحاد والوحدة في الأقنومية
وما نقلته رواة الأناجيل الأربعة وشهدت به. فأنكرت العقول والفكر الجمع
بين النقائض وقال العقلاء:" كيف يتفق أو يليق بهذا المسمّى إلهًا وابنًا للإله
أن يلى بمثل هذا البلاء؟ ولأيّ معنى كان ذلك؟"

وفطن أصحاب القوانين وأهل المجامع الرواة لذلك الإنكار من العقلاء،
فقرّروا أنّ ذلك إنما كان لخلاص آدم وذرّيته من الجحيم ولخلاصنا[166] معشر
النصارى. واستدلّوا بقول المسيح: "أبونا الذي في السموات،[167] وافعلوا الخير
يفرح بكم أبوكم الذي في السماء،[168] وإني صاعد إلى أبي وأبيكم وإلهي
وإلهكم"[169] ومثل ذلك. ثم رتّبوا كلامًا كالعقيدة وسمّوه الأمانة الكبيرة ،
فقالوا في أوّلها: "نؤمن بإله واحد آب ضابط الكلّ خالق السموات والأرض
صانع ما يُرى ومالا يُرى" ، ثمَّ قالوا: "ونؤمن بيسوع المسيح ابن   * 22v *
الله الوحيد وأنه إله حقّ من إله حقّ من جوهر أبيه" ، ثمَّ قالوا: "وأنه جاء
لخلاصنا معشر البشر وخلاص آدم وذرّيته من الجحيم" ، ثمَّ قالوا: "وأنه
صلب وأولم وذاق الموت كما هو مكتوب في كتب النبوّات" ، ثمَّ قالوا:
"ونؤمن بقيامة أبداننا وأننا نصير إلى الحياة الأبدية" ، ثمَّ قالوا عن المسيح:
"ونؤمن أنه قام في اليوم الثالث وصعد إلى السماء وجلس عن يمين أبيه وأنه
سيأتي مرة ثانية ليفصل بين الأحياء والأموات".

32. ولمّا قرّروا هذه الأمانة سخر من تقريرها

---

[166] A and B: ولاخلاصنا; cf. f. 22v.   [167] Mtt VI: 9.   [168] Cf. *Ibid.*: 14.   [169] Jn XX: 17.

Constantine made Christianity public and brought people into it willy-nilly. They were told about matters connected with Christ, such as the crucifixion, killing, suffering and humiliation, as well as what the canonical experts claimed about fatherhood, sonship, indwelling, uniting, unity in hypostaticity, and what the transmitters of the four Gospels had narrated and attested. Rational minds and intellects rejected contradictory ideas being combined, and reasonable people said, 'How can it be right or fitting for this being, who is named God and Son in divinity, to suffer such tribulations as these? And for what purpose did this happen?'

The canonical experts and members of the Councils who had passed this on became aware of what reasonable people rejected, and they insisted that it was expressly to save Adam and his seed from hell and to save their community of Christians. As proof they adduced Christ's words, 'Our Father who is in heaven', 'Do good and your Father who is in heaven will rejoice in you', 'I am ascending to my Father and your Father, to my God and your God', and the like.[84] Then they compiled a statement like a declaration of faith, which they named the Great Creed. At the beginning of it they said: We believe in one God and Father, Preserver of all, Creator of the heavens and earth, (22v) Maker of what is seen and unseen. Then they said: And we believe in Jesus Christ, the only Son of God, that he is true God from true God, of the substance of his Father. Then they said: And that he came to save us humans, and to save Adam and his seed from hell. Then they said: And that he was crucified, was made to suffer and experienced death, as is written in the books of the prophets. Then they said: And we believe in the resurrection of our bodies and that we will attain everlasting life. Then they said about Christ: And we believe that he rose on the third day, ascended into heaven and was seated at the right hand of his Father, and that he will come again to separate the living and the dead.[85]

32.   When they had established this Creed, reasonable people

---

[84] The quotation from Jn XX: 17 is surprising, because for Muslims this was the most popular proof-text of Jesus being human like the disciples; cf. M. Accad, 'The Ultimate Proof-Text: The Interpretation of John 20. 17 in Muslim-Christian Dialogue (second/eighth-eighth/fourteenth centuries)', in D. Thomas, ed., *Christians at the Heart of Islamic Rule, Church Life and Scholarship in 'Abbasid Iraq*, Leiden, 2003, pp. 199-214.

[85] This resembles the parts of the Nicene Creed that refer to God the Father and God the Son.

العقلاء وحكى بعضهم لبعض حكاية كالمثل وكالأضحوكة المحزنة المبكية من وجه والمضحكة المعجبة من وجه ، فقال في جملتها: "زعم النصارى أنّ آدم ونوح وابراهيم وموسى وسائر المرسلين وجميع بني آدم وذريّته قهرهم الشيطان الرجيم وسلّط عليهم جنده وحبسهم في جحيمه وأنهم استغاثوا بإله السماء وسألوه خلاصهم من يد الشيطان الحاكم في الأرض ففكر إله السماء طويلاً وأوسع * الحيلة حتى اختار امرأة من البشر اسمها مريم فنفخ فيها من روحه نفخة لا خالقة ولا مخلوقة فامتزج لاهوته بناسوتها وتركّب من هذا المزاج مولود من طبيعتين ومشيئتين إلهًا تامًا وإنسانًا تامًا يسمّى المسيح ، ولمّا بلغ أشدّه قصد إلى جحيم الشيطان لإخراج آدم والذرّية من الجحيم فعندما فتحه ومدّ يده ليخرجهم فطن الشيطان به فنهض إليه وسلّط عليه اليهود فمسكوه وصلبوه وقتلوه وذاق الموت لاهوته وناسوته المتحد غير المنفصل[170] هذا عن هذا كما زعمت النصارى".

قال الحاكي: "وكان مع المسيح روح القدس وملائكة السماء فهربوا إليها صاعدين فوجدوا إله السماء قد علم ووصل إليه الألم من لاهوته المتحد بناسوت المسيح ووجدوا ملائكة العرش والسموات حزانى باكين يقولون بالحال: "صلب ابن الإله ، قتل ابن الإله وعجز الآب عن خلاص الإبن من أيدي اليهود وبقي آدم وذريّته في الجحيم على ما كانوا عليه من العذاب وأشرّ ممّا كانوا".

قال الحاكي لهذه الأضحوكة * المبكية: "ثمّ إنّ الشيطان بزعم النصارى لمّا علم بأنّ المسيح قد سرقته ملائكة السماء بعد الموت وأحياه أبوه وأطلعه إليه خفية من اليهود قال الشيطان في نفسه: "لابدّ أن أعرّف أهل الأرض كلهم بما فعلت اليهود بهذا الابن"، فظهر للنصارى في صورة عالم من علمائهم وزيّن لهم تصوير تمثال المسيح

---

[170] A and B: الغير منفصل

laughed at what they had done and one narrated it to another as a tale, a sad, tragic joke on the one hand, and on the other as something amazing to laugh at. He told the whole story thus: 'The Christians claim that accursed Satan had victory over Adam, Noah, Abraham, Moses, all who were sent, and all the children of Adam and his seed; he gave his army power over them and shut them up in his hell. Then they sought help from the god of heaven,[86] and begged him to save them from the power of Satan, who held sway in the earth. The god of heaven thought for a long time, and devised (23r) a trick: from humankind he chose a woman whose name was Mary and breathed into her a breath from his spirit, which was neither Creator nor created, so that his divinity mingled with her humanity. From this mingling was composed a being born with two natures and volitions, perfect God and perfect man, named Christ. And when he had reached maturity he went to the hell of Satan in order to liberate Adam and his seed from hell. But just as he was about to open it and stretch out his hand to liberate them, Satan noticed him. He pounced on him, and he gave the Jews power over him. They seized him, crucified him and killed him, and his divinity and humanity, which as the Christians claim were united and indivisible from each other, both tasted death.'

The teller said, 'The Holy Spirit and angels of heaven were with Christ; they fled upwards and found that the god of heaven already knew, and that the pain from his divinity which was united with Christ's humanity had stricken him. And they found the angels of the throne and the heavenly beings mourning and weeping, and saying about the affair, "The Son of God has been crucified, the Son of God has been killed. The Father could not save the Son from the hands of the Jews, and Adam and his seed remain in hell with punishment afflicted upon them as before, and more viciously than before."'

The teller of this tragic (23v) joke said, 'Then, according to the Christians' claim, when Satan discovered that the angels of heaven had stolen Christ after death and that his Father had revived him and raised him up to himself in secret from the Jews, Satan said to himself, "I must tell all the people of the earth what the Jews have done to this Son." And he appeared to the Christians in the form of one of their scholars and conjured up in their minds the image of Christ

---

[86] The story is being mockingly transmitted within the dualistic framework of a god of heaven and god of the earth that is referred to at the beginning of this *Illustration*, § 31.

مصلوبًا مقتولاً مسلوبًا كل شيء فصوّروه على الحوائط والألواح وفي الكنائس وانتشر ذلك في الأرض مبالغة في الهوان وفي الاشتهار و لم يستنكفوا من هذه الشهرة الشنيعة والحالة الفظيعة ، واستمرّوا على ذلك وإلى الآن .

فالتفت ذوو العقول والرحمة للنصارى وقالوا لهم تعريفًا وتعنيفا: يا هؤلاء لو حكى لكم حاك عن قوم آخرين بعض هذه الأضحوكة المبكية وأخبر أنهم بزاوية من زوايا الأرض منفردين فيها عن الناس وأنّ هذا المذهب مذهبهم وهذه الأمانة أمانتهم وهذا الظنّ ظنّهم بربّ العالمين أفكنتم تعدّونهم من العقلاء أو تسمّونهم أهل دين أو * تقولون إنهم متمسّكون بدين بني من الأنبياء أو هم على شيء؟ لا والله بل كنتم تعجبون من حلم الله وإمهاله لهم وتجزمون بضلالهم وجهلهم وتقولون تنزيهًا: "سبحان ربّنا وتعالى عمّا يشركون هؤلاء وعمّا يصفون".

وتعلمون من ذلك الحين من هو الرسول الذي بشّر به المسيح وأخبرهم عنه بأنه يوبّخ العالم على الخطيئة والحكم والعدل معرفة لا جهالة معها وتشهدون أنه محمّد وليس هو ما زعم أهل القوانين في روح القدس المتوهّمة غير المحسوسة[171] كما تقدّم القول فيها وتحقون أنه مرسل إلى العرب الجاهلية وأهل الكتاب "الضالّين" و"المغضوب عليهم[172]" وسائر العالمين الجنّ والأنس أجمعين.

33.   نكتة: لمّا كان لكلّ شيء وسط وطرفان[173] كما المشرق والمغرب ووسط السماء كان للنصارى جهة المشرق وفيها إشارة إلى أنهم قاصدون الحقّ والخير والطاعة والاستسلام لكل ما يظنّونه حقّاً وأنه من أمر الله ، ولكنهم في حضيض الأفق وأوّل التوجّه إلى * الشرف والعلو لم يبلغوا

* 24r

* 24v

_____

وسطا وطرفين :A and B [173]   S. I: 7. [172]   الغير محسوسة :A and B [171]

crucified, killed and shorn of everything. So they painted this on walls and panels and in the churches, and it was made known throughout the world with its humiliation and notoriety exaggerated. They made no attempt to deny this repugnant infamy and odious situation, and they have persisted in it to the present.

'People with understanding and compassion took some consideration for the Christians and said to advise and admonish them, "If anyone were to relate to you part of this tragic joke from other people, and reported that they had cut themselves off from humankind in a corner of the earth, and that this doctrine was theirs, this creed theirs, and this supposition about the Lord of the worlds was theirs, would you people regard them as reasonable, call them people of religion, (24r) say that they followed the religion of any prophet, or had any serious purpose? No, by God! Instead, you would be amazed at God's gentleness and forbearance towards them, and you would conclude that they were in error and ignorance. And as a declaration that he is above all this you would say, 'Our God is holy, and is far above the things with which these people associate him and characterise him'."'

From this time on you will know fully without any ignorance at all who is the messenger whom Christ announced and declared to them would rebuke the world about sin, judgement and justice. And you will witness that he is Muḥammad, and not the one whom the canonical experts claim is the imagined Holy Spirit, which is intangible, as the preceding argument has shown. And you will confirm that he was sent to the pagan Arabs, to the People of the Book, 'those who go astray' and 'those who earn anger', and to all the other races of jinn and humankind together.[87]

33. *Illustration*: Everything has a middle and two ends, like the sunrise and sunset and the midpoint of heaven. Hence, the Christians had the direction of sunrise, which indicates that they were moving towards truth, goodness, obedience and submission in everything they supposed was true and according to the command of God. But they were at the lowest point of the horizon, and the first to have to move towards (24v) eminence and elevation, and they have not reached the

---

[87] Since the Christians are still addressed in the second person it would seem natural to take this concluding paragraph as a continuation of the direct address begun in the previous paragraph. But the summary of points made in earlier arguments and the reference to 'the preceding argument' indicate that al-Dimashqī has resumed in his own person and is addressing the Cypriot Christians directly. Cf. the latter part of the next *Illustration*.

الغاية. وكانت اليهود جهة المغرب وفيها إشارة إلى إدبارهم وإعراضهم عن الحقّ والخير والطاعة وإشارة أيضًا إلى اليأس من روح الله ومن الفلاح .

وكانت القبلة وسط السماء لنا معشر المسلمين وهي موضع الوسط والاستعلاء على الطرفين ولذلك قال الله تعالى في القرآن: ﴿كنتم خير أمّة أخرجت للناس تأمرون بالمعروف وتنهون عن المنكر وتؤمنون بالله ولو آمن أهل الكتاب لكان خيرًا لهم منهم المؤمنون وأكثرهم الفاسقون﴾[174] وقال تعالى: ﴿وكذلك جعلناكم أمّة وسطًا لتكونوا شهداء على الناس ويكون الرسول عليكم شهيدًا﴾[175]. فالوسط الخيار وقد قيل: "خير الأمور أوسطها" .

وممّا يوضّح توسّطنا واستقامتنا على الطريقة المثلى وانحراف الأمتين عن الحقّ والتوسّط أنّ اليهود حرّمت على أنفسها طيّبات أحلّت لها وكلّ ما ذبح بيد مستبيح السبت أو ذبحوه و لم يجدوا فيه شرائط لهم كثيرة ممّا يطول شرحه كاللحم مع اللبن ولحوم كلّ ذي ظفر ، فقابلت النصارى هذا التحريم * بأن أكلت لحم الخنزير ولحوم كلّ حيوان فيما بين الدودة والفيل وأكلت المقتول قتلاً والمذبوح ذبحًا والمنحور نحرًا والمخنوق خنقًا.

وأن اليهود بالغت في التنجيس حتى حبست النساء عزلة في مدّة حيضهن واختتنوا طلبًا للطهارة وبجّسوا الهواء المحيط

* 25r

---

goal. And the Jews had the direction of sunset, which indicates that they were withdrawing and turning away from truth, goodness and obedience, and also indicates that they have lost hope of the spirit of God or success.[88]

The *qibla* is the middle of heaven for us Muslims; it is the midpoint and stands above the two ends. Thus God the exalted has said in the Qur'an, 'Ye are the best community that hath been raised up for mankind. Ye enjoin right conduct and forbid indecency; and ye believe in Allah. And if the People of the Scripture had believed, it had been better for them. Some of them are believers; but most are evil-livers.' And the exalted One has said, 'Thus we have appointed you a middle nation, that ye may be witnesses against mankind, and that the messenger may be a witness against you.' So, the middle is the best; as has been said, 'The best position is the middlemost'.

That we are the middlemost and are set on the perfect way, and that the two communities have deviated from the truth and middle position is shown clearly by the fact that the Jews have forbidden to themselves things that are good and have been made permissible to them, or whatever has been slaughtered by a hand that has been given permission to do so on the sabbath, or they have slaughtered but not found in it the many stipulations they have (that would take too long to explain), such as flesh with milk, or any form of flesh with hooves.[89] But the Christians follow the opposite to this prohibition, (25r) because they eat pork and the flesh of any animal from a worm to an elephant. They eat anything that has been killed, slaughtered, had its throat cut, or been strangled.

The Jews have gone to such lengths over pollution that the women are kept in seclusion throughout their monthly period, they are circumcised as a requirement of purity, and they regard the air around

---

[88] The connection of the three religions with these particular positions of the sun is not immediately obvious, though since the Muslims must be at its highest point the other two religions must be at its rising and setting. Al-Dimashqī maybe links the Christians with the fresh start along the path to the full light of truth because of Christ's anticipation of the coming of Muḥammad which he has repeatedly mentioned earlier. Likewise, he links the Jews with the darkness of evening because they completely rejected Muḥammad during his lifetime and hindered his ministry. But his main point is that the Muslims are at the highest, midmost position, as the following quotations from the Qur'an demonstrate.

[89] Cf. Deut XIV: 7-8 and 21 and parallels. In contrast to the criticisms against these self-imposed privations, S. VI: 146 explicitly states that it was God who 'forbade every animal with claws, *dhī ẓufur*'.

بالميت إذا كان في بيت ، فقابلت النصارى ذلك بإباحة وطء الحائض من غير
طهر وتركوا الختان وتركوا استعمال الماء من الجنابة والوطء واكتفوا بالتعميد
طهرًا، وإن اليهود عطّلت معاشها وأسبابها يوم كلّ سبت فجعلت النصارى يوم
لعبها وانفساحها ودخولها الحمّام وتنعيمها بالملاذ كله يوم السبت ، وإن اليهود
بالغت في تكذيب الأنبياء وقتلهم وعصيانهم لله تعالى وكثرة العنت[176] فبالغت
النصارى في الغلوّ في الأنبياء وإفراط المحبة حتى اتخذوهم أربابًا من دون الله
وتضرّعوا إلى تماثيلهم في الكنائس وانقادوا لكلّ مخبر يخبر عن الله ، سواء كان
الخبر حقًّا أو باطلاً، وغلوا أشدّ غلوّ في المسيح حتى أخرجوه عن البشرية
واتخذوه * إلهًا.

* 25v

وقالت اليهود عند استماع كلّ حقّ وباطل: "لا نسلم"، فقالت النصارى
عند استماع كلّ باطل وكذب:" آمنّا وصدّقنا"، فجاء الله بالأمّة الوسط
بين هؤلاء وهؤلاء وجعلها شاهدة على أفعال هؤلاء وهؤلاء ومفضّلة عند
هؤلاء وهؤلاء قائمة بالقسط معروفة في الأمم الأول بالحمادين أهل الختان ،
أناجيلهم في صدورهم وقرابينهم دماؤهم ، أولئك المحمّديون الابراهيميون
أهل الله وخاصته الذين أكمل لهم الدين وأتمّ عليهم النعمة ورضي لهم
الإسلام دينًا وحبّب إليهم الإيمان وزيّنه في قلوبهم وكرّه إليهم الكفر
والفسوق والعصيان أولئك هم الراشدون .

وعلى الجملة[177] قد لزمكم اتباع هذا النبي العربي بمقتضى قولكم إنكم
علمتم أنه لم يأت إليكم بل إلى جاهلية العرب فأقررتم بأن الله أرسله إلى
العرب والنبي ثابت الصدق والتصديق وقد أخبر هذا النبي العربي الثابت
الصدق والتصديق الذي علمتم أنه رسول من عند الله إلى العرب أنّ الله تعالى
أرسله إلى الناس كافة فلزمكم اتباعه * .بمقتضى قولكم .

* 26r

---

[176] A and B: العبث   [177] A note in the margin of A reads: من قوله وعلى الجملة إلى
الفصل زيادة من الناسخ ليست في الأصل

a corpse, if it is in a house, as unclean. But the Christians follow the opposite to this in permitting intercourse with a menstruating woman without purification, they have abandoned circumcision, they have abandoned using water for major impurity and intercourse, and they are content with baptism for purification. And while the Jews suspend their way of living and means of livelihood every sabbath day, the Christians have made the sabbath a day for their amusement and leisure, for going into baths on the sabbath with the pleasures they hold and all their enjoyments. The Jews have gone to the extreme in repudiating the prophets and killing them, in their rebellion against God the exalted and increasing iniquity, while the Christians have gone to the extreme in making too much of the prophets and immoderate love, to the extent that they take them as lords in place of God, bow down before the portraits of them in churches, and lend credence to anyone who comes with a communication from God, whether it is truthful or false. They have gone to the extreme of exaggerating about Christ, to the point that they have removed him from humankind and made him into (25v) a god.

When the Jews hear any truth or falsehood they say, 'We do not accept'; and when the Christians hear any falsehood or lie they say, 'We believe and trust'. So God has brought the middle community between the two of them, and made it a witness to the actions of them both, pre-eminent in comparison with them, promoting justice, known among the nations as the first of those who give praise, a people of circumcision, their gospels in their breasts, and their sacrifices their blood. They are the people of Muḥammad and Ibrāhīm, the people of God, and his elite: he completed religion for them, perfected blessedness on them, approved Islam as a religion for them, made faith beloved to them, set it in their hearts, and made them hate unbelief, sinfulness and disobedience. They are the rightly guided.

In short, you should follow this Arabian Prophet in accordance with your statement that you know he did not come to you but to the pagan Arabs. For you do acknowledge that God sent him to the Arabs. A prophet confirms what is truthful and trustworthy, and this Arabian prophet, who confirmed what is truthful and trustworthy and whom you recognise was a messenger from God to the Arabs, declared that God the exalted sent him to all people. So you should follow him (26r) in accordance with your statement.[90]

---

[90] Al-Dimashqī here turns the Christians' polemical ploy back upon them. He

34. وثبتت عليكم الحجّة بما استدللتم به من الآيات الكريمة على تخصيص الرسالة المحمدية على زعمكم الكاذب لأنكم توهّمتم أنّ الأعجمين في قوله تعالى ﴿ولو نزلناه على بعض الأعجمين﴾[178] الآية من عدا العرب فيكون الإنزال خاص بالعرب وليس كذلك ، فإنّ الأعجمين جمع أعجم والأعجم كلّ من كان في لسانه عجمة وإن كان من العرب والعجمي منسوب إلى العجم وإن كان فصيحًا ، وأنّ قوله تعالى: ﴿كما أرسلنا فيكم رسولاً منكم﴾[179] خطاب خاص بالعرب وليس كذلك بل الميم في "فيكم" ضمير الجمع المخاطبين وهم الناس كافة ومعنى ميم "منكم" أي إنسان من جنسكم ليس بمَلَك ولا جنّي وكذلك قوله: ﴿إذ بعث فيهم رسولاً من أنفسهم﴾[180]. ويعضد ذلك قراءة مَن قرأ: "من أنفسهم" بفتح الفاء أي من أشرفهم وأنّ قوله تعالى ﴿لتنذر قومًا ما أتاهم من نذير من قبلك﴾[181] هم العرب خاصة وليس كذلك بل القوم كلّ حيّ كان في زمن بعثته صلم بدليل قوله تعالى: ﴿لينذر من كان حيًّا﴾[182] وأيضًا فإنه[183] تصدّق على كلّ حيّ في زمنه إنه لم يأته نذير إذ كان بعثه صلم على فترة من الرسل وكذلك قوله تعالى: ﴿لتنذر قومًا ما أنذر آباؤهم﴾ الآية[184]

---

[178] S. XXVI: 198. [179] S. II: 151. [180] S. III: 164. [181] S. XXVIII: 46. [182] S. XXXVI: 70. [183] These two words are added in the margin in A. [184] Ibid.: 6.

34. The argument by which you have sought to prove from the noble verses the restricted nature of Muḥammad's apostleship can be proved against you, against your lying claim. For you imagine that 'the nations' in the words of the exalted One, 'And if we had revealed it unto one of any other nation'[91] and the rest of the verse, excludes the Arabs, so that the sending down is restricted to the Arabs. But it is not thus: 'the nations' is the plural of 'nation', and 'nation' is anyone who has incorrectness in his speech, whether Arab or foreigner from among the non-Arabs, even though he may be an eloquent speaker.[92] Also that the words of the exalted One, 'Even as we have sent unto you a messenger from among you', is an address to the Arabs alone; though it is not thus: the 'you' in 'unto you' is a plural pronoun for those who are addressed, and they are all people, and the meaning of 'you' in 'from among you' is 'a man from your kind', rather than an angel or a jinn. And similarly his words, 'By sending unto them a messenger of their own, *min anfusihim*'; the reading *min anfasihim* with a vowel 'a' on the 'f', meaning 'from the most distinguished among them', gives strength to this.[93] And that the exalted One's words, 'That thou mayest warn a folk unto whom no warner came before thee', are the Arabs alone; though it is not thus: 'the folk' are all who were living at the time he was sent (may God bless him and give him peace), as is proved by the words of the exalted One, 'To warn whosoever liveth', which also confirms that it was to everyone living at his time, for no warner had come to them when his mission (may God bless him and give him peace) occurred, at an interval after the messengers. Similarly, the exalted One's words, 'That thou mayest warn a folk whose fathers were not warned, *mā undhira ābā'uhum*' and the rest of the verse, for he

---

argues that if they acknowledge Muḥammad as a prophet, which they have indicated they do, though only for the Arabs, then on the grounds that prophets are true and trustworthy they should accept him when he says he was sent to the whole world.

[91] The Christians cite this and the following verses in the portion of their *Letter* quoted above in § 5.

[92] This argument depends on the semantic distinction between *aʿjam/aʿjamūn*, one who has difficulty in speaking Arabic, and *ʿujma*, lack of correctness in speaking Arabic. Thus, for al-Dimashqī the verse does not mean non-Arabs but anyone not proficient in Arabic language.

[93] Al-Dimashqī reads the elative form of the adjective *nafīs*, 'excellent', 'costly', rather than the plural of *nafs*, 'individual'. This gives a general meaning to the verse that Muḥammad was the most noble of all those to whom he was sent, rather than that he was an Arab like those to whom he was sent. According to al-Zamakhsharī, *Kashshāf, ad* S. IX: 128, this was said to be the vocalisation of the word approved by the Muḥammad himself, as well as by Fāṭima and ʿĀʾisha.

* 26v   لأنه يصدق على أبائهم الحقيقة * أنهم لم ينذرهم نبي بلسانه ، هذا إذا سلّمنا أنّ "ما" للنفي فإن لم نسلّم ذلك كانت للإثبات فيكون معناها "الذي" وتقدير الكلام: لتنذر قومًا الذي أنذره أباؤهم ، لتنذر قومًا الذي أتاهم به النذر من قبلك. وتعدى الفعل بنفسه من غير حرف جرّ وتصدّق على آدم فمن بعده أنهم آباء لهم فيكون ذلك تصديقًا للرسل وتوكيدًا لما جاؤوا به بدليل قوله تعالى: ﴿ألم الله لا إله إلا هو الحيّ القيوم نزل عليك الكتاب بالحقّ مصدّقاً لما بين يديه﴾ [185]. ونحو ذلك، سلّمنا أن القوم هنا هم العرب لكن لا يلزم من ذلك أن يكون إنما أرسل إليهم خاصة لأنه لم يأت في ذلك بأداة من أدوات الحصر وكيف وقد قال تعالى: ﴿يا أيها الناس قد جاءكم الرسول بالحقّ من ربّكم﴾ [186] ، ﴿قل يا أيها الناس إني رسول الله إليكم جميعًا﴾ [187] ، ﴿وما أرسلناك إلا كافة للناس﴾ [188] ، ﴿يا أهل الكتاب قد جاءكم رسولنا يبيّن لكم كثيرًا مّما كنتم تخفون من الكتاب ويعفو [189] عن كثير﴾ [190] ، ﴿يا أهل الكتاب قد جاءكم رسولنا يبيّن لكم على فترة من الرسل﴾ [191] وغير ذلك من الآيات الدالة على عموم دعوته.

وأمّا قوله تعالى: ﴿وما أرسلنا من رسول إلا بلسان قومه﴾ [192] وقوله تعالى: ﴿ولقد بعثنا في كلّ أمّة رسولاً﴾ [193] وقوله تعالى: ﴿ولقد أرسلنا من قبلك رسلاً إلى قومهم﴾ [194] فهو إخبار * من الله تعالى عن ما تقدّم ليس لكم   27r * فيه دليل بل هو حجّة عليكم لأنّ مّما جاءت به الرسل

---

[185] S. III: 1-3.   [186] S. IV: 170.   [187] S. VII: 158.   [188] S. XXXIV: 28; يا أيها الناس [189] A …كافة للناس : these words are supplied in the margin in A in the same hand. [189] A and B: وتغفوا (wrongly).   [190] S. V: 15.   [191] Ibid.: 19.   [192] S. XIV: 4.   [193] S. XVI: 36.   [194] S. XXX: 47.

spoke truly to their fathers (26v) that no prophet had warned them in his language. This is so if we accept that *mā* is the negative 'not'. But if we do not accept this then it is the affirmative, so that its meaning becomes 'what', and the sense of the words is, 'That you may warn a folk what their fathers had been warned', 'That you may warn a folk what warners had brought them before you', the verb being used transitively alone without a preposition. This also confirms that Adam and those after him were fathers to them, and so it affirms the messengers, and bears out what they brought, according to the proof of the exalted One, 'Alif. Lam. Mim. Allah! There is no god save him, the alive, the eternal. He hath revealed unto thee the scripture with truth, confirming that which was before it'. Furthermore, we might allow that 'the folk' here are the Arabs, but it does not follow from this that he was only sent to them alone, because he did not include any restrictive particle in it.[94] So how could it be thus, when the exalted One has said, 'O mankind! The messenger hath come to you with the truth from your Lord', 'Say: O mankind! Lo! I am the messenger of Allah to you all', 'And we have not sent thee save unto all mankind', 'O people of the scripture! Now hath our messenger come unto you, expounding unto you much of that which ye used to hide in the scripture, and forgiving much', 'O people of scripture! Now hath our messenger come unto you to make things plain unto you after an interval of the messengers', and other verses that prove the universality of his call.

As for the words of the exalted One, 'And we never sent a messenger save with the language of his folk', 'And verily we have raised in every nation a messenger', and 'Verily we sent before thee messengers to their own folk', these are notifications (27r) from God the exalted that the above contains no proof to support you, but is rather an argument against you. For what the messengers brought was an

---

[94] I.e. even if the verse does refer to the Arabs, it does not refer to them alone because there is no restrictive term such as 'only' or 'specifically' present. This verse appears to raise a particular difficulty for al-Dimashqī, so he counters the reading of the Christians with two arguments. His first is that it is not a negative statement (the *mā* being construed as a relative pronoun) so that its meaning is not that Muḥammad came to people who had never been sent a warner from God, but that he came to all people with a warning that others (earlier prophets) had already given. His second is that even if the verse is read in the way the Christians understand it, with its primary reference the Arabs who had not been sent a previous warner, there is nothing in it to confine Muḥammad's activity to the Arabs alone.

التبشير بمحمّد صلم والتحريض على اتباع دينه إذ أظهر على ما تقدّم بدليل قوله تعالى: ﴿ومن يبتغ غير الإسلام دينًا فلن يقبل منه وهو في الآخرة من الخاسرين﴾ [195]، و"من" للعموم في كلّ من يعقل بالاتفاق لا لما ادعيتموه من التخصيص بالاختلاف.

---

[195] S. III: 85.

announcement of Muḥammad (may God bless him and give him peace) and an incitement to follow his religion. For the exalted One has explained the above by the attestation of his words, 'And whoso seeketh a religion other than the Surrender it will not be accepted from him, and he will be a loser in the hereafter'. 'Whoso' refers to everyone, by agreement of all who are reasonable, and not to the particular few that you spuriously make them out to be.

35.   **فصل**

ثمّ قلتم في رسالتكم:

وليعلم أنّ الله عدل وليس من عدله أن يطالب قومًا أو أمّة من الأمم يوم القيامة باتباع إنسان لم يأت إليهم ولا وقفوا له على كتاب بلسانهم ولا من جهة داع من قبله.

ثمّ وجدنا أيضا في هذا الكتاب من يعظّم السيّد المسيح وأمّه حيث يقول في سورة الأنبياء: ﴿والتي أحصنت فرجها فنفخنا فيها من روحنا وجعلناها وابنها آية للعالمين﴾[1]. وقال في سورة آل عمران: ﴿وإذ قالت الملائكة يا مريم إنّ الله اصطفاك وطهّرك﴾ الآية[2] مع الشهادات للمسيح بالمعجزات وأنه حبلت به أمّه لا من مباضعة بل ببشارة ملاك الله لأمّه، وأنه تكلّم في المهد وأحيا الموتى وأبرأ الأكمه ونقّى الأبرص، وأنه خلق من الطين كهيئة الطير ونفخ فيه فكان طيرًا بإذن الله * وأنّ الله رفعه إليه لقوله في سورة النساء: ﴿وما قتلوه وما صلبوه﴾ الآية[3]، وقوله في سورة آل عمران: ﴿إذ قال الله يا عيسى إني متوفيك ورافعك إليّ﴾ الآية[4]، وقوله في سورة البقرة: ﴿وآتينا عيسى ابن مريم البيّنات﴾ الآية[5]، وقوله في سورة الحديد: ﴿وقفينا بعيسى ابن مريم وآتيناه الإنجيل﴾ الآية[6] وقوله في سورة آل عمران: ﴿من أهل الكتاب أمّة قائمة يتلون آيات الله آناء الليل وهم يسجدون﴾ الآية[7].

ثمّ وجدناه يعظّم إنجيلنا ويقدّم صوامعنا ويشرّف مساجدنا ويشهد بأنّ اسم الله يذكر فيها كثيرًا وذلك قوله في سورة الحجّ: ﴿ولولا دفع الله الناس...﴾ الآية[8]، وهذا وغيره أوجب لنا التمسّك بديننا.

36.   فالجواب: لا شكّ أنّ الله تعالى عادل ولا يطالب قومًا ولا أمّة باتباع رسول لم يأت إليهم ولا وقفوا له على كتاب بلسانهم. هذا صحيح في دعوة الأنبياء الخاصة المبعوثين إلى قوم بعينهم

* 27v

---

[1] S. XXI: 91.   [2] S. III: 42.   [3] S. IV: 157.   [4] S. III: 55.   [5] S. II: 87.   [6] S. LVII: 27.   [7] S. III: 113.   [8] S. XXII: 40.

35.   *Section [Two]*

Then you say in your *Letter*,

> It is known that God is just, and it is not part of his justice to demand on the day of resurrection that a people or any community should have followed a man who had not come to them, or whose book they were not familiar with in their language, or without the authority of any herald preceding him.
>
> Further, we also find in this book one who extols the lord Christ and his mother in what he says in *The Prophets*, 'And she who was chaste, therefore we breathed into her of our Spirit and made her and her son a token for peoples'; and in *The Family of 'Imrān* he says, 'And when the angels said: O Mary! Lo! Allah hath chosen thee and made thee pure' and the rest of the verse.
>
> There are also the testimonies to Christ in the miracles, that his mother conceived him not through intercourse but by the annunciation of an angel of God to his mother,[1] that he spoke in the cradle,[2] brought the dead back to life, healed those born blind, made lepers whole,[3] created from clay the likeness of a bird, breathed into it, and it was a bird by the permission of God,[4] (27v.) that God raised him up to himself, according to his word in *Women*, 'They slew him not nor crucified him' and the rest of the verse; his word in *The Family of 'Imrān*, 'When Allah said, O Jesus! Lo! I am gathering thee and causing thee to ascend unto me' and the rest of the verse; his word in *The Cow*, 'And we gave unto Jesus son of Mary clear proofs' and the rest of the verse; in *Iron*, 'And we caused Jesus son of Mary to follow, and gave him the gospel' and the rest of the verse; and in *The Family of 'Imrān*, 'Of the people of the Scripture there is a staunch community who recite the revelations of Allah in the night season, falling prostrate' and the next verse.
>
> Then we find him extolling our Gospel, favouring our hermitages, honouring our places of worship, and bearing witness that the name of God is mentioned in them often. This is through his word in *The Pilgrimage*, 'For had it not been for Allah's repelling some men' and the rest of the verse. This and other things oblige us to keep to our religion.

36. *Response*: There is no doubt that God the exalted is just and does not demand that a people or community should follow a messenger who did not come to them and whose book they were not familiar with in their language. This is true as regards the specific preaching of the prophets who were sent to a particular nation and

---

[1] SS. XIX: 16-22; III: 45.
[2] SS. XIX: 29-33; III: 46; V: 110.
[3] SS. III: 49; V: 110.
[4] SS. III: 49; V: 110.

دون غيرهم . وأمّا الرسول المرسل إلى الناس كافة أبيضهم وأسودهم

وعربهم وعجمهم وكلّ ذي رأي ونحلة وكتاب وملّة وبشّرت به التوراة

والإنجيل والزبور وكتب النبوّات * وأسفار الملوك كما تقدّم من القول فإنّ   28r *

دعوته شملت وعمّت وبلغت زوايا العالم .

وقد أقررتم بتحصيل كتابه عندكم وأنكم قرأتموه وتدبّرتموه وشهدتم أنه

أخبر عن المسيح وأمّه بالتعظيم وأنه ذكر صوامعكم ومعابدكم واستشهدتم

ببعضه دون بعض فدخلتم بذلك مدخل اليهود لمّا أرسل إليهم المسيح

فقالوا: "لا نسمع منه ولا نصدّقه وحسبنا التوراة وشريعة موسى"، فذمّهم

الله في كتابنا بقوله تعالى: ﴿أفتؤمنون ببعض الكتاب وتكفرون ببعض﴾

الآية[9] إلى قوله: ﴿ولا هم ينصرون﴾[10].

وأعندكم[11] من ذلك فإنكم أقرب إلينا معشر المؤمنين مودّة كما قال

الله تعالى عن أصحوى النجاشي ملك الحبشة وأهل مملكته حين آمنوا

وبكوا لمّا سمعوا القرآن وشهدوا أنه كلام الله تعالى ، فإن كنتم كما قلتم

مصدّقين بهذا الكتاب الكريم وهو عندكم فاقرأوا ما في سورة الأعراف من

ذكر موسى وهارون وسؤال موسى لربّه بقوله: ﴿فاغفر لنا وارحمنا وأنت

خير الغافرين﴾[12] إلى قوله تعالى: ﴿فآمنوا بالله ورسوله النبي الأمّي الذي

يؤمن بالله وكلماته واتبعوه لعلكم تهتدون﴾[13] واقرأوا أيضاً قوله: * ﴿ومن   28v *

يبتغ غير الإسلام

---

[9] S. II: 85-6.   [10] إلى...ينصرون : these words are added in the same hand in the margin in A.   [11] A and B: وأعندكم (sic).   [12] S. VII: 155.   [13] Ibid.: 158.

no others. But as for the messenger who was sent to all people, white and black, Arabs and foreigners, everyone with discernment, faith, book and confession, whom the Torah, Gospel, Psalms, writings of the Prophets (28r) and Books of Kings foretold, as the discussion above has shown, his preaching encompassed, embraced and spread through the entire world.

You acknowledge that his book has reached as far as you, and that you have read it and reflected upon it,[5] and you witness that it reports about Christ and his mother with reverence, that it mentions your hermitages and your places of worship, though you cite only some parts of it and not others. In this you align yourselves with the Jews when Christ was sent to them, for they said, 'We have not heard about him and do not believe in him, we remain loyal to the Torah and Law of Moses.' So God the exalted censured them in our Book by the words of the exalted One, 'Believe ye in part of the scripture and disbelieve in part thereof?' and the rest of the verse, to his words, 'Neither will they have support'.

How obstinate you are in this, you who are nearest to us Muslims in love,[6] as God the exalted said about Aṣḥawā the Negus, king of Ethiopia, and the people of his realm when they believed and wept upon hearing the Qur'an, and witnessed that it was the word of God the exalted.[7] So if you believe in this noble book, as you have said, and you possess it, then read what is said in *The Heights* about Moses and Aaron and Moses' request to his Lord,[8] when he said, 'Therefore forgive us and have mercy on us, Thou, the best of all who show forgiveness', to the exalted One's words, 'So believe in Allah and his messenger, the prophet who can neither read nor write, who believeth in Allah and in his words, and follow him that haply ye may be led aright.' And read also his words, (28v) 'And whoso seeketh as religion

---

[5] Cf. § 5 above, where the Christians affirm this. Al-Dimashqī repeatedly reminds them of these words in his *Response*.

[6] S. V: 82.

[7] Cf. Ibn Isḥāq, *Sīra*, pp. 220-1, 223-4/*Life*, pp. 152, 154-5. Ibn Kathīr, *Bidāya*, vol. III, p. 77/*Life of the Prophet*, vol. II, p. 18, gives his name as Aṣḥama, with the variant Maṣhama; cf. also *EI²*, vol. VII, p. 862.

[8] The verses that follow all emphasise the point that the truth of Islam has been revealed to the Jews and others, even though they demur from it. The implication is that the Christians should take such verses into account, as well as the verses they select to support their own views, and accept the Qur'an as a whole like the Negus and his people.

دينًا فلن يقبل منه﴾ الآية[14] إلى قوله: ﴿والله لا يهدي القوم الظالمين﴾[15].
وقوله تعالى لليهود الذين هم أقدم شريعة منكم وأكثر علمًا واحتجاجًا:
﴿يا بني إسرائيل اذكروا نعمتي التي أنعمت عليكم وأوفوا بعهدي أوف
بعهدكم وإيّاي فارهبون وآمنوا بما أنزلت مصدّقًا لما معكم ولا تكونوا أوّل
كافر به﴾[16] إلى قوله: ﴿وتكتموا الحقّ وأنتم تعلمون﴾[17]، وقوله تعالى:
﴿لم يكن الذين كفروا من أهل الكتاب والمشركين منفكّين حتى تأتيهم
البيّنة﴾[18] إلى قوله: ﴿وذلك دين القيّمة﴾[19]، وقوله تعالى: ﴿شهد الله أنه
لا إله إلا هو﴾[20] إلى قوله: ﴿فإن الله سريع الحساب﴾[21]. ومعنى الإسلام
الانقياد لأمر الله والطاعة له والاستسلام والدخول في السلم من غير مجاذبة
ولا ممانعة ولا تردّد كما تردّدت اليهود في ذبح البقرة مرّات وذمّهم الله
على ذلك بقوله: ﴿فذبحوها وما كادوا يفعلون﴾[22].

37. وكم من آية في هذا الكتاب العزيز شاهدة بأنّ رسول الله مرسل إلى
جميع العالم وقد قرأتموه وتدبّرتموه واطلعتم منه كما قلتم على ذكر المسيح
وأمّه ووصفهما بأوصاف الكمال والشرف والاصطفاء والقرب من الله
عزّ وجلّ، واطلعتم فيه أيضًا على * قصص الأنبياء وأخبار الأمم السالفة   * 29r
ولو تعقلتم وتدبّرتم بغير زيغ ولا تحريف لوجدتم فيه خبر ما كان وما نبأ ما
يكون وتعريف الأمّة بما هو كائن لها من ظهور دين الإسلام على الدين كله،
ومن هلاك الكفرة والمشركين الجاهلية الجهلاء، ومن خلو جزيرة العرب
من الأصنام، ومن دخول الناس ﴿في دين الله أفواجًا﴾[23]، ومن إرث الأمّة
الأرض مشرقها ومغربها واستخلاف الله لهم فيها، ومن أخذ الجزية من أهل
الكتاب المخالفين

---

[14] S. III: 85.   [15] *Ibid.*: 86: الظالمين ... إلى قوله: these words are supplied in the same hand in the margin in A.   [16] S. II: 40-1.   [17] *Ibid.*: 42.   [18] S. XCVIII: 1. [19] *Ibid.*: 2-5.   [20] S. III: 18.   [21] *Ibid.*: 19.   [22] S. II: 71.   [23] Cf. S. CX: 2.

other than the Surrender it will not be accepted from him' and the rest of the verse to 'And Allah guideth not wrongdoing folk'; and the exalted One's words to the Jews who preceded you in the Law and have greater knowledge and forms of argument, 'O People of Israel, remember my favour wherewith I favoured you, and fulfil the covenant toward you, and fear me. And believe in that which I reveal, confirming that which ye possess already, and be not first to disbelieve therein' to his words 'nor knowingly conceal the truth'; and the exalted One's words, 'Those who disbelieve among the People of the Scripture and the idolaters could not have left off till the clear proof came unto them' to his words 'That is true religion'; and the exalted One's words, 'Allah is witness that there is no God save him, [and the angels and the men of learning. Maintaining his creation in justice, there is no god save him, the almighty, the wise. Lo! religion with Allah is the Surrender. Those who received the Scripture differed only after knowledge had come unto them, through transgression among themselves. Whoso disbelieveth the revelations of Allah] lo! Allah is swift at reckoning.' The meaning of 'the Surrender' is to yield to the command of God, to obey and surrender oneself to him and to find peace, without struggling, objecting or wavering, as the Jews wavered repeatedly when they sacrificed the cow. For this God censured them in his words, 'So they sacrificed her, though almost they did not.'

37.   How many verses in this esteemed book witness that the messenger of God was sent to the whole world? You have read it and reflected upon it and, as you say, you know all about its references to Christ and his mother, the description of them as perfect, noble, chosen and near to God, great and mighty. And you also know all about (29r) the stories of the prophets in it, and the accounts of bygone nations. If you were to apply your minds and consider without deflecting or distorting, then you would find in it reports of what had been, news of what was to be, and an announcement to the community of what was to happen to it, namely the triumph of the religion of Islam over every other religion, the destruction of unbelievers and the ignorant pagan polytheists, the clearing of idols out of Arabia, the entry of masses of people into the religion of God, the community inheriting the earth both east and west and God's appointing them as successors there,[9] the exacting of the tribute from hostile People of the Book in

---

[9] Cf. S. XXIV: 55.

المجاورين وغير ذلك ممّا وقع وممّا سيقع كما أخبر فيه به . ولعلمتم أيضًا
من صولة ألفاظه وخطابة العليّ فيه تارة للنبي وتارة للأمّة وتارة للناس
كافة عظمة الإلهية وصولة كبرياء المتكلم به وجلاله كقوله تعالى: ﴿قل
هو الله أحد﴾[24] إلى آخرها، وقوله: ﴿يأيها الرسول بلّغ ما أنزل إليك
من ربّك﴾ الآية[25] ، وقوله: ﴿قل للمؤمّنين يغضّوا من أبصارهم﴾ الآية[26] ،
وقوله: ﴿قل يأهل الكتاب تعالوا إلى كلمة سواء بيننا وبينكم﴾ الآية[27] ،
وقوله: ﴿يا معشر الجنّ والأنس﴾ الآية[28] ، وقوله ﴿ألم أعهد إليكم يا بني
آدم﴾ الآية[29].

* 29v   وهكذا من أوّله إلى آخره يخاطب عباده * طورًا يصف جلاله وعظمته
ونعوت الكمال الأكمل والكبرياء الأعظم وطورًا يسمّي نفسه بأسمائه
الحسنى الذاتية التي منها اسمه الله الإله الحقّ وبأسمائه الصفاتية التي منها اسمه
الحيّ القيوم العليّ العظيم ، وبأسمائه الفعلية التي منها اسمه الخالق الباري
المصوّر الرزّاق ، وبأسمائه الإضافية التي منها اسمه الأوّل الآخر الظاهر الباطن ،
وبأسمائه النسبية المتخلّق بمسمّياتها عباده طلبًا لكمالهم التي منها اسمه الحنّان
المنّان الرؤوف الرحيم الودود الشكور الغفور ، وبأسمائه الأفعلية للمبالغة التي
منها اسمه الأعزّ الأكرم الأرحم .

وتارة ينعت لهم تنزيهه وعزّته ووحدانيته وأحديته ، ويحذّر[30] من الشرك
به وإنه ممّا لا يغفره ولا يسامح به وتارة يعرّف الأمّة أمر دينهم وكيفية الصوم
والصلاة والحجّ والزكاة وتارة يأمر بالعدل والإحسان والمعروف ويحذّر من
الظلم والبغي وينهي عن الفحشاء والمنكر ويندب إلى أدب الدين والدنيا وإلى
مكارم الأخلاق ويدعو إلى دار

surrounding areas,[10] and other things that had taken place and were to take place as are reported in it. And you would also know from the incisiveness of its words and the exalted form of address in it, sometimes to the Prophet, sometimes to the community and sometimes to all people, the divine majesty, and the irresistible grandeur and greatness of the One speaking through it, such as the words of the exalted One, 'Say he is Allah, the one' to its end, his words, 'O messenger, make known that which hath been revealed unto thee from thy Lord' and the rest of the verse, his words, 'Tell the believing men to lower their gaze' and the rest of the verse, his words, 'Say, O people of the scripture! Come to an agreement between us and you' and the rest of the verse, his words, 'O company of jinn and men' and the rest of the verse, and his words, 'Did I not charge you, O ye sons of Adam' and the rest of the verse.

He addresses his servants in this way from its beginning to its end. (29v) At times he describes his glory and greatness, and the qualities of most perfect perfection and most sublime grandeur, and at times he names himself by his beautiful essential names, such as God, the Divinity and the Truth; by his attributive names, such as the Living, the Self-subsistent, the Exalted and the Sublime; by his active names, such as Creator, Initiator, Shaper and Sustainer; by his relative names, such as the First, the Last, the Evident, the Hidden; by his imputed names of relation, upon hearing which his servants attempt to perfect themselves, such as the Tender, the Gracious, the Benevolent, the Merciful, the Loving, the Praiseworthy and the Forgiving; by his names which are in the superlative for the sake of intensiveness, such as the most Majestic, the most Noble and the most Merciful.[11]

Sometimes he describes to them his transcendence, power, unity and singleness, warns about associating with himself as something he will not forgive or tolerate. Sometimes he introduces to the community the decrees of their religion and the manner of fasting, praying, pilgrimage and charity. Sometimes he commands justice, right action and fairness, warns against wrongdoing and injustice, forbids vileness and abomination, enjoins proper conduct in affairs of religion and the world and the good qualities of morality, invites to the abode of

---

[10] Cf. S. IX: 29.

[11] This categorisation of God's attributes resembles trends evident in later classical Islamic creeds, such as those of al-Nasafī, al-Ījī and al-Sanūsī; cf. W.M. Watt, *Islamic Creeds*, Edinburgh, 1994, pp. 80–97.

السعادة ويذكر ما أعدّ الله لأهل الطاعة من الكرامة والنعيم الدائم * مفصّلاً

موضّحًا للذي أجمله المسيح بقوله في الإنجيل: "إنكم صائرون إلى حياة أبدية "

ولم يذكر كيفيتها بل أحال التفصيل[31] والبيان على نبيّنا المسمّى منه أركون

العالم كما تقدّم ذكره ، فإن نبيّنا صلم القائل في الدار الآخرة وفي وصف

الجنّة والنار ما لم يقله المسيح فيهما[32] لأن المسيح كان عالمًا بقصور أذهان

أهل زمنه واليهود وتكذيبهم وكثرة جدلهم ومحاجتهم واختلافهم على

أنبيائهم بالاعتراضات كما بيّناه قبل .

وتارة يبيّن في هذا الكتاب أمر الحلال والحرام والمشتبه وتبيين أحوال

النساء والرضاع والولادة وقسمة المواريث وكلّ ما هو في سير[33] الأولين من

التشريع وكلّ ما يقتضيه العقل السليم من تكملة النفوس البشرية بأمر المعاش

والمعاد ومثل ذلك .

---

[31] A: على تفصيل   [32] A: فيها   [33] This word is corrected in the margin from زير
in A; B: زير

bliss, and recalls the everlasting munificence and grace that God has promised to the obedient. (30r) This gives detail and clarity to what Christ speaks about in general terms when he says in the Gospel, 'You will obtain everlasting life'.[12] He does not mention the manner of this, but leaves the detailed exposition and explanation to our Prophet, whom he calls the Ruler of the world, as has been mentioned above.[13] For our Prophet (may God bless him and give him peace) said things about the hereafter and the description of paradise and hell that Christ never did, because Christ was aware of the modest intellects of the people of his time, and of the Jews with their denials and many disputes, arguments and opposition to their prophets with protests, as we have explained above.

Sometimes in this book he makes clear the decree concerning what is permitted, what is forbidden and what is uncertain, and gives clear details about the circumstances of women, fostering, childbirth, the divisions of inheritance, all the legislation that is in the writings of those before, and everything that sound reason requires concerning the perfection of human souls in the conduct of this life and the hereafter, and suchlike.

---

[12] Cf. e.g. Mtt XIX: 29.
[13] Cf. § 8 above.

فصل

في هذا الكتاب العزيز مع ذلك حجج قطعية مسكتة وبراهين قطعية مبهتة وإلزامات مفحمة ومبكية ودلالات واضحة يعجز عن الإتيان بمثلها الفيلسوف المبرهن والجدلي المحتجّ ، ولا يوجد في التوراة ولا الإنجيل مثلها لا في الإيجاز والبلاغة والجمع للمعاني ولا في الإعجاز والعزّة والصولة .

فمن ذلك إخباره للنبي صلم عن اليهود المنكرين نزول الإنجيل * والقرآن من السماء بقوله: ﴿وما قدّروا الله حقّ قدره﴾ ، أي عرفوه حقّ معرفته ، ﴿ إذ قالوا ما أنزل الله على بشر من شيء﴾[1] إلى قوله: ﴿ثمّ ذرهم في خوضهم يلعبون﴾[2] أي بالمقاييس الفاسدة والعقول المكادة المحجوبة بالنظر في الأصوات والحروف والأدوات الجسمية والكتفية والقارع والمنقرع والتجويز وكلّ ما هو من صفات المخلوقين، فإنّ القياس به باطل والحكم به لعب وما هو فوق أطوار العقول فإنه لا يتعقّل.

ومن ذلك قوله للنبي أيضًا: ﴿ألم تر إلى الذي حاجّ ابراهيم في ربّه﴾ الآية[3] ، ومن ذلك قوله تعالى: ﴿وأسروا قولكم أو اجهروا به﴾[4] إلى قوله: ﴿الخبير﴾ [5]، وقوله تعالى: ﴿وضرب لنا مثلاً ونسي خلقه﴾[6] إلى آخر السورة ، وقوله تعالى: ﴿أم اتخذوا آلهة من الأرض هم ينشرون﴾[7] إلى قوله: ﴿معرضون﴾ [8]، وقوله: ﴿ما اتخذ الله من ولد﴾[9] إلى قوله: ﴿فتعالى عمّا يشركون﴾[10] ، وقوله: ﴿وما أمروا

---

[1] S. VI: 91. [2] *Ibid.* [3] S. II: 258. [4] S. LXVII: 13. [5] *Ibid.*: 14 [6] S. XXXVI: 78. [7] S. XXI: 21. [8] *Ibid.*: 22-4. [9] S. XXIII: 91. [10] *Ibid.*: 92.

38.   *Section [Three]*

In addition to such things in this esteemed book, there are decisive
arguments that impose silence, decisive proofs that cause bewilder-
ment, compelling points that evoke perplexity and ruefulness, and
demonstrations so clear that the philosopher, the dialectician and the
contentious debater cannot produce anything similar. And their like
is not to be found in the Torah or the Gospel, either in conciseness,
comprehensiveness and all-embracing significance, or in inimitability,
power and incisiveness.

An example is his declaration to the Prophet (may God bless him
and give him peace) about the Jews who denied that the Gospel
(30v) and Qur'an were revealed from heaven, in his words, 'And
they measure not the power of Allah its true measure (that is, have
full awareness of it) when they say, Allah hath nought revealed unto
a human being. [Say: Who revealed the book which Moses brought,
a light and guidance for mankind, which ye have put on parchments
which ye show, but ye hide much, and ye were taught that which ye
knew not yourselves nor your fathers? Say: Allah.] Then leave them to
their ploy of cavilling', that is, by false gauging and crafty speculation
concealed from sight, about sounds and letters, organs of the body and
shoulders, striking and being struck, the permitted, and everything by
which created beings are characterised.[1] Drawing analogy from such
is futile, and judging by it is a waste, and what is above the limits of
intellects cannot be comprehended.

Other examples are also his words to the Prophet, 'Bethink thee
of him who had an argument with Abraham about his Lord' and the
rest of the verse; likewise the words of the exalted One, 'And keep
your opinion secret or proclaim it' to his word 'the Aware'; the words
of the exalted One, 'And he hath coined for us a similitude, and hath
forgotten the fact of his creation' to the end of the *Sūra*; the words
of the exalted One, 'Or have they chosen gods from the earth who
raise the dead?' to his words, 'they are averse'; his words, 'Allah hath
not chosen any son' to his words, 'and exalted be he over all that
they ascribe as partners'; and his words, 'When they were bidden to

---

[1] Al-Dimashqī appears to be referring to quibbles over methods of reciting
scripture. If this is so, his general argument may refer to the Jews making contrasts
between the Torah and the Qur'an on the basis of the different ways in which they
are articulated.

إلا ليعبدوا إلهًا واحدًا لا إله إلا هو سبحانه عمّا يشركون﴾[11]، إذ من المستحيل عقلاً وشرعًا أن يكون للعالم إلهان اثنان قديمان واجبا[12] الوجود معًا أو يكون أحدهما محدثاً فلا يكون إلهًا.

ومن ذلك أيضًا قوله تعالى عن ابراهيم عليه السلام لمّا كسر الأصنام وقال له قومه: ﴿أنت فعلت هذا بآلهتنا يا ابراهيم. قال: بل فعله كبيرهم هذا﴾ الآية[13] فرجعوا إلى أنفسهم ونكسوا رؤوسهم * حياءً واعترافًا وقالوا: ﴿لقد علمت ما هؤلاء ينطقون﴾[14] ، قال: ﴿أفتعبدون ما تنحتون؟﴾ الآية[15] ، وقوله تعالى: ﴿أفعيينا بالخلق الأوّل﴾ الآية[16] ، وقوله تعالى: ﴿ومن يدع مع الله إلهًا آخر لا برهان له به﴾[17] ، وقوله تعالى: ﴿وقضى ربّك ألا تعبدوا إلا إيّاه﴾ إلى آخر الوصيّة التي جمعت ما في سائر الكتب المتقدّمة[18] ، وقوله تعالى: ﴿يأيها الناس إن كنتم في ريب من البعث﴾[19] إلى قوله: ﴿وأنّ الله يبعث من في القبور﴾[20] ، وقوله تعالى: ﴿ولقد خلقنا الإنسان من سلالة من طين﴾[21] إلى قوله: ﴿فتبارك الله أحسن الخالقين﴾[22]. وكثير مثل هذه الآيات البيّنات في هذا الكتاب المجيد.

ثمّ فيه للأمّة من التشريع والتعاليم والتعريفات ما وصّى به الله سبحانه وتعالى رسله الكرام نوحًا وابراهيم وموسى وعيسى ونادى منادي إعجازه على رؤوس الأشهاد: قل يا محمّد لأهل الكتاب والجحود والعناد وجمع الكفرة والأضداد إئتوا بمثل هذا القرآن أو بعشر سور مثله أو بسورة واحدة من مثله ﴿وادعوا من استطعتم﴾ الآية[23] ، ﴿فلو اجتمعت الإنس والجنّ﴾ الآية[24] فعجزوا وأفحموا وخسئوا وخسروا خسرانًا مبينًا.

39. فتدبّروه أيها المدّعون أنهم قد حصلوه عندهم وطالعوه وفهموه بحسب مبلغهم من العلم به

* 31r *

---

[11] S. IX: 31. [12] A and B read: إلهين اثنين قديمين واجي [13] S. XXI: 62-3. [14] *Ibid*.: 65. [15] S. XXXVII: 95-6. [16] S. L: 15. [17] S. XXIII: 117. [18] S. XVII: 23; وقوله تعالى ... المتقدمة: these words are supplied in the same hand in the margin in A. [19] S. XXII: 5. [20] *Ibid*.: 6-7. [21] S. XXIII: 12. [22] *Ibid*.: 13-14. [23] S. XI: 13. [24] Cf. S. XVII: 88.

worship only one God. There is no God save him, be he glorified from all that they ascribe as partner', since it is impossible in terms of reason and revelation for the world to have two eternal gods who would both be necessarily existent, or for one of them to be temporal and therefore not a god.

Further examples are the words of the exalted One concerning Abraham (peace be upon him), when he broke the idols and his people said to him, 'Is it thou who hast done this to our gods, O Abraham? He said, But this, their chief hath done it' and the rest of the verse. 'Then gathered they apart,' and 'they were utterly confounded' (31r) in shame and admission, and they said, 'Well thou knowest that those speak not'. He said, 'Worship ye then that which you yourselves do carve?' and the next verse; the words of the exalted One, 'Were we then worn out by the first creation?' and the rest of the verse; the words of the exalted One, 'He who crieth unto any other god along with Allah hath no proof thereof'; the words of the exalted One, 'Thy Lord hath decreed that ye worship none save him' to the end of the counsel that brings together what is in all the earlier books;[2] the words of the exalted One, 'O mankind! If ye are in doubt concerning the resurrection' to his words ' and because Allah will raise those who are in the graves'; the words of the exalted One, 'Verily, we created man from a product of wet earth', to his words 'So blessed be God the best of all creators', and many others like these clear verses in this glorious book.

It also contains legislation, instructions and directions to the community which God, blessed and exalted, entrusted to his noble messengers Noah, Abraham, Moses and Jesus and to the Summoner who publicly proclaimed its inimitability: Say, Muḥammad, to the People of the Book, the repudiators, the obstinate and all the unbelievers and antagonists, Produce a like to this Qur'an, or ten *Sūras* like it, or one *Sūra* like it, 'and call on all ye can' and the next verse. Even if 'mankind and the jinn should assemble' and the rest of the verse, they would be incapable, dumbfounded, forced to retract and made to suffer the most palpable loss.

39. So reflect on it, you who claim you have obtained it, read it and comprehended it,[3] according to your immense knowledge about

---

[2] This and the verses in the *Sūra* down to 39 contain ethical teachings similar to those in Jewish and Christian scripture.

[3] Once again he refers back to the very opening of the Christians' *Letter*, § 5.

وانصفوا لأنفسكم من أنفسكم في ما ذكرته وبيّنته لكم من بعض ما
في القرآن المجيد ، هل إذا قرأتم التوارة والإنجيل وتدبّرتم ألفاظهما * بأيّ   * 31v
لغة شئتم تجدونهما مثلما وصفت في كتابنا أو قريبًا منه؟ بل تجدون التوراة
حكايات من حاك يحكي عن الله تعالى عن موسى في حياته وبعد موته وعن
أشياء منكورة لا ينبغي أن تحكى عن الأنبياء كفلان وزناه بابنته وفلان
وفعله.

ومع ذلك ففيها كلام الله تعالى متفرّق ومحرّف وسبب ذلك خيانة اليهود
وتحريفهم ﴿الكلم عن مواضعه﴾[25] بحسب أغراضهم ولأن بخت نصّر الذي
هو بوخذ ناصر الكلداني البابلي المخرّب أحرق التوراة عند خراب البيت
المقدّس وقتل اليهود حتى أنه لم يبق[26] منهم يحفظ التوراة إلا رجل واحد[27]
أملاها من صدره ، وكذلك الملك أنطهيوس أحرقها أيضًا وأقام صنمه
بالقدس ولأن موسى عليلم ألقى الألواح من يده غضبًا على قومه بني إسرائيل
حين عبدوا العجل ، فغاص بعضها في أرض البيت المقدّس وصار بعضها
إلى السماء ، ولأنّ اليهود جاءتهم العشر كلمات الوصايا بدلاً ممّا ذهب من
التوراة ولأنه بين توراة السامرة وتوراة اليهود اختلاف في اللفظ والمعنى وهم
يزعمون أنّ التوراة التي بأيديكم مبدّلة مغيّرة ، ولأنّ اليهود يزعمون أنّ عزرا
الكاهن استجدّ لهم التوراة وكتبها بأرض بابل ، ويزعم السامرة أنّ عزرا
المذكور كتبت الملائكة * بيده   * 32r

---

[25] S. IV: 46; S. V: 13.   [26] A and B: تبق   [27] A and B: رجلا واحدا

it, and accept with fairness among yourselves what I have mentioned and explained to you about some of what is in the glorious Qur'an. If you read the Torah and Gospel and consider the words in them in any language you wish (31v), will you find that they are comparable to the things I have described in our book or similar to them? On the contrary, you will find that the Torah comprises reports from a narrator who tells about God the exalted, about Moses during his lifetime and after his death and about abominable things which should not be reported about prophets, such as a certain one and his intercourse with his daughter,[4] and another and his doings.

In addition to this, it contains the word of God the exalted in piecemeal and corrupted form. The reason is the Jews' treachery and their altering 'the words from their places' in accordance with their own purposes. Further, Bakht Naṣṣar, who was Bukhdh Nāṣir the Chaldean from Babylon, the destroyer, burnt the Torah during the destruction of Jerusalem and killed so many Jews that there was no one left among them who could remember the Torah, except one man who dictated it by heart.[5] In the same way, king Antiochus also burnt it and erected an image of himself in the holy place.[6] Further, Moses (peace be upon him) threw down the tablets from his hand in anger at his people, the children of Israel, when they were worshipping the calf, and some parts fell into the land of Jerusalem and others flew up to heaven.[7] Further, the Ten Commandments came to the Jews in place of what was lost of the Torah. Further, between the Torah of the Samaritans and the Torah of the Jews there is difference in wording and meaning, with them claiming that the Torah which you possess has been changed and altered.[8] Further, the Jews claim that Ezra the priest made a new Torah for them and wrote it in Babylon, and the Samaritans claim that the angel (32r) wrote the Torah by

---

[4] This appears to be an allusion to the incident of Lot and his daughters in Genesis XIX: 30-8.

[5] Cf. Ezra VII: 6, 10, 14, 25, and 2 Esdras XIV: 23-43, and further n. 9 below.

[6] Cf. 1 Maccabees I: 54-7, and Daniel XI: 31 and XII: 11, referring to the desecration of the Jerusalem temple under the Seleucid king Antiochus IV Epiphanes (175-163 BCE) in 168, when copies of the Torah were burnt and an altar to Zeus was set up, with maybe an image of Antiochus as the god.

[7] Cf. Exodus XXXII: 19-20. The scattering of the pieces, as described here, must have been known to al-Dimashqī through oral legend.

[8] Al-Shahrastānī, *Milal*, p. 171, says that the Samaritans claim the Torah was originally written in their language and later translated into *Sūriyāniyya*.

التوراة بلا اختياره ، وأنّ الذين كانوا حوله ينظرون إلى أصابعه تتحرّك رقمًا للحروف وهم ينقلونها أوّلاً فأوّلاً ، ولأنّ في تواريخ اليهود أيضًا أنّ التوراة لمّا عدمت جاءهم بالتوراة أناس من مدينة ماسّة بأقصى المغرب ، كانت في مغارة هناك على ما يزعمون ، ومثل هذه الأشياء التي ينبغي السكوت عنها إجلالاً لما في التوراة يومنا هذا من بقيّة كلام الله تعالى.

40.   وكذلك إذا طالعتم الإنجيل المجموع من البشارات الأربع[28] وليس لكم اليوم إنجيل غيره تجدونه أربعة[29] تواريخ أرّخها[30] متى ولوقا ومرقس ويوحنا ، فأمّا متى فابتدأ بذكر مولد المسيح ونسبه إلى داود وذكر بشارة الملك لمريم

---

[28] A and B: الأربعة   [29] A and B: أربع   [30] A and B: ورخها

the hand of this Ezra without his having free choice, and that those who were around him saw his fingers moving to write the letters and they took them away one by one.[9] Further again, in the histories of the Jews, when the Torah was lost people from the town of Māssa in the furthermost west brought the Torah to them: according to what they claim it was in a cave there.[10] There are things similar to these, but we should be silent about them out of respect for what remains of God the exalted's word in the Torah today.

40. In the same way, when you read the Gospel assembled from the four versions—and you have no Gospel apart from this today—you find that it is four histories compiled by Matthew, Luke, Mark and John.[11] Matthew begins with the birth of Christ and his descent from David, then he mentions the angel's annunciation of him to Mary

---

[9] Cf. 2 Esdras XIV: 23-43. In Rabbinic literature Ezra was regarded almost as a second Moses (L. Ginzberg, *The Legends of the Jews*, Philadelphia, 1911-38, vol. IV, p. 355: 'If Moses had not anticipated him, Ezra would have received the Torah'), though the Samaritans execrated him because they considered he had corrupted the script of the Torah (R.J. Coggins, *Samaritans and Jews*, Oxford, 1975, pp.72f.). Al-Dimashqī appears to be following accepted Muslim tradition in what he says, since al-Thaʿlabī, *Qiṣaṣ al-anbiyāʾ*, Beirut, 1994, p. 346, similarly describes Ezra tying a pen to each finger and writing with all of them until he had finished the Torah; cf. further H. Lazarus-Yafeh, *Intertwined Worlds, Medieval Islam and Biblical Criticism*, Princeton, 1992, ch 3.

Almost as an anticipation of this criticism, Peter the Venerable in the sixth/twelfth century argues that Ezra could not have established a false law suddenly and so the original law must have been returned from Babylon, *Liber contra Sectam sive Haeresim Saracenorum*, ed J. Kritzeck, *Peter the Venerable and Islam*, Princeton, 1964, pp. 254-5 (cf. p. 179).

[10] In the *Nukhba*, p. 23.8, al-Dimashqī mentions Māssa as a town in Morocco beyond Marrākash, Draʿa and Sijilmassa. This identifies it as the present-day Massa on the Atlantic coast south of Agadir, as far west from Damascus as anyone could travel on land. But what of the Torah in the cave? Jewish scriptures hidden in this way were known to a number of earlier authors, including the Patriarch Timothy I (cf. O. Braun, 'Der Brief des Katholicos Timotheus I über biblische Studien des 9-Jahrhunderts', *Oriens Christianus* 1, 1901, pp. 304-5, Syriac text and German translation; there is an English translation in C. Thiede, *The Dead Sea Scrolls and the Jewish Origins of Christianity*, London, 2000, p.48), and the Muslim theologian Abū ʿĪsā al-Warrāq, who mentions a Jewish sect intriguingly called the *Maghāriba* or *Maghāriyya* (cf. D. Thomas, 'Abū ʿĪsā al-Warrāq and the History of Religions', *Journal of Semitic Studies* 41, 1996, pp. 277f., and notes).

[11] Al-Dimashqī again refers to these four reconstructions of the original *Injīl* in §§ 43 and 47. Cf. al-Jāḥiẓ, *Fī al-radd ʿalā al-Naṣārā*, ed. J. Finkel in *Thalāth rasāʾil li-Abī ʿUthmān al-Jāḥiẓ*, Cairo, 1926, p. 24, and ʿAbd al-Jabbār, *Al-mughnī fī abwāb al-tawḥīd wa-al-ʿadl*, vol. V, ed. M.M. al-Khuḍayrī, Cairo, 1965, pp. 142f., who both regard the evangelists as unreliable and possibly liars.

عليلم به ، وساق بعض ما جاء في كتابنا في سورة مريم ثمّ ذكر وصايا ووقائع وبلغ إلى ذكر ليلة الفصح وسهر المسيح ووصيّته للتلاميذ ثمّ ذكر الصلب والقتل والهوان والدفن والقيام بعد الموت والتراءي لبعض التلاميذ في العليّة وفي مركب الصيد ببحر طبرية أو البحر ، وختم كلامه.

وأمّا لوقا ومرقس فإنهما تقاربا في حكايتيهما عن المسيح ونسبه ووصاياه وما جرى له وساقاه إلى السهر ليلة الفصح والتضرّع إلى الله تعالى والعهد إلى التلاميذ وتعريفهم بأنه ذاهب عنهم ، ثمّ أبلغاه إلى الصلب والقتل والقيام

* 32v   كما ذهب إليه متى مع اختلاف ومناقضات في الشهادة والخبر.

وأمّا يوحنّا فإنه ابتدأ كلامه بما معناه أنه في البدء كانت الكلمة وأنّ الكلمة صفة تابعة للموصوف والموصوف قديم خالق ، فالكلمة كذلك . يريد بقوله الكلمة أنها المسيح ، ثمّ ساق من الخبر قريبًا ممّا ساقوه الثلاثة قبله بزيادة في القول ونقص[31] ومناقضة فيه ، ثمّ لمّا بلغ إلى الصلب والموت والدفن والقيام قال ما معناه أنّ مريم المجدلانية قامت يوم الأحد على مدفن المسيح بعد الصلب فرأت الحجر مدهوهًا ، و لم تَرَ جسد المسيح فبكت وقالت: "أين ربّي؟ من أخذ ربّي؟ أين ذهبوا بربّي؟" فهي كذلك في بستان الفاخوري إذ سمعت صوت المسيح قائلاً: "مريم" فالتفتت فرأته في طرف البستان فقالت له: "رابوني" أي "يا معلّم" ، وقصدت إليه فمنعها وأوصاها وصيّة إلى التلاميذ وأن يجتمعوا به قبل أن يصعد إلى السماء.

---

[31] Or perhaps read ونقض, 'contradiction'.

(peace be upon her), and continues with some of *Mary* in our Book.[12] Then he mentions instructions and incidents, and reaches the account of the night of the Passover, Christ's vigil and his instruction to the disciples. Then he mentions the crucifixion, the killing and disgrace, the burial and resurrection after death, and the appearance to some of the disciples in the upper room and in a fishing boat on the Sea of Tiberias or the sea. Then he ends his story.[13]

Luke and Mark are close to each other in their accounts about Christ, his descent, instructions, and what happened to him. They follow him to the vigil on the night of the Passover, the impassioned prayer to God the exalted, the testimony to the disciples and disclosure to them that he was departing from them. Then they bring him to the crucifixion, death and resurrection, (32v) as Matthew does, though with differences and contradictions in the witness and report.

John begins his story with what in essence is, 'In the beginning was the Word, and the Word was an attribute belonging to the One attributed, and the One attributed was eternal and Creator. This was the Word.'[14] He means by his reference to the Word that it was Christ. Then he closely follows in the report the three before, with additions, omissions and contradictions in what he says. Then when he reaches the crucifixion, death, burial and resurrection, he says what in essence is that on the Sunday Mary Magdalene came to stand near Christ's sepulchre after the crucifixion, and she saw that the stone had been removed. She could not see Christ's body and she wept, saying, 'Where is my lord? Who has taken my lord? Where have they gone with my lord?' She was in this state in the potter's garden when she heard Christ's voice say, 'Mary'. She turned around and saw him at the end of the garden, and she said to him, '*Rābbūnī*', which means 'Master'. She made straight for him but he stopped her, and gave her instructions for the disciples, that they should all come to him before he ascended into heaven.[15]

---

[12] The annunciation story only appears in Lk I: 26-38 (cf. Mtt I: 18).

[13] These post-resurrection appearances do not occur in the Gospel of Matthew, and are more reminiscent of John.

[14] Cf. Jn I: 1. Al-Dimashqī evidently knows more about the Gospel of John than the other Gospels.

[15] Cf. Jn XX: 1 and 11-17. Al-Dimashqī summarises the Gospel text closely, though he introduces two references from Mtt, XXVII: 7-10, to the Potter's field which the Jewish priests bought with Judas' returned pieces of silver as a burial ground for foreigners, and XXVIII: 7, to the angel's instruction to Mary of Magdala

فيا[32] هؤلاء العقلاء ، أين كلام الله العظيم وكلام المسيح من هذه الحكاية المخبّر بها امرأة كانت مجنونة يصرعها سبعة[33] شياطين وبرئت بزعمكم؟ وهلّا ذكر هذه القصّة متّى ولوقا ومرقس فيما ذكروه ، وهو مهمّ عظيم جدًا ، مع أن يوحنا أصغرهم وأبعدهم عهدًا بالمسيح؟ فتدبّروا ذلك واعرفوا الحقّ في خلال التدبّر ، واعلموا أنّ الرسول[34] * صلم أرسل إلى العالم كافة لإصلاح ما فسدوا وللتوبيخ لهم على ما أحدثوا وأشركوا وظنّوا وغلطوا واختلفوا وتصديقًا للمسيح في خبره عن أركون العالم المسمّى بارقليطس أي رسول الله الآتي من عنده والمنبثق من فيه روح الحقّ الذي هو القرآن المجيد ، كلام ربّ العالمين.

* 33r

41. ولمّا صدّق الإنجيل التوراة وصحّحها وصدّقت التوراة الإنجيل وصحّحته وصدّقهما القرآن المجيد وصحّحهما وصدّقاه من قبل وصحّحاه شهد البعض للبعض على تطاول المدد وامتداد الدهور ، فإنّ بين التوراة والإنجيل ألف سنة ، وذلك من خروج موسى من مصر ببني إسرائيل وإلى ولادة المسيح عليهما السلام وبين ظهور المسيح وظهور نبيّنا محمّد نحو ستماية وبضع وثلاثين سنة. وجاء القرآن مبيّنًا ما كان قبل في هذه المدّة وفيما قبلها إلى آدم عليكم وذاكرًا كيفية بدء الخليقة وكيفية عودها بالإنطواء وعلم ما كان وعلم ما يكون ونبّأ ما بين الأمّة

---

[32] B:فيه (wrongly). [33] A and B: سبع [34] A and B: رسول

People of intelligence, how different are the words of God the almighty and those of Christ from this account given by a woman who had been possessed, seized by seven devils and recovered, according to your claim! And why do not Matthew, Luke and Mark include this story in what they recount, since together with them he is of such great importance, although John was younger than them and after them in coming to know about Christ?[16] Reflect on this, and recognise the truth as you do so. And know that the Messenger (33r) (may God bless him and give him peace) was sent to the whole world in order to put right what they had made wrong and to rebuke them for their invention, polytheism, presumption, mistakenness and disagreement, and to confirm that Christ was true in his announcement about the Ruler of the world named Paraclete, the messenger of God who would come from him and from whose mouth would proceed the spirit of truth, which is the glorious Qur'an, the words of the Lord of the worlds.[17]

41. Since the Gospel confirms and corrects the Torah, the Torah confirms and corrects the Gospel, and the glorious Qur'an confirms and corrects them both, and they both correct and confirm it in advance, each witnesses to each over the extent of time and lengthening of the ages.[18] For between the Torah and the Gospel there were a thousand years, which was from the exodus of Moses out of Egypt with the People of Israel up to the birth of Christ (peace be upon them both), and between the appearance of Christ and that of our Prophet Muḥammad there were about six hundred and some thirty years.[19] The Qur'an came to explain what had taken place in that period, and in what had preceded that up to Adam (upon him be peace). It recounted the manner in which the natural order began and the manner of its structure in its complexity, it taught about what has been and what will be, informed about what is within the community,

---

and her companion when they came to the tomb to tell the disciples to join Jesus in Galilee.

[16] Mtt XXVIII: 1 and parallels.

[17] Cf. § 8 above.

[18] SS. V: 46, III: 3.

[19] The figure of a round thousand years for the period between Moses and Christ's birth is understandable on symbolic grounds, but the figure of about 630 years between the appearance of Christ and of Muḥammad is less easy to square. In § 56 al-Dimashqī gives the figure of about 640 years between the birth of Christ and the birth of Muḥammad; cf. Section 5, n. 32.

ووصف المسيح وأمّه بما لا يحسن³⁵ الغلاة أن يصفوهما بمثله من الشرف
والفخار والعلو والإصطفاء والنزاهة والتطهير الذي لا يليق غيره بهما
والشهادة للمسيح بأنه أحد أولي العزم من الرسل أصحاب الرسالة العامة
كما * نبّأ إرميا برؤية الشعوب والربوات بين يديه ويدي نبيّنا صلم.

ومن البيّن الواضح أنّ المسيح لم يرسل رسله إلى الناس تبرعًا منه بل بإذن
الله وأمره له ، وكذلك محمّد صلم لم تنقد³⁶ الأمم³⁷ إلى³⁸ دعوته والدخول
في دينه وشرعته وهابته ملوك الأرض قاطبة تبرعًا منه واستحبابًا من غير أن
يأمره الله تعالى بذلك ، بل بأمره وإرساله له وتأييده إيّاه.

وفيما استشهدت به لكم بأنه لم يأت بغتة ولا مفاجأة للعالم ولا رسالته
إلى العرب خاصة بل إلى الناس كافة كفاية ومقنع. ولو بسّطنا القول في ذكر
محاسن الشريعة وجوامع الآداب والكمالات في الصلاة والصيام والحجّ
والإذكار والتسبيحات لجاء في كتب عديدة وفيما أوضحناه وبيّناه كفاية.

---

³⁵ A and B: يحسنوا   ³⁶ A and B: تنقاد   ³⁷ Corrected in A from الأمة; B: الأمة.
³⁸ A and B: لي (wrongly).

described Christ and his mother in terms that exaggerators would not
see fit to employ, such as nobility, glory, exaltedness, election, purity
and chastity, because nothing more is appropriate for them,[20] and
bore witness that Christ was one among the messengers, the holders
of universal apostleship most entitled to greatness, as (33v) Jeremiah
prophesied in his vision of the people and myriads who were before
him and before our Prophet (peace be upon him).[21]

It is quite clear that Christ did not send his apostles to the people
on his own account, but with God's permission and his ordering him.
Similarly with Muḥammad (peace be upon him), the nations did not
yield to his call, or enter into his religion and revealed law, or the
kings of the whole world stand in awe of him on his own account or
out of love, without God the exalted ordering him to do this, but by
his ordering, sending and supporting him in it.

What I have presented to you about him, that he did not come suddenly or unexpectedly to the world, and that his apostleship was not to
the Arabs specifically but to all people, is sufficient and convincing.[22]
If we were to make our exposition any longer by stating the virtues
of the revealed law, and the host of elegances and perfections in worship, fasting, pilgrimage, remembrances, and hymns of adoration, it
would take up numerous books. What we have explained and made
clear is sufficient.

---

[20] By the name *ghulāh*, 'exaggerators', al-Dimashqī means the Christians who go
further than these attributions of excellence, in imputing divinity to Jesus and semi-
divinity to Mary; cf. S. IV: 171.

[21] Cf. §§ 10 and 25 above. The allusion to the prophecy here is a reminder that
if Jesus is the rider on the ass he is succeeded by the rider on the camel, and thus
cannot be the last one sent by God. Al-Dimashqī's gloss that he was accompanied
by a multitude underlines the idea that he was only one among many.

[22] This is another reference back to the Christians' remark at the beginning of
their *Letter*, that Muḥammad had been sent to the pagan Arabs alone, § 5.

فصل

ثمّ قلتم في الرسالة سياقًا:

وهذا وغيره أوجب لنا التمسّك بديننا وأن لا نهمل مذهبنا ولا نرفض ما معنا ولا نتبع غير السيّد المسيح كلمة الله وحواريّيه[1] الذين أرسلهم[2] إلينا أنذرونا بلغاتنا وسلّموا إلينا ديننا الذي قد عظّمه هذا الكتاب بقوله في سورة الحديد: ﴿لقد أرسلنا رسلنا بالبيّنات وأنزلنا معهم الكتاب والميزان﴾ الآية[3]. وقال في سورة

البقرة: ﴿فبعث الله النبيّين مبشّرين ومنذرين﴾ * الآية[4]، فأعنى بقوله أنبياءه المبشّرين ورسله المنذرين الحواريّين الذين داروا في جميع العالم وبشّروا بالكتاب الواحد الذي هو الإنجيل المقدّس، لأنّه لو كان أعنى عن ابراهيم وموسى وداود ومحمّد لكان قال: "ومعهم الكتب" لأنّ كلّ واحد منهم جاء بكتاب دون غيره ولم يقل إلّا الكتاب الواحد الذي هو الإنجيل الطاهر.

ثمّ يشهد هذا الكتاب أنّهم أنصارالله، حيث يقول: ﴿كما[5] قال عيسى ابن مريم للحواريّين من أنصاري إلى الله قال الحواريّون نحن أنصار الله﴾[6] إلى قوله: ﴿ظاهرين﴾[7].

وأمّا تعظيمه لإنجيلنا وكتابنا الذي في أيدينا فيقول: ﴿وأنزلنا إليك الكتاب بالحقّ مصدّقًا لما بين يديه﴾ الآية[8]، وقال: ﴿ألم الله لا إله إلّا هو الحيّ القيوم﴾[9] إلى قوله: ﴿للناس﴾[10]، وقال: ﴿ألم ذلك الكتاب لا ريب فيه هدى للمتقين﴾[11] إلى قوله: ﴿المفلحون﴾[12]، فأعنى بالكتاب الإنجيل وبالذين يؤمنون بالغيب نحن النصارى ثمّ أتبع بالقول: ﴿والذين يؤمنون بما أنزل إليك﴾ الآية[13]، فأعنى بهم المسلمين الذين آمنوا بما

---

[1] A and B: وحواريه   [2] B: أرسلها   [3] S. LVII: 25.   [4] S. II: 213.   [5] A and B: إذ
[6] S. LXI: 14.   [7] *Ibid.*   [8] S. V: 48.   [9] S. III: 1.   [10] *Ibid.*: 2-4.   [11] S. II: 1-2.
[12] *Ibid.*: 3-5.   [13] *Ibid.*: 4.

42.   *Section [Four]*

Then you next say in the *Letter*:

> This and other things have obliged us to adhere to our religion, and
> not to forget our doctrine, abandon what we have, or follow anyone
> other than the lord Christ, the Word of God, and his disciples whom
> he sent to us to warn us in our languages and to pass on to us our
> religion, which this book extols in its words in *Iron*, 'We verily sent our
> messengers with clear proofs, and revealed with them the scripture and
> the balance' and the rest of the verse. And in *The Cow* it says, 'And Allah
> sent prophets as bearers of good tidings and as warners' (34r) and the
> rest of the verse, meaning by its words his 'prophets of good tidings'
> and his messengers 'as warners' the disciples, who spread throughout
> the world and proclaimed the one book, the holy Gospel. For if it had
> meant Abraham, Moses, David and Muḥammad it would have said,
> 'and with them the scriptures', because each of them brought a scripture
> different from others.[1] But it only refers to 'the scripture', which is the
> unblemished Gospel.
>
> This book also witnesses that they were helpers of God, for it says,
> 'Even as Jesus son of Mary said unto the disciples: Who are my help-
> ers for Allah? The disciples said: We are Allah's helpers' to his words
> 'the uppermost'.
>
> As for its extolling our Gospel and the book which we possess, it says,
> 'And unto thee have we revealed the scripture and the truth, confirm-
> ing whatever was before it' and the rest of the verse. And it says, 'Alif.
> Lam. Mim. Allah! There is no god save him, the alive, the eternal.
> [He hath revealed unto thee the Scripture with truth, confirming that
> which was before it, even as he revealed the Torah and the Gospel
> aforetime, for a guidance] to mankind'; also 'Alif. Lam. Mim. This is
> the scripture whereof there is no doubt, a guidance to those who ward
> off evil [who believe in the unseen and establish worship, and spend of
> that we have bestowed upon them; and who believe in that which was
> revealed unto thee and that which was before thee, and are certain of
> the hereafter. These depend on guidance from their Lord. These are]
> the successful'. By 'the scripture' it means the Gospel,[2] and by 'who
> believe in the unseen' us Christians. Then it follows with the words,
> 'And who believe in that which is revealed unto thee' and the rest of
> the verse, and by them it means the Muslims who believed in what he

---

[1] For the sake of their argument the Christians accept without question the
Muslim doctrine of the line of messengers and revelations.

[2] The Arabic (translated by Pickthall, the translation we employ throughout, as
'this is the scripture') reads *dhālika al-kitāb*. This unelaborated statement recalls Paul
of Antioch's much more explicit argument that since the verse specifically refers to
'that book' and not 'this book', it cannot mean the Qurʾan but another scripture;
Paul of Antioch, *Risāla*, § 16, and p. 4 above.

أتى به وما أتى من قبله ، وقال في سورة المائدة: ﴿وقفينا على آثارهم بعيسى ابن

مريم﴾[14] إلى قوله: ﴿الفاسقون﴾[15]، وقال في سورة آل عمران: ﴿فإن كذّبوك

فقد كذب رسل من قبلك الآية﴾[16]، فأعني أيضًا بالكتاب المنير[17] الإنجيل * المقدّس *34v

وبالرسل الحواريّين ، وقال أيضًا: ﴿فإن كنت في شكّ ممّا أنزلنا إليك الآية﴾[18]،

فثبت بهذا ما معنا ونفى عن إنجيلنا وكتبنا التي في أيدينا التّهم[19] والتبديل لها .

فقال لكم القائل ، وكليام حاضر: إن قال قائل إن التبديل والتغيير[20] يجوز

أن يكون بعد هذا القول ، فقلتم: إنا نعجب من هذا القول ومن هؤلاء القوم

على علمهم وذكائهم ومعرفتهم كيف يحتجّون علينا بمثل هذا القول. فلو قلنا إنّ

الكتاب الذي في أيديهم هذا قد غيّروه وبدّلوه وكتبوا فيه ما أرادوا واشتهوا

أفكانوا يجوّزون كلامنا؟ فقال لكم: هذا ما لا يجوز ولا يمكن لأحد[21] أن يقوله

أبدًا ولا يمكن أن يتغيّر منه حرف واحد ، فقلتم: فإذا كان الكتاب الذي في أيديهم

باللسان العربي الواحد لا يمكن تغييره ولا تبديل حرف واحد منه ، فكيف يمكن

تغيير كتابنا الذي هو مكتوب باثنين وسبعين لسانًا؟[22]

---

[14] S. V: 46. [15] *Ibid*: 46-7. [16] S. III: 184. [17] So in P1 and P2; B and P3, however, read: المبين [18] S. X: 94. [19] B: اليهم (wrongly). [20] B: والتغيين (wrongly). [21] A and B: أحد . So in P1, P2 and P3. [22] A and B: لسان

brought and what came before him. And it says in *The Table Spread*, 'And we caused Jesus, son of Mary, to follow in their footsteps' to his word 'evil-livers', and in *The Family of 'Imrān*, 'And if they deny thee, even so did they deny messengers who were before thee, [who came with miracles and with the Psalms and with the scripture giving light]', meaning by 'the scripture giving light' the holy (34v) Gospel, and by 'the messengers' the disciples. It also says, 'And if thou art in doubt concerning that which we reveal unto thee [then question those who read the scripture before thee. Verily the truth from thy Lord hath come unto thee. So be not thou of the waverers]', confirming by this what we have, and rejecting any suspicions about the Gospel and books which we possess, and any substitution.

Someone said to you in the presence of Kilyām,[3] 'What if someone should say that substitution and alteration could have taken place after this statement?' You said, 'We are amazed at such a remark and at how these people, despite their knowledge, intelligence and perception, can confront us with such a remark. For if we were to say that they had made alterations and substitutions in the book which they possess today, and had written in it what they wanted and desired, would they tolerate our words?' He said to you, 'This cannot be tolerated, nor should anyone ever say it. It is impossible for a single jot of it to have been altered.' So you said, 'If in the book which they have in the one language of Arabic not one letter can have been altered or substituted, how can our book which is written in seventy-two languages be altered?[4]

---

[3] The *Letter* itself reads *fa-qultu lahum: in qāla qā'il*, in which the author is speaking to the Cypriot scholars he is supposedly consulting. Al-Dimashqī is compelled to change this to an anonymous speaker and add the reference to Kilyām, the messenger who brought the *Letter* from Cyprus (cf. Author's Introduction, n. 9), in order to give some meaning to what has become an intrusion.

[4] This number agrees neatly with the number of Christian sects in some versions of the Ḥadīth about the divisions in Judaism, Christianity and Islam (e.g. Ibn Māja, *Sunan, Kitāb al-fiṭra* no. 17; al-Tirmidhī, *Sunan, Kitāb al-īmān* no. 18; al-Dārimī, *Sunan, Kitāb al-siyar* no. 75). But the source here is most likely the list of nations enumerated in Gen X: 2-31 according to the Septuagint (not the Massoretic text), and the number of disciples sent out by Jesus according to Lk X: 1 and 17 (in some MSS), on which is built the inference that all these nations were evangelised and possess a copy of the Gospel; cf. further, B. Metzger, 'Seventy or Seventy-Two Disciples?', *New Testament Studies* 5, 1958, pp. 299-306, especially p. 302, where he interestingly observes that many Syrian witnesses of Luke prefer the number seventy-two.

As early as the seventh century CE, Isidore of Seville, *Etymologiae*, Book IX, 2.2, ed. and trans. M. Reyellet, *Isidore de Séville, Étymologies, Livre IX*, Paris, 1984, pp. 42-3, stated as fact that there were originally seventy-two nations in the world, comprising the descendants of Japhet, Ham and Shem.

On the general point that the spread of the Gospel text ruled out uniform corruption, cf. Peter the Venerable, *Liber contra Sectam sive Haeresim Saracenorum*, ed Kritzeck, *Peter the Venerable and Islam*, pp. 257-60 (English summary pp. 180-2), and also Fakhr al-Dīn al-Rāzī, *Muḥaṣṣal afkār al-mutaqaddimīn wa-al-muta'akhkhirīn*, Cairo, 1905, pp.153f. (quoted in Perlmann, *Ibn Kammūna's Examination of the Three Faiths*).

ومن يقدر على جمعها من أقطار الأرض وزوايا العالم حتّى نغيّرها؟ وإن أمكنه
تغيير بعضها فلا يمكنه تغيير كلها ، فإنّ هذا لا يمكن أن يكون لأن كونها بالألسن
قولاً واحدًا ولفظًا واحدًا [23]، فهذا ما لا يجوز لنا أبدًا تسليمه ولا يجوز لقائل * أن * 35r
يقوله أبدًا. ثمّ وجدنا ما هو أعظم من هذا برهانًا قوله في سورة الشورى[24]: ﴿قل
آمنت بما أنزل الله من كتاب﴾[25] إلى قوله: ﴿المصير﴾[26]، وأمّا لغير أهل[27] الكتاب
يقول: ﴿قل يأيها الكافرون﴾[28] إلى آخرها.

43. فالجواب لمن كان له قلب أو ألقى السمع وهو شهيد: إن كنتم أنتم
المؤمنون بالغيب وقد صدّقتم بكتابنا ، ﴿فلا تقولوا ثلاثة انتهوا[29] خيرًا
لكم﴾[30] وإلا فلستم بمؤمنين كما زعمتم ، ولكنكم كما سمّاكم الله في
الكتاب الذي احتججتم به بقوله: ﴿لقد كفر الذين قالوا إنّ الله هو المسيح
ابن مريم﴾.[31] وأمّا زعمكم بأنّ الكتاب المنزل بالحقّ هو الإنجيل فغير مسلّم
لكم ولكنّه القرآن المجيد، بدليل قوله تعالى: ﴿ألم ذلك الكتاب لا ريب
فيه﴾ الآية.[32] وقوله: ﴿طسم[33] تلك آيات الكتاب المبين﴾[34]، وقوله: ﴿حمّ
تنزيل من الرحمن الرحيم﴾[35] إلى قوله: ﴿ونذيرًا﴾[36]، حيث أنزلت هذه
الحروف المقطّعة في أوّل سور منه كالعلامة له وأشار بها إلى أنّ هذا الكتاب
مع إعجازه لجميع العالمين أن يأتوا بسورة من مثله أنزل منظم من هذه
الحروف العربية على هذا النبيّ الأمّي الذي لا يحسن الكتابة ولا الحساب ولا
تعلّم علمًا من غير الله تعالى، وهو قرآن عربي مبين.

---

[23] A and B: قول واحد ولفظ واحد [24] A and B: شورى [25] S. XLII: 15. [26] *Ibid.*
[27] A and B: هذا [28] S. CIX: 1. [29] عن الشرك : A adds these two words in the
margin in the same hand. [30] S. IV: 171. [31] S. V: 17. [32] S. II: 1-2. [33] B: طسم
(wrongly). [34] S. XXVI: 1-2. [35] S. XLI: 1-2. [36] *Ibid.*: 4

Who would have been able to gather them from the regions of the world and corners of the earth for us to alter? And even if he were able to alter one of them, he could not have altered them all. But such a thing could not have taken place, because the existence of this as a single version would have been a single utterance and single expression. So we can never tolerate this, nor should the person (35r) ever say it. Indeed, we have found a proof that is more impressive than this in his words in *al-Shūrā*, 'Say: I believe in whatever scripture Allah hath sent down, [and I am commanded to be just among you. Allah is our Lord and your Lord. Unto us our works and unto you your works; no argument between us and you. Allah will bring us together, and unto him is] the journeying'. As for those who are not People of the Book, it says, 'Say: O disbelievers! [I worship not that which ye worship; nor worship ye that which I worship. And I shall not worship that which ye worship. Nor will ye worship that which I worship. Unto you your religion, and unto me my religion.]'[5]

43.   The *Response* to anyone who has a mind or will give ear and is reliable: If you are believers in the unseen and you place trust in our Book, then 'Say not "Three"—Cease [from polytheism]—it is better for you', otherwise you will not be believers as you claim. But you are as God has named you in the Book from which you argue, in his words, 'They indeed have disbelieved who say: Lo! Allah is the Messiah, son of Mary'. As for your claim that the book which was sent down with the truth is the Gospel, you cannot be allowed this, for it is the glorious Qur'an, according to the evidence of the exalted One's words, 'Alif. Lam. Mim. This is the scripture whereof there is no doubt, [a guidance unto those who ward off]', his words, 'Ta. Sin. Mim. These are revelations of the scripture that maketh plain', and his words, 'Ha. Mim. A revelation from the Compassionate, the Merciful, [a scripture whereof the verses are expounded, a lecture in Arabic for people who have knowledge, good tidings] and a warning'. For these single letters at the beginning of its *Sūras* were revealed as its distinguishing marks, and by means of them he explained that this is the Book, and made the whole world incapable of producing a *Sūra* like it. He revealed an arrangement of these Arabic letters to this unlettered Prophet who had mastered neither writing nor arithmetic, and had learnt nothing other than from God the exalted, and this was the clear Arabic Qur'an.

---

[5] The force of these two verses together is that Muslims should accept any revealed scripture as it is, for the possession of a scripture distinguishes true believers, among them Christians, from others.

وليس الإنجيل منه بشيء ولا التوراة وإن كان فيهما من كلام الله ما

فيهما ، إذ[37] التوراة ، كما تقدّم القول عنها بشهادة تواريخ * اليهود   * 35v

وما زعموه من الحريق لها ومن استجدادها بعد عدمها مرّتين واختلافهم

في المستجدّة التي بأيديهم اليوم وأيدى السامرة وأيديكم ، وأمّا الإنجيل

فإنكم معشر النصارى تعلمون وتشهد تواريخكم وتواريخ اليهود أنّه جمع من

حكايات الحاكين للملك قسطنطين في المجمع ما حكوه من سيرة المسيح

ووصيّته وما جرى له ، وإنه – أعني الإنجيل المحكي – كان إحدى عشرة[38]

بشارة حكاية تاريخًا بعدد تلاميذ المسيح غير يهودس[39] الشبيه المصلوب ،

فاستكثرها قسطنطين وعاين ما فيها من الاختلاف ، فاختار منها الأربعة

التي هي اليوم الإنجيل وأحرق الباقي إلا واحدًا منها يعرف بإنجيل الصبوة،

حكايات عن[40] المسيح أنه فعلها كالعجيبيات والمعاجز حسب لا غير. وهذا

الإنجيل في أيدي اليعاقبة ظاهر وعند غيرهم من النساطرة والملكيّة والمارونيّة

موجود ومكتوم عن العامة.

وتعلمون أيضًا أنّ أصحاب القوانين[41] في المجامع قنّنوا دين النصرانية

لقسطنطين وضمّوا البشارات الأربع[42] بعضها إلى بعض وسمّوها إنجيلاً ،

ومعنى الإنجيل في اللغة العربية الأمر الظاهر بعد الخفاء. يقال: نجل الشئ إذا

ظهر وبان ، ومنه تسمية النجيل نجيلاً ، وتسمية الولد

The Gospel is not at all like this and neither is the Torah, even though they both contain such words of God as they do. With regard to the Torah, as has been said above[6] this is borne out by the witness of the Jewish histories (35v), and also their claims about its being burnt and attempts to renew it after it had perished twice, and their disagreements over the new version which both they, the Samaritans, and you still possess. As for the Gospel, you Christians know, and your histories and those of the Jews testify, that it is a collection of the accounts given by narrators to king Constantine at the Council about the life of Christ, his injunctions, and what happened to him. This—the Gospel that was narrated—comprised eleven testimonies and historical accounts, according to the number of Christ's disciples, except for Judas who bore a resemblance and was crucified.[7] Constantine thought these were too many and examined the differences in them. He chose four of them, and these are today the Gospel. He burnt the rest, except for one which is known as the Infancy Gospel, accounts about what Christ did such as wonders and miracles, and nothing else at all. This Gospel is held openly by the Jacobites, and it can be found among others such as the Nestorians, Melkites and Maronites, but it is kept hidden from the common people.[8]

You also know that the canonical experts in the Councils determined the Christian religion for Constantine and collected together the four witnesses one with another and called them a 'Gospel'.[9] In Arabic the meaning of 'gospel' is 'what becomes apparent after being concealed': you say 'The thing was produced' when it appeared and became evident. From this the grass *najīl* is named, and a son is named

---

[6] Cf. § 39.

[7] This appears to be al-Dimashqī's own hypothesising. The reference to Judas assumes the traditional Muslim explanation of S. IV: 157, that he was mistaken for Jesus and crucified instead of him; cf. Section 1, n. 69 above.

[8] These details indicate that al-Dimashqī had some first-hand knowledge of this text, in which case he is probably referring to the *Arabic Infancy Gospel* which consists largely of miracle stories from Jesus' boyhood (see the summary in M.R. James, *The Apocryphal New Testament*, Oxford, 1969, pp. 80-2). The date of its composition, probably from a Syriac original, is unknown, though if the earliest surviving MS from 1299 is at all indicative (cf. G. Graf, *Geschichte der Christlichen Arabischen Literatur*, vol. I (*Studi e Testi* 118), Vatican City, 1944, pp. 225-7), it may have been newly in circulation among Arabic readers only a few decades before al-Dimashqī was writing.

[9] Although this can be understood as a reference to assembling the four Gospels and according them canonical status, the use of the verb *damma*, which can mean 'to compress' as well as 'to collect', might suggest a harmonisation of the Gospels such as Tatian's *Diatessaron*.

نحلاً لظهورهما بعد الخفاء.

* 36r *

وممَّا كان في إنجيل الصبوة * ومتى[43] أنَّ المسيح لم يكن له آلة النسل بل كان أمسحًا قار الوها وعملوا القلندس الذي معناه الختان لئلا ينسب إلى ناسوته نقص خلق ولأن الإنجيلات شاهدة بأنَّ أمّ المسيح ختنته ثامن يوم ولادته.

44. ثمَّ إنَّ أصحاب القوانين لم يجدوا في هذا الإنجيل المجموع تشريعًا كافيًا ولا تعريفًا شافيًا ، فاستعانوا بما في التوراة من الأحكام والتشريع وسمّوها العتيقة والقدميّة[44] لمعنيين ، أحدهما كون المسيح كان عالمًا بها عاملاً بما فيها ، والثاني لما فيها من التشريع الغير موجود في الإنجيل المجموع المذكور.

ثمَّ رتّبوا صلوات في اليوم والليلة ورتّبوا صيامًا تابعوا فيه صيام المسيح وقصدوا أن يكون آخره أبدًا يوم الأحد ليوافق قيام المسيح في يوم الأحد من القبر بعد الصلب ويكون لهم عيدًا بزعمهم ، فاستعانوا بأهل الحساب الفلكيّين ، فاتّفق لهم بالحساب النجومي أنَّ الشمس والقمر متى اجتمعا بين السرار والإستهلال في أيّام معدودة أوّلها ثاني يوم من شباط وآخرها رابع يوم من آذار صاموا يوم الإثنين الذي يأتي بعد اجتماع الشمس والقمر أو مع اجتماعهما ، فصار ذلك قاعدة في الصيام والفطر ، يتقدّم تارة يسيرًا ويتأخّر تارة يسيرًا ، ولا ينفكّ فيما بين شباط وآذار ونيسان أشهر الربيع ، وزمن إقبال السنة. ثمَّ نظروا * في عدّة الأيام التي صامها المسيح فوجدوها أربعين يومًا ووجدوا آخرها لا يوافق أن يكون يوم الأحد دائمًا ، فزادوا عليها أيامًا عشرة أو أكثر أو أقلّ بيسير وجعلوا الزيادة صومًا

* 36v *

---

43 A: ومتا   44 A and B: والقرمية (wrongly).

'offspring', *najl*, because they each appear after being concealed.[10]

Included in the Infancy Gospel (36r) and Matthew is that Christ did not have an organ of procreation but was neuter [*2 words untranslatable*].[11] They performed the *qalandis*, which means 'circumcision', so that no human deficiency could be ascribed to his humanity, and because the Gospels witness that Christ's mother had him circumcised on the eighth day after his birth.[12]

44. Moreover, the canonical experts could not find in this collected Gospel sufficient legislation or clear instruction. So they turned to the rules and legislation of the Torah, and called it the old and former, for two reasons, one because Christ was familiar with it and carried out what it contained, and the other because of the legislation in it which was not found in this collected Gospel.

Then they arranged prayers for the day and night and arranged a fast, in this following Christ's fast. They intended that it should always end on a Sunday in order to coincide with the resurrection of Christ from the tomb after the crucifixion on a Sunday, which is a festival for them as they claim. They turned to experts in astronomical calculation, and by means of calculations based on the stars it was agreed that when the sun and the moon were in conjunction between the end of the month and the beginning of the month on days calculated, the earliest being the second day of February and the latest the fourth day of March, they would fast on the Monday that followed or coincided with the conjunction of the sun and moon. This formed the basis for fasting and breaking the fast, sometimes being put forward a little and sometimes put back a little, though it never falls outside the period of February, March and April, the spring months, the time of the start of the year. Then they checked (36v) the number of days during which Christ had fasted and discovered they were forty. And they also discovered that the last of these did not always fall on a Sunday. So they added ten days or so to them, making these extra a fast and

---

[10] The point of this derivation is that the Christian Gospel was introduced into the community rather than being transmitted uninterruptedly from Jesus, who according to Muslim belief would have passed it on after receiving it as revelation.

[11] This may be a confused reference to Mtt XIX: 12, where Jesus says that some are born eunuchs. Dozy, *Supplément aux dictionnaries arabes*, vol. II, p. 590, gives the meaning of *amsaḥ* as '*chatré* [= emasculated], *privé du membre et des testicules*'. Al-Dimashqī appears to have a less drastic form of impotence in mind.

[12] The only reference in the canonical Gospels to Jesus being circumcised occurs in Lk II: 21.

وقسّموها على الجمع يومين يومين سبت وأحد ، سبت وأحد.

وجعلوا الصيام إمساكًا عن الأكل دورة من دورات الفلك وخيّروا الصائم في وقت فطره وأباحوا له فيه الوطء واللعب والعبث [45] ومنعوه [46] من أكل لحوم الحيوان البري ، وقصدوا بذلك ثلاثة [47] معان ، أحدها موافقة الصابئة في الصيام للكواكب بترك أكل كلّ روح ، فإنَّ عهدهم بمذهبهم كان قريبًا ، ولذلك اتخذوا التماثيل والدخنات أمامها بحصى اللبان وكشف الرؤوس للقسيسين في الصلاة وإيقاد الشمع والمصابيح ليلاً ونهارًا بالقرب منها ، والثاني تسهيل الصوم على الصائم ، فإنّه إمساك عن اللحوم وما منها وإباحته شرب الخمر نيابة عن اللحم وأكل النبات وما فيه وبذلك تقلّ النفقات وتجتمع المال مدّة شهرين في كلّ سنة ، وجمع المال محبوب للنفوس ، والمعنى الثالث فصل الربيع تغزر فيه الدماء وتقوى الحيوانيّة التي هي الشهوة والغضب في الإنسان ، والخمر تثير ما يجده مع أنها أبدًا تهدي إلى نفوس الشاربين لها مسرّة كاذبة وتهدى إلى عقولهم مضرّة صادقة ، فبترك أكل اللحوم * في الفصل ومداومة أكل النبات تنكسر تلك الأخلاق الحيوانية   * 37r قليلاً وهو المراد.

45. ثمّ [48] أنّ أصحاب القوانين منعوا من كثرة قراءة الإنجيل ومن حفظه في الصدور وقسّموه فصولاً فصولاً وجعلوا كلّ فصل مختصّاً في القراءة بيوم أحد أو يوم عيد أو موسم أو وقت حادثة تحدث من عدو أو من آفة سماوية وطابقوا بين معنى ذلك الفصل ومعنى ذلك اليوم أو الحادث ورتّبوا له لحنًا وصوتًا

---

distributing them through the weeks as pairs of days, Saturday and Sunday, Saturday and Sunday.[13]

They made the fast an abstinence from eating for one complete day, and they permitted the person fasting to choose the time of breaking his fast. They placed no restrictions upon him regarding sexual intercourse, amusement and frivolity, but they forbade him to eat the flesh of any land animal. In doing this they had three purposes in mind. One was to conform to the Ṣābians in their fasting for the stars by abstaining from what had life. For they were very familiar with the doctrine of these people, and so they had adopted images with incense smoke before them, and priests with their heads uncovered in worship, and candles and lamps lit near them both night and day. The second was to make fasting easy for the person fasting. For it was abstaining from flesh and anything to do with it, while allowing him to drink wine in place of flesh, and to eat vegetables and the like. By this means expenditure was reduced and money saved for a period of two months every year; and saving money is attractive to people. The third purpose was the season of spring, in which blood and animal vigour surge, which in the human are desire and rage. Wine makes whatever he encounters stimulating, though it always induces in the souls of those who drink it false pleasure while in their intellects it induces real harm. So by abstaining from flesh (37r) in the season and continuing to eat vegetables, animal characteristics are subdued a little, and this is the intention.

45. Furthermore, the canonical experts forbade frequent reading of the Gospel and learning it by heart. They divided it up into portions and they specified each portion for reading on Sundays, festivals, feast days, or times when enemies or heavenly afflictions struck. They made the intent of the particular portion correspond to the intent of the particular day or event, and they set a measure and tune accord-

---

[13] The development of the Lenten fast in early Christian history is complicated, to say the least; cf. T. Talley, *The Origins of the Liturgical Year*, Collegeville, MN, 1991, pp. 214-17. Al-Dimashqī presents his explanation on the assumption that the end of Lent always coincided with Easter, though in starting from the spring equinox and showing how days had to be added in order to bring it to its conclusion on Easter Sunday, he could be preserving vestiges of the primitive form of the fast, which began from Epiphany and was only later moved forward to connect it with Easter. On the point of Sunday fasting, however, he seems to be mistaken, since Sunday was always regarded as a non-fasting day.

يقرأ به ذلك الفصل ، واستعملوا في أعيادهم ومواسمهم الأرغون وسماع
أنغامه أوقاتٍ صلواتهم كذلك ، ولأنّ التلحين يهزّ النفوس البشريّة ويحرّك
طباعها بالطرب ويشوّقها إلى معناها ويثير منها الساكن الملكاني فتحنّ حنينًا
لطيفًا ساذجًا[49] إلى معهدها القديم وتجد وجدانًا بحسب إشراق جوهرها وقوّة
ضياء حسّها. ويكون لسماع ذلك الفصل المقروء من الإنجيل موقع عظيم[50]
وسيّما ما فيه من الوصايا والإشارات اللطيفة المسيحيّة.

ولأنه[51] متى تكرّرت قراءة الإنجيل وسمعت ساذجة بغير تلحين ، اطّلعت
العقول الواعية على ما ذكرناه وحصل الفحص والتفكّر ، فيكون ذلك شيئا
موجبًا للإنحلال عن تعظيمه والاطّلاع على أنّه من جمع الجامعين المؤرخين ،
وأين ذلك من كتابنا "الشفاء لما في الصدور"[52] و"الميسّر للذكر"[53] والمحرّض
نبيّنا صلم على دراسته وتدبّره والتفكّر فيه ، والذي لعلماء الأمّة اليوم
سبعماية سنة يتدبّرونه ويستخرجون من معانيه ويستنبطون منه ويكتبون
شروحه ولم يبلغوا منه الغاية ولا انتهوا في العلم به إلى النهاية وتفسيره نحو
المايتين وستين تفسيرًا مطوّلة ومبسوطة ، فمن المطوّلة ما هو خمسون مجلّدًا
فما دونها.

ثمّ أنّ أصحاب القوانين لمّا لم يجدوا في الإنجيل تفصيل حلال من حرام
ولا تعليم عبادة ولا قسمة ميراث ولا تشريع كما بيّنّا واضطرهم التقنين إلى
ذلك كلّه جعلوا أمر الميراث إلى الميت يخصّ ميراثه من أراد

* 37v *

---

[49] B: ساذجاء   [50] A and B: موقعًا عظيمًا   [51] B: والآية (wrongly).   [52] Cf. S. X:
57.   [53] Cf. S. LIV: 17, 22, 31, 40.

ing to which this portion should be read out.[14] Similarly, at the times of worship on their festivals and feast days they were accustomed to playing organs and to listening to melodies on them.[15] Musical settings stir human souls and move their natures with delight, filling them with desire for their true being and stimulating the latent angelic natures within. So, with a subtle and simple yearning they yearn for their former abode, and they discover a longing in accord with the radiance of their substance and the power of the brilliance of their sensations, and a profound impression is made when this portion recited from the Gospel is heard, particularly by the sublime instructions and counsels of Christ within it.

But then when the reading out of the Gospel is repeated, and it is heard simply without musical arrangement, attentive minds become aware of what we have stated,[16] and questioning and considering begin. For this reason we are compelled to disentangle ourselves from thinking it impressive, and to be aware that it is only a collection by historians who collected it together. For what is it compared with our Book? This is 'a balm for that which is in the hearts', and is made easy to remember. Our Prophet (may God bless him and give him peace) instigated study of it, reflection upon it, and consideration of it, (37v) and scholars of the community today and for seven hundred years have been studying it,[17] bringing out its meaning, extracting things from it, and writing expositions of it. They have not even now reached the end of this, nor come to full knowledge of it. There are about 260 commentaries on it, elaborate and detailed, among the elaborate alone there being some which comprise 50 volumes.

Furthermore, the canonical experts could not find in the Gospel any distinction between what is permitted and what is forbidden, nor any instruction about worship, or the division of inheritance, or any legislation, as we have explained. So they were forced to make laws for all this. They made the matter of inheritance something for the dying person, who could fix his inheritance upon anyone he wished

---

[14] Cf. *The New Grove Dictionary of Music and Musicians*, London, 1980, vol. XVIII, 'Syrian Church Music'.

[15] On this point in general, cf. *The New Grove Dictionary*, vol. XIII, 'Organ, § IV, 2. The Byzantine Organ, and 3. The Organ of the Arabs'.

[16] I.e. that the Gospel which is read out in churches was compiled long after the time of Jesus; cf. § 43 above.

[17] Al-Dimashqī is of course writing this in 721 AH.

من الأقارب والأجانب ، وجعلوا المرأة لرجل واحد وحرّموا الطلاق والجمع
بين زوجتين وأغفلوا الطهر من الحيض والجنابة والوطء وندبوا إلى أنّ كلّ
امرأة من نسائهم تتخذ لها إشبينًا كالمؤاخي لها، وتشبّهوا في ذلك بيوسف
النجّار ومريم البتول عليهم ، وكلّ ذلك شرعوه ورتّبوه وقنّنوه من عند
أنفسهم وبما اقتضته آراؤهم مع رأي قسطنطين ، وليس[54] لكم أن تنكروا
ذلك ، وكيف تنكرونه وتواريخ اليهود مع تواريخكم شاهدون به؟

46.   وأمّا زعمكم في قول الله تعالى[55] لنبيّه عليلم: ﴿فإن * كنت في شكّ   * 38r
ممّا أنزلنا إليك﴾ الآية[56]، أنّ ذلك تثبيت[57] للإنجيل وشهادة له بأنّه ما بدّل ولا
غيّرت منه كلمة واحدة فليس كذلك وإنما هذا خطاب العين والمراد به الغير ،
ولقد أحسنت النساء في قولهنّ: "الحديث لك يا جارة ، واسمعي يا كنّة" ،
فالمقصود من ذلك تعريف العرب الكفّار أنّ اسمه ووصفه وعلاماته في التوراة
والإنجيل كما بيّناه قبل. وكما كانت اليهود يتواعدون الكفّار الجاهلية به
وبمحبته ، وأنهم سوف يكونون أنصاره والمنتصرون به على العرب ، حتى
إذا بعثه الله تعالى كفروا به ، فلعنة الله على الكافرين المهدّدين المنذرين بقوله
تعالى: ﴿يا بني إسرائيل اذكروا نعمتي التي أنعمت عليكم وأوفوا بعهدي﴾[58]
إلى قوله: ﴿وأنتم تعلمون﴾[59].

---

[54] B: ولسن (wrongly).   [55] في ... تعالى: these words are supplied in the same hand in the margin in A.   [56] S. X: 94.   [57] B: تثبّت (wrongly).   [58] S. II: 40.   [59] Ibid.: 40-2.

whether relatives or strangers; they restricted a woman to one man and forbade divorce and possessing two wives together; they made no provision about purification after monthly periods, major impurities or sexual intercourse, and they stipulated that every one of their women should take a protector for herself like a brother, in this following the example of Joseph the carpenter and Mary the Virgin (peace be upon them). They legislated, arranged and made all this as law on their own initiative, and as their opinions, together with Constantine's, dictated. You are in no position to deny this, and how can you deny it when the histories of the Jews and your own attest to it?[18]

46.   As for your claim about the words of God the exalted to his Prophet (peace be upon him), 'And if (38r) thou art in doubt concerning that which we reveal unto thee [then question those who read the scripture before thee. Verily the truth from thy Lord hath come unto thee. So be not thou of the waverers]', that this is a confirmation and attestation that the Gospel has not been substituted nor a single word of it altered, this is not the case. For this is a specific statement and its intention is different—indeed, women get it right when they say, 'These words are meant for you, neighbour, so listen sister-in-law'. For its purpose was to inform the unbelieving Arabs that his name, description and indications of him were in the Torah and Gospel, as we have shown above, and because the Jews had given assurances to the unbelieving pagans about him and about loving him, and that they would be his helpers and be helped by him against the Arabs. And then when God the exalted sent him they did not believe in him. So the curse of God is upon the unbelievers who were threatened and warned, in the words of the exalted One, 'O Children of Israel! Remember my favour wherewith I favoured you, and fulfil your part of the covenant' to his words, 'nor knowingly conceal the truth'.[19]

---

[18] These concluding remarks are a reminder that all the preceding details in §§ 43-5 contribute to the point that the Gospels and all the numerous aspects of Christian life and legislation were human contrivances. Therefore, the Christians have no grounds for arguing as they do that the scripture to which the Qur'an refers is the Gospels which they possess.

[19] This interpretation of S. X: 94 in the light of II: 40-2 reverses the Christians' interpretation by suggesting that since the scripture of the Jews (and Christians) contains references to Muḥammad they should be true to it and accept his prophetic status. Thus the verse ceases to be a proof of the reliability of the Bible and turns out to be a reminder that the Bible, when it is read correctly, urges its readers to accept Muḥammad.

وأمّا التبديل والتغيير فقد تقدّم فيه من القول رمزًا وإشارة[60] ما فيه كفاية ومقنع، وسأجاوب عن ذلك آخر الجواب[61]، وفي قصّة شطبير المزوّر عيّنة لمن يفهم. وأين يا قوم ما هو منقول بالتواتر؟ نقلته الألوف عن الألوف حتى إلينا من منقول عن آحاد مجهولين مختلفين في النقل غير موثوق بهم، كامرأة معتوهة وصيّاد للسمك وأربعة مجتمعين ليلاً في مكان متحيّرين فيه من عدوهم، ومعنى قولي النقل المتواتر * هو كالخبر المتواتر من أهل التجر أنّ أصقلية جزيرة كبيرة بالبحر مسكونة ببني آدم يشهد الشاهد بوجودها وإن لم يرها، بل بالنقل المتواتر عنها ممّن لا يحتمل تواطئهم على الكذب ولا ما يحتمل من أجله التواطؤ.

* 38v

وأمّا زعمكم في قوله تعالى: ﴿ألم ذلك الكتاب لا ريب فيه﴾ الآيات[62] أنّ المؤمنين بالغيب أنتم وأنّ المؤمنين بما أنزل الله إلى نبيّنا وما أنزل من قبله نحن المسلمون وأنّ الكتاب الذي لا ريب فيه الإنجيل لا غيره، فليس كذلك من حيثكم وحيث الإنجيل إذ من يقول في الله إنه ثالث ثلاثة وإنه هو المسيح وإنه اتخذ المسيح ولدًا

---

[60] رمزا وإشارة: these two words are supplied in the margin in A in the same hand, but are lacking in B.   [61] وسأجاوب ... الجواب: these words are supplied in the margin in A in the same hand, but are lacking in B.   [62] S. II: 1-2.

As for substitution and alteration,[20] there are enough convincing hints and allusions about this in the earlier discussion on it. I shall reply to it at the end of the response, though in the story of Shaṭbīr the falsifier is an instance for anyone who understands.[21] But, my friends, what has been transmitted uninterruptedly? It has been transmitted by thousands to thousands down to us, from a thing transmitted by individuals who are unknown, who differ in their transmitting and who are untrustworthy, such as an insane woman, a fisherman, and four who gathered together by night in a place and were confused over it because of their enemy.[22] The meaning of my term 'uninterrupted transmission' (38v) is like uninterrupted reports from traders that Sicily is a great island in the sea inhabited by humans. Thus, even though he has not seen it, a person can witness to its existence through uninterrupted transmission about it from those who could not conceivably be in conspiracy to lie, and from what could not conceivably be conspiracy about it.[23]

As for your claim about the exalted One's words, 'Alif. Lam. Mim. This is the scripture whereof there is no doubt' and the following verses, that those 'who believe in the unseen' are you, that those who believe in what God revealed to our Prophet and in what he revealed to those before him are us Muslims, and that 'the scripture whereof there is no doubt' is the Gospel and nothing else, it is not the case concerning you or the Gospel. For whoever says that God is the third of three, that he is Christ, and that he took Christ as a son,[24]

---

[20] Referring back to the passage of the *Letter* he has just quoted in § 42, al-Dimashqī picks up the Christians' brief reference to this, which they make immediately after the point he has just refuted.

[21] The unelaborated mention of this figure suggests that he was well known in circles where corruption of Christian scripture was discussed.

[22] These are references to Mary Magdalene, who has already been mentioned as one of those who stood at the cross and also witnessed Jesus' first post-resurrection appearances (Jn XX: 11-17), to Peter who was the first to enter Jesus' tomb and find it empty (Jn XX: 6f.), and to the four evangelists. On these last, cf. ʿAbd al-Jabbār, *Mughnī*, vol. V, p. 143, though he argues that the evangelists must have consciously lied, while al-Dimashqī imputes the errors in the Gospels to the circumstances in which he melodramatically imagines the evangelists composed their works following the execution of Jesus.

[23] Of course, al-Dimashqī has in mind the test of uninterrupted and multiple transmission by which the most genuine prophetic Ḥadīths are guaranteed. When applied to the Gospels, this test exposes the shakiness of their connection with the events of Jesus' life.

[24] Cf. e.g. SS. V: 73, V: 72 and II. 116 respectively.

فليس بمؤمن بالغيب ولا بالشهادة بل كافر مشرك ضالّ مسمّى في كتاب الله تعالى كافر من كفرة أهل الكتاب المستحقين أليم العذاب.

وأمّا زعمكم في الإنجيل أنه الكتاب المنزّل "هدى للمتقين"[63] فقد تقدّم القول بأنه القرآن المجيد لا الإنجيل بالدليل الواضح ، ولو سلّمنا أنه الإنجيل لكان حجّة عليكم مثبتاً فسقكم لأنكم ضلّيتم به فلم تكونوا متقين. ولو فطنتم من هذه الآيات الكريمة في أوّل هذه السورة أنّ الله تعالى ذكر المؤمنين وصفاتهم وذكر المنافقين وصفاتهم وذكر الكفّار وصفاتهم ، وهو من أوّل قوله: ﴿* ألم ذلك الكتاب لا ريب فيه﴾ وإلى آخر قوله: ﴿الله يستهزئ بهم * 39r ويمدّهم في طغيانهم يعمهون﴾[64]، قابلوا[65] ذلك من الكتاب الذي حصلتموه وتدبّروه تجدوا ذلك ظاهرًا باللفظ والمعنى.

وأمّا زعمكم في قوله تعالى لنبيّه عليلم: ﴿وقل آمنت بما أنزل الله من كتاب الآية﴾[66] ، أنه ما أمره بذلك إلا ليقرّركم[67] على دينكم وأعمالكم وليعرّفكم أنه إنما أرسل إلى العرب خاصّة فليس كذلك ، بل رسالته عامة ودعوته شاملة للأنس والجنّ كافة بشهادة القرآن العزيز له وإظهار دينه واستعلائه على الدين كلّه ، واقرأوا ما في سورة الكهف من قوله تعالى: ﴿الحمد لله الذي أنزل على عبده الكتاب﴾[68] إلى قوله:

---

63 Cf. *Ibid.*: 2; S. III: 138; S. V: 49.   64 S. II: 1-15.   65 B: قابوا (wrongly).   66 S. XLII. 15.   67 B: لقرّكم   68 S. XVIII: 1.

cannot be a believer in the unseen or the seen. He is an unbeliever, a polytheist and in error, named in the Book of God the exalted as an unbeliever among the unbelievers of the People of the Book who deserve the painfulness of punishment.

As for your claim about the Gospel that it is the book revealed, 'guidance to those who ward off evil', the explanation that it was the glorious Qur'an and not the Gospel has already been given, with clear proof. But if we were to grant that it was the Gospel, it would be a substantial argument against you of your error, because you have become misguided over it and do not ward off evil. If you could see in the noble verses at the beginning of this particular *Sūra* that God the exalted refers to the believers and their characteristics, to the hypocrites and their characteristics, and to the unbelievers and their characteristics—this is from the beginning of his words (39r) 'Alif. Lam. Mim. [This is the scripture whereof there is no doubt]' to the end of his words, 'Allah doth mock them, leaving them to wander blindly on in their contumacy'; compare this in the book that you have obtained and reflected upon—then you would find it obvious in word and meaning.[25]

As for your claim about the words of the exalted One to his Prophet (peace be upon him), 'But say: I believe in whatever scripture Allah hath sent down' and the rest of the verse, that he only commanded him to do this in order to confirm you in your religion and practices, and in order to inform you that he was only sent to the Arabs and no-one else, this is not the case. In fact, his apostleship was general and his call was comprehensively intended for humans and jinn all together, according to the esteemed Qur'an's witness to him, the prevalence of his religion, and its supremacy over all religions.[26] Read the exalted One's words in *Al-Kahf*, 'Praise be to Allah who hath revealed his scripture unto his slave, [and hath not placed therein any crookedness, (But hath made it) straight, to give warning of stern punishment from him, and to bring unto the believers who do good works the news that theirs will be a fair reward, wherein they will abide for ever; And to warn those who say: Allah hath chosen a son, whereof they had no

---

[25] The Christians do not measure up to the teachings of their own scripture because, as these verses from the beginning of S. II show, they are deceptive in their faith.

[26] Proofs of the veracity of the Prophet based on the triumph of Islam are found from early times; cf. 'Alī al-Ṭabarī, *Dīn wa-dawla*, pp. 50-4/ *Religion and Empire*, pp. 57-60.

﴾إِن يَقُولُونَ[69] إِلَّا كَذِبًا﴿[70]. وليس إلا النصارى القائلون ذلك والمنذرون منه والموبّخون على لسانه ، إذ هو الموبّخ والنذير لهم ، ولأنّ الله أمره بالعدل بينهم كما في الآية وبتعريفهم أنّ الإله واحد ، والمعدلة لا تكون إلا من حكم حاكم يحكم به على محكوم عليه أو له. وهم الأمّة للرسول المأمور بالعدل فيهم لا ريب ، وكذا إذا أقرّهم على حكم أو حدّد لهم حكمًا أو حكم فيهم بكتابهم الأوّل ، فإنه حكم منه كما كان المسيح يحكم بما في التوراة وكتب النبوءات وأقرّ اليهود على * أشياء وتبع شريعتهم في أشياء وهو مرسل إليهم ودعوته شاملة لهم لا شكّ في ذلك.

39v

47. وأمّا قولكم: إنه لا يمكن تغيير كتابكم لكونه باثنين وسبعين لسانًا وهو مفرّق في أربع زوايا العالم إلى آخر ذلك.

فالجواب: قد علمتم من تواريخكم وتواريخ اليهود أنه لم يكن على وجه الأرض يوم ظهور دين النصرانية بقيام قسطنطين في ظهوره إنجيل[71] غير البشارات الأربع[72] المجموعة باتّفاق أصحاب القوانين إنجيلاً واحدًا وهو هذا الذي بين أيديكم يومنا هذا لا غيره سوى إنجيل الصبوة وقد تقدّم القول فيه ، فإن كانت دعواكم بأنّه لما جمع كتب باثنين وسبعين لسانًا واثنين وسبعين قلمًا[73] فيحتمل أن يكون ذلك مع أنه أغرب من عنقاء مغرب كما يقال في المثل ، ولو سأل سائل عن

---

[69] A and B: تقولون   [70] S. XVIII: 1-5.   [71] A and B: إنجيلا   [72] A and B: الأربعة
[73] B: كلما (wrongly).

knowledge, nor their fathers. Dreadful is the word that cometh out of their mouths.] They speak nought but a lie'. It is only the Christians who say this. And they are the ones who were warned by him and rebuked by his tongue, because he was their rebuker and warner, and because God commanded him to show justice among them, as in the verse, and to inform them that God is one. Equity can only come from the judgement of a judge who judges by it either for or against the one judged. And they are without doubt the community among whom the messenger was ordered to show justice. Thus if he confirmed them according to a judgement, or came to them with a judgement, or judged them according to their original book, he judged on the basis of it as Christ had judged according to what was in the Torah and books of the prophets. The latter confirmed the Jews (39v) in certain things and followed their law in certain things, for he was sent to them and his proclamation was intended for them, and there is no doubt about this.[27]

47. As for your words that there cannot have been any alteration of your book because it is in seventy-two languages and is dispersed throughout the four corners of the world, to the end of this, the response is: You know from your histories and those of the Jews that on the day when Christianity became public, when Constantine undertook to make it public, nowhere on the face of the earth was there a gospel other than the four witnesses collected together by the agreement of the canonical experts into a single Gospel, and this is what you possess today.[28] There is nothing beside it except the Infancy Gospel, which has already been mentioned. So if your claim is that when it was collected it was written in seventy-two languages and seventy-two hands, this may be possible, though it is more remarkable than the fabulous bird as is mentioned in the parable.[29] And if someone were to ask about

---

[27] Al-Dimashqī turns the argument back upon the Christians by adducing S. XVIII: 1-5, which not only shows that the Qur'an was sent to warn Christians, and so was more general in its application than the Cypriot Christians claim, but also that the Christians can be shown to be wrong in imputing a son to God on the basis of their own scripture. His presupposition is that the Gospels in their original form proclaimed the oneness of God in the same way as the Qur'an.

[28] Cf. § 43 for al-Dimashqī's account of the selection of the Gospel from the eleven versions circulating before the time of Constantine.

[29] Cf. Lane, *Lexicon*, p. 2177, where the *'anqā' mughrib* is variously explained as: a great bird that is seldom seen (and so the term is generally used to refer to a calamity); a bird found in the west; a bird that no-one has seen; and the 'swarms of flying creatures' referred to in S. C: 3 that were sent by God against the army of Abraha.

هذه الإثنين وسبعين لساناً وطلب أسماء أمّها ، كان مثل مدّعيها كمثل طبّاخ أدّعى صناعة ماية طعام فاخر ثم أخذ يعدّها فتلجلج لسانه بعد عدد عشرة أو عشرين ، فقيل له: "هذا التلجلج ينبغي أن يكون في عُشر الماية".

فإن قلتم إنّ قسطنطين حشر الأمم من أقصى صين الصين وإلى أقصى ساحل أوقيانوس المحيط المغربي شرقًا وغربًا برًا وبحرًا وحشرهم كذلك [*] من وراء خطّ الاستواء وإلى أوّل إقليم الظلمة و كتبوا بجملتهم هذا الإنجيل بلغاتهم الإثنتين[74] وسبعين ففي ذلك ما فيه.

[*] 40r

وإن قلتم إنّ الأربعة الإنجيليين ألقوه إلى أهل المجامع باثنين وسبعين لساناً كان كمن يقول: "نصف العشرة ثلاثة". وإن قلتم إنّ التلاميذ أخذوه عن المسيح بهذه اللغات كلّها كان مكابرة للمحسوس.

وإن لم تجدوا جوابًا فحسب العاقل علمه بالشيء إن كان حقًا أو باطلاً ، مع أنّ قوله:"نحكم نشهد بأنّ شخصًا يسمّى شطبير زوّر الإنجيل وأمكنه الزيادة فيه والنقصان منه ، وكيف لا يمكنه ويمكن غيره الزيادة والتنقيص؟" وبين كل لغة ولغة ولسان ولسان من هذه اللغات والألسن من التباين والبعد كما بين اللغة العربية واللغة التركية ، فارجعوا إلى عقولكم لتعلموا ما نحن به عالمون.

وحاشا العقلاء أن يدّعوا أمرًا باطلاً ويقولوا[75] إنهم متمسّكون به تمسّكًا دينيًا ، والتجازف ممجوج منكور ، والإلباء أجلّ عند نفوسهم من أن يستعينوا في بصيرة دينهم ومذهبهم بباطل ، حيث تقولون إنكم متمسّكون بدين المسيح الذي سلّمه إليكم أصحاب القوانين والتلاميذ كما تسلّموه هم من المسيح. وتعلمون أنّ بين أيام قسطنطين وتقنين دين النصرانية وبين زمن المسيح نحو الماية سنة [*] أو أزيد ،

[*] 40v

---

⁷⁴ A and B: الإثنين   ⁷⁵ A and B: وتقولون

these seventy-two languages and inquired about the names of their communities, the one making the claim would be just like the chef who boasted he could make a hundred delicious dishes: he started to itemize them, but then his tongue faltered after ten or twenty, and he was told, 'This was bound to happen after a mere tenth.'

If you say that Constantine mustered communities from the furthermost parts of China to the furthest coast of Ocean towards the west, east and west, land and sea, and also mustered them (40r) from beyond the equator to the edge of the region of darkness, and together they wrote this Gospel in their seventy-two languages, well this speaks for itself.

And if you say that the four evangelists presented it to the members of the Councils in seventy-two languages, this is like the man who says, 'Half of ten is three'. And if you say that the disciples received it from Christ in all of these languages, this is a violation of what is physically possible.

If you cannot find a reply, then for a reasonable person his knowledge of whether a thing is true or false is enough, though he might say, 'We judge and witness that an individual named Shaṭbīr falsified the Gospel and was able to add to it or remove from it'. And why could not he or someone else add to it or remove from it when there are differences and distances between all of these languages and tongues, like between Arabic and Turkish? So refer to your intellects in order to know what we know.[30]

It is out of the question for reasonable people to claim something is false and then say they follow it with religious devotion, for recklessness is ruled out and debarred, while the intelligent have too much self-respect to depend upon anything worthless in discerning their religion and doctrine. In that you say you follow Christ's religion, which the canonical experts and disciples handed on to you just as they received it from Christ, even though you know that between the age of Constantine when Christianity was legalised and the time of Christ there were about a hundred years (40v) or more,[31] and you

---

Dozy, *Supplément*, p. 182, gives 'griffon'. Al-Dimashqī uses the image to suggest that the idea of seventy-two versions of the Gospel story being in existence before the time of Constantine is so far-fetched as to be effectively impossible.

[30] Al-Dimashqī methodically piles up objections to the probability of the Christians' claim about the seventy-two translations of the Gospel. Again, he mentions the strange figure of Shaṭbīr in familiar terms.

[31] Constantine gave public recognition to Christianity in 313 CE.

وتعلمون أيضًا بشهادة معقولكم أنّ اليهود الفريسيّين[76] أعني علماء اليهودية لم يكونوا ليصلبوا المسيح ويقتلوه بسبب ما ادّعاه ، ثم تكونوا بعد هلاكه تبّاعه من إظهار دعوته وإعلان ما أنكرته اليهود عليه وقتله به ، وهذه قضيّة لا يقبلها العقل السليم.

ألا ترون[77] إلى بطرس كيف أنكر المسيح وحلف أنه ما صحبه ولا يعرفه؟ وكيف هربت التلاميذ إلى كلّ مخبأ؟ وكيف بقيت النساء حائرات ييكين؟ وكلّ من كان مؤمنًا بالمسيح كتم إيمانه وبقي عليه إلى أن استدعى قسطنطين بأهل مدينة الناصرة ، وكان ما كان من تقنين دين النصرانية.

---

76 A and B: الفريسيّون   77 A and B: تروا

also know according to the witness of your own common sense that the Jewish Pharisees, I mean the Jewish scholars, had no authority to crucify Christ or to kill him on the basis of the claims he made,[32] but then you became his followers after his passing because his preaching was made known and the Jews' denial of him and reason for killing him were made public—no one with sound intelligence would accept such a case.

Can you not see how Peter denied Christ and swore that he was not his companion and did not know him? And how the disciples fled to any hiding place? And how the women remained, confused and weeping?[33] Anyone who believed in Christ concealed his faith and kept it so until Constantine called the people of Nazareth for questioning, and the legalisation of Christianity resulted.

---

[32] The Synoptic passion narratives make it clear that Jesus' accusers could not find any substantial charge against him, e.g. Mtt XXVI: 59-66, though the nearest Gospel reference to this comment is Jn XVIII: 31.

[33] Cf. Mtt XXVI: 69-75, XXVI: 56, XXVII: 55f.

فصل

ثمّ قلتم في الرسالة سياقًا ، مستشهدين بقوله تعالى: ﴿ولا تجادلوا أهل الكتاب﴾ الآية¹،

أنه أعني بقوله: ﴿ونحن﴾ أي عنه كنّا ونحن العرب التابعين لما جاء في كتابه. وأمّا الذين ظلموا فما يشكّ أنهم اليهود الذين سجدوا لرأس العجل فكفروا بالله مرارًا كثيرة وقتلوا أنبياءه وعبدوا الأصنام وذبحوا للشياطين حسبما شهد الله عليهم قائلاً على لسان نبيّه داود النبي في كتاب الزبور في مزمور ماية وخمسة² يقول: "ذبحوا

     * 41r

بنيهم وبناتهم للشيطان * وأراقوا الدماء لمنحوتات كنعان وقد نجست الأرض بالدماء وتنجّست أعمالهم وزنوا وسخط الرب عليهم ورذل ميراثهم"³.

وقال أيضًا على لسان أشعياء النبي صلم: "يقول الله في بني إسرائيل سمعوا كلامي ووصاياي فلم يحفظوها وغيّروا كلّما أوصيتهم ونقضوا الميثاق الذي كتبت عليهم وجعلته لهم إلى الأبد فلذلك أجلستهم على الخزي والخراب وأهلكتهم وانقطع عمّن بقي منهم الفرح والسرور". هكذا قال الله على سكّان أورشليم بني إسرائيل: "سأبدّدهم بين الأمم وفي تلك الأيام يرفعون الأمم أصواتهم ويمجّدون الله ويسبّحونه بأصوات عالية ويجتمعون من أقطار الأرض ومن جزائر البحر ومن البلدان البعيدة ويقدّسون اسم الله ويرجعون إلى الله إله إسرائيل ويكونون⁴ شعبه ، وأمّا بنو إسرائيل⁵ فيكونون مبدّدين في الأرض"⁶.

وقال أيضًا على لسان أشعياء النبي: "يقول الله: يا بني إسرائيل نجّستم الجبل المقدّس ، فإني سأفنيكم بالحرب وتموتون وذلك لأني⁷ دعوتكم فلم تجيبوني وكلّمتكم فلم تسمعوني وعملتم الشرّ بين يدي".

وقال أشعياء النبي أيضًا: "إنّ الله قد بغض بني إسرائيل من بيته قد أخرجهم ولا يغفر لهم لأنه لعنهم * وقد جُعلوا لعنة الناس ، فلذلك

     * 41v

أهلكهم الله وبدّدهم بين الأمم ولم يعد يرحمهم ولا ينظر إليهم برحمته إلى أبد الآبدين ولا

---

¹ S. XXIX: 46.   ² Psalm 106.   ³ Psalm CVI: 37-40; A and B: ميزانهم (wrongly).   ⁴ A and B: ويكونوا   ⁵ A and B: فيكونوا   ⁶ A reminiscence of Isaiah XXIV: 13-16.   ⁷ B: التّي (wrongly), a misreading of A.

48. *Section [Five]*

Then you say in your Letter following this, citing the words of the exalted One, 'And argue not with the People of the Scripture [unless it be in (a way) that is better, save with such of them as do wrong; and say: We believe in that which hath been revealed unto us and revealed unto you; our God and your God is one, and we surrender unto him]':

By his words 'and we' he meant himself, 'ourselves and we Arabs' who followed what came in his book. As for 'such of them as do wrong', they are without doubt the Jews who bowed down before the heifer's head, and repeatedly refused to believe in God, killed his prophets, worshipped idols and sacrificed to satans, according to what God declares against them, saying on the tongue of his prophet the prophet David in the Book of Psalms, in Psalm 105, 'They sacrificed their sons and daughters to Satan, (41r) and shed blood to the hewn images of Canaan. The earth was polluted with blood, and their deeds became polluted, they committed fornication, and the Lord was angry with them and he despised their inheritance'.

Also on the tongue of the prophet Isaiah (peace be upon him) he says, 'God says concerning the People of Israel: They hear my word and my injunctions, but they do not remember them. They alter everything I have given them in instruction and they cancel the covenant which I wrote for them and made with them for ever. For this I will make them dwell in shame and desolation; I will put an end to them, and joy and happiness will be cut off from those of them that are left. Thus says God about the inhabitants of Jerusalem, the People of Israel: I will scatter them among the nations, and in these days the nations will raise their voices and will give glory to God and praise him with a loud voice. They will gather from the ends of the earth, from the islands of the sea and from the distant lands, and will praise the name of God, and they will return to God the God of Israel and will be his people. As for the People of Israel, they will be scattered over the earth.'

He also says on the tongue of the prophet Isaiah, 'God says: People of Israel, you have defiled the holy mountain, therefore I will destroy you with war and you will die; this is because I called you and you did not answer me; I spoke to you and you did not listen to me, but you did evil in my sight.'

The prophet Isaiah also says, 'Indeed God has hated the People of Israel, he has expelled them from his house, and he will not forgive them because he has cursed (41v) them and they have been made a curse to the people. Because of this, God has destroyed them and scattered them among the nations. He will no longer have compassion on them and he will never again look on them with his compassion. They will not be

يقرّبون لله قرباناً ولا ذبيحة في ذلك الزمان ولا يفرح قلوبهم لأنهم قد ضلّوا من الله".

وقال أرميا النبي: "قال الله: كما أنّ الحبشي لا يستطيع أن يكون أبيض فكذلك بنو إسرائيل لا يتركون عادتهم الخبيثة ، ولذلك إني لا أرحمهم ولا أشفق عليهم ولا أرق على الأمّة الخبيثة ولا أرثي لها"[8].

وقال حزقيل النبي: "قال الله : إنما رفعت يدي عن بني إسرائيل وبدّدتهم بين الأمم لأنهم لم يعملوا بوصاياي ولم يطيعوني وخالفوني فيما قلت لهم ولم يسمعوا إليّ" [9].

ومثل هذا القول في التوراة وكتب الأنبياء وزبور داود شيء كثير يقرأونه اليهود اليوم في كنائسهم ويصدّقون[10] به ولا ينكرون[11] منه حرفًا واحدًا ، وأمّا نحن النصارى فلم نعمل شيئاً ممّا عملته اليهود فلذلك كان في هذا الكتاب قوله: ﴿لتجدنّ أشدّ الناس عداوة﴾ الآيات[12] ، فذكر القسيسين والرهبان لئلا يقال إنّ هذا عن غيرنا [13]، ودلّ بهذا على جميع أفعالنا وحسن نيّاتنا[14] ونفى عنّا اسم الشرك بقوله: ﴿اليهود والذين أشركوا أشدّ عداوة للذين آمنوا والنصارى أقربهم مودّة﴾[15]

49. ٭ وقال أيضًا في سورة البقرة:[16] ﴿ إنّ الذين آمنوا والذين هادوا﴾ ٭ 42r الآية[17]، فساوى بهذا القول بين سائر الناس المسلمين وغيرهم ثمّ مدح قرابيننا وتواعدنا إن أهملنا ما معنا وكفرنا بما أنزل إلينا يعذّبنا عذابًا لا يعذّبه أحدًا من العالمين ، وذلك قوله في سورة المائدة: ﴿إذ قال الحواريون يا عيسى ابن مريم﴾[18] وإلى قوله: ﴿من العالمين﴾[19]، فالمائدة[20] هي القربان المقدّس الذي نتقرّب به في كل قدّاس.

ولما تقدّم به القول فإنه غير لائق بذوي الألباب أن تهمل روح القدس وكلمة الله الذي شهد له في هذا الكتاب بالمعظمات وقال عنه:

---

[8] Cf. Jeremiah XIII: 14, 23. [9] Cf. Ezekiel VI: 8. [10] A and B: ويصدّقوا [11] A and B: ينكروا. [12] S. V: 82-4. [13] B: غيرها [14] B: بناتنا [15] Cf. S. V: 85. [16] في سورة البقرة: [17] S. II: 62. [18] S. V: 112. [19] Ibid.: 112-15. [20] B: قال لمايدة (wrongly), a misreading of A. these words are supplied in the same hand in the margin in A.

able to draw near to God with offering or sacrifice in those days, and their hearts will not be gladdened for they have erred from God.'

The prophet Jeremiah says, 'God says: Just as the Ethiopian cannot be white, so the People of Israel will not abandon their evil way. Because of this I will not show them compassion, nor have pity on them, nor will I relent towards the evil nation or feel sorrow towards them.'

The prophet Ezekiel says, 'God says: Indeed I have withdrawn my hand from the People of Israel and have scattered them among the nations because they have not acted according to my injunctions and have not obeyed me. They have offended me in what I said to them and they have not listened to me.'

There are many things in the Torah, the books of the prophets and Psalms of David like these words. The Jews read them today in their synagogues, and they believe them and do not deny a single word. But we Christians have never done a single thing such as the Jews did. And for this reason there are in this book his words, 'Thou wilt find the most vehement of mankind in hostility [to those who believe the Jews and the idolaters. And thou wilt find the nearest of them in affection to those who believe those who say: Lo! We are Christians. That is because there are among them priests and monks, and because they are not proud. When they listen to that which hath been revealed to the messenger, thou seest their eyes overflow with tears because of their recognition of the Truth. They say: Our Lord, we believe. Inscribe us among the witnesses. How should we not believe in Allah and that which hath come unto us of the Truth? And (how should we not) hope that our Lord will bring us in along with righteous folk?]'. He mentions priests and monks, so that it cannot be said that this is about anyone other than us. In this he points to all our deeds, presents the goodness of our intentions positively, and denies the name of polytheist with regard to us, in his words, 'The Jews and the idolaters are the most vehement in hostility to those who believe, and the Christians are closest to them in affection.' (42r)

49. Furthermore, he says in *The Cow*, 'Those who believe, and those who are Jews' and the rest of the verse. Here he makes all people, Muslims and others, equal. He also commends our communions and warns us that if we abandon what we have and do not believe in what was revealed to us he will punish us with a punishment which he has not meted out to any creatures. These are his words in *The Table Spread*, 'When the disciples said: O Jesus, son of Mary!' and to his words 'any creatures'. For 'the table' is the holy communion which we receive in every communion service.

Therefore, in the light of these arguments, it is not appropriate for reasonable people to abandon the Holy Spirit and Word of God, whom he witnesses to in this book with great exaltation. For he says about

﴿وإنّ من أهل الكتاب إلاّ ليؤمننّ[21] به قبل موته﴾ الآية.[22] ثمّ شهد هذا الكتاب لقرابيننا وذبائحنا أنها مقبولة لدى الله وشهدت بذلك كتب اليهود التي بأيديهم يومنا هذا المنزّلة من عند الله على أفواه الأنبياء ، ومن ذلك قول أشعياء النبي: "قال الله: إني أعرف لبني إسرائيل قلوبهم القاسية الخبيثة ، فإذا أنا ظهرت إلى[23] الأمم فنظروا إلى كرامتي أقيم منهم أنبياء وأبعث منهم مخلّصين يخلّصون الأمم من البلدان القاصية للذين لم يسمعوا بسماعي ولم يعرفوه من قبل كرامتي ، ويكون اسمي فيهم ويجيئون[24] بقرابين لله * على الدواب والمراكب إلى جبل قدس أورشليم فيقرّبون لي القرابين بالسميد كما كانوا بني إسرائيل من قبل ، وكذلك باقي الأمم وتقرّب القرابين بين[25] يدي فهم[26] وزرعهم إلى الأبد يحجّون في كل شهر ومن سنة إلى سنة إلى بيت القدس بيت الله وكلهم يقرّبون لله ربّهم فيه قرابين زكية نقية وينظرون إلى الأمّة الخبيثة المارِدة بني إسرائيل لا يلى حزنها ولا ينقطع بلاؤها إلى الأبد".[27]

وقال دانيل النبي: "سيأتي على شعبك وقرية قدسك سبعون[28] سابوعًا وتنقضي الذنوب وتفنى الخطايا وغفران الإثم ويؤتى بالحقّ الذي لم يزل من قبل ، ولتتمّ نبوءات[29] الأنبياء وكتب الرسل وتشيّد[30] قرية القدس وتخرب مع مجيء المسيح ويفنى الميثاق العتيق من الناس ومن بعد أسبوع ونصف تبطل ذبائح اليهود وقرابينهم وتصير على كفّ النجاسة والفساد إلى انقضاء الجرمة".[31]

وقال ميخا النبي: "قال الله في آخر الزمان إذا أتى المسيح يدعو الأمم المبدّدة ويصنعهم شعبًا واحدًا ويبطل قتال بني إسرائيل وسلاحهم وملكهم وقرابينهم إلى الأبد".[32]

وقال عاموص النبي: "لا تذبحوا بعد العجول ، فإنّ الربّ سيأتي إلى صهيون * ويحدث وصيّة جديدة طاهرة من الخبز النقي والخمر الزكي ويعبرون[33] بنو إسرائيل مطرودين".[34] وهذا أيضًا يقرأونه اليهود في كنائسهم ولا ينكرون منه حرفا واحدًا.

وأيضًا من قول هذا بما أتى به في كتابه حيث أتبع القول إنه لم يرسل إلينا مع تشككه فيما أتى به بقوله في سورة سبأ: ﴿وإنّا أو إيّاكم لعلى هدى أو في ضلال مبين﴾،[35] وأيضًا في سورة الأحقاف: ﴿وما أدري ما يفعل بي ولا بكم﴾،[36] مع الأمر له في سورة الفاتحة

---

him, 'There is not one of the People of the Scripture but will believe in him before his death' and the rest of the verse. This book also witnesses that our offerings and sacrifices are acceptable before God, as do the books of the Jews which they possess today, and which have come down from God through the mouths of the prophets. For example, the words of the prophet Isaiah, 'God says: Indeed I know the hearts of the People of Israel that they are hard and evil. But when I appear to the nations and they see my glory, I will raise up from them prophets and from them I will send liberators who will liberate the nations from the distant lands, to those who have never heard tell of me and have never before acknowledged my glory, and my name will be among them. They will bring offerings to God (42v) on riding animals and conveyances to the holy mountain of Jerusalem, and they will make grain offerings to me as the People of Israel did before. And the other nations will do likewise, they will make offerings before me, and they and their seed for ever will make pilgrimage in every month and year after year to the holy house, the house of God. And they will all make pure, clean offerings to God their Lord there, and they will look on the evil rebellious nation, the People of Israel, whose sorrow never lightens, whose affliction is never relieved.'

The prophet Daniel says, 'Seventy weeks will be completed for your people and holy city, and offences will come to an end, transgression will cease, there will be forgiveness of sin, everlasting truth will be brought in, the prophecies of the prophets and books of the messengers will be fulfilled, and the holy city will be built and destroyed with the coming of Messiah. The old covenant will be brought to an end before the people, and after a week and a half the sacrifices and offerings of the Jews will cease, and impurity and iniquity will be curbed until there is an end of sin.'

The prophet Micah says, 'God says: In the latter time behold the Messiah will come; he will call the scattered nations and will make them into one people; he will abolish the murderousness of the People of Israel, their weapons, dominion and offerings for ever.'

The prophet Amos says, 'Do not sacrifice heifers any more. For the Lord will come to Zion (43r) and he will make a new covenant which is fresh and pure, in unblemished bread and clear wine, and the People of Israel will depart in exile.' The Jews also read this in their synagogues and they do not deny a single jot of it.

Also among the words of this individual that he brought in his book is where he next says that he was not sent to us, and his own doubts about what he was bringing, in his words in *Sabā'*, 'Lo! we or you assuredly are rightly guided or in error manifest', and also in *The Wind-Curved Sandhills*, 'Nor know I what will be done with me or with you', together

أن يسأل الهداية للصراط المستقيم ﴿صراط الذين أنعمت عليهم﴾[37] إلى آخرها ،

فأعني بقوله: ﴿المنعم عليهم والمغضوب عليهم والضالّين﴾[38] هم الثلاث أمم الذين كانوا في عصره وهم النصارى واليهود وعبّاد الأصنام ، ولم يكن في زمانه غير هذه الثلاث[39] أمم ، فالمنعم عليهم هم نحن النصارى والمغضوب عليهم فلا شكّ أنهم اليهود الذين غضب الله عليهم في كتب النبوءات والضالّين[40] هم عبّاد الأصنام الذين ضلّوا عن معرفة الله ، فهذا أمر واضح بيّن ظاهر عند كلّ أحد سيّما ذوو[41] العقول. والصراط هو المذهب وهذه لفظة روميّة لأن الطريق بالروميّة أسراطا بقول * الأسقف دميان .

* 43v

50. فالجواب: أمّا اليهود فإنهم مذمومون في كتابنا وعلى لسان داود وعيسى ابن مريم ومضروبة عليهم الذلّة والمسكنة وبائون بغضب من الله وأين ما بغضوا أخذوا وقتلوا تقتيلاً إلا بحبل[42] من الله وحبل من الناس وذلك لعتوّهم وعنادهم وقتلهم الأنبياء بغير حقّ وافترائهم على المسيح وأمّه ولأنهم آمنوا بموسى ثمّ كفروا به مرّات ثمّ آمنوا بعيسى ثمّ كفروا به عند مجيئه ثمّ آمنوا بمحمّد قبل ظهوره ثمّ كفروا به عند إتيانه وكانوا أشدّ الناس عداوة له ولمن آمن به ، وهذا هو الظلم الفاحش والكفر المكرّر ، إذًا الظلم معناه الخروج عن الحقّ ووضع الباطل موضع الحقّ ، ولمّا كان هذا الغي هو الظلم كانوا المخالفين لكتابنا والخارجون عن الحقّ الذي جاء من ربّنا.

والقائلون إنّ الواحد الأحد ثالث ثلاثة هم الظالمون الضالّون[43] وهم المشركون وكفرة أهل الكتاب كما سمّاهم الله تعالى ورسوله

---

[37] S. I: 7. [38] Cf. *Ibid.* [39] A and B: الثلاثة [40] B: والضلين [41] A and B: ذوا [42] B: الإنجيل (wrongly). [43] B: الضلون

with the command to him in *The Opener* to ask for guidance on the
straight path, 'The path of those whom thou hast favoured' to its end.
By his words, 'Those who are favoured, those who are the object of
anger, and those who go astray' he means the three communities that
existed in his day, Christians, Jews and idol worshippers; there were no
other communities than these three in his time. Now, 'those who are
favoured' are we Christians, 'those who are the object of anger' are
undoubtedly the Jews upon whom God directed anger in the books of
the prophets, and 'those who go astray' are the idol worshippers who
went astray from knowing about God. This is a clear, evident and
manifest fact to everyone, particularly intelligent people. And 'the path'
is a road followed: it is a Latin word, for 'highway' in Latin is *strata*, as
(43v) Bishop Damian says.[1]

50.   *Response:* As for the Jews, they are reproached in our Book and
on the tongue of David and of Jesus, son of Mary; baseness and
humility are inflicted upon them, and they are placed under the wrath
from God. Were it not for restraint on the part of God and on the
part of people, they would be seized and put to slaughter wherever
they are hated. This is because of their stubbornness and wilfulness,
their killing of the prophets unlawfully, their false accusation against
Christ and his mother, and because they believed in Moses and then
repeatedly disbelieved him, they believed in Jesus and then disbelieved
him at his coming, and then they believed in Muḥammad before his
appearance and then disbelieved him at his arrival and were the most
hostile people towards him and to those who believed in him. This is
shameless injustice and repeated unbelief, for the meaning of injustice
is to abandon the truth and to put falseness in its place. And since
this transgression is injustice they have offended against our Book and
have departed from the truth which came from our Lord.

   Those who say that the one and unique is the third of three are
unjust and astray; they are polytheists and the unbelievers amongst the
People of the Book, as God the exalted and his messenger have called

---

   [1] Significantly, there is no mention of this figure in either P1 or P2, indicating
that he was unknown to the copyists, the earlier of whom was working on Cyprus less
than twenty years after the *Letter* was sent. Assuming the reference to him is original
to the version of the *Letter* sent to al-Dimashqī, and not inserted by al-Dimashqī
himself, he was obviously a local scholar, since he had some knowledge of Arabic
and the text of the Qur'an.
   Unaccountably, P1, f. 56r, alters the reading here to say that *sirāṭ* is derived
not from the Latin but from the Greek *isṭirāṭ*. P2, f. 55r, restores the reading in
al-Dimashqī.

و لم يكونوا بالمؤمنين الأقربين إلينا مودّة والفائضة أعينهم من الدمع ممّا عرفوا
من الحقّ والذين آمنوا بالله ورسوله النبيّ الأمّي وباليوم الآخر أي يصدّقون
بما جاء به نبيّنا * من خبر القيامة والجنّة والنار والحساب والمجازاة بل أولئك   44r *
هم النصارى الحبوش النجاشي وأهل مملكته الذين آمنوا بالنبيّ وبما جاء به
وأووا من هاجر إليهم من المسلمين وأرسلوا أولادهم وهداياهم إلى النبي كما
أخبر داود نبيّه به صلم فهؤلاء هم المؤمنون الذين ۞ لا خوف عليهم ولا هم
يحزنون ۞ [44] لا الذين هم باقون على تهوّدهم وتنصّرهم وصابئتهم ، فإنّ هؤلاء
مردودة عليهم أعمالهم لن تقبل منهم غير الإسلام [45] دينًا.

ومثلهم في إقامتهم على التهوّد والتنصّر والتمجّس كمثل [46] إنسان مرض
بالحمّى المحرقة وغلبة الصفراء فجاءه طبيب ذلك الزمان ووصف له شراب
السكنجبين واللينوفر وكلّ قامع للصفراء مبرّد للحرارة المفرطة ، فاستعمله
المريض فبرأ ومضت عليه سنون ومرض مرضة ثانية بالفالج وغلبة البلغم
فجاءه طبيب [47] ثان عارف بالمرض والعلاج فوصف له شراب الأسطوخودس
والزنجبيل المربّى وكلّ ما هو محلّل للبلغم مسخّن للبدن فأبى ذلك المريض
أن يستعمل إلا ما وصفه له الطبيب الأوّل وغاب عن هذا المريض الصواب
في أنّ مرضه الثاني غير الأوّل وأن لكلّ مرض دواء وعلاجًا [48] وأنه * لو كان   44v *
الطبيب الأوّل معاصرًا للثاني لم يخالفه فيما وصف.

وكذلك أهل الكتاب لمّا مرضوا المرض الروحاني طبّبهم موسى بما.

[44] S. II: 62.   [45] B: السلام   [46] B: وكمثل (wrongly), a misreading of A.   [47] A and B: ثاني   [48] A and B: وعلاج

them.[2] They are not the believers who are nearest to us in affection, with their eyes overflowing with tears for what they recognise as the truth, who believe in God and his messenger, the unlettered Prophet,[3] and the last day, in other words those who trust in the communication our Prophet brought (44r) about the resurrection, paradise, hell, the reckoning and the reward. Such people are the Christians of Ethiopia, the Negus and the people of his realm, who believed in the Prophet and what he brought, and gave shelter to the Muslims who migrated to them, and sent their sons to the Prophet together with gifts, as his prophet David (peace be upon him) had announced.[4] These are the believers 'on whom no fear shall come neither shall they grieve', not those who remain in their Judaising and Christianising and Ṣābianism.[5] As for these, their deeds will return to them and nothing will be accepted from them as a religion other than Islam.

In maintaining their Judaising, Christianising and Magianising they are like a man ill with a burning fever and an excess of bile; a doctor comes to him at this time and prescribes for him a potion of vinegar syrup, water-lily and all the things that suppress bile and cool a raging temperature. The ill man takes it and gets better. Then years pass and he falls ill a second time with semi-paralysis and an excess of phlegm. A second doctor comes to him, an expert in illness and cure, and prescribes for him a potion of lavender, preserved ginger and all the things that relieve the phlegm which is causing fever in the body. But the ill man refuses to take anything except what the first doctor has prescribed for him, having no awareness of the fact that his second illness is different from the first, that each illness has a remedy and cure, and that (44v) if the first doctor were contemporary with the second he would not differ from him in his prescription.

The People of the Book are just like this: when they suffered from a spiritual sickness, Moses treated them according to what their condi-

---

[2] Cf. S. V: 73.

[3] Cf. SS. V: 82f., VII: 157f.

[4] Ibn Kathīr, *Bidāya*, vol. III, p. 78/*Life of the Prophet*, vol. II, p. 19, mentions the Negus' nephew being sent. Al-Dimashqī maybe relates this to Psalm LXVIII: 31.

[5] Cf. SS. II: 62, V: 69. In his refutation of Christianity, 'Alī al-Ṭabarī shows the same attitude with regard to true Christians who followed Christ and the Gospels (and so accepted Islam) and others who falsified Christ and the first disciples' teachings with 'Christian inventions'; 'Alī al-Ṭabarī, *Radd ʿalā-n-Naṣārā*, p. 120; trans. Gaudeul, *Riposte*, p. 2.

اقتضاه حالهم فبرئوا ثمّ مرضوا ثانيًا وبلغوا الموت فجاءهم عيسى بطبّ
روحاني غير ما جاءهم به موسى فأنكروه وقالوا: "ما نسمع[49] غير قول
موسى ولا نترك مذهبنا المأخوذ عنه" ، فهلكوا إلا من آمن بعيسى وتلقّى
طبّه بالقبول[50] ، ثمّ مرضوا مرضة ثالثة بالكفر والشرك والابتداع لما ابتدعته
النصارى في زمن قسطنطين[51] وفيما بعده ، فجاءهم نبيّنا محمّد صلم بالطبّ
الأكبر[52] والمعرفة لمرض هؤلاء وهؤلاء أعني اليهود والنصارى ووصف لهم
أحسن وصف وعرّفهم أبلغ تعريف ونصح الجميع أعظم نصح فمنهم من
آمن وصدّق وقبل الوصف فبرئ وتعافى قلبه وسلمت نفسه وفُصل من الكفر
والنفاق ، ومنهم من أصرّ على كفره وشركه وجحوده فطال مرضه وأزمن[53]
حتى هلك وقيل له: "أدخل النار مع الداخلين".[54]

51.   وأمّا قولكم إنّ المائدة هي قرابينكم فليس كذلك لأنّ القرابين
مذكورة في القرآن العزيز والمائدة * مذكورة أيضًا وهي غيرها ، وتواريخكم   * 45r
تشهد أنّ المائدة غير القربان وأنه كان عليها خبز وبقل وسمكات وزيتون
وأكل منها قدّام المسيح خلق كثير يتداولون عليها ، قوم يشبعون ويقومون
وقوم يجلسون ويأكلون وذلك معنى العيد "لأوّلهم وآخرهم"[55] أي المعاودة
للأكل عليها وعلامة قرب المسيح من الله تعالى وإجابته لدعائه.

ثمّ لما كان في علم الله تعالى أنّ بعض تلاميذ المسيح يكفر بعده ويشرك
ككفر يهودس[56] أسخريوطي وهلاكه وكفر من

---
[49] B: يسمع   [50] B: بالقول   [51] A: قسنطين   [52] B: الأكفر (wrongly).   [53] B: وإن من
(wrongly), evidently a misreading of A.   [54] Cf. S. LXVI: 10.

tion required, and they recovered. Then they fell ill a second time and came close to death, and Jesus came to them with spiritual medicine different from what Moses had brought them. But they rejected him and said, 'We will only listen to what Moses said, and we will not abandon our belief which has come down from him.' They perished, except the ones who believed in Jesus and were prepared to receive his medicine. Then they fell ill from a third sickness of unbelief, polytheism and innovation, because of the innovations the Christians made in the time of Constantine and afterwards. Our Prophet Muḥammad (may God bless him and give him peace) brought them the greatest medicine and knowledge about both their sicknesses, that is of the Jews and Christians. He made for them the best prescription, imparted to them the most complete instruction, and gave all of them the most significant advice. Some among them believed and trusted and accepted the prescription, and they recovered, they were restored to health in their innermost being, made whole in their spirits, and they cut themselves off from unbelief and hypocrisy. But some of them persisted in their unbelief, polytheism and infidelity, and their illness lingered and continued until they perished and were told, 'Enter the fire along with those who enter'.

51. As for your statement that 'the table' is your offerings, this is not so, because the offerings are referred to in the esteemed Qurʾan and so is the table (45r), and they are different from these. Your histories bear witness that the table was different from the offering, and that on it were bread, herbs, fish and oil. A large crowd ate these in front of Christ, each in turn, people eating their fill and getting up, and people sitting down and eating.[6] And this is the meaning of 'the feast for the first of them and for the last of them', that is returning time and again to eat upon it, and a sign of Christ's nearness to God the exalted and of God's response to his call.

It was known to God the exalted that some of Christ's disciples would stop believing after him and would become polytheists, such as Judas Iscariot's unbelief and his destruction, and the unbelief of

---

[6] This is an allusion to Jesus' miracles of feeding large crowds in Mtt XIV: 13-21 || Mk and Lk, and Mtt XV: 32-9 || Mk, which al-Dimashqī sees as the Gospel equivalent to the table sent down in S. V: 112-15. The details of the herbs and oil on the table are additions to the Biblical and Qurʾanic accounts.

افترى على المسيح وزعم أنه قال: "عمّدوا العالم باسم الثالوث[57]" وأمر بالشرك بالله وككفر من اتخذه إلهًا من دون الله.

﴿قال الله إني منزّلها عليكم﴾ ، يعني المائدة ، ﴿فمن يكفر بعد منكم﴾ الآية[58]، فالمائدة كانت من معجزات المسيح لا ممّا زعم أنّه قال عن خبز السميد النقيّ: "هذا لحمي فلوكوه وهذا دمي فاشربوه" ، يعني الخمر المحرّم سكره في جميع الشرائع حتى يكون قربانًا يتقرّب به إلى الله تعالى بالأكل له.

ولقد كان للمسيح من المعجزات ما هو أعجب من المائدة من إطعام الخلق * الكثير من الخبز اليسير وأطعم في قرية الطابغة من ستّ سلال خبز أو سبع سلال ألوفًا من الناس وأخرج الله له من شجرة التين العريانة من الورق والثمر تينًا حلوًا نضيجًا أكل منه وأطعم التلاميذ وذلك ببيت عيانا ، وكما أمر الله تعالى بلسان الملك لأمّه مريم عند ولادته أن تهزّ إليها بجذع النخلة ، فتساقط عليها من الجذع رطبًا جنيّاً ، وكما كان من زكريّا يدخل عليها فيجد عندها الفاكهة[59] الغريبة والرزق الشهي فيقول: ﴿أنى لك هذا؟﴾ فتقول: ﴿هو من عند الله﴾ الآية[60].

وكما فعل نبيّنا صلم

* 45v

---

[55] A reminiscence of S. V: 114. [56] A and B: هيرودس [57] A adds الأقدس in the margin in a different hand. [58] S. V: 115. [59] B: الفاهة (wrongly), evidently a misreading of A. [60] S. III: 37.

those who invented lies against Christ and claimed that he had said,
'Baptize the world in the name of the Trinity',[7] and had ordered them
to associate others with God, and the unbelief of those who took him
as a god besides God.

'Allah said: Lo! I send it down to you [that is, the table]. And whoso
disbelieveth of you afterward' and the rest of the verse. So the table
was one of Christ's miracles, and was not, as is claimed, what he said
about the unblemished grain bread, 'This is my body, eat it; this is
my blood, drink it'[8] (meaning wine with which it is forbidden to get
drunk in all forms of law), so that it became the offering by means of
eating which one is brought close to God the exalted.[9]

Christ performed more impressive miracles than the table, such as
feeding a great many (45v) people with a little bread;[10] in the town
of al-Ṭābagha he fed thousands of people from six or seven baskets
of bread;[11] and from a fig tree that was bare of leaves and fruit God
produced for him figs sweet and ripe, and he ate them and fed the
disciples. This was in Bethany.[12] Similarly, God the exalted through
the tongue of the angel ordered his mother Mary at his birth to shake
the trunk of the date palm towards herself, and then they fell on her
from the palm fresh and ripe.[13] And also when Zakariyyā used to go
in to her, he found she had exotic fruits and tasty food, and he said,
'Whence cometh unto thee this?' and she said, 'It is from Allah' and
the rest of the verse.

In the same way, our Prophet (may God bless him and give him

---

[7] Cf. Mtt XXVIII: 19. Al-Dimashqī strongly implies that this is an example of
corruption of the original *Injīl*.

[8] Cf. Mtt XXVI: 26f.

[9] This is another casual indication that al-Dimashqī knew about Christian worship.

[10] This is a general reference to Jesus' miracles of feeding large crowds; cf. n.
6 above.

[11] The nearest Gospel equivalent is Mtt XV: 32-9 || Mk VIII: 1-10, in which
Jesus feeds the crowd from seven loaves and some fish, after which seven baskets of
pieces were collected. There is no reference there or in the other feeding miracle
accounts to al-Ṭābagha. Al-Dimashqī does not refer to it in the *Nukhba*, and there is
no sign of it in Yāqūt, *Muʿjam al-buldān*.

[12] Cf. Mtt XXI: 18-22 || Mk XI: 12-14 and 20-5, in which Jesus while on his
way from Bethany to Jerusalem curses a fig tree because it has no fruit and it withers.
Al-Dimashqī reverses the meaning of the story.

[13] Cf. S. XIX: 24-6.

مرّات كثيرة معجزات باهرة ضبطها العلماء وحرّروها فكانت ألفًا وتسعين معجزة منها أطعم ألوفًا من المسلمين في غزاة تبوك فأشبعهم وملأ أوعيتهم تمرًا ودقيقًا من كومة تمر ما يحجب القاعد إليها عن القاعد إليها ثمّ فضل منها بعد كفايتهم فضلة وسقاهم أيضًا ورواهم في تلك الغزوة وهم ألوف من مزادة على جمل لامرأة ودلّهم عليها وأنّها بوادي⁶¹ كذا تسير⁶² فأحضروها إليه فسمّى الله تعالى وفتح المزادة وسكب الماء منها على يده الشريفة إلى الحوض * الجلد وأمر أن يردوه بعد عشرة حتى اكتفوا وسقوا دوابهم ثمّ سدّ عزازيل المزادة فإذا هي ملآنة كما كانت ، فقال للمرأة: "خذي مالك واذهبي فقد سقانا الله تعالى وماؤك ماؤك"⁶³.

* 46r *

ولمّا وصل إلى تبوك لم يكن بها ماء إلا ما يروي الشفة ، فأخرج سهمًا وغرسه في تلك العين فثجّت وانفجرت نهرًا فقال : "من عاش منكم سيرى هنا حدائق وأعنابًا" ، فكان ذلك وهذه العين إلى يومنا هذا تفجّ بالماء وتسقي نخيلاً وزروعًا بتبوك ، وهذا ومثله غير منكور من الأنبياء عليهم السلام أن يأتوا بمثله بإذن الله تعالى.

52. وأمّا قولكم: وإنه كان مأمورًا بطلب الهداية إلى الصراط المستقيم⁶⁴ واستشهادكم بفاتحة الكتاب وبآيتي سبأ والأحقاف فليس كذلك ولا يدلّ عليه لا ظاهر لفظ الآيات ولا معانيها المعقولة ولا يقتضيه القياس ، ولكنكم لمّا لم تفهموا المعنى ولا تدبّرتم القول ولا عرفتم المراد به زعمتم ما زعمتم⁶⁵ وسأبيّن لكم الحقّ فيه وأنّ المراد خلاف ما قلتموه.

---

⁶¹ B: بوادن ⁶² B: لتسير ⁶³ A and B: وماؤك ماءك ⁶⁴ B: المتقيم ⁶⁵ ما زعمتم :B omits these two words.

peace) many times performed brilliant miracles which scholars have recorded and put down. There were one thousand and ninety miracles, among them his feeding thousands of Muslims during the raid on Tabūk.[14] He satisfied them, and filled their bags with dried dates and flour from a heap of dates that one person sitting near it was able to screen from another sitting nearby, then after they were satisfied there was still some left over. On this raid, he also quenched their thirst and satisfied them with water from a water bag on a woman's camel, and they were thousands. He told them about her and that she was walking in a certain valley. They brought her to him and, pronouncing the name of God the exalted, he opened the water bag and poured water from it over his noble hand into a cool (46r) pool. He ordered them to come to him ten by ten until they were satisfied and their horses had been watered. Than 'Azāzīl closed the provision bag and, indeed, it was as full as it had been before. He said to the woman, 'Take what is yours and go, for God the exalted has given us water, and your water belongs to you.'

When he arrived at Tabūk, there was no water there except what can moisten the lip, so he took out an arrow and thrust it into the spring there; it gushed forth and poured out in a stream. He said, 'Whoever of you lives will see here gardens and grapes.' This happened, and the spring still flows with water today and waters date palms and fields in Tabūk. This and similar things cannot be denied in the case of prophets (peace be upon them); they produce such things with the help of God the exalted.[15]

52.   As for your statement, He was ordered to seek guidance on the 'straight path', and your quotation from *The Opener* and of verses from *Sabā'* and *The Wind-Curved Sandhills*, it is not like this, because neither the actual words in the verses nor their clear meaning point to it, nor does logical thinking demand it. But since you have no conception of the meaning, have not reflected on the words and have no notion of its intention, you make the claim that you do. But I will show you the truth of it and that the intention is different from what you say.

---

[14] This took place in 9/631.

[15] The miracles of multiplying food and increasing the flow of the spring are found in slightly different forms in Ibn Kathīr, *Bidāya*, vol. V, pp. 9-10 and 12/*Life of the Prophet*, vol. IV, pp. 1-12 and 15; cf. Perlmann, *Ibn Kammūna's Examination of the Three Faiths*, p. 133.

أمّا الفاتحة فإنها من أوّل المنزّل[66] من القرآن ، ولذلك [67] سمّيت فاتحته
وأمّه. حمد الله تعالى * نفسه وأثنى[68] عليها فقال: ﴿الحمد لله ربّ العالمين﴾[69]
أي قولوا: الحمد لله وتمام الثناء عليه سبحانه ، وقولوا: ﴿إيّاك نعبد وإيّاك
نستعين﴾[70] وقولوا: ﴿اهدنا الصراط المستقيم صراط الذين أنعمت عليهم﴾[71]
يعني من النبيّين والصديقين والشهداء والصالحين المذكورين للتعريف بهم في
قوله تعالى في سورة النساء: ﴿ومن يطع الله ورسوله﴾ الآيات[72] إلى قوله:
﴿عليمًا﴾[73].

ولقد سئل رسول الله صلم عن المغضوب عليهم من هم؟ فقال: "هم
اليهود" أي الجاحدون الحقّ مع علمهم به والمعاندون الأنبياء حسدًا وبغيًا ،
وكذا كلّ ملحد ومنكر ومحرّف لكلام الله تعالى عن مواضعه، وسئل عن
الضالّين من هم؟ فقال: "هم النصارى" أي أنهم ضلّوا عن طريق الهدى
وأشركوا بالله خلقه وكفروا بما جاءهم من الحقّ بلسان الرسول الموبّخ للعالم
على الخطيئة بقول الثالوث واعتقاد الأقانيم.

53. وسأبيّن فصلاً في الشرك يظهر لكم منه ما أنتم عليه فاسمعوه وعوه.
إنه لما كان المشرك بالله تعالى منقسمًا إلى شرك تعمّده المشرك القاصد له وإلى
شرك خطأ من المشرك الغير قاصد له بل قصده التوحيد ولكنه ضالّ * غير
مهتد إليه ولا راجع إلى هدى من يهديه إليه ، كان العامدون هم المشركون
الجاهلية عبدة الأصنام والأوثان والنصب والشياطين والجنّ والطاغوت عمدًا
من غير انتماء إلى ملّة ولا قيام بشريعة ولا تمسّك

* 46v

* 47r

[66] B: المنز (wrongly). [67] B: وكذلك [68] A and B: وأبنى [69] S. I: 2. [70] Ibid.: 5
[71] Ibid.: 6-7. [72] S. IV: 69. [73] Ibid.: 69-70.

The Opener is among the first of the Qur'an revealed, and for this reason it is called its opening and 'mother'.[16] God the exalted (46v) praises and exalts himself, saying, 'Praise be to Allah, Lord of the worlds', that is, say, 'Praise be to Allah, and perfect exaltation be to him, may he be blessed'; and say, 'Thee we worship, thee we ask for help'; and say, 'Show us the straight path, the path of those whom thou hast favoured' meaning 'of the prophets, the saints, the martyrs and the righteous' who are mentioned in the exalted One's words in *Women* so that they may be recognised, 'Whoso obeyeth Allah and [his] messenger, [they are with those unto whom Allah hath shown favour, of the prophets and the saints and martyrs and the righteous. The best of company are they! That is bounty from Allah, and Allah sufficeth] as Knower'.

The messenger of God (may God bless him and give him peace) was asked who 'those who earn thine anger' were, and he said, 'They are the Jews', that is, those who reject the truth despite knowing it, and oppose the prophets with envy and jealousy, and in the same way all who turn away, or deny, or change God the exalted's words from their places.[17] And he was asked who 'those who go astray' were, and he said, 'They are the Christians', that is, they went astray from the path of guidance, associated his creature with God himself, and did not believe in the truth that came to them on the tongue of the messenger who rebuked the world about wrongdoing in speaking about the Trinity and believing in the Persons.

53.   I will explain polytheism separately, so that it will be plain to you what you believe. So listen and take heed. Those who have polytheistic beliefs about God the exalted are divided into polytheism which is committed by the polytheist who intends it, and polytheism which is a mistake on the part of the polytheist who does not intend it but intends to declare the unity of God, though he has gone astray (47r) and is not properly guided, and does not come back to the guidance from the one who guides him. Those who deliberately committed it were the polytheists of the time of ignorance, worshippers of idols, images, statues, devils, jinn and false gods, who had no adherence to a religion, no respect for a religious law, and no commitment to the

---

[16]   *Umm al-kitāb*, mentioned in SS. III: 7, XIII: 39 and XLIII: 4, is often identi-fied as the first *Sūra*.

[17]   Cf. SS. IV: 46, V: 13 and 41.

بإثارة من علم منسوبة إلى رسول مطلق الرسالة مثل نوح وابراهيم وموسى وعيسى ومحمّد صلوات الله عليهم أجمعين ، فهؤلاء العامدون الشرك هم الكفرة الأنجاس الفجرة المحرّمة ذبائحهم ، ونكاحهم وإنكاحهم على المسلمين حتى يؤمنوا.

وكان الخاطئون خطأ العمد بطلبهم معرفة الله تعالى بما تقتضيه آراؤهم وقصدهم تنزيهه وتوحيده بحسب ما رأته عقولهم وحسنته نفوسهم ، فقسّموا الإله الواحد الأحد ثلاثة آلهة أقانيم ثالوثاً وسمّوها آباً وابناً وروحًا واتخذوها إلهًا واحدًا وكان مثل خطأ هؤلاء العمد وشركهم مع قصدهم التوحيد وعدم الاهتداء إليه كمثل من أراد رمي صيد بسهم والصيد حوله أناس قيام فقيل له: "لا ترم سهمك فربّما يصيب أحدًا من الناس القيام" ، فقال: "إنما أرمي الصيد" ثمّ رماه قاصدًا له دون من حوله فأصاب بسهمه إنسانًا منهم فقتله بغير قصد لقتله ولم يصب الصيد الذي كان قاصدًا له ، وهؤلاء هم المشركون الضالّون * كفرة أهل الكتاب المباحة للمؤمنين ذبائحهم بذكر اسم الله عليها دون ما يقتلونه قتلاً ودون صيد الحيوان البري والمباح لنا نكاح المحصّنات الكتابيّات منهم دون إنكاحهم.

47v *

فاليهود مغضوب عليهم وهم كتابيّون والنصارى ضالّون[74] مشركون وهؤلاء وهؤلاء منتمون[75] إلى ﴿الذين أنعم الله عليهم من النبّيين﴾ الآية[76] انتماءً غير صادق فامتازوا عنهم وعن النعمة وذكر الله بسبب امتيازهم ولم يذكر الجاهلية

---

[74] B: ضلون   [75] A and B: منتميون   [76] S. IV: 69.

traditions of knowledge ascribed to a messenger whose apostleship was absolute, such as Noah, Abraham, Moses, Jesus and Muḥammad (may God's blessings be upon them all). These people who committed polytheism were the unclean unbelievers, the wicked, whose slaughtered meat and giving and taking in marriage with them was forbidden for Muslims until they came to believe.[18]

Those who were mistaken were mistaken in what they committed through searching for knowledge of God the exalted under the guidance of their opinions and their intention to declare his transcendence and unity following what their minds perceived and their own selves approved. Hence, they divided the one, single Divinity into three Divinities, hypostases in a Trinity, and named them Father, Son and Spirit, accepting them as one Divinity. In trying to declare divine unity and not arriving at it, their mistake of commission and polytheism is like someone who wishes to shoot an arrow at a prey. Around the prey there are people standing, and someone says to him, 'Don't shoot your arrow because it may hit one of the people here', but he says, 'I am only going to shoot at the prey.' Then he fires, aiming at it and not those around it, but he hits one of the men with his arrow and kills him unintentionally, and does not hit the prey which he was aiming at. These are the polytheists who 'go astray', (47v) unbelievers among the People of the Book, whose slaughtered meat is permitted to believers if the name of God is pronounced over it, although not what they kill in the way they do nor the wild animals which are their prey.[19] And taking from them in marriage chaste women of the scripturalists is permitted to us, although not giving to them in marriage.[20]

So the Jews are 'those who earn thine anger' although they are scripturalists, and the Christians are 'those who go astray', polytheists. Both are related to 'those unto whom Allah hath shown favour, of the prophets [and the saints and the martyrs and the righteous. The best of company are they!]', though not by a true relationship, because for their various reasons they separated from them and from the grace and remembrance of God. He does not mention the pagan

---

[18] Cf. SS. LXXX: 42, II: 221.

[19] This is an oblique reference to pork and other animals which Christians eat but Muslims reject.

[20] S. V: 5.

الكفّار لأنهم غير منتمين إلى رسول لله ولا إلى كتاب.

54.   وأمّا تكرار طلب المهتدين للهدى إلى الصراط المستقيم وهم عليه سالكون متبعون فلمعان تشدّ عن غير المؤمنين أحدها شدّة رغبة المؤمنين في الهدى ولمحبّتهم للإيمان والطاعة وطلبهم الثبات والدوام على ذلك ، والثاني لكونهم شهداء على الناس ومطّلعون على ما فتن به الشيطان اليهود والنصارى وغيرهم واستدرجهم إلى الكفر بعد الإيمان[77] وإلى الشرك بعد التوحيد وإلى الضلالة بعد الهدى. ومن ذلك ما قرّروه أصحاب القوانين من الصيام التطوّع والمفروض لأسماء رجال ونساء بأعيانهم ولم يخلصوا لله[78] منها صوم يوم واحد * بل قالوا: "صيام يوحنا ، صيام بطرس وبولص ، صيام جرجس ، صيام تادرس، صيام مركيس ، صيام بربارة ، صيام السيّدة ، صيام الميلاد ، صيام المسيح للصوم الكبير" ، فعزوا كلّ صوم إلى من أشركوا به وهم لا يشعرون ، فكرّر المؤمنون طلب الهداية خشية من مثل ذلك وسألوا الله الثبات عليها لأنه مقلب القلوب والأبصار والفعّال لما يريد.

   والثالث أنّ المؤمنين ندبوا إلى تلاوتها في كلّ صلاة ليتدبّروا ما فيها من معاني القرآن وجوامع أسماء الله الحسنى العشرة وذكر

* 48r

---

[77] B: اليمان (wrongly), a misreading of A.   [78] B: الله

unbelievers, because they are not related to any messenger of God nor to any book.

54. As for the repeating of the request for guidance along 'the straight path' from those who were guided and were walking along it one after another, for a number of reasons this rules out those who are not believers.[21] The first is the intensity of the believers' desire for guidance, their yearning for faith and obedience, and their quest for steadfastness and permanence in this. The second is the fact that they are testifiers about people, being aware of the temptations that Satan has laid before the Jews, Christians and others, and his enticing of them into unbelief after faith, into polytheism after declaring divine unity, and into error after guidance. An example of such is the canonical experts' stipulation of voluntary and obligatory fasting in the names of men and women who are important among them. They have not dedicated one day among these to God, (48r) but have said instead: the fast of John, of Peter and Paul, of George, of Theodore, of Markīs, of Barbara, of our Lady, of Christmas, and of Christ which is Lent, relating each fast to the person whom they make a partner with him, and they do not realise.[22] The believers seek guidance time and again out of fear of doing the same, and they implore God for steadfastness in following it, because he can transform hearts, attitudes and deeds as he wills.

The third is that the believers apply themselves to reciting it in every prayer, so that they can reflect upon the themes of the Qur'an it contains: the collection of the ten beautiful names of God, the ref-

---

[21] This refers to the point made by the Christians at the end of the passage from their *Letter* quoted at the beginning of this section, § 49. The three reasons that follow show how true believers could not request guidance from Christians because: they are inconsistent, they have abandoned monotheism, and the believers themselves seek this guidance from God as in their daily prayers they meditate upon the *Sūra* which contains it.

[22] These fasts appear to fall into three groups: firstly, those preceding the festivals of great figures from the founding period of Christianity; secondly those preceding the festivals of saints connected with warfare (that is, if Theodore is identified as Theodore of Heraclea, a Roman general martyred by command of the emperor Licinius, often mentioned together with George the model soldier saint, and Markīs is taken as a representation of the name of the soldier martyr Mercurius, on whom cf. S. Baring-Gould, *The Lives of the Saints*, London, 1898, vol. XIV, p. 540, and J.J. Delaney, *Dictionary of Saints*, London, 1982; Barbara, one of the four patrons of the Eastern Church, was recognised as the patron saint of armourers and artillery-man); and thirdly those associated with the principal feasts of Mary and Jesus.

العالمين المشتق من المعاملة أعني أنّ كلّ ذرّة من ذرّات العالم معلَّمة بدلالتها
على صانعها ربّ العالمين الربّ لكلّ مربوب وذكر أهل السعادة والشقاوة
وتعريف العباد بسعة رحمة الله ورحمانيته بتكرار اسمه الرحمن الرحيم وطلب
المؤمنين المهتدين للهداية الخاصة الخالصة من شوائب الرقائق السارية في
الأمّة بالمشابهة بين قلوب السالفين[79] من الأمم وقلوب الخالفين من الأمّة في
العقائد والآراء كالرقيقة اليهودية والنصرانية التي أهل هذه استسلموا وصدَّقوا
وانقادوا لكلّ ما يقال حتى غلوا في المسيح وظنّوه إلهاً مع الله وتلقوا[80] كلما * 48v *
سمعوه عنه من حقّ وباطل وصدق وكذب بالقبول ، فلو قيل لهم ما عسى أن
يقال قالوا: "آمنّا وصدَّقنا" ، وعلى مثل هذا تأسَّست قواعد دين النصرانية
ولم يكن ذلك من العدل ، وأهل هذه تابوا وأنكروا وامتنعوا عن قبول
كل شيء من حقّ وباطل وصدق وكذب فلم ينقادوا ولا استسلموا لأمر
إلهي إلا بعد جدل وبحث وسؤالات واقتراحات وإيرادات شكوك محتملات
وغير محتملات حتى لو قيل لهم: "إنّ الجزء أصغر[81] من الكلّ" لقالوا: "لا
نسلم" ، وبمثل ذلك قتلوا الأنبياء وكذَّبوا الرسل ولُعنوا في الدنيا والآخرة ،
وكالرقائق المجوسيّة والصابئية والفلسفيّة والواقفيّة وغيرها من الرقائق
السارية في الأمـم.

---

79 السالف :B   80 وتاقوا :B   81 الحذاء صغر :B

erence to 'the worlds', which is derived from 'indication' (meaning that every single particle of the world is an indicator in that it points to its Maker, the Lord of the worlds, the Lord of everything beneath his lordship), the reference to the people of bliss and misery, the announcement to humanity of the extent of God's compassion and compassionateness by repeating his name 'the Compassionate, the Merciful', and the request on the part of believers who are guided for guidance which is particular and purified from the traces of the flaws that spread in the community, because the minds of those in earlier communities are similar to the minds of those in a later community as regards beliefs and opinions. Such is the trace among the Jews and the Christians, who submit to, trust and obey everything that is said, to the extent that they have gone too far over Christ and thought he is a god besides God, and have readily accepted everything (48v) they have heard about him, whether right or wrong, true or lying. If someone were to say to them 'It could be said...', they would reply, 'We believe and trust'. In a way such as this were the foundations of Christianity established. And it is not just, for these people turn away, deny and refuse to acknowledge all that is right and wrong, true and false. They only obey or submit to a divine command after dispute, discussion, raising questions, making suggestions and introducing matters of doubt both probable and improbable, to such an extent that if someone said to them, 'The part is smaller that the whole', they would say, 'We will not concede this'. In the same way they killed the prophets and called the messengers liars, and they are cursed in this world and the next. The traces among the Zoroastrians, the Ṣābians, the philosophers, the *Wāqifiyya*[23] and other traces that spread in communities are similar.

---

[23] These groups evidently corrupted monotheism in various ways, the Zoroastrians through dualism, the Ṣābians, as al-Dimashqī has made clear already, through polytheism, and the philosophers through favouring natural processes over divine power. The *Wāqifiyya* are less easy to identify. The name is used variously within Islam, for Kharijites who 'hesitated' or 'desisted' from following ʿAlī after the Battle of Ṣiffīn, and for Shīʿa groups who 'desisted' from giving allegiance to anyone after a particular Imām, and especially the seventh. It could also be levelled at those Ṣūfīs who appeared to refer to themselves alone as the authority of their knowledge and insight into God (cf. A. Arberry, *The Mawāqif and Mukhātabāt of Muhammad ibn ʿAbdi 'l-Jabbār al-Niffarī*, London, 1935, pp. 14-16), and so would desist from accepting revelation or reason. But none of these identifications seems appropriate in the case of the group al-Dimashqī has in mind, because here, and even more obviously at the end of § 56,

ومعنى الرقيقة هو انطباق قلوب المتأخّرين على ما كانت عليه المتقدّمون⁸²
من العقائد والديانات والميل إلى شيء دون شيء فيأتي الرجل المتأخّر على
مثل ما كان عليه المتقدّم من طبع وجبلة وخير وشرّ وعلم وعمل وإدراك لمعان
دون غيرها. ولهذه المشابهة القلبية مثال حسّي يضرب لأولى الألباب وهو أنَّ
المطر تصبّ على الأرض فتنبت به نباتا مختلفًا في الطباع والخاصة والصورة ،
والمطر في نفسه طبيعة واحدة ثمّ ينزل مرّة أخرى * في وقت نزوله فتنبت

* 49r

به تلك الأرض نباتًا كالأوّل في تنوّعه واختلاف طباعه وخواصه حتى يكاد
أن يكون هو هو ، وكذلك القلوب والعقول هداها الوحي الإلهي من سماء
العزّة وهو واحد فتنبت به ضروبًا من العقائد والأمانات باصطلاح النصارى ،
فإنهم يسمّون العقيدة أمانة ثمّ يأتي قرن بعد مضي قرن فتختلف منهم القلوب
بالعقائد ويكون الاختلاف من الخالف كالاختلاف من السالف وتكون
المشابهة له منه في الآراء والنِحَل كالمشابهة بين النبات الأوّل الكائن نباته
في الزمن الخالي وبين النبات الثاني الآتي نباته في الزمن المستقبل فهما سواء في
المشابهة وفي المطابقة وبينهما ما بينهما في الأعصر والدهور.⁸³

فلمّا كانت هذه الرقائق سارية في الأمّة ولا يكادون يشعرون بها علّمهم
الله تعالى قول: ﴿أهدنا الصراط المستقيم﴾⁸⁴ أي الطريق الأقصد ﴿صراط
الذين أنعمت عليهم﴾⁸⁵ أي بالسلامة من غفلة النصارى وتسليمهم للباطل
ومن عصيان اليهود وجحودهم للحقّ مع علمهم أنه الحقّ ومن كلّ ما
يشوب التوحيد الخالص الإبراهيمي المحمّدي من ...⁸⁶

55.   وأمّا ما أمر الله به لنبيّه أن يقوله ويقولونه الأمّة معه ، فالآيات التي في
سورة * الأنعام وهي قوله: ﴿إنَّ صلاتي

* 49v

---

⁸² A and B: المتقدّمين   ⁸³ B: والدهار   ⁸⁴ S. I: 6.   ⁸⁵ *Ibid.*: 7.   ⁸⁶ A word (or perhaps a phrase) appears to have been dropped here in both A and B; read perhaps: شوائب

The meaning of 'trace' is that the minds of later people conform to the beliefs and religious opinions held by earlier people and favour one thing over another, so that the later man emulates the earlier man in such things as character, temper, goodness, wickedness, knowledge, action and understanding of one matter over another. There is a physical comparison of this affinity of minds that can be applied to the leading thinkers: the rain pours down onto the earth which as a result brings forth plants different in nature, character and form, though in itself the rain has one nature. Then it falls a second time (49r) and as a result the earth beings forth plants that are like the first in their variety, difference of nature and character, so that these are almost the same as those. It is the same with minds and intellects: from the height of heaven the divine revelation, which is one, guides them, and as a result they grow into forms of beliefs and creeds (to use a Christian expression, for they call the statement of belief the creed). Then, after centuries pass a century arrives when minds among them differ over beliefs, and the difference between the later becomes like the difference between the earlier, and the affinity to the one of the other with regard to opinions and sects is like the affinity between the first plants which grew in earlier times and the second plants which grew in later times: they have a close affinity and conformity, even though there is a great gap of times and ages between them.

Since these traces spread in the community, and people were hardly aware of them, God the exalted taught them the words, 'Show us the straight path', that is, the most direct path, 'the path of those whom thou hast favoured', that is, in security from the heedlessness of the Christians and their submission to falsehood, and from the rebelliousness of the Jews and their denial of the truth despite their knowing that it is the truth, and from all that contaminates the pure Abrahamic, Muḥammadan unity of God ...

55.   As for what God commanded his Prophet and the community with him to say,[24] the verses in (49v) *Cattle*, 'My worship and my

---

he makes clear that he regards them as a group outside Islam. Maybe he means agnostics, those who hesitate to put faith in a Divinity because they have no positive proof. Cf. also § 56 and n. 38 below, and § 99 and Section 13, nn. 9 and 29.

[24] This refers back to the beginning of the part of the *Letter* quoted at the start of this section (§ 48), where the Christians suggest that the words from S. XXIX: 46, 'And say: We believe in that which hath been revealed unto us and revealed unto you', command Muḥammad and his followers to acknowledge Christian as well as Muslim scripture.

ونسكي﴾ الآية[87]، إلى قوله: ﴿وهو ربّ كلّ شيء﴾[88] وقوله: ﴿قل أغير[89] الله اتّخذ وليّاً﴾ الآية[90]، وقوله: ﴿قل هذه سبيلي﴾ الآية[91]، فهذا ومثله هو الذي أمر الله أن يقوله لا ما زعمتموه بغير علم ولا تدبّر للقول. وأمّا زعمكم أنه كان مشكّكًا فيما يأتيه من الوحي غير عالم ولا واثق بما وعده الله به وبما يكون منه واستشهادكم ببعض الآيتين فزعم باطل ومثلكم فيه كمثل قوم امتنعوا من الصلاة وقالوا: "إنّ الله قال في القرآن: ﴿يأيها الذين آمنوا لا تقربوا الصلاة﴾[92] فقيل لهم: ﴿إنما قال: ﴿لا تقربوها[93] وأنتم سكارى﴾ الآية[94]، فقالوا: "لا يحتاج إلى ذكر سبب المنع بل نمتثل"، وكذلك أنتم استشهدتم بقوله: ﴿وإنّا أو إيّاكم﴾ الآية[95] وقوله: ﴿وما أدري ما يفعل﴾ الآية[96]، ولم تتلوا الكلام من أوّله حيث يقول لنبيّه[97]: ﴿قل من يرزقكم[98] من السموات والأرض قل الله﴾[99] إلى قوله: ﴿بل هو الله العزيز الحكيم وما أرسلناك إلا كافة للناس﴾ الآية[100]، والمراد المفهوم القول للكفّار بأنّ الله رازقكم ورازقنا جميعًا وسواء كنّا على هدى أو في ضلال مبين، وذلك برحمانيته العامة لجميع العالمين كما أنه يطلع شمسه وقمره وينزل غيثه ومطره على سائر الخلق برًّا وبحرًا فهو رحمن الدنيا ورحيم الآخرة والقول للكفّار سياقًا: ﴿قل * أروني الذين ألحقتم[101] به شركاء﴾[102] أيرزقكم أحد منهم أو يرزق نفسه أو تملكون لكم أو لأنفسهم ضرًّا أو نفعًا أو موتًا أو حياة[103] أو نشورًا[104] ﴿كلا بل هو الله﴾ الآية[105]. ولقد قال نبيّنا في مثل هذا المعنى: "الله أصبر على أذى يسمعه من الناس يجعلون له أندادًا ويجعلون له ولدًا وهو مع ذلك يرزقهم ويمدّهم"[106].

* 50r

---

[87] S. VI: 162. [88] *Ibid.*: 162-4. [89] A and B: أفغير [90] S. VI: 14. [91] S. XII: 108. [92] S. IV: 43. [93] تقربوها ... فقيل: these words are supplied in the same hand in the margin in A. [94] S. IV: 43. [95] S. XXXIV: 24. [96] S. XLVI: 9. [97] B: لنبيه [98] B: برزقكم [99] S. XXXIV: 24. [100] *Ibid.*: 24-8. [101] B: الحقيم (wrongly). [102] S. XXXIV: 27. [103] A and B: حياتاً (wrongly). [104] Cf. S. XXV: 3. [105] S. XXXIV: 27. [106] B: وعمدهم (wrongly).

sacrifice' and the rest of the verse, to his words 'When he is the Lord of all things', his words, 'Say: Shall I choose for a protecting friend other than Allah?' and the rest of the verse, and his words, 'Say: This is my way' and the rest of the verse, these and the like are what God ordered him to say, not what you claim without knowledge or reflection upon the words.[25] And as for your claim that he was in doubt about the revelation that came to him, not knowing or being sure about what God had promised him and what would happen to him, and your citing of parts of two verses, it is a false claim.[26] In it you are just like people who refuse to pray, and say, 'God has said in the Qur'an, "O ye who believe! Draw not near unto prayer".' And they are told, 'In fact he has said, "Draw not near... when ye are drunken" and the rest of the verse.' So they say, 'He does not need to give a reason for the ban, we just obey.' In the same way you cite his words, 'Lo! We or you' and the rest of the verse, and his words, 'Nor know I what will be done' and the rest of the verse, but you do not read the words from the beginning, where he says to his Prophet, 'Say: Who giveth you provision from the sky and the earth? Say: Allah' to his words, 'For he is Allah, the mighty, the wise. [And we have not sent thee save unto all mankind]'. The words are obviously intended for unbelievers: God nourishes you and us in common, equally whether we are being guided or in clear error. This is an outcome of his universal compassionateness to all the worlds, just as he causes his sun and moon to rise and sends down his rain and showers on all creation, both land and sea; he is the Compassionate in this world and the Merciful in the hereafter. And the words to the unbelievers that come after, (50r) 'Say: Show me those whom ye have joined unto him as partners'—will one of them nourish you or nourish himself? Do they possess harm or good, death or life or resurrection, either for you or for themselves?—'Nay! For he is Allah' and the rest of the verse. Our Prophet said something the meaning of which is similar, 'God is very forbearing in the face of the insult he hears from people who make rivals to him and make him sons; for despite this he nourishes them and provides for them.'

---

[25] These three verses all draw a distinction between belief in God and belief in other beings. Al-Dimashqī adduces them to prove that Muslims cannot be commanded to accept Christians, because the latter do just this by associating Jesus with God.

[26] This refers back to the last argument quoted from the Christians in this section, § 49, where they employ SS. XXXIV: 24 and XLVI: 9.

وكذلك أيضًا لم تتلوا قوله تعالى عن كفّار قريش: ﴿أم يقولون أفتراه﴾،
يعني القرآن، ﴿قل إن افتريته فلا تملكون لي من الله شيئًا﴾[107] إلى قوله: ﴿وما
أنا إلا نذير مبين﴾[108]. ولم تتدبّروا القول فيتبيّن لكم أنه صلم نذير وبشير
للناس كافة ولليهود والنصارى عامة وللعرب الجاهلية خاصة وتجدون معنى
قوله: ﴿وما أدري ما يفعل بي ولا بكم﴾[109] مثل معنى قول المسيح ليلة
الفصح: "المشيئة مشيئتك لا مشيئتي، فإن شئت أن تصرف عنّي هذا الكأس
وإلا فالمشيئة مشيئتك"[110]، والقصد إنما هو تفويض الأمر إلى الله والرجوع
بالحول والقوّة إليه سبحانه وتعالى.

وبالجملة فكلّ ما في القرآن الكريم من الصفح عن المشركين والإعراض
عن الجاهلين والموادعة لهم وشبهه كقوله تعالى: ﴿وأعرض عن الجاهلين﴾[111]،
وقوله تعالى: ﴿ولا تجادلوا أهل الكتاب﴾ الآية[112]، وقوله تعالى: ﴿فاعف
عنهم وأصفح﴾[113]، وقوله: ﴿لا حجّة بيننا وبينكم﴾[114] وقوله: ﴿لكم
دينكم ولي دين﴾[115] وما شابه ذلك كلّه منسوخ الحكم بآية السيف وهي
قوله تعالى: ﴿يأيها النبي جاهد الكفّار والمنافقين واغلظ عليهم * ومأواهم
جهنّم وبئس المصير﴾[116] وما شابهها كقوله تعالى: ﴿فاقتلوا المشركين
حيث وجدتموهم وخذوهم واحصروهم﴾ الآية[117]، وقوله: ﴿قاتلوا الذين لا
يؤمنون بالله ولا باليوم الآخر﴾ الآية[118].

56.   وأمّا ما زعمتم في قوله تعالى: ﴿كان الناس أمّة واحدة﴾

* 50v

---

[107] S. XLVI: 8.   [108] *Ibid.*: 8-9.   [109] *Ibid.*: 9.   [110] Cf. Lk XXII: 42.   [111] S. VII:
199.   [112] S. XXIX: 46; الآية ... والموادعة: these words are supplied in the same hand
in the margin in A.   [113] S. V: 13.   [114] S. XLII: 15.   [115] S. CIX: 6.   [116] S. IX:
73.   [117] *Ibid.*: 5.   [118] *Ibid.*: 29.

In the same way also you have not read the words of the exalted One concerning the Quraysh unbelievers, 'Or say they: He hath invented it (that is, the Qur'an)? Say: If I have invented it, still ye have no power to support me against Allah' to his words, 'And I am but a plain warner'. And you have not reflected on what is said so that it might become plain to you that he (may God bless him and give him peace) was a warner and herald to all people, to Jews and Christians in general, and to the pagan Arabs in particular. And you will find the meaning of his words 'I do not know what he is doing to me or to you' like the meaning of Christ's words on the night of Passover, 'Yours is the will not mine; if you will you can take this cup from me; if not, yours is the will.'[27] The intention is nothing more than to commit the matter to God and to yield might and power to him, may he be praised and exalted.

In a word, all that is in the noble Qur'an about pardoning the polytheists and relenting towards the pagans, moderation towards them and the like, such as the exalted One's words, 'And turn away from the ignorant', 'And argue not with the People of the Scripture' and the rest of the verse, 'But bear with them and pardon them', 'No argument between you and us' and 'Unto you your religion, and unto me my religion', and all that is like this, it is all cancelled in legal judgement by the verse of the sword, which is the exalted One's words, 'O Prophet! Strive against the disbelievers and the hypocrites! Be harsh with them. (50v) Their ultimate abode is hell, a hapless journey's end',[28] and others that are similar to it, such as the words of the exalted One, 'Slay the idolaters wherever ye find them, and take them captive, and besiege them' and the rest of the verse, and 'Fight against such of those who believe not in Allah nor the Last Day' and the rest of the verse.[29]

56.   As for what you claim about the words of the exalted One, 'Mankind were one community, [and Allah sent prophets as bearers of good tidings and as warners, and revealed therewith the scripture

---

[27] Cf. § 28 above for a different form of this prayer.

[28] Various other verses are also given this title, particularly S. IX: 5.

[29] In this paragraph al-Dimashqī has developed an argument that is effectively based on the principle of *tafsīr al-Qur'ān bi-al-Qur'ān*, allowing the whole context of scripture to provide a meaning for single verses. The result in this case is that the individual verses which the Christians claim could be made to give them and their scripture equality with Muslims and the Qur'an are shown by many others not to bear this meaning.

الآية[119] أنّ النبيّين هم التلاميذ رسل المسيح لا غيرهم ، وأنّ الكتاب المنزل معهم هو الإنجيل لا سواه فليس كذلك وإنما النبيّون المذكورون سائر رسل الله وأنبيائه فأوّلهم آدم وآخرهم محمّد صلم ﴿وأولو العزم منهم﴾[120] والأئمّة العظماء رؤساء العالمين خمسة سمّاهم الله تعالى في القرآن وهم نوح وابراهيم وموسى وعيسى ومحمّد ، وبين كلّ رسول ورسول من هؤلاء الخمسة أنبياء ومرسلون مؤيّدون لرسالتهم داعون إليها فيما بين نوح وابراهيم وبين ابراهيم وبين موسى وموسى وعيسى وبين عيسى وبين محمّد صلوات الله عليهم أجمعين.

فمن نوح والطوفان وإلى ابراهيم ونمرود نحو ألف وثلاثماية سنة ، ومن ابراهيم وإلى موسى نحو ألف وماية سنة ، ومن مخرج موسى ببني إسرائيل من مصر وإلى تجلّي المسيح بجبل تابور ألف سنة وثلاث[121] وثلاثون سنة ، ومن مولد المسيح وإلى مولد سيّدنا محمّد * صلم نحو ستماية وأربعين سنة.

* 51r

والدليل على أن النبيّين المذكورين هم سائر الأنبياء والرسل من آدم وإلى آخر وقت وليس هم بطرس وبولص وتوما ومن زعمتم أنهم رسل المسيح الذين أرسلهم بعد موته وقبل رفعه إلى السماء وانفصاله عن الدنيا قوله تعالى في أوّل الآية: ﴿كان الناس أمّة واحدة فبعث الله النبيّين﴾ الآية[122] وقدّم ذكر البشارة على النذارة للافتتاح و لم يكن[123] الناس أمّة واحدة قطّ إلا في زمن آدم وعند

[119] S. II: 213.   [120] S. XLVI: 35.   [121] A and B: وثلاثة   [122] S. II: 213.   [123] A and B: و لم يكون

with the truth that it might judge between mankind concerning that wherein they differed]', that 'the prophets' were the disciples, Christ's apostles and no others, and that 'the scripture' that was sent down with them was the Gospel and not another, it is not so.[30] Rather, the prophets mentioned are all the messengers and prophets of God; the first of them was Adam and the last Muḥammad (may God bless him and give him peace). The 'stout of heart' among them, the leaders in resolution and chiefs of the worlds were five whom God the exalted names in the Qur'an, Noah, Abraham, Moses, Jesus and Muḥammad. Between each of these five messengers were prophets and those sent to confirm their apostleship, to call to it during the time between Noah and Abraham, Abraham and Moses, Moses and Jesus, and Jesus and Muḥammad (may God's blessings be upon them all). From Noah and the flood to Abraham and Nimrod[31] there were about one thousand three hundred years; from Abraham to Moses there were about one thousand one hundred years; from Moses' Exodus from Egypt with the People of Israel to the Transfiguration of Christ on Mount Tabor there were one thousand and thirty-three years; and from the birth of Christ to the birth of our lord Muḥammad (51r) (may God bless him and give him peace) there were about six hundred and forty years.[32]

The evidence that these prophets are the only prophets and messengers there will be from Adam to the end of time, and not Peter, Paul, Thomas and those you claim were apostles of Christ whom he sent after his death and before his ascension into heaven and departure from the world,[33] are the words of the exalted One at the beginning of the verse, 'Mankind were one community, and Allah sent prophets [as bearers of good tidings and as warners]' and the rest of it. The reference to 'good tidings' precedes 'warning' as a first stage,[34] and people were not a single community at all except at the time of Adam and the

---

[30] Al-Dimashqī refers back to the part of the *Letter* he quotes at the beginning of the previous section, § 42, which he has not yet answered directly.

[31] Nimrod is identified throughout Muslim literature as the unnamed opponent of Ibrāhīm referred to in S. II: 258. Al-Dimashqī refers to him a number of times in this *Response*.

[32] Cf. Section 3, n. 19. There is a rather awkward overlap between the dating of the period from the Exodus to the Transfiguration of Christ, and then from the birth of Christ to the birth of Muḥammad.

[33] This is an allusion to Mtt XXVIII: 16-20.

[34] I.e. prophets bringing good news from God would logically precede those who came to warn people who had not heeded it.

أوّل النشوانيّة والتناسل منه وكان من هابيل وقابيل ما كان ومن قنيات وعنق ما كان لا الحواريّون المدّعون الرسالة كما تقدّم.

ولئن قلتم إنّ الناس كانوا في زمن الحواريين أمّة واحدة قيل لكم إنّ بني إسرائيل كانوا أمّة كبرى والصابئون كانوا[124] ثلاث أمم كبار ، أحدها الفرس[125] والثانية الهنود والثالثة الصابئة عبدة الكواكب ، وكانت الجاهليّة عبدة الأصنام أمّة سادسة وكانت الفلاسفة اليونان أمّة سابعة كالجنس العالي لما تحته من أنواع أممهم مثل الطبيعيّين والرياضيّين والإلهيّين وأصحاب الوقفة ، فلم يكن الناس في زمن الحواريّين أمّة واحدة.

57.   وسأذكر فصلاً معقولاً برهانه لأولي الألباب في سبب بعثة الأنبياء إلى الناس ، أوّلهم وآخرهم * في زمن بعد زمن ونبيّ بعقب نبيّ. وإنه أعني إرسال الرسل من ضروريات مصالح الناس وكمال نفوسهم وسياستهم وإرشادهم إلى صلاحهم في الدنيا والآخرة وإن انضمّ إلى ذلك سياسات أخر ، فأقول: إنّ النوع الإنساني لمّا كان مدنيّاً بالطبع ولا يمكن أن يربي فريدًا ولا ينشأ وحيدًا من

* 51v *

---

124 أمّة كبرى ... كانوا: these words are supplied in the same hand in the margin in A.   125 B: الغرس

first intoxication and the procreation from him, and what happened to Abel and Cain and to Qaniyāt and 'Unuq,[35] not the disciples for whom apostleship is claimed, as is mentioned above.

And lest you should say that at the time of the disciples the people were one community, you will be told that the People of Israel were a great community, and the Ṣābians were three great communities, the first of them the Persians, the second the Indians and the third the Ṣābians, the worshippers of stars.[36] The pagan Arabs who worshipped idols were a sixth community,[37] and the Greek philosophers were a seventh, like a superior genus with species of communities beneath it such as the naturalists, the mathematicians, the theologians and the supporters of *waqfa*.[38] Thus, at the time of the disciples people were not one community.

57. I will devote a part-section, with a proof comprehensible to the foremost minds, to the reason why the prophets were sent to people, the first and last of them, (51v) period after period and prophet following prophet. This was, so to say, the sending of messengers for the necessary purposes of benefiting people, perfecting their persons and their communal affairs, leading them to what is beneficial for them in this world and the hereafter, and whatever other communal affairs could be added to these. So I say: The human species, since it is sociable by nature, cannot grow up alone or increase in isolation because of

---

[35] These individuals can all be related to the dawn of creation, and in some way were involved in the first sins: according to Jewish legend, Adam was the first to become intoxicated on the juice of the grapes he grew after his expulsion from Eden (Ginzberg, *The Legends of the Jews*, vol. I, p. 168); according to both the Bible and Qur'an, Cain shed the first blood when he slew his brother Abel (Genesis IV: 8; S. V: 30); in Numbers XIII: 33, the Anakim (of which 'Unuq may be the Arabic plural form) are identified with the Nephilim, who according to Genesis VI: 4 were the product of the sinful intercourse between the sons of God and the daughters of men, which occasioned the Flood (cf. Ginzberg, *The Legends of the Jews*, vol. I, p. 151). If this is so, Qaniyāt is possibly a reference to these daughters of men, Canaanite women. Although this identification fits into al-Dimashqī's list of the first sins, it must be accepted with some hesitation in light of the fact that the Islamic tradition records the name 'Unuq as a daughter of Adam and the first prostitute (al-Tha'labī, *Qiṣaṣ al-anbiyā'*, p. 241, and p. 44, where her name is given as 'Unāq; cf. Ibn Kathīr, *Qiṣaṣ al-anbiyā'*, Beirut, 1972, pp. 101f.).

[36] In *Nukhba*, pp. 44-7, al-Dimashqī lists the communities influenced by Ṣābianism as: two groups of the Ṣābians themselves, the Indians, the Chaldeans, the Greeks, the Egyptians and the Arabs.

[37] So far he has only listed five, though maybe he also includes the Christians without thinking it necessary to mention them.

[38] Cf. n. 23 above.

شدَّة احتياجه وضرورته من حين يولد وإلى أن يموت إلى نوعه ممّن يحضنه ويربّيه ويرضعه ويكسوه ويسوسه ويقوم بمصالحه ويذبّ عنه ويميط أذاه ويعالجه في مرضه وعرضه ويعينه على قيامه بمصالحه.

قضى العقل أن يكون الإنسان مع الأناس أبدًا لتربّيه الحواضن في صغره ويسوسه المعلّمون في أوّل نشوئه ويعينه الباقون على إصلاح شأنه فيكون منهم الغارس والزارع والذابّ والدافع والغازل والنسّاج والخيّاط والحنّاط والخبّاز والجزّار والحدّاد والنجّار والفاخوري والعطّار والحجّام والبيطار والحطّاب والحلّاج والتاجر والحمّال والساعي والسائس والراعي والمعلّم والكاتب والمهندس والحاسب والكاحل والمتطبّب والمتعيّش والمتسبّب والفقير المستعطي والمتطوّل المعطي ، ويكون أيضًا فيهم الأمين والخائن والصدوق والمائن والداهية والأبله * واللبيب والأعته والغشوم والمغتال والظلوم والمحتال والقوي والضعيف والمشروف والشريف ليقوم بعضهم لبعض بالمصالح.

والعقل يقضي أنّ فيهم غير الصالح وأنهم لا يستغنون عن التبايعات[126] والمشاركات والمزارعات والمناكحات ، وفي ذلك كله التنازع والمطالبة والتجاذب والمغالبة وقهر القويّ للضعيف وشبه ذلك، وذلك موجب إثارة الشرور واتصال الفتن بين القاهر والمقهور فيصيرون بذلك شرّ الدواب وأشبه بالكلاب والذئاب وتذهب فضيلة الإنسانية عنهم ويعود خسيس الحيوان أفضل منهم.

فقضى العقل أن لا يترك هذا النوع الشريف المستخلف على ما في الأرض بالتصريف ، فلا يوجد فيها مقدار الشبر فما دونه إلا وله خلفاء من هذا النوع يملكونه مهملاً بل يكون لهم شرع يرجعون إليه ويعوّلون في

* 52r

---

126 B: الثبايعا

its acute need and necessity from the time it is born until it dies for those in its species who can nurse it, help it grow, suckle it, dress it, direct it, look after its concerns, defend it, remove its hurt, tend it in sickness and disease, and assist it as it goes about its affairs.

Reason concludes that the human will always be among people. Thus, nursemaids nurture him when he is young, teachers direct him in his first development, and others assist him in order to improve his affairs. Among them will be the sower, the planter, the watchman, the guardian,[39] the spinner, the weaver, the tailor, the miller, the baker, the butcher, the smith, the carpenter, the potter, the perfumer, the cupper, the farrier, the wood gatherer, the cotton ginner, the merchant, the carrier, the courier, the groom, the shepherd, the teacher, the secretary, the engineer, the mathematician, the optician, the physician, the scrounger, the street trader, the needy who begs, and the generous who gives. There are also among them the trustworthy and the betrayer, the truthful and the liar, the resourceful and the simple, (52r) the agile-minded and the weak-minded, the brutal and the murderous, the treacherous and the fraudulent, the powerful and the weak, the low-born and the high-born, so that some will be preoccupied with concerns against others.

Reason concludes that among them will be those who are not virtuous, and that they cannot do without commercial compacts, co-partnerships, agricultural agreements and marriage contracts. All these are opportunities for disputes, demands for restitution, heated exchanges, struggles, the victory of the powerful over the weak, and so on. And this inevitably leads to maliciousness being stirred up and discord arising between the victor and the vanquished, so that they both become as malicious as riding animals, and just like dogs and wolves. The superiority of humanity deserts them, and the lowliest animal becomes their superior.

Reason concludes that this noble species which has been appointed vicegerent over everything in the earth should not be given an entirely free hand, for then there would be no single inch of it that did not have vicegerents from this species ruling it undirected. Rather, there should be a revealed way for them which they might consult and rely upon in

---

[39] This and the preceding job are not readily identifiable. Both terms appear to denote people who repel or ward off, and in the context could refer to those who in different ways protected the growing crops from predators, maybe thieves or even birds or pests.

المنازعة والتجاذب عليه وأن يكون من بارئهم العليم بمصالحهم والخالق لصالحهم وطالحهم ، وأن لا يأتي بهذا الشرع حيوان ولا ملك بل إنسان يعرفونه ويفهمون عنه ويألفونه ولا ينفرون منه وأن يكون معه من المعجز ما يشهدون به صدقه ويذعنون له ويثبتون حقّه وأن يأتي مع المعجز بكتاب يتلونه ويدينون * له ويحكمون به ويتشارعون به في التظالم فينصف مظلومهم من ظالمهم ويحكم بينهم فيما يختلفون فيه ويهتدى إلى مكارم الأخلاق والحقّ ويبيّن[127] أمر الحلال والحرام ويعرف تنزيه ذي الجلال والإكرام وأنه الواحد الأحد الفرد الصمد الذي لا يتجزّأ أقانيم ولا يتعدّد.

* 52v *

وقضى العقل أن لا يأتي هذا الرسول في زمن واحد بل في أزمنة متعاقبة وأن لا يكون رسولًا واحدًا بل رسل طاعتهم واجبة ، وأن يأتي كلّ واحد بما أتى به الأوّل ويزيد عليه وأن يكون لهم رسولًا خاتمًا يُنهى التعليم[128] على يديه ويكمل التشريع والدين ويتمّ النعمة على الموحدين وأن يكون هذا الرسول الخاتم للنبيّين[129] جامعًا برسالته كلّ ما أتى به المتقدّم من المرسلين لأنه يلزم من كمال التشريع وتمامه تمام النبوّة وليس بعد الرسول الخاتم ختام.

وقضى العقل أن لا يكون هذا النبي[130] الخاتم منتسبًا إلى ملّة كاليهودية والنصرانية فيكون عند إظهار دعوته كافرًا بملّته فتنفر[131] منه النفوس وتأبى تصديقه وما جاء به فكان ذلك كذلك. وجاء النقل بما قضى به العقل ، فلم يكن خاتم النبيّين ﴿يهوديًا ولا نصرانيّاً ولكن كان حنيفًا مسلمًا وما كان من المشركين﴾[132] ولم يكفّره أهل ملّة لو نسب إليها حين أظهر

---

[127] A: وتبين; B: وبنين [128] B: اليعليم (wrongly). [129] B: للبنيّين (wrongly). [130] B: البني (wrongly). [131] B: فيتفر (wrongly). [132] S. III: 67.

dissension and heated exchanges. And it should be from their Maker,
who knows their interests in full, and the Creator of the good and bad
among them. No animal or angel should deliver this revealed way, but a
man whom they could know, discover about, be familiar with and not
fear. And there should be miracles accompanying him by which they
could recognise his trustworthiness, so that they would submit to him
and declare that he was true. Together with the miracles, he should
deliver a book, which they could read out, accept as authority, (52v),
take as a basis for judgements and derive laws from for wrong-doings.
Thus, it would give justice to the wronged over the wrong-doer among
them, judge between them in what they disputed, give guidance towards
the excellent qualities of morality and truth, make clear the permitted
from the forbidden, and make known the transcendence of him who is
glorious and honoured, and that he is the One, the Single, the Alone
and the Self-subsistent, who is not divided into hypostases and is not
plural.[40]

Reason concludes that this messenger should not appear at one time
but at successive times, and that there should not be one messenger but a
number, to whom obedience would be obligatory. Each should deliver
the same as the first and add to it, and they should have a messenger
who would be a seal,[41] through whom instruction would be brought
to a conclusion, legislation and religion completed, and grace upon
the monotheists perfected. This messenger who would be a seal to the
prophets should include in his apostleship all that those who had been
sent before had delivered, because the completeness and perfection of
revealed legislation is a prerequisite of the perfection of prophethood.
There would be no seal after the sealing messenger.

Reason concludes that this sealing Prophet should not belong to
a faith such as Judaism or Christianity, so that he would become an
unbeliever in his faith when he began to make his proclamation known,
with the people turning from him and denying his trustworthiness and
what he delivered. And this is what happened: the report of events
follows what reason concludes, for the Seal of the prophets 'was not
a Jew or a Christian, but a *Ḥanīf* and Muslim, nor was he from the
polytheists'.[42] The people of a faith to which he would have belonged
could not declare him an unbeliever when he began to make known

---

[40] Cf. S. CXII: 1 and 2, and its implied denial of the Trinity.
[41] Cf. S. XXXIII: 40.
[42] S. III: 67, referring to Abraham.

دعوته وخالف * تلك الملّة كما جرى للمسيح مع اليهودية إذ كان عالمًا
من أكبر علمائهم بالتوراة عالمًا بما فيها ، ثمّ لمّا أرسله الله تعالى بما أرسله
واستجدّ ما استجدّه أنكرت اليهود ذلك وكفرت به وكفّرته بزعمها الفاسد
، فهذا سبب إرسال الرسل إلى الناس وانضمّ إلى ذلك أسباب كثيرة ليس
هذا موضع إيرادها وذكرها.

58.   ولقائل أن يقول لكم: "إنّ العقل السليم فطن[133] وأدرك بسبب
تخصيصكم للحواريين أنهم هم النبيّون المبعوثون مبشّرين ومنذرين" وأنّ
"الكتاب المنزل بالحقّ" هو الإنجيل وبما أوردتموه ونحوتموه ما سنوضّحه لكم ،
ولمطالعي[134] هذه الأجوبة إن شاء الله تعالى. وهو أنكم لمّا اقتضت آراؤكم
القول بالأقانيم وأن تجعلوا في الأرض إلهًا شبيهًا بالإنسان يفعل أفعال البشر
لتكون بين أظهرهم ظاهرًا كما زعمتم أنّ أشعيا نبّأ بذلك واتخذتم المسيح
الإله المجعول وعبدتموه كما يعبدون الله المؤمنون الموحّدون.

ثمّ فكّرتم في الإله الحقّ ربّ العالمين فحجبت عنكم معرفته فجعلتم بين
الذي جعلتموه إلهًا مختصرًا وبين ربّ العالمين علاقة نسبيّة بزعمكم وسمّيتموها
روح القدس ، ثمّ أقدمتم على الأقانيم التي اصطلحتم على الصفات الثلاث[135]
بها فقسّمتموها * ثلاثة أقسام وسمّيتموها آبًا وابنًا وروحًا وقلتم إنّ الثلاثة

واحد ولم تفطنوا لتعجّب العالمين منكم وسخرتهم[136] من جهالة من جهل
شأن الإلهيّة وما يجب لها ويطلق عليها وما يجوز أو يستحيل إعزاؤه إليها،[137]
ثمّ فطنتم بأنّ الآب والابن اسمان متغايران متباينان وأنّ التوالد قسمان:
معقول

---

[133] B: فطن   [134] B: والمطالعي   [135] A and B: الثلاثة   [136] B: وسخر بهم (wrongly).
[137] A and B: إليه

his proclamation and opposed (53r) this faith, such as happened to Christ with Judaism. For the latter was one of the greatest scholars on the Torah and knew what it contained. Then, when God the exalted sent him for the purpose he did, and he introduced the new teachings that he did, the Jews repudiated this and cursed him and called him an unbeliever, with their false allegation.

So this was the reason for the sending of the messengers to the people, and there are many other reasons as well, though this is not the place to raise them or refer to them.[43]

58. Someone may say to you: Sound reason will fully see why you identify the disciples as the prophets who were sent 'as bearers of good tidings and as warners' and the Gospel as 'the Scripture revealed with truth', and what you are intending and aiming at, as we will make clear to you and to anyone reading these responses, if God the exalted wills. This is that your opinions drove you to speak about the hypostases,[44] and to make a god on earth similar to humankind and performing human actions, 'so that you may be manifest among the most manifest of them' which you claim Isaiah prophesied, and to take Christ as a god who is made and to worship him as the monotheist believers worship God.

Then you contemplated the true God, Lord of the worlds, and comprehension of him was hidden from you. So between the one whom you made a limited god and the Lord of the worlds you made a connecting link, as you claim, and you called this the Holy Spirit. Then you rashly introduced the hypostases, for which you adopted three attributes, dividing them (53v) into three and calling them Father, Son and Spirit. You said that the three are one, not realising the whole world's marvelling at you and laughing at the ignorance of people who had no idea of what divinity is, or what is requisite to it and repudiated of it, what is possible and impossible to impute to it. Then you thought that 'father' and 'son' were two separate and distinct names, and that there were two forms of generation, rational

---

[43] Al-Dimashqī concludes this short excursus on the logical reasons for the line of prophets and now returns to the immediate point, begun in § 56, of refuting the Christians' claim that S. II: 213 refers to the disciples and the Gospel.

[44] The change from *wa-qaḍā al-ʿaql*, 'reason concludes', in the previous paragraphs to *iqtaḍat ārāʾukum*, 'your opinions drove you', signals a clear change of attitude as al-Dimashqī turns from his own arguments, which he presents as objective proofs, to the more partial and subjective ideas of the Christians.

ومحسوس ، فالمحسوس كتوالد الحيوان وتوالد النبات والمعقول كلقاح
عقل إنسان بعقل إنسان فينتج عن ذلك اللقاح نتاج حكمي وهو من باب
الإستعارة لا الحقيقة ولا يطلق على غير المخلوقين فاستنكفتم من التثليث.

ثمَّ قلتم لأنفسكم: قد سمَّى المسلمون كلمة الله وروحًا منه وسمَّاه بعض
أنبيائنا بالكلمة، والكلام فهو صفة المتكلّم والصفة تابعة للموصوف فالكلمة
حلَّت بمريم واتحدت[138] بناسوتها وتجسّمت وصارت بشرًا سويّاً ولاهوتًا إلهيًا
إنسانًا تامًّا وإلهًا تامًّا يفعل فعل أبيه.

ثمَّ لزمكم أن تكملوا إلهية هذا المجعول منكم[139] إلهًا فكان من كمالها أن
يكون له أنبياء مرسلون[140] يرسلهم إلى العالمين في زمن إلهيّته وإن كان زمنًا
قصيرًا بالنسبة إلى الدهور والأعصر ، فزعمتم أنه بعث أنبياء إلى العالم إمّا
ثلاثة أنفار وهم: توما وبطرس وبولص البديل بدل يهودس[141] وإمّا الأحد
عشر تلميذًا بعدتهم وأنَّ[142] بعثهم لم يكن إلا بعد أن صلب ومات وبعد
أنْ[143] * قام من القبر حيّاً كما ذكرت مريم المجدلانيّة في إنجيل يوحنّا.

* 54r

وللقائل الأوّل أن يقول لكم: أتعبتم نفوسكم وكلَّفتموها فوق طاقتها ،
حيث صنعتم إلهًا مألوهًا وجعلتموه خالقًا وهو مخلوق وأقمتموه على وفق[144]
مرادكم وأرسلتم له رسلاً باثنتين[145] وسبعين لغة وهم أحد عشر نفسًا ويا
لله[146] العجب كيف تعلَّموا الرسل المشار إليهم هذه اللغات التي تفصل[147] في
التقسيم على سائر الأمم في ساعة واحدة من متخفّ مترقّب خائف متستر[148]
عن أعدائه القائلين له: يا هؤلاء ، دونكم وعقول العقلاء.

---

138 B: واتّخذت (wrongly).   139 This word is supplied in the margin in A.   140 A
and B: مرسلين   141 A and B: هيرودس   142 وأنَّ: this word is supplied in the margin in
A.   143 أنْ: this word is repeated in A and B.   144 B: وقف (wrongly).   145 A and B:
باثنين   146 B: وبالله   147 B: تفعل   148 A and B: متسيّر

and physical. The physical is like the generation of animals and plants, and the rational is like one person's intelligence being impregnated by another's, with the result that it produces intellectual issue. But this is metaphorical not real, and it should not be applied to beings who are not created. You should desist from making God three.

Then you said to yourselves: The Muslims name the Word of God and a Spirit from him, and some of our prophets name him Word, while Speech is the attribute of one who is speaking, and the attribute is the adjunct of the one whose attribute it is. The Word came to dwell in Mary and united with her human nature. It became incarnate and was fully man and godly divine, perfect human and perfect divinity, and he did the work of his Father.

Then you had to complete the divinity of this god manufactured by you, so his being complete entailed his having prophets who were sent out, whom he sent to the worlds during the time he was divine, even though this was brief in comparison with ages and eras. So you claimed that he sent prophets to the world, either three individuals, Thomas and Peter and Paul, who replaced Judas,[45] or eleven disciples in a group, and that their being sent was only after he was crucified and died, and after (54r) he rose from the tomb alive, as Mary Magdalene recounted in the Gospel of John.[46]

This someone may say to you:[47] Are you not troubling and bothering your souls beyond their ability, in turning one who is below divinity into a divinity, making him into a Creator when he was created, having him resurrected according to your purpose, and sending out in his name apostles in seventy-two languages,[48] although they were eleven individuals? In God's name, it is a wonder how these apostles learnt these languages which had been separated out over the nations, at the very time each was hiding, watchful and fearful, concealed from his enemies who might say to him, 'Hey you, beware of the scholars and their intellects!'

---

[45] Strictly speaking, the disciples chose Matthias to take Judas' place among them, as Acts I: 15-26 recounts, though Paul was recognised as an Apostle, Acts XIII: 1-3, 1 Cor. XV: 8-11.

[46] Jn XX: 18.

[47] This supposedly sympathetic and understanding character whom al-Dimashqī introduces here actually compounds the predicament in which the Christians are placed by detailing the very absurdities he says he does not want to challenge them to explain, and condescendingly talking about them as spiritually unstable.

[48] Cf. Section 4, n. 4.

وللقائل أيضًا أن يقول: من كان هذا حذوه وذا الرأي رأيه لا يقال له:
ما الحكمة في وضع المخارف بالكنائس والمعابد كنزول النار يوم سبت النور
وإمساك الصليب في الهواء بالمغناطيس بقبرص وماء ميرون وحمل الزرازير
للزيتون إلى ديرهم وظهور الخنافيس بديرهم والزيت الفاير بصيدنايا ظاهر
دمشق ، وفيض أعين التماثيل بالدمع وأشياء مثل هذه المخارف لا تكاد تعدّ
كثيرة ، ولكنه يعذر من كون نفسه تماريت[149] واستقرّ عندها هذا، ولبعد
عهدها عن المعقولات وتعقّلها والمنقولات الحقّ والتفقّه فيها ورؤية الحق حقّاً
والباطل باطلاً ظنّت * أنّ العالم لم يزل خاليًا من التدبير الإلهي والسياسة   * 54v
الربانيّة إلى أن ظهر الإله المصنوع فبعث إلى العالم رسلاً مبشّرين ومنذرين
وداموا ثلاث سنين أو أربع أو مائة سنة

---

[149] A and B: تمرّيت

Someone may also say: The one who has this facing him and with this opinion that he holds should not be told, 'What is the wisdom in placing childish things in churches and places of worship, such as the descent of fire on Holy Saturday,[49] the cross being suspended in the air by means of magnets in Cyprus,[50] chrism oil,[51] starlings carrying olives to one of their monasteries, beetles appearing in one of their monasteries, oil gushing forth at Seidnaya outside Damascus, the eyes of images flowing with tears, and so many things similar to these childish notions that they can hardly be counted?' But someone whose soul is wavering may be forgiven should this come to lodge in it. It is far from grasping rational things and understanding them, and true things that are passed down and reflecting upon them, or seeing the true as true and the false as false. So it might think (54v) that the world had never had divine control and lordly rule until this artificial god appeared and sent messengers into the world as bearers of good tidings and warners, remained for three, four, or a hundred

---

[49] This is a reference to the climax of the Holy Week ceremonies in the Church of the Holy Sepulchre in Jerusalem, when fire is believed to be miraculously kindled as a sign of the resurrection of Christ. According to one version of the sermon he preached at Clermont in 1095, Pope Urban II referred to this miracle as part of his crusading call to recover the Holy Places for Christendom.

[50] Al-Dimashqī seems to be showing knowledge of his opponent's own homeland: in the mid eighth/fourteenth century the French poet William of Machaut wrote as follows, 'In Famagusta there is a cross which, if you are in your right mind, you must believe to be the cross of the Good Thief: for it stands on no stone or plinth, but floating unsupported in the air', *La prise d'Alexandrie*, quoted in E. Hallam, ed., *Chronicles of the Crusades*, Godalming, Surrey, 1989, p. 294.

There was a widespread belief among Christians at this time that Muḥammad's tomb was likewise suspended in mid-air; cf. e.g. Alexandre du Pont, *Li Romans de Mahon*, written in 1258:

They have forged an iron sarcophagus
Wherein they lay Muhammad's corpse.
They build a vaulted maisonette
Of lodestone constructed
So that they leave the body, which is attached
To nothing, in its centre:
It remains in the air with no connecting mechanism (ll.1902-8);

R. Hyatte ed. and trans., *The Prophet of Islam in Old French, 'The Romance of Muhammad' (1258) and 'The Book of Muhammad's Ladder' (1264)*, Leiden, 1997, pp. 91-2. For further examples, cf. Tolan, *Saracens*, pp. 122 and 143.

[51] In popular belief chrism oil, which is used at the baptism of new believers, might be thought to have the power of restoring to life, not just of giving new life. The remaining miracles were presumably known locally in Damascus. Cf. the *Rothelin* continuation of William of Tyre, in Shirley, *Crusader Syria in the Thirteenth Century*, p. 28, where the miracle of the oil gushing from the image at the monastery of 'Sardenay' near Damascus and other miracles are mentioned.

ثمّ خلت الأعصار والدهور[150] من التدبير الإلهي ومن السياسة الربّانية كما كانت خالية من قبل والله أكبر وأجلّ وأعظم سبحانه وتعالى ربّ العالمين.

[150] B: والدبور (wrongly).

years, and then the ages and eras were without divine control and lordly rule as they had been before.

God is most great, sublime and mighty, may he be praised and exalted, the Lord of the worlds.

فصل

ثمَّ قلتم في الرسالة نسقًا بعد ذلك إنَّ كليام وجماعة من ذوي الفطنة
والمعرفة قالوا لكم عنّا معشر المسلمين إننا ننكر على النصارى قولهم: "آب
وابن وروح قدس" وقولهم: "إنهم ثلاثة أقانيم"، وقولهم: "إنَّ المسيح ربّ
وإله وإنّه خالق". وإنكم أجبتم قائلين:

لو علموا قولنا هذا إنما نريد به تصحيح القول إن الله شيء حيّ
ناطق لما أنكروا ذلك علينا لأنّا معشر النصارى لمّا رأينا حدوث الأشياء
علمنا أنّ شيئاً غيرها أحدثها ، إذ لا يمكن حدوثها من ذاتها لما فيها
من التضادّ والتقلّب، فقلنا: إنه شيء لا كالأشياء المخلوقة إذ هو خالق
لكلّ شيء وذلك لننفي العدم عنه، ورأينا الأشياء تنقسم قسمين: شيء حيّ وشيء
غير حيّ ، فوصفناه بأجلّ القسمين لنفي الموت عنه ، فقلنا: هو شيء حيّ، ورأينا[1]
الحيّ ينقسم قسمين: حيّ ناطق وحيّ غير ناطق فوصفناه بأفضل القسمين لننفي
الجهل عنه، والثلاثة أسماء شيء حيّ ناطق الذات والنطق والحياة ، فالذات عندنا
الآب والنطق الإبن والحياة الروح القدس .

وهذه الأسماء لم نسمّه نحن النصارى بها من ذوات أنفسنا بل الله سمّى لاهوته
بها ، وذلك أنه قال على لسان موسى النبي في التوراة مخاطبًا لبني إسرائيل قائلاً:
"أليس هذا الآب الذي صنعك وبراك واقتناك؟" [2] وعلى لسانه أيضًا قائلاً: "وكان
روح الله ترفّ على الماء"[3]، وقوله على لسان داود النبي: "روحك القدس لا تنزع
مني" [4]، وأيضًا على لسان داود: "بكلمة الله تشدّدت السموات والأرض وبروح
فيه[5] جميع قواهنّ" [6]، وقوله على لسان أيّوب الصدّيق: "روح الله خلقني وهو
يعلّمني"[7]، وقوله على لسان أشعيا: "ييبس القتاد ويجفّ العشب وكلمة الله باقية
إلى الأبد"[8]، وقول

---

    [1] This word is repeated in A and B.   [2] Deut XXXII: 6.   [3] Genesis I: 2.
[4] Psalm LI: 11.   [5] A and B: فاه   [6] Psalm XXXIII: 6.   [7] Cf. Job XXXIII: 4.
[8] Isaiah XL: 8.

59. *Section [Six]*

Then you say in the *Letter* immediately after this that Kilyām and a group of clever and acute people said to you on behalf of us Muslims[1] that we disapprove of the Christians saying 'Father, Son and Holy Spirit', 'They are three hypostases', and 'Christ is Lord, God and Creator'.

You answered them saying:

> If only they knew this teaching of ours, that we only intend by it to refine the teaching that God is a thing, living and articulate,[2] they would not disapprove of us saying this. For when we Christians see that things come into being, we know that something other than them has brought them into being, since they could not come into being of themselves, because of the contradictions and inconstancy within them.[3] So we say: He is a thing unlike created things because he is the Creator of all things. This is to deny non-existence of him.
>
> And we see things divided into two kinds: Things living and things not living. So we ascribe to him the more exalted of the two kinds in order to deny death of him, and we say: He is a thing that is living. We see (55r) living things divided into two kinds: Living things that are articulate and living things that are not, so we ascribe to him the more superior of the two kinds, in order to deny ignorance of him. The three names, thing, living and articulate, are the essence, speech and life. As we see it, the essence is the Father, the speech is the Son and the life is the Holy Spirit.
>
> It is not at the behest of our own authorities that we Christians have called God by these names, for in fact God calls his divine nature by them. He actually says on the tongue of the prophet Moses in the Torah, speaking to the People of Israel, 'Is this not the Father who formed you, made you and got you for his own?'; also on his tongue, 'The Spirit of God was hovering over the water'; his words on the tongue of the prophet David, 'Do not take your Holy Spirit from me'; also on the tongue of David, 'By the Word of God were the heavens and the earth established and by the breath of his mouth all their powers'; on the tongue of Job the upright, 'The Spirit of God created me and he teaches me'; on the tongue of Isaiah, 'The bush dries up and the grass withers away, but the word of God remains for ever'; and the words

---

[1] It appears that Kilyām is something of a representative for the Muslims, explaining the blessing al-Dimashqī pronounces on him when introducing him, § 3.

[2] This proof is given by Arab Christians from the third/ninth century onwards; cf, ʿAmmār al-Baṣrī, *K. al-Burhān*, pp. 46-65 and particularly pp. 48.18-49.2; and further the summary given by al-Nāshiʾ al-Akbar, *K. al-awsaṭ fī al-maqālāt* in J. van Ess, *Frühe muʿtazilitische Häresiographie*, Beirut, 1971, p. 87.

[3] Cf. ʿAmmār, *Burhān*, pp. 21-22.15.

السيّد المسيح في الإنجيل المقدّس للتلاميذ الأطهار: "إذهبوا إلى جميع العالم وعمّدوهم باسم الآب والابن والروح القدس إله واحد وعلّموهم أن يحفظوا جميع ما أوصيتكم به"[9].

وقد قال في هذا الكتاب: ﴿ولقد سبقت كلمتنا لعبادنا المرسلين﴾[10]. وقال أيضًا: ﴿يا عيسى بن مريم أذكر نعمتي عليك وعلى والدتك﴾ * الآية[11]، وقال أيضًا: ﴿وكلّم الله موسى تكليماً﴾[12]، وقال في سورة التحريم: ﴿ومريم ابنت عمران﴾ الآية[13]، وسائر المسلمين يقولون: إنّ الكتاب كلام الله ولا يكون كلام إلا لحيّ ناطق.

* 55v

وهذه صفات جوهرية تجري مجرى أسماء، وكلّ صفة منها غير الأخرى والإله واحد لا يتجزّأ ولا يتبعّض.

60.   فالجواب: أمّا ما ذكرتم من استدلالكم على معرفة الإله الخالق وأنه شيء لا كالأشياء فهو حقّ وعرفان، أمّا قولكم: إنه حيّ بحياة هي روح القدس لولاها لم يكن حيّاً ولولاه بموجدها[14] لم تكن موجودة فقول باطل ينقض بعضه بعضًا، إذ الموجد للحياة لولاه ما وُجدت غنيّ عنها والذي هو حيّ بها لولاها لم يكن حيّاً فقيراً إليها فاستحال أن يكون حيّاً بها وهو الموجد[15] لها، واستحال أن تكون حيّة لذاتها وموجودة به.

ولو قلتم إنه شيء لا كالأشياء وحيّ لا كالأحياء لصدقتم ونزّهتموه عن القياس بكلّ حيّ بحياة عرضيّة ولم يضطركم القياس والتشبيه إلى القول بالنطق وبالتثليث وأنّ الناطق المقاس عليه أفضل من غير الناطق الشبيه، فوصفتم الخالق بوصف المخلوق ولم تفرّقوا بين القديم الواجب المطلق الوجود وبين المحدث الممكن المقيّد الوجود.

---

9 Mtt XXVIII: 19-20.   10 S. XXXVII: 171.   11 S. V: 110.   12 S. IV: 164.
13 S. LXVI: 12.   14 A and B: يوجدها   15 B: الوجد (wrongly).

of the lord Christ in the holy Gospel to the pure disciples, 'Go into all
the world and baptize them in the name of the Father and of the Son
and of the Holy Spirit, one God, and teach them to observe all that I
have commanded you'.

And he says in this book, 'And verily our word went forth of old unto
our bondmen sent'; he also says, 'O Jesus, son of Mary! Remember my
favour unto thee and unto thy mother[; how I strengthened thee with
the holy Spirit]' (55v) and the rest of the verse; he also says, 'And God
spake directly unto Moses'; and he says in *Banning*, 'And Mary, daughter of 'Imrān [, whose body was chaste, therefore we breathed therein
something of our Spirit]'. All the Muslims say that the book is the word
of God, and only one who is living and articulate possesses word.

These are attributes of the substance which are just like names, and
each one of the attributes is different from the other, though God is
one, unpartitionable and indivisible.

60.   *Response*: As for what you mention concerning your inference
about knowing God the Creator, and that he is a thing unlike things,
this is true and perceptive. But as for your remark that he is living
by life which is the Holy Spirit, and that without it he would not be
living, and that without him as its source of existence it would not
exist, this is a false claim, and one part of it contradicts the other. For
the source of existence of life, without whom it would not exist, will
be independent of it, and one who is living by it, without which he
would not be living, will be dependent upon it. So it is impossible for
him to be living by it while being the source of its existence, and it is
impossible for it to be living by its own essence and existent by it.

And if you said that he is a thing unlike things and living unlike
the living, then you would be telling the truth, and elevating him
above analogy with anything that is living by an accident of life,[4] and
analogy and anthropomorphism would not have forced you to speak
about Word and Trinity, and that the articulate being with whom an
analogy is drawn is superior to an inarticulate being who is similar.
For you have described the Creator in terms of the created, and you
have not distinguished the eternal, who is necessary, absolute Being,
from the temporal, which is potential, qualified being.[5]

---

[4]   This is the classic Ash'arite position that, like creatures, God has attributes,
but whereas their attributes are endowed by accidents superadded to their beings,
his attributes are integral to his being though discrete from it: *Lā hiya Allāh wa-lā hiya
ghayruh*, as Ibn Kullāb summed it up in the early third/ninth century (Abū al-Ḥasan
al-Ash'arī, *Maqālāt al-Islāmiyyīn*, ed. H. Ritter, Istanbul, 1930, p. 169).

[5]   This terminology, which is reminiscent of Ibn Sīnā, shows the extent to which
philosophical vocabulary had become part of theological discourse by this time.

وألزمكم اختصاركم على التثليث أن تسوقوا بواقي الأسماء والصفات
القياسيّة كما' ابتدأتموها بالقياس وإثبات الأفضل ونفي الأرذل ، فقولوا: * 56r *
ورأينا الشيء الحيّ الناطق فمنه ما هو ناطق بلسان وصوت وحروف ومخارج[16]
لها وأدوات يسمع السامع منه نطقه وكلامه ، ومنه ما هو ناطق بضميره
لضميره ولا يسمع متكلّمًا كالمتكلّم بالأدوات التي يسمع بها المخاطبين خبره
وأمره ونهيه ، ومنه ما هو ناطق بالحال نطقًا مجازيًّا كما قيل في الموجودات ،
فكلّ بكلّ ناطق وهو صامت يخاف ويرجو فهو يدعو أو يسأل. هذا إذا
أردتم بالنطق الكلام وإن كنتم أردتم به العلم والإدراك فتصفوه بأكمل
النطقين وهما الكلام المسموع أو العلم الذي هو ضدّ الجهل.

وقولوا أيضًا: ورأينا الناطق ذا وجود في الذهن وفي الخارج وذا وجود
مفروض في الذهن دون الخارج فوصفناه بأكمل الوصفين فقلنا[17]: هو
شيء حيّ ناطق موجود في الذهن وفي الخارج ، وتقولون[18] أيضًا لزومًا
واضطرارًا: ورأينا الشيء الحيّ الناطق الموجود في الذهن وفي الخارج منقسمًا
إلى حسّاس مدرك للمحسوسات وغير حسّاس ، والحسّاس أكمل فوصفناه
بإدراك المحسوس ، وتقولون[19]: ورأينا الحسّاس منقسمًا إلى متحرّك باختياره
ومتحرّك مجبر على الحركة ومتحرّك بغيره وليس بحيّ ، والمتحرّك بالاختيار
أفضل فوصفناه * بأنه حسّاس متحرّك بالاختيار لا ساكن[20] عطل عنها. * 56v *

وتقولون[21] أيضًا ورأينا الشيء الحيّ الناطق الموصوف المشار إليه منقسمًا
إلى ذي خواصّ كالتخيّل والتفكر والتذكّر والحفظ ، وإلى غير ذي خواصّ ،
وذو الخواصّ أفضل وأكمل فوصفناه بالأكمل الأفضل .

---

[16] A and B: ونقوا ;وتقولوا :B. [17] B: قتلنا (wrongly), a misreading of A. [18] A: ومخارح
(wrongly), evidently a misreading of A which supplies the consonants لو of the word
in the margin. [19] A and B: وتقولوا [20] B: ساكي (wrongly), evidently a misreading
of A. [21] A and B: ويقولوا

Your restriction to a Trinity forces you to pursue the remaining analogous names and attributes in the same way (56r) that you treated them at the beginning, to confirm the most excellent and deny the meanest.[6] So say: We see things that are living and articulate; among them are those who articulate by tongue, voice, syllables, utterance and organs, from whom we can hear their speech and words; and among them are those who articulate from heart to heart, and are not heard forming words like those who form words by organs through which those addressed hear the being's information, commands and prohibitions; and among them are those which articulate in a form of metaphorical speech, as one says about everything in existence, for, even though it may be silent, every single thing articulates when it is afraid or wants something, for then it calls out or asks. Whether by speech you mean words, or whether you mean knowledge and perception, you must attribute to him the more perfect of the two forms of articulation, words that are heard or knowledge that is the opposite of ignorance.

Say as well: We see articulate things who possess it internally and externally, and those who are assumed to possess it internally and not externally, and we attribute to him the more perfect of the two descriptions. So we say: He is a living thing with articulation existing internally and externally. You must also by force of necessity say: We see living things with articulation existing internally and externally divided into those which are sensitive and perceptive to sensory stimuli and those which are not. And those which are sensitive are the more perfect, so we attribute to him the ability to perceive a sensory stimulus. And say: We see sensitive beings divided into those which move voluntarily, those which move by compulsion, and those which move through something other than themselves and are not living. Those which move voluntarily are superior, so we attribute him (56v) as being sensitive, moving voluntarily, not still or devoid of them.

You say also: We see these living, articulate things described earlier divided into those who possess specific qualities such as imagination, contemplation, recollection and memorisation, and into those without specific qualities. Those with qualities are superior and more perfect, so we attribute him with these.

---

[6]   The lengthy argument that occupies the rest of § 60 retraces Muslim refutations of this defence of the Trinity occurring from the third/ninth century onwards; for details cf. D. Thomas, 'The Doctrine of the Trinity in the early Abbasid Era', in L. Ridgeon ed., *Islamic Interpretations of Christianity*, London, 2001, pp.78-98.

وتسلسلون هذه الرواية القياسيّة إلى أن تدلّكم على الإنسان الجامع لهذه الأوصاف لا غيره من سائر الحيوان والملائكة والجان ، والجدّ له أن يقال: هو شيء حيّ ناطق مائت أو يقال هو حيوان ضاحك عريض الأظفار حيّ ناطق مائت ، وسبحان الله ربّ العالمين عمّا وصفتموه وتصفون وتعالى عن أن يقال له من خلقه أبدًا: "لولا أوامره".

وكذلك أيضًا يلزمكم في هذا الفحص والنظر بآرائكم أن تقولوا: ورأينا الموصوف[22] بما وصفناه من الصفات الأكمليّة والأفضليّة منه ذو اختيار وقدرة ومنه ما لا اختيار له ولا قدرة ، والقادر أفضل فوصفناه بالقدرة على الفعل وعلى الترك وتقولون[23] في القدرة إنّها صفة[24] تابعة لموصوفها وهو قديم لم يزل فقدرته لم تزل ، والقادر بقدرة لغير مقدور لا يكون بل قادر بقدرة * لمقدور لم يزل ، فيلزمكم القياس والتشبيه الذي أسّستم عليه التثليث * 57r أن تقولوا في الموصوف بأنه قادر وأنه قدرة وأنه مقدور وكذلك يلزمكم أن تقولوا: هو المريد وهو الإرادة وهو المراد وهو الفاعل وهو الفعل وهو المفعول ، وأيّ قول أظهر استحالة من هذا أن يكون ربّ العالمين قادرًا وقدرة ومقدورًا؟[25] تعالى الله وسبحانه عن ذلك.

61. ثمّ قلتم إنّ مرادكم إنما هو تعداد أسماء صفات للذات ثلاثة أسماء صفات شيء حيّ ناطق ، أسماء مسمّاها واحد: إله واحد ، ربّ واحد ، خالق واحد. ثمّ أتبعتم هذا الشرح بقولكم: الذات والحياة والنطق ، فالذات عندنا الآب والنطق الإبن والحياة روح القدس ، تعنون أنكم اصطلحتم على هذا الهزء[26] اصطلاحًا لأنفسكم منكرًا عقلاً وشرعًا ، وكنتم بهذا القول شارحين صدور اليهود مفرحين قلوبهم، مثبتين

‏‫‏‫‏22 B: الموه صوف (wrongly), evidently a misreading of A.   23 A and B: وتقولوا
24 This word is supplied in the margin in A.   25 B: ومقدور   26 A: الهزا؛ B: الهزاء

You continue this analogous portrayal until it leads you to the human, who combines together these descriptions, and no other being among animals, angels or jinn, though in all seriousness it can be said either that he is a living, articulate, mortal thing, or that he is a grinning beast with talons, living, articulate and mortal. God, the Lord of the worlds, is blessed beyond what you have attributed him with and continue to. And he is exalted above it ever being said to him by his creatures, 'If only it had not been for his commands!'

In the same way also you have to say in this investigation and inquiry based upon your opinions: We see that some of those who are attributed with the most complete and superior attributes which we have been given possess choice and power, and some are without choice and power. The powerful is superior, so we attribute to him power over acting and not acting. Then say that power is an attribute which belongs to the one attributed with it. He is eternal and has always been, so his power has always been. One who is powerful by a power over no object cannot exist; rather, he is powerful by a power (57r) over an object that is eternal. So the analogy and anthropomorphism on which you establish the Trinity forces you to say about the One who is attributed: He is Powerful, Power and Object of power; and likewise it forces you to say: He is Willer, Will and Willed, Agent, Act and Acted upon. What words could be more patently impossible than these, that the Lord of the worlds should be Powerful, Power and Object of power? God is more exalted and blessed than this![7]

61. Then you say that your intention is only to list the names of the attributes of the essence, the three names of the attributes, thing, living and articulate, as names of the one Being named by them, one God, one Lord, and one Creator. Then you follow this explanation by saying, 'Essence, Life and Speech—to us the Essence is the Father, the Speech is the Son, and the Life is the Holy Spirit.' You are fully aware that you have chosen this mockery entirely yourselves in the face of reason and revelation, and that by what you have said you have delighted the hearts of the Jews and gladdened their minds, confirm-

---

[7] This is precisely the position of the fourth/tenth century Christian apologist Yaḥyā Ibn ʿAdī (E. Platti, *Yaḥyā Ibn ʿAdī, théologien chrétien et philosophe arabe*, Leuven, 1983, pp. 109-10). Cf. Perlmann, *Ibn Kammūna's Examination of the Three Faiths*, p. 85, where Ibn Kammūna refers to Yaḥyā's triad of the Father as God's reason, the Son as God's knowing himself, and the Holy Spirit as God's knowledge of his essence.

لهم ما زعموا في المسيح وزعموا في ما بسببه قتلوه.

صادق عليكم تسميتكم كفرة[27] أهل الكتاب بشهادة القرآن وواضح البرهان به حيث ابتدأتم في النظر ، وفحصتم عن معرفة الله تعالى بالمعقول ودلّكم * الدليل الواضح من الموجودات شيئاً [28] ، على أنه سبحانه موجود ثابت الوجود أزلاً وأبداً ، وعلى أنه تعالى لولا وجوده الحقّ وإيجاده لمّا أوجد لم يكن موجودًا وعلى أنه سبحانه حيّ عالم مريد قادر سميع بصير متكلّم ، وسمّيتم كلامه علمًا ونطقًا ثمّ أعرضتم عن المعقول والمنقول وقلتم في ربّ العزة الأحد الصمد إنّه ثلاث ذوات أقانيم جوهرية ثوابت الوجود ولم يزالوا ولا يزالون[29] أبدًا مشتركين في إلهيّتهم المتحدة.

وقلتم بالمعنى إنّ هؤلاء الثلاثة هم الشيئية والحياة والنطق متفقون في الإلهية والربوبيّة والخلق ، فهم إله واحد: آب وابن وروح ، كلّ مسمّى منهم غير المسمّى الآخر ، إذ الآب غير الإبن ومباين له لا محالة والروح غيرهما كذلك.

فصرّحتم بالكفر والشرك كما قلتم في شرح معناها إنّ الآب موجود لذاته أي لم يزل حيّ بالروح ناطق بالابن وإنّ الروح حيّة لذاتها أي لم تزل وإنها موجودة بالآب ناطقة بالإبن ، وإنّ الابن ناطق لذاته أي لم يزل موجود بالآب حيّ بالروح ، فأفصحتم بالشرك وأعظمتم الفرية على الذي هو شيء لا كأشياء.

ولم يكن لكم حجّة تحتجّون بها ولا إثارة من علم ولا مخلص ولا مخرج[30] ممّا أتيتم به من الشرك * الصريح إلا أن تستندوا إلى ما زعمتم أنه في التوراة والإنجيل مكتوب ، تعنون قوله لبني إسرائيل: "أباك الذي صنعك وبراك واقتناك"[31] ، وقول المسيح: "أبونا الذي في السموات"[32] ، وقوله: "يفرح بكم أبوكم الذي في السموات" ، وقوله لمريم المجدلانيّة: "إني صاعد إلى أبي وأبيكم وإلهي وإلهكم".[33] مع علمكم بأنّ لفظة الأب في اللغتين العبرانيّة والسريانيّة

57v

58r

---

[27] B: كفر [28] B: وذلكم من الموجودات شياء الدليل الواضح (wrongly), evidently a misreading of A; شيئا ...من الموجودات: these words are supplied in the margin in A. [29] A and B: ولا يزالوا [30] A and B: ولا مخلصًا ولا مخرجًا [31] Deut XXXII: 6. [32] Cf. Mtt VI: 9. [33] Cf. Jn XX: 17.

ing for them what they claimed with regard to Christ and what they claimed with regard to the reasons for killing him.

This apportioning names of yours proves that the moment you embark on speculation and search for understanding about God the exalted through intellectual means you truly are the unbelievers among the People of the Book, according to the witness of the Qur'an and clear proof of it. For clear evidence (57v) based upon all that exists proves to you one thing, that the blessed One exists and is constant in existence, eternal and everlasting, that if the exalted One did not exist in reality and did not bring into existence what he did it would not exist, and that the blessed One is living, knowing, willing, powerful, hearing, seeing and speaking. You call his word knowledge and speech, and then you turn away from the reasonable and reported and say that the Lord of might, the one and self-subsistent, is three substantial essences and hypostases constant in existence, which ever have been and ever will be in eternity, sharing in their single divinity.

With regard to the meaning, you say that these three are the Thing itself, Life and Speech, coincident in divinity, lordship and creation, one God, Father, Son and Spirit, each named being among them different from another named being, in that the Father is different from the Son and utterly distinct from him, and similarly the Spirit is different from both of them.

In this way you declare unbelief and polytheism, as you do when you explain the meaning of them, that the Father exists by his essence, that is, he has always been, and that he is living by the Spirit and articulating by the Son; that the Spirit is living by its essence, that is, it has always been, and that it exists by the Father and is articulating by the Son; and that the Son is articulating by his essence, that is, he is eternal, is existent by the Father and living by the Spirit. Thus you give the clearest indication of polytheism and you increase the enormity of the lie against the One who is a living thing unlike other things.

You have no proof or any trace of knowledge that you can produce, you have no refuge or escape from manifest (58r) polytheism in what you have adduced, other than placing your trust in what you claim is written in the Torah and Gospel. You refer to his words to the People of Israel, 'Your Father who made you, shaped you and got you for his own', and Christ's words, 'Our Father in heaven', 'Your Father in heaven is delighted in you', and his words to Mary Magdalene, 'I am ascending to my Father and your Father, to my God and your God'. This despite your knowing that in Hebrew and Syriac the word

معناها معنى الربّ ، وفي اللغة العربية الربّ هو السيّد المالك الرابّ المربّي لكل مربوب كما بيّناه في غير هذا الموضع.

ومنه قول بعضكم لبعض في المخاطبة بالتعظيم: "يا أبونا ، يا أبونا"، وكقولكم في أوّل الأمانة الكبيرة: "نؤمن بإله[34] واحد أب ضابط للكلّ خالق السموات والأرض صانع ما يُرى وما لا يُرى"، ثمّ قرنتم إلى اسم الآب اسم الإبن جزمًا باعتقادكم الوالد والولد[35] وذلك قولكم في الأمانة بعد القول الأوّل: "ونؤمن بيسوع[36] المسيح ابن الله الوحيد الإله الحقّ من الإله الحقّ من جوهر أبيه"[37] تصريحًا بالوالديّة والولديّة[38] وتبعيض الإله إذ لفظه من يقتضي التبعيض والتجزئ كما يقال: "الجزء من الكلّ ، واعطني من هذا" أي من بعض هذا.

62. ثمّ أكّدتم إفراد الآب عن الإبن * والابن عن الآب وصرّحتم بالتجسيم ، * 58v فقلتم في أمانتكم هذه إنّ المسيح صُلب وعُذّب وذاق الألم والموت وقام في اليوم الثالث وصعد إلى السماء وجلس عن يمين أبيه وسيأتي مرّة ثانية لفصل القضاء بين الأموات والأحياء.

وكأنّما أنتم مشاهدون لما تخبرون به وتقتضونه من هذا الهزء[39] ، إذ حكم معقولكم عندما وجدتم في التوراة قوله: "أباك الذي صنعك" أنها أبّوة حقيقية وأنها معنويّة لا محسوسة وأنّ الآب لابدّ وأن يكون والدًا وإلا فلا يسمّى أبًا ، وقد سمّى نفسه في التوراة أبًا ، فلا بدّ له من ابن مولود منه وعنه تكون ذاته من ذاته وصفاته كصفاته وليس إلا النطق والحياة الصفتان للشيئية ولا يليق بالحياة إلا أن يكون ابنًا للآب وهو حيّ بها. فالنطق هو الإبن لأن النطق كلام متولّد عن المتكلّم به وقائم في نفسه الناطقة مولود[40] منه باللسان والأدوات قارع للسمع يتلقّاه السمع المتقرّع به تلقيًّا معنويًّا كتلقي الفرج[41] نطفة[42] الولد الحسّي.

---

[34] A and B: بالإله   [35] B: والوالد   [36] A and B: يا يسوع   [37] B: جوهرائية   [38] B: والولديّة   [39] A: الهزا؛ B: الهزاء   [40] A and B: مولودة   [41] A and B: الفرح   [42] B: لنطفة

'father' means 'lord', and that in Arabic the lord is the master, owner, stepfather and bringer-up of all under his responsibility, as we have shown elsewhere.[8]

An example of this is the words addressed by you to one another when showing esteem, 'Reverend father, reverend father', and like your words at the beginning of the great Creed, 'We believe in one God, Governor of all, Creator of the heavens and earth, Maker of what is seen and unseen'; upon which you peremptorily join the name Son to the name Father in your belief about the Begetter and the begotten: this in your words following the first words in the Creed, 'And we believe in Jesus Christ, the only Son of God, true God from true God, of the substance of his Father'. You speak directly about begetting and being begotten and about partitioning of God, since the term for this connotes partitioning and division, as is said, 'The part from the whole', and 'Give me some of this', that is, a part of it.

62.   Then you confirm the separation of the Father from the Son (58v) and the Son from the Father, and you speak directly about the Incarnation. For in this Creed of yours you say that Christ was crucified, tortured, suffered pain and death, rose on the third day, ascended into heaven and was seated at the right hand of his Father, and that he will come again to judge the dead and the living.

It is as though you simply witness to this mockery which you relate and lay claim to because your minds have judged that his words which you find in the Torah, 'Your Father who made you', are fatherhood in reality, though of the mind and not of the senses, and that the Father must be a begetter, otherwise he could not be called Father, for indeed he calls himself Father in the Torah. So he must have a Son begotten from him and out of him, his essence from his essence and his attributes like his attributes. Speech and life are two attributes of the thing itself alone, so the latter cannot be associated with life unless he is the Son of the Father and is living by it. This speech is the Son, because speech is the word begotten from the one who utters it. It subsists in his articulate soul, and it is produced from him through the tongue and organs. It pours into the ears and the ears receive it and are filled with it in an abstract sense, just as the vagina receives the seed of a physical child.

---

[8]   Cf. 'Alī al-Ṭabarī, *Radd*, pp. 147.2-148.20. This demonstration is not found earlier in the *Response*, so al-Dimashqī must either be referring to another work, or he has forgotten what he has argued so far.

وحسن القياس الفاسد هذا لكم والإسناد بالتأويل الغير صحيح إلى قول داود في المزامير: "بكلمة الله خلقت السموات والأرض" [43]، وقول أشعيا: "يجفّ العشب وكلمة الله باقية إلى الأبد" [44]، فقلتم في أنفسكم: "هذه الكلمة هي * النطق ولم تعلموا أنّ المراد تعريف العباد بأنّ الله يقوم السموات والأرض بأمره وبكلمته قامتا وخرجتا من العدم إلى الوجود وكلمته قوله للشيء: "كن فيكون".

* 59r

ولمّا سمّيتم الكلمة نطقًا وجعلتم النطق ابنًا ولم يكن كتابنا الكريم نزل ولا ديننا الحقّ ظهر عاودتم النظر في التوراة وكتب النبوءات لعلكم تجدون شبهة تستندون إليها في زعم الأبوّة والبنوّة ، إذ زعمهما من أنكر المنكرات في العقل وإن كانت معنويّة لا حسيّة ، فوجدتم في التوراة القول لإسرائيل: "أنت ابني بكري الذي ارتضيت" [45]، فجزمتم بما زعمتم في الكلمة أنها النطق وأنّ النطق ابن. [46]

ووجدتم في التوراة أيضًا القول بما معناه: "وكان روح الله ترفّ على الماء" [47]، وقول أيّوب الصدّيق: "روح الله خلقني وهو يعلّمني" [48]، وقول داود النبيّ: "روحك القدس لا تنزع مني" [49]، فجزمتم بأنّ الحياة التي هي أحدى [50] الصفات الثلاث روح القدس وجعلتموها ذاتا متوسّطة بين الآب والابن رابطة بينهما بقوّتها وأنّ المسمّى أبًا والمسمّى ابنًا والمسمّى روحًا كمثل من يقول: الإنسان وروحه ونطقه أو الشمس وشعاعها وضوؤها ، فإنه يسمّي ثلاثة أسماء والمسمّى والحقيقة واحد. هذا غاية ما دلّكم عليه معقولكم * ومنقولكم.

* 59v

63. ومن أعجب ما ادّعيتموه وأغرب ما تحرّيتموه إلى المسيح زعمكم المنكر أنه قال في الإنجيل لتلاميذه: "إذهبوا إلى جميع العالم وعمّدوهم

[43] Psalm XXXIII: 6.   [44] Isaiah XL: 8.   [45] Exodus IV: 22; cf. also Ben Sira XXXVI: 12. See Patrick Skehan *The Wisdom of Ben Sira*, New York, 1987, p. 413; Israel Levi, *The Hebrew Text of the Book of Ecclesiasticus*, Leiden, 1969, p. 38.   [46] A: ابنا   [47] Genesis I: 2.   [48] Job XXXIII: 4.   [49] Psalm LI: 11.   [50] A and B: أحد

This foul analogy seems proper to you, as does the ascription of an incorrect interpretation to the words of David in the Psalms: 'By the Word of God were the heavens and the earth created', and the words of Isaiah, 'The grass withers, but the Word of God remains for ever'. You say among yourselves: This Word is (59r) Speech, without knowing that the intention is to appraise humankind that by his command and his word God raised up the heavens and the earth to stand and emerge from nothing into existence. His word and saying to a thing is 'Be' and it is.

When you called the Word Speech and made Speech the Son, and our noble book had not been revealed nor our true religion appeared, you went back to examine the Torah and the prophetic books in the hope that you might find some obscurity to rely on in the claim about fatherhood and sonship. For the claim about both of these is denied most vehemently by reason, even though it may be abstract and not sensory. So you found in the Torah the words to Israel, 'You are my first-born son in whom I am pleased',[9] and you decided definitely about your claim that the Word was Speech and speech was the Son.

You also found in the Torah words the meaning of which is, 'The Spirit of God was hovering over the water', the words of Job the upright, 'The Spirit of God created me and he teaches me', and the words of the prophet David, 'Do not take your Holy Spirit from me'. So you asserted that Life, which was one of the three attributes, was the Holy Spirit, and you made it an essence intermediate between the Father and the Son, through its power a link between them, and that the One named Father, the One named Son and the One named Spirit were like someone saying, 'The man, his spirit and his speech', or 'The sun, its rays and its brightness':[10] he is called by three names, though what is named and the actuality is one. This is the point to which your intelligence (59v) and tradition lead you.

63. One of the most surprising things you allege, and most far-fetched things you impute to Christ is your unacceptable claim that he said in the Gospel to his disciples, 'Go out to all the world and baptize

---

[9] The sentiment expressed in this verse was a familiar element of Muslim polemic against Christianity; cf. S. Pines, '"Israel, my Firstborn" and the Sonship of Jesus', in E.E. Urbach, R.J. Zwi Werblowsky and C. Wirzubski, eds, *Studies in Mysticism and Religion presented to Gershom G. Scholem*, Jerusalem, 1967, pp. 177-90.

[10] These analogies of the Trinity are Patristic in origin, and they appear among Muslim authors as early as the third/ninth century, e.g. in al-Qāsim b. Ibrāhīm, *Radd*, p. 315.7-22.

باسم الآب والإبن والروح القدس إله[51] واحد" [52]، فنسبتموه إلى ما
لا ينتسب إليه الضالّون من الجهل والضلال والشرك الصريح والكفر .بما في
التوراة والإنجيل والزبور والفرقان ، وبما قاله هو في الإنجيل وأمر به من القول
بالتوحيد والتفريد واعتقاد أحديّة الإله وصمديّته وتنزيهه عن كلّ ما سواه،
وصدّقتم اليهود وزكّيتم قولهم عنه "إنه كان ضالاً مضلًّا ، ولذلك قتلناه
وصلبناه وأنّ المسيح الذي نبّأت به الأنبياء لم يأت بعد وأننا في انتظاره وإذا
أتى صدّقناه وتبعناه ، فنسأل الله العافية ونحمده على الهداية".

ثمّ لما جاء الله بالإسلام وأنزل القرآن المجيد على نبيّنا عليه السلام واتّصل
بكم لترتيب الحجّة عليكم كما قلتم إنكم قرأتموه وفهمتموه ووجدتم فيه
وصف المسيح بأنه رسول الله وكلمته ألقاها إلى مريم وروح منه وأنه عبد الله
آتاه الكتاب والحكمة وجعله نبيّاً مباركًا أينما كان وأوصاه بالصلاة والزكاة ،
* وأيّده بروح القدس وجعله وأمّه آية للعالمين وأنه لن يستنكف أن يكون
عبدًا لله ولا الملائكة المقرّبون أي الذين هم الملأ الأعلى ، ووجدتم فيه أيضًا
تحريم الشرك والتحذير منه وأنه ظلم فاحش وضلال بعيد وإثم عظيم وذنب لا
يُغفر وأقررتم بأنّ نبيّنا صلم رسول الله أرسله إلى العرب واستشهدتم ببعض[53]
آيات[54] من القرآن الذي أنزل عليه ، لزمتكم حجّة الله تعالى .بما علمتموه من
وحيه هذا وبما بيّنه لكم والعالم من أمر المسيح واختلاف أهل الكتاب فيه.

فجذبكم الغلوّ إلى التمسّك بظاهر قوله تعالى عن المسيح إنه كلمته ألقاها
إلى

* 60r

---

[51] A and B: إلاه   [52] Mtt XXVIII: 19.   [53] This word is supplied in the margin in A.   [54] B: اياب (wrongly).

them in the name of the Father and of the Son and of the Holy Spirit, one God'. You link with him things that no people who are astray have done, ignorance, error, clear polytheism and unbelief about what is in the Torah, the Gospel, the Psalms and the Criterion,[11] and about what he himself said and enjoined in the Gospel, namely to declare the unity and individuality of God, and to believe in the singularity, self-subsistence and transcendence of God above all that is other than him. You have affirmed that the Jews are right, and have vouched for the truth of their words about him: 'He was false and deceiving, and so we killed him and crucified him. The Messiah about whom the prophets prophesied has not yet come. We still expect him, and when he does come we will believe in him and follow him. So we request protection from God, and we praise him for guidance'.

Since God has delivered Islam and revealed the glorious Qur'an to our Prophet (peace be upon him), and it reached you as a set of proofs arrayed against you—as you say, you have read it and comprehended it—and you have found in it the description of Christ, that he was the messenger of God, his word which he cast into Mary and a spirit from him; that he was a servant of God, who gave him the Book and the Wisdom and made him a prophet blessed wherever he was, and imparted to him the prayers and alms-giving, (60r) supported him with the holy spirit and made him and his mother a sign to the worlds;[12] that he 'will never scorn to be a slave unto Allah, nor will the favoured angels', those who are the heavenly host; and you have also found in it the condemnation of polytheism and a warning against it, and that it is repugnant wrongdoing, eccentric error, monstrous misdeed and unforgivable sin; and you have acknowledged that our Prophet (may God bless him and give him peace) was the messenger of God whom he sent to the Arabs; and you have attested to some of the verses from the Qur'an which was revealed to him—then the proof of God the exalted is binding upon you in what you have discovered from this revelation from him and in what he has made clear to you and the world about Christ and the disagreement of the People of the Book over him.

But your excessive preference for the literal meaning of the exalted One's words about Christ, that he was his word whom he cast into

---

[11] Cf. S. III: 4, etc. 'The Criterion' is identified as the Qur'an.
[12] Cf. SS. V: 110, XIX: 31, II: 253, XIX: 91.

مريم وروح منه من غير تدبّر لمفهوم الكلمة ولا تفقّه[55] لمعنى الإلقاء ، فجسّمتم المعنى اللطيف ونزّلتم التسمية للكلمة منزلة الولد المولود من الوالد و لم تفطنوا أنّ التسمية للمسيح بالكلمة تكرمة له وتشريف من الله تعالى وتخصيص خصّصه به كتخصيص آدم أبي[56] البشر بتسميته النفخ فيه من روحه وسجود الملائكة له والإشارة إليه في التوراة عند ذكر بدء[57] الخليقة بالشبه والمثال وتخصيص ابراهيم * بالخلّة وتخصيص موسى بالتكليم وتخصيص محمّد بالمحبّة والرؤية.[58] و لم يكن آدم إلهًا مسجودًا له من دون الله تعالى ولا كان ابراهيم متخلّلاً بذاته ذات الله ولا كان موسى سامعًا لكلام الله كسماعه للكلام الإنساني لأنه لو كان كذلك لم تكن له مزيّة ولا تخصيص ولا كان عيسى المسيح كلمة الله وروحًا منه متبعّضة منفصلة كانفصال الأجسام أو متّصلة كاتصال الكلام والأرواح المعلومة للمعقول ولا كان محمّد رائياً ربّه كرؤية البصر للمبصرات ، بل شرّف الله سبحانه كلّ واحد منهم بتشريف خاص مناسب به متميّز عليه يلوح لأهل الذوق لائحة سناء برق ذلك الاختصاص ويفهمون منه الإشارة بعبارة تلك التسمية التي اختصّ بمسمّاها.

كما فهمنا نحن المسلمون الإشارة إلى هذه التخصيصات الستة لهؤلاء الرسل الكرام الستة من عبارة الكلمات الستّ[59] التي علّمنا إياها نبيّنا صلم وهي قول: "سبحان الله والحمد لله ولا إله إلا الله والله أكبر ولا حول ولا قوة إلا بالله العليّ العظيم"، والمعنى المفهوم من إشارتها أنّ موسى بن عمران عليلم لم يزل قائلاً بالحال والقال[60]: * سبحان الله سبحان الله

* 60v

* 61r

[55] B: نفقة [56] B: لي (wrongly), evidently a misreading of A. [57] A and B: بدو [58]
B: والمقال [59] A and B: الستة [60] B: والروبة

Mary and a spirit from him, have captivated you, though you have not considered the significance of 'word' nor reflected on the meaning of 'casting'. Thus you have made something refined into something material, and have reduced the designation 'word' to the level of child born of a parent, without the insight to see that the designation of Christ as word is a mark of honour and distinction upon him from God the exalted. It is a token by which he distinguished him, like that of Adam the father of mankind, whom he designated as the one whom he breathed into with his spirit, the one to whom the angels bowed, and the one mentioned in the Torah in the account of the beginning of creation as the resemblance and image.[13] The token of Abraham (60v) was friendship, that of Moses was being spoken to, and that of Muḥammad was love and the vision.[14] But Adam was not a god bowed down to in place of God the exalted; Abraham's essence was not pervaded by the essence of God;[15] and Moses did not hear God's speech as he heard human speech, for if he had it would not have been a privilege or token for him. Neither was Jesus Christ God's word or a spirit from him, partitioned and segmented in the way that bodies are segmented, nor combined as speech and spirits in normal understanding are combined with intelligence; nor did Muḥammad see his Lord as the eye sees visible things. Rather, the blessed God distinguished each of them by a particular distinction that was appropriate to him and by which he was set apart; to people of perception it shone on him with the brilliance of a lightning flash. It was a characteristic from which they understood the significance of the words in the phrase by which he was particularly named.

In the same way we Muslims understand the significance of the six tokens of the six noble messengers in the six phrases which our Prophet (may God bless him and give him peace) taught us. These are: Blessed be God, Praise be to God, There is no god but God, God is most great, There is no power and there is no strength except in God the august and mighty. The obvious meaning of their significance is that Moses son of 'Imrān (peace be upon him) never ceased saying at every opportunity, (61r) 'Blessed be God, blessed be God' to the

---

[13] Cf. e.g. S. XV: 28-9, Genesis I: 26-7.
[14] S. IV: 125 and 164. As is made clear in what follows, the third is a reference to the Prophet's vision of God during his heavenly journey.
[15] Ibn 'Arabī says exactly this in *Fuṣūṣ al-ḥikam*, ed. A. 'Afīfī, Beirut, 1946, pp. 80-4.

تعجّباً من سماعه الخطاب من النار والشجرة ومن انقلاب العصا في يده حيّة تسعى وانقلاب الحيّة عصاً[61] كما كانت ومن شهوده لضرباته العشر[62] التي ضربها فاعلاً بذلك فعل الإله كما رمى نبيّنا التراب والحصى بكفّه في أعين الكفّار فهزمهم وقال الله في ذلك: ﴿وما رميت إذ رميت ولكن الله رمى﴾.[63]

وأنّ المسيح عليلم لم يزل بالحال والمقال قائلاً: "الحمد لله الحمد لله" على تعداد النعمة عليه وعلى أمّه بإلقاء الكلمة إليها وتأييده بروح القدس وإحيائه للموتى مثل العازر وغيره ممّن أحياهم بإذن الله وإبرائه الأكمه وتنقيته الأبرص ونفخه في الطير الطين فيكون حيًا بإذن الله.

وأنّ نبيّنا صلم لم يزل بالقال والحال قائلاً: "لا إله إلا الله لا إله إلا الله" حتى خلت جزيرة العرب من الأصنام وعُبد الله وحده في أقطار الأرض وأذلّ المشركين كفرة أهل الكتاب في غالب الأرض ﴿فأعطوا الجزية عن يد وهم صاغرون﴾[64] ورفع عَلَم الهُدى للعالمين ، وأعلى الله به دين الإسلام وكلمة التوحيد على كلّ دين ، حتى أنه في كلّ يوم من أيام الدهر ينادي مناديه: لا إله إلا الله بأعلى مكان بكلّ بقعة * على كلّ شرف بأحسن صوت من أشرف قائل ومخلوق أعني الإنسان ، في كلّ يوم وليلة خمس مرّات.

* 61v

وأنّ ابراهيم عليلم لم يزل قائلاً بالحال والمقال: "الله أكبر الله أكبر" إعلاناً بالحقّ وتبكيتا لنمرود وتعريفًا للصابئة عبدة الكواكب ، حتى دان العالم في زمنه بدين الحنيفيّة ،

---

[61] A and B: عصى   [62] A and B: العشرة   [63] S. VIII: 17.   [64] S. IX: 29.

astonishment of everyone who heard him declaring about the fire
and the bush, about the transformation of the staff in his hand into
a slithering snake and the transformation of the snake into a staff as
it had been, and about his witnessing to his ten plagues that he had
inflicted, it being God who performed it as he was performing it. In
the same way our Prophet threw the dust and pebbles in his palm into
the eyes of the unbelievers and routed them, about which God said,
'And thou threwest not when thou didst throw, but Allah threw'.[16]

And Christ (peace be upon him) never ceased saying at every opportunity, 'Praise be to God, praise be to God' for the host of blessings
upon him and his mother, for the word cast into her, his being supported by the holy spirit, his raising the dead such as Lazarus and
others whom he raised with the help of God, his restoring sight to the
blind, his cleansing the leper, and his breathing into the clay bird so
that it came to life with the help of God.

Our Prophet (may God bless him and give him peace) never ceased
saying at every opportunity, 'There is no god but God, there is no god
but God', until Arabia was emptied of idols and God and no other was
praised throughout the earth; he humbled the polytheist unbelievers
among the People of the Book through most of the earth, so they paid
the poll-tax 'readily, being brought low', and he raised up the banner
of guidance for the worlds. Through him God exalted Islam and the
declaration of divine unity above all religions, so that on every single
day without stop his herald proclaims 'There is no god but God' from
the highest point in every place (61v) and every eminence, with most
melodious voice by the most noble user of speech among creatures—I
mean mankind—five times every day and night.

Abraham (peace be upon him) never ceased saying at every
opportunity, 'God is most great, God is most great', proclaiming the
truth, a reproach to Nimrod and announcement to the Ṣābians, the
star-worshippers,[17] until the world in his time yielded to the Ḥanīfite

---

[16] This is a reference to Muḥammad's action of throwing dust into the air at the
battle of Badr and miraculously blinding the Meccan army; cf. Ibn Kathīr, *Bidāya*,
vol. III, pp. 283-4/*Life of the Prophet*, vol. II, pp. 288-9.

[17] Cf. S. II: 258, where 'he who had an argument with Abraham' is identified
in Muslim tradition as Nimrod, the king who persecuted and tortured the prophet
because of his persistence in monotheism; cf. Ibn Kathīr, *Bidāya*, vol. I, pp. 147-9.
Abraham's association with Ḥarrān in Muslim literature provides an additional link
with the Ṣābians, who were identified as the star-worshippers known to Muslim
authors in that city; Ibn Kathīr, *Bidāya*, vol. I, pp. 149-50.

شاهدين بأنّ الله هو المعبود الحقّ لا إله إلا هو الكبير المتعال.

وأنّ آدم أبا البشر لم يزل قائلاً بالحال والمقال: "لا حول إلا بالله"، وذلك عند رؤية كلّ بليّة ومحنة وفتنة، إذ خُلق هو وذرّيته للإمتحان والتكليف والإبتلاء وأُخرج من الجنّة مع حوّاء إلى الأرض، وسُلّط عليه إبليس وعلى ذرّيته وعصا آدم وإبليس بمعصية مشتركة، فآدم نُهي عن الشجرة فخالف، وإبليس أُمر بالسجود لآدم فخالف ثمّ تاب الله على آدم وهداه.

وأنّ نوحًا عليكم[65] لم يزل قائلاً بالحال والقال: "لا قوّة إلا بالله، لا قوّة إلا بالله" تفويضًا إلى الله تعالى وتوكّلاً عليه واستعانة به على كفّار قومه بالله وتكذيبهم لنوح وصبره على أذاهم له ﴿ألف سنة إلا خمسين عامًا﴾[66] وعمله للسفينة وحشر سائر الحيوان إليها ليحمل فيها ﴿من كل زوجين اثنين﴾[67]، وعلى هول الطوفان وجريان السفينة ﴿في موج كالجبال﴾[68]، ومثل هذه الأهوال.

64. فالمسيح كلمة الله بمعنى أنه مخلوق * بكلمة الله التي هي قوله للشيء ٭ 62r الذي يريد[69] كونه: "كن فيكون" وتخصّص بالتسمية[70] لذلك، ولأنّ مثله كمثل آدم، ولأنها اسم تكرمة له من الله تعالى.

وأيّ فرية على الله وعلى المسيح أعظم من القول بتجسّم كلمة الله التي هي من صفات ذاته وانقلابها وهي خالقة بزعمكم انقلابًا بالتدريج والممازجة والحلول والاتحاد بناسوت مريم إلى ناسوت المسيح المخلوق المولود بالكلمة من مريم أمّه إلهًا[71] تامًّا وإنسانا تامًّا مولودين معًا مع استحالة هذا القول أصلاً وفرعًا وعقلاً وشرعًا واستحالة الممازجة[72] والحلول والانقلاب من الربوبيّة إلى العبودية ومن القدم[73] والواجبيّة إلى الحدث والممكنيّة وامتناع ذلك، إذ الربّ ربّ لذاته والعبد عبد لغيره، والربّ لا يكون[74] عبدًا.

---

    [65] B: عليكم (wrongly), evidently a misreading of A which has a diagonal stroke over the second *lām* to indicate a marginal reading.　[66] S. XXIX: 14.　[67] S. XI: 40.　[68] *Ibid.*: 42　[69] A and B: يريده　[70] B: بالشمية (wrongly).　[71] B: إلهتا (wrongly).　[72] B: المزجة　[73] B: القوم (wrongly).　[74] B: اليكون (wrongly), evidently a misreading of A.

religion, witnessing that it was God who was to be worshipped in truth and that there is no god but him, the great and sublime.

Adam, the father of mankind, never ceased saying at every opportunity, 'There is no power except in God', and this when he went through every trial, ordeal and tribulation. For he and his seed were created to be put to the test, given burdens and afflicted with distress: he was driven out of paradise with Eve to the earth; the devil was given power over him and his seed, for both Adam and the devil were joint partakers in disobedience, because Adam was forbidden the tree but he disobeyed, and the devil was ordered to prostrate before Adam but he disobeyed. But then God forgave Adam and gave him guidance.

Noah (peace be upon him) never ceased saying at every opportunity, 'There is no strength except by God, there is no strength except by God', committing himself to God the exalted, relying totally upon him, seeking his help against the unbelievers among his people and their accusation that Noah was a liar; his steadfastness at their insulting him for 'a thousand years save fifty years'; his constructing the ship and gathering all animals into it in order to carry in it 'two of every kind, a pair' on the terror of the flood when the ship sped along 'amid waves like mountains'; and there were also further terrors.

64.   Christ was the word of God in the sense that he was created (62r) by the word of God, which is his saying to a thing that he wills to be, 'Be!' and it is. He was given the specific title for this reason, and because his likeness was the likeness of Adam, and because it is a name which is a bestowal of honour upon him from God the exalted.

What slander against God and Christ is greater than to talk about the word of God, one of the attributes of his essence, becoming flesh and, even though it is a creator by your claim, being transformed by coming into proximity, mixing, indwelling and uniting through the human nature of Mary with the human nature of Christ, who was created, born by word from Mary his mother, fully God and fully man together? This is despite the impossibility of such a statement in root and branch, in reason and revelation, and the impossibility of mixing, indwelling, and being transformed from lordship to servanthood, and from eternal and what is necessary to temporal and what is potential. Such a thing is inadmissible, because the Lord is Lord by virtue of his essence, and the servant is servant by virtue of something extraneous, and the Lord does not become a servant.[18]

---

[18] This is an eloquent summary of the reasons given by Muslims for rejecting

فاستحال أنّ المسيح ربّ خالق[75] وهو[76] مربوب مخلوق ولدته أمّه طفلاً
وأرضعته وربّته بحضانتها محمولاً على الأيدي من قضاء التلهّي يبكي
ويضحك وينام ويبول ويتغوّط، وكان له اخوة واخوات كما هو مكتوب
في الإنجيلات "انّ يسوع وامّه واخوته وتلاميذه صعدوا للعيد" و"مرّوا إلى
العرس". وكان يسوع أصغر اخوته واخواته "وختنته أمّه وهو ابن ثمانية
أيام" على سنّة موسى. وفي الإنجيلات أنّ * مريم لمّا جاءها المخاض وهي
في الفندق ببيت لحم وليست عندها قابلة، فذهب يوسف النجّار وأتاها
بامرأة رابية اسمها سليمة فقبلت يسوع وأرضعته وملحته ولفته بخرق ونوّمته
في مذود حمار في الفندق.

وفي إنجيلاتكم[77] أنّ يسوع رقد في السفينة، وهاجت الرياح وكان
معه تلاميذه فنبّهوه وقالوا له: "قم اطلب فينا إلى الله تعالى"[78]. وفي إنجيلاتكم
أيضًا أنه دخل العرس أكل وشرب ورقد سكرانا في منزل سمعان كصفا[79]
وهو مريض فجاءت إليه الزانية امرأة سامرية وقبّلت رجليه ولم يعلم بها[80].
وفي أناجيلكم أيضًا أنه لمّا بلغ عمر يسوع ثمانية أيام ذهبت به أمّه إلى الكاهن
ليقرّب عنه قربانًا كما أمر الله

* 62v

---

[75] A and B: ربأ خالقأ.   [76] This word is supplied in the margin in A.   [77] B: إنجيلايكم
(wrongly).   [78] Cf. Mtt VIII: 23-6, Mk IV: 35-9 and Lk VIII: 22-5.   [79] Cf. Mtt VIII:
14-15, Mk I: 29-30 and Lk IV: 38.   [80] Cf. Mtt XXVI: 6-13, Mk XIV: 3-9, Lk VII:
36-48 and Jn XII: 1-8.

So it was impossible for Christ to be Lord and Creator and also subservient and created, born of his mother as a baby, suckled and brought up by her nurture, picked up in arms at the end of play; he cried, laughed, slept, urinated and defecated, and he had brothers and sisters, as is written in the Gospels, 'Jesus, his mother, brothers and disciples went up for the festival', 'They went into the wedding', 'Jesus was the youngest of his brothers and sisters', and 'His mother had him circumcised when he was eight days old, according to the Law of Moses'.[19] It is also in the Gospels that (62v) when Mary's labour pains came upon her in the inn at Bethlehem and there was no midwife at hand, Joseph the carpenter brought her a wet nurse named Salīma.[20] She delivered Jesus, suckled him, fed him with her milk, wrapped him in cloth bands, and laid him to sleep in an ass' manger in the inn.

It is also in your Gospels that Jesus was asleep in the boat when the storm blew up, and his disciples who were with him roused him and said to him, 'Rise up and implore God the exalted for us'. Also in your Gospels is that he went to the wedding and ate and drank, and went to sleep drunk in the house of Simon Peter. He was ill, and a Samaritan woman who was an adulteress came to him and kissed his legs, though he was not aware of her. It is also in your Gospels that when Jesus was eight days old his mother took him to the priest for him to make a sacrifice on behalf of him, as God had commanded

---

the doctrine of the Incarnation. As early as the third/ninth century al-Qāsim b. Ibrāhīm argued that the divine and human are so utterly distinct that they cannot be related in any way, while Abū ʿĪsā al-Warrāq argued that metaphysical explanations such as mixing, indwelling, etc., offered no solution to the fundamental problem of the doctrine.

Al-Dimashqī's last comment reflects the theologians' principle that God's characteristics are endowed by attributes that are internal to his being, while those of creatures are endowed by accidental attributes that are superadded to their essences. This emphasises the radical distinction that prevents the one becoming the other.

[19] There are references to Jesus' brothers in Mtt XII: 46, || Mk III: 31, Lk VIII.19, and Jn II: 12, and to his brothers and sisters in Mtt XIII: 55-6, || Mk VI: 3.; to his brothers going up to the festival in Jn VII: 8; to Jesus and his mother being at the wedding in Jn II: 2; and to his circumcision in Lk II: 21-2. Here and in the following paragraphs al-Dimashqī employs the form Yashūʿa rather than the more familiar ʿĪsā.

[20] Cf. *The Protoevangelium of James*, in E. Hennecke, *New Testament Apocrypha*, trans. R. McL. Wilson, vol. I, *Gospels and Related Writings*, London, 1963, pp. 384-5, where Salome acts as midwife at the birth of Jesus. According to Mk XV: 40-1 Salome looked after Jesus when he was in Galilee, and in Mk XVI: 1 she was one of the three women who came to the tomb of Jesus.

لبني اسرائيل، فلما رآه[81] سمعان الإمام بان له فقال سمعان: "أيّ بلاء يظهر من هذا الصبيّ[82] على بني إسرائيل".[83]

وأنه لمّا بلغ هيرودس أو هذورس الملك خبر يسوع طلبه ليقتله[84] فهرب به يوسف النجّار إلى مصر ومعه سليمة الرابية وأمّه مريم وعلّمه بمصر الصباغة وعالج أعمالا وصنائع كثيرة حتى مات هذورس الملك، فعاد به يوسف إلى الشام[85]، وأنه أوّل عجب عمله يسوع بعد قدومه من مصر أن حوّل الماء خمرًا.[86]

وإنّ في إنجيلاتكم أيضًا * نسبة باختلاف واضطراب، ففي إنجيل متى هو يشوع بن يوسف بن يعقوب بن متان بن العازر بن أليهود بن امون بن صادوق ابن عازور. وساق إلى أربعين أبا.[87]

وفي الإنجيل أيضًا هو يشوع بن يوسف بن هيلي[88] ابن مطون[89]. وفي إنجيل لوقا ومرقس أنّ يسوع بن يوسف من قرية ناصرة الجليل[90] واخوته واخواته عندهم مزوجات[91].

وفي الإنجيل أيضًا أنّ المسيح لمّا دخل البلد كان يقف في جماعتهم يروي ويخبر فيقول الناس: "من أين هذه الأحكام والآيات لهذا؟ أليس هو ابن يوسف النجّار؟ اسم أمّه مريم واخوته سمعان ويوسف ويعقوب ويهوذا". حقّا إنّ قد قال: "لا يُحقَّر نبي إلا في مدينته"[92].

فهذه الروايات كلها مع اختلافها وبطلانها وافتراء الزاعمين لها بقولهم: إنّ المسيح بن يوسف

81 B: راءه   82 A and B: هذه الصبر (wrongly).   83 Cf. Lk II: 21-35.   84 B: ليقبله   85 Cf. Mtt II: 13-23.   86 Jn II: 1-11.   87 A and B: أب; cf. Mtt I: 1-16.   88 Cf. Lk III: 23.   89 Cf. Mtt I: 15.   90 A and B: الخليل   91 Cf. Lk IV: 22, and VIII: 19; Mk III: 31 and VI: 3.   92 Mtt XIII: 53-7; Mk VI: 1-4.

the People of Israel. When Simon the leader of prayers saw him, he came up before him and said, 'Oh the tribulation for the People of Israel that will arise from this child!'

When news about Jesus reached Herod, or Hadhūrus, the king, he searched for him to kill him. So Joseph the carpenter fled with him to Egypt, together with Salīma the wet nurse and his mother Mary, and she taught him the dyer's trade in Egypt.[21] He took up many trades and occupations until King Hadhūrus died, when Joseph returned with him to Syria. The first miracle that Jesus performed after coming back from Egypt was to turn the water into wine.[22]

Also in your Gospels (63r) are diverging and clashing genealogies. For in the Gospel of Matthew he is Yashū'a son of Joseph, son of Jacob, son of Matthan, son of Eleazar, son of Eliud, son of Amun, son of Zadok, son of Azor, continuing to forty ancestors. But in the Gospel also he is Yashū'a son of Joseph, son of Heli, son of Matim. And in the Gospel of Luke and Mark is that Jesus was the son of Joseph from the village of Nazareth in Galilee, and that his brothers and sisters had spouses.

Also in the Gospel is that when Christ entered the district and stayed in their community telling stories and giving accounts, the people said, 'Where has he got these instructions and miracles from? Is he not Joseph the carpenter's son? His mother's name is Mary and his brothers are Simon, Joseph, Jacob and Judah.' Truly, he himself said, 'A prophet is scorned only in his own town.'

All these reports, with their disagreements, untruths and the lies of those who purvey them when they say, 'Christ was the son of Joseph

---

[21] Cf. §§ 72 and 79 below. Jesus' association with dyeing cloth had become a commonplace of Muslim tradition by the time of al-Dimashqī. Al-Tha'labī, *Qiṣaṣ al-anbiyā'*, pp. 389-90, recounts how Mary apprenticed him to a dyer for whom he performed the miracle of producing cloths of different colours from one vat, as does Ibn al-Athīr, *Al-kāmil fī al-ta'rīkh*, Beirut, 1998, vol. I, p. 241, while Jalāl al-Dīn al-Rūmī twice briefly refers to him dipping a multi-coloured cloth into a vat of dye and pulling it out white, *The Mathnawī of Jalālu'ddin Rūmī*, ed. and trans. R.A. Nicholson, London, 1977, Books I. 500-1, VI, 1855.

A much earlier reference in the Christian tradition occurs in the apocryphal Gospel of Philip, which dates from the second or third century CE: 'The Lord went into the dye-works of Levi. He took seventy-two colours and threw them into the vat. He took them out all white'; R. McL. Wilson, *The Gospel of Philip*, London, 1962, p. 39. The reference here to seventy-two colours tantalisingly recalls the number of versions of the Gospels referred to in the Cypriot *Letter*, above Section 4, n. 4.

[22] Al-Dimashqī's purpose in listing all these details about Jesus' birth and infancy is to emphasise his humanity.

النجّار وإنّ له اخوة واخوات كلهم أكبر منه سنًّا، وهم إمّا من مريم وإمّا من امرأة غيرها مزوجة ليوسف استولدها هؤلاء الأولاد، فإنّ ذلك بشهادة كتابنا الحقّ المبين حديث باطل مفترى وقول زور، ولم يكن لمريم البتول زوج[93] ولا مسّها بشر ولا كانت[94] بغيًّا، بل كانت كما أخبر الله تعالى قائلاً: ﴿ومريم ابنت عمران﴾ الآية[95]، وقائلاً في * سورة مريم عنها حين أرسل إليها الملك على صورة إنسان واستعاذت بالله منه، فقال لها: ﴿إنّما أنا رسول ربّك﴾، إلى آخر قصّتها[96]. والعقل السليم يقضي أنّ مريم لا تكون[97] غير بكر مطهّرة بتول لنفي[98] سوء الظنّة بها لو كانت مزوجة أو ذات ولد غير المسيح قبله وبعده، إذ لا يليق إلا ذلك.

    لا كما جاء في الإنجيل أنّ مريم لمّا حبلت بيشوع بعث أغوسطس أو أغسطس الملك فكتب الناس كلهم فوجدوا مريم حبلى في فندق في بيت لحم، فسألوها: "ممّن أنت حبلى؟" فقالت: "من يوسف النجّار"، فكتبوا: "مريم والذي في بطنها من يوسف النجّار"[99]. وفي إنجيل متى أنّ جبريل الملاك قال ليوسف: "إذهب وخذ امرأتك ولا تخف"[100].

  65.   وهذه أقوال ظاهرة التناقض مردودة عقلاً وشرعًا، وكالذي زعمتم من تجسيم كلمة الله وصيرورتها مسيحًا متحدًا بناسوته المربّى المولود إلهًا وربّا خالقًا وفعّالاً للعجائب التي لا يفعلها إلا الإله وليس كذلك، فإن زعمكم في الكلمة وتجسّمها زعم باطل لا يقوله عاقل ولا يقبله عاقل، لأنّ المعقول لا يمازج المحسوس والكلام لا ينفصل عن * المتكلّم المعلوم لنا انفصالاً ذاتيًّا ولا يتجسّم ومن المحال تجسّمه وهو معنى لطيف يُسمع ولا يُرى، فكيف ما لا يحيط به علم ولا أين له ولا كيف ولا كم؟ ولأنّ الكلام صفة ذاتية للموصوف قائمة به، ومن أمحل المحال تجسّمه، فهذا والله هو عين الجهل المركّب:

* 63v

* 64r

---

[93] A and B: زوجًا [94] B: كاتب (wrongly). [95] S. LXVI: 12. [96] S. XIX: 19. [97] B: يكون [98] B: لبقي (wrongly). [99] Lk II: 1-5. [100] Mtt I: 20.

the carpenter, and he had brothers and sisters, all of them older than himself, and they were either from Mary or another woman married to Joseph from whom he wanted these children', according to the witness of our true and clear Book they give an untrue and lying account and false statement. For the Virgin Mary never had a husband, no man ever touched her, and she was not unchaste. Rather, she was as God the exalted teaches when he says, 'And Mary daughter of 'Imran [whose body was chaste, therefor we breathed therein something of our spirit]' and the rest of the verse. And he says about her in (63v) *Mary*, that when the angel was sent to her in the form of a man and she sought God's protection from him, he said to her, 'I am only a messenger of thy Lord' to the end of the account about her. Sound reason concludes that Mary was no other than a pure virgin and intact when denying the foul suspicion against her that she may have been married or the parent of a child before or after Christ, for only this is fitting.

It is not as given in the Gospel, that when Mary conceived Jesus, Augustus, or Aghuṣṭus, the king sent out for all people to be registered. They discovered Mary pregnant in an inn in Bethlehem, and they asked her, 'By whom did you conceive?' She replied, 'By Joseph the carpenter.' So they registered Mary and the child in her womb from Joseph the carpenter. And according to the Gospel of Matthew the angel Gabriel said to Joseph, 'Go, take your wife and do not be afraid.'

65.　These are clear statements of contradiction, rejected by both reason and revelation. They are like your claim about the incarnation of the Word of God and its becoming Christ, united in his nurtured, born human nature, with Divinity, Lord, Creator and Agent of miracles which only God can perform. But the matter is not like this. For your claim about the Word and its incarnation is a false claim, which no reasonable person would make or allow. For what is intellect does not mingle with what is perceptible to the senses, and speech is not separated from (64r) the speaker as known to us in any essential way, nor does it become flesh. This is quite impossible for it, since it is a refined entity which is heard but not seen, and even more than this it cannot be encompassed by knowledge and does not possess where, why or how much. Further, speech is an essential attribute which subsists in the one it characterises. So its becoming flesh is utterly impossible. By God, this is the very being of compounded ignorance!

من الجهالة بالمعبود يا لكع	يا من يقال لهم: كونوا على ثقة
مركّب من صغير باللها قطع	ويحكم، هل كلام الله ذو جسد
مع الهواء بتصريف فيستمع	صوت يصوّته تجويف قائله
ورجعه قارع للسمع، منقرع	نطق يموّجه حمل الهواء له
مجسّمًا، ويل قوم ربّهم صنعوا	حتى تظنّوا كلام الله صنعتكم
وبئس من قنّنوا هذا ومن شرعوا	بئس المقالة ما قلتم، وبئسكم
ابن كلام؟ لهذا مفترى شنع	يا للعقول، أربّ العالمين له
من ذاته ولد كالخلق مخترع؟	يا للعقول، أربّ العالمين له

ولله درّ نسطور إذ يقول وأنتم تعرفون قوله: "كفرت بربّ يسكن الرحم"، وخلّى دينكم واتبع رأي نفسه.

وما مثل قولكم في الكلمة إنها تجسّمت بانسان مخلوق واتحادها به الاتحاد الجوهري البريء من التغير والاستحالة، وإنها خرجت مولودة * من مريم إنسانًا تامًّا وإلهًا تامًّا يفعل المعجز بلاهوته ويظهر العجز بناسوته إلا كقول من يقول حكاية كان كنونو برغش وصنونو العسل طريح والبصل بطيخ طارت الجمال حبلت الرجال، وأمثال هذه الأضحوكات المبكيات.

وأعجب العجب استشهادكم بآيات من القرآن وقول من التوراة وبما في كتب النبوءات على ما ذهبتم إليه من القول بالأقانيم المشتركة في الإلهية والخلق للعالم والربوبية مشاركة بتواطئ إغضاب [101] وتساهل، حيث قلتم إنّ في القرآن ذكر الكلمة والروح وهو

                * 64v

---

[101] A and B: واغضبا (sic).

O you who are told, 'Keep trusting
   in the follies of what you worship', O wretches,
Woe to you, has the word of God a body
   composed of little bits, and severed from God,
Is it a sound which is made by a sounding hollow
   with air as it is exhaled and is heard,
Speech which the air carrying it bears along,
   And its echo penetrates deep into the ear?
And do you imagine that the word of God is your making,
   with a body, the affliction of people who made their lord?
What evil words you speak, so woe to you,
   and woe to those who have laid this down and legislated.
People of intelligence, does the Lord of the worlds have
   a son, his word? Such is truly a slanderous lie.
People of intelligence, does the Lord of the worlds have
   from his essence a child, contrived in the manner of men?

How excellent was Nestorius when he said—and you know his words—'I refuse to believe in a lord who dwelt in a womb'. He withdrew from your religion and followed his own opinion.[23]

Your statement that the Word became incarnate in a created man, that its uniting with him was a uniting of substance though excluding change or transformation, that it emerged born (64v) from Mary's womb perfect man and perfect God, in his divine nature performing works of which others are incapable, and in his human nature displaying incapacity—all this is no different from the teller of the unlikely tale of Kunūnū the gnat and Ṣunūnū, of honey unwanted and onion as water melon, of camels flying and men falling pregnant, as well as other ridiculous and sorrowful things.[24]

Most surprising of all is your quoting of verses from the Qur'an, teachings from the Torah, and what is in the prophetic books in support of what you believe concerning the teaching about the hypostases which share completely in divinity, creation of the world and lordship. You do this connivingly, provocatively and sloppily, because you have said that the Qur'an contains references to the Word and Spirit, in

---

[23] This is a simplified summary of the fifth century CE schism caused by the Patriarch of Constantinople Nestorius (d. *ca* 451), who refused to call Mary 'Mother of God' or to accept that the divine nature shared in the human experiences of Christ, for which he was anathematised by the Council of Ephesus in 431, and many of whose teachings the church in the Persian Empire later accepted; cf. S.H. Moffett, *A History of Christianity in Asia, volume I: Beginnings to 1500*, New York 1998, pp. 172-80.

[24] These were presumably proverbial examples of impossibility.

قوله تعالى: ﴿ومريم ابنت عمران﴾ الآية[102]، وقوله: ﴿وآتينا عيسى ابن مريم البيّنات﴾ الآية[103]، وهذا لا يدلّ على أنّ الروح هي الحياة التي بها حيّ الموجد لها من قبل أن يوجدها وكانت حيّة لذاتها من قبل إيجاده لها كما زعمتم، ولا يدلّ على أنّ روح القدس المؤيّد بها المسيح هي الروح الشريكة للإبن والناطقة به مع الآب والحيّ بها الآب الموجد لهما من قبل أن يكون حيّا ناطقًا بها، ولا يدلّ على أنّ الكلمة المسمّاة الإبن الشريك الثالث الذي به ينطق الآب والروح وبهما يحيا[104] ويوجد هي الكلمات التي صدقت بها مريم وسبقت لعباد الله المرسلين، ﴿ولو كان البحر مدادًا * لها وأمده سبعة أبحر ما نفدت كلمات الله﴾[105].

* 65r

وليس المؤيّد بروح القدس هو روح القدس بل غيرها، والذي أيّده بها فإنّه غيره وغيرها وهو الله تعالى.

وقلتم أيضًا إنّ في التوراة أسماء الأقانيم الثلاثة: الآب، وهو قوله لإسرائيل: "أباك الذي صنعك"[106]، والإبن هو قوله لإسرائيل: "أنت ابني الذي ارتضيت"[107]، والروح وهو قوله: "وكان روح الله ترفرف على الماء".[108] ولا دليل في ذلك على الشرك والثالوث، إذ الآب بمعنى الربّ وقد تقدّم شرحه مع قوله: "صنعك وبراك واتقنك"[109] لا ولدك ولا تولّدت منه. وكذا ترفرف الروح لا يدلّ[110] على الشرك بل له معنى في كتابنا يفهم منه وهو قوله تعالى[111]: ﴿وكان عرشه على الماء﴾.[112]

ولله قول بعض أهل التحقيق، شعر:

سفينة تجري بأسمائه	أنظر إلى العرش على مائه

---

[102] S. LXVI: 12.   [103] S. II: 87.   [104] A and B: يحيى   [105] A reminiscence of S. XVIII: 109.   [106] Deut XXXII: 6.   [107] Exodus IV: 22; Ben Sira XXXVI: 12 (cf. p. 336 above and n. 45).   [108] Genesis I: 2.   [109] *Sic* in A and B; possibly read واقتناك; cf *supra*, f. 58r and Deut XXXII: 6.   [110] B: الروح لي لا يدلّ, evidently a misreading of A.   [111] B: تعا, evidently a misreading of A.   [112] S. XI: 7.

the words of the exalted One, 'And Mary, daughter of 'Imrān [whose body was chaste, therefor we breathed therein something of our Spirit]' and the rest of the verse, and his words, 'And we gave unto Jesus, son of Mary, clear proofs [and we supported him with the holy Spirit]' and the rest of the verse. This does not prove that the Spirit is the life by which the One who gave it existence lived before he gave it existence, or that it lived by its essence before he gave it existence, as you claim. And it does not prove that the holy Spirit by which Christ was supported was the Spirit that participated in the Son and spoke through him as with the Father, or that the One who was living by it was the Father who gave existence to the two of them before he was living and speaking by them. And it does not prove that the Word, which is called the Son, the third participant, by whom the Father and Spirit spoke, and who was given life and existence by the two of them, was the words by which Mary spoke true, and which had previously been given to the servants of God who had been sent. 'Though the sea became ink (65r) spread through the seven seas, the words of God would not be exhausted.'

The one who was supported by the holy Spirit was not the holy Spirit itself but different from it, and the One who supported him by it was neither him nor it, but he was God the exalted.

You have also said that the names of the three hypostases are in the Torah: Father, in his words to Israel 'Your Father who made you'; Son, in his words to Israel 'You are my son, in whom I take delight'; and the Spirit, in his words 'The spirit of God was hovering over the water'. But there is no proof here for sharing or Trinity. For 'Father' has the meaning of 'Lord', and the explanation of this has been given earlier, in God's words 'He made you, shaped you and got you for his own', not 'he begot you' or 'you were begotten from him'. Similarly, the hovering of the Spirit does not prove sharing, but rather it has a meaning in our Book by which it can be understood, in the words of the exalted One, 'And his throne was upon the water'.[25]

Indeed, one of the people of true knowledge has a word of poetry:

See the throne above his waters,
   It is a vessel proceeding by means of his names.

---

[25] Al-Dimashqī's first point is that the verses in the Torah refer to God creating and making rather than begetting, while his second seems to be that this is a metaphorical reference with no idea of a real entity implied.

فصل

ثمّ قلتم:

وأمّا تجسّم كلمة الله الخالقة بإنسان مخلوق وولودتهما معًا أي الكلمة مع
الناسوت، فإنه لم يخاطب الباري أحدًا إلا وحيّا أو من وراء حجاب حسبما[1] جاء
في هذا الكتاب يقول: ﴿وما كان لبشر﴾ الآية[2]. وإذا كانت اللطائف لا تظهر
إلا في الكثائف، فكلمة الله التي بها خلقت اللطائف تظهر في غير كثيف * كلا، * 65v
ولذلك ظهرت في عيسى ابن مريم، إذ الإنسان أشرف ممّا خلق الله[3] تعالى، ولهذا
خاطب الخلق وشاهدوا منه ما شاهدوا.

وقد قال الله على أفواه الأنبياء المرسلين الذين نبئوا على تجسّده وولادته وجميع
أفعاله التي فعلها في الأرض. وهذه النبوءات أيضًا عند اليهود مقرّين معترفين بها
ويقرؤنها في كنائسهم، وسبيلنا أن ندلّ على بعض الأنباء.

قال عزرا الكاهن[4] حين سباهم بخت نصر إلى أرض بابل "إلى أربعمئة سنة
واثنتين وثمانين سنة يأتي المسيح ويخلّص الشعوب والأمم" ، وفي كمال هذه المدّة
أتى السيّد المسيح.

وقال إرميا النبي عن ولادته: "في ذلك الزمان يقوم[5] لداود ابن وهو ضوء[6] النور
يملك الملك ويعلّم ويفهم ويقيم الحقّ والعدل في الأرض ويخلّص من آمن به من
اليهود ومن اسرائيل ويبقى بيت المقدس بغير قتال ولا مقاتل واسمه الإله"[7].

وقال أشعيا: "قل لصهيون هنا تفرح وتهلّل بأنّ الله يأتي ويخلّص من آمن
به وبشعبه ويخلّص مدينة بيت المقدس ويظهر الله ذراعه الطاهر فيها لجميع أهل
الأرض وجميع المبدّدين ويجعلهم أمّة واحدة ويبصرون جميع أهل الأرض خلاص
الله لأنه يمشي معهم وبين يديهم ويجمعهم إله اسرائيل"[8].

* وقال زكريا النبي: "افرحي يا بنت[9] صهيون لأني آتيك وأحلّ فيك وأتراءى * 66r
ويؤمن بالله في ذلك اليوم الأمم الكثيرة ويكونون له شعبًا واحدًا ويحلّ هو وهم
فيك وتعرفين[10] أني أنا الله القويّ الساكن فيك، ويأخذ الله في ذلك اليوم الملك من
يهوذا ويملك عليهم إلى الأبد"[11].

وقال عاموص النبي: "ستشرق الشمس على الأرض

---

[1] B: حسبها (wrongly), a misreading of A.   [2] S. XLII: 51.   [3] This word is repeated
in A and B.   [4] B: الكاهر (wrongly), a misreading of A.   [5] B: تقوم   [6] B: ضواء
[7] Jeremiah XXXIII: 15-16.   [8] Cf. Isaiah LXVI: 10-18.   [9] A and B: بيت   [10] A and
B: وتعرف   [11] Zechariah II: 10-13.

66.   *Section [Seven]*

Next you say:

As for the Word of God, which was creator, becoming flesh through a created human, and their being born together, the Word with the human nature, the Creator never addressed any individual except from behind a veil, as is given in this book, saying, 'And it was not for any mortal' and the rest of the verse. If refined things are only manifest in physical things, then how could the Word of God, by which refined things were created, be manifest in anything entirely different from a physical thing? (65v) Thus it was manifest in Jesus, son of Mary, because humankind is more noble than anything which God the exalted has created, and in this way he spoke to creation and they beheld something of him.[1]

God spoke through the mouths of the prophets who had been sent, who prophesied about his incarnation and birth and all his actions that he performed on earth. These prophecies are also possessed by the Jews who acknowledge and confess them, and read them in their synagogues. We will now proceed to adduce some of their utterances.

When Nebuchadnezzar led them into exile in the land of Babylon, Ezra the priest said, 'In four hundred and eighty-two years the Christ will come to free the people and the nations', and at the completion of this period the lord Christ did come.

The prophet Jeremiah spoke about his birth, 'In those days a son of David will rise up, the brightness of light, he will rule the kingdom, he will teach and instruct, he will establish truth and justice in the land and he will redeem those who believe in him among the Jews and Israel, and Jerusalem will remain without warfare or warriors, and his name will be God.'

Isaiah says, 'Say to Zion, behold, be happy and rejoice, for God is coming to redeem those who believe in him and his people. He will redeem the city of Jerusalem and God will show there his holy arm to all the people of the earth and all those who are scattered, and he will make them a single nation. All the people of the earth will behold the salvation of God, for he will walk with them and before them, the God of Israel will unite them.' (66r)

The prophet Zechariah says, '"Rejoice, O daughter of Zion, for I am coming to you, and will dwell among you and show myself." Many nations will believe in God that day, and they will become one people before him, and he and they will dwell within you, and you will know that I, God the almighty, am residing within you. On that day God will appoint a king from Judah, and he will rule over them for ever.'

The prophet Amos says, 'The sun will rise over the earth, and those

---

[1] Cf. 'Ammār al-Baṣrī, *K. al-Burhān*, pp. 62.15-68.10.

ويهتدي بها الضالّون[12] ويضلّ عنها بنو[13] اسرائيل".

وقال في السفر الثالث من أسفار الملوك: "والآن يا ربّ اله اسرائيل ليحقّق كلامك لداود أبي لأنه حقّ أن تكون آية[14] سيسكن الله مع الناس على الأرض، اسمعوا أيها الشعوب كلكم[15] ولتنصت الأرض وكلّ من فيها فيكون الربّ عليها شاهدًا، وينزل ويطأ على مشارق الأرض في شأن بني يعقوب" [16]، هذا كله.

وقال ميخا النبي: "وأنت يا بيت لحم قرية يهوذا بيت افراتا[17] منك يخرج لي رئيس[18] يرعى شعبي اسرائيل وهو من قبل أن تكون الدنيا لكنه لا يظهر إلا في الأيام التي تلده فيها الوالدة، وسلطانه من أقاصي الأرض إلى أقاصيها". [19]

وقال حبقوق النبي: "إنّ الله في الأرض يتراءى ويختلط مع الناس ويمشي معهم". [20]

وقال إرميا النبي: "الله بعد هذا في الأرض يظهر، ويتقلّب مع البشر فيقول أنا الله ربّ * الأرباب". [21]

* 66v

وقال إرميا النبي وأشعيا النبي: "ها هي العذراء تحبل وتلد ابنًا ويدعى عمانوئل" [22]، وهذه الكلمة عبرانية ترجمتها "إلهنا معنا".

وقال أشعيا أيضًا: "من أعجب الأعاجيب أنّ ربّ الملائكة سيولد من البشر" [23].

فماذا يكون أوضح من هذا وأبين وأعظم من هذا القول إذ قد أوردناه من قول الله ولا سيّما واليهود الضالّون عن الحقّ والمخالفون لقول النبوءات جميعًا يشهدون لنا بصحّة ذلك ويقرأون هذه النبوءات في كنائسهم ولا ينكرون منها شيئا. وعندهم في التوراة وكتب النبوءات مثل ذلك شيء كثير، وإنما ذكرنا البعض لنورد بذلك تثبيت ديننا[24] وما نعتقده في السيّد المسيح.

67. والجواب: أمّا قولكم في تجسّم الكلمة واللطائف والكثائف فسيأتي الجواب عنه إن شاء الله تعالى، وفيما تقدّم كفاية. وأمّا بشارة عزرا الكاهن فلا تعلّق لها بما قلتم. وأمّا قول إرميا في الإبن فهو سليمان الملك النبي الآتي البيت المقدّس والمعلّم لغة الطير ومنطقها والمفهم الحكومة في الغنم والزرع لا المسيح، فإنه لم يملك ولا طالت مدته وجرى ما جرى.

وأمّا قول أشعيا وقول زكريا وقول ميخا في المسيح

---

[12] B: الضلّون [13] A and B: بنوا [14] B: انه [15] B: كلهكم, a misreading of A.
[16] Cf. I Kings VIII: 26-30. [17] A and B: اقراما [18] A and B: رئيس [19] Micah V: 2.
[20] Habakkuk III: 3. [21] A reminiscence of Jeremiah XXIII: 5-6. [22] Isaiah VII:
14. [23] Isaiah IX: 6-7. [24] B: دين

who are astray will be guided by it, but the children of Israel will stray from it.'

In the third Book of Kings it says, '"Lord God of Israel, now may your word to David my father be confirmed." For it is true that the sign will be that God will reside with mankind on the earth; all you peoples take heed of it, and let the earth and all in it give ear, and the Lord will be a witness against it; he will come down to subjugate the eastern parts of the earth for the sake of the children of Jacob.' All of this.

The prophet Micah says, 'And you, O Bethlehem, city of Judah, house of Ephrātā, from you will come out for me a leader; he will protect my people Israel. He existed before the earth was, but he will only appear in the days when a woman with child gives birth to him. And his rule will be from one end of the earth to another.'

The prophet Habakkuk says, 'God will appear on earth; he will mingle with the people and will walk with them.'

The prophet Jeremiah says, 'After this God will appear on the earth; he will commune closely with man so that he may say "I am God, the (66v) Lord of lords".'

The prophets Jeremiah and Isaiah say, 'Behold, the virgin will be with child and will give birth to a son, and he will be called Emmanuel'—this is a Hebrew word, the translation of which is 'our God with us'.

Isaiah also says, 'It is the greatest miracle that the Lord of the angels should be born of humankind.'

What could be clearer than this or more mightily evident than these words which we have quoted from God's word, particularly since the Jews, who have erred from the truth and have altogether diverged from the words of the prophecies, acknowledge to us that this is correct. They read these prophecies in their synagogues, and do not deny any part of them. They have many things similar to these in the Torah and prophetic books, though we have only referred to some so that by means of them we may set out the validation of our religion and what we believe about the Lord Christ.

67. *Response*: As for what you say about the incarnation of the Word, and refined and physical things, an answer will be given, if God the exalted wills, though enough has been said about it above. As for Ezra the priest's proclamation, it has no connection with what you say. And as for Jeremiah's words about the son, this is Solomon the king and prophet who came to Jerusalem, knew the speech and discourse of birds, and was expert in right judgement regarding cattle and crops.[2] This was not Christ, because he never ruled, he did not have a long span of life, and so on.

As for the words of Isaiah, Zechariah and Micah about Christ, his

---

[2] Cf. SS. XXVII: 16-19, XXI: 79.

وملكه واستيلائه وجمعه المبدّدين أمّة واحدة إنما هو إذا جاء المرّة الثانية آخر
الزمان كما أخبر الله * تعالى في كتابه العزيز بقوله: ﴿وإنّ من أهل الكتاب * 67r
إلا ليؤمننّ به﴾ الآية[25]، وأخبر نبيّنا صلم أنّ المسيح ينزل من السماء متهاديًا
بين ملكين من الملائكة إلى الارض ويقتل المسيح الدجّال ويقتل اليهود معه
ويكسر الصليب ويقتل الخنزير ويجعل الناس أمّة واحدة ويملأ الأرض قسطًا
وعدلاً.

وأمّا قول عاموص النبي فهو نبيّنا صلم أنسب ممّا هو بالمسيح، فإنه صلم
كان كالشمس في ظهوره ونور هداه وآمن به الناس كافة إلا اليهود.

وأمّا قول حبقوق وإرميا أيضًا فلا يصحّ حمله على ظاهره الذي استدللتم
به، إذ في ذلك ما فيه. وأمّا قول إرميا وأشعيا أيضًا فمعناه أنهما بشّرا بالمسيح
وأنّ الغلاة فيه يقولون عمانويل لا إنه كذلك كما أخبر نبيّنا صلم لابن عمّه
علي عليلم[26] أنه يهلك فيه طائفتان من الأمّة: محبّ مفرط ومبغض مفرط،
فكانت الغلاة الزاعمون[27] فيه زعمكم في المسيح هم الهالكون بالغلوّ وكانت
النكارة الخوارج هم الهالكون بالبغضاء والخروج عليه.

وأمّا قولكم: "وإنّ اليهود يتلون هذا ويصدّقون به إذ هو مكتوب عندهم
ثمّ لا يؤمنون"، فالجواب منّا ومنهم عن[28] ذلك. أمّا اليهود فيقولون: "إننا
لم نمتنع من الإيمان بالمسيح إلا لمعان منها أنّ المسيح الذي نبّأت به الأنبياء له
شرائط وعلامات ودلائل وهي * أنه يأتي بعد موسى * 67v

---

[25] S. IV: 159.   [26] B: عليكم (wrongly).   [27] A and B: الزاعمين   [28] B: من

rule, his assumption of power and gathering up scattered people into one community, this is actually about his second coming at the end of time, as God the exalted announced (67r) in his esteemed Book, saying, 'There is not one of the People of Scripture but will believe in him [before his death, and on the day of Judgement he will be a witness against them]'. Our Prophet (may God bless him and give him peace) also announced that Christ will descend from heaven, advancing between two hosts of angels to the earth; Christ will kill the Antichrist and the Jews with him, smash the cross, kill the swine, make the people one community, and fill the earth with justice and equity.[3]

As for the words of the prophet Amos, this is more appropriately our Prophet (may God bless him and give him peace) than Christ, for it was he (may God bless him and give him peace) who was like the sun in his rising up and the light of his guiding, and all people believed in him except the Jews.

As for the words of Habakkuk and also Jeremiah, it is not right to take literally what you attempt to prove by them, for they have their own meaning. And as for the words of Jeremiah and Isaiah too, their purport is that they both proclaim Christ, though the exaggerators about him say 'Emmanuel'. It is not thus, but as our Prophet (may God bless him and give him peace) informed his cousin 'Alī (peace be upon him) about the two parties in the community that would be destroyed because of him: 'Excessively loving and excessively hating.' The *Ghulāt*, who made the same claims about him as you do about Christ, they were the ones who were destroyed through exaggeration, while the ignorant Kharijites were the ones who were destroyed through hatred and deserting him.[4]

As for your words, 'The Jews read this and accept it because it is written in what they possess, but they do not believe it', the response from them and us is as follows. The Jews say, 'We have never ceased believing in the Messiah, though the significance of this is that the Messiah about whom the prophets spoke would have portents, signs and proofs. These (67v) would be that he would come after Moses, he

---

[3] These are references to well-known Ḥadīths concerning Jesus' part in the end-time; cf. M. Hayek, *Le Christ de l'Islam*, Paris, 1959, pp. 247-8 and references.

[4] In early Islamic heresiographies the *Ghulāt* were characterised as virtually divinising 'Alī and his descendants (cf. M. Momen, *An Introduction to Shi'i Islam*, Yale, 1985, pp. 65-8), while the Kharijites broke with him and denied his leadership in consequence of what they regarded as vacillation at the Battle of Ṣiffīn; 'Alī routed them at the Battle of Nahrawān a little later.

ويجعل الناس أمّة واحدة ويظهر سلطانه على كلّ سلطان ويجدّد دينًا وتشريعًا
جديدًا، ويخلّص النفوس من أسر الشيطان والشهوات ويبلغ ملكه أقاصي
الأرض كلّها ويطل السبوت والأعياد ويملأ الأرض قسطًا وعدلاً وفضلاً"،
ويطل قتال اليهود وقرابينهم وملكهم فانتظروه وتوطّأت[29] نفوسهم لإتباعه.
فلمّا جاءهم المسيح ورأوا منه في مبادئ أمره عجائب ومعاجز قالوا: هو
هو، ولم يكن إلا يسير حتى ثاروا عليه وجرى ما جرى، ولم يروا في زمنه
ممّا أشارت إليه النبؤات شيئا بل كانوا هم الظاهرون[30] عليه والقاهرون له
والرادّون دعوته والمشتتون شمله كما زعمتم وشهدت أناجيلكم ولم تكونوا[31]
أنتم أيّها القائلون: إنا نصارى موجودين ولا ظاهرين بالنصرانية إلى أن ظهر
قسطنطين وزعم أنّ المسيح أرسل إليه وإلى أصحاب القوانين روح القدس
مؤيّدة لهم في ترتيب الدين وتقنينه وفي جمع الإنجيل وتدوينه.

فهذا الذي أوجب لليهود أن لا يتبعوه ولا يصدّقوه مع ما هم عليه من
الأوصاف الذميمة في الكتب المنزلة على ألسنة الأنبياء عليهم.[32]

68.   وأمّا نحن المسلمون فنقول: إنّ كلّ ما استشهدتم * به أيها النصارى   * 68r
من ظواهر هذه الألفاظ المحرّفة عن مواضعها والمغيّر معانيها والمبدّلة بنقل
ناقليها من لغتين وثلاث لغات إلى اللغة العربية، والمصطلحون على ما وجدوه
فيها من الأسماء والصفات اصطلاحًا مخالفاً لمعانيها مع اختلاف أفهام النقلة
وعدم تحرّيهم وتحريرهم للألفاظ اللغوية لا تبقى مع ذلك معنى على ما كان
عليه، ولا أسماء ولا صفات كما كان بلغة الآتي به، ولا ينبغي الاستشهاد به
وسمّى على الشرك الصريح ومخالفة الكتب والرسل

---

[29] A and B: وتوطيت   [30] B: الظاهر من   (wrongly).   [31] A and B: تكوانوا   [32] B: عليكم
(wrongly).

would make the people one community, he would manifest his authority above all authority, he would renew religion and give a new law, he would liberate souls from Satan's chains and carnal desires, his rule would reach to all the ends of the earth, he would bring to an end sabbaths and holy days, he would fill the earth with justice, equity and goodness, and he would bring an end to the fighting, sacrifices and rule of the Jews.' Thus they wait for him, and their souls are ready to follow him. So when Christ came to them and they saw wonders and miracles at the start, they said, 'This is he', and all went smoothly until they were roused up against him, and so on. They did not see in his time any of the things that the prophecies had mentioned about him. Rather, they themselves rebelled against him, overthrew him, rejected his call and scattered his following, as you claim and your Gospels witness. This was not you, you who say, 'We Christians were in existence but did not make Christianity public until Constantine appeared and claimed that Christ had sent the Holy Spirit to him and to the canonical experts as a help to them in framing and legislating the religion, and collecting and recording the Gospel'.[5]

This is what compels the Jews not to accept him or believe in him, nor to speak of the objectionable references to him which they have in the books that were revealed on the tongues of the prophets (peace be upon them).

68. As for us Muslims, we say: Christians, all the literal readings you adduce (68r) from these words that have been moved from their places, their meanings altered and replaced with accounts translated from two or three languages into Arabic,[6] the generally accepted names and attributes which they found there differing in their meaning according to the different understandings of the translators, their carelessness and imprecision with linguistic terms, have meant that the original meaning no longer remains, nor the names and attributes as they were in the language of the one who delivered it. It is therefore inevitable that you should adduce readings and give names that are clearly polytheistic and contrary to the books and messengers, and to

---

[5] Cf. § 16 above.

[6] This is an allusion to the long-standing accusation that Christians, as People of the Book, corrupted their scriptures; cf. SS. II: 75, X: 15 etc. In what al-Dimashqī says here, it appears that this corruption was mainly a consequence of translation from the original Hebrew and Greek (and maybe Syriac or Latin unless he is talking casually), rather than of any calculated malicious intent.

والمعقول والمنقول الحقّ، فلا التفات إلى زوره وباطله ولو أسند إلى من أسند وهو شرك وباطل عددناه ﴿هباءً منثورًا﴾[33].

مع علمكم أنّ جدّ الخبر عند العقلاء ما احتمل الصدق والكذب، إلا أن يقوم به بيّنة على الصدق أو يكون منقولاً بالتواتر وقد تقدّم شرح معناه، وإنّ خبر الآحاد لا يفيد يقينًا ولا يبنى عليه حكم ولو كان مطابقًا للمعقول الحقّ وموافقًا للمنقول الصدق، فكيف بدعوى أربعة أنفار مختلفين فيما تزعمون من حياة بعد موت وصعود إنسان سويّ إلى السماء وحرق الأفلاك بالبدن الطيني ومخالطة أملاك بالجسم البشري وجلوسًا على العرش واعتقادًا للشبه والمثال والأبوّة والبنوّة * وإرسالاً لأنبياء مرسلين أُرسلوا من مرسل أرسلهم بعد موته ودفنه ليعمّدوا الناس باسم الثالوث: الآب والإبن وروح القدس إله واحد، ويدعونهم إلى الشرك والتجسّم والتشبيه واستناد من المدّعين ذلك إلى حكايات مدوّنة في كتب مجهولة منسوبة إلى حاكين قد مضت عليهم أحقاب ودهور ومسخت تلك الحكايات النقلة لها والناسخون لها ولمعانيها من لغة الى لغة ومن اصطلاح إلى اصطلاح.

وتعلمون أيضًا أنّ الله تعالى خاطب البشر بحسب عقولهم وأنزل كتبه وجعل لكلّ آية من آياتها ظهرًا وبطنًا، وفهّمهم من ذلك ما في إمكانهم فهمه وأمرهم أن يردّوا تأويل ما يشكل عليهم فهمه إليه وإلى رسله، فاختلفتم معشر النصارى أهل الكتاب الآمنين[34] في المسيح وأمّه وفي أشياء، وزعمتم أنّكم على الصواب دون اليهود، وكذلك زعموا في كلّ ما اختلفتم فيه وفاتكم جميعًا المطلوب، فإنكم صدّقتم ما نسب إلى المسيح من الصلب والموت والتعذيب، واليهود كذّبوا بما جاء به المسيح وأنكروه وانتظروا غيره حملاً على ما أخبرت الأنبياء عنه وحكمًا بمقتضى فقد الشرائط المشروطة في المسيح.

ورجعنا، نحن المسلمون، إلى كتابنا فوجدنا المسيح يأتي مرّتين: الواحدة إتيانه * وغيبته، والثانية

* 68v

* 69r

what is reasonable and truly revealed, because there is no awareness of its falseness and meaninglessness. Even though it is ascribed to the one to whom it is ascribed, because it is polytheistic and false we regard it as 'scattered motes'.

Now, you know that according to people of intelligence any new report must be regarded as truthful or untruthful unless there exists some clear sign of its truthfulness, or it has been transmitted by multiple attestation and it has a clear explanation of its meaning; also that a singular report does not give any reliable information, and no judgement can be founded upon it, even though it may conform to clear reason and agree with trustworthy transmissions. So, how much more the pretensions of four solitary individuals, according to what you claim, about life after death, the ascension of a single man into heaven, the skies set ablaze by a body of clay, sovereigns mingling with human physicality, being seated on the throne, belief in resemblance and likeness, fatherhood and sonship, (68v) sending prophets as messengers from one sent who sent them after his death and burial in order to baptize people in the name of the Trinity, Father, Son and Holy Spirit, one God, and to call them to polytheism, corporealism, anthropomorphism and, according to those who allege this, dependence on accounts written in anonymous books ascribed to narrators from times and ages long past, accounts which those who had passed them and their meanings on and copied from language to language and terminology to terminology had falsified.

You also know that God the exalted addresses humankind in accordance with their intelligence, revealing his books and giving every single verse an outward meaning and an inner meaning. He gives them to understand of this what is in their ability to understand, and he orders them to leave the interpretation of what hinders them understanding it to him and his messengers. But you Christians differ from the People of the Book who believe in Christ, his mother and other things, and claim that you and not the Jews are correct, while they claim the same with regard to everything over which you differ, though what you hope for has eluded you all. For you accept crucifixion, death and torture with regard to Christ, and the Jews condemn what Christ proclaimed. They deny him and wait for another, accepting the reports of the prophets about this latter, and judging according to the fact that the conditions stipulated for the Messiah are lacking.

But we Muslims refer to our Book and find that Christ is to come twice. The first is his coming (69r) and concealment, and the second,

التي يؤمن به فيها أهل الكتاب قبل موته وتصدق عليه نبوّات الأنبياء في العزّ
والحكم والسلطان والقهر وجمع سائر الناس على التوحيد والإيمان، فيكونون
أمّة واحدة، وتبيّن لنا ما جاء منه وما جاء عنه صلّى الله على نبيّنا وعليه.

فأمّا الذي جاء منه فدعوته إلى الله وإلى توحيده والبراءة[35] من الشرك
ورسالته بالإنجيل وتلويحه بما لوّح من ذكر الحياة الأبدية والتشويق إليها ومن
ذكره لأبناء السماء وأبناء الأرض ومن تعظيمه للحقّ واحترامه للخلق وأمره
للحواريين بالذلّة والخضوع والتجريد والانقياد والرحمة للعالم واقرأهم عنوان
السعادة من فوق ختم كتاب ختم لهم الحسنى وزيادة واشهدهم تعلّق اللطائف
والمعاني بمظاهر الكثائف والمباني وتخلّق الكثائف والمباني بمباطن اللطائف
والمعاني، وقال الذائق تنبيهًا:

فتسمّى لتثنية الأنس إنسان	يا من تأنس لطيفة بكثيفة
والمخاطب بالتورية والإنجيل والقرآن	يا خليفة الرحمن وزبدة[36] الأكوان
كان ما كان	والذي من أجله وأجل استخلافه
إطرح أنفالك واطلب كمالك	إعرف معناك واذكر مغناك
أحطط رحالك	لاحظ مآلك
ذاته من غيره لكنه لا يعلم	يا من تخاطبه حقيقة

* 69v

---

35 A and B: والبراة   36 B: وزيدة

which the People of the Book believe about him, is before his death. The prophecies of the prophets attest that this will be in might, judgement, authority and victory, and bringing together all the people into belief in God's oneness and faith, so that they will be one community. This was made plain to us in what was said by him and what was said about him, may God bless our Prophet and him.[7]

As for what was said by him, this was his call to God, to declare his unity, and to abandon polytheism; his being a messenger with the Gospel, the intimations he gave in alluding to everlasting life and kindling desire for it, his mentioning of sons of heaven and sons of earth, and his glorification of truth and honouring creatures; the commandments he gave to the disciples about humility, submissiveness, giving up possessions, obedience and compassion for the world. He taught them that beyond what is in a book the principles of blessedness would be for them 'the best and more', and he witnessed to them to prefer refined and higher qualities over the public show of material and lower qualities, and to reform material and lower qualities into the secret desire for refined and higher qualities.[8] One who has sampled this has said in explanation of it:[9]

> O you who have brought the refined close to the physical,
>   And from the doubling of closeness are named man,
> O vicegerent of the Merciful, and distillation of being,
>   Who are addressed in Torah, Gospel and Qur'an,
> The one for whom and for whose becoming vicegerent
>   What was was,[10]
> Recognise your significance and recall your worth,
>   look at what you were given and seek your perfection,
> See what you possess
>   and cease your wandering.
> O you whose true (69v) essence addresses him

---

[7] Cf. e.g. SS. IV: 159, XLIII: 61, III: 55, and the discussions in Hayek, *Le Christ de l'Islam*, pp. 241-71, and N. Robinson, *Christ in Islam and Christianity*, New York, 1991, pp. 78-105.

[8] This summary of Jesus' teachings draws on both the Qur'an and the Gospels, particularly echoing the Sermon on the Mount, Mtt V-VII.

[9] The choice of the distinctly Ṣūfī term *al-dhā'iq*, 'one who tastes', here gives some indication about the author of this poem; it may in fact be al-Dimashqī himself. On the significance of Jesus in Ṣūfism, cf. T. Khalidi, *The Muslim Jesus*, Cambridge, Mass. and London, 2001, pp. 41-3, and Robinson, *Christ in Islam and Christianity*, pp. 53-8.

[10] This is a play on such verses as SS. III: 47 and 59, and XIX: 35, which refer to the manner in which Jesus was created by the divine command, 'When he decreeth a thing, he saith unto it only: Be! And it is', *kun fa-yakūnu*.

فهو المكلّم عنه والمتكلّم	وهو المخاطب ذاته من غيره
ألا ترى ذاك وأنت نائم؟	في روحك الأرواح والعوالم
فالكلّ أنت عالم وعالم	والكلّ فيك حاضر في غيبه
للتعريف والبون	منادى بلسان الكون
ولا دعوى النصارى ولا دعوى اليهود	فلا يدّعى دعوى فرعون ونمرود
أو يتخيّل أو يتوهّم بالحدوس	بل نزّه البارئ عن كلّ ما يخطر في النفوس
ولا فرّقت بين الأوّل الأحد والواحد الثاني	لا كالذي جسّمته النصارى من المعاني

فهذه الإشارات والتلويحات مصرّحة بمعنى ما جاء به المسيح.

وأمّا ما جاء عنه فقد تقدّم فيما أوردته من الأجوبة من وصاياه وتعبّده وتذلله وصلاته لربّ العالمين.

From outside, though he does not know,
The one whose essence addresses him from outside,
   The one talked about and talking,
In your spirit are the spirits and worlds;
   Do you not see this, slumbering as you are?
All is within you, present in its concealment,
   You know it all in full.
One summoned by the mouth of being
   To understanding and excellence,
Does not make the claims of Pharaoh or Nimrod,
   Nor the claims of the Christians or Jews.[11]
But he raises the Creator far above all that is conceived in the souls,
   Or fancied and imagined in surmise.
Not like the one whom the Christians made physical from abstract,
   Failing to distinguish the Single and Alone from the first and second.

These indications and intimations explain the significance of what Christ brought.

As for what was said about him, this has already been covered in his injunctions, worshipping, self-abasement and praying to the Lord of the worlds that I have referred to in my responses.

---

[11] Pharaoh and Nimrod, the enemies of Moses and Abraham, are singled out in Islamic history as tyrants who claimed to place themselves on the level of God; cf. SS. XXVIII: 38 and XL: 36-7 for Pharaoh, and II: 258 for Nimrod, where he is identified as the opponent of Abraham who claims 'I give life and death'. The two can thus be grouped with Christians and Jews who claim that Christ and Ezra are sons of God, S. IX: 30.

فصل

ثمّ قلتم سياقًا:

إنّ أشعيا قال أيضًا: "إن غلامًا ولد لنا وابنًا أعطيناه ، رئاسته على عاتقه ومنكبيه، ويدعى ملكًا عظيم المشيئة بشرًا ملكًا عجيبًا إلهًا قويًا مسلط رئيس السلامة أبًا لكلّ[1] الدهور وسلطانه كامل ليس له فناء"[2] وإنه قال أيضًا: "تخرج عصاه من أصل يشي وينبت نوْر منها وتحلّ فيه روح القدس روح الله روح الحكمة والفهم روح الحِيل والقوّة * روح العلم وخوف الله. وفي تلك الأيام يكون أصل يشي للأمم وبه يؤمنون وعليه يتوكلون ويكون لهم النياح والكرامة إلى دهر الداهرين".[3] واليهود مقرّون بهذه النبوّات، معترفون أنّها حقّ وأنّها عتيدة أن تكمل عند مجيء المسيح.

70r

فقال لكم كليام: إذا كانت اليهود عالمون بذلك، فأيّ حجّة لهم يحتجّون بها عن الإيمان به؟ فقلتم:

إنّ الله اختار بني إسرائيل واصطفاهم له شعبًا في ذلك الزمان دون كلّ العالم، وحيث كانوا في أرض مصر في عبودية فرعون[4] أرسل إليهم موسى النبي دلّهم على معرفة الله تعالى ووعدهم أنّ الله يخلّصهم من عبودية فرعون ويخرجهم من مصر إلى أرض الميعاد التي هي أرض بيت المقدس ويريهم آيات. فطلب موسى من الله وعمل العجائب أمامهم وضرب أهل مصر العشر ضربات وهم يرون ذلك جميعًا وأخرجهم من مصر بيد قوية وشقّ لهم البحر وأدخلهم فيه وصار لهم الماء حائطًا عن يمينهم وحائطًا عن شمالهم، ودخل فرعون وجميع جنوده في البحر وبنو[5] إسرائيل ينظرون ذلك.

فلمّا غاب عنهم موسى إلى الجبل[6] ليناجي ربّه وأخذ لهم التوراة من يد الله تركوا عبادة الله ونسوا جميع أفعاله وكفروا به وعبدوا رأس العجل بعد ذلك.

70v

ثمّ عبدوا * الأصنام بعده ليس مرّة واحدة بل مرارًا كثيرة، وذبحوا لها الذبائح ليست حيوانات بل بنيهم وبناتهم حسبما ذكر فيما قبل ذلك، وجميع أفعالهم مكتوبة في أخبار بني اسرائيل.

فلمّا رأى[7] الله قساوة قلوبهم وغلظ رقابهم وكفرهم به ورأى أفعالهم النجسة الخبيثة غضب عليهم مردولين مهانين في جميع الأمم وليس لهم نبي ولا كاهن ولا ملك إلى الأبد حسبما نبّأت عنهم الأنبياء على ما ذكرنا قبل وتشهد به كتبهم التي في أيديهم يومنا هذا.

وكذا قال الله لأشعيا: "إذهب قل لهذا الشعب:

---

[1] A and B: كل   [2] Isaiah IX: 6.   [3] Cf. *ibid.* XI: 1-10.   [4] B: فرعو   [5] A and B: وبنوا   [6] B: الجبال   [7] A: رأ

69.   *Section [Eight]*

Directly following you say:

Isaiah also said, 'A child has been born to us, a son we have been given. His government is on his neck and shoulders, and he will be called king mighty in will, man, wonderful king, powerful and mighty God, prince of peace, father of all time. His dominion is perfect and will know no decline.' He also said, 'His rod will go forth from the root of Jesse, and a shoot will spring up from it. In him will dwell the Holy Spirit, the Spirit of God, the Spirit of wisdom and understanding, the Spirit of strength and power, (70r) the Spirit of knowledge and the fear of God. In those days the root of Jesse will be for the nations: in him they will believe and on him they will depend. He will be for them tranquillity and honour for ever and ever.' The Jews acknowledge these prophecies, granting that they are true and will be realised in full when the Messiah comes.

Kilyām said to you: If the Jews are aware of this, then what argument have they put forward against believing in him? And you said:

God chose the People of Israel and made them a people for himself from all the world at that time. When they were in the land of Egypt in slavery to Pharaoh, he sent the prophet Moses to them to lead them to the knowledge of God the exalted, and to promise them that God would free them from slavery to Pharaoh and lead them out of Egypt to the promised land, which is the land of Jerusalem, and would show signs to them. Moses supplicated God and worked miracles before them: he struck the people of Egypt with the ten plagues, and they saw it all; he led them out of Egypt with a mighty hand and parted the sea for them; he led them through it and the water became a wall for them on their right and on their left. Pharaoh and all his army went into the sea, and the People of Israel saw this.

When Moses withdrew from them onto the mountain to converse with his Lord, and took the Torah from the hand of God for them, they abandoned the worship of God and forgot all his acts, deserting him after this and worshipping a heifer's head.

Then after this they worshipped (70v) idols, not once but many times. They made sacrifices to them, not animals but their sons and daughters. This is according to what has been mentioned above, and all their acts are written in the chronicles of the People of Israel.

When God saw the hardness of their hearts, their stubbornness and their disbelief in him, and saw their vile, abominable acts, he grew angry with them and made them contemptible and insignificant among all the nations, and they have had no prophet, priest or king ever again. This is as the prophets prophesied about them, as we have already mentioned, and as their books, which they have in their possession today, bear witness.

To this effect God said to Isaiah, 'Go, say to this people: You will

ستسمعون سمعًا ولا تفهمونه، وتنظرون ولا تبصرون لأنّ قلب هذا الشعب قد غلظ وقد سمعوا بآفهامهم سمعًا ثقيلًا، وقد غمضوا أعينهم لئلّا يبصروا بها وسمعوا بآذانهم ولم يفهموا بقلوبهم ويرجعوا إليّ فارحمهم".[8]

وقال أشعيا هكذا: "مقتت نفسي سبوتكم ورؤوس شهوركم وصارت عندي مرذولة".[9] وقال: "في ذلك اليوم سأبطل السبوت والأعياد كلّها وأعطيكم سنّة جديدة مختارة كالسنّة التي أعطيتها لموسى عبدي يوم حوريب يوم الجمع الكبير، سنّة آمر بها وأخرجها من صهيون"[10]، فصهيون هي أورشليم والسنّة الجديدة * المختارة هي السنّة التي تسلّمناها نحن معشر النصارى من أيدي الرسل الأطهار على ما تسلّموها هم من السيّد المسيح، وهذه النبوّات مثلما هي عند اليهود وكذلك هي عندنا معشر النصارى في اثنين وسبعين لسانًا يقرؤها جميع الأمم قولاً واحدًا وإنّها قول الله.

وقالت اليهود عتيدة أن تكمل عند مجيء المسيح، لكنّ المسيح البعيد[11] ما جاء وأنّ الذي جاء ليس هو المسيح، هذا قولهم وكفاهم أنّهم يكفرون ويفجرون مع الكفر ويقولون إنّ المسيح كان ضالاً مضلًا، وإنّما المسيح عتيده أنه يأتي ويكمل نبوّات الأنبياء، فإذا ما أتى تبعناه وكنّا أنصاره.

وهذا رأيهم واعتقادهم في السيّد المسيح، فماذا يكون أعظم من هذا الكفر الذي[12] هم عليه، ولأجل ذلك سمّاهم في هذا الكتاب ﴿المغضوب عليهم﴾[13] لأجل خلافهم لقوله الذي أنطق به أنبياءه. ولمّا كنّا نحن معشر النصارى مستمسكين بما أمرونا به الرسل الأطهار سمّانا في هذا الكتاب ﴿المنعم عليهم﴾.[14]

70. وأمّا قولنا في الله ثلاث أقانيم إله واحد، فهو أنّ الله تعالى نطق به، وأوضحه لنا في التوراة وفي كتب الأنبياء، ومن ذلك[15] ما جاء في السفر الأوّل من التوراة، يقول: "حيث شاء الله أن يخلق آدم قال الله: لنخلق خلقًا على شبهنا ومثالنا"[16]، فمن شبهه ومثاله غير كلمته وروحه؟ وحين * خالف آدم وعصى ربّه قال الله: "ها آدم قد صار كواحد منّا"[17]، وهذا قول واضح أنّ الله قال هذا القول لابنه أي كلمته وروح قدسه. وقال هذا القول يهزئ بآدم، أي أنه طلب أن يكون كواحد[18] منّا، صار هكذا عريانًا مفتضحًا.

وقال الله عندما أخسف بسدوم وعامورة قال في التوراة: "وأمطر الربّ من عند الربّ من السماء على سدوم وعامورة نارًا وكبريتًا".[19] أوضح بهذا

* 71r

* 71v

---

[8] Isaiah VI: 9-10. [9] *Ibid*. I: 13-14. [10] *Ibid*. II: 3. Cf. also Jeremiah XXXI: 31-3, Micah IV: 2, Malachi IV: 4 and *supra*, f. 8r. [11] A and B: البعد [12] A and B: الذين [13] S. I: 7. [14] Cf. *ibid*. [15] A gloss in the same hand in the left margin of A reads: الجواب عن هذا يأتي في الكراس الثاني ان شاء الله تعالى [16] Genesis I: 26. [17] *Ibid*. III: 22. [18] B: لواحد (wrongly), a misreading of A. [19] Genesis XIX: 24.

hear but not understand, you will look but not see, because the minds of this people have been dulled and they understand little of what they hear; they have closed their eyes so that they cannot see; they hear with their ears but do not understand with their minds or turn to me to heal them.'

Isaiah says likewise, 'Your sabbaths and new moons are abominable to me and have become despicable in my eyes', and 'On that day I will put an end to all sabbaths and festivals, and I will give you a new chosen law like the law I gave to my servant Moses on the day of Horeb, the day of the great assembly, a law which I will enjoin and will send out from Zion.' Now Zion is Jerusalem, and the new chosen (71r) law is the law which we Christians have received from the hands of the pure Apostles, as they received it from the lord Christ. Just as these prophecies are in the possession of the Jews, so they are in the possession of us Christians in seventy-two languages,[1] which all the nations read as one teaching, the teaching of God.

The Jews say that they will be fulfilled when the Messiah comes, though the Messiah is far off and has not come, and he who has come is not the Messiah. This is what they say. And not only do they not believe, but they wantonly compound the unbelief by saying that Christ was deceived and deceiving, for the Messiah is still to come and will fulfil the prophets' words, at which time 'we will follow him and be his helpers'.

This is what they think and believe about the lord Christ, though what greater disbelief could there be than theirs? It is because of this that he has called them in this book 'those who earn thine anger', because of their disputing over his words which he gave his prophets to utter. And since we Christians adhere to what the pure Apostles commanded us, he called us in this book 'those whom thou hast favoured'.[2]

70. Turning to our teaching that God is three hypostases, one God, this is because God the exalted spoke about it and made it clear to us in the Torah and the books of the prophets. For example, there is what he says in the first book of the Torah, 'When God willed to create Adam, God said, "Let us make a creature in our own image and likeness", and what are his image and likeness other than his Word and Spirit? And when (71v) Adam disobeyed and defied his Lord, God said, 'Adam has become like one of us'; these words are clearly spoken by God to his Son, that is, his Word, and his Holy Spirit. He said them in derision of Adam, that he should seek to be 'like one of us', and he thus became naked and exposed.

And when God caused Sodom and Gomorrah to be destroyed, he said in the Torah, 'And the Lord rained down from the Lord from heaven fire and brimstone on Sodom and Gomorrah', thus making clear the

---

[1] Cf. Section 4, n. 4 above.

[2] The Cypriot Christians' awareness of the traditional interpretation of S. I: 7 is a sign of some knowledge on their part of Muslim exegetical norms.

ربوبية الآب والابن.

وقال أيضًا في السفر الثاني من التوراة: "وكلّم الله لموسى من العلّيقة قائلاً: "أنا إله ابراهيم، أنا إله اسحق، أنا إله يعقوب"[20] ولم يقل: "أنا إله ابراهيم واسحاق ويعقوب"، بل كرّر اسم الإله ثلاث دفوع قائلاً: "أنا إله وإله وإله" ليحقّق مسألة الثلاث أقانيم في لاهوتيته.[21]

وقال داود النبي في المزمور الثاني: "الربّ قال لي: أنت ابني، وأنا اليوم ولدتك"[22]. وقال أيضًا في مزمور ماية وتسعة: "قال الربّ لربّي: إجلس عن يميني حتى أضع أعداءك تحت موطأ قدميك"[23]، وكذلك أشعيا يشهد بتحقيق الثالوث ووحدانية جوهره، وذلك بقوله: "ربّ القوات"، وبقوله: "ربّ السموات والأرض".

ومثل هذا القول في التوراة والمزامير شيء كثير حتى أنّ اليهود إلى هذا الوقت يقرّون هذه النبوّات ولا يعرفون لها * تأويلاً، وهم معترفون بذلك ولا ينكرون منه كلمة واحدة، وإنما قلوبهم مغلقة عن فهمه لقساوة قلوبهم على ما ذكرنا قبل ذلك.

* 72r *

وإنّهم إذا اجتمعوا في كنيستهم كلّ سبت يقف الحزّان أمامهم ويقول كلامًا عبرانيًا هذا تفسيره ولا يجحدونه: "نقدّسك ونعظّمك ونثلّث لك تقديسًا مثلّثا كالمكتوب على لسان نبيّك أشعياء. فيصرخ الجميع مجاوبين له: "قدّوس قدّوس قدّوس ربّ القوات وجميع السموات والأرض". فما أوضح إقرارهم في الثالوث وأشدّ كفرهم به وبمعناه، فنحن...

71.   والجواب:[24] أنّ حديث أشعيا لا يدلّ معناه في تعداد الحيل والقوّة والعلم والفهم على أنها روح القدس ولكنها تسمية مجازية واستعارة لطيفة للممدوح. ويكفيكم تهافتا إجماع كلمتكم في الأقانيم وإن لم تفطنوا له أنّ كلّ واحد منها ربّ مربوب، إله مألوه، خالق مخلوق، قادر عاجز، غنيّ فقير، فاعل مفعول، واحد ثلاثة، والد مولود. وما مثلكم في احتجاجكم بقوله تعالى في التوراة: "وكلّم الله موسى من العلّيقة"[25] إلى آخره، وقول حزّان اليهود وغير ذلك مما تحتجّون[26] به على تحقيق التثليث وبيان مسألة الأقانيم إلا كمثل من قال

---

[20] Exodus III: 6.   [21] B: الهويته   [22] Psalm II: 7.   [23] Psalm CIX (CX): 1.   [24] B: فالجواب   [25] Exodus III: 4.   [26] A and B: يحتجون

lordship of the Father and the Son.

He also says in the second book of the Torah, 'God spoke to Moses from the burning bush saying, "I am the God of Abraham, I am the God of Isaac, I am the God of Jacob".' He did not say, 'I am the God of Abraham, Isaac and Jacob', but he repeated the name 'God' three times, saying, 'I am God, and God, and God' in order to substantiate the issue of three as hypostases in his divine nature.

The prophet David says in Psalm 2, 'The Lord said to me, "You are my son, today I have begotten you".' He also says in Psalm 109, 'The Lord said to my Lord, "Sit at my right hand until I cast your enemies beneath your footstool".' In the same way Isaiah witnesses to the reality of the Trinity and the singleness of his substance when he says, 'Lord of hosts' and 'Lord of the heavens and earth'.

There are many things like this in the Torah and Psalms. Thus the Jews even now read these prophecies and do not recognise (72r) the interpretations of them, though they acknowledge them and do not deny a single word. But their hearts are obscured from understanding it because of the hardness of their hearts, as we have said above.

Despite this, when they assemble in their synagogues each sabbath, the cantor[3] stands before them and says in Hebrew (of which this is a version), and they do not object to it, 'We glorify you, we exalt you, and we confess three times your threefold holiness, as is written on the tongue of your prophet Isaiah.' And the whole assembly cries out in answer to him: 'Holy, holy, holy, Lord of hosts and of all the heavens and earth.' How openly do they acknowledge the Trinity, and how gravely do they disbelieve in it and its significance! We however...

71. *Response*: When it lists force, power, knowledge and understanding, what Isaiah says does not prove in its meaning that this is the Holy Spirit, but rather it is figurative attribution and subtle metaphor for the One praised. You are content with the incoherence in all your references to the hypostases, although you are quite unaware that each of them is Master and mastered over, Divinity and subservient, Creator and created, Powerful and weak, Self-sufficient and needy, Agent and recipient, One and three, Begetter and begotten.[4] And in your argument concerning the exalted One's words in the Torah, 'God spoke to Moses from the burning bush...' to the end, and the words of the Jewish cantor, etc., by which you argue that the Trinity is real and the issue of the hypostases evident, you are just like someone who says

---

[3] *Al-ḥazzān* is a transliteration of the Hebrew.

[4] Put this briefly the argument is not obvious, though al-Dimashqī appears to be saying that if there are three beings they cannot logically be equal, and so must be respectively superior and inferior in their relationships.

لمدّعي معرفة الكتابة والتهجّي: "تهجّ لي اسم عليّ"، فقال:
"عليّ خمسة أحرف: ط ـــ ح ـــ م"، فتبسّم السائل وقال له: "مليح، تهجّيت
ولكنك أغفلت حرف الصاد"، أو كمثل من قال عند استواء الشمس * 72v *
وسط السماء: "هذا ثلث الليل، والدليل على ذلك غيبوبة النجوم وشدّة حرّ
الشمس". ويا حسرة عليكم من العقلاء! ويا استحياءهم[27] عنكم من اليهود
لو سمعوا هذا الاستشهاد والاحتجاج الذي لا يحوج الخصم معه إلى غيره في
بيان الجهالة والضلالة من خصمه.

72. ولقد حضر بعض أهل الذمّة إلى المجاوب لكم وسمع تلطّفه في الأجوبة،
فأقسم عليه أن يذكر لكم بعض مناظرة الأسقف الذي أسلم، فأبرّ المجاوب
القسم وقال حاكيًا مناظرته للنصارى قائلاً: "أيها النصارى، إني لمّا رأيتكم
على ملل شتّى وكلّ فرقة منكم تشهد بضلالة الفرقة الأخرى وكلكم يزعم
أنّ المسيح وحوارييه أهينوا وعذّبوا أربعة[28] أيّام، فإن كان ذلك عن كره منهم
وقهر لهم فليس بإله قادر من يكره ويعذّب، وإن كان برضى منهم فقد نالوا
أغراضهم ومناهم". وقال الحاكي:[29]

وإلى أيّ والد نسبوه؟   عجبًا للمسيح بين النصارى

ثمّ قالوا إنّ اليهود قد صلبوه.   نسبوه للإله افتراء

---

[27] A and B: استحياؤهم   [28] A and B: أربع   [29] A and B: الحاك

to a person claiming he can write and spell, 'Spell the name 'Alī for me', and he says, "Alī is five letters, *ṭa'*, *ḥa'*, *mīm*'. The person asking the question smiles and says to him, 'You have spelt it well, (72v) but you have forgotten the letter *ṣād*'. Or you are like someone who says when the sun has mounted to the middle of the sky, 'A third of the night has passed, and the proof is that the stars are faint and the sun's heat is strong'. What tribulations lie in store for you from the experts! What shame would be inflicted on you by the Jews if they heard these quotations and pretexts which give one antagonist all he needs to show the ignorance and error of another!

72. A *Dhimmī* was in the presence of someone who was responding to you and heard how polite he was in his response, so he made him vow to tell you part of the debate of the bishop who became a Muslim.[5] The person responding obliged, and narrated the debate to the Christians as follows: Christians, I notice that you are divided into separate denominations and each sect among you declares that another sect is in error, and all of you claim that Christ and his disciples were insulted and made to suffer for four days. If this happened to them, despite disliking it and being forced, then one who feels dislike yet is made to suffer cannot be a powerful God. And if they did it willingly, then they fulfilled their desires and purpose.[6]

The narrator said:

> How strange is Christ among the Christians;
>   To which begetter do they relate him?
> They relate him to God, though falsely,
>   And then say the Jews crucified him.

---

[5] The three characters mentioned here, the *Dhimmī*, the controversialist, and the bishop, remain anonymous, though the incident of the bishop converting and his identity would presumably be known to Muslim readers in Damascus, if not to the Cypriot Christians. This presupposes that an actual event is being referred to and not a popular literary topos, though cf. D. Thomas, 'Two Muslim-Christian Debates from the Early Shi'ite Tradition', *Journal of Semitic Studies* 33, 1988, pp. 54-65, for an account of a much earlier debate supposedly between the Shī'ī theologian Hishām Ibn al-Ḥakam and a bishop named Barīha, which led to the latter's conversion to Islam.

In this introduction, the *Dhimmī's* wish to embarrass the Christians by having this conversion story recounted and to abandon politeness is easily explained if he is identified as a Jew.

[6] This simple argument proves that Christ could not be God because either he was forced to suffer and so could not be omnipotent, or enjoyed suffering and so must be insane. The reference to four days of suffering could be to the period between Christ's entry into Jerusalem and his arrest, during which he and his disciples were in constant danger.

ويزعمون أنّ الله هو المسيح وأنّ المسيح هو الله، وأنّ المسيح نزل إلى الأرض واستتر عن عيون الآدميين ليهدي الناس من ضلالاتهم، فهل كان يهديهم لسنّته او لسنّة غيره؟ فإن قلتم: "لسنّة غيره" لم يكن إلهًا، وإن قلتم: "لسنّة نفسه" كذّبتم أناجيلكم إذ قول المسيح فيها: "إني لم أجئ لأنقض توراة موسى بل أثبّتها"[30] وأقول لكم: أخبروني عمّن عمل بسنّة المسيح، هل اهتدى أو ضلّ؟ فإن قلتم: "اهتدى"، فقد ضللتم حيث لم تعملوا بسنّته إذ كان على سنّة موسى، وإن قلتم: "ضلّ" فقد كفرتم بالله وبالمسيح إذ خالفتم قولهما في السبت والختان وغير ذلك.

وهل كان المسيح رسولاً أو راسلاً؟ فإن قلتم: "إنه رسول" كذّبتم إنجيلاتكم الشاهدة بأنه إله معبود، وإن قلتم: "إنه راسل" كذّبتم المسيح في قوله: "هذه الكلمة ليست منّي بل هي ممّن أرسلني"[31] وقوله في أوّل جزء من إنجيل يوحنا: "قد علموا أنك أنت الذي أرسلتني وقد بيّنت[32] اسمك لهم"،[33] وقوله: "لا أدين الناس وحدي بل أنا والذي أرسلني"[34]، وقوله أيضًا: "إذا هم شهدوا اثنين صادقين إني أشهد على نفسي والله الذي أرسلني"[35]، وقوله في إنجيل يوحنّا: "الأعمال التي عملتها تشهد عليّ بأنّ الله الذي أرسلني والله الذي يرسلني إلى خلقه"[36]، وقوله للذي قال له: "أيها المعلّم الصالح، أيّ عمل صالح تأمرني أفعله أنال به الحياة الدائمة"، فقال للرجل: "لا تدعني صالحا، فإنما الصالح هو الله وحده"[37]، وقوله أيضًا طالبًا من الله: "إن شئت يا ربّ أن تنزع كأس هذا الموت عني فهو بأمرك ليس هو بأمري"[38]، وقوله أيضًا: "ليس أتكلّم بأمري، ولكن بأمر الذي أرسلني وأعطاني الأمر بما أقول وأتكلّم به، واعلموا[39] أنّ كلّ من يطيع أوامره ويقبل ما يرسمه ينحله الحياة الدائمة"[40]، وقوله لهم حين قالوا له: "اذهب واهرب من ها هنا فإنّ هدورس يريد يقتلك"، فقال لهم: "إني أخرج الشيطان من أجسام الناس بآيات كثيرة، فإذا أنا أتممت ما أنا فيه خرجت منطلقا إلى الله من أجل أن لا يستطيع نبي يتلف خارج دار السلام"[41]، وقوله: "إني لم أجيء لأنقض توراة موسى ولا كلام الأنبياء، بل جئت[42]

73r *

73v *

---

[30] Mtt V: 17.   [31] Cf. Jn V: 30.   [32] B: بنيت   [33] Jn XVII: 8.   [34] Ibid. VIII: 15-16.   [35] Ibid. 17-18.   [36] Ibid. V: 36.   [37] Lk XVIII: 18-19.   [38] Ibid. XXII: 42. [39] B: وعلموا   [40] Jn XII: 49-50.   [41] Lk XIII: 31-3.   [42] B: حيث (wrongly), a misreading of A.

They claim that God is Christ and Christ is God, and that Christ descended to earth, being concealed from the eyes of the descendants of Adam, in order to lead people out of their sins. But did he lead them to his own law or to someone else's? If you say: To someone else's law, he was not divine. And if you say: To his own, (73r) then you are denying your Gospels, because Christ's words in them are, 'I have not come to do away with the Torah of Moses but to confirm it'. And I say to you: Tell me about the one who acts according to Christ's law, is he guided or gone astray? If you say: He is guided, you yourselves have gone astray because you do not act in accordance with his law, for he followed the law of Moses. And if you say: He has gone astray, you have disbelieved in God and Christ because you have offended against the words of both of them over the sabbath, circumcision, and so on.

Was Christ sent or Sender? If you say that he was sent, you deny your Gospels which witness that he was divine and worshipped. And if you say that he was Sender, you deny Christ's words, 'This word is not from me but from the One who sent me'; his words in the early part of the Gospel of John, 'They know that you are the One who sent me, and I have announced clearly to them your name'; his words, 'I do not judge people on my own, but I and the One who sent me'; also his words, 'If they require two trustworthy witnesses, I witness to myself and God who sent me'; his words in the Gospel of John, 'The actions I have performed witness to the fact that it was God who sent me, and it is God who sends me to his creatures'; his word to the man who said to him, 'Good teacher, what good works can you command me to do so that I may obtain everlasting life through them?', and he said to the man, 'Do not call me good, for the one who is good is God alone'; also his words when he was imploring God, 'Lord, if you will to (73v) take the cup of this death from me—but it is by your authority not mine'; also his words, 'I do not speak on my own authority, but on the authority of the One who sent me and gave me the authority by which I utter and speak; and know that to everyone who obeys his commands and accepts what he lays down he will give eternal life'; his words to them when they said to him, 'Get away, escape from here, for Herod wants to kill you', he said to them, 'I will be expelling the devil from people's bodies by many signs, and if I complete what I am about I shall go away to God, because a prophet cannot meet his end anywhere but Jerusalem'; his words, 'I have not come to abolish the Torah of Moses nor the words of the prophets, rather I have come

أتمّمها بعمل الحقّ آمين"[43]، وقوله حين قام بطرس ليغسل رجليه بالماء: "لم يجيء ابن البشر لِيُخدم وإنّما جاء لِيَخدم"[44]، وقوله لتلاميذه: "اجلسوا ها هنا حتى أصلّي"[45]، وقام وتنهّد وقال: "بلغت نفسي إلى الموت"[46]، وقوله لسمعان ويوحنا ويعقوب: "أنا يسوع قد بلغت نفسي إلى الموت، أنظروني وتيقظوا حتى أتقدّم قليلاً وأسجد على الأرض وأصلّي لله تعالى حتى ينجّيني، ويصرف عنّي هذا السوء"، ثم إنه خرّ على الأرض سجودًا وطلب من الله أن يصرف عنه كأس الموت وقال: "يا ربّ، اصرف عنّي هذا الكأس بمسرّتك لا بمسرّتي ولا بأمري"[47]، ثم قال لسمعان كصفا * "أنت راقد وتراني في هذه الشدّة والعاقة والضيق، وقد أسلمت بيد الخطاة"[48]، وحين قال الشيطان ليسوع: "أسجد سجدة واحدة وخّر على وجهك لي حتى أفوّض إليك الدنيا وأبيحها لك"، فقال يسوع للشيطان: "أليس مكتوب في التوراة: الله إلهك خف[49] وإيّاه فاعبد وباسمه المقدّس فاقسم وبطاعته وعبادته التزم"[50]. وفي الإنجيلات أيضًا أنّ يسوع[51] قام وصلّى ثلاث دفعات ونبّه تلاميذه وقال لهم: "ألا تنتبهون وتصلّون معي وتطلبون[52] لي من الله على هذه الشدّة العظيمة والمصيبة الزائدة التي قد وقعت فيها في هذا اليوم؟"[53] فناموا وودروا كلامه.

ومن إنجيلاتكم المخالفة بالشهادة لهذه الأقوال، الشاهدة على المسيح بأنه عبد الله ورسوله قول لوقا في إنجيله إنّ يسوع أقبل إلى الجليل[54] إلى يوحنا وطهّره في الأردن وخرج صوت ينادي: "أنت ولدي وحبيبي وابني"[55]. وفي الإنجيلات أيضًا أنّ يسوع أقبل من الجليل[56] إلى يوحنا إلى الأردن ليطهّره، ولمّا طهّره، انفتحت السماء ونزلت روح الله ترفرف عليه، وخرج صوت ينادي: "هذا ابني وحبيبي الذي * ارتضيت وهويت"[57]، وفي الإنجيل أيضًا أنّ فيلفوس قال ليسوع: "أريد أن تريني[58] الآب حتّى أموت"، فقال له يسوع: "هذا اليوم كله أنا معك وما يكفاك، ومن نظر إليّ فقد نظر إلى الآب، وأنا وأبي سواء"[59].

---

[43] Mtt V: 17. [44] Mtt XX: 28, Mk X: 45. Cf. also Lk XXII: 27. [45] Mtt XXVI: 36. [46] Ibid.: 38. [47] Cf. Mtt XXVI: 37-9; Mk XIV: 33-36. [48] Mtt XXVI: 41; Mk XIV: 37. [49] A and B خاف [50] Mtt IV: 8-10; Lk IV: 5-8. [51] A and B: يسوع [52] A and B: تنتبهوا وتصلوا وتطلبوا [53] Cf. Mtt XXVI: 40-6. [54] A and B: الجليل [55] Lk III: 21-2. [56] A and B: الجليل [57] Mtt III: 13-17. [58] A and B: توريني [59] Jn XIV: 8-10.

to fulfil them by actions of truth indeed'; his words when Peter was standing for him to wash his feet with water, 'The Son of Man has not come to be served but to serve'; his words to his disciples, 'Stay here while I pray', then he got up and sighed, and he said, 'My soul is close to death'; his words to Simon, John and James, 'I Jesus am close to death, so stay by me and keep watch while I go apart a little and prostrate on the ground and pray to God the exalted to deliver me and take this torment away from me', then he fell to the ground in prostration and implored God to take away from him the cup of death, saying, 'Lord, take this cup away from me, according to your will not according to my will or authority', then he said to Simon 'the Rock', (74r) 'You sleep when you can see me in this distress, strain and anxiety, for I have been given into the hands of sinners'; when Satan said to Jesus, 'Make one prostration and fall on your face before me, and I will give you authority over the world and make it yours', but Jesus said to Satan, 'Is it not written in the Torah: It is God your God whom you should fear, him whom you should serve, by his holy name you should swear, and in obedience and worship to him you should be bound?'; it is also in the Gospels that Jesus rose and prayed three times, and he roused his disciples and said, 'Can you not stay awake and pray with me, and implore God for me about this great affliction and overwhelming disaster which I must face today?', but they slept on and did not heed what he said.

Among your Gospels, which contain divergent attestations of these words and attest that Christ was the servant and messenger of God, are the words of Luke in his Gospel that Jesus came to Galilee to John who cleansed him in the Jordan, and a voice called out saying, 'You are my begotten, my beloved, my Son'. And it is in the Gospels also that Jesus came from Galilee to the Jordan to John for him to cleanse him, and when he had cleansed him the heavens opened and the Spirit of God descended and hovered over him, and a voice called out saying, 'This is my Son, my beloved, in whom (74v) I am pleased and delight'. And also in the Gospel is that Philip said to Jesus, 'I would like you to show me the Father before I die', and Jesus said to him, 'This very day I am with you, and is this not enough? He who has seen me has seen the Father, for I and my Father are the same.'[7]

---

[7] The three contradictions arise from the fact that on the one hand Jesus presents himself as a human, and on the other is acclaimed or acclaims himself as Son of God.

أخبروني عن هذا التناقض في شهادات الأناجيل بأنّ المسيح نبي مرسل تارة وولد للإله تارة وإله بذاته تارة، هل له مستند في المعقول؟ كلا والله ولا من المنقول.

وكذا شهادتكم في أمانتكم[60] بأنّ المسيح إله حقّ من إله حقّ من جوهر أبيه، وأنكم آمنتم بإله واحد آب ضابط الكلّ خالق السموات والأرض صانع ما يُرى وما لا يُرى. وهذا تناقض[61] في الإيمان، فإنّ المسيح إن كان في السموات أو في الأرض أو منهما، أو كان يُرى أو لا يُرى، أو كان من الكلّ فإنه مخلوق لا خالق ولا إله، ولا هو من جوهر أبيه الذي لا يتجزّأ ولا ينقسم ولا ينسب إليه ما ينسب إلى المخلوقين من الجسمية والجوهرية المتحيزة والكيفية والأينية. فكانت هذه الأمانة منكم خيانة لله ولرسله وللمسيح في زعمكم فيه أنه إله وأنه نزل إلى الأرض لخلاصكم معشر البشر.

وكيف يكون إلهًا ربًّا خالقًا، وقوله في الأناجيل قوله المتقدّم؟ وكيف يجوز أن يُعبد وهو بشر وابن البشر وأفعاله كلها أفعال البشر في الخلق والخُلق والنشوء والنموّ والتغذّي والنوم والسُّكر بالخمر والتهوّر[62] والجزع والفزع والهروب والجوع والعطش وتعلّم[63] الصنائع الدنية كالصباغة للثياب ومثلها؟ وكيف تزعمون أنه الله وأنّ الله هو، وتعلمون أنه قال: "وجدت العصافير وكرًا يسكنونه، ووجدت الثعالب موضعًا يختبئون فيه وابن البشر لم يجد موضعًا يسكن فيه إلا خشبة يركب عليها؟"[64] وأين هذا القول والاعتراف بالعبودية والانقهار والتذلّل والانكسار من زعمكم فيه وتكذيبكم لأناجيلكم المذكور فيها قوله إنه رسول لا راسل وعبد لا ربّ ومألوه لا إله؟

* 75r

---

[60] B omits في أمانتكم   [61] A and B: يناقض   [62] A and B: والتهو   [63] A and B: وتعليم
[64] Cf. Mtt VIII: 20; Lk IX: 58.

Explain to me about this contradiction in the attestations of the Gospels, that in one place Christ is a prophet sent, in another the Son of God, and in another God himself. Is there any proof of this that reason would accept? No, by heavens, nothing at all, nor in what has been passed down.

It is the same with your attestation in your Creed, that Christ is true God from true God, of the substance of his Father, and that you believe in one God who is Father and Master of all, Creator of the heavens and earth, Maker of what is seen and unseen. This is self-contradiction in belief. For even though Christ may have been in the heavens or on earth or from both, or was seen or unseen, or was all these, he was created and not Creator or God, nor of the substance of his Father, who cannot be split or divided, nor can anything be ascribed to him that is ascribed to created beings, such as corporeality, substantiality, limitation, modality or directionality. So this creed of yours is a betrayal of God, of his messengers and of Christ inasmuch as you claim that he was God and that he descended to earth for your salvation as human beings.

How could he be God, Lord and Creator, when his words in the Gospels are such as given above? How can it be right for him to be worshipped when he was a man and the Son of Man, and all his actions were the actions of a man in inner and outer make-up, growing, development, being nourished, sleeping, being drunk with wine, high spirits, fear, alarm, (75r) running away, hunger, thirst, learning lowly trades such as cloth dyeing, and so on?[8] How can you claim that he was God and God was him, when you know that he said, 'The sparrows have found a nest to rest in, and the foxes have found a place to hide, but the Son of Man has found no place to rest except the beam of wood to which he is fastened'? How do these words, and the recognition of humanity, defeat, self-abasement and dejection, relate to your claim about him and to your denial of your Gospels, with their references to his words that he was sent and not Sender, servant and not Lord, subservient and not Divine?

---

[8] The two remarks about Jesus being drunk and being apprenticed as a dyer repeat remarks made by al-Dimashqī earlier, § 64 (and also the end of § 74 below, where there is another mention of Jesus being drunk still in this passage from the *Dhimmī*). So either al-Dimashqī is there anticipating elements of this argument, or he and this speaker employ details about Jesus that must be commonplace knowledge among Muslims at this time.

73. ولئن قلتم إنه فعل العجائب قلت لكم إنّ غيره من الأنبياء فعل ما هو أعجب من فعله و لم يتخذوه إلهًا ولا أشركوا به كما اتخذتم المسيح إلهًا وأشركتم به. خلق الله آدم أبا البشر من غير أب ولا أمّ وهو أعجب من خلقه المسيح من أمّ بغير أب ، ورفع الله أخنوخًا إلى السماء ورفع آلياهو النبي إلى السماء كما قلتم إنه رفع المسيح إلى السماء. وسمّى الله إسرائيل في التوراة ابنًا قال: "ابني بكري إسرائيل"[65]، كما سمّى المسيح نفسه ابنًا وسمّى الحواريين أبناء في الإنجيلات بقوله: "أحبّوا أقرباءكم وابغضوا[66] اعداءكم وباركوا على من لعنكم واصنعوا الحسنات إلى من أساء[67] عليكم وصلّوا على من يتكلّم عليكم لكيما تكونوا بني أبيكم الذي في السماء"[68]، وقوله أيضًا فيها: "إن أنتم كافأتم السيئة بالسيئة فأيّ أجر لكم عند أبيكم الذي في السماء"[69]، فإمّا أن تعبدوا إسرائيل وتعبدوا أنفسكم حيث جعلكم أبناء الله بالتسمية المجازية أو ترجعوا عن الشرك بالله وعن قولكم: "المسيح ابن الله".

* 75v

وإن كان الشرك بالمسيح لأجل أنه أشبع ألف رجل من ثمانية أرغفة مع سمكتين وأحيا الميت وكشف السقم عن المريض، فإنّ أليسع النبي والياهو النبي أحيا كلّ واحد منهما الموتى[70]

---

[65] Exodus IV: 22; Ben Sira XXXVI: 12. [66] *Sic* in A and B; cf. Mtt V: 44 and Lk VI: 35 where Jesus' saying is given as احبّوا [67] A and B: اسي [68] Mtt V: 44-5. [69] Cf. Lk VI: 32-4. [70] Cf. II Kings IV: 19-35 and I Kings XVII: 17-24.

73.   In case you should say that he performed miracles,[9] I say to you that other prophets performed greater miracles than he did, but they have never been taken as gods nor made partners with him in the way that you take Christ as God and make him a partner. God created Adam, the father of humankind, without father or mother, and this is more miraculous than his creating Christ from a mother without a father. God raised Enoch to heaven, and he raised the prophet Elijah to heaven, just as you say he raised Christ to heaven. In the Torah God calls Israel son, saying 'My elder son Israel', just as in the Gospels Christ calls himself son and the disciples sons, saying 'Love those who are nearest to you, hate your enemies, ask blessing on those who curse you, do good to those who wrong you, and pray for those who speak against you, so that you may become sons of your Father who is in heaven';[10] and also his words there, 'If you return wrong for wrong, what reward will you have with your Father who is (75v) in heaven? He will forgive you your wrongdoings'. So you should either worship Israel and yourselves, since in a figurative form of address he has made you sons of God, or you should abandon associating others with God and saying 'Christ is the Son of God'.

If associating Christ arises from his feeding a thousand men with eight loaves and two fish,[11] raising the dead and removing the illness of the sick, the prophets Elisha and Elijah each raised dead people,

---

[9] The comparison of the miracles of Jesus and other prophets, to show that while theirs were more impressive than his they did not attract attributions of divinity, was a popular motif in Muslim anti-Christian polemic from as early as the third/ninth century; cf. D. Thomas, 'The Miracles of Jesus in early Islamic Polemic', *Journal of Semitic Studies* 39, 1994, p. 221-43, with further references in Thomas, 'Abū Manṣūr al-Māturīdī on the Divinity of Jesus Christ', pp. 60f., n. 15. The comparisons given here repeat the same prophetic miracles as many earlier versions but give no clue about any clear relationship with a predecessor.

A noticeable omission from this comparisons argument is any reference to the mode of performance of the miracles, whether Christ himself performed them 'with the help of God', *bi-idhni Allāh*, or whether God produced them as signs of Christ's prophetic status. This significant theological point is a prominent feature of many earlier versions.

[10] Cf. Mtt V: 43-4, though Jesus' revision of the Jewish teaching to love one's enemies rather than hate them in v. 44 has been catastrophically confused with the original teaching given in v. 43.

[11] The canonical Gospels mention either five loaves and five thousand people, Mtt XIV: 17 || Mk VI: 38 and 44, and Lk IX: 13 and 14, or seven loaves and four thousand people, Mtt XV: 36 and 38 || Mk VIII: 4 and 9.

وحزقال النبي أحيا ألفًا في بقعات دورا[71]، وألياهو دعا في كفّ دقيق وفي
قليل زيت فكفى خلقًا كثيرًا ثلاث سنين إلى أن نزل المطر، ثمّ دعا فأنزل
المطر، ودعا الله على جبل الكرمل[72] فنزلت له النار وأحرقت القربان ولقلقت
ست وثلاثون[73] جرّة ماء[74]. وأليسع جعل بكلمته في يسير من السويق والخبز
بركة عظيمة حتّى قام .بماية نبي[75]، وموسى بن عمران بعثه الله إلى فرعون
بالضربات المشهورة قلب مياههم دمًّا، وسلّط عليهم الطوفان والجراد والقمل
والضفادع والظلمة العجيبة وقتل أبكارهم في الضربة العاشرة، وتحويله العصا
تنّينًا والتّين عصًا، أعجب من إحياء الموتى. وأخرج بني إسرائيل وشقّ
بين أيديهم البحر، وسيّرهم بعمود نار وعمود غمام، وفجّر له عيون الماء
وطعمهم المنّ والسلوى وأمر الأرض ففتحت فاها وابتلعت قارون وأهله بأمر
الله.[76] ويوشع ابن نون وقفت له الشمس والقمر يومًا * تامًّا[77] وضرب ماء
الأردن فيبس إلى أن عبر صندوق عهد الله[78]، وكذا حزقياهو الداوودي ردّ
الشمس درجات إلى وراء وعاد الظلّ إلى عشر درجات[79].

* 76r

وأنتم فلا تقدرون تكذبون بشيء ممّا ذكرته من آيات الأنبياء المذكورين
وبراهينهم ولم يضع المسيح أعجب منها، فإمّا تتخذونه نبيًّا رسولاً كما شهد
لنفسه في أناجيلكم، وإمّا تعبدون هؤلاء الأنبياء وتشركون بهم كما أشركتم
به.

74. وقلتم: الآب والإبن وروح القدس، كانوا جميعًا ولم يكن منهم واحد
قبل الآخر من وجه وكان قبله من وجه. وإنهم يعنون الثلاثة بقدرة واحدة
وسلطان واحد وأقنومية واحدة. فإن قلتم

---

[71] Cf. Ezekiel XXXVII: 1-10.   [72] A and B: الكرمد   [73] A and B: ستة وثلاثين   [74] Cf. I Kings XVII: 7ff., XVIII: 34-8.   [75] Cf. II Kings IV: 42-4.   [76] Exodus VII: 8ff.   [77] Joshua X: 12-13.   [78] *Ibid.* III:15-17.   [79] In fact it was Isaiah the prophet, and not King Hezekiah, who performed this miracle; cf. II Kings XX: 8-11.

while the prophet Ezekiel raised a thousand in the fields of Dura;[12] during a shortage of flour and scarcity of oil Elijah prayed, and he satisfied many people for three years until the rains fell; he prayed and the rains fell; and he prayed to God on Mount Carmel and fire came down to him, consuming the offering, and thirty-six jars of water simmered away;[13] Elisha spoke a great blessing over a little corn porridge and bread until it proved enough for a hundred prophets; Moses son of 'Imrān, God sent him to Pharaoh with the well-known plagues, turned their rivers to blood and inflicted on them flood, locusts, lice, frogs, mysterious darkness, and the killing of their first-born sons in the tenth plague;[14] his turning the staff into a serpent and the serpent into a staff is more wonderful than raising the dead; he brought out the People of Israel, parted the sea before them, and led them with a pillar of fire and a pillar of cloud; he made water springs gush forth for him, he fed them with manna and quails, and he commanded the earth and it opened its mouth and swallowed Korah and his family as God commanded; and Joshua son of Nun, the sun and moon stood still for him for a whole (76r) day, he struck the waters of the Jordan and it remained dry until the ark of the covenant had been carried across; likewise Hezekiah of the line of David, he made the sun go backwards a few steps and the shadow moved back ten steps.

You are in no position to refute a single one of the signs or proofs of the above-mentioned prophets which I have referred to, and Christ did not produce anything more miraculous. So either you have to accept him as a prophet and messenger as he attested of himself in your Gospels, or you have to worship these prophets and associate them as you associate him.

74. You say: Father, Son and Holy Spirit, they all exist jointly and no one is or has been before another in any way, three regarded as possessing one power, one authority, one hypostatic nature. If you

---

[12] According to Daniel III: 1, the plain of Dura is in the province of Babylon. Since Ezekiel is traditionally located there, Ezekiel I: 1-3, this must be an inference based on the Biblical text, together with some personal knowledge.

[13] According to translations of 1 Kings XVIII: 34-5, Elijah ordered four jars of water to be poured on the altar on Mount Carmel three times, making twelve in all, though it is possible that this author understood the reference in verse 35, 'They did it a third time', to mean that they repeated the whole triple pouring of the four jars three times, rather than pouring the four jars a third time.

[14] S. XXVII: 12 mentions nine signs (and cf. Yusuf 'Ali's translation *ad* S. VII: 133 for a list). This reference clearly follows the Biblical account.

إنّ الإبن نسب إلى أبيه حين ولده وتولّد منه نقضتم الباطل بالباطل، وإن قلتم كان الأب أبًا والإبن ابنًا أبدًا وأزلاً⁸⁰ كان من أمحل المحال ذلك.

وكذلك قولكم: إنه بديمار واحد لاهوت وديمار واحد ناسوت وإنه صعد إلى السماء بالإثنين فاستوى على العرش مع الآب، فصورة شهادة منكم. من أين لكم هذا؟ وكيف تشهدون الزور وتقولون على الله الكذب؟ ويا لها فضيحة وأضحوكة!

وقولكم أيضًا إن أقنوم الإبن نزل من السماء إلى مريم العذراء، فهل نزل معه الآب وروح القدس أو الإبن وحده نزل؟ فإن قلتم: "نزل وحده والتحم" فقد أبطلتم الباطل الأوّل بباطل غيره، وإن قلتم: "نزلوا * جميعًا" كان باطلاً **76v** وجنونًا وتلعّبًا ممّن لا يفقه قولاً ولا يهتدي سبيلاً.

ويكفيكم ويل وبعد عن الإنسانية زعمكم في المسيح أنه إله وربّ وخالق. وتشهد أناجيلكم أنه كان في الأرض حيث لا منتهى له، وفي البحار حيث لا نهاية، وفي الجبال والمغرب كذلك، كما أنّ الربّ في كلّ مكان. وتشهد أناجيلكم أيضًا أنه كان جسد المسيح كأجساد الناس. وتعلمون أنّ الآية الثانية من العشر كلمات: "لا يكون لك معبود⁸¹ دوني. ولا تتخذوا صنمًا مصوّرًا لا في السماء العليا ولا في الأرض السفلى ولا في المياه التي تحت الأرض"⁸². ولمّا انتهى في إسماعهم الآية العاشرة قالت الأئمّة لموسى: "سمعنا وأطعنا" وقرّوا بجملتهم أنّ

---

say that the Son is related to his Father inasmuch as the latter begot
the former and the former was begotten from the latter, you are refuting one falsehood with another. And if you say that the Father was
Father and the Son was Son in eternity and before time, this is the
most extreme impossibility.

It is the same with your words: He had one aspect which was divine
nature and one aspect which was human nature,[15] and he ascended
as both to heaven and was seated on the throne with the Father, as
a visible testimony on your part. But where did you find this? And
why do you testify to what is untrue, and speak lies about God? How
shameful and ridiculous this is!

And also your statement that the hypostasis of the Son descended
from heaven to the Virgin Mary, did the Father and Holy Spirit
descend with him, or was it the Son alone? If you say: He descended
alone and took flesh, you cancel out the first falsehood with another.
And if you say: They all descended, (76v) it would be untrue, mad
and a game on the part of someone who had no understanding of
language and was not guided along any way.[16]

Your claim that Christ was God, Lord and Creator is sufficient
woe to you and is improbable for the human nature. Your Gospels
bear witness that he was on the earth because there was no limitation
for him, and on the seas because there was no end, and likewise in
mountains and remote places, in the same way that the Lord is in
every place. Your Gospels also bear witness that Christ's body was
like the bodies of other people. You know the second saying of the
Ten Commandments: You shall have no being to worship other than
me. You shall not take an image or form of anything in the heavens
above or the earth below, or in the water which is under the earth.
And when he had finished reading out to them the tenth saying, the
leaders said to Moses, 'We hear and obey', and they all affirmed that

---

[15] The term *dīmār* is not found in the dictionaries, and the closest term that makes
sense is the Persian *dīmar*, 'face', 'aspect', which would correspond to the Arabic *wajh*,
a term occasionally found in Christian Arabic texts as a translation for 'hypostasis'.

[16] Like the miracles comparison above, this argument is employed from the third/
ninth century onwards; cf. D. Thomas, 'Early Muslim Responses to Christianity',
in D. Thomas, ed., *Christians at the Heart of Islamic Rule, Church Life and Scholarship in
'Abbasid Iraq*, Leiden, 2003, pp. 236-9. The two impossible alternatives are that either
the Son alone became flesh, in which case he must be distinct and not one with the
other hypostases, or all three hypostases became flesh, which violates both Christian
doctrine itself and any conception about the nature of divinity.

الله واحد ليس سواه. وتعلمون أيضًا أن داود النبي قال لربّه: "أريد أن أبني لك يا ربّ بيتاً"، فقال له: "يا داود، أيّ بيت يسعني؟ وأيّ مكان؟ السموات والأرض لا تحويني"[83].

وأنّ يسوع لمّا أصابه الجهد والعرق استغاث وقال: "قد بلغت نفسي إلى الموت"، وأنّه قال لبطرس: "إذهب واسرق لي هذا الفلو ولا تعلم صاحبه"، فذهب بطرس إلى صاحب الفلو لحلّه[84] وسرق الفلو وأركبه يسوع وهرب به[85]. وتعلمون أيضًا أنّ يسوع دعوه إلى العرس ومعه أمّه مريم، فأكل وشرب وسكر ونام، فأيقظته أمّه وقالت له: "قم يا ولدي فقد فرغ الخمر"، فانتبه وقال: "إنّ الذي * ينبغي أن يدعوا به إلى الله أن يرزقنا خمرًا نشربه"[86]، فيا خسران من زعم في من هذه صفاته أنه ربّ وإله وخالق ويا هلاكه.

75. وتعلمون أيضًا مع هذا أنّ موسى بن عمران رسول الله سأل أن ينظر إلى الله تعالى، فقال له الله: "يا موسى عبدي[87]، لا يقدر أحد ينظر إليّ فيعيش"[88]. وسئل مرة عن الإله ورؤيته فقال: "لم يره أحد ولا يراه أحد قطّ، ومن رآه مات". فكيف تزعمون أنّ يسوع إله وربّ خالق[89] وتعبدونه وتعبدون الصليب وتقبّلونه وتجعلونه قدّامكم في المذابح أوقات صلواتكم المردودة عليكم، وكلّ ذلك من شرككم به، مع أنكم تعلمون وتجزمون[90] وتشهدون أنّ يسوع أقام أربعين يومًا هاربًا في الجبل جزعًا فزعانًا وهو يصلّي ويسجد ويطلب الخلاص من الله تعالى كما قال لوقا في الإنجيل، وأنّ الشيطان ما زال يطلب يسوع حتى وجده مختبئًا[91] في موضع كادت روحه تذهب من الجوع والعطش والجهد، فقال ليسوع لمّا وافاه: "إن كنت إلهًا كما قد زعمت فقل لهذه الصخور والكهوف تنفجر عيونًا وتشرب منها الماء"، فقال يسوع للشيطان: "إنه مكتوب في التوراة: ليس على الخبز وحده يحيا الإنسان ولكن بكلام الله يعيش إبن آدم"، فجرّ الشيطان ليسوع جرًّا عنيفًا حتى أتى به إلى مدينة القدس فأخذه وأصعده إلى أعلى

* 77r

---

83 A reminiscence of II Samuel VII: 1-7.   84 A and B: كحلّه   85 Cf. Mk XI: 1-7; Lk XIX: 29-35.   86 Cf. Jn II: 3-4.   87 B: عندي (wrongly), a misreading of A.   88 Exodus XXXIII: 20.   89 A and B: إلهًا وربًّا وخالقًا   90 B: تجزمون   91 A and B: مختني

God is one, with none beside him. You also know that the prophet David said to his Lord, 'O Lord, I wish to build you a house', but he said to him, 'David, what house would be big enough for me, and what place? The heavens and the earth cannot contain me'.

And when Jesus was experiencing strain and perspiration he called for help saying, 'My soul is close to death'. And he said to Peter, 'Go and steal this colt for me and do not tell its owner'. So Peter went to the owner of the colt, untied it, and stole the colt. And Jesus got on it and escaped on it.[17] You also know that Jesus was invited to the wedding, and with him his mother Mary. He ate, drank, got drunk and fell asleep. Then his mother roused him and said to him, 'Get up, son, the wine has run out'. He woke and said, 'Then what (77r) they have to do is pray to God to give us wine to drink'. How injurious to the one who claims that someone with these attributes could be Lord, God and Creator! What ruin for him!

75. You also know in addition to this that Moses son of 'Imrān, the messenger of God, asked to look on God the exalted, and God said to him, 'Moses my servant, no one can look on me and live'. Once he was asked about God and seeing him, and he said, 'No one has ever seen him and no one can see him at all, for whoever sees him will die'. So how can you claim that Jesus was God, Lord and Creator, worship him, worship the cross, kiss it and place it before yourselves on the altars at the times of your prayers (which rebound on you)? All of this is because you associate him with God, even though you know without any doubt and you testify that Jesus spent forty days as a fugitive in the mountain in fear and dread, worshipping, prostrating and seeking salvation from God the exalted. As Luke says in the Gospel, Satan kept on looking for Jesus until he found him hiding somewhere, with his spirit almost spent from hunger, thirst and strain. He said to Jesus when he came up to him, 'If you are God as you have claimed, tell these rocks and hollows to burst out in springs, and drink the water from them'. Jesus said to Satan, 'It is written in the Torah: Man does not live by bread alone but mankind is fed by God'. Satan dragged Jesus roughly along until he brought him to the city of Jerusalem, and he took him and carried him up to the highest point

---

[17] Cf. Mtt XXI: 1-9 || Mk XI: 1-10 and Lk XIX: 28-38, where Jesus sends two disciples to bring the colt. There is an ingenious twist to the story here, where rather than publicly entering Jerusalem on the colt and inviting almost certain arrest and execution, Jesus completes the theft by using it to escape arrest.

الهيكل وقال: * "يا يسوع، إن سجدت لي سجدة واحدة ملّكتك هذه الدنيا
بكلّ ما فيها"، فقال يسوع للشيطان: "أليس مكتوب في توراة موسى: الله
إلهك خفه وإيّاه اعبد وباسمه المقدّس أقسم وبعبادته وطاعته التزم؟". [92]

وتعلمون وتخبرون وتؤرّخون في كتبكم ما أنا ذاكره وحالف عليه بالله
العظيم الأحد أنني لو لم أره مدوّنًا في إنجيل ومكتوبًا في كتبكم ما ذكرته
ولا حكيته لما فيه من القبح والشناعة والبهتان، وذلك إن قلتم: "ذاكرون [93]
له".

ولمّا كان يوم الجمعة أصبحوا اليهود جاؤوا إلى يسوع إلى الحبس
فأخرجوه منه وجعلوا على رأسه إكليلاً من الشوك [94] والعوسج وأسقوه الخلّ
وماء الحنظل وعذّبوه وأهانوه وأنزلوه المنازل القبيحة وغطوا رأسه بذيله
وجعلوا يلطمونه بأيديهم، ويقول اللاطم له: "يا يسوع، إن كنت إلهًا كما
تزعم ويزعمون أصحابك، أعلمنا من ذا يلطمك؟" وهو يستغيث وييكي
ويقول: "ما أعلم الغيب ولا يعلم الغيب إلا الله وحده . وأقسم بالله العظيم
أنّ هذا الفعل القبيح لو فعل بحمار أو ثور لكان منكرًا ومستقبحًا"، [95] فضلاً
عن أن تصفون هذا في إنجيلكم عمّن زعمتم أنه خالق ربّ فعّال لما يريد،
فيا بئس قوم هذا مذهبهم وهذا اعتقادهم.

ثمّ سقتم * تمام هذه الحكاية القبيحة، فقلتم: ثمّ إنّ اليهود لم يزالوا
يطوفون بيسوع يوم الجمعة إلى نصف النهار وعلى رقبته خشبة الصلب حتى
كاد يموت من ثقلها وتعذييهم له بها وبالسحب والمناداة عليه واللطم له،
فوقعت الخشبة من فوق كتفه إلى الأرض حتى جاء سمنون او سميون وحملها
عن يسوع بزعمكم ومشوا بيسوع إلى أن جاؤوا به إلى موضع يريدون صلبه
فيه وهو موضع خارج البلد وصلبوه في الشمس وصار يستغيث ويضجّ من
عظم الألم من فوق الخشبة ويقول: "يا إلهي لم خليتني وسلّمتني بيد أعدائي؟
ربّ أغثني وخلّصني". [96]

واختلفت إنجيلاتكم في أمره، فقوم يقولون: "مات فوق الخشبة" وقوم
يقولون: "طعن برمح

---

[92] Lk IV: 2-8.   [93] A and B: ذاكرين   [94] B: الشون (wrongly), evidently a misreading
of A.   [95] Cf. Mtt XXVII: 27ff.   [96] Mtt XXVII: 46.

of the temple and said, (77v) 'Jesus, make one prostration before me and I will give you the world and all that is in it for your kingdom'. But Jesus said to Satan, 'Is it not written in the Torah of Moses: God is your God, him shall you fear and him shall you worship, by his holy name shall you swear, and to his devotion and obedience shall you be bound?'.

You know, you broadcast and you have recorded in your books what I have mentioned. And I swear by the one great God that if I had not seen it set down in the Gospel and written in your books, I would not have mentioned it or recounted it because of the foulness, hideousness and lies that it contains. And this is in case you say, 'We are quite aware of this'.

When Friday came the Jews went early to Jesus in prison. They brought him out and placed on his head a crown of spines and thorns, and gave him vinegar and the juice of colocynth to drink. They tortured him, humiliated him, threw him down in filthy places, put his garment over his head and kept on striking him with their hands. One said as he struck him, 'Jesus, if you are God as you and your companions claim, tell us who is striking you.' He called for help and cried, saying, 'I do not know the unknown, for no one knows the unknown except God. I swear by God almighty that if this foul treatment was inflicted on an ass or an ox, it would be disallowed and thought shameful.' This is to say nothing of the fact that you give this description in your Gospel of the one you claim is God, Creator, Lord and performer of what he wills. How wretched are the people who hold such a doctrine and belief!

Then you pursue this foul account to its (78r) climax and say, The Jews went on leading Jesus around throughout Friday until the middle of the day, on his neck the cross-beam for crucifixion, so heavy that he almost died from it and their torturing him with it, from being dragged along and from the shouting against him and blows upon him. The cross-beam fell from his shoulder to the ground, so Simnūn (or Simeon) came and carried it for Jesus, as you claim. They went with Jesus and took him to a place where they intended to crucify him. It was outside the city, and they crucified him under the sun. He began to call for help, and to cry out upon the cross from the intensity of his pain, and he said, 'My God, why have you forsaken me and given me into the hands of my enemies? Lord, help me and save me!'

Your Gospels differ over what happened to him. Some people say he died upon the cross-beam, others that he was pierced with a spear

فمات، و لم يزل مصلوبًا مدّة طويلة" وقوم يقولون: "سعى في خشبته أبوه يوسف النجّار واستغاث إلى فيلاطس الملك حتى وهبت اليهود له جسد يسوع وأنزلوه من الخشبة ولفّوه في ثوبين ودفنوه في المقبرة" كما زعمتم في إنجيل متى ويوحنا.

فهذا قولكم في معبودكم الذي زعمتم أنه إله، وحسبكم ما تراه عقولكم ويكفيكم. ثمّ زعمتم مع هذا الجنون واختلاط العقول أنّ يسوع بعد صلبه وموته ودفنه قام وأرسل إليكم من جهته * رسلاً يأمرونكم بالشرك بالله ويعلّمونكم أنّ الآب والإبن والروح القدس إله واحد ويوصونكم عنه بوصايا مخالفة للتوراة وبين كل واحد وواحد منهم ماية سنة وأكثر وكتبوا لكم التوراة والشرائع وفرضوا عليكم فرائض كلها زور وبهتان وأسندوها إلى يسوع فقبلتها عقولكم وجعلتموها قوانينكم.

ومن ذلك قوله في الأناجيل الأربعة: "تصدّقوا بكلّ شيء يكون لكم واجعلوا كنوزكم حيث لا تُسرق ولا تسوّس".[97] وقوله: "لا تجمعوا في بيوتكم ذهبًا ولا فضّة ولا نحاسًا، فإنّكم لا تستطيعون[98] تعبدون إلهين ولا تخدموا ربّين[99]، ومن ترك هذه الوصايا فقد عصاني"، وقوله: "من لطم خدّك اليمين فحوّل له اليسار ومن سخّرك ميلاً فامش معه ميلين ومن ظلمك فاغفر له ومن ضحك عليك[100] صلّ عليه ومن أذنبت إليه لا تبت[101] أن تستغفره فإن لم تستغفره غضبت عليك". وقوله: "من سألك تعطيه فلا تمنعه ومن أراد أن يأخذ قميصك فلا تمنعه"، وقوله: "أعطوا أقرباءكم وابغضوا[102] اعداءكم وباركوا على من

* 78v

---

[97] Mtt VI: 19-21.   [98] A and B: تستطيعوا   [99] Mtt VI: 24.   [100] A and B: ضحلكك (wrongly).   [101] A and B: أو   [102] Sic in A and B; cf. Mtt V: 44 and Lk VI: 35, where Jesus' saying is given as احبّوا. Cf. also supra, f. 75v.

and died, remaining crucified for a long time, and others say that his father Joseph the carpenter tried to get him off the cross-piece and asked Pilate the king for help.[18] So the Jews let him have the body of Jesus. They brought him down from the cross-beam and, wrapping him in two pieces of cloth, they buried him in the sepulchre, as you claim in the Gospel of Matthew and John.

This is what you say about the one you worship, whom you claim is God, and the opinion your intellects arrive at. For you this is satisfactory. Then, in addition to this folly and intellectual confusion, you claim that after his crucifixion, death and burial, Jesus rose and sent to you on his behalf (78v) apostles who instructed you to associate him with God, taught you that the Father, Son and Holy Spirit are one God, and gave into your keeping from him directions that differ from the Torah. Between any two of them there were a hundred years and more. They wrote for you the Torah and the Laws, appointed religious duties for you, all of them untrue and lying, and they ascribed them to Jesus as authority.[19] Your intellects accepted them and you made them your legal guidelines.

Among these are his words in the four Gospels: 'Give alms on everything you own, and put your treasure where it cannot be stolen or eaten by worms'; his words, 'Do not put gold, silver or copper in your houses, for you cannot worship two gods nor serve two masters; whoever neglects these instructions has rebelled against me'; his words, 'Whoever strikes your right cheek turn the left to him, whoever makes you go a mile walk with him two miles, whoever wrongs you forgive him, whoever scorns you pray for him, whoever you wrong do not let a night pass without asking his forgiveness, for if you do not I will be angry with you'; his words, 'Whoever asks you to give him something do not refuse him, whoever wishes to take your shirt do not stop him'; his words, 'Give to those near you, hate your enemies, bless those who

---

[18] Cf. Mtt XXVII: 57-8 || Mk XV: 43 and Lk XXIII: 50-2, and Jn XIX: 38, where Joseph of Arimathea requests the body of Jesus from Pilate. While it is understandable that he and Joseph the carpenter should be conflated into one person because of their shared name, the appearance of Joseph as Jesus' father here admirably serves the anonymous author's polemical purpose.

[19] The author must have in mind not the Apostles whom Jesus is recorded sending out directly after his resurrection, cf. e.g. Mtt XXVIII: 16-20, but the major figures of the early church whom he would know as the originators of the main sects of Christianity. He recognises these teachers as the real authors of the two parts of the Bible which Christians possessed.

لعنكم واصنعوا الحسنات إلى من أساء[103] إليكم"، وقوله: "إن أنتم كافأتم
السيئة بسيئة فأيّ أجر لكم؟" [104]

وأغفلتم ما جاء في التوراة[105] * وفي المزامير وكتب النبوءات من الحكم * 79r
والوصايا والتشريع والسنن التي سنّها موسى ابن عمران وتبعها المسيح،
فحسبكم علمكم بأنفسكم ومعرفة العالم بأسرهم لكم.

ثمّ كلام الذمّي الذي أقسم "أني أحكي ما يليق[106] أن يحكى منه لا كله،
فإنّ فيه ما يصكّ السمع ويذهب بالبصر ويورث أحناء وضغائن، وسواء إن
كان وقع أو لم يكن وقع".

76. ثمّ لنرجع إلى ما كنّا بسبيله من المجاوبة. فنقول إن تواريخ اليهود
أيضًا وتواريخ العلماء منكم أنّ بولص لم يعاصر المسيح ولا صحبه ولا
كان من تلاميذه وكان بينه وبين زمن المسيح نحو المائة والخمسين سنة أو
دونها أو أكثر منها، وأنه كان يهوديًا مسلطًا على النصارى ولم يزل قائمًا
عليهم بالقتل والمحاربة حتى أجلاهم عن الشام إلى الروم وأنه بعد ذلك لبس
المسوح وأظهر التوبة والرغبة في النصرانية ولحق بأهل الروم النصارى فقبلوه
ودخل معبدًا وأقام فيه سنة لا يظهر لأحد وأنه كان يخدمه أربعة من علماء
النصارى، فقال لهم:

---

[103] A and B: أسي   [104] Cf. Mtt: V: 17–48; VI: 19–24 and Lk VI: 27–38.   [105]
B: التورح (wrongly), evidently a misreading of A.   [106] B: يلتو (wrongly), evidently
a misreading of A.

curse you, do good to those who do evil to you';[20] his words, 'If you return evil for evil what reward will this be for you?'

You neglect what the Torah, (79r) Psalms and prophetic Books contain about the orders, instructions, regulations and exemplary practices which Moses son of 'Imrān established and Christ followed. For your knowledge is enough for you, and worldly wisdom in all its forms is yours!

There is also the argument of the *Dhimmī* who vowed, 'I will relate the part that is suitable, but not all of it because it contains matters to deafen the ears, take away sight, and instil hatred and grudges, no matter whether they took place or not.'[21]

76.   Now let us return to the reply we have been engaged in. So we say that the annals of the Jews and the annals of your experts [confirm] that Paul was neither a contemporary, nor a companion, nor a disciple of Christ, and between him and the time of Christ there were almost a hundred and fifty years, give or take a few;[22] that he was a Jew given authority over the Christians, and that he kept on harassing them with killing and attacks until he forced them out of Damascus into Byzantine territory; that after this he put on sack-cloth and displayed repentance and a desire for Christianity; he joined with the Byzantine Christians who received him; he went into a place of worship and remained there a year without appearing to anyone; and that four Christian scholars used to serve him.[23] He said to them, 'I

---

[20] Cf. n. 10 above.

[21] This brief quotation from an anonymous *Dhimmī* concludes the summary of the arguments requested by another *Dhimmī* from a controversialist which was begun in § 72.

[22] Paul is traditionally thought to have been martyred under Nero in 62 CE, about thirty years after the crucifixion; cf. Section 1, n. 38 above.

[23] Cf. Galatians I: 13-17 and Acts IX: 1-19. Al-Dimashqī summarises the New Testament story of Paul accurately until he reaches the four scholars, from where the story is clearly constructed to explain the origin of the doctrinal disagreements among Christians. In its most general outlines it bears resemblance to two evidently polemical traditions in Islam given in commentaries on S. XIX: 37 (also S. XLIII: 65), 'The sects among them differ'. On this cf. C. López-Morillas, 'The Moriscos and Christian Doctrine', in M.D. Meyerson and E.D. English, eds, *Christians, Muslims and Jews in Medieval and Early Modern Spain, interaction and cultural change*, Notre Dame, Ind., 2000, pp. 290-305, and particularly nn. 9 and 11, where she quotes al-Ṭabarī, *Jāmiʿ al-bayān*, and Ibn Kathīr, *Tafsīr*, on this verse. The latter's comment, that the People of Israel asked the views of four wise men about Jesus and they gave four different beliefs, approximates closely enough to al-Dimashqī's version here to suggest that the latter was recasting this tradition for his own purpose.

But there is also a second tradition, traceable to al-Kalbī in the second/eighth

"نوديت من السماء أن يا بولص اسمع ما أوحيه إليك فأنا المسيح واحفظه

وأعلم به فلانًا يعني أحد الأربعة خدّامه، ولا تعرف الثلاثة رفاقه معه"، ولم

يسمّ المشار إليه فظنّ كلّ واحد منهم أنه هو المخاطب بالسرّ.

ثمّ أنّ بولص خلا بواحد وأوصاه على الكتمان وأن يلقي إلى الفرقة

القائلة به من النصارى ما يلقيه بولص إليه وأن يكتموه[107] مع التديّن به، ثمّ

قال له: "المسيح هو الله والله هو المسيح طبيعة واحدة ومشيئة واحدة، ظهر

لخلقه[108] رحمة لهم واحتجب عن خلقه بخلقه رحمة لهم". ثمّ قال للثاني مع

الوصيّة له كالأوّل: "إنّ المسيح وأمّه إلهان قوّتان ظهرا في الأرض رحمة للناس

ولخلاصهم من الجحيم، طبيعتان ومشيئة واحدة ظاهرهما مخلوق وباطنهما

خالق"، وقال للثالث بعد الوصيّة: "إنّ الله ثلاث أقانيم صفات وخواص

آب وإبن وروح القدس متوسّطة والثلاثة واحد لاهوت وناسوت طبيعتان

ومشيئتان"، وقال للرابع كذلك بعد الوصيّة: "إنّ الله لابس صورة العالم كله

وأنّ هو الانسان القديم وإنّ المسيح نسخته كالمركّب المحيط دائرة عظمى

ونقطة جامعة، طبيعة واحدة ومشيئتان".

---

[107] A and B: يكتمونه   [108] B: كخلقه

was spoken to from heaven, "Paul, listen to what I am revealing to you. I am Christ. Remember this and teach it to so and so (that is, one of his four servants), and do not tell his three companions with him."' He (79v) did not name the person concerned, so each of them thought that he was the one addressed secretly.

Then Paul got one alone and commanded him to keep the secret, and to impart to the Christian sect that would acknowledge him what Paul was going to impart to him, and that they should conceal it while placing belief in it. Then he said to him, 'Christ is God and God is Christ, one nature and one volition; he appeared to his creation as a mercy to them, and he veiled himself from his creation in his creation as a mercy to them.'[24] Then he commanded the second like the first, saying to him, 'Christ and his mother are two powerful divinities who appeared on earth as a mercy to people and to save them from hell fire; they had two natures with one volition, in appearance created, in their inner nature Creator.'[25] To the third he said, after giving him the command, 'God is three hypostases, attributes and characteristics, Father, Son and Holy Spirit between; the three are one divinity and humanity, two natures and two volitions.'[26] He said something similar to the fourth, after giving him the command, 'God put on the form of the entire world, the eternal man, of whom Christ was a version, like an all-encompassing container with huge dimensions and room for everyone, one nature and two volitions.'[27]

---

century, that Paul only pretended to convert to Christianity and then taught three men, Nestor, Jacob and Malkān, different versions of faith. In the form in which this is retold by al-Qarāfī in the seventh/thirteenth century there is a fourth disciple, Mu'min, though he rejects Paul's teaching. On this cf. S.M. Stern, "Abd al-Jabbār's Account of how Christ's Religion was falsified', pp. 177-81.

[24] This approximates to Jacobite/Monophysite Christology as it was summarised by Muslims; cf. Thomas, *Early Muslim Polemic*, p. 92.8-19.

[25] The Christological model of two natures and one volition was associated with the Nestorians (cf. Thomas, *Early Muslim Polemic*, p. 90. 21-6), though neither they nor other major denominations made the claims given here about Mary. This may well be al-Dimashqī's own reconstruction on the basis of S. V:116, where God asks Jesus, 'Didst thou say unto mankind: Take me and my mother for two gods beside Allah?'

[26] This is evidently an attempt to explain the origin of the doctrine of the Trinity. It incorporates the assumption that the three Persons of the Godhead were all involved in the Incarnation and so all possessed double natures.

[27] Cf. the teaching attributed to the Melkites by Abū 'Īsā al-Warrāq, that the divine Son united with the universal human, *al-insān al-kullī*, 'the substance which is common to all human individuals', in order to save the whole of humanity (Thomas, *Early Muslim Polemic*, p. 86. 11-15).

وأنهم خرجوا من عنده وكلّ واحد منهم يظنّ أنه هو صاحب السرّ
وحده. وتكلّم كلّ واحد منهم مع طائفته بذلك حتى استقرّ كلامه في
أذهانهم، فاختلفوا وصاروا أربع فرق * لذلك.[109]

* 80r

وإنّ بولص احتجب بعد ذلك سنة ثانية وخرج رسولاً ظاهرًا يزعم أنّ
المسيح أرسله مع بطرس وصدّقوه النصارى، وجعلوه بدلاً عن يهودس[110]
الإسخريوطي المشبّه بالمسيح والمسمّى الشقي. وإنّ بولص أباح للنصارى
أكل المقتول والمخنوق والمنحور وجعل القربان من الخبز والخمر جسد
الربّ، ورقم صورة وجه المسيح وعنقه في منديل ودفعه إلى بطرس فزعم
بطرس أنّ المسيح دفعه إليه في النوم، وكان هذا أوّل تمثال وضعته النصارى
في كنائسها، وإنه هو الدافن لخشبة جعلها خشبة الصلب. وإنّ هيلان أمّ
قسطنطين الصغير نبشتها وحملتها وصفّحتها بالذهب، وكان ذلك أوّل عبادة
النصارى للصليب وتعظيمهم له.

وإنّ النصارى أنكروا رسالة بطرس ونقموا عليه وعذّبوه وطافوا به مخلوق
الذقن مقلّدًا بمصارين الغنم متوّجًا بالكرش، ثمّ تابوا وصدّقوه بتصديق بولص
له، وكان ذلك سبب حلق الفرنج ذقونهم ولبسهم ما هم لابسوه. وكذلك[111]
لبسوا القسيسون الأقماع المائلة تشبّها بالكرش الذي لبسه بطرس تعزيزًا .

They went out from him, each of them with the impression that he alone possessed the secret. Each told it to his group until his words were taken into their thoughts, and they disagreed with one another. And in this way they became four sects. (80r)

After this Paul hid himself for a second year, and then he emerged as a manifest apostle, claiming that Christ had sent him as well as Peter. The Christians believed in him and put him in place of Judas Iscariot, who resembled Christ and was known as 'the wretched'.[28] Paul permitted the Christians to eat what had been slaughtered, strangled and butchered, and instituted the communion of the bread and wine as the body of the Lord. He traced Christ's face and neck on a handkerchief and gave it to Peter, who claimed that Christ had given it to him in his sleep. This was the first representation that the Christians placed in their churches.[29] He was also the one who buried a cross-beam and called it the cross-beam of the crucifixion. Helen, the mother of the young Constantine, unearthed it, took it away, and covered it with gold. This was the first Christian worship and reverencing of the cross.[30]

The Christians spurned Peter's apostleship and grew hostile towards him. They subjected him to torture, led him around with his beard shaved and adorned with the intestines of a sheep and crowned with its stomach. Then they repented and, following Paul putting trust in him, they gave him their trust. This is the reason why the Franks shave their beards and dress in the way they do. In the same way, out of esteem the priests wear sloping funnel-shapes which strongly resemble the sheep's stomach worn by Peter.[31]

---

[28] Cf. § 58 above for a previous mention of Paul replacing Judas. The reference to the latter resembling Christ echoes the traditional interpretation of S. IV: 157, *wa-lākin shubbiha lahum*, that Judas was made to look like Christ and crucified in his place.

[29] 'Abd al-Jabbār, *Tathbīt*, pp. 157-8, earlier accuses Paul of introducing many customs that distorted pristine Christianity. The particular reference here is clearly to the Mandylion, the supposed portrait of Christ that was venerated at Edessa until its transfer to Constantinople in 944 CE (the Greek *mandylion* is often thought to have been derived from the Arabic *mandīl*, the word used here); cf. J.B. Segal, *Edessa, 'The Blessed City'*, Oxford, 1970, pp. 76-8, 214-16. There is no association of this image with Paul in Christian tradition.

[30] The story of the Empress Helena discovering the true cross derives from the fourth century, and ultimately the historian Eusebius, *Vita Constantini*, 3. 41-7. It is mentioned briefly by Ibn Kathīr, *Kāmil*, vol. I, p. 253.

Veneration of the cross was a point of controversy between Muslims and Christians from early times; cf. *EI²*, vol. VIII, p. 981, art. 'al-Ṣalīb'.

[31] It is hard to imagine al-Dimashqī being entirely serious in these fanciful explana-

وأنّ بطرس وضع كتابًا كالملحمة وعزاه إلى المسيح وإنه بجملته كذب وزور. وإنّ بولص وضع رسائل كذلك معروفة به112 معانيها أشبه بلعب الصبيان وحديث النسوان، وإنّ ذلك كله * كان بعد المسيح بنحو من ماية وخمسين سنة أو حولها.

* 80v

77. وكان في هذا التاريخ أشياء لا يليق ذكرها أعرضت عنها احترامًا للملّة والدعوة ولأجل ما هو في كتابنا العزيز من ذكر الإنجيل وذكر النصارى وأنّ ﴿فيهم قسيسين ورهبانًا وأنهم لا يستكبرون﴾113 ولأنه ليس بيننا وبينهم إلا الشرك الذي أحدثوه:

| قل للذي يزعم من جهله | أنّ النصارى يعملون الحساب |
| لو صحّ ذا ما جعلوا واحدًا | ثلاثة، وهو خلاف الصواب. |

وتجسيمهم المعاني المبتدع واتخاذهم دينهم لهوًا ولعبًا كالمرافع قبل صومهم والشعانين والهجمة وتسقية عظام الموتى114 بالزيت وتدويرهم على المسيح في آخر

---

112 B omits this word.   113 S. V: 82.   114 B: المولى (wrongly), evidently a misreading of A.

Peter wrote a book in the form of an epic and imputed it to Christ, though it is entirely false and untrue.[32] In the same way Paul wrote letters known as from him, the import of which is like a children's game or women's chatter.[33] All (80v) this was about a hundred and fifty years after Christ, or thereabouts.

77.   In this account there are things which it is not suitable to mention, and I have avoided them out of respect for religion and mission, and because of what our esteemed Book mentions about the Gospel and the Christians, because among them are 'priests and monks, and because they are not proud', and because between us and them there is nothing more than this associating with God which they have made up:

> Say to the one who claims in his ignorance
>   that the Christians can do their sums,
> 'If this were so they would not make one
>   three, which is far from right.'

There is also the way in which they make much of innovatory elements and take their religion as amusement and game, such as carnivals before their fast, the palm branches, the rush forward, dousing the bones of the dead with oil, their searching for Christ at the end

---

tions of clerical dress. His description of headgear is probably of a bishop's mitre.

[32] While the existence of a Gospel of Peter is attested from early Christian sources (a third/ninth century fragment from Egypt survives, and it is possible that the work was known in Syria; cf. Hennecke, *New Testament Apocrypha*, vol. I, pp. 183-7), the work to which al-Dimashqī refers is likely to be the mysterious book containing revelations given by Peter to his disciple Clement which some sixth/twelfth century Christian authors mention as having been translated into Arabic (cf. Tolan, *Saracens*, pp. 200 and 212). Among these authors, the German canon Oliver of Paderborn (d. 1227), who accompanied the Fifth Crusade, wrote in his *Historia Damiatina*, composed between 1217 and 1222, that this *Liber Clementis* began from the creation and continued until the end of the world, gave prophecies about the capture of cities including Alexandria and Damascus, and predicted the appearance in Jerusalem of two kings from the east and west (*Die Schriften des Kölner Domscholasters, späteren Bischofs von Paderborn und Kardinal-Bischofs von S. Sabina, Oliverus*, ed. O. Hoogweg, Tübingen, 1894, pp. 258-9; trans. J.J. Gavigan, *The Capture of Damietta, by Oliver of Paderborn*, Philadelphia, 1948, p.72). Nearer al-Dimashqī's own time, the book was also known in the late seventh/twelfth century to Fidentius of Padua, who significantly says he was brought it by a Syrian monk; *Liber recuperationis Terrae Sanctae*, in G. Golubovich, *Biblioteca bio-bibliographica della terra sancta e dell' oriente francescano*, 5 vols, Quaracchi, 1906-27, vol. II, p.26. Such a work might appropriately be called a *malḥama*, 'epic' or 'tale of fighting'.

[33] Cf. 2 Peter III: 15-16, where Paul's 'obscure passages' are already a matter for comment.

الصوم وازدرادهم للقطايف العجين بعدد مخصوص وعلوقهم على الخمر ليلاً نهارًا وتركهم الفحص عن الحقّ والعرفان له.

وهذا التاريخ وما ذكر من اللائق ذكره منه، فإنه إن كان حقًّا أو باطلاً فإنما إثمه على المؤرّخ وعهدته على المدوّن منكم أيها النصارى ومن اليهود، لأننا معشر المسلمين متمسّكون بوصيّة نبيّنا صلم حين أوصانا أن "لا تكذّبوا أهل الكتاب ولا تصدّقوهم في ما يذكرونه عن أنبيائهم وفي كتبهم من الموافق لا المخالف الذي هو شرك وجحود وكفر وفسوق"، فإننا[115] نردّه ونلعن قائله * ومعتقده.

* 81r

وسأبيّن لكم أيها النصارى العقلاء الرؤساء في ما أذكره على سبيل الحكاية أنكم إذا أردتم أن تدعوا الله مخلصين له الدين وتطلبوا منه حوائجكم تقولون بأصواتكم وألسنتكم: يا الله، يا ربّنا، يا آب، يا إبن، يا روح القدس، يا مسيح، يا ثلاث أقانيم، يا ثالوث مقدّس، يا إله واحد، يا إنسان تام وإله تام إرحمنا ونجّنا يا من صُلب وقُتل بالحربة، أنت معبودنا ولك سجودنا يا من لم يدفع لاهوته عن ناسوته العذاب والهوان والصلب والموت، بل كان اللاهوت هو الذائق لذلك، فإنّ الناسوت جسم موات مع الأجسام الغير حسّاسة، يا قادر على كلّ شيء، يا عاجز عن خلاص نفسه من إهانة اليهود وصلبهم له، يا من صُلب ومات قدّام العالم ثمّ حيي وقام بشهادة مجنونة وصيّاد واثنين ثلاثة أخبروا أنهم رأوه مختفيًا مستترًا خائفًا من اليهود أن لا يمسكوه مرّة أخرى، نسألك بعجزك عن سلامة نفسك وخلاصها من الصلب آلامًا نجّيتنا ممّا نخاف يا غني يا فقير، يا واحد يا اثنين يا ثلاثة، يا من هو النطق وهو الحياة وهو الروح المرفرفة على الماء سلّمنا.

---

115 B: بآفاتنا (wrongly), evidently a misreading of A.

of the fast, their swallowing a particular number of specially made dough cakes,[34] their dependence on wine night and day, and their abandoning the search for truth and insight into it.

The offence in this account, or the parts that are appropriate to mention whether true or false, is due to its author, and the responsibility for it lies with the one who wrote it down, who is from among you, Christians, and from among the Jews. For we Muslims remain loyal to the command of our Prophet (may God bless him and give him peace), when he instructs us, 'Do not call the People of the Book liars, neither believe them in what they relate from their prophets. For in their books are things that agree, not only things that disagree, such as polytheism, lack of faith, unbelief and iniquity'—we reject it and condemn the one who says it (81r) and the one who takes it as belief.

Christians, leading thinkers, I will show you from what I recall from reports that when you want to pray to God, faithfully worshipping him, and seeking your needs from him, you say with your voices and tongues, 'O God, O our Lord, O Father, O Son, O Holy Spirit, O Christ, O three Persons, O holy Trinity, O one God, O perfect man and perfect God, have mercy on us and rescue us, you who were crucified and killed with the spear, you who are the one we worship and bow before, O you whom suffering, shame, crucifixion and death did not sever your divinity from your humanity, but whose divinity tasted this, whose humanity was a mortal body like other bodies and endowed with senses, O you who have power over all things, O you who were unable to save yourself from humiliation and crucifixion by the Jews, O you who were crucified and died with the world looking on, then came to life and rose, as a deranged woman and fisherman witnessed, and two or three people reported that they saw you in secret and hiding afraid that the Jews might take you a second time,[35] we ask why you were too weak to free your soul and save it from crucifixion, how far can you rescue us from what we feared? O rich, O poor, O one, O two, O three, O you who are Speech, Life and Spirit hovering over the water, save us!'

---

[34] These are elements in the observance of Lent and Holy Week which al-Dimashqī presumably knew from first hand observation.

[35] Cf. Jn XX. 1-9, referring to Mary Magdalene and Peter the fisherman, and also the resurrection appearances in Matthew, Luke and John, where Jesus appears only to the disciples.

وكذلك إذا تضرّعتم ودعوتم بأمّ المسيح او استشفعتم بها في حوائجكم، تقولون: "يا ستّ يا حنونة يا أمّ الإله، يا من ولدت الله بلا زرع، يا عروس لا عرس لها إشفعي لنا * الى ابنك الذي جسمه منك وروحه هي الله وهي من الله"، وكذلك تقولون عند تمثالها في ليلة عيد البشارة وليلة الميلاد، فيا قوم أين تذهبون؟ وما الذي تقولون يا نيام العقول ومخالفين المنقول والمعقول؟ أيّ دين تدينون؟

* 81v

وهذا ومثله رأيكم ومذهبكم. وتدّعون أنكم تسلّمتموه من المسيح وتعالى الله ربّ العالمين.

Similarly, if you entreat and pray to the mother of Christ or ask her intercession for your needs, you say, 'O Lady, O tender one, O mother of God, O you who bore God without seed, O bride without groom, pray for us (81v) to your Son whose body was from you, whose soul is God and from God.'[36] You say similar things before portraits of her on the Eve of the Annunciation and Christmas Eve. But what can you be thinking of, people? And what are you saying, you whose intellects slumber, who clash with what is related and what is reasonable? What religion are you following?

This and the like of it are your ideas and teachings, and you say that you have received it from Christ! God be exalted, Lord of the worlds!

---

[36] This is a fuller form of the prayer quoted in § 20 above.

فصل

ثمّ قلتم سياقا:

فنحن لأجل هذا البيان الواضح الذي قاله الله في التوراة وفي كتب الأنبياء نجعله
ثلاث أقانيم جوهرًا واحدًا طبيعة واحدة إلهًا واحدًا خالقًا واحدًا ربًا واحدًا،
وهذا الذي بقوله: آب وابن وروح قدس. وقد علمنا أنه لا يلزمنا إذا قلنا: ليس
هذا عبادة ثلاثة آلهة بل إله واحد كما لا يلزمنا إذا قلنا الإنسان ونطقه وروحه
ثلاثة أناس ولا إذا قلنا: لهب النار وحرارة النار وضوء النار ثلاث[1] نيران، ولا إذا
قلنا: قرص الشمس وضوء الشمس وشعاع الشمس ثلاث شموس، وإذا كان هذا
رأينا في الله تقدّست اسماؤه فلا لوم علينا ولا ذنب لنا، إذ لم نهمل ما تسلّمنا ولا
نرفض ما تقلّدناه ونتبع ما سواه، ولا سيّما لنا هذه الشهادات البيّنات والدلائل
الواضحات من الكتاب الذي في أيدي هؤلاء القوم، وأعظم حجّتنا ما وجدنا
فيه من الشهادة لنا بأنّ الله جعلنا فوق الذين كفروا إلى يوم القيامة بإتباعنا السيّد
المسيح روح الله وكلمته.

وأمّا تجسيم كلمة الله الخالقة التي بها خلق الله كلّ شيء بإنسان مخلوق، يعني
الذي أخذ من مريم العذراء ﴿المصطفاة على نساء العالمين﴾[2] واتحدت الكلمة
به اتحادًا بريًا من اختلاط[3] أو تغيّر أو استحالة. وخاطب الناس كما خاطب الله
موسى النبي من العوسجة ففعل المعجز بلاهوته وأظهر العجز بناسوته، والفعلان
هما في المسيح الواحد.

وقد جاء أيضًا في هذا الكتاب الذي في أيديهم يقول: ﴿يا عيسى إني متوفيك﴾
الآية[4]، وقال: ﴿وكنت عليهم شهيدًا﴾ الآية[5]، فأعني بموته عن موت الناسوت
الذي أخذ من مريم العذراء. وقال أيضًا: ﴿وما قتلوه وما صلبوه﴾ الآية[6]، فأشار
بهذا القول إلى اللاهوت الذي هو كلمة الله الخالقة.

وقد سمّاه أيضًا في هذا الكتاب خالقًا حيث قال: ﴿وإذ علّمتك الكتاب
والحكمة﴾ الآية[7]، فأشار بالخلق إلى كلمة الله المتحدة في الناسوت المأخوذ من
مريم

---

[1] A and B: ثلاثة   [2] Cf. S. III: 42.   [3] Corrected in A from: الاختلاط; B: الاختلاط
[4] S. III: 55.   [5] S. V: 117.   [6] S. IV: 157.   [7] S. V: 110.

78. *Section [Nine]*

Then, next you say:

> On the basis of this clear demonstration that God gives in the Torah and Books of the Prophets, we make him three hypostases and one substance, one nature, one God, one Creator, one Lord. This is what is meant by Father, Son and Holy Spirit. We know that it does not follow for us from saying this that it is the worship of three gods but of one God, just as it does not follow from saying a man, his speech and his spirit that they are three people, nor from saying a fire's flame, heat and radiance that they are three fires, nor from saying the sun's disk, brightness and beams that they are three suns.[1] If this is our view concerning God, holy be his names, no blame or offence attaches to us for not abandoning what we have received or rejecting what we have been given to hold, and following something else, especially since we have these clear witnesses and obvious proofs from the Book which these people possess. Our most important proof is the witness (82r) in our favour that we find in it, that God has placed us above those who disbelieve until the day of resurrection because we follow the Lord Christ, God's Spirit and Word.[2]
>
> On the matter of the Incarnation of God's creative Word, by which God created all things, in a created man, that is the one taken from the Virgin Mary 'who was chosen above earthly women', and the Word united with him in a union free from mixing, altering or changing, and addressed people as God addressed the prophet Moses from the thorn bush, he performed miracles by his divine nature and exhibited weakness by his human nature, both actions being in the one Christ.
>
> Furthermore, in this Book which they possess occur his words as follows: 'O Jesus! Lo! I am gathering thee' and the rest of the verse; and it says, 'I was a witness of them' and the rest of the verse—by his death it means the death of the human nature which was taken from the Virgin Mary; it also says, 'They slew him not nor crucified' and the rest of the verse, referring by these words to the divine nature which is the creative Word of God.
>
> He has also called him Creator in this Book, because it says, 'How I taught thee the Scripture and Wisdom [and the Torah and the Gospel; and thou didst shape of clay as it were the likeness of a bird by my permission]' and the rest of the verse—by 'shaping' it refers to the Word of God which united in the human nature that was taken from Mary.

---

[1] Analogies of this kind can be traced back to Patristic authors and are known among Muslim polemicists from the time of the earliest encounters with Christians; cf. e.g. al-Qāsim b. Ibrāhīm, *Radd*, p. 315.7-22, and Abū ʿĪsā al-Warrāq's passing reference to them in Thomas, *Anti-Christian Polemic*, pp. 68. 1-3, and 196, n. 8.

[2] Cf. S. III: 55.

لأنه كذا قال على لسان داود النبي: "بكلمة الله خلقت السموات والأرض"[8] لأنه
ليس خالق إلا الله وكلمته وروحه. وهذا ما يوافق رأينا واعتقادنا في السيّد المسيح

* 82v * لذكره السجود لأنه حيث قال: ﴿وخلق من الطين كهيئة الطير ونفخ فيه فكان
طيرًا بإذن الله﴾[9] أي بإذن لاهوت الكلمة المتحدة بالناسوت.

وقال أيضًا: ﴿إنّ مثل عيسى عند الله﴾[10] الآية فأعني بقوله: ﴿مثل آدم﴾[11]
إشارة إلى الناسوت المأخوذ من مريم الطاهرة. وكما أنّ آدم خلق من غير جماع
ولا مباضعة، وكما أنّ جسد آدم[12] ذاق الموت فكذلك جسد المسيح ذاق الموت،
وعلى هذا القياس يقول إنّ المسيح صلب ناسوته ولم يصلب لاهوته.

وقد برهن أيضًا بقوله في موضع آخر قائلاً: ﴿إنّ الله ألقى كلمته إلى مريم﴾[13]
وذلك حسب قولنا معشر النصارى إنّ كلمة الله الخالقة الأزلية حلّت في مريم
وتجسّدت بإنسان كامل. وعلى هذا المثال نقول:[14] في السيّد المسيح طبيعتان:
طبيعة لاهوته التي هي كلمة الله وطبيعة ناسوته الذي أخذ من مريم العذراء واتحدت
الكلمة به.

وأمّا ما تقدّم به القول من الله على لسان موسى إذ يقول: "أليس هذا الآب
الذي خلقك وبراك وأقتناك؟"[15] وعلى لسان داود أيضًا: "بكلمة الله تشدّدت
السموات والأرض وبروح فيه[16] جميع قواهن"[17] فليس يدلّ هذا على ثلاثة خالقين
بل خالق واحد الآب وكلمته أي نطقه وروحه أي حياته.

79. فالجواب: أمّا قولكم في الثلاث أقانيم إنها كالإنسان أو النار أو
الشمس فسيأتي الجواب عنه إن شاء الله، وقد تقدّم من الرمز والإشارة ما فيه

* 83r * كفاية. وأمّا قولكم إنّ كلمة الله تجسّدت وولدتها مريم متحدة بالناسوت
الذي هو الجسم اتحادًا بريًا من إختلاط أو تغيير[18] أو استحالة، وخاطب
الناس كما خاطب الله موسى من العوسجة أو العلّيقة وأنه حلول أو اتحاد،
فتعالى الله عن ذلك وسأبيّن لكم جليّة الحال من كتابنا الذي حصلتموه
عندكم وتدبّرتموه كما قلتم.

فاتلوا[19] قوله تعالى في سورة النمل: ﴿إذ قال موسى لأهله إني آنست
نارًا سآتيكم منها بخبر أو آتيكم بشهاب قبس لعلكم تصطلون فلمّا جاءها
نودي أن بورك من في

---

[8] Psalm XXXIII: 6. [9] Cf. S. III: 49. [10] S. III: 59. [11] *Ibid.* [12] A and B: المسيح
(wrongly). [13] Cf. S. IV: 171. [14] A and B: يقول [15] Deut XXXII: 6. [16] A and B:
فاه [17] Psalm XXXIII: 6. [18] A and B add: أو اختلاط [19] B: قاتلوا (wrongly).

For he says the same on the tongue of the prophet David, 'By the Word of God were the heavens and the earth created', for the only Creator is God, his Word and his Spirit. This is consistent with our opinion and belief about the Lord Christ (to whose mention be reverence), (82v) since he says, 'He created from clay the shape of a bird and breathed into it, and it was a bird by God's leave', that is, by the leave of the divine nature, the Word which united with the human nature.

He also says, 'Lo, the likeness of Jesus with God [is as the likeness of Adam]' and the rest of the verse. By his words 'as the likeness of Adam' he means to refer to the human nature taken from Mary the pure one. Just as Adam was created without intercourse or intimacy, and just as the body of Adam tasted death, so the body of Christ tasted death. By analogy with this, he says that Christ's human nature was crucified but not his divine nature.

This is further proved by his words elsewhere, when he says, 'God conveyed his Word unto Mary.' This is in agreement with the teaching of us Christians that the eternal creative Word of God came to dwell in Mary and was incarnate through a complete human. Accordingly, we say that there were two natures in the Lord Christ, the nature of his divinity which was the Word of God, and the nature of his humanity which he took from the Virgin Mary and the Word united with it.

And concerning the earlier words of God about him on the tongue of Moses, when he says, 'Is not this the Father who created you, restored you and made you his own?', and also on the tongue of David, 'By the Word of God were the heavens and the earth set fast, and by the breath of his mouth all their strength', these do not imply three creators but one Creator, the Father, his Word, that is his speech, and his Spirit, that is his life.

79. *Response*: As for your contention that the three hypostases are like a man or fire or the sun, if God wills a response will be given to this, though there is enough in the suggestions and references above. And as for (83r) your contention that the Word of God was incarnate and Mary gave birth to it united with the human nature, which was the body, in a manner free from mixing, altering or changing, and that it addressed people as God addressed Moses from the thorn bush or burning bush, and that this was indwelling or uniting, well, God is too exalted for such a thing! I will show the true state of affairs clearly to you from our Book which, as you say, you have in your possession and have reflected upon.

So read the exalted One's words in *The Ant*, 'When Moses said unto his household: Lo! I spy afar off a fire; I will bring you tidings thence, or bring to you a borrowed flame that ye may warm yourselves. But when he reached it, he was called, saying: Blessed is Whosoever is in

النار ومن حولها وسبحان الله ربّ العالمين يا موسى إنه أنا الله العزيز الحكيم﴾. ²⁰ أخبر سبحانه وتعالى أنّ الذي في النار وحولها مبارك مقدّس وأنه فعل ما لم يسمّ فاعله بقوله أن بورك الآية، ونزّه نفسه سبحانه عن الحلول فيها والاتحاد بها أو أنه جسم شبيه بالنار أو النار والشجرة مظهر له بقوله: ﴿وسبحان الله ربّ العالمين﴾. ²¹ ونبّه على عظمته العظمى ونفى عن نفسه كلّ ما يخطر في نفوس السامعين من توهّم الكيفية والخبر²² والحصر والحركة والأينية بوصف نفسه بالعزّة والحكمة فالعزيز هو الممتنع جنابه عن الدروك والأوهام والأفهام فلا يرام ولا ينال بتوهّم ولا تخيّل ولا تعقّل ولا يُحاط بعلم، والحكيم المحكم الأشياء المتقنها المرتّب لها على أكمل نظام وأفضل إتقان وأحسن تقويم سبحانه وتعالى.

وأمّا قولكم عمّا * جاء في التوراة من ذكر الشبه والمثال، وهو قوله في السفر الأوّل من التوراة: "فأردنا أن نخلق خلقًا على شبهنا ومثالنا"²³ وأنّ المراد بذلك المسيح لا غيره فليس كذلك بل المراد أن يخلق خليفة في الأرض شبيهًا بالمستخلف له في التصريف في الأرض والتمكين وأن يكون موجودًا حيًا عالمًا مريدًا قادرًا سميعًا بصيرًا متكلّمًا مشيئاً فاعلاً أفعالاً شبيهة بأفعال مستخلفه لا من كلّ وجه، وأن يستدلّ الخليفة بما هو فيه من هذه الصفات المحدثة المقيّدة على الصفات العلية القديمة المطلقة، ونعلم الفرق بين قدرته وقدرة مستخلفه وكذا جميع صفاته، فإذا ظهر له الفرق والبون لم²⁴ يكن كنمرود وفرعون

* 83v

²⁰ S. XXVII: 7-9. ²¹ *Ibid.*: 8. ²² A and B: والخير ²³ Genesis I: 26. ²⁴ B: ولم

the fire and Whosoever is round about it! And glorified be Allah the
Lord of the worlds! O Moses! Lo! It is I, Allah, the Mighty, the Wise!'
May he be praised and exalted, he intimates that the One in the fire
and round about it is blessed and holy, and by his words 'Blessed' and
the rest of the verse that this is a verb whose subject is not named.
He places his exalted self above dwelling within it and uniting with
it, and above being an object similar to fire, or fire with the tree his
outward manifestation, by his words, 'And glorified be God the Lord
of the worlds'. He draws attention to his stupendous greatness, and
dismisses from himself all that might spring up in the souls of those
who listen, such as wondering about manner, advantage, restriction,
movement and direction, by ascribing to himself power and wisdom.
One who is powerful is one who in his honour cannot be apprehended,
imagined or understood at all, he cannot be attained or reached by
imagination, he cannot be conceptualised, grasped or comprehended
by knowledge. And one who is wise is one who is the arbitrator of
things, the one who perfects them and arranges them according to
the most consummate organisation, the most sublime precision and
the most splendid ordering, may he be praised and exalted.

As for your comments about (83v) the reference to resemblance
and likeness that occurs in the Torah, which is his words in the first
book of the Torah, 'We intend to create a human according to our
resemblance and likeness', and that the intention of this is Christ and
no other, this is not so.[3] The intention is that he was going to create
a vicegerent on the earth, bearing a resemblance to the One who
appointed him as vicegerent with full responsibility and delegation
on earth, that he should be existing, living, knowing, willing, powerful, hearing, seeing, speaking, intending and performing acts which
resemble those of the One who appointed him vicegerent, though not
in every respect, and that from the created, limited attributes that are
in him the vicegerent should be able to draw inferences about the
elevated, eternal, unlimited attributes. We know the distinction between
his power and that of the One who appointed him vicegerent, and
the same with all his attributes. If the distinction and difference was
made obvious to him, he would not be like Nimrod and Pharaoh who

---

[3] This reference occurs in the previous quotation from the *Letter* at the start of
Section Eight, § 70, though there the Christians employ it as evidence for the Trinity,
not that Christ was uniquely like God.

الغالطين في الاستخلاف والكافرين بالخلاف بغير خلاف.

80. ولم يذهب[25] مذهبكم الباطل ولا مذهب الثنوية الباطل[26] الذي جذبكم الشيطان إليه جذبًا عنيفًا وأنتم تبصرون وساقكم إلى التثليث به وأنتم لا تشعرون فأراكم إلهين اثنين: إلهًا في السماء وإلهًا في الأرض ووسوس[27] لكم أنّ إله الأرض قويّ على إله السماء فحبس أنبياءه ورسله وحزبه في الجحيم أي آدم وذرّيته.

كما زعمتم في سبب نزول المسيح أنه لم ينزل إلى الأرض إلا لخلاص آدم وذرّيته من الجحيم، فوسوس لكم أنّ إله السماء فكّر طويلًا في كيفية خلاص حزبه من حبس إله الأرض فلم يجد في الملائكة من يقوم بذلك، ففصل كلمته التي هي * صفة ذاته وخالقة معه كما زعمتم وأرسلها مع أمين الملائكة إلى الارض وأمره أن يختار لها ذاتًا حسّاسة من البشر القريبين إلى إله الارض بالمشابهة له فيمازجها بها ويتلطف ما أمكنه حتى تمتزج الكلمة التي هي في الحقيقة لا أين لها ولا كيفية ولا كمية امتزاجًا تامًا بتلك الطينة الأرضية العنصرية ويكون منها إذا اتحدت بها ولدًا إلهًا ممزوجًا من الكلمة والذات الحسّاسة كما زعمتم، فخرج من بين الفرث والدم ومجرى الأنجاس والأثقال إلهًا تامًا وإنسانًا تامًا ابنًا ممزوجًا متحدًا فيه اللاهوت[28] بالناسوت ففعله المعجز بجوهر أبيه وعجزه وبشريّة من أمّه الذات الحسّاسة كما زعمتم.

فلما نزل الملك[29] بالكلمة المفصولة عن المتكلّم بها وبقي المتكلّم بزعمكم بلا كلمة لان كلمته الخالقة التي بها "تشدّدت السموات

---

took their positions as vicegerent wrongly, and rejected the difference as not being different.[4]

80.   Neither your false faith nor the false faith of the dualists which Satan has harshly attracted you to, even though you can see, has ceased to exist.[5] And he has driven you to Trinitarian belief in it, although you are not aware, and has shown you two gods, a god in heaven and a god on earth. He has seduced you into believing that the god of earth has power over the god of heaven and has shut up in hell his prophets, messengers and supporters, that is, Adam and his descendants.

This is what you claim about the reason for the descent of Christ: he descended to earth expressly to free Adam and his offspring from hell. So he seduced you into believing that the god of heaven thought for a long time as to how his supporters might be freed from the god of earth's imprisonment. He could not find among the angels any who would undertake this, so he divided off his Word, which as you claim was (84r) an attribute of his essence and Creator with him, and sent it together with the foremost of the angels to earth.[6] He ordered the latter to chose for it a perceptive essence from the humans who were closest to the god of earth in likeness. He should mix it with her as secretly as he could until the Word, which in reality has no origin, mode or quantity, was blended completely with this being of clay and earthly elements, and when it had united with her she should have a divine child who would be a mixture of the Word and the perceptive essence, as you claim. So, from undigested waste and blood, and the passage of filth and soil he emerged as perfect god and perfect man, a son in whom were mixed and united divine and human natures, his performance of miracles coming from the substance of his Father, and his weakness and humanity from his mother the perceptive essence, as you claim.

When the angel descended with the Word which was separated off from the One who spoke through it, the One who spoke was left without Word, as you claim. For his creative Word, 'by which the heavens

---

[4] Cf. the poem in § 68 and Section 7, n. 11. Nimrod and Pharaoh are both depicted in the Qur'an and Muslim tradition as attempting to usurp God's position.

[5] This account repeats the main points of the earlier account in § 32, though here al-Dimashqī concentrates more on the theological implications of the Incarnation and the death of Jesus.

[6] As the context implies, this must be the angel Gabriel, cf. Lk 1.26.

والأرض" وهي ثلث إله السماء أي النطق الذي هو أحد الأقانيم الثلاثة انفصلت عن الآب وعن روح القدس الأقنومين الباقيين. وانحلَّ بذلك تركيبهم الجوهري عند انفصالها واتصالها بالذات الحسّاسة وتجسّدها إنسانًا كما زعمتم في أمانتكم وكما ذكرتم الآن في رسالتكم هذه.

ثمَّ إنَّ الشيطان وسوس لكم بعد ذلك أنَّ إله السماء لمّا صار له هذا الولد السمائي والأرضي وحضنته أمَّه وزيّنته لم يفطن به إله الأرض حتى شبَّ وعمل العجائب مثل أنه قلب الخمر وصبغ * الثياب ألوانًا من صبغ واحد وظهر للفرس المرسلين إليه في صورة شيخ للشيخ منهم وصورة شاب للشاب منهم وصورة صبي للصبي منهم، ومثل هذه الأشياء التي زعمتم أنها عجيباته.

*84v

ثمَّ فطن له بعد ذلك فاختطفه[30] كما زعمتم وجرّه جرًّا عنيفًا وذهب به ليهلكه بالجوع والعطش، ثمَّ أمره أن يسجد له سجدة واحدة فأبى الولد أن يسجد له وقال له: "لا أسجد إلا لإله السماء" كما زعمتم في أناجيلكم.

ثمَّ إنَّ هذا الولد الممزوج سعى في خلاص آدم وذرّيته من الجحيم وأراد فتح بابها فما مكنه إله الأرض ولكنَّه سلَّط عليه طائفة من اليهود، مسكوه وحبسوه ثمَّ عزروه وشهروه ثمَّ قتلوه وصلبوه. وفرح إله الأرض حيث

---

30 B: فأخطفه

and the earth were established', which was one third of the god of heaven, Speech which was one of the three hypostases, was detached from the Father and the Holy Spirit, the two remaining hypostases.[7] In consequence their construction as substance was weakened by its detachment and joining to the perceptive essence and its incarnation as a man, as you claim in your Creed and as you have now mentioned in this *Letter* of yours.

Then, after this Satan seduced you into believing that when the god of heaven had this heavenly and earthly child, and his mother nursed him and gave him comeliness, the god of the earth did not become aware of him until he grew up and performed miracles, such as transforming the wine,[8] colouring (84v) cloths differently with one colour,[9] appearing to the Persians who were sent to him in the form of an old man to the old man among them, in the form of a young man to the young man among them, and in the form of a youth to the youth among them,[10] and similar things that you claim were his miracles.

After this he did become aware of him and snatched him away, as you claim, dragging him harshly along and taking him off to destroy him with hunger and thirst. Then he commanded him to prostrate before him once, but the child refused to do this, saying to him, 'I will only prostrate before the god of heaven', as you claim in your Gospels.[11]

Then this child who was a mixture tried to free Adam and his descendants from hell and attempted to open its doors, but the god of earth did not make this possible for him. Rather, he gave a group of Jews power over him; they grabbed him and put him in jail, they heaped blame and insults on him, and then they killed and crucified him. The god of earth was delighted at the fact that they had cruci-

---

[7] This notion of a portion of the Godhead being detached from it is referred to by al-Māturīdī in the fourth/tenth century; cf. Thomas, 'Abū Manṣūr al-Māturīdī', p. 50. 2-11.

[8] Cf. Jn II: 1-11.

[9] Cf. Section 6, n. 21 above. The reference here is fuller than previously, and indicates that al-Dimashqī knows a similar version of the miracle to that given by al-Thaʿlabī, *Qiṣaṣ al-anbiyāʾ*, pp. 389-90.

[10] Cf. Mtt II: 1-12. The miracle of Jesus changing appearance was sufficiently widespread at this time for Marco Polo to have heard it in Persia during his travels about fifty years before al-Dimashqī wrote; cf. Marco Polo, *La divisement du monde*, vol. I, ed. Marie-Luce Chênerie *et al.*, Geneva, 2001, pp. 151 and 204 n. 30.17.

[11] Cf. Mtt IV: 1-11 ‖ Mk I: 12-13, Lk IV: 1-13, and the earlier reference to this in § 72 above.

صلبوا الجسد بالكلمة وقتلوها به، إذ لم تزل متحدة به كما قلتم في أمانتكم: "إنَّ المسيح ألم وصلب وذاق الموت"، فذوق الموت ليس للجسد دون الروح ولا للناسوت دون اللاهوت لأنَّ الجسد موات من حيثه لا حياة له ولا إحساس وإنما الحياة والإحساس للروح بواسطته كما قلتم في اللطائف: وإنها لا تظهر إلا في الكثائف.

وقلتم أيضًا في الكلمة: "وإنها تجسَّمت من مريم فكانت جسمًا مع الجسم متحدة به بغير انفصال"، فلمَّا صلب هذا الولد الممزوج بزعمكم وذاق الموت اتصل ذوقان ذلك إلى الحياة وإلى الآب الأقنومين الباقيين * ونقض 85r * تركيب الإله المثلّث بزعمكم عند فقده للنطق وعاد أمر آدم وذرِّيته إلى شرٍّ ممَّا كانوا عليه وعطَّلت إلهية إله السماء بزعمكم وعظم إله الأرض عند قتله لإبن إله السماء.

فتدبَّروا هذه الأضحوكات المبكيات وابكوا منها أو اضحكوا على عقول رأت هذا الرأي وذهبت هذا المذهب.

81. وأمَّا قولكم إنَّ المسيح لمَّا خرج من مريم فعل المعجز بلاهوته وفعل العجز بناسوته وإنه في موته كآدم في موته مات ناسوته ولم يمت لاهوته إذ الناسوت طبيعة واللاهوت طبيعة، فقد قدَّمنا من البيان ما فيه كفاية في أنَّ كلمة الله صفة ذاتية لا تتجسَّم ولا تتكيَّف ولا تتحد بالجسم ولا تحلَّ في جسد، وأغلطنا القول عليكم وصدعنا بالحقّ شفقة عليكم ومحبّة للنوع الإنساني ورحمة وبيانًا لبطلان هذه الدعوى وإنذارًا لكم من الشرك فإنه ظلم عظيم، وكيف يصحّ ما قلتم والناسوت باصطلاحكم جسم موات داخل في جنس الأجسام لا يحسّ ولا يتحرَّك ولا يحيا

fied the body with the Word and killed the Word with it because it remained united with it, as you say in your Creed: Christ suffered, was crucified, and experienced death. To experience death is not something for the body without the spirit, nor for the human nature without the divine nature. For the body is lifeless when it has no spirit or sensation, and life and sensation belong to the spirit by means of it; as you say about refined entities, they are only apparent through the physical.

You also say about the Word: It took flesh from Mary and was a physical object together with the physical object with which it was united without separation. When this child which was a mixture was crucified, as you claim, and experienced death, the experiences that affected him also affected Life and the Father, the two remaining hypostases, (85r) and the structure of the Trinitarian God, as you claim it, was destroyed when it lost Speech. The condition of Adam and his descendants returned to a worse state than before, the god of heaven's divinity was paralysed, as you claim, and the god of earth grew powerful when he killed the son of the god of heaven.

Think about all this lamentable ridiculousness, and either lament it or ridicule the minds that harbour this opinion and maintain this doctrine.

81.   As for your words that when Christ emerged from Mary he performed miracles through his divine nature and exhibited weakness through his human nature, and that in his death he was like Adam in his death, his human nature dying but not his divine nature because the humanity was one nature and the divinity was another, we have already given enough explanation about this above to show that the word of God is an essential attribute which does not become flesh, take on a shape, unite with a physical object or inhere within a body.[12] We have shown by argument that you are in the wrong, and we have uttered the truth openly out of sympathy for you, love for the human species, compassion to make plain the falseness of this claim, and as a warning to you against associating with God, which is profound wickedness.

And how can what you say be true, when according to your convention the human nature was physical and mortal, included in the genus of physical things which have no sensation, do not move or live

---

[12] Cf. § 65 above.

إلا بالروح؟ فالحياة والموت واللذة والألم والحركة و السكون والإحساس،
كلّ ذلك من صفات الروح لا الجسم ولا يتصف الروح بالحياة المعلومة
والصفات المذكورة إلا بعد تركيبها مع الجسد ونفخها فيه واتّحادها به
بالوصف لا بالذات، فإنّ ذات الروح بسيطة * روحانية وللمتكلّمين على * 85v
ماهيتها ومعناها آراء أحدها أنها جسم لطيف سار[31] في جميع أجزاء الجسم
محمول على بخار الدم اللطيف وتسمّى روحًا وأرواحًا وأنها الموجودة في
النبات والحيوان والإنسان وكلّ حيّ ذي حياة كذلك وأنها تموت بموت
البدن وتدثر بدثوره وهي غير نفس الإنسان الناطقة.

هذا رأي الثاني: إنها حياة سارية في أجزاء العالم العلوي والسفلي كسريان
النار في زيرة الحديد الحامية بها، وأنها جوهر لطيف حيّ روحاني مفاض على
كلّ جزء من أجزاء العالم بحسبه مستعلن بفيضه في الحيوان وفي الإنسان
استعلانًا بالحسّ والحركة ومستعلن في النبات بالنموّ والتصوير والتغذّي، وفي
بواقي الأشياء بحسب تلك الأشياء محمولة على كلّ موضوع ولا يقال فيها
إنها تموت ولا إنها تحيا ولا إنها العقل ولا النفس ولا الحرارة المنبعثة ولا
الطبيعة الفاعلة ولا إنّ لها وجودًا بعد موت البدن كوجودها به.

الثالث: إنها جنس روحاني تحته أنواع روحية كلّ نوع غير نوع من
وجه وكأنه هو من وجه، فمن هذا الجنس روح كلّية حاملة نظام العالم
بجزئياته وكلّياته وتسمّى الطبيعة الفاعلة المنفعلة في كلّ شيء ومنها روح
المعدن * وتسمّى الخاصية وهي يعنون هذا الروح في المولدات الثلاثة[32] وفي * 86r
الإنسان، ومنها روح النبات وتسمّى النفس النامية، وهذه هي في النبات
والحيوان والإنسان دون المعدن، ومنها روح الحيوان وتسمّى النفس الحيوانية
ولها الحسّ والحركة وهي في الحيوان والإنسان دون النبات والمعدن، ومنها
روح الإنسان التامة الإحساس والحركات والمتصفة بسائر أوصاف الإنسان
الحيوانية التي هي الحبّ والبغض والرضاء والغضب والخوف والأمن والإقبال
والإدبار والشهوة والكراهية وسائر صفاته الحيوانية المتفرّقة في

---

[31] A and B: ساري [32] A and B: الثلاث

except through the spirit? For life, death, pleasure, pain, movement, rest, sensation, are all attributes of the spirit not of a physical body, and the spirit is only described as life in the acknowledged way, and as the attributes just mentioned, after it has been put together with the human body, been breathed into it and been united with it in the form of property not of essence. For the essence of the spirit is simple (85v) and immaterial, and theologians have many views about its nature and significance.

One is that it is a refined physical entity which moves through all the parts of physical things carried on the vapour of the light blood, and is called breath and breaths. It is found in plants, animals, humans and every living thing that has life in this sense. It dies with the death of the body and becomes extinct with it, and it is different from the rational soul of the human being.

Here is a second view: It is the life that moves through the parts of the higher and lower world in the way that fire moves throughout an iron vessel that has been heated by it. It is a refined substance, living and immaterial, which is spread through every part of the world: in proportion to its being spread through the animal or human it is revealed in sensation and movement, revealed in plants in growth, taking form and nutrition, and in remaining things in proportion to these things. It is carried to every place, and cannot be said to die or to live, to be intellect or soul, to be the heat given off or the active nature, or to have existence after the death of the body as it has with it.

A third: It is an immaterial genus which includes immaterial species each one of which differs from another in some aspect, although it is identical in another aspect. To this genus belongs the universal spirit which supports the arrangement of the world in its parts and its whole and is called the active nature which operates in every thing. There is also the originating spirit (86r) which is called specific, the one they think of in the three forms of generation, and in humans. There is also the spirit of plants, which is called the soul that gives growth, the one that is in plants, animals and humans in addition to the originating. There is also the spirit of animals, which is called the animal soul and to which feeling and movement are due, the one that is in animals and humans in addition to the growing and originating. There is also the spirit of humans of perfect sensations and movements, which is characterised by all the animal properties of the human, love, hate, delight, anger, fear, contentment, attentiveness, indifference, attraction, repulsion and all his animal qualities which are naturally dispersed

الحيوان بالطبع والمجموعة في الإنسان بالخاصية والقصد كالكيد والمكر والحسد والتخيّل والغيلة. وإذا تحلّل تركيب الإنسان ذهبت عنه وبقي منها الروح الحاملة للنظام والمسمّاة الطبيعة الفاعلة المنفعلة فقط، ومنها الروح النفساني المختصة بالإنسان وتسمّى النفس الإنسانية المشتركة بين الحيوانية والناطقة والمتصفة بالفضائل والرذائل وليست بموجودة في الحيوان ولا في النبات ومنها النفس الناطقة الحيّة الداركة لذاتها ولغيرها والعاقلة الشاعرة ببعض المغيب والفاعلة بقواها ما لا يفعله الحيوان والنبات ولها سبع قوى خواص باطنة وخمس قوى حواس ظاهرة، فالباطنة * الحسّ المشترك والمتخيّلة والمتوهّمة والمفكرة العاقلة والمتفهّمة والذاكرة والحافظة، والظاهرة السمع والبصر والذوق والشمّ واللمس ومنها روح الأرواح المدركة القابلة للفيض الإلهي والوحي الإلهامي والكلام الربّاني المسموع لها بواسطة حجاب من الحجب المعنوية الروحانية أو رسول من الملائكة الأقدسين النورية أو وحي أو نوم أو بنفث في الروح أو خطاب باللسان المطلق، وهذه الروح هي العقل والجوهر المفارق والملك الكروبي الذي به ظهور التدبير في المملكة الإنسانية وبه الأخذ والعطاء وهو المخلوق في أحسن تقويم وعند أصحاب هذا الرأي أنه لا يموت [33]بموت البدن بل يبقى جوهرًا مجردًا حيًّا مرتسمًا فيه وله وبه مكتسباته ومستفاداته ومعلوماته أبدًا وأنه من المخلوقين للبقاء فعّال بقابليته المستعدة للفيض العلي وللاتصاف بالصفات الفعلية الإضافية كما قال الحكماء إنّ النفس معبودة للجسم، فإذا اتصف بصفاتها كان هو هي من غير اتحاد لأن الاتحاد محال وإنّ العقل معبود للنفس، فإذا اتصفت بصفاته كانت هي هو من غير اتحاد * وإنّ الحقّ معبود للعقل فإذا اتصف بصفاته كان هو هو من غير اتحاد.

فقولكم أيها النصارى إنّ المسيح مات ناسوته ولم يمت لاهوته ولا عجز بعجزه ولا وجد الألم بوجدانه الألم غير مسلّم لأن الجسد من حيث هو فإنه موات لا إحساس له ولا حياة إلا بالروح وهي الواجدة الذائقة والمدركة بالحواس والخواص

* 86v

* 87r

---

in animals, and specifically and intentionally collected in the human, such as cunning, wiliness, envy, fancifulness and destructiveness. If the composition of the human is dissolved they depart from him, and there remains only the spirit that preserves the arrangement, also called the active, operative nature. There is also the mental spirit which is specific to the human, called the human soul, sharing the animal and the rational, characterised by virtues and vices, not found in animals or plants. There is also the rational living soul that is aware of itself and others, understanding and seeing into some of the unknown. By its power it performs what animals and plants cannot, endowed with seven specific hidden powers and five manifest sensory powers, the hidden (86v) being collective sense, fancy, imagination, rational reflection, comprehension, memory and retention, and the manifest being hearing, sight, taste, smell and touch. There is also the highest spirit which is perceptive of and receptive to divine emanation and instinctive revelation, and to the word of the Lord which is audible to it through one of the abstract, immaterial veils, or a messenger from one of the most holy angels of light, or revelation during sleep or through an inspiration in the spirit, or a direct, oral address. This spirit is intelligence, a separate substance, and the cherub angel through whom control in the human realm and receiving and giving are made manifest. It was created in the most splendid rank and, according to the advocates of this opinion, it does not die at the death of the body but continues as a free and living substance, with all the person's characteristics, traits and marks of distinction for ever impressed within it, upon it and beside it. Of created things it is directed towards the active eternal because of its predisposed receptivity towards the sublime emanation, and because of its being distinguished by the active, relative attributes. As the philosophers say, the soul is served by the body, so if the latter is characterised by the soul's attributes it is identical with it, though without uniting because uniting is impossible; the intellect is served by the soul, so if the latter is characterised by the intellect's attributes it is identical with it, though without uniting; (87r) truth is served by the intellect, so if the latter is distinguished by its attributes it is identical with it, though without uniting.

So, Christians, your teaching that Christ's human nature died but not his divine nature, that it was not weak as he was weak, and did not feel suffering as he did, is not beyond dispute. For in itself the body is mortal, and only possesses senses and life through the spirit. It is this that experiences, tastes and perceives all the rational and sensory

منه سائر المدركات المعقولة والمحسوسة دونه إذ هو موات داخل في حكم الجسمية بالنوعية والشخصية.

ولا يخلو المسيح من أن يكون فيه هذه الأرواح المذكورة والنفس الناطقة مع اللاهوت الذي زعمتم، أو يكون اللاهوت وحده أو المجموع دونه، وللائق أن يكون اللاهوت متحدًا بعقل المسيح ونفسه الناطقة وروحه اللطائف الثلاث دون الجسد الكثيف العنصري. وإذا كان ذلك لزم أن يكون اللاهوت هو المدرك للألم والذائق للموت دون الناسوت، فإنّ الناسوت موات لم يزل ميتاً بالذات وحياته عرضية فيه طارئة عليه فانتفى [34] أن يكون الناسوت واجدًا للموت والألم والتعذيب بل اللاهوت الذي سمّيتموه إلهًا ربًا خالقًا، والذي شهدتم بشهادة أناجيلكم * شهادة عيب محض وشرك صريح وأضحوكة يعجب منها العقلاء، إذ تستشهدون بجلوس المسيح الإبن عن يمين ربّ العالمين الآب بزعمكم مع تقدّم الشهادة منكم بأنهما واحد لا اثنان ولا شخصية لهما [35] ولا تجزئ ولا تبعيض ولا أبوّة تناسل كالمعروفة ولا بنوّة كالمعهودة، فالله أكبر وأجلّ وأعظم "وسبحانه عما يشركون"، فلو فحصتم عن الشيء الحيّ الذي هو لا كالأشياء فحصًا بالحقّ لثبت بالدليل القطعي أنّ ذاته لا كالذوات وصفاته لا كالصفات ولخررتم بعقولكم له ساجدين واجدين قائلين بالحال والمقال (شعر):

* 87v

وصفاته التلويح والتصريح	يا من تعالى أن يحوز بذاته
لكن تنزّلك اللطيف يبوح	أنت العلي عن الصفات بأسرها
وتخيّل وتوهّم سبوح	والقول منّا عند كلّ تعقّل

---

[34] B: فانتفاء (wrongly), a misreading of A.   [35] B: لها

stimuli by means of the former's senses and particular properties, though it is distinct from it since this is mortal and included within the category of corporeal under species and individual.

Christ must have had in him these spirits just mentioned and a rational soul as well as the divine nature you claim, or else he must have been the divine nature alone or a composite without it. It would be appropriate for the divine nature to be united with Christ's intellect, rational soul and refined spirit, the three separate from the physical, elemental body. If this was so, the divine nature must have been susceptible to pain and able to suffer death separate from the human nature, and the human nature must have been without life, was always mortal in its essence, and its life was accidental in it and extraneous to it. Thus it could not have been the human nature that felt death, pain and torture but the divine nature, which you call God, Lord and Creator. You confirm this by the witness of your Gospels, (87v) a witness that is utterly defective and is obvious associating with God, that causes mirth and amazement among scholars. For you cite the fact that Christ, the Son, was seated at the right hand of the Lord of the worlds, the Father in your claim, in the face of the earlier witness of yours that they are one not two,[13] do not have individuality, separation or division, and do not have fatherhood through reproduction in the acknowledged way nor sonship in the accepted manner. But God is most great, glorious and powerful, and 'is exalted above their associating him'. For if you were to investigate the Living who is not like other things, and you did this conscientiously, it would be confirmed by incontrovertible proof that his essence was not like other essences and his attributes not like other attributes. And then you would fall down with your intellects prostrate and entranced, saying directly and affirmatively (poem):

> O you who are too exalted for your essence
>   and attributes to be explicated or explained,
> You are high above attributes altogether,
>   though your delicate stooping down is known;
> And words from us, all attempts at reason,
>   fancy and supposition, are praise.

---

[13] This is a reference to the two articles in the Nicene Creed that the Son was 'of one being with the Father', and that after his ascension he was 'seated at the right hand of the Father'.

فصل

ثمّ قلتم سياقًا إنّ كليام وجماعته قالوا لكم إنّ المسلمين يقولون: "إذا كان اعتقادكم في الباري أنّه واحد متصف بثلاث صفات ، فما حملكم على أن تقولوا: آب وابن وروح قدس ؟، فتوهمون السامعين أنكم تعتقدون في الله أنه ثلاثة أشخاص أو مجزّءاً ثلاثة أجزاء أو أنه ثلاثة آلهة أو أن يكون له ابن من المباضعة." * فيظنّ من لا يعلم قولهم ولا يعرف اعتقادهم أنهم يظنّون ذلك فيطرقون على أنفسهم تهمة هم منها بريئون. وإنكم أجبتم كليام وجماعته قائلين لهم:

فالمسلمون مع اعتقادهم في الباري أنه غير جسم وغير ذي[1] أعضاء وغير محصور في مكان يقولون إنّ لله عينين ويدين ووجهًا ونفسًا وساقًا[2] يكشفه للسجود وأنه يأتي في ﴿ظلل من الغمام﴾[3] ومع الملائكة وينتقل من مكان إلى مكان، ويوهمون التجسيم، ويظنّ من لا يعرف اعتقادهم أنهم مجسّمة ومشبّهة فيتهمهم بما هم منه بريئون.

وإنّ كليام وجماعته قالوا لكم إنّ المسلمين يقولون إنّ العلة في قولنا: ما عددتموه من الصفات هو أنّ القرآن نطق به وأنّ ذلك على غير ظاهره وأنّ كلّ من يحمل ذلك على ظاهر اللفظ أو يعتقد أنّ الله جسم ذو جوارح وأعضاء وانتقال وحركة وغير ذلك ممّا يقتضي التجسيم والتشبيه فنحن نلعنه ونكفّره، وإننا إذا كفّرنا من يعتقد ذلك فليس لمخالفينا أن يلزمونا به بعد أن لا نعتقده.[4]

وإنكم قلتم لكليام وجماعته مجاوبين:

وكذلك نحن أيضًا العلّة في قولنا إنّ الله ثلاثة أقانيم: آب وابن وروح قدس أنّ الإنجيل نطق به والمراد بالأقانيم غير الأشخاص المركّبة والأجزاء والأبعاض

---

[1] B: أي (wrongly), a misreading of A.   [2] A and B: عينان ويدان ووجه ونفس وساق
[3] S. II: 210.   [4] A and B: يعتقده

82.   *Section [Ten]*

Then following this you say that Kilyām and the people with him[1]
told you that the Muslims said, 'If your belief about the Creator is
that he is one characterised by three attributes, then what has induced
you to say: Father, Son and Holy Spirit? For you cause those who hear
you to suppose that you believe either that God is three individuals,
or is divided into three parts, or is three gods, or that he has a son
through sexual intercourse.' (88r) Anyone who does not know their
teaching or is unacquainted with their belief might think that this
is what they hold, so that they will bring suspicion upon themselves
even though they are innocent of it. You answered Kilyām and the
people with him, saying to them:

> Despite their belief that the Creator is not a physical object, has no organs
> and is not limited by place, the Muslims say that God has two eyes, two
> hands, a face, a soul and a thigh which he reveals when he bows, and
> that he comes in the darkness of the clouds and with the angels, and
> moves from place to place.[2] They give an impression of believing that
> God has a body, and anyone who was not acquainted with their belief
> might think they were corporealists and anthropomorphists, suspecting
> them of something of which they are innocent.

Kilyām and the people with him told you that the Muslims said: The
reason why we say, 'Why have you multiplied him in accordance with
the attributes?' is that while the Qur'an speaks about this it is not
literal, and we condemn and accuse of unbelief everyone who takes
this literally or believes that God is a body, with limbs, organs, change
of position, movement and other features that necessitate corpereal-
ism and anthropomorphism. If we accuse anyone who believes this
of unbelief, then our opponents are in no position to impose it upon
us when we do not believe it!

You also said to Kilyām and the people with him in answer:

> It is exactly the same with us. The reason we say that God is three
> hypostases, Father, Son and Holy Spirit, is that the Gospel speaks about
> it. What is intended by 'hypostases' is not composite individuals, parts or
> divisions and everything required by (88v) partnership and plurality, for
> the Father and Son are not the fatherhood of wedlock, procreation or

---

[1] These are the 'clever and acute people' accompanying Kilyām referred to in
§ 59.

[2] Al-Dimashqī identifies these anthropomorphic references in § 85 below.

وكلّ ما تقتضيه * الشركة والتكثير، فالآب والابن غير أبوّة نكاح أو تناسل
أو جماع وكلّ من يعتقد أنّ الأقانيم الثلاثة آلهة مختلفة أو متفقة أو ثلاثة أشخاص
مركّبة أو قوى أو أعراض أو كلّ ما يتقضيه الإشتراك والتكثير والتحسيم والتبعيض
فنحن نلعنه ونحرّمه ونكفّره ونكفر به، وإذا لعنّا من يعتقد ذلك فليس لمخالفينا أن
يلزمونا بما لا نعتقده.

فإن الزمونا الشرك والتشبيه لأجل قولنا إنّ الله جوهر واحد ثلاث أقانيم
آب وابن وروح قدس ألزمناهم نحن أيضًا التحسيم والتشبيه لقولهم إنّ
الله له عينان ويدان ووجه وجنب وإنه ﴿استوى الى السماء﴾[5] ﴿واستوى
على العرش﴾[6] بعد أن لم يكن عليه وغير ذلك ممّا يقتضي ظاهرة التحسيم
والتشبيه.

83.   فالجواب: أمّا قولكم إنّ الباري جلّ جلاله ثلاثة أقانيم آب وابن
وروح قدس وبراءتكم مع ذلك من الشرك ومن اعتقاد الجسمية والتشبيه
وإنكم لم تريدوا بقولكم: الآب والإبن والروح[7] إلا تعداد صفات الإله
الواحد وإنكم من علمتم منه ذلك لعنتموه وكفّرتموه وحرمتموه، فافتحوا
أعينكم واصغوا بأسماعكم واحضروا بقلوبكم واعقلوا ما قلتم.

فإنكم لن تحدوا على وجه الأرض من لدن قسطنطين وإلى يومنا هذا
نصرانيًّا إلا وهو يقول في الإله إنه ثلاثة آلهة شركاء في الإلهية إله واحد وهم *
الآب المغاير للإبن[8]، والإبن المغاير للآب في اللفظ والمعنى والتسمية والمسمّى،
وروح القدس المغايرة لهما والثلاثة واحد في الكيان مثلّث في الكيفية، فالآب
أصل وعلّة والابن فرع ومعلول والروح متوسّطة بينهما كتوسّط النفس بين
العقل والجسد مع ألوف ألوف مؤلّفة في كلّ زمن من الأزمنة عامّة وجاهلية
النصارى يعتقدون المباضعة والجماع والتناسل، ويصوّرون[9] صورة تمثال كبير
الجبهة ويخرجون[10] من فيه خطًا أحمر[11] ممتدًا من صورة الفم نازلاً إلى جوف
تمثال مريم حكاية للمباضعة الروحية الجسمية. ولا شرك ولا تحسيم

---

[5] S. II: 29.   [6] S. VII: 54, S. X: 3, S. XIII: 2, S. XX: 5, S. XXV: 59.   [7] B omits
this word.   [8] A and B add: في   [9] A and B: وتصورون   [10] A and B: وتخرجون   [11] A
and B: أحمراً

reproduction. We curse, excommunicate, accuse of unbelief and show no gratitude towards everyone who believes that the three hypostases are three different or coincident gods, three composite individuals, powers or accidents, or anything required by partnership, plurality, corporeality or division. And if we curse anyone who believes this, our opponents are not in any position to impose upon us what we do not believe.

Thus, if they force us to acknowledge polytheism and anthropomorphism on account of our teaching that God is one substance and three hypostases, Father, Son and Holy Spirit, we in turn force them to acknowledge corporealism and anthropomorphism because of their teaching that God has two eyes, two hands, a face and a side, that he is seated in heaven, sat on the throne after not being on it,[3] and other things that necessitate obvious corporealism and anthropomorphism.

83. *Response*: As for your teaching that the Creator, great is his glory, is three hypostases, Father, Son and Holy Spirit, and despite this your being innocent of polytheism and belief in corporealism and anthropomorphism, that you only intend by your words Father, Son and Spirit to enumerate the attributes of the one God, and that you curse and accuse of unbelief and excommunicate anyone from whom you ascertain this, open your eyes, listen closely, concentrate, and realise what you have said.

Nowhere on the face of the earth, from the time of Constantine to the present, could you find a Christian who would not say that God is three gods who share in divinity as one God, (89r) the Father who is distinct from the Son, the Son who is distinct from the Father in word, meaning, designation and appellation, and the Holy Spirit who is distinct from both of them; the three are one in being and triple in modality, for the Father is origin and cause, the Son is derived and caused, and the Spirit is central between them as the soul is central between the intellect and the body. And thousands upon thousands of Christians from every single period in the common era and before have expressed belief in sexual intercourse, reproduction and procreation. They have painted a picture of a figure with a great forehead, and have traced from his mouth a red line extending from the mouth-shape down to the womb of the figure of Mary as a representation of spiritual and physical intercourse.[4] There is no polytheism, corporealism

---

[3] Verses such as SS. VII: 54, X: 3 and XIII: 2 appear to suggest that God mounted the heavenly throne after completing the creation.

[4] The precise details of this description suggest that al-Dimashqī is recalling a particular painting he has seen. In Annunciation scenes from this period it is conven-

ولا فرِيّة على الله أعظم من هذا، فالعنوا هؤلاء من البحر إلى البحر.

وما مثلكم في جحودكم الشرك[12] وبراءتكم منه مع القول بالثالوث واصطلاحكم على الأقانيم وتفسيركم لما في التوراة من قوله عن آدم وإنه طلب أن يكون كواحد منّا تعنون الآب والابن حيث أصعدتموه من الأرض إلى أبيه وأجلستموه عن يمين أبيه معه على العرش إلا كمثل امرأة شكت إلى الحاكم من أخيها لكثرة لعنه لها، فأحضره الحاكم فحلف له أنه ما لعنها قطّ، ثمّ التفت إليها فقال لها: "يا ملعونة يا بنت الملاعين أنا قطّ لعنتك". فقال الحاكم: "لوحدها لا بل لآبائها معها".

أو كمثل جرّار باع جرّة للماء على أنها صحيحة فوجدها مشتريها مكسورة لا تمسك الماء، فحلف الجرّار أنها ليست * مكسورة ولكن الماء يسيل من سقوفها وجوانبها.

89v *

84. وأمّا التفاتكم إلينا معشر المسلمين وتشبيثكم بنا معشر المسلمين حيث قلتم إننا نلتزم بمثل ما ألزمكم به المعقول والمنقول من اعتقاد الجسمية والتشبيه والشرك الصريح والجمع بين النقائض وتجويز الممتنعات كالحلول والاتحاد والوحدة، فإنه غير لازم لنا ولا وجه لإلزامنا بشيء منه وبيننا وبينكم العقلاء.

أمّا زعمكم في الإنجيل أنه أمركم بالشرك على ألسنة بطرس وبولص وتوما وسمعان وغيرهم وزعمكم أنّ المسيح قال لكم: قولوا ثالث ثلاثة وعمّدوا العالم باسم الآب والابن والروح فزعم كاذب ودعوى باطلة، وحاشا وكلا أن يأمر المسيح العالم بالشرك بالله، وقد جمعت في هذه الأجوبة قبل هذا الفصل من كلام المسيح وتوحيده

---

[12] B: الشراك (wrongly), evidently a misreading of A.

or slander against God greater than this, and hence you should curse these people from sea to sea.

In your denial of polytheism and protestation of innocence from it, despite the teaching about the Trinity, the terms you have for the hypostases, and your exegesis of his teaching in the Torah about Adam's attempt 'to be like one of us' as meaning the Father and the Son because you have raised him from the earth to his Father and have seated him at the right hand of his Father on the throne, you are just like a woman who complains to a judge about her brother because of all his many curses upon her. The judge brings him before himself, and the latter swears in his presence that he has never cursed her, whereupon he turns round to her and says, 'Accursed one, daughter of accursed ones, I have never cursed you.' The judge remarks, 'Not only her, but her parents as well!' Or you are like a potter who sells a water pot with the assurance that it is sound: its purchaser finds it is cracked and cannot hold water, but the potter swears that it is not (89v) broken even though the water is flowing from its mouth and sides.

84.   As for the way you turn round to us Muslims and keep on at us, saying that we have to accept the same things that you have to concerning rational and reported beliefs such as corporealism, anthropomorphism, unadorned polytheism, holding together mutually contradictory notions and allowing impossibilities such as indwelling, uniting and singleness, actually we do not have to accept these, for there is no reason why we should accept any of it while there are intelligent people between us and you.

As for your claim that the Gospel commands you to accept polytheism through the mouths of Peter, Paul, Thomas, Simon and others,[5] and your claim that Christ said to you, 'Say the third of three, and baptize the world in the name of the Father and the Son and the Spirit',[6] this is a lying claim and false allegation. It is completely out of the question that Christ would have commanded the world to associate any other with God. I have brought together in an earlier section of these responses enough statements from Christ concerning his belief

---

tional to depict the mode in which the Virgin conceives by a beam of light directed from above onto her head or breast, though this is usually white or gold.

   [5] The Cypriot *Letter*, § 82, simply says that the Gospel gives justification for the doctrine of the Trinity. Al-Dimashqī betrays some uncertainty about his facts in claiming that these early Christians transmitted the Gospel, and that Peter and Simon are different individuals.

   [6] This is a subtle synthesis of S. V:73 and Mtt XXVIII: 19.

وإقراره بأنه رسول وأنه نبي وأنه ابن البشر وأنه غير الله وأن الله غيره، ما أغنى عن الإعادة والتطويل. وكذلك تضرّعه وبكاؤه ودعاؤه وصلاته وسجوده وسيّما ليلة الفصح وخميس العهد وغسله لرجلي بطرس وكذلك التوراة والزبور وكتب النبوءات شاهدة بالتوحيد آمرة به ناهية عن الشرك محذّرة منه، فاقرأوها ان كنتم في شكّ من ذلك.

مع علمكم اليقين بزعمكم أنّ المسيح صلب ومات بمشهد من أهل البيت المقدّس أورشليم وهم إذّاك خلق[13] كثير، فيهم الملك فيلاطس * والسوقة والرعيّة والشريف والمشروف، و لم يكن للمسيح إنجيل مكتوب مدوّن[14] مثل التوراة والزبور وكتب نبوءات الأنبياء المترّلة قبل التوراة وبعدها، ولو كان موجودًا أو معروفًا لليهود أو محفوظًا في الصدور لحصّلته اليهود ولو من تحت تخوم الأرض وأحرقوه وذرّوا رماده في الهواء و لم يتركوا لحرف واحد منه أثرًا في العالم ولكانوا قتلوا من وجدوه معه أو عنده أو كان تلميذًا أو غير تلميذ كما فعلوا بالتلاميذ ومزّقوهم كلّ ممزّق حتى أنكروا المسيح واسمه وذكره ومعرفته وتبرّأوا منه ومن دعواه وزعمه الذي نسبته إليه اليهود من المخالفة لشريعة موسى وسنّته كتحليل السبت واتباعه لتحريمه لنفسه والختان كذلك والفصح والعاشور.

وبقي[15] الأمر كذلك حتى جاء الملك قسطنطين وظهرت الأناجيل بالأقوال المختلفة والمناقضات الظاهرة، وقد قدّمنا من ذكر ذلك ما فيه مقنع، فلا تحتجّوا به في القول بالشرك الصريح وعظّموا حرمة المسيح، واعرفوا حقّه ومنزلته

* 90r

---

[13] B: خلوّ (wrongly), evidently a misreading of A.   [14] A and B: مكتوبًا انجيلاً مدونًا   [15] B: ونفي (wrongly).

in the oneness of God and his confession that he was a messenger, a prophet, the son of a human, and other than God and God other than him, to render repetition and elaboration unnecessary.[7] There is also his supplicating, weeping, calling out, worshipping and bowing down, particularly on the Night of the Passover, Maundy Thursday, and his washing Peter's feet.[8] The Torah, Psalms and prophetic Books similarly attest to belief in the oneness of God, enjoining it, forbidding polytheism and warning about it. If you are in doubt about this, read them.

This also applies to your certain knowledge, as you claim, that Christ was crucified and died in the presence of the people of al-Bayt al-Maqdis, Jerusalem, who at that time were numerous, including King Pilate, (90r) the populace, citizens, nobles and ordinary people. Christ never possessed a written, recorded Gospel like the Torah, Psalms or Prophecies of the Prophets which were revealed before and after the Torah. If it had existed, been known to the Jews, or been memorised, the Jews would have got hold of it no matter where in the world it was, and would have burnt it and scattered its ashes to the wind. They would not have left the trace of a single letter of it in the world. They would have killed whoever they found with it or possessing it, whether a disciple or not a disciple. They did this to the disciples, torturing them in every way until they denied Christ and his name and any mention of him or knowledge of him, washed their hands of him and of any pretension or claim that the Jews imputed to him. These consisted of divergences from the revealed law and practice of Moses, such as breaking the sabbath and its observance and banning it on his own authority, and likewise circumcision, Passover, and the tithe.[9]

The situation remained like this until King Constantine came and the Gospels were published with different and clearly contradictory teachings, about which we have already spoken convincingly above.[10] So do not use this to support any teaching about naked polytheism. Exalt the holiness of Christ, recognise who he truly was and his status

---

[7] Cf. § 72 above.

[8] Cf. Mtt XXVI: 39-44 || Mk XIV: 35-9, Lk XXII: 41-5 and Jn XIII: 6-9.

[9] Cf. Mtt XII: 1-14 for breaking the Sabbath; Jn VII: 22-3 for Jesus referring to circumcision, though Paul is the main New Testament opponent of this ritual; 1 Corinthians V: 6-8 for what might be taken as a rejection of the Jewish Passover, though by Paul not Jesus; and Mtt XXIII: 23 for Jesus' condemnation of the Scribes and Pharisees' over-preoccupation with the details of tithes.

[10] Cf. §§ 16, 43 and 47 above.

عند الله تعالى، ولا يحملكم الحصر والفحم والتبكيت على أن تجعلوا

* 90v لأنفسكم فينا أسوة لكم إذ نسبتم إلينا ما لا يصحّ * أن ينسب إلى مثلنا، ولا

يُظنّ بنا ولا جاءت معانيه في كتابنا ما أنتم قائلونه ومعتقدونه ومخالفون به

سائر الملل والآراء والنحل.

وأين زعمكم أنّ المسيح أمركم بالشرك وأرسل تلاميذه إلى زوايا العالم

ليعمّدوا العالم باسم الآب والابن وروح القدس من قول الله تعالى لنبيّه محمّد

صلم: ﴿قل هو الله أحد...﴾[16] إلى آخر السورة، وذلك حين سألته اليهود

أن يصف لهم الله عزّ وجلّ.

85. مع أنّ كتابنا أنزل بلسان أفصح العرب البلغاء النبغاء الألباء وعلى

لغتهم معجزًا لهم ولسائر أهل الأرض والأنس والجنّ تعجيزًا ببلاغته وإيجازه

وبيانه وجوامع كَلِمه ومعانيه وقصصه وحكمه وأحكامه، وفيه من تحرير

الكلمَ وتحقيق الحكمَ وإثبات ذات الله وتنزيه صفاته عن المثلية والشبهية

والجسمية ما لم يأت في غيره من الكتب المنزّلة مثله، وذلك قوله تعالى:

﴿ليس كمثله شيء وهو السميع البصير﴾[17] وصف وتنزيه ونفي وإثبات

وقوله: ﴿لا تدركه الأبصار﴾ الآية[18]، وقوله: ﴿يعلم ما بين أيديهم وما

خلفهم﴾ إلى قوله: ﴿العظيم﴾[19]، وقوله: ﴿ولا يحيطون به علمًا﴾[20]، وقوله:

﴿هو الحيّ لا إله إلا هو﴾ الآية[21]، ولم يقل الحيّ بحياة وروح فيؤذن قوله

بتشبيهه ومثيلته وافتقاره[22] إلى صفة زائدة * على ذاته بما هو حيّ كما زعمتم *** 91r**

في الحياة بروح القدس الغني تعالى على الإطلاق وجلّ جلاله.

وفي كتابنا النور المبين أيضًا من الأمثال الصادقة المطابقة والاستعارات

الرائقة والكنايات والتضمينات والمقدّرات المحذوفة والألفاظ المجازيات

المستعملة في اللسان العربي ما يفهمه المخاطبون به ويعلمون مراد الله منه من

ظاهر اللفظ، واستعمالها للتفهيم وللتأنيس وللتعريف ليوهم بالإشارة إلى ما

يعرفون ويعهدون

---

[16] S. CXII: 1. [17] S. XLII: 11. [18] S. VI: 103. [19] S. II: 255. [20] S. XX: 110.
[21] S. XL: 65. [22] B: وافتقان (wrongly), evidently a misreading of A.

before God the exalted and do not be carried along by inability to speak, being nonplussed, or desire to apportion blame to make us the same as yourselves. For you have imputed to us things that cannot rightly (90v) be imputed to anyone like us nor thought of us. The meaning of what you say and believe does not appear in our Book, and all the faiths, opinions and sects disagree with it.

Your claim that Christ commanded you to accept polytheism and sent his disciples throughout the world to baptize the world in the name of the Father and the Son and the Holy Spirit—how very far is this from the words of God the exalted to his Prophet Muḥammad (blessings and peace be upon him), 'Say: He is Allah the one' to the end of the *Sūra*. This was when the Jews asked him to describe God, great and mighty, to them.

85.   For our Book was revealed in the purest language of the most eloquent, distinguished and intelligent Arabs, and in their speech, as a miracle to them and to the whole world, mortals and jinn, stupendous through its eloquence, succinctness and clarity, and the comprehensiveness of its expression, meaning, stories, maxims and judgements. It contains apposite arguments, precise judgements and confirmations of God's essence and the transcendence of his attributes above likeness, similarity or physical connotations that are not found in other books revealed like it. These are the words of the exalted One: 'Naught is as his likeness; and he is the hearer, the seer', which is a description, a declaration of transcendence, a negation and affirmation; his words, 'Vision comprehendeth him not' and the rest of the verse; his words, 'He knoweth that which is in front of them and that which is behind them' to 'the tremendous'; his words, 'While they cannot compass it in knowledge'; his words, 'He is the living one. There is no god save him' and the rest of the verse. He does not say 'Living by life and spirit', so as to imply in what he says similarity and likeness on his part, or his need for an attribute added (91r) to his essence by which he is living, as you claim about life through the Holy Spirit. He is exalted and utterly independent, and great is his glory.

Also in our Book, which is light and clarity, are reliable and appropriate similes, fine metaphors, records, matters of significance, abbreviated references and figurative expressions used in Arabic which those who speak it can understand, and by which they can comprehend God's intention according to the plain meaning of the language. These are employed in order to help them understand, recognise and comprehend by means of allusion, so that they may comprehend, grasp and

ويعلمون مراد الله منهم من غير حمل المعاني على ظواهر الألفاظ.

كقوله تعالى: ﴿هل ينظرون إلا أن يأتيهم الله في ظلل من الغمام﴾[23] أي

يأتيهم أمره، وقوله: ﴿وجاء ربّك﴾[24] أي جاء أمر ربّك، وقوله: ﴿فأين ما

تولوا فثمّ وجه الله﴾[25] أي المشرق والمغرب لله وسائر الجهات لله ، فحيث

ما توجّهتم بالعبادة والسجود له فأنتم على الحقّ والله مطّلع عليكم، وذكر

الوجه فهو من باب الاستعارة كما تقال لغة وجه الصبح ووجه القوم ووجه

الصواب ووجه السماء ووجه الماء، وقوله: ﴿كلّ شيء هالك إلا وجهه﴾[26]

أي إلا هو فإنه الباقي بلا زوال، وقوله لموسى وهارون: ﴿إنني معكما أسمع

وأرى﴾[27] أي أعلم ما يكون منكما ومن فرعون وأنصركما * عليه، وقوله:

﴿ما يكون من نجوى ثلاثة إلا هو رابعهم﴾ الآية[28] أي علمًا وإحاطة ثمّ

تنبيهم بما عملوا، وقوله عن قول عيسى: ﴿تعلم ما في نفسي﴾ الآية[29]،

أي تعلم غيبي ولا أعلم غيبك، وقوله: ﴿يد الله فوق أيديهم﴾[30] أن يبعثهم

وثيقة وبها لهم رضوان الله، وقوله: ﴿بل يداه مبسوطتان﴾[31] أي إنه كريم

جوّاد منعم بإرادة واختيار لا بالطبع والقبض كما زعمت اليهود أنّ عطاءه لا

بالقصد، ولذلك قالوا: ﴿يد الله مغلولة غلّت أيديهم﴾ الآية[32]، وذكر اليدين

من باب الاستعارة والمجاز وتعريف العباد أنه فاعل مختار يرزق من يشاء

بغير حساب، وقوله: ﴿أو لم يروا أنّا خلقنا لهم ممّا عملت أيدينا أنعامًا﴾

الآيات[33] أي أنعم على العباد بذلك لا إنّ له أيد متعددة تعالى الله وسبحانه،

وقوله لإبليس: ﴿ما منعك أن تسجد لما خلقت بيدي﴾ الآية[34] أي اعتنيت

بآدم وجعلته خليفة في

* 91v

[23] S. II: 210.   [24] S. LXXXIX: 22.   [25] S. II: 115.   [26] S. XXVIII: 88.   [27] S. XX: 46.   [28] S. LVIII: 7.   [29] S. V: 116.   [30] S. XLVIII: 10.   [31] S. V: 64.   [32] *Ibid.* [33] S. XXXVI: 71.   [34] S. XXXVIII: 75.

know God's intention for them, without taking the meanings of the words literally.

Hence the words of the exalted One, 'Wait they for naught else than that Allah should come unto them in the shadows of the clouds', meaning that his command came to them; his words, 'And thy Lord shall come', meaning that the command of your Lord came; his words, 'And whithersoever ye turn, there is Allah's countenance', meaning that the east and the west and all other directions belong to God, so that wherever you turn in worship and prostration before him you are right and God will be observing you—the mention of 'face' is metaphorical, as is said 'the face of dawn', 'the face of the nation', 'the face of what is right', 'the face of the heaven' and 'the face of the water'; his words, 'Everything will perish save his countenance', meaning 'except him', because he is the inextinguishable Everlasting; his words to Moses and Aaron, 'Lo! I am with you twain, hearing and seeing', meaning 'I know what the outcome between you two and Pharaoh will be, and I will help you (91v) against him'; his words, 'There is no secret conference of three but he is their fourth' and the rest of the verse, meaning 'knowing and comprehending and then informing them of what they did'; his words concerning Jesus' words, 'Thou knowest what is in my mind' and the rest of the verse, meaning 'you know what I conceal but I do not know what you conceal'; his words, 'The hand of Allah is above their hands', that he sent them a deed by which they were given God's approval; his words, 'Nay, but both his hands are spread out wide in bounty', meaning that he is kind, generous and gracious by will and free choice, and not involuntarily or grudgingly—as the Jews claim, his giving was unintentional saying, 'Allah's hand is fettered. Their hands are fettered' and the rest of the verse—and the mention of 'two hands' is metaphorical and figurative, an indication to humanity that he acts freely to nourish whom he wills without reckoning; his words, 'Have they not seen how we have created for them of our handiwork the cattle'[11] and the following verses, meaning 'he is gracious to humanity in this way' not that he has a number of hands, may God be exalted and blessed; his words to Iblīs, 'What hindereth thee from falling prostrate before that which I have created with both my hands?' and the rest of the verse, meaning 'I have provided for Adam and have made him a vicegerent in the

---

[11] Literally, 'of what our two hands performed'.

الأرض على ما فيها، وقوله: ﴿والأرض جميعًا قبضته يوم القيمة والسموات مطويّات بيمينه﴾[35] أي إنّ السموات أشرف من الأرض وكلاهما ملكه وفي قبضته وتصريفه، وقوله عن السفينة ﴿ذات ألواح ودسر تجري بأعيننا﴾[36]، أي مع كونها ألواح ودسر فهي محمولة محفوظة محروسة من الغرق والكسر محاطة بالعناية الإلهية، وقوله لموسى: * ﴿ولتصنع على عيني﴾[37] أي[38] أسخّر لك فرعون وزوجته وأجيبك إلى كلّ من يراك وأردّك إلى أمّك مستورًا عليك حالك، وقوله: ﴿وكتبنا عليهم فيها﴾[39] يعني التوراة والكتابة. بمعنى القضاء وهو الحكم، وقوله: ﴿كتب ربّكم على نفسه الرحمة﴾[40] أي ختمها وحكم بها، وقوله: ﴿يوم يكشف عن ساق﴾ الآية[41] فهو من باب الاستعارة والمجاز كما يُقال: قامت الحرب على ساق والمعنى كشف الغطاء وشهود ما تواعدتهم الرسل به ثمّ يدعون إلى السجود تهزئًا بهم وقد منعوا منه فلا يستطيعون، وقوله: ﴿ثمّ استوى على العرش﴾[42] هو كقوله: ﴿خلق الله السموات والأرض﴾[43] أي أبدعهما وأوجدهما بعد أنّ لم يكونا وكذلك العرش لا إنّ الله جسم متمكّن بالقعود على العرش ولا إنّ له ساقًا يكشفه للسجود ولا إنّ له نفسًا منفوسة كنفوس المخلوقين ولا إنّ له عينًا حبّب بها موسى إلى فرعون وعيونا جرّب بها سفينة نوح ويدًا يقبض بها جملة الأرض ويمينًا عظيمة[44] يطوي بها السموات ويدين على قدر آدم خلقه بهما ويدين مبسوطتان أبدًا بهما ينفق ويرزق وأيد كثيرة خلق بها الأنعام ولا إنه[45] جسم متجزّأ جزّاً مع كلّ فرد فردًا[46] من البشر * ولا إنّ له وجهًا وقفًا وجسمًا كالأجسام ولا إنه يأتي تارة مع الملائكة وتارة في ظلل من الغمام،

*92r

*92v

---

[35] S. XXXIX: 67.   [36] S. LIV: 13-14.   [37] S. XX: 39.   [38] B omits this word.
[39] S. V: 45.   [40] S. VI: 54.   [41] S. LXVIII: 42.   [42] S. VII: 54.   [43] S. XXIX: 44.
[44] B: عظيم   [45] B: والانه (wrongly), a misreading of A.   [46] A and B: فرد

earth over everything in it'; his words, 'When the whole earth is his
handful on the day of resurrection, and the heavens are rolled in his
right hand', meaning the heavens are higher than the earth, and both
are his possession to hold and dispose of; his words about the ship, 'a
thing of planks and nails that ran in our sight', meaning that although
it was of planks and nails it was carried, preserved and protected from
being submerged and breaking up, surrounded by divine concern; his
words to Moses, (92r) 'That thou mightest be trained according to my
will',[12] meaning 'I have made Pharaoh and his wife subservient to you,
I have granted your request against all who see you, I have returned
you to your mother with your well-being preserved'; his words, 'And
we prescribed for them therein'[13]—he means the Torah, and the
writing means the decree which is the judgement; his words, 'Your
Lord hath prescribed for himself mercy', meaning 'he has sealed it
and ruled on it'; his words, 'On the day when it befalleth in earnest
[and they are ordered to prostrate themselves but are not able]',[14]
this is metaphorical and figurative, as is said, 'war flared up', and the
meaning is of drawing aside the veil and revealing what the messengers
warned them about, then they were summoned to worship, by way
of mockery, but they were prevented from it and were not able; his
words, 'Then he mounted the throne', which are like his words, 'Allah
created the heavens and the earth', meaning 'he brought them into
being and gave them existence after they were not', and similarly with
the throne—it is not that God has a body able to sit on the throne,
nor that he has a thigh which he reveals when he bends, a breathing soul like the souls of creatures, an eye by which he made Moses
loveable to Pharaoh, eyes by which he tested Noah's ship, a hand in
which he holds all the earth, a great right hand with which he folds
up the heavens, two hands suited to creating Adam and he created
him with them, two hands ever outstretched with which he provides
and sustains, and many hands with which he creates living things, a
body divided into parts with every part a part from a human, (92v) a
face, nape of the neck, or body like other bodies, that he will come
at one time with the angels and at another in the darkness of clouds.

---

[12] Literally, 'under my eyes'.

[13] In this and the following quotation, 'prescribe' is literally 'write'.

[14] This verse is more literally 'The day that the shin shall be laid bare' (Yusuf 'Ali's
translation). Clearly this is what the Christians point to, as al-Dimashqī's discussion
of the next verse makes clear.

بل كلّ ذلك مثله في التفهيم والإشارة والعبارة كمثل ما[47] يقول أحدنا لصاحبه: "أنا وأنت بعين الله وبين يديه، والذي ذهب منّا ففي جنب الله" فيفهم عنه مراده وهو تعريفه بأنّ الله مطّلع عليهما وأنه يخلف عليهما ما ذهب منهما من بقته أو غيرها.

ومن كلام علمائنا رحمهم الله تعالى عند تلاوة الآيات التي زعمتم أنّ ظواهر ألفاظها مؤذنة بما يوهم التجسيم والتشبيه، إنهم يقولون: "آمنّا بالله وبما جاء عن الله على مراد الله وآمنّا برسل الله وبما جاء عن رسل الله على مراد رسل الله"؛ ومن أقوالهم كذلك: "التوحيد إثبات ذات غير مشبّهة بالذوات ولا معطّلة من الصفات، وجلّت الذات القديمة أن يكون لها صفة حديثة، كما استحال أن يكون للذات الحديثة صفة قديمة، فليس كذاته ذات ولا كاسمه اسم ولا كصفته صفة ولا كفعله فعل".

ولقد قال أمير المؤمنين عثمان لأعرابي وحشي حافٍ[48]: "أين[49] ربّك؟" فقال له: "بالمرصاد يا عثمان"، فكاد عثمان أن يموت فرقًا من خشية الله تعالى.

وما مثلكم * أيها النصارى في قولكم: إن أنكروا علينا الشرك أنكرنا عليهم التجسيم إلا كمثل امرأة صوّتت وإلى جانبها طبل فضربت عليه لتستر بصوته تصويتها، فقيل لها: "أين الرنّة من الرنّة والريح من الريح؟" وكذلك أنتم يقال لكم: أين قول ربّ العالمين بنون العظمة: ﴿نحن قسمنا بينهم معيشتهم﴾

* 93r

---

[47] This word is repeated in A and B.   [48] B: في جاء (wrongly), evidently a misreading of A.   [49] B: ابن (wrongly).

Rather, all this is to be taken as a form of referring, expressing and speaking in the same way as one of us will say to his companion, 'You and I are under the eye of God and in his hands, and what we have lost is at God's side.' The latter understands his intention, which is to tell him that God watches over them both and will compensate them for what they have lost at his own expense or otherwise.

In the teaching of our scholars (may God the exalted be merciful to them) concerning the reading of the verses in which, as you claim, the literal meaning of the words allows one to imagine Incarnation and anthropomorphism is that they say, 'We believe in God and what comes from God according to what God intends, and we believe in God's messengers and what comes from them according to what they intend.'[15] Among their teaching is also, 'To believe in God's unity is to confirm his essence uncompared with other essences and not shorn of the attributes, for the eternal essence is too glorious to possess a temporal attribute, just as it is impossible for a temporal essence to have an eternal attribute; there is no essence like his essence, no name like his name, no attribute like his attribute and no action like his action.'[16]

The Commander of the faithful 'Uthmān said to a wild, barefoot desert Arab, 'Where is your Lord?', and he replied, 'Lying in wait along the road, 'Uthmān!' 'Uthmān almost died of terror from dread of God the exalted.[17]

Christians, (93r) when you say, 'If they deny that we are guilty of associating, we will deny that they are guilty of anthropomorphism', you are just like a woman shouting, who has at her side a drum which she beats upon in order to conceal her noise with the noise from it; someone says to her, 'What is one noise next to another, and one clamour next to another?' In the same way someone could say to you, What are the words of the Lord of the worlds, in the plural of majesty, 'We have apportioned among them their livelihood' and the

---

[15] In other words, the teachings of scripture and the prophets must be understood according to guidelines set by God and the prophets themselves. Al-Dimashqī does not attempt to resolve the hermeneutical problem implicit in these words by identifying how these guidelines are to be discerned, though he would presumably abstract them from the dominant tenor of scriptural teaching.

[16] Their principle is that God and his attributes are unlike creatures and their attributes, and any statement about God must be understood in conformity with this.

[17] The Caliph was evidently stricken by the over-familiar anthropomorphic way in which the Bedouin talked about God.

الآية[50]، ﴿إِنَّا نَحْنُ نَزَّلْنَا الذِّكْرَ﴾[51]، ﴿إِنَّا كُلَّ شَيْءٍ خَلَقْنَاهُ بِقَدَرٍ﴾[52] من قولكم الآفك القبيح: بسم الآب والإبن وروح القدس إله واحد؟ وله مثال قول المنادي: معشر الناس الخاص والعام والجيّد والرديء والجهاوات وغيرها، من تأخّر لا يسأل ما يجري عليه، فالله الله في أنفسكم أيها النصارى قبل الموت.

[50] S. XLIII: 32.   [51] S. XV: 9.   [52] S. LIV: 49.

rest of the verse, 'Lo! We, even we, reveal the reminder', and 'Lo! We have created everything by measure', next to your false, shameful words, 'In the name of the Father and the Son and the Holy Spirit, one God'?[18] Just like it are the words of someone calling, 'People, distinguished and ordinary, good and bad, local and others, no one will care if you come late!' God must be God in your souls, Christians, before you die.

---

[18] The three verses from the Qur'an emphasise God's transcendence and might in dealing with creatures, while the Trinitarian statement depicts his internal disorder. The significance of the following cry may be that it is common street language, calling people to hurry to some event, far distant from the exalted language of the Qur'an, but not so different from Trinitarian statements.

فصل

86.

ثمّ قلتم عقب ذلك إنّ كليام قال لكم إنهم ينكرون علينا في قولنا: إنّ الله تعالى جوهر، وإنكم أجبتموه قائلين:

إننا نسمع عن هؤلاء القوم أنهم أهل فضل وعلم وأدب ومعرفة[1]، ومن هذه صفته وقد قرأ شيئاً من كتب الفلسفة والمنطق والحكمة فما حقّهم ينكرون هذا علينا؟

وذلك أنّ[2] ليس في الوجود شيء إلا وهو إمّا جوهر وإمّا عرض، لأنّ أي أمر نظرنا فيه وجدناه إمّا قائمًا بنفسه غير مفتقر في وجوده إلى غيره وهو الجوهر وإمّا مفتقر في وجوده إلى غيره * ولا قيام له بنفسه وهو العرض. ولا يمكن أن يكون للقسمين قسم ثالث.

فأشرف هذين القسمين القائم بذاته الغير مفتقر في وجوده إلى غيره وهو الجوهر. ولمّا كان الباري تقدّست أسماؤه أشرف الموجودات أو هو سبب سائرها أوجب أن يكون أشرف الأمور والأعلى منها الجوهر، ولهذا قلنا إنه جوهر لا كالجواهر المخلوقة، كما نقول إنه شيء لا كالأشياء المخلوقة وإلا لزم أن يكون قوامه بغيره ومفتقر في وجوده إلى غيره، وهذا فمن أقبح الأقاويل أن يقال على الباري سبحانه وتعالى.

ثمّ[3] قلتم إن كليام قال لكم عنا إننا إنما ننكر من أن نسميه جوهرًا لأن الجواهر ما قبلت أعراضًا وما شغلت حيّزات، فلهذا لم نطلق القول بأنه[4] تعالى جوهر. فقلتم له:

إنّ الذي يقبل العرض ويشغل الحيّز إنما هو الجوهر الكثيف، فأمّا الجوهر اللطيف فلا يقبل

* 93v

---

[1] B: ومعروفة   [2] A and B: إذ   [3] Over three lines of text (from ثمّ to كلّا) are added in the margin of A.   [4] B: بأنه الله

86.   *Section [Eleven]*

Then immediately after this you say that Kilyām said to you: 'They criticise us for saying that God the exalted is substance';[1] and that you answered him saying:

> We have heard about these people that they are refined, knowledgeable, cultured and experienced. People of this character will have done some reading in works of philosophy, logic and wisdom, so can they really criticise us for this?
>
> The point is that things that exist must either be substance or accident. For, whatever entity we examine we find either that it subsists in itself without need of anything else for its existence, and this is a substance, or that it does need something else for its existence (93v) and it has no subsistence in itself, and this is an accident. There is no possibility of a third category in addition to these two.
>
> So the more noble of these two categories is what subsists in itself without need of anything else for its existence, and this is a substance. And since the Creator, holy be his names, is the most noble of existent things, or alternatively is the reason for all others, it necessarily follows that he is the most noble of entities and the highest of them, substance. Thus we say that he is a substance unlike created substances, as we say that he is a thing unlike created things. Otherwise his subsistence would have to derive from something else and he would need something else for his existence. This is one of the most infamous things that can be said about God the Creator, blessed and exalted.[2]

Then you say that Kilyām told you about us, that we refuse to call him substance because substances are what receive accidents and occupy space, and thus we do not utter the words, 'The exalted One is a substance'. You said to him:

> That which receives an accident and occupies space is indeed a physical substance. But refined substance, on the other hand, does not receive

---

[1] Kilyām's reference to 'us' here in the presence of the Cypriot Christians indicates clearly his own Christian allegiance.

[2] Christians were accustomed to calling God substance for the reason given here, that the term denoted a self-subsistent entity. But Arabic-speaking Christians encountered difficulties when they employed the term *jawhar* to translate it. For, as al-Dimashqī says immediately below, this was precisely the term used in *kalām* to designate the fundamental composite of physical matter that bore and was characterised by accidents. This led Muslim theologians to assume easily that Christians regarded their God as material. For an earlier instance of the disagreement that arose from the two different understandings of the term, cf. al-Bāqillānī, *Kitāb al-tamhīd*, pp. 75.5–79.3.

عرضًا ولا يشغل حيّزًا مثل جوهر العقل وجوهر النفس وجوهر الضوء وما يجري هذا المجرى من الجواهر اللطيفة المخلوقة. وإذا كانت الجواهر اللطيفة المخلوقة لا تقبل عرضًا ولا تشغل حيّزًا فيكون خالق الجواهر اللطائف والكثائف ومركّب اللطائف في الكثائف يقبل عرضًا ويشغل حيّزًا كلاّ.

87.   فالجواب: أمّا قولكم إنّ الله جوهر بمعنى أنه موجود واجب الوجود فلا بأس به مع القول بالاستحالة المتناهي[5] على وجوده ونفي الحيزية عنه وتنزيهه عن مشابهة ما سواه من الجواهر المحيزية والقائمة بها الأعراض، وإن كان بعض علمائنا ينكرون هذه التسمية تنزيهًا للربّ تعالى كما بيّناه.

وأمّا قولكم إنّ الجوهر اللطيف لا يشغل حيّزًا ولا يقبل عرضًا مثل جوهر النفس وجوهر العقل وجوهر الضوء وكلّ جوهر لطيف مثل ذلك فإنه قول مدخول مزلزل، وذلك أنّ كلّ واحد من النفس والعقل والروح فإنّ العلماء مختلفون في ماهيتهم بمبحث هل الروح جسم أو قوّة من القوى أو خاصية من الخواص أو معنى ما من المعاني الغيبية التي لا تدرك ولا يدرك وجودها * الحيّ إلا بالحسّ والحركة؟ وبمبحث هل النفس والعقل الدارك المدبّر المستفاد كلّ واحد منهما جوهر لطيف روحاني متصف بالصفات؟ أو هما صفتان من صفات الإنسان المشار إليه بقول أنا؟

والقول في البحث عن النفس أن يقال فيها إنها إمّا أن تكون جملة مزاج البدن أو يكون المزاج آلة لها وأخلاقها تابعة له، والقول في البحث عن العقل فهو أن يقال: إمّا أن يكون جملة مزاج الدماغ أو مزاج الدماغ ببطونه الثلاثة آلة له، أو إنه صفة للعاقل الموصوف به يعقل به المعقولات ويدرك به المدركات .

ثمّ من البيّن أنّ هذه النفوس والعقول على كلّ تقدير

* 94r

---

[5] B: اليناهي (wrongly).

accidents or occupy space, for example the substance of the intellect, the substance of the soul, the substance of brightness, and other refined, created substances to which the same applies. So if there are refined, created substances which do not receive an accident or occupy space, then it can be that the Creator of refined and physical substances who sets the refined in the physical does not at all receive an accident or occupy space.

87. *Response*: As for your statement that God is a substance in the sense that he exists and is the Necessary Existent,[3] there is no objection to this. But any limitation upon his existence must be declared impossible, his occupying space must be rejected, and he must be distanced from any resemblance to substances other than him, which occupy space and in which accidents subsist. However, some of our scholars have rejected the terminology in order to distance the exalted Lord, as we have shown.

As for your statement that refined substance does not occupy space or receive accidents, such as the substance of the soul, of the intellect, of brightness and any similar refined substance, this is a feeble and shaky statement. For scholars are in disagreement over the nature of the soul, the intellect and the spirit respectively, and they inquire whether the spirit is a physical object, one of the powers, one of the particular characteristics, or one of the unseen entities which cannot be detected and the existence of which a living being can only detect (94r) by sensation and movement. And they inquire whether the soul and the intellect which discern, direct and employ are both refined, immaterial substance characterised by attributes, or whether they are two of the attributes of the human who is referred to as 'I'.

The discussion about the inquiry into the soul is that people say either that it belongs entirely to the constitution of the body or that the constitution is its instrument and the natural dispositions of the latter are subject to it. The discussion about the inquiry into the intellect is that people say either that it belongs entirely to the constitution of the brain, or that the constitution of the brain with its three inner parts is its instrument, or else that it is an attribute of the thinking being who is characterised by it, and by means of which he thinks about intellectual things and perceives perceptible things.

It is quite clear by any estimate that souls and intellects are different

---

[3] The term *wājib al-wujūd*, designating God as existing by virtue of his own essence rather than an external cause, is characteristic of Ibn Sīnā's philosophy.

مختلفات بالماهيات، ولو لم تكن مختلفات لكان مثلاً عقل نمرود عقل ابراهيم وعقل فرعون عقل موسى ونفس يهودس[6] نفس المسيح، والذي يراه زيد بعقله يراه عمرو بعينه، و لم يكن الأمر كذلك فثبت الاختلاف بين ماهيات العقول والنفوس ولزم من ذلك تباين ذواتها ولزم من تباينها أن تكون كلّ نفس محيّزة بحيّز، محاطة بمحيط نسبي روحاني، متناهية في ذاتها إلى ذاتها، وأن يكون كلّ عقل من العقول وكلّ جوهر روحاني كذلك، وأن يكون العقل الأوّل مغايرًا بذاته لذات المبدع له، مباينًا له محدودًا بحصره محصورًا بحدّه، محاطًا مع إحاطته، محتوشًا بين طرفي الأولية والآخرية والوجود والعدم والابتداء والانتهاء، * متناهيًا في ذاته إلى ذاته، قابلاً للعدم والوجود معًا ممكنًا تقابله الحدوث.

* 94v

وإنّ الله سبحانه شيء لا كالأشياء، وموجود مطلق الوجود، وجوهرٍ لا في حيّز، وذات [7] بجرّدة، وصمد لا في موضوع، وواجب الوجود أزلاً وأبدًا، حيّ قيوم ليس بذي حياة مستفادة له من روح القدس التي أوجدها بعد أن لم تكن موجودة وحيّ بها بعد أن أوجدها كما زعمتم، وليس بذي نطق استفاده من الابن الموجود به من جوهره كما زعمتم، والذي لولاه بعد إيجاده له لم يكن ناطقًا به قبل إيجاده

---

[6] A and B: هيرودس   [7] A and B: وذوات

in their natures. For if they were not, then, for example, Nimrod's intellect would be like Abraham's, Pharaoh's intellect like Moses', and Judas' intellect like Christ's,[4] that what Zayd observed with his intellect ʿUmar could observe with his eye. But this is not the case, and so the difference between the natures of intellects and souls is confirmed. It necessarily follows that their essences are dissimilar, and it follows from their dissimilarity that every soul is bounded within a space, encompassed by a proportional, immaterial periphery and limited in its essence to its essence; also that every intellect and every immaterial substance is such, and that the First Intellect is different in its essence from the essence of the One who produces it and is distinct from it, is bounded by its restriction, restricted by its boundary, encompassed with its encompassment, enclosed between the two extremes of the first things and last things, existence and non-existence, beginning and end, (94v) limited in its essence to its essence, capable of non-existence and of existence together, possible and susceptible to temporal occurrences.[5]

Thus God, may he be praised, is a thing unlike others, is existent absolutely, is a non-spatial substance, is a pure essence, is self-subsistent not in any object,[6] the Necessary Existent, eternal, unending, living, subsistent. He is not the possessor of life conferred on him from the Holy Spirit which he brought into existence after it did not exist, nor living by it after he brought it into existence, as you claim. And he is not the possessor of speech which he acquired from the Son who exists with him and is of his substance, as you claim, and, after he brought him into existence for himself, without whom he could not be speaking through him before he brought him into existence from

---

[4] Nimrod, Pharaoh and Judas have been portrayed a number of times in the *Response* as villainous foils to the three prophets with whom they are linked.

[5] Al-Dimashqī develops his point about the distinction between individual souls and intellects in order to emphasise the strict distinction between separate beings and, most importantly, between contingent beings and God. The occurrence of more terms from Ibn Sīnā's cosmology, *al-ʿAql al-awwal* and *al-Mubdiʾ*, suggests that he is arguing within the framework that the contingent universe, of which the Intellects were the highest beings and among them the First Intellect highest of all, was an emanation from the One rather than his creation. Within this framework the ontological distinction between God and the contingent order could be more easily blurred than within the theological framework in which God created by command without any notion of outpouring from his essence.

[6] I.e. God does not subsist in a substrate in the way that accidents do, making him dependent on another entity for his existence.

منه كما زعمتم. وقلتم: الآب موجود لذاته، والابن ناطق لذاته، والروح حيّة لذاتها، وكلّ واحد من الثلاثة غنيّ قديم من وجه وفقير حادث من وجه، والثلاثة واحد بزعمكم الفاسد، فيا خسران من هذا رأيه ومذهبه وظنّه بربّه! والحمد لله على الهداية.

فثبت أنه لا بدّ لكلّ جوهر لطيف من حيّز لطيف روحاني يمتاز به عن باقي الجواهر اللطيفة المختلفة بالماهيات.

وأمّا تسميتكم للضوء جوهرًا لا حيّز له فغير مسلّم، وإنما الضياء عرض قائم بعرض وهو الشعاع أو النور المحمول على موضوع الشمس، أعني ضوءها الباهر، وهو الجوهر لا النور القائم به ولا الضياء القائم بالنور، فإنهما عرضان لازمان له معلولان عنه وهو جسم الشمس الشاغل حيّزه المكاني، فليس الضوء ولا النور بجوهر لا حيّز له كما * زعمتم بل عرضان كما تبيّن.

* 95r

وأمّا قولكم في الله تعالى إنه سبب لسائر الأشياء فقول خطأ، وافقتم به قول الفيلسوف ذلك في موضعه، وكان الصواب أن تقولوا إنه سبحانه مسبّب سائر الأسباب كما أنه تعالى طابع الطبيعة ومعلّل العلل ومكوكب الكواكب وخالق كلّ شيء، لا إله إلا هو سبحانه وتعالى عمّا تشركون.

himself, as you claim. You say, the Father exists by his essence, the Son speaks by his essence and the Spirit lives by its essence, and each of the three is independent and eternal in one respect, and dependent and temporal in another. The three are one, according to your false claim, but what a scoundrel to hold such an opinion, belief and thought about his Lord! Praise be to God for guidance!

So it is confirmed that every refined substance must have a refined, immaterial space by which it is marked off from the rest of the refined substances which are differentiated by their natures.

As for the designation you give to brightness as a substance without space, this is not sound. Radiance is an accident and no more, subsisting in an accident which is the rays or light that can be traced to the object of the sun—in other words, its dazzling brightness—and it is this that is the substance, not the light subsisting in it and not the radiance which subsists in the light. They are both accidents intrinsic within it and derived from it, and it is the physical object of the sun which occupies its delimited space. So neither radiance nor light are substances without space as (95r) you claim, but accidents, as has been shown.

As for your statement that God the exalted is the reason for all things, this is wrong. In making it you concur with the statement of the philosopher, which will have its appropriate place.[7] You would be more correct to say that the blessed One is the instigator of all reasons as he is the imprinter of all character, the initiator of all causes, the One who fashions the stars, the Creator of all things. There is no god but he, blessed and exalted above your associating.

---

[7] Cf. §§ 93-9 below, and particularly §§ 98-9.

فصل

88.

ثمّ قلتم سياقة:

وإنّا لنعجب من هؤلاء القوم، تعنوننا[1] معشر المسلمين، الذين مع أدبهم وفضلهم كيف لم يعلموا أنّ الشرائع شريعتان: شريعة عدل وشريعة فضل، لأنه لمّا كان الباري تعالى عدلاً وجوّادًا وجب أن يظهر عدله على خلقه، فأرسل موسى إلى بني إسرائيل فوضع شريعة العدل وأمر بفعلها إلى أن استقرّت في نفوسهم.

ولمّا كان الكمال الذي هو الفضل لا يمكن أن يأتي به ويضعه إلا أكمل الكمال وجب أن يكون هو تقدّست أسماؤه الذي يضعه لأنّ ليس شيء أكمل منه، ولأنه جوّاد وجب أن يجود بأجلّ الموجودات، وليس في الموجودات أجلّ من كلمته، فلذلك وجب أن يجود بكلمته، فعلى هذا وجب أن يتخذ ذاتًا محسوسة يظهر منها قدرة جوده، ولمّا لم يكن في المخلوقات أشرف من الإنسان اتخذ الطينة البشرية من السيّدة مار مريم المصطفاة على نساء العالمين.

وبعد هذا الكمال لم يبق * شيء يوضع لأنّ جميع ما تقدّمه يقتضيه وما يأتي   * 95v
بعده غير محتاج إليه.

وفي هذا القول مقنع[2] والسلام.

89.   فالجواب: أمّا قولكم لكليام إنكم عجبتم منّا كيف لم نعلم شريعة العدل وشريعة[3] الفضل الآتي بها موسى وبهذه عيسى وإنهما أغنيا العالم بتشريعهما عن كلّ ما جاءت به الأنبياء أو يأتي به قبلهما وبعدهما، فإننا بحمد الله تعالى نعلم أنّ لله تعالى شريعتين كلّيتين عاميتين شاملتين إحداهما[4] شريعته الإرادية وهي شريعة الفضل الشاملة لأحكام إيجادنا وإيجاد العالم وإمدادنا بالمواد وإمداد العالم وتشريعها من حضرة الربوبية للمربوبين أهل السموات وأهل الأرض وسائر الخلق أجمعين وهي سنّة الله التي فطر الناس عليها وأراد لهم ومنهم وبهم

---

[1] A and B: يعنوننا   [2] B: منع (wrongly), a misreading of A.   [3] B omits شريعة العدل و: these words.   [4] A and B: احدهما

88. *Section [Twelve]*

Following this you say:

> We are frankly surprised why these people (you mean us Muslims), in spite of their culture and refinement, do not know that there are two revealed laws, the law of justice and the law of grace.[1] For since the exalted Creator is just and generous, he must reveal his justice to his creatures. So he sent Moses to the People of Israel to institute the law of justice and to order its implementation until it became established in their souls.
>
> When perfection came, which was grace, it could be only the most perfect of the perfect who would bring it and institute it. And so he himself, holy be his names, was necessarily the one to institute it, because there is nothing more perfect than he. And since he is generous, he necessarily showed his generosity through the most glorious of existing things. And there is nothing among existing things more glorious than his Word, and thus he necessarily showed his generosity through his Word. For this purpose, he necessarily took an essence perceptible to the senses and revealed through it the power of his generosity. And since among created things there is nothing more noble than humankind, he took human clay from the saintly lady Mary who was chosen above the women of the world.
>
> After this perfection there was nothing left (95v) to institute, because everything that preceded it led up to it and what succeeded it was not required.
>
> This teaching is sufficient, so farewell.

89. *Response*: As for your words to Kilyām that you are surprised at us not knowing about the law of justice and law of grace, the former brought by Moses and the latter by Jesus, and that with the regulations they gave they exempted the world from all that the prophets brought, or what was brought before them and after, praise God the exalted, we know that God the exalted has two universal, general and comprehensive laws. One of them is his law of will, the law of grace, which comprehends the ordinances of our existence and the existence of the world, and of our material support and the support of the world. Its regulations are from the lordly presence to those who are under lordship, dwellers in the heavens, dwellers on earth and the whole entirety of creation. It is God's customary way, and he endowed people with it and intended for them, from them, to them,

---

[1] Cf. Jn I: 17.

وعنهم وفيهم ما هم فاعلوه وقائلوه وواجدوه من خير وشرّ ونفع وضرّ
وإيمان وكفر وطاعة وعصيان وسعادة وشقاوة وغني وفقر وقوّة وضعف
وصحّة وسقم وخَلْق وخُلْق وعلم وعمل ومذهب وملّة ورأي ونحلة وموت
وحياة لا تبديل لخلق الله، وهي كلمة الله التي بها خلقت السموات والأرض
وتشدّدت كما في مزامير داود[5]، وليست بالمسيح كما زعمتم ولا هي دين
النصرانية الذي ادّعيتم * وابتدعتم. وقد دللنا في ابتداع النصرانية وبيّنا فساد   * 96r
باطلها فيما تقدّم.

وأمّا الشريعة الثانية فشريعته الأمرية الواردة من حضرة الإلهية وهي التي
جاءت بها الأنبياء والمرسلون عليهم السلام، وهي شريعة العدل المشروعة
لأولي الألباب المكلّفين والتي لم يأت فيها من التشريع[6] إلا ما يثبته العقل
أو يجوّزه، وأحكامها الأصولية تعريف العباد أحدية الخلق وتعليمهم مكارم
الأخلاق وتكميل النفوس بحسن الاستعداد واتخاذ المعارف والعبادة كالزاد
وقراءة عنوان السعادة من فهرسة[7] شريعة الإرادة إذ الإنسان مريد مراد له
محمل ودليل وزاد وتهيّؤ للمصير إلى الحياة الأبدية والنعيم المفضّل للأمّة
المحمدية أهل الإسلام بدار السلام.

فهاتان الشريعتان مشروعتان من الله تعالى عدلاً وفضلاً من مبدأ الخلق
وإلى إعادته، لا ما حصرتموه من القسمة في ما جاء به موسى وجاء به عيسى
وأضمرتم ما أضمرتم من

---

[5] Cf. Psalm XXXIII: 6. [6] B: التشريع [7] B omits this word.

of them and among them what they should do, say and produce, the good, bad, benefit, harm, belief, unbelief, obedience, disobedience, success, misery, wealth, poverty, strength, weakness, health, sickness, bodily build, personal character, knowledge, action, confession, religion, opinion, creed, death and life. It is not an alternative to God's creation, but God's word, and it is by this that the heavens and earth were created and established, as is in the Psalms of David, not by Christ as you claim.[2] It is not the religion of Christianity which you have alleged (96r) and contrived: we have already given the proof that Christianity is contrived, and have shown the error of its falsehood in what is above.

Concerning the second law, this is his law of command, which appears from the divine presence, and it is this that the prophets and those who were sent (peace be upon them) brought. It is the law of justice given as law to the foremost intellects of those charged with it, and no regulation has come in it that cannot be confirmed or sanctioned by reason. Its fundamental decrees are an intimation to humankind of the unity of creation, information to them about the noble qualities of moral virtues, and the perfection of souls by means of suitable preparation, acquiring knowledge and such observances as 'provision', and perusing the principles of felicity from the compilation of the law of will.[3] For the human seeks for a purpose which has an intention, direction, 'provision' and preparation for progress towards the everlasting life and supreme blessedness that is given to the community of Muḥammad, the people of Islam, in the abode of safety.

These are the two laws that have been instituted from God the exalted as justice and grace from the beginning of creation to its returning, not the portion you have condensed down from what Moses and Jesus each delivered, nor what you have schemingly conceived in say-

---

[2] In al-Dimashqī's Muslim view the law of grace is something placed by God within the human make-up at creation, unlike the Christian view that it is something distinct from this and drawing against it. Thus it is not a *tabdīl li-khalq Allāh*, 'an alteration to God's creation', since it is something that God *faṭara al-nās ʿalayhā*, 'endowed people with', as an innate tendency that did not require drastic change. Here, he briefly and somewhat obliquely alludes to a fundamental difference between Muslim and Christian anthropology.

[3] In S. II: 197 'the best provision' is defined as *taqwā*, 'to ward off evil'. Al-Dimashqī envisages the prophetic law of command as both supplementing the innately endowed law by directing minds to the nature of creation and the higher virtues, and also complementing it by directing them to use the faculties they have been given to reflect upon the nature of the life prepared for them.

قول: "لا حاجة إلى إرسال أحد بعدهما"، تعنون الجحود لما جاء به نبيّنا محمّد
صلم وابتعثه الله إلى العالمين بالهدى ودين الحقّ وكلّ⁸ ما جاءت به الأنبياء
والرسل من قبل، وليس لهذا جواب، إذ أنتم عارفون* به.

* 96v

---

⁸ B omits this word.

ing, 'There is no need for anyone to be sent after these two', meaning to repudiate what was delivered by our Prophet Muḥammad (may God bless him and give him peace). God sent him to the worlds with guidance, the religion of truth and everything that the prophets (96v) and messengers had brought earlier. There is no response to this, because you know it full well.

90.

فصل

ثمّ قلتم ختامًا:

وهذا الذي عرفنا من رأي النصارى الذين رأيناهم وفاوضناهم، والذي يحتجّون به عن أنفسهم، فإن يكن ما ذكروه صحيحًا فلله والمنة إذ وفّقهم لذلك[1]، وإن كان بخلاف ذلك[2] فينعم مولانا الشيخ المعظّم فلان بما نوضّحه لننبئه للقوم ولنوقفهم عليه.

فقد سألونا ذلك وجعلوا كليام فيه سفيرًا والحمد لله حمدًا كثيرًا.

91. فالجواب: هداكم الله للصواب، فقد أنصفتم في القول وأتيتم بما عندكم، وقد سمعتم عن كلّ فصل جوابًا فيه مقنع وكفاية. وإني والله والله لكم من الناصحين، فانظروا ما أوردته عليكم وتدبّروه وأحسنوا النظر فيه ترشدوا إلى الحقّ وإلى طريق الرشاد، ولا تكونوا كالذين دعوا إلى الهدى فأبوا وقالوا: ﴿إنّا وجدنا أباءنا[3] على أمّة وإنّا على آثارهم مهتدون[4]﴾[5].

ولقد فكّرت في قولكم: إنّ لا حاجة إلى من يأتي بعد المسيح، وإنه جحود للرسالة المحمدية ولكلّ نبي ورسول ممّن تقدّم على موسى عليم، ثمّ فطنت[6] إلى أنكم أخذتم هذا النكر من السامرة[7] المنكرين سائر النبوءات إلا نبوّة موسى ورسالته. ومن قولهم الهزاء في ذلك: "إن كان الذي جاء به موسى مثل الذي جاء به من تقدّمه فلا فائدة في مجيء موسى ومجيئه ثابت، وإن كان دونه فمحال فبطل أن يكون قبله غيره * شريعة مشروعة. وإن كان الذي يأتي بعده يأتي بمثل ما أتى به فلا حاجة إليه إذ هو من تحسين تحصيل الحاصل. وإن كان أنقص منه فكذلك، وإن كان أزيد فمحال إذ ليس بعد الكمال كمال. وإن كان نسخًا أو عن بدأ فمحال على

* 97r

---

[1] B: وإن كان بخلاف ذلك: these words are repeated in B.   [2] كذلك   [3] A and B: أبانا   [4] A and B: مقتدرون   [5] S. XLIII: 22.   [6] B: لم وطنت (wrongly), evidently a misreading of A.   [7] B: السائرة (wrongly).

90.   *Section [Thirteen]*

Then in conclusion you say:

> This is what we have discovered about the views of the Christians whom
> we have met and conversed with, and the arguments which they them-
> selves put forward. If what they have said is at all right, it is from God
> and a blessed gift, because he has granted them the success of this.
> If it is otherwise, then may our revered master So and So graciously
> consider what we have explained, so that we may tell the people and
> instruct them about it.

They asked us to do this, and made Kilyām a mediator for it. Praise
God with all praise!

91.   Response: May God guide you to what is right, for you have
spoken fairly and have put forward your views. And you have heard a
decisive and sufficient response to each section of it. By God indeed,
I am acting towards you as an adviser, so examine what I have written in answer to you, think about it and give it full consideration,
and you will be directed to the truth and to the way of instruction.
Do not be like those who are called to guidance but refuse and say,
'Lo! We found our fathers following a religion, and we are following
their footprints.'

I have thought about your words, 'There is no need for anyone
to come after Christ',[1] and indeed it is a rejection of Muḥammad's
apostleship and every prophet and messenger who preceded Moses
(peace be upon them). Then I realised that you had taken this denial
from the Samaritans, who deny all prophethood except the prophethood and apostleship of Moses. Their disdainful words about this
include: 'If what Moses delivered was like what anyone before him
delivered, there was no advantage in Moses' coming. But his coming
is confirmed, and if it is impossible that he did not come, it is false
that any law other than it (97r) was revealed before it. If those who
came after him delivered the same as he did, there would be no need
of this because it would be an embellished, condensed condensation:
if it was briefer than that, the same applies, and if it was fuller, this
is impossible because there cannot be completeness after completeness; if it was an abrogation or something new, it is impossible for

---

[1] This refers to the point the Christians make in the previous portion of their
Letter quoted in § 88.

الله أن يبدو له ما لم يكن، فبطل أن يأتي بعد موسى نبي آخر". والسامرة أخذوا هذا الكفران والجحود من منكري[8] النبوءات براهمة الهنود.

ويلزمكم أيها النصارى الردّ على السامرة في جحودهم رسالة المسيح أو الاعتراف منكم بتسليم ما ادّعوه. وأمّا نحن فقد أجبنا عن هذا الهذيان الملفّق في أوّل كلامنا عند ذكركم لرسل المسيح واقتصاركم عليهم.

وأمّا قولكم بأنّ أفاضلكم سألوا إيضاح ما نعلمه ممّا ذكروه وادّعوه لتوقفوهم عليه، فقد تقدّم من القول ما هو كفاية. وأقول وأقسم بالله العظيم إنه لولا مراعاة المجاوب جناب النبوءة الشريفة، وانتمائكم إليها بالمحبّة والتعظيم، وملاحظته لمقتضى الشريعة الإرادية وجريان أحكامها، وعلمه بصحّة رسالة المسيح السيّد وما جاء به من عند الله تعالى، واطّلاعه على الأغلوطات ومخزاتها الواقعة من أتباعه أهل دين النصرانية، ومعرفته للمبتدعين ما ابتدعوه ممّا لم يكتبه الله عليه، وشهوده لقصور أفهامكم وجمودها * على تجسيم المعاني، وتقليد الخالف للسالف تقليدًا بغير تدبّر ولا تعقّل[9] ولا معرفة بما يجب ويجوز ويستحيل عقلاً وشرعًا وعادة، لكشفت الغطاء وبيّنت الصواب والخطأ.

٩٢. وسأذكر نبذة حسنة تركّ العارف الفطن وتوقظ الغافل الأيسر، فأقول: إنّ السيّد المسيح عليلم لمّا أرسله الله تعالى إلى

* 97v

---

anything that had not been to become manifest to God. So it is false that any other prophet came after Moses.' The Samaritans adopted this unbelief and rejection from those deniers of prophecy the Indian Brahmins.[2]

Christians, you should either answer back the Samaritans in their rejection of Christ's apostleship, or else confess that you concede what they allege. For our part, we have answered this contrived delusion at the beginning of our argument in connection with your reference to Christ's apostles and your limitation to them.[3]

As for your words that your scholars have asked for an explanation of what we know about the things they mention and allege, wanting you to inform them about it, enough has been said above. And I say and swear by God almighty that if it were not for the correspondent's consideration for the esteemed noble prophethood and for your close ties with it in love and respect,[4] his attention to what is required by the law of will and the principles that issue from it, his knowledge about what is correct in the apostleship of the lord Christ and what he delivered from God the exalted, his awareness of pointless questions and the disgrace in them resulting from his familiarity with the followers of Christianity, his acquaintance with notions devised by heretics which God never wrote about, all his evidence for the inadequacy and inflexibility of your minds (97v) concerning the incarnation of entities and those who came later imitating those who were before without reflection, reason or knowledge of what is required, allowed and forbidden in reason, revealed law and custom, then I would take the wraps right off and make clear what is right and what is wrong.

92. I will mention an apt example that will enfeeble the alert and intelligent, and arouse the inattentive and simpleton. So I say: when God the exalted sent the lord Christ (peace be upon him) to

---

[2] The Brahmins were stock deniers of all prophethood in Muslim theological writings; cf. e.g. al-Bāqillānī, *Tamhīd*, pp. 104-31; Ibn Ḥazm, *Kitāb al-fiṣal fī al-milal wa-al-ahwā' wa-al-niḥal*, Cairo, 1903, vol. I, pp. 69-70. Al-Dimashqī's speculative connection between them and the Samaritans evidently arises from the similarities he sees in their dismissal of prophethood.

[3] Cf. §§ 56-8 above, where al-Dimashqī counters the Cypriot exegesis of S. II: 213.

[4] The Christians have shown respect for the status of Muḥammad as an authentic prophet, though have restricted his relevance to the Arabs and have interpreted his message in the Qur'an in conformity with their own beliefs. Al-Dimashqī shows here some of the politeness and decorum he notes is absent from the beginning of the Christian *Letter*, § 6.

الأمم الأربع الذين كانوا في زمنه، أعني اليهود والمجوس والصابئة والفلاسفة أولي الآراء والنحل، وأظهر لهم ما أظهره من العجائب والمعجزات، وألاح لعقولهم ما ألاحه من بهر نور العرفان القدسي الخاطف للبصائر كخطف البرق اللامع للبصراء، غشّى أعين بصائر بني إسرائيل بما غشاها من بهر ذلك النور اللائح لهم وهم في ظلم أكوانهم وعمه حيلاتهم، وحجب عوائدهم الحاجبة عقولهم عن النفوذ في العرفان إلى ما هو من وراء طورها وفوق شهودها، وجذبهم بقوّة بهر ذلك النور عن الصابئة عبدة الكواكب وروحانياتها وأصنامها الموضوعة لها كالمظاهر بزعم عبدتها، وعن تجسيم اليهودية المستقرّ اعتقاده في نفوسهم بما فهموه الفهم المعكوس من ظواهر ألفاظ التوراة وكتب أنبيائهم كالإخبار بالشبه والمثال وذكر الاستراحة والاستلقاء والوضع لرجل على أخرى وكالإشارة إلى أنّ آدم يريد أن يكون كواحد منّا والقول بأنه جاء * من سيناء وأمثال هذه.

* 98r

ونزعهم[10]، أعني المسيح، عن مهلكة غلط الثنوية القائلين بإلهين اثنين، وحذّر من قولهم واعتقادهم، وأوضح دهش الفلاسفة وحيرتهم ونهى عن الإصغاء إليهم، فثبت بصائر المؤمنين به والتابعين له لرؤية ذلك البهر العرفاني، وفهموا بالحال والذوق معنى قول الله تعالى في كتابنا المبين: ﴿سنريهم آياتنا في الآفاق وفي أنفسهم حتى يتبيّن لهم أنه الحقّ﴾ الآيتان[11]، ولمّا فهموا ذلك وتحقّقوا معناه

---

[10] B: وترعمهم (wrongly), evidently a misreading of A.   [11] S. XLI: 53-4.

the four communities of his day, the Jews, Zoroastrians, Ṣābians and philosophers, the holders of opinions and sects,[5] and he revealed to them his wonders and miracles and displayed for their minds the dazzling light of holy perception that communicates to insight in the way that lightning communicates flashes to those who can see, the eyes of insight among the People of Israel were covered from the dazzle of this light displayed to them, for they were under the oppression of their souls, the confusion of their wiliness, and the veils of their habitual ways which veiled their minds from piercing perceptively into what lay beyond their condition and above their present situation. By the force of the dazzle of this light he won them away from the Ṣābians who worshipped the stars, their spiritual forces and their idols that had been set up to them as visible forms, as their worshippers claimed; also from the Jewish belief in corporealism which was lodged in their hearts, according to which they held an understanding contrary to the literal reading of the Torah and the books of their prophets. These include the report about similarity and likeness, the reference to taking rest and reposing, crossing one leg over another, and also the allusion to Adam wanting to become 'like one of us', the statement 'he came (98r) from Sinai', and similar notions.[6]

And he—I mean Christ—took them away from the dangerous error of the dualists, who talked of two divinities, and he warned about their teachings and beliefs. He exposed the bafflement and confusion of the philosophers, and forbade anyone to listen to them. And he fixed the eyes of those who believed in him and followed him on the vision of this dazzling perception, and they came to understand by trial and taste the meaning of God the exalted's words in our clear Book, 'We shall show them our portents on the horizons and within themselves until it will be manifest unto them that it is the truth' this and the following verse.[7] When they understood this and were convinced of its meaning,

---

[5] Cf. §§ 25 and 54, and also § 56, where al-Dimashqī earlier mentions four communities, or these four among others.

[6] These anthropomorphisms in the Old Testament are identifiable as: the reference to God creating humans in his image, Gen I: 26-7; God resting after completing the creation, Gen II: 2-3, Exodus XX: 11; Adam and Eve becoming like gods after eating the forbidden fruit, Gen III: 22; and Moses' declaration that God came to his people from Sinai, Deut XXXIII: 2 (the reference to God crossing his legs is not so evident). Al-Dimashqī has previously referred to Adam becoming like a god in §§ 70 and 83, and to God coming from Sinai in §§ 7 and 73.

[7] The appearance of the typically Ṣūfī terms ḥāl and dhawq underlines the general

سكروا بعد الصحو، وغرقوا في لجّة بحر المحو ثمّ أفاقوا قائلين: نحن أنصار الله آمنّا بالله.

ورأى ذلك الضوء الباهر طائفة منهم فظنّوه نارًا أو نورًا معهودًا، فاقتحموا الفحص عنه بآرائهم وكان مثلهم عند رؤيته واقتحام العرفان به كمثل الفراش عند رؤية المصباح في الظلمة يقتحم النور والإشراق، ولا يخشى اللهب والإحراق فيهلك حرقًا وغرقًا.

ثم أخبر بعض هذه الطائفة لتابعيهم عن رؤية ذلك الضوء الباهر وما اقتضته آراؤهم في معناه، فجسّم التابعون السامعون لذلك¹² الخبر معانيه، وألحدوا في آيات الله تعالى وفيه، وغلوا غلوّا كبيرًا وأعماهم الحبّ وأصمّهم فأطروا وتماروا، وظنّوا المعاني مباطن المباني وسمّوا المباني مظاهر المعاني، واختلطت أفهامهم فشبّهوا الأوّل بالثاني واستنتجوا بالثاني، * فكانوا من الأخسرين أعمالاً، وجلّ الله وسبحانه وتعالى.　* 98v

ومن هؤلاء التابعين من تحيّر وقال بالوقفة، وسرت فيهم رقيقة الصابئة فقالوا باتخاذ آلهة كثيرة مشتركين في الإلهية بزعمهم وفي الخلق¹³ والأمر، وصنعوا لها تماثيل مظاهر يتعبّدون لها ويتضرّعون عند المهمّات والملمّات إليها، ويقرّبون لها الدخنات وينذرون إليها النذور، وحكوا الصابئة في كثير من أفعالهم.

ومن هؤلاء التابعين المذكورين من سرت فيه رقيقة الثنوية فثنّوا، وأشاروا إلى

---

¹² B: كذلك　¹³ B: الخلو (wrongly), evidently a misreading of A.

they became intoxicated after being alert, and they foundered in the depths of the sea of oblivion. Then they recovered consciousness and said, 'We will be Allah's helpers, we believe in Allah.'[8]

A group of them saw this dazzling brightness and thought it was a familiar fire or light, and they jumped to hasty conclusions about it. Their seeing it and jumping to assumptions about it is just like a household servant who sees a glow in the dark; he rushes to the light and radiance without any fear of the blaze and conflagration, and he is utterly burnt up and consumed.

Then a part of this group told its followers about the vision of this dazzling brightness and what their own opinions had concluded about its meaning. Their followers who heard this account gave body to the meanings in it, fell into error about the signs from God the exalted and about him, and committed gross exaggeration. Love blinded and deafened them, so they grew excessive in their praise and argued with one another. They thought the meanings were the core of the structures and called the structures the surface of the meanings. Their minds became confused, so they made the former similar to the latter and drew conclusions from the latter, (98v) and thus grew utterly degenerate in their conduct. God is glorious, blessed and exalted!

Among these followers some became bewildered and advocated non-commitment.[9] They had lurking among them a trace of Ṣābianism, so they taught about having many gods who, according to their claim, shared in divinity, creation and command. They made pictures in representations of them and venerated them, and they prayed to them when grave crises and misfortunes befell, bringing incense before them and making vows to them. And they copied the Ṣābians in many of their actions.[10]

Among these followers mentioned were some in whom a trace of dualism was lurking. So they proclaimed dualism and signified the

---

tenor of this passage that Jesus' teachings afforded insight into the deeper significance of faith. For the portrayal of him as a mendicant critic of the status quo, cf. Khalidi, *Muslim Jesus*, especially pp. 32-43.

[8] This group are the true Christians as al-Dimashqī sees them, who recovered from their first overwhelming experience of Christ and followed the path of strict monotheism.

[9] Cf. Section 5, n. 23.

[10] This vivid reference to the veneration of icons could well derive from first-hand witnessing of the practice. Al-Dimashqī has already condemned this as an imitation of Ṣābianism in § 44.

الإلهين المزعومين بالتصليب على وجوههم بإصبعين، واتخذوا رؤوس تيجانهم شعبتين وقالوا بالطبيعتين والمشيئتين، وحكوا المجوس الثنوية والتحشية في تشويهيهم لصورهم وحلقهم لذقونهم وأوساط رؤوسهم، ووقود القناديل والشمع ليلاً ونهارًا، والتحلّي بالذهب والجواهر، ولبس المصبغ عند العبادة اقتفاء بالمجوس.

ومنهم أيضًا من سرت فيهم هذه الرقيقة فتحيّروا ووقفوا عن القول بإلهين فجمعوا لهم بآرائهم إلهًا واحدًا مثلثًا في الكنه مركبًا، وسمّوا تثليثه آبا وابنًا وروحًا، ومنهم من سمّى آبا وابنًا وأمّاً يعنون الشيء والحياة والنطق، فالشيئية الواجبة والحياة مريم والنطق الممكن المسيح الصالح لأن يكون * إلهًا، ولا يكون إنسانًا، ولأن[14] يكون قادرًا ولا يكون عاجزًا.

* 99r

ومن هؤلاء التبّاع من سرت فيهم رقائق عدّة وتزاحمت فاندهشوا[15]، ووسوست لهم نفوسهم فرجعوا إلى الفلسفة الفجّة البتراء، ورأوا رأيًا فلسفيًا في الإنسان أنه زبدة الأكوان وفيه بالقوّة وبالفعل ما في سائر العالم من معقولات ومحسوسات، مندرجة فيه بادية منه، ظاهرة عليه شاهدة له، محصّلة عنده صادرة عنه، وأنه يعلم بعض الكليات علمًا بكلية القائم به، فقالوا: إنه مُظهر للعقل والعقل مَظهر الباريئ، وخصّصوا المسيح بذلك لما ظهر منه من العجائب والمعجز وسيّما كونه

---

two alleged gods by making the sign of the cross on their faces with two fingers. They divided the tops of their mitres into two, taught about two natures and wills, and resembled the dualist Zoroastrians and *Taḥshiyya*[11] in disfiguring their faces and shaving their chins and the middle of their heads, burning lamps and candles night and day, and using gold and precious stones for adornment and dyed clothes during worship in imitation of the Zoroastrians.[12]

Among them were also those in whom this trace lurked, though these people hesitated and held back from teaching about two gods. They assembled for themselves, according to their opinions, a God who was one in name but triple and composite in being, naming his tripleness Father, Son and Spirit. Among them some gave the names Father, Son and Mother, meaning the Thing, the Life and the Speech, the Thing being the Necessary One, Life being Mary, and the possible Speech being the righteous Christ, for he was (99r) divine and not human, powerful and not weak.[13]

Among these followers were those in whom lurked a number of traces. These kept welling up and the people became perplexed; their souls wheedled away within them and thus they reverted to the defective, primitive philosophy. They espoused the philosophical view of mankind, that he is the quintessence of existent things, and in himself contains in potential and actuality things of the intellect and of the senses that are in the rest of the world, integral to him and issuing from him, visible upon him and indicative of him, originating around him and arising from him, and that he has knowledge of some of the universals by virtue of a knowledge of the universal subsistent within him. They said, 'He manifests reason, and reason is a manifestation of the Creator.' They particularly referred to Christ in this way because wonders and miracles were manifest from him, and especially his speak-

---

[11] This would appear to be a variant form of *Ḥashwiyya*, the name given to scholars of low repute, particularly those who accepted Ḥadīths of questionable origin with crude anthropomorphic contents. Al-Dimashqī places them with the Zoroastrians because they allow distorted teachings about the one, transcendent God, and compares the Christians to both because they accept the shallow, incorrect teachings that have been imparted to them and act on them with uncritical vigour.

[12] These further examples of attempts at aetiology are evidently based on observation of Christian beliefs and practices. In § 76 al-Dimashqī has explained the origin of shaving beards among the Franks differently, as a commemoration of the ignominy inflicted on St Peter.

[13] Cf. S. V:116 which can be understood to identify the Trinity as comprising God, Jesus and Mary.

تكلّم في المهد، و لم يعلموا أنّ صبي يوسف تكلّم في المهد شهادة ببراءة يوسف، وصبي التمامة تكلّم في المهد شهادة بأن محمدًا رسول الله، ثمّ لم يتكلّم بعدها حتى شبّ كما في التواريخ من كلامه.

ومنهم أيضًا من سرت فيه الرقيقة اليهودية فجسّموا وأغلظوا التجسيم فركّبوا الإله تركيب الجسوم وقالوا بحلوله واتحاده بالأبدان و لم يفرّقوا بين معنى القدم وبين معنى الحدث ولا بين الواجب والممكن.

93.   وكان هؤلاء شرّ مكانًا وأضلّ سبيلاً، ولو أنّ هذه الفرق الضالّة سمعوا ما أنزل إلى الرسول النبي الأميّ [16] خاتم النبيّين وصاحب التمام والذي وجب عليهم أن يسمعوا منه * ويطيعوه لاهتدوا [17] من الضلالة وأنقذوا من الجهالة وكانوا مع ﴿الذين أنعم الله عليهم من النبيين﴾ الآية [18] القائلين في الإله من حيث المعقول المبرهن والأدلّة القطعية والحقّ الصرف: " نؤمن أنّ الله سبحانه شيء لا كالأشياء واجب الوجود لذاته لا يتصل به شيء من الممكنات ولا تحلّ به [19] ولا يتحد به منها شيء ولا يحلّ بها ولا يمتزج بشيء منها ولا تمتزج به، ولا ذاته علّة لذواتها ولا ذواتها معلولة لذاته"، وإنه سبحانه أوجدها بقصده واختياره لا بالطبع والقوّة وإنه لا متصل بالعقل الأوّل ولا متحد به ولا ممتزج به لأنه لو كان متصلاً بالعقل

* 99v

---

[16] B: إلا في (wrongly), evidently a misreading of A. [17] B: لا يمتدوا (wrongly), evidently a misreading of A. [18] S. XIX: 58. [19] ولا تحلّ به: A adds these words in the margin; B omits them.

ing in the cradle,[14] though they were ignorant of the fact that Joseph's baby spoke in the cradle to witness that Joseph was innocent,[15] and that the perfect baby spoke in the cradle to witness that Muḥammad was the messenger of God, and then did not speak after this until he grew up, as is in the histories concerning his speaking.[16]

Among them also were those in whom lurked a trace of Judaism. They developed a crude form of corporealism and gave to God the composition of composite physical bodies. They talked about his indwelling in and uniting with human bodies, and they made no distinction between the meaning of the eternal and of the temporal, nor between the necessary and the possible.

93. These people were wicked in their position and most erroneous in their way. If only these erring sects had heard what was revealed to the messenger, the unlettered Prophet, Seal of the prophets, Master of perfection, the one whom they should have heeded (99v) and obeyed, they would have been guided out of error and rescued from ignorance, and they would have been together with those 'unto whom Allah showed favour from among the prophets' and the rest of this verse, who say about God only what is demonstrably reasonable, definitively provable and absolutely true: We believe that God, blessed is he, is a thing unlike things and exists necessarily by his essence; none of the possibles is connected with him, none of them dwells in him or unites with him; he does not dwell in them, or mingle with any of them, and they do not mingle with him; his essence is not a cause of their essences, and their essences are not caused by his essence; he, blessed is he, brought them into existence by his intention and choice, not instinctively or inherently;[17] he is not connected with the First Intellect nor united or mingled with it.[18] For if he were connected with the First

---

[14] Cf SS. III: 46, V: 110 and XIX: 29-33.

[15] Cf. S. XII: 26, where 'a witness of her own folk' testifies that it was the Egyptian's wife who tried to tempt Joseph and that he was innocent. In later tradition this witness is often identified as a baby in a cradle, according to Ibn ʿAbbās one of the four babies who spoke; cf. Ibn al-Athīr, *Al-kāmil fī al-tārīkh*, Beirut, 1998, vol. I, p. 108.

[16] Jalāl al-Dīn al-Rūmī, *Mathnawī*, Book III. 3220-37, recounts the story of the babe in arms who greeted the Prophet and acknowledged his prophethood.

[17] I.e. God creates by an intentional act rather than by an unconscious process in which his being inexorably gives rise to created beings by its very nature, or in which they are potentially in existence and necessarily come to be.

[18] Al-Dimashqī has already referred in passing to the Necessary Existent and the First Intellect (cf. Section 11, nn. 3 and 5). They are characteristic of Ibn Sīnā's Neoplatonic cosmology, in which all beings other than God exist by virtue of causes

الأوّل اتصالاً لازم الثبوت لزم منه ما ذهب إليه القائلون بالعلّة والمعلول وهو
محال كما ندلّ عليه، وإن كان منفصلاً عن العقل الأوّل بالانفصال²⁰ اللازم²¹
الثبوت لزمه الحصر بذلك الانفصال اللازم الثبوت، وثبوت الانفصال المطلق
إن كان واجبًا معه قديمًا لزم منه قدم المنفصل عنه وهو محال. وإن كان ليس
بقديم ولا واجب فهو ممكن وإذا كان الانفصال ممكنًا استحال لزوم ثبوته
على الإطلاق فهو لا متصل به على الإطلاق ولا منفصل عنه على الإطلاق،
وكذلك مجموع الممكنات فإنها في قبضة الإحاطة الوجودية لا متصلة بذاته
ولا منفصلة عن إحاطته لأنّ * الذاتين القائمتين بنفسيهما لا تدخل إحداهما²² * 100r
في الذات الأخرى .بمعنى الامتزاج والاتحاد لأنّ الذاتين لا تكونان واحدًا
والقائمين بنفسيهما لا يكونان في حيّز واحد، لكن عند حلول أحدهما في
الحيّز ارتفع²³ الثاني من ذلك الحيّز فيمتنع الحلول القديم والممكنات في حيّز
واحد معًا²⁴، فلزم أن لا يكون حالاً في ذاته ولا ذاته حالة في حيّز العالم لأنّ
القديم لا يمازج الحوادث ولا يقبل الحلول بها ولا تقبل القائمات بأنفسها
القيام بغيرها، فالعالم بأسره وحيّزه خارج عن ذاته تعالى منفصل عنه مباين
له بالذات والحقيقة.

ومن الدليل على ذلك أننا تأمّلنا العالم علويه وسفليه وكلّياته وجزئياته
وجواهره وأعراضه²⁵ وسائر الموجودات فوجدناها ممكنات الوجود والعدم
ووجدنا لها محيطًا حاويًا تناهى إليه ولم نجد وراءه وجودًا ممكنًا ولا وراء خلقه
خلقًا، لأنه لو كان وراء الممكنات ممكنات ووراء الممكن ممكن²⁶ لتسلسلت
الممكنات إلى غير

---

²⁰ B: بالافصال   ²¹ A and B: الازم   ²² A and B: يدخل إحديهما   ²³ A and B: ارتفاع
²⁴ A and B add: ذات (sic).   ²⁵ B: وجواهر وأعرا منه (wrongly), evidently a misreading
of A.   ²⁶ A and B: ممكناً

Intellect in a connection that entailed permanence, then the cause and effect that speakers refer to would have to apply to him. And this is impossible, as we will demonstrate about him. But if he was separated from the First Intellect by a requisite, permanent separation, then he would have to be restricted by this requisite, permanent separation. And if the permanence of the absolute separation was necessary and eternal with him, then he would have to be eternally separated from it, which is impossible. But if it is not eternal or necessary then it will be possible; and if the separation is possible, then its requisite permanence cannot at all be absolute, and he will neither be connected with it absolutely nor separated from it absolutely.

The same can be said about all possibles: in the grip of the surrounding of existence they are neither connected with his essence nor severed from his surrounding. For (100r) one of two self-subsistent essences cannot enter the essence of the other in the sense of mingling or uniting, because two essences cannot be one, and two self-subsistent entities cannot occupy one space. On the contrary, when either of them comes to dwell in a space the second is removed from it. So it is inconceivable for the eternal and possibles to dwell in one space simultaneously. It follows that nothing can dwell in his essence, and that his essence will not dwell in the space of the world, because the eternal does not mingle with temporal things and cannot be indwelt by them, and self-subsistent things cannot admit things that subsist through another. So the world in its totality and in its space is outside the exalted One's essence, separate from it and distinct from it in essence and reality.

A proof of this is that when we consider the world, its upper and lower, its whole and parts, substances and accidents, all existent things, we find that they are existent and non-existent by possibility, and we find that they have an encircling encompasser at which they reach their limit. We do not find any possible existent beyond this, nor any creation beyond its creation, for if there were possibles beyond the possibles or any possible beyond a possible, then there would be an unlimited

---

lying outside themselves and are hence potentially existent, *mumkin al-wujūd*, while he alone exists by virtue of himself as the *wājib al-wujūd*. The coming into existence of the contingent universe is through a process of emanation from God in his self-contemplation, the highest contingent forms being the Intellects which govern the heavenly spheres, with the First Intellect supreme among these. Al-Dimashqī goes on to criticise aspects of this cosmology.

نهاية وللزم من إيجاد الممكنات إلى غير نهاية عدم الواجب الوجود إلى غير نهاية لأنّ الغيرين لا يجتمعان في ما لا يتناهى معًا. والوجود حكم لازم لثبوت واجب الوجود فلا يوجد وجود إلا به، فإذا لم يكن واجب الوجود ثابتًا فلا يثبت وجود الممكنات، فثبوت وجود الممكنات في الشاهد دليل على * ثبوت واجب الوجود.

* 100v

94.   وقولنا واجب الوجود أي لازم الثبوت حكم ضروري وذلك أنّ الوجودات المسلسلة إلى غير نهاية لا تتحصل إلا بالوجود الواجب الذي يتناهى وجودها إلى وجوده وهو غير متناه[27] لغيره لمّا كان مجموع الممكنات محصورًا بين طرفي الآخرية والأولية والبداية والنهاية كان أوّلها مسبوقًا بعدم وجودها، فإن كان السابق أيضًا مسبوقًا بعدم وجوده تسلسلت الوجودات السابقة إلى غير نهاية. ولمّا كانت عدمات الموجودات سابقة للموجودات وأنّ كلّ موجود يتقيّد بالأولية فأولية وجوده مسبوقة بعدمها.[28]   فإذا طرّت الموجودات السابقة إلى غير نهاية لزمها عدمات إلى غير نهاية عكسًا لأنّ عدم الموجودات سابق[29] لوجودها إلى غير نهاية. وإذا لم تتناه[30] عدماتها فلا يتحصّل وجودها، ولمّا تحصّل وجودها في الشاهد لزم من ذلك تناهي عدمها إلى وجودها ويلزم من تناهي عدمها إلى وجودها تناهي وجودها إلى عدمها.

---

[27] A and B: متناهي   [28] B: بعدها (wrongly), evidently a misreading of A.   [29] A and B: سابقاً   [30] A and B: يتناها

succession of possibles. But if unlimited possibles were brought into being the non-existence of the Necessary Existent would be unlimited because two different things do not meet together at the same time in what has no extent.[19] What exists is an inevitable condition for the permanence of the Necessary Existent because no existent is brought into existence except through him, for if the Necessary Existent was not enduring the existence of possibles could not be confirmed. Hence the permanence of the existence of possibles in the visible world is a proof of the (100v) permanence of the Necessary Existent.

94. Our statement that the Necessary Existent, the Intrinsically Constant, is an unavoidable condition means that existent things in a limitless succession cannot result except from an Existent who is necessary,[20] to whose existence their existence extends but whose existence does not extend to anything outside himself. For since the totality of possibles is confined between the two extremes of final and initial, primary and ultimate, the first of them must be preceded by the absence of their existence, for if there was a preceding one in turn preceded by the absence of its existence, there would be an unlimited succession of preceding existent things. And since the absences of existent things precede existent things, and every existent thing is restricted by the initial, then the initial point of its existence will be preceded by the absence of this. If preceding existent things continued to multiply without limit they would in turn have to have absences of existence without limit, because the absence of existent things would precede their existence without limit. But if their absence of existence had no limit, their existence could not result. Since their existence in the visible world does result, it follows from this that their absence of existence is limited by their existence, and it follows from the absence of existence being limited by their existence that their existence is limited by their absence of existence.[21]

---

[19] If there is no limit to the number of possible existents there is no room for the Necessary Existent because the possible and Necessary, being different from each other, cannot simultaneously occupt the same space. This is why al-Dimashqī is intent on establishing that there must be a boundary to the contingent universe.

[20] Strictly speaking this cannot be the case because a limitless succession would be infinite.

[21] In this argument al-Dimashqī contends that since contingent things come into existence at some point, their existence must be preceded by their non-existence. If there were a limitless succession of existences they would always be preceded in existence by non-existence, which means that they could never actually come into existence. So since things do exist, there cannot be this limitless succession.

والوجود والعدم المتناهيان مسبوقان بوجود غير مسبوق وبعدمه وهو المشار إليه بالوجود المطلق الذي لا أوّل له ولا هو محصور بين طرفي الأولية والأخرية ولا هو مسبوق بعدم ذاته ووجوده، وإنّ عدم، الممكنات مسبوق بوجوده الواجب ووجودها مسبوق بعدمها فذلك هو المشار إليه بواجب الوجود * والربّ المعبود الذي لولا وجوده الواجب لم يكن يتحصّل لما بعده * 101r * وجود.

هذا معنى قولنا إنّ الوجود حكم لازم الثبوت أزلاً وأبدًا والممكنات بين أزليته وأبديته في أوّليتها وأخريتها، لأنه لمّا استحال أن تكون الممكنات غير متناهية الطرفين فثبت أنها متناهية إلى منتهى محيط بها ممكن الوجود وهو العقل الأوّل والحجاب الأعظم. عاد الكلام على المحيط بالعقل الأوّل الذي إليه المنتهى فرأيناه واجب الوجود لا غيره لأننا دلّلنا على أن لو كانت الممكنات أخذت في الوجود إلى غير نهاية استحال أن يجتمع الواجب والممكن في ما لا يتناهى معًا أو تكون الممكنات غير متناهية الوجود فيكون الواجب معدومًا إلى غير نهاية أو يكونان[31] موجودين في ما لا يتناهى معًا وذلك أعظم استحالة لأنّ اتحاد متغايرين في ما لا يتناهى محال لاستحالة الجمع بين الضدّين وتداخل الوجود في الوجودين، كما لا تكون الذات الواحدة ذاتين.

95.   فلزم من ذلك أنّ الممكنات متناهية إلى الواجب وأنّ الواجب ليس بمنته[32] إلى غيره كما أنّ وجوده ليس بمتناه[33] إلى عدمه ولا إلى وجود غيره لأنه لو تناهى إلى

---

[31] A and B: يكونا   [32] A and B: بمنتهي.   [33] A and B: بمتناهي.

Existence and absence of existence, which are both limited, are preceded by an Existence who is not preceded by his non-existence. He is the one referred to as absolute existence who has no beginning, is not confined between the two extremes of initial and final, and is not preceded by the non-existence of his essence and existence, while the non-existence of possibles is preceded by the existence of the One who is necessary, and their existence is preceded by their non-existence. This is the one referred to as the Necessary Existent, (101r) Lord and the One worshipped, without whose being necessarily existent there could never have resulted what existed beside him.

This is the meaning of our saying that the Existent is a condition, inevitably permanent, timeless and eternal, and that the possibles are between timelessness and eternity in having beginnings and ends. For since it is inconceivable for the possibles not to be limited by extremes, it is certain that they are limited by a termination that surrounds them which is a possible existent, namely the First Intellect, the greatest veil.[22] So the discussion returns to the Encompasser of the First Intellect, who is its termination, and we see that he is the Necessary Existent and no other. We have shown that if the possibles were to begin existence without limit, it being inconceivable for the necessary and possible to join together in what had no extent, or for the possibles to be without limit of existence, then either the Necessary would be non-existent without limit, or both of them would be existent together in what has no extent. This is the greatest implausibility, because the uniting of two different things in what has no extent is inconceivable due to the implausibility of two opposites joining together or of an existent entering two existent things, just as one essence cannot be two essences.

95. It follows from this that possibles have their limit at the Necessary and that the Necessary does not terminate at something other than himself, just as his existence is not limited by his non-existence or by the existence of something other than himself. For if he extended to

---

His point is that since a limitless succession of contingents would preclude the Necessary Existent, there would be no agent or cause to bring them from non-existence into existence. Thus, since things exist there must be a Necessary Existent and there is a limit to the number of contingents.

[22] Al-Dimashqī's reference to the highest of the heavenly Intellects shows again that he is arguing within an Avicennan framework, in which the First Intellect controls the highest heavenly sphere which surrounds the lowest sphere and the earth and conceals the One from the contingent universe.

غيره للزم أن يكون محصورًا بين حاصرين وللزم أيضًا أن يكون ذلك الغير متناهيًا إلى الغير وما تسلسل فلا يتحصّل. وذلك بأن واجب * الوجود لمّا * 101v لم يكن إلا واحدًا لزم أن لا يحيط به غيره لأنّ ذلك الغير إن كان واجب الوجود لزم أن يكون ثمّ واجبين وهو محال. وإن كان حادثًا فالحادث لا يحصر القديم ولا يحيط به لأن الواجب الوجود هو الذي لا يتقيّد بالحصر لأنه مطلق الوجود، فلزم أن يكون محيطًا بالمتناهيات ولا تحيط به وأن لا يكون في مكان لاستحالة النهاية عليه لأنّ المكان عبارة عن الظرف الحاوي للموجود المحوى، وواجب الوجود مطلق لا يحويه المكان والزمان لأنّ المكان لا يخرج عن تحديد الجهات الستّ، فهو إمّا أن يكون فوقًا لما تحته أو عكسه أو محاذيًا لما وراءه أو مقابلاً لما هو أمامه أو متناهيًا نحو يمينه أو شماله، وكلّ هذه الأقسام باطلة لأنه لو كان فوقًا لما تحته لزمه الحدّ والحصر والتناهي إلى ذلك التحت وبه، فإن كان ذلك التحت قديمًا لزم منه وجود واجبين وهو محال، وإن كان حادثًا تبيّن أن القديم محصور بالحادث وهو محال وكذلك القول في ما فوقه ولو أنه تحت لما فوقه أيضًا للزم التقسيم الأوّل والتقدير الأوّل وهو محال، وكذلك القول باستحالة حصره في سائر جهاته فلزم من ذلك أن يكون وجوده تعالى منزهًا لذاته عن المكان والجهة والحيّز والتناهي والحصر والفوق والتحت وهو في ذاته مطلق الوجود ليس معه في ذاته غير ذاته ولا محصور بغير لوجوده الحاصر غيره.

ولا * تدرك الأفهام لوجوده نهاية ولا تبلغ الأوهام لذاته غاية لأنّ * 102r الأفهام والأوهام إنما تتصوّر ما دخل تحت الحدود والتناهي والمقدار والحيّز والمكان

something other than himself, he would have to be confined between two confines, and also this other would have to extend to another, and there would be this continuing series.[23] This is because, since the Necessary (101v) Existent is only one, anything other than him cannot surround him, for if this other were a necessary existent there would then have to be two necessary beings, which is inconceivable; and if it were temporal, the temporal cannot confine the Eternal or surround him, because the Necessary Existent is the one who cannot be restricted by being confined since he is the Absolute Existent.

So it follows that he surrounds finite things and they do not surround him, and that he is not in any location because limits are inconceivable for him. For a limit implies a container that holds what exists inside it, but the absolute Necessary Existent is not held by location or time, since a location cannot be separated from the demarcation of the six directions, and is thus either above what is beneath it, or opposite it, or immediately before what is behind it, or opposite what is before it or extending to its right or left. All these alternatives are wrong, because if he were above what is beneath him he would have to have a limit, restriction and extension towards and up to this thing beneath him. If this thing beneath were eternal, the existence of two necessary things would inevitably ensue, and this is inconceivable; if it were temporal, it would be clear that the Eternal was restricted by the temporal, and this is inconceivable.

The same can be said about what might be above him: if he were beneath what was above him then similarly the previous set of alternatives and estimation would apply, and this is inconceivable. The same applies to the argument concerning the inconceivability of his being restricted in the other directions applying to him. And it follows from this that the existence of the exalted One is by his essence, free from location, direction, space, extension, restriction, and being above or beneath. In his essence he is absolutely existent, there is nothing with him in his essence other than his essence, and he is not restricted by any other thing on his existence, for it is he who restricts others.

Intellects cannot (102r) perceive an end to his existence, nor imaginations attain his essence, for intellects and imaginations can only form what is included within limits, extension, measurement, space, location

---

[23] This is because there would no longer be the one, unique Necessary Existent as the origin of all else.

والزمان وما لا يتصل[34] بهذه التقسيمات فلا يدركه إلا هو ولا يعلمه سواه، وذلك لأنّ العلم به وحقيقته لا يطابقه من جميع الوجوه لأنّ حقيقة العلم إنما هو معنى يطابق ماهية المعلوم على ما هو المعلوم عليه وقيام معنى المطابق لما لا يتناهى في علم المتناهى محال، لأنّ العقول متناهية بحدّ الحدود والكمية والتناهي فلا يتعدى طوره، ولا يدرك ما هو خارج عن حصره، فالعلم به لا يطابقه من جميع الوجوه لأحد من خلقه كلّياتها وجزئياتها.

96.   فإن قال قائل: إنّ قولكم هذا يدلّ على واجب الوجود محيط. منتهى إحاطة العقل الأوّل وبما سواه من العقول والجواهر الروحانية والأفلاك والعالم كلّه من جميع الوجوه وذلك يؤدّي الى محالات أحدها أنه يكون متناهيًا[35] إلى المحيط بها، أعني العقول الأولى[36] المتناهية إليه، والمحيط[37] بالشيء فإنه محاط بمحيطه لأنّ وجود المحاط مقابل لوجود المحيط من سائر جهاته، والثاني أنّ ذلك يلزم المقابلة من جميع الجهات والمقابلة يلزم منها أن يكون ذا جهات من ذاته وقد دلّلتم على أن الجهات في حقّه محال، والثالث أنّ الإحاطة بالجهات الستّ[38] يلزم منها التجويف لذات * المحيط بالمتناهيات، فالجواب * 102v أنّ الحصر الضروري ألزم الإحاطة وهو أنّا دلّلنا على استحالة كون واجب الوجود فوق لما تحته أو تحتاً لما فوقه أو محصورًا بجهاته لأنّه تعالى منزّه عن ذلك، ودلّلنا على أنه سبحانه قائم بذاته لا في مكان وليس له في ذاته جهة ولا لغيره لاستحالة النهاية على ذاته إلى غيره، ورأينا العالم بأسره متناهيًا محصورًا في ما لا يتناهى فرأيناه لا يتصف بالمكان والحصر والجهات فلم نر تلك الصفات من صفات الممكنات المتناهية، وليس وراء الممكنات وجود ثان سوى وجود الواجب الوجود فلزمنا الحصر الضروري ثبوت الإحاطة، لأنّه تعالى إذا لم يكن[39] فوقها ولا

---

[34] This word is illegible in A; B: يتعد (wrongly), a misreading of A.   [35] A and B: متناهي   [36] A and B: الأوّل   [37] B: المحيط   [38] A and B: الستة   [39] A and B omit this word.

and time. He alone perceives what is not related to these categories, and none knows it other than him. This is because knowledge of him and his reality in whatever respect is not equivalent to him, since the actuality of knowledge is nothing more than that it is a meaning which is equivalent to the essence of the thing known as it is something that is known. But the existence of a meaning that is equivalent to what has no finitude in the knowledge of the finite is inconceivable. This is because intellects are limited by a particular limit or quantity, and what is finite cannot exceed its bounds and cannot perceive what is outside its restriction. So, knowledge of him does not correspond to him in any respect on the part of anything in his creation, either in its entirety or in its constituents.

96. If someone should say: This account of yours proves that the Necessary Existent surrounds the limit of what is surrounded by the First Intellect, and in addition the Intellects, the immaterial substances, the heavens and the whole universe in all ways. And this leads to a number of impossibilities. One is that he will extend to what surrounds them, that is the First Intellects, which will extend to him. For what surrounds a thing is surrounded by what it surrounds, because the presence of what is surrounded will be equivalent to the presence of what surrounds in all its directions. The second is that this necessitates equivalence in all directions, and as a consequence of equivalence he must by his essence be the possessor of directions, though you have shown that directions are inconceivable in his actuality. The third is that it follows from surrounding in the six directions that the Encompasser of spatial objects must be hollow in his essence. (102v)

The response is that necessary restriction must entail surrounding. Now we have shown that it is inconceivable for the Necessary Existent to be above what is beneath him, or beneath what is above him, or restricted in his directions, because the exalted One is free from this. And we have shown that the blessed One subsists by his essence not in any location because he has no direction in his essence, and not through another because it is inconceivable for his essence to have a limit in anything other than itself. We see the world in its entirety extending to and being restricted by what has no extent, and we see that this is uncharacterised by place, restriction or directions, and we do not see such attributes as the attributes of spatial possibles. Behind the possibles there is no second existent other than the Necessary Existent. So restriction that is unavoidable requires us to accept surrounding as something that is fixed. If the exalted One was not above them or

تحتها ولا في جهة من جهاتها ولا خارج عنها ولا داخل فيها فيتبيّن أنه
تعالى ليس بموجود لأنّه لا يكون موجودًا داخلاً في الوجودية يخرج عن
هذه التقسيمات اللازمة إلا ما ذهبت إليه المعطلة من القول بالوجود الذهني
الذي لا حقيقة له في الخارج بوجه من الوجوه أو الاتحادية القائلون بأنه هو
العالم والعالم هو ظاهره خلق وباطنه حقّ، فظاهر العالم بأسره أسماء للواجب
وصفات. وقد دلّلنا على استحالة هذه المذاهب واستحالة القول بالحلول
كذلك، فلمّا لم تحط الممكنات به تعالى أحاطها ولمّا لم تحصره الجهات   * 103r *
حصرها، ولمّا استحال عليه الحلول بحيّزها لزم مباينته بالذات عن ذوات
الممكنات والحلول بها. فهذه الأقسام الضرورية لا ريب فيها ولا مخرج عنها.
وأما قول القائل: إنه يلزم من إحاطته بالجهات بمعنى الإحاطة
مقابل الجهات فإنّ ذلك لا يضرّ لأن الوجود والمحيط بسائر الممكنات تعتبر
في بحر ذاته الغير متناه[40] كنقطة ماء[41]، ولا يمنع أن يقابل بنقطة ماء من وجود
إحاطته بسائر الممكنات بمجموعها، وهذا دليل على الكمال. وأمّا قول
القائل إنه يلزم من إحاطته بالمتناهيات التناهي إليها من جميع الجهات فإنه
محال لأنّ التناهي عبارة عن الدخول تحت حصر الكمية وحدّ الماهية وتحديد
الأينية وتناهي الذات والوجود إلى أن يتناهى طرفاه من جميع الجوانب حتى
تحدّد له جهات ستّ[42] وتحيط به من فوقه ومن تحته وحوله وهو سبحانه منزّه
هنالك عن الفوقية والتحتية والجهات والحدّ حتى تلزمه هذه المحالات، فلا
فوق له ولا تحت، ولا جهة له ولا حدّ[43]، ولا مقدار ولا تناهي لذاته.

97.   فإن قال قائل إنّ الإحاطة تلزم * أن يكون الوجود الذي هو محيط بجهة   * 103v *
الفوق فوقًا لما تحته، والمحيط بجهة التحت للممكنات تحتًا لما فوقه وكذلك
حتى تتحدد له بالمقابلة جهات ستّ[44] محيطة لمقابلة الجهات الستّ[45]

---

[40] A and B: متناهي　[41] B omits this word.　[42] A and B: ستة　[43] B: واحد (wrongly).
[44] A and B: ستة　[45] A and B: الستة

beneath them or in any of their directions, or outside them or inside them, then it would be clear that the exalted One did not exist. For nothing could exist and be included in existence but excluded from these unavoidable alternatives except in the doctrine of those who deny all attributes of God and teach about hypothetical existence which has no external reality of any kind, or those who make God united and say that he is the world and the world is him, his manifestation is creation and his interior is truth: the manifestation of the world in its entirety is the names and attributes of the necessary One. We have already shown how inconceivable such doctrines are, and how inconceivable is the teaching about indwelling (103r) in the same way. So, since possibles do not surround the exalted One he surrounds them, and since directions do not restrict him he restricts them, and since indwelling in their space is not conceivable for him then he must be distinct in essence from the essences of possible things and from indwelling in them. For there is no doubt about these unavoidable alternatives and no escape from them.

As for the person's saying: Since the exalted One surrounds directions then in the sense of surrounding he must have directions, this presents no difficulty, because existence and surrounding all possibles must be regarded as a drop of water in the limitless sea of his essence. There is no objection to his having contact with a drop of water as a result of surrounding all possibles in their entirety, for this is a proof of perfection.

As for the person's saying: Since he surrounds limits he must be limited by them in all directions, this is inconceivable because being limited is an expression that comes from being included within the restriction of quantity, the confine of quality, the confinement of direction, and the limitation of essence and existence, to the point that the two extremities of a thing will be limited on all sides until six directions confine it and surround it from above, beneath and around it. But in that respect the blessed One is exalted so far beyond being above or being beneath, or having directions and confine, that these impossibilities cannot affect him. For he has no above or beneath, direction or confine, measurement or limit to his essence.

97.   If someone should say: Surrounding requires (103v) the being who surrounds the direction of above to be above what is beneath him, and one who surrounds the direction of beneath possible things to be beneath what is above him, and so on until through bearing the six directions of surrounding he will be circumscribed by bearing the

المحاطة ، فالجواب: أمّا تحديد الجهات فإنها من حيث توجّه الجهات إليه لا
من حيث أنه ذو جهات لذاته والثاني أنّ الجهات المتوجّهة إلى إحاطته بها
إنما هي محدودة لنقطة الإحاطة بها، ونقطة الإحاطة جزء، والماهية والإحاطة
بالجزء والتحديد له لا يلزم منه الإحاطة بالكلّ ولا تحديد الكلّ.

وسآتيكم بنبأ غريب وفصل أذكره للتأنيس عجيب فأقول: يا أيها
القائل والمعترض ويا أيها السامعون اسمعوا وعوا. إنّ الأفهام إذا سارت بسير
الأوهام في وسع وجود لا يتناهى فهي تسير إلى أن ينقطع، فإذا انتهى سيرها
في تلك العظمة الغير متناهية ثمّ التفتت الأذهان إلى ما وراءها[46] نحو الممكنات
لرآها الذهن في حيّزها نقطة مختفية في إحاطة بحر غير متناه.[47] وإذا سرت
في ما لا يتناهى تلاشت هنالك النقطة المتلاشية إلى أن لا يدرك لها وجود
أصلاً، فينطمس معناها المحاط ومعنى الإحاطة، كانطماس نقطة في ذاتية
البحر المحيط، وكانطماس الطائر في الجوّ عن النظر بسبب البعد المفرط،
فمن أين يقال إنّ الطائر المختفي في الجوّ والنقطة المطموسة في البحر أحاطا في
الطواميس الواسعة؟ * ولا معنى للإحاطة إلا الحصر المجموع المجمّع ماهية المحاط   104r *
وذاتيته ووجوده من كلّ الوجوه. وأمّا مجموع الممكنات فإنها فوق نقطة
الإحاطة بحسب وسعها، لا بحسب وجود المحيط بها. فإنّ الوجود والذات
لا تحت له ولا فوق لاستحالة التناهي عليه. وأمّا الفوق والتحت والجهات
والحدّ فهي بالنسبة إلينا وإلى المتناهيات المحصورة بحدودها والمحدودة
بحصرها.

وأمّا قول القائل بأنه لو كان محيطًا بالجهات الستّ[48]

---

[46] A: وارها; B: واتها   [47] A and B: متناهي   [48] A and B: الستة

six directions of being surrounded, the response is: As for the confinement of directions, the sense is that directions may be applied to him, but not that he possesses directions in his essence. The second is that the directions which apply to his surrounding are only confined to a drop enclosed by them, and the drop enclosed is a small part, while the quality and surrounding of a small part and confining it do not necessitate his surrounding the whole or confining the whole.

I will give you some curious information and an amazing piece of news, which I will recount to ensure calm, so I say: You who are speaking in opposition, and you who are listening, listen and take heed. If thoughts could lead imaginations in progress through the vastness of being without end, they would come to the point where they would be halted. If their progress stopped at the Sublimity which has no limitations, then minds would become aware of what lay beyond it such as the possibles, and the mind would see them in their space like a drop concealed in the hold of a limitless sea.[24] And if they continued into where there was no extent, the ephemeral drop would in a sense vanish to the point that no existence of any kind could be understood of it. So the idea of it being surrounded and the idea of surrounding it would be obliterated like a drop being obliterated in the essence of the surrounding sea, or like a bird being obliterated from sight in the sky through gathering distance. How can it be said that the bird hidden in the sky and the drop obliterated in the sea are surrounded in vast obliteration? (104r) There is no meaning to surrounding except that of total restriction in every respect of the quality, the being and the existence of what is surrounded. In the case of the totality of possibles, they are only more than the drop that is surrounded because of their extent not because of the existence of One who surrounds them. For there is no above or beneath to his existence and essence because of the impossibility of his having finitude. Above, beneath, directions and confine, these relate to us and to things that are finite and restricted by their limitations and limited by their restrictions.

As for the person's saying: If he surrounded the six directions he

---

[24] Al-Dimashqī is attempting here to visualise the physical universe, with its contingent or possible parts, from the viewpoint of the divine. Seen thus, it is no more than a tiny drop in the ocean of God's being, and it becomes meaningless to think of him having dimensions or being at all restricted simply because human minds can imagine him encompassing the comparatively insignificant universe in the vastness of his being.

لزمه التجويف المحدّد بالإحاطة فذلك محال من وجوه أحدها أنّ الإحاطة[49]
تلزم التجويف للأجسام أو الجواهر المحيّزة، فمن ليس هو بجسم ولا جوهر
ذي حيّز ولا محصور بمماثل من أين يلزمه التجويف بالإحاطة كما يلزم
الأجسام والجواهر المحيّزة التجويف بالإحاطة إذ الإحاطة وجودها الداخل في
الحيّز لما في إحاطته؟ ولمّا استحال كونه جسمًا أو جوهرًا ذا حيّز استحال أن
يدخل عليه بالإحاطة من التجويف ما يدخل على الأجسام والجواهر المحيّزة.
ولمّا كان مغايرًا للأجسام والجواهر المحيّزة فكذا إحاطته بالممكنات مغايرة
لإحاطة الأجسام بالأجسام والجواهر بالجواهر، والمغاير بالذات والحقيقة
والإحاطة بالأجسام مغايرها بالأحكام، فإذا لزمها بالإحاطة التجويف لم

* 104v

يلزم المغاير * لها من الحكم ما لزمها[50]، فلا يلزمه التجويف.

الوجه الثاني أنه إن صحّ بأن تدرك ماهيته وحقيقته وكنهه أو
تعقل، لزم أن يعقل لإحاطته بالممكنات التجويف، وإذا لم يصحّ إدراك الماهية
والحقيقة لا يتصوّر التجويف أبدًا بوجه من الوجوه، وكذلك إذا لم يكن
محصورًا باتصاله بمنتهى الممكنات والأجسام كيف تدخل عليه هذه المحالات
المتخلّية عن الأفهام، وهو أنه تعالى لمّا استحال عليه الحلول بالذات والحقيقة
في حيّز العالم لزم الذات التباين لاستحالة الحلول. ولمّا كانت الممكنات
بأجسامها وجواهرها وأعراضها ومجموعها متناهية لزم أن تتناهى إلى
الواجب لأنها لو تناهت إلى ممكن آخر والممكن إلى ممكن فلا بدّ أن تتناهى
الممكنات على كلّ تقدير، فإن لم يتناهى عدم وجود الواجب وعدم وجود
الواجب محال فاستحال أن تكون الممكنات غير متناهية.

والوجه الثالث أننا لمّا عقلنا الموجودات بأسرها والممكنات
بمجموعها ورأيناها متناهية بين طرفي الأولية والأخرية ومحصورة تحت الكمية
والحدود والماهية وأنّ مجموعها محصور تحت

---

[49] B: للإحاطة (wrongly), evidently a misreading of A. [50] B adds: فلا يلزمها

would have to be hollow and delimited through surrounding, this is inconceivable for many reasons. One is that for physical bodies or spatial substances surrounding necessitates being a hollow, so for what reason must One who is not a physical body or substance, spatial or similarly restricted be a hollow because of surrounding, in the way that physical bodies and spatial substances are necessarily hollow through surrounding? Surrounding is their being which corresponds to the space they surround, but since it is inconceivable for him to be a physical body or substance with space, the surrounding through being hollow that applies to physical bodies and spatial substances cannot apply to him. And since he is different from physical bodies and spatial substances, then his surrounding possibles is different from the surrounding by bodies of bodies and by substances of substances. One who is different in essence, reality and surrounding of bodies will be different from them in properties, so although they must be hollow because of surrounding, the property that applies to them does not necessarily apply (104v) to one who differs from them, and so being hollow does not necessarily apply to him.

The second respect is that if it is correct that his quality, reality and essential being could be perceived or comprehended, it would necessarily follow that hollowness could be comprehended because he surrounds possibles. But if it is not correct that this quality and reality can be perceived, hollowness cannot ever be imagined in any respect at all. Similarly, if he is not restricted by his connection with the termination of the possibles and physical bodies, how can these impossibilities that defy understanding apply to him when, because indwelling in an essence and actual presence in the space of the world are inconceivable for him, he in his exaltedness must be an essence that is distinct because of the inconceivability of indwelling? And since possibles, in the form of physical bodies, substances, accidents and everything else, are finite, they must reach their limit at the necessary One, because if they reached their limit at another possible and this possible at a possible, then by any estimation the possibles must inevitably reach their limit. If they did not reach a limit, the Necessary Existent would not exist, and the non-existence of the Necessary Existent is inconceivable. So it is inconceivable for the possibles to be infinite.

The third respect is that since we can understand existent things in their entirety and possibles in their totality, and we see them limited between the two extremes of initial and final, and restricted by quantity, limitations and quality, and in their totality restricted by the

إحاطة العقل الأوّل المحيطة بالعقول والنفوس والأرواح والجواهر الروحانية وسائر الممكنات. ورأينا تلك الإحاطة العظيمة الحاوية للكلّ ذات حيّز لا يخرج عن الماهية والكيفية * وكلّ داخل تحت الماهية والكيفية فإنه معقول * 105r للعقول ومحصور بالحدّ، محدود للذهن متناهٍ[51] بحاضره محاط بماهيته، فلزمه التناهي الذاتي، وذلك التناهي الذاتي محاط بغيره لا ريب.

98.   وذهب الفيلسوف ها هنا إلى القول باتحاد ذات المحيط المشار إليه بالمحاط ولزوم اتحاد ذاته بذاته أزلاً وأبدًا فهما واحد[52] بالوجود والقدم. وإنّ الرتب ألزمت التسميات الممتازة فاصطلحوا، أعني الفلاسفة، على رتبة بالعناصر، وعلى أخرى بالهيولى والصورة، وعلى أخرى بالنفس حيث هي محلّ المدبرات، واصطلحوا على المحيط بها بالعقل، وعلى الوجود المحيط بالعقل بالباري، وقالوا بارتباط الذوات الجامعة معًا أزلاً وأبدًا، واصطلحوا على المحيط أيضًا بالعلّة، وعلى المحاط بالمعلول وقالوا: "إنّ الأجسام مظاهر العقل الفعّال، والعقل مظهر الباري ومعلول ذاته اندفع عنه بالقوّة والطبع لا بالقصد والاختيار". وقالوا: "إنّ العلّة والمعلول والمظهر والمبطن منهما وجود الأزل" وإنّ "العقل الأوّل حامل صفات الإلهية ليس فوقه صفة بعقل والقصدية بتحصّل ثبوت وجود فرد فرد أي يفيد العقل المادّة الثبوتية والقوّة الوجودية طبعًا بالخاصة والقوّة

---

[51] A and B: متناهي   [52] A and B: واحداً

surrounding of the First Intellect which surrounds the Intellects, souls, spirits, spiritual substances and all other possibles; and we see this great surrounding which embraces all spatial being that cannot escape from quality and quantity (105r) but is included entirely within quality and quantity, and can thus be grasped by intellects and restricted by limit, limited by the mind, finite in its presence, and surrounded in its quality, it must therefore be finite in essence, and this finite in essence must undoubtedly be surrounded by One other than itself.

98. With regard to this, the philosopher prefers the view that the essence of the One who surrounds (referred to above) unites with what is surrounded, and that his essence is necessarily united with its essence eternally and for ever so they are one in existence and eternity, and that the orders necessitate distinct designations.[25] Thus they, I mean the philosophers, agree on an order according to origin, on others according to matter and form, and on others according to soul, because that is the location of directing forces. They also agree that what surrounds them is the Intellect and the being that surrounds the Intellect is the Creator. They say that all essences together are eternally and forever related, and they agree further that the One who surrounds is the cause and what is surrounded is the effect. They say: 'Physical bodies are the outward manifestation of the Agent Intellect, and the Intellect is the outward manifestation of the Creator and the effect of his essence, flowing from him instinctively and inherently, not by intention or choice'. They say: 'From both the cause and the effect, the manifest and the concealed, comes eternal existence', and: 'The First Intellect bears the attributes of divinity, and above it there is no attribute of Intellect or of intention to produce a concrete, specific existent. This is to say that the Intellect influences concrete matter, and the potential that exists naturally as a characteristic, potential,

---

[25] Al-Dimashqī moves from a general theological-philosophical defence of the distinctiveness of God who is nevertheless related to the contingent universe, to a specific refutation of what philosophers say on this. As the rest of this paragraph shows, the system proposed by the Islamic philosophers on the basis of their Neoplatonic Aristotelianism is comprised of orders of being all controlled and regulated in systematic rigidity by the First Intellect who governs the highest of the heavens. God, or the One, is outside this system and unrelated to it, except that the First Intellect emanates from him as a result of the One's self-contemplation. For al-Dimashqī, like al-Ghazālī two centuries earlier, this system restricts God and removes him so far from the created world that he ceases to resemble the Deity depicted in the Qur'an.

The philosopher who al-Dimashqī mentions here by title is almost certainly Ibn Sīnā.

والأحكام * والتدبيرات والاختيارات إنما تتجلّى من ذات العقل لذاته، وإنّ * 105v *
رتّبه العقل محلّ الاختيارات والتدبيرات والتصوّرات، وإنّ الباري منزّه عن
قيام ذلك بذاته بل هو ذات مجرّدة ووجود مطلق لا يحدّ بحصر ولا يحصر
بحدّ".

فنظرنا، نحن المسلمون، في ما ذهبوا إليه، فظهر لنا خطأهم في كثير منه،
ودليلنا على ذلك أن الربّ ربّ لذاته والعبد عبد لغيره، والربّ لا يكون
عبدًا، فلو كان الربّ هو العقل والعقل هو الفلك لم يكن بين حقيقة العقل
وحقيقة الفلك تغاير [53] في الذات والحقيقة، وكذلك لم يكن بين ذات الفلك
وحقيقته وبين عالم العناصر القابلة الاستحالات تغاير. [54] ولمّا ظهر في الشاهد
تغاير الفلك وذات العقل عن حقيقتيهما وعن حقيقة ذوات العناصر دلّ
ذلك على التغاير، وإذا لزم التغاير من هذا الطرف أمكن تغاير ذلك الطرف
المتناهي للعقل إلى وجود الباري تعالى. وإذا أمكن التغاير لزم الانفصال
الذاتي، والانفصال الذاتي يمنع الاتحاد وثبوت الاتصال المطلق بالعقل الأوّل
أزلاً وأبدًا.

ودليل ثان [55] أنّ عالم العناصر قابل للتغيّر والاستحالة، وتلك التغيّرات
تلزم تغيّر صفات العقول المتعلقة بها، وتغيّر صفات * العقل المعلولة [56] يلزم * 106r *
منه تغيّرات حدثت في علّته الأولى لأنّ العلّة تفيد المعلول للكون والفساد
والتغيّرات، والمعلول لا يفيد العلّة فكان يلزم أن تكون العلّة المغيّرة صادرة
عن العلّة الأولى، وقبول تغيّرات صفات العلّة الأولى يلزم عنه تغيّر الحقيقة
عمّا هي عليه، وثبوت العلّة الأولى على حقيقة واحدة يلزمهم ثبوت حقيقة
المعلول على حالة واحدة مع كون تغيّر المعلولات وقبولها للاستحالات محال
وما يقضي إلى المحال

---

[53] A and B: تغايراً   [54] A and B: تغايراً   [55] A and B: ثاني   [56] B: الملولة (wrongly).

properties, (105v) controls and choices, is made apparent only from the essence of the Intellect to its essence, and it is the Intellect that fixes it as a location for choices, controls and concepts. The Creator is too transcendent to accomplish this by his essence, for he is pure essence, absolute existence, unlimited by any restriction and unrestricted by any limitation.'

We Muslims have examined the position they favour, and their errors in a great part of it have become plain to us. Our proof for this is that the Lord is Lord by virtue of his essence, and the servant is servant by virtue of something extraneous, and the Lord is not a servant. If the Lord were the Intellect and the Intellect the celestial sphere, there would be no distinction in essence or reality between the reality of the Intellect and the reality of the celestial sphere, and likewise there would be no distinction between the essence or reality of the celestial sphere and the world with its changeable constituents.[26] But since the distinction between the celestial sphere and the essence of the Intellect from their respective realities and from the reality of the essences of the constituents is apparent to observation, this proves distinction. And if there is a necessary distinction at this extremity, there is a possibility of distinction at that extremity extending from the side of the Intellect to the existence of the exalted Creator. If distinction is possible, then there must be a disjunction of essence, and disjunction of essence prohibits uniting and the permanence of the absolute relationship with the First Intellect eternally and for ever.

A second proof is that the world of constituents is susceptible to alteration and transformation. These alterations require alteration in the attributes of the Intellects to which they are attached, and alteration in the caused attributes (106r) of an Intellect requires alterations that occur in its first cause, because the cause influences the effect with respect to existence, decay and alterations, while the effect does not influence the cause. Now it necessarily follows that the cause that alters proceeds from the first cause, and for the first cause to be susceptible to alterations in its attributes necessitates alterations in its original reality. To affirm that the first cause is one in reality compels them to affirm that the reality of the effect is one state despite alteration of effects, and for it to change is inconceivable. What has been decided is inconceivable

---

[26] These distinct entities would effectively be identical with one another if, as the philosophers state in the preceding paragraph, they were united with one another necessarily and eternally.

محال، لأنه كيف يحلّ التغيّر في المعلول ولا يكون ذلك التغيّر مبدلة عن العلّة الأولى؟ وكما كانت العلّة مفيدة المادة والثبوت والبقاء، وكلّ ذلك منبعث عنها بالقوّة كيف لا تكون تلك التغيّرات منبعثة عنها بالقوّة؟ ولا فرق، فإن كانت التغيّرات في المعلولات انبعثت عنها بالقوّة والطبع لزم أن يكون أصل التغيّر في ذات العلّة الأولى وتغيّر المعلولات تبع لها. وإن كان محلّ التغيّر في المعلولات ولا تشعر العلّة به ولا هو صادر عنها فكذلك أيضًا لا يشعر المعلول بالعلّة، ولا يتصل بالمادة كما لا تتصل العلّة الأولى بالتغيّر، فإن ألزمونا اتصال المادة والقوّة من العلّة إلى المعلول ألزمناهم اتصال التغيّر * 106v * من المعلول إلى العلّة.

فإن قالوا إنّ المعلول يقبل المادة طبعًا والعلّة تقبل التغيّر طبعًا وقوّتها دافعة التغيّر على الإطلاق، فالجواب: إنّ قوابل المعلولات متعلّقة بخاصيّة عللها بالقوّة، والعلّة متّحدة القوّة بالمعلول طبعًا والاتحاد يلزم الاشتراك في سائر الأحكام لأنّ اتحاد قوابل المعلول بقوّة العلّة وخاصتها المقبولة باعثة أحكام التغيّرات إلى العلّة بواسطة العلّة المجرّدة المتعلّقة بالذاتين كما هي باعثة المادة والثبوت الوجودي أزلاً وأبداً.

99.   وقالوا أيضًا إنّ وجود المعلول متولّد عن العلّة وفائض عنها بالقوّة وإنّ الفيض المعلول[57] لم يزل متعلقًا بعلّته وإنه لا يصدر عن الواحد إلا واحد، ولا يجوز أن يصدر عن الواحد اثنان وذلك لأنّ المعلول الفائض عن العلّة بالطبع والخاصة

---

57 B: الملول (wrongly).

is inconceivable, for how can alteration inhere in an effect when this alteration has not been brought about by the first cause? And just as the cause influences matter, constancy and permanence, and all this emanates from it inherently, why should these alterations not emanate from it inherently?[27] There is no difference, for if the alterations in effects emanate from them inherently and instinctively, the origin of alteration in the essence of the first cause and the alteration of effects must pertain to it. If alteration dwells in effects and the cause is not aware of this and it does not originate from it, then similarly again the effect will be unaware of the cause and will not be connected with matter, just as the first cause is not connected with alteration. If they force us to accept the connection of matter and potential between the cause and the effect, we will force them to accept the connection of alteration (106v) between the effect and the cause.

If they say, The effect is susceptible to matter naturally and the cause is susceptible to alteration naturally, while above this any alteration is absolutely ruled out, the response is: Things that are susceptible to effects are attached to the characteristics of their causes by potential, and the cause unites the potential with the effect naturally. Uniting necessitates sharing in all properties, because the uniting of what is susceptible to an effect with the potential of the cause and the characteristic to which it is susceptible gives rise to considerations of alteration on the part of the cause through the single cause being connected to two essences, and also emitting matter and concrete existence eternally and forever.[28]

99.　　They also say that the existence of the effect is generated and flows from the cause inherently, that the flowing out of the effect is eternally related to its cause, that only one can issue from one, and that it is impossible for two to issue from one. This is because the effect which flows out from the cause by nature and characteristic

---

[27]　A consequence of this intimate unity between all orders of the universe is that the changes and alterations seen all around must be the effects of higher causes which must themselves change in order to bring about these effects. On the basis of the close unity which the philosophers declare, this necessitates alteration at the highest level of the heavenly Intellects, which defies their own logic.

[28]　The argument continues to turn on the mutual influences between effects and causes in the philosophers' system where all entities are intimately united. Al-Dimashqī persists in his point that causes cannot be free when their effects undergo change, which ultimately means that God himself will be susceptible to change. This is self-evidently nonsensical.

لا يغاير طبيعة العلّة أبدًا بوجه من الوجوه. كما أنّ الحرارة المدفوعة عن النار لا تغاير طبع النار.

فقلنا لهم كان يلزم من هذا أن يكون طبع آخر المعلول ملائمًا لطبيعة أوّل العلل، ويلزم من ذلك استحالة التغاير بين العلّة والفيضة بالطبع وبين معلولها الفائض عنها لأنه هو نفس طبيعتها بعينه كما أنّ الحرارة نفس طبيعة النار بعينها، ووجود تغاير طبع المعلولات * في الشاهد يدلّ على * 107r استحالة هذا القول وكذلك استحالة أنه لا يصدر عن الواحد إلا واحد، فذلك الواحد الصادر إن كان مغايرًا لطبيعة علّته لزم أن لا يكون صادرًا عنه بالطبع والقوّة لأن الطبع لا يخالف نفسه وهو المطلوب. وإن كان صادرًا عنه وهو ملائم لطبعه كملاءمة الحرارة لطبيعة النار فكان يلزم أن لا يصدر عن الواحد إلا واحد بملاءمة الطبع، وذلك يلزم استحالة التغاير بين العلّة والمعلول والصادر والصادر عنه، ووجود تغاير طبائع الموجودات في الشاهد وتغاير حقائقها وذواتها يدلّ على استحالة هذه الدعوى الباطلة، وذلك بأنّ تغاير الحقائق وذوات الممكنات وتغاير طبائعها يدلّ على انفصال ذواتها لأن الغيرين لا يتلاءمان بالطبع والميلين[58] لا يتقاطعان لأن الطبيعة لا تفارق نفسها.

فواجب الوجود لمّا كان مغايرًا للعقل الأوّل امتنع أن يكون علّته وإذا امتنع أن يكون علّته لزمه الانفصال واستحال الاتحاد والممازجة والتعلّق اللازم أزلاً وأبدًا وهو المطلوب.

ولمّا علمنا هذا وفهمناه حقّ فهمه ودلّلنا عليه بالأدلّة القاطعة لم يأخذنا شبه الحلولية ولا الاتحادية ولا الوحدية * ولا المعطلة ولا المشبّهة ولا المجسّمة * 107v ولا الدهرية ولا أهل الحيرة والوقفة بل قلنا كما قال

---

58 A and B: والميلان

never differs from the nature of the cause in any respect at all, just as the heat that is radiated from the fire does not differ from the nature of the fire.

We say to them: It follows from this that the nature of the last of effects must conform to the nature of the first of the causes, and it follows necessarily from this that any difference between the cause and natural pouring forth and its effect that pours forth from it is inconceivable because this is exactly the very nature of that, just as the heat is the very nature of the fire. The existence of difference in the natures of effects (107r) in the observable world proves how inconceivable this statement is, and also how inconceivable it is for only one to issue from one. For if this one that issues forth is different from the nature of its cause, then it cannot issue from it naturally and inherently because the nature does not differ from itself, which is what was in question. But if it does issue from it and conforms to its nature as the heat conforms to the nature of the fire, then it will necessarily follow that only one could issue from one in view of the conformity of the natures. And this necessarily shows how inconceivable it is for there to be differences between the cause and the effect, and what issues forth from what it issues from. The existence of difference in the natures of existent things in the observable world and the difference in their realities and essences proves the inconceivability of this false claim. This is because difference in the realities and essences of possibles and difference in their natures proves that their essences are distinct, because two different things will not conform in nature, and two things that conform will not be counter to each other because nature will not divide from itself.

Since the Necessary Existent is different from the First Intellect, he cannot possibly be the cause of it. And if he cannot possibly be the cause of it he must be distinct, and so uniting, adjacency and necessary attachment must be inconceivable eternally and for ever. And this is what was in question.

Since we know this and comprehend it truly, and have proved it with unassailable proofs, no similarity to supporters of indwelling, uniting, or oneness, (107v) of the strippers of attributes, of the anthropomorphists, of the corporealists, of the materialists, or of the confused and indecisive can attach to us.[29] But we will say what our

---

[29] These are all beliefs and groups that appear to blur the radical distinction

أبونا وأبوكم ابراهيم عليكم﴾59: ﴿ووجّهنا وجوهنا للذي فطر السموات والأرض حنفاء مسلمين وما نحن من المشركين﴾60، وقال كلّ واحد منّا ما أمر الله سبحانه لنبيّه محمّد صلم أن يقوله بقلبه ولسانه ونقوله نحن كذلك: ﴿قل إنّ صلاتي ونسكي﴾61 الآيتان.

إنقضى الكلام على معرفة الإله جلّ جلاله من حيث المعقول والرأي البادي للعقل السليم وما يجب للإله من الوصف وما يجوز وما يستحيل.

100. وواحسرة عليكم أيها النصارى الأخوان في النوعية والشخصية لو أنكم تعقلون هذا القول الذي ذكرته لكم ودلّلت به وأوضحته وأرجو إن شاء الله تعالى أنكم تعقلونه62 ليتبيّن لكم ما بان لنا، وتعلمون أنّ لا إله إلا الله وحده لا شريك له، وإن كان لكم مخرج وبرهان مخالف63 للحقّ فأتوا به. ولا برهان لكم ولا مستند ولا إنارة علم ولا سابقة ممّن تقدّمكم من الأمم تجعلون لأنفسكم فينا أسوة ولا أسوة

59 B: عليكم (wrongly). 60 A reminiscence of S. VI: 79. 61 Ibid.: 162. 62 A and B: تعقلوه 63 A and B: مخالفا وبرهانًا ومخرجًا

father and your father Abraham (peace be upon him) said, 'We have turned our faces to him who created the heavens and the earth, as those by nature upright, Muslims, and we are not of the associators.' And each of us says what God the blessed commanded his Prophet Muḥammad (may God bless him and give him peace) to say with his heart and tongue, and so we say, 'Say, Lo! my worship and my sacrifice' and the rest of the two verses.[30]

Here concludes the argument concerning the knowledge of God, great is his majesty, with respect to the rational, to opinion that is plain to sound reason, to what must be ascribed to God, and to what is permissible and not plausible.[31]

100. What a shame it is for you Christians, brothers in kind and in person![32] If only you would understand these words I have put before you, the things I have proved and made plain! But I hope, if God the exalted wills, that you will understand it, so that what is clear to us will become clear to you, and you will know that there is no god but God alone with no partner. If you have any excuse and proof that differs from the truth, produce it. But you do not have any proof or plausible evidence, no enlightenment of knowledge, nor any predecessors among the communities that have gone before you. You make yourselves an example for us, though you have no example to

---

between God and contingent being or to threaten his divinity. Most have been mentioned at various stages in the *Response* already, including the enigmatic *Ahl al-waqfa*, who were probably agnostic; cf. Section 5, n. 23. The name *Dahriyya* was applied in general ways to groups who advocated the eternity of the world and had no doctrine of God.

[30] The relevance of these two verses to the argument is that they inculcate worship of the one, unchanging God, on the part of Abraham when he recognises that all the heavenly bodies decline and realises that God alone remains firm, and on the part of Muḥammad when he in enjoined to declare that God is one and the supreme Disposer of all.

[31] This brings to a close the long theological-philosophical discussion about the relationship of God with the creation that began at § 93. Starting from the beliefs of the Christian group that favoured the doctrine of God indwelling and uniting with humans and blurring the distinction between Creator and creatures, al-Dimashqī embarks on this elaborate and often tortuous series of technical arguments intended to demonstrate both that any claim to intimate relationship collapses on itself since it deprives God of his distinctive attributes of divinity, and also that any notion that he is remote from the creation and indifferent to it also breaks down.

The arguments do not arise from anything said explicitly in the Cypriots' *Letter*, and their relevance to the defence is not immediately apparent.

[32] This closing address to the Cypriot Christians comes almost as an aside, following the long discussion about the distinction between God and the creation.

لكم. والسلام على من اتّبع الهدى.

تمَّ الجواب بالنفثات السبوحية عن رسالة أهل الملّة المسيحية على يد العبد الفقير إلى من هو بالعفو جدير أبي بكر بن علي رعوض التروحي في خامس عشرين ربيع الأوّل من عام ٧٧٢.

give. Peace be upon those who follow guidance!

The response to the accusations that have flowed out from the Letter of the Christians is concluded. It was written down by the servant who has need of the One who can grant pardon, Abū Bakr Ibn ʿAlī Raʿūḍ al-Trūḥī, on 25 Rabīʿ I in the year 772.[33]

---

[33] On 17 October 1370 CE, forty-nine years after its composition.

BIBLIOGRAPHY

'Abd al-Jabbār al-Hamadhānī, *Al-mughnī fī abwāb al-tawḥīd wa-al-ʿadl*, vol. V, ed. M.M. al-Khuḍayrī, Cairo, 1965.
—— *Tathbīt dalāʾil al-nubuwwa*, ed. ʿA.-K. ʿUthmān, Beirut, 1966.
Accad, M., 'The Ultimate Proof-Text: The Interpretation of John 20. 17 in Muslim-Christian Dialogue (second/eighth—eighth/fourteenth centuries)', in D. Thomas, ed., *Christians at the Heart of Islamic Rule, Church Life and Scholarship in ʿAbbasid Iraq*, Leiden, 2003.
ʿAlī, M. Kurd, *Kunūz al-ajdād*, Damascus, 1950.
ʿAlī al-Ṭabarī, *Kitāb al-Dīn wa-al-dawla*, ed. A. Mingana, Manchester, 1923, trans. A. Mingana, *The Book of Religion and Empire*, Manchester, 1922.
—— *Al-radd ʿalā al-Naṣārā*, ed. I.-A. Khalifé and W. Kutsch, 'Ar-Radd ʿalā-n-Naṣārā de ʿAlī aṭ-Ṭabarī', *Mélanges de l'Université Saint Joseph* 36, 1959; trans. J.-M. Gaudeul, *Riposte aux Chrétiens par ʿAlī al-Ṭabarī*, Rome, 1995.
ʿAmmār al-Baṣrī, *K. al-Burhān*, in M. Hayek, *ʿAmmār al-Baṣrī, theologie et controversies*, Beirut, 1977.
Arberry, A., *The Mawāqif and Mukhātabāt of Muhammad ibn ʿAbdi 'l-Jabbār al-Niffarī*, London, 1935.
al-Ashʿarī, Abū al-Ḥasan, *Maqālāt al-Islāmiyyīn*, ed. H. Ritter, Istanbul, 1930.
al-ʿAsqalānī, Ibn Ḥajar, *Al-durar al-kāmina fī aʿyān al-miʾa al-thāmina*, Hyderabad, 1349.
Bacon, Roger, *Opus Maius*, ed. J. Bridges, *The 'Opus Maius' of Roger Bacon*, Oxford, 1897-1900.
al-Bāqillānī, Abū Bakr, *Kitāb al-tamhīd*, ed. R.J. McCarthy, Beirut, 1957.
Baring-Gould, S., *The Lives of the Saints*, London, 1898.
Blau, J., *A Grammar of Christian Arabic (Corpus Scriptorum Christianorum Orientalium*, 267, 276, 279; *Subsidia*, 27, 28, 29), Louvain, 1966-7.
Braun, O., 'Der Brief des Katholicos Timotheus I über biblische Studien des 9-Jahrhunderts', *Oriens Christianus* 1, 1901.
Buffat, L., 'Lettre de Paul Évêque de Saïda, moine d'Antioche, à un Musulman de ses amis demeurant à Saïda', *Revue de l'Orient Chrétien* 8, 1903.
Burchard of Mount Zion, *Descriptio Terrae Sanctae*, ed. C.J. Lauren, *Perigrinationes medii aevi quatuor*, Leipzig, 1864.
Busse, H., "Omar's Image as Conqueror of Jerusalem', *Jerusalem Studies in Arabic and Islam* 8, 1986.
Cheikho, L., 'Risālat Bawlus Usquf Ṣaydā al-Rāhib al-Anṭākī qad arsalahā li-baʿḍi maʿārifihi alladhīn bi-Ṣaydā min al-Muslimīn', in *Vingt traités théologiques d'auteurs arabes chrétiens*, Beirut, 1920.
Coureas, N., *The Latin Church of Cyprus, 1195-1312*, Aldershot, 1997.
De Statu Saracenorum, ed. P. Engels, *Notitia de Machometo (Corpus Islamo-Christianorum, Series Latina)*, Wurzburg, 1992.
Delaney, J.J., *Dictionary of Saints*, London, 1982.
al-Dhahabī, Muḥammad b. Aḥmad, *Taʾrīkh al-Islām wa-ṭabaqāt al-mashāhīr wa-al-āʿlām*, Cairo, 1367.
al-Dimashqī, Shams al-Dīn, *Nukhbat al-dahr fī ajāʾib al-barr wa-al-baḥr*, ed. A.F. Mehren, *Cosmographie de Chems-ed-Din Abou Abdallah Mohammad ed-Dimachqui*,

St Petersburg, 1866; trans. Mehren, *Manuel de la Cosmographie du Moyen Age*, Copenhagen, 1874.

Ebied, R., 'Inter-Religious Attitudes: al-Dimashqī's (d. 727/1327) *Letter to the People of Cyprus*', ARAM 9-10, 1997-8.

Edbury, P., *The Kingdom of Cyprus and the Crusades, 1191-1374*, Cambridge, 1991.

Fidentius of Padua, *Liber recuperationis Terrae Sanctae*, ed. G. Golubovich, *Biblioteca bio-bibliographica della terra sancta e dell' oriente francescano*, Quaracchi, 1906-27, vol. II.

Fritsch, E., *Islam und Christentum im Mittelalter: Beiträge zur Geschichte der Muslimischen Polemik gegen das Christentum in arabischer Sprache*, Breslau, 1930.

Fück, J., *Arabiya: Untersuchungen zur arabischen Sprach- und Stilgeschichte (Abhandlungen der Sachsischen Akademie der Wissenschaften zu Leipzig*, Phil. hist. Kl., Bd. 45, Ht. 1), Berlin, 1950.

Gimaret, D., *Une lecture muʿtazilite du coran*, Louvain-Paris, 1994.

L. Ginzberg, *The Legends of the Jews*, Philadelphia, 1911-38.

de Goeje, M.J., *Catalogus Codicum Orientalium, Bibliothecae Academiae Lugduno–Batavae*, vol. V, Leiden, 1873.

Graf, G., *Geschichte der Christlichen Arabischen Literatur (Studi e Testi* 118, 133, 146, 147, 172), Vatican City, 1944-52.

Griffith, S.G., 'Muslims and Church Councils: the Apology of Theodore Abū Qurrah', *Studia Patristica* 25, Leuven, 1993.

The New Grove Dictionary of Music and Musicians, London, 1980.

Hallam, E., ed., *Chronicles of the Crusades*, Godalming, 1989.

Hayek, M., *Le Christ de l'Islam*, Paris, 1959.

Hennecke, E., *New Testament Apocrypha*, trans. R. McL. Wilson, vol. I, *Gospels and Related Writings*, London, 1963.

Hillenbrand, C., *The Crusades: Islamic Perspectives*, Edinburgh, 1999.

Holt, P., *Early Mamluk Diplomacy (1260-1290), Treaties of Baybars and Qalāwūn with Christian Rulers*, Leiden, 1995.

Housley, N., *The Later Crusades, from Lyons to Alcazar 1274-1580*, Oxford, 1992.

—— *Documents on the Later Crusades, 1274-1580*, Basingstoke, Hampshire, 1996.

Hyatte, R., *The Prophet of Islam in Old French, 'The Romance of Muhammad' (1258) and 'The Book of Muhammad's Ladder' (1264)*, Leiden, 1997.

Ibn ʿArabī, *Fuṣūṣ al-ḥikam*, ed. A. ʿAfīfī, Beirut, 1946.

Ibn al-Athīr, ʿIzz al-Dīn, *Al-kāmil fī al-tārīkh*, Beirut, 1998.

Ibn Ḥazm, Abū Muḥammad, *Kitāb al-fiṣal fī al-milal wa-al-ahwāʾ wa-al-niḥal*, Cairo, 1903.

Ibn Isḥāq, *Sīrat sayyidnā Muḥammad rasūl Allāh*, ed, F. Wüstenfeld, Göttingen, 1858-60; trans. A. Guillaume, *The Life of Muhammad*, Oxford, 1955.

Ibn Kammūna, Saʿd ibn Manṣūr, *Tanqīḥ al-abḥāth li-al-milal al-thalāth*, trans. M. Perlmann, *Ibn Kammūna's Examination of the Three Faiths*, Los Angeles and London, 1971.

Ibn Kathīr, ʿImād al-Dīn, *Al-bidāya wa-al-nihāya*, Beirut-Riyadh, 1966; trans. T. Le Gassick, *The Life of the Prophet Muḥammad*, Reading, 2000.

—— *Qiṣaṣ al-anbiyāʾ*, Beirut, 1972.

Ibn Taymiyya, Taqī al-Dīn, *Al-jawāb al-ṣaḥīḥ li-man baddala dīn al-Masīḥ*, Cairo, 1905; ed. ʿA. B. Ḥasan b. Nāṣir et al, Riyadh, 1999.

Isidore of Seville, *Etymologiae*, Book IX, ed. and trans. M. Reyellet, *Isidore de Séville, Étymologies, Livre IX*, Paris, 1984.

al-Jāḥiẓ, Abū ʿUthmān, *Fī al-radd ʿalā al-Naṣārā*, ed. J. Finkel in *Thalāth rasāʾil li-Abī ʿUthmān al-Jāḥiẓ*, Cairo, 1926.

James, M.R., *The Apocryphal New Testament*, Oxford, 1969.

Jeffery, A., *A Reader on Islam*, 's Gravenhage, 1962.

de Jong, P., 'Een Arabisch Handschrift, behelzende eene Bestridjing van 't Christendom', *Verslagen en Mededeelingen der Koninklijke Akademie van Wetenschappen*, Afdeeling Letterkunde, Tweede Reeks, Achtste Deel, Amsterdam, 1878.

Khalidi, T., *The Muslim Jesus*, Cambridge, Mass., and London, 2001.

Khalifé, I.-A., '*Makhṭūṭ al-ʿilm al-ṭabīʿī wa-mīzātuh al-lughawiyya*', *Al-machriq* 62, 1968.

Khoury, P., *Paul d'Antioche, évêque melkite de Sidon (xiiᵉ s.)*, Beirut, 1964.

Kritzeck, J., *Peter the Venerable and Islam*, Princeton, 1964.

Lazarus-Yafeh, H., *Intertwined Worlds, Medieval Islam and Biblical Criticism*, Princeton, 1992.

Levi, I., *The Hebrew Text of the Book of Ecclesiasticus*, Leiden, 1969.

López-Morillas, C., 'The Moriscos and Christian Doctrine', in M.D. Meyerson and E.D. English, eds, *Christians, Muslims and Jews in Medieval and Early Modern Spain, interaction and cultural change*, Notre Dame, Ind., 2000.

A. Luttrell, 'The Hospitallers in Cyprus after 1291', *Acts of the I International Congress of Cypriot Studies, II. Nicosia, 1972*, repr. in A. Luttrell, *The Hospitallers in Cyprus, Rhodes, Greece and the West 1291-1440*, Aldershot, Hampshire, 1978.

—— 'The Hospitallers in Cyprus: 1310-1378', *Kypriakai Spoudai* 50, 1986, repr. in A. Luttrell, *The Hospitallers of Rhodes and their Mediterranean World*, Aldershot, Hampshire, 1992.

Marco Polo, *La divisement du monde*, ed. Marie-Luce Chênerie *et al.*, Geneva, 2001.

al-Masʿūdī, Abū al-Ḥasan, *Murūj al-dhahab*, ed. and trans. C. Barbier de Meynard and Pavet de Courteille, Paris, 1861-77.

Metzger, B., 'Seventy or Seventy-Two Disciples?', *New Testament Studies* 5, 1958.

Michel, T., 'Ibn Taymiyya's *Al-Jawāb al-Ṣaḥīḥ*, a Muslim Theologian's Response to Christianity', PhD Dissertation, Chicago, 1978.

—— *A Muslim Theologian's Response to Christianity, Ibn Taymiyya's al-Jawab al-Sahih*, Delmar, New York, 1984.

Michot, J.R., *Ibn Taymiyya, Lettre à un roi croisé*, Louvain-la-Neuve and Lyons, 1995.

Mingana, A., 'The Apology of Timothy the Patriarch before the Caliph Mahdi', *Bulletin of the John Rylands Library* 12, 1928.

Moffett, S.H., *A History of Christianity in Asia, volume I: Beginnings to 1500*, New York 1998.

Momen, M., *An Introduction to Shīʿi Islam*, Yale, 1985.

al-Nadīm, Abū al-Faraj, *Kitāb al-Fihrist*, ed. M. Riḍā-Tajaddud, Tehran, 1971.

al-Nāshiʾ al-Akbar, *K. al-awsaṭ fī al-maqālāt*, ed. J. van Ess, *Frühe muʿtazilitische Häresiographie*, Beirut, 1971.

Nicoll, A., *Catalogi Codicum Manuscriptorum Orientalium Bibliothecae Bodleianae pars secunda*, Oxford, 1835.

Oliver of Paderborn, *Die Schriften des Kölner Domscholasters, späteren Bischofs von Paderborn und Kardinal-Bischofs von S. Sabina, Oliverus*, ed. O. Hoogweg, Tübingen, 1894; trans. J.J. Gavigan, *The Capture of Damietta, by Oliver of Paderborn*, Philadelphia, 1948.

Pines, S., '"Israel, my Firstborn" and the Sonship of Jesus', in E.E. Urbach, R.J. Zwi Werblowsky and C. Wirzubski, eds, *Studies in Mysticism and Religion presented to Gershom G. Scholem*, Jerusalem, 1967.

Platti, E., *Yaḥyā Ibn ʿAdī, théologien chrétien et philosophe arabe*, Leuven, 1983.

al-Qarāfī, Shihāb al-Dīn, *Al-ajwiba al-fākhira ʿan al-asʾila al-fājira*, ed. B.Z. ʿAwad, Cairo, 1987.

al-Qāsim b. Ibrāhīm, *Al-radd ʿalā al-Naṣārā*, ed. I. di Matteo, 'Confutazione contro i Cristiani dello zaydita al-Qāsim b. Ibrāhīm', *Rivista degli Studi Orientali* 9, 1921-2.

Rahmé, G., '*Risāla fī faḍīlat al-ʿafāf*', *Al-machriq* 62, 1968.

al-Rāzī, Fakhr al-Dīn, *Muḥaṣṣal afkār al-mutaqaddimīn wa-al-muta'akhkhirīn*, Cairo, 1905.

Renard, J., *All the King's Falcons, Rumi on Prophets and Revelation*, Albany, NY, 1994.

Robinson, N., *Christ in Islam and Christianity*, New York, 1991.

Roggema, B., 'A Christian Reading of the Qur'an: the legend of Sergius-Baḥīrā and its use of Qur'an and Sīra', in D. Thomas, ed., *Syrian Christians under Islam, the first thousand years*, Leiden, 2001.

Rubin, U., *The Eye of the Beholder, the Life of Muhammad as viewed by the early Muslims* (*Studies in Late Antiquity and Early Islam* 5), Princeton, 1995.

al-Rūmī, Jalāl al-Dīn, *The Mathnawī of Jalālu'ddin Rūmī*, ed. and trans. R.A. Nicholson, London, 1977.

al-Ṣafadī, Ṣalāḥ al-Dīn, *Al-wāfī bi-al-wafayāt*, Weisbaden, 1931-99.

—— *Āyān al-'aṣr wa-a'wān al-naṣr*, ed. 'A. Abū Zayd *et al.*, Beirut/Damascus, 1998.

Sahas, D.J., *John of Damascus on Islam, the "Heresy of the Ishmaelites"*, Leiden, 1972.

Samir, S.K., 'Notes sur la "Lettre à un musulman de Sidon" de Paul d'Antioche', *Orientalia Lovaniensia Periodica* 24, 1993.

—— 'The Prophet Muḥammad as seen by Timothy I and some other Arab Christian Authors', in D. Thomas, ed., *Syrian Christians under Islam, the first thousand years*, Leiden, 2001.

Schmeider, F., '*Nota sectam maometicam atterendam a tartaris et christianis*, The Mongols as non-believing apocalyptic friends around the year 1260', *Journal of Millenial Studies* 1, 1998.

Segal, J.B., *Edessa, 'The Blessed City'*, Oxford, 1970.

al-Shahrastānī, Abū al-Fatḥ, *Kitāb al-milal wa-al-niḥal*, ed. W. Cureton, London, 1846.

Shirley, J., *Crusader Syria in the Thirteenth Century, the Rothelin Continuation of the History of William of Tyre with part of the Eracles or Acre Text* (*Crusader Texts in Translation* 5), Aldershot, 1999.

Skehan, P., *The Wisdom of Ben Sira*, New York, 1987.

Steinschneider, M., *Polemische und apologetische Literatur in arabischer Sprache, zwischen Muslimen, Christen und Juden nebst Anhangen verwandten Inhalts* (*Abhandlungen fur die Kunde des Morgenlandes* 6, no. 3), Leipzig, 1877.

Stern, S.M., "Abd al-Jabbār's Account of how Christ's Religion was falsified by the Adoption of Roman Customs', *Journal of Theological Studies* new series 19, 1968.

al-Ṭabarānī, Abū al-Qāsim, *Al-mu'jam al-kabīr*, ed. H. 'Abd al-Majīd al-Salafī, Beirut, 1984-.

al-Ṭabarī, Abū Ja'far, *Ta'rīkh al-rusul wa-al-mulūk*, ed. M.J. de Goeje *et al.*, Leiden, 1879-1901.

Talley, T., *The Origins of the Liturgical Year*, Collegeville, MN, 1991.

al-Tha'labī, Aḥmad b. Muḥammad, *Qiṣaṣ al-anbiyā'*, Beirut, 1994.

Thiede, C., *The Dead Sea Scrolls and the Jewish Origins of Christianity*, London, 2000.

Theophanes Confessor, *The Chronicle of Theophanes Confessor*, trans. C. Mango and R. Scott, Oxford, 1997.

Thomas, D., 'Two Muslim-Christian Debates from the Early Shi'ite Tradition', *Journal of Semitic Studies* 33, 1988.

—— *Anti-Christian Polemic in Early Islam, Abū 'Īsā al-Warrāq's 'Against the Trinity'*, Cambridge, 1992.

—— 'The Miracles of Jesus in early Islamic Polemic', *Journal of Semitic Studies* 39, 1994.

—— 'Abū 'Īsā al-Warrāq and the History of Religions', *Journal of Semitic Studies* 41, 1996.

—— 'Abū Manṣūr al-Māturīdī on the Divinity of Jesus Christ', *Islamochristiana* 23, 1997.

—— ed., *Syrian Christians under Islam, the first thousand years*, Leiden, 2001.

—— 'Paul of Antioch's *Letter to a Muslim Friend* and *The Letter from Cyprus*', in Thomas, ed., *Syrian Christians under Islam, the first thousand years*, Leiden, 2001.

—— 'The Doctrine of the Trinity in the early Abbasid Era', in L. Ridgeon ed., *Islamic Interpretations of Christianity*, London, 2001.

—— *Early Muslim Polemic against Christianity, Abū ʿĪsā al-Warrāq's 'Against the Incarnation'*, Cambridge, 2002.

—— ed., *Christians at the Heart of Islamic Rule, Church Life and Scholarship in 'Abbasid Iraq*, Leiden, 2003.

—— 'Early Muslim Responses to Christianity', in Thomas, ed., *Christians at the Heart of Islamic Rule, Church Life and Scholarship in 'Abbasid Iraq*, Leiden, 2003.

Tiele, P. and A. Hulshof, *Catalogus Codicum Manuscriptorum Bibliothecae Universitatis Rheno-Trajectinae*, Leiden, 1887.

Tolan, J.V., *Saracens, Islam in the Medieval European Imagination*, New York, 2002.

Troupeau, G., *Catalogue des manuscrits Arabes*, Paris, 1972.

al-Warrāq, Abū ʿĪsā, *Al-radd ʿalā al-thalāth firaq min al-Naṣārā*, cf. Thomas, *Anti-Christian Polemic in Early Islam*, and *Early Muslim Polemic against Christianity*.

Uri, J., *Bibliothecae Bodleianae Codicum Manuscriptorum Orientalium*, Oxford, 1787.

Vriemoet, E.L., *Arabismus; Exhibens Grammaticam Arabicam Novam & Monumenta quaedam Arabica, cum Notis Miscellaneis & Glossario Arabico-Latino*, Franequerae, 1733.

William of Tripoli, *Notitia de Machometo*, ed. P. Engels (*Corpus Islamo-Christianorum, Series Latina*), Wurzburg, 1992.

Wilson, R. McL., *The Gospel of Philip*, London, 1962.

Watt, W.M., *Islamic Creeds*, Edinburgh, 1994.

al-Zamakhsharī, Maḥmūd b. ʿUmar, *Al-kashshāf ʿan ḥaqāʾiq ghawāmiḍ al-tanzīl wa-ʿuyūn al-aqāwīl fī wujūh al-taʾwīl*, 4 vols., ed. M. ʿAbd al-Salām Shāhīn, Beirut, 1995.

al-Ziriklī, Khayr al-Dīn, *Al-aʿlām*, Beirut, 1999.

QUOTATIONS AND REFERENCES FROM THE BIBLE

Biblical quotations in both the *Letter* and *Response* are not always easy to identify precisely. In instances where a direct correspondence cannot be found we have given the nearest approximation, and in the case of sayings and stories which appear in more than one of the Synoptic Gospels, we have given references to Matthew only unless the Gospel is named.

QUOTATIONS AND REFERENCES FROM THE QUR'AN

INDEX